THE NEW JERUSALEM BIBLE
NEW TESTAMENT

The
New Jerusalem
Bible

New Testament

READER'S EDITION

DARTON · LONGMAN + TODD

Darton, Longman & Todd Ltd
1 Spencer Court
140–142 Wandsworth High Street
London SW18 4JJ

New Testament: Reader's Edition first published 1991

2/5

ISBN 0–232–51966–8

Phototypeset by Intype, London
Printed and bound in the United Kingdom
at the University Press, Cambridge.

CONTENTS

THE NEW TESTAMENT

SUPPLEMENTS

EDITOR'S FOREWORD

Admiration of the view of an iceberg must never lead the viewer to forget that only the tip is visible; the visible tip must never be thought to be self-explanatory. So it is a dangerous project to present the New Testament on its own, for the New Testament is the record of the fulfilment of God's promises made to the People of Israel in what we now call the Old Testament, and can be truly understood only as the fulfilment of the yearnings of Israel. The New Testament frequently quotes the Old (and these quotations are here given in italics) and much more frequently alludes to it. So, while it is useful to have a conveniently portable New Testament, the reader should be aware that it is like carrying round a torch which exerts its full power only if it is replaced frequently on its charger.

Another warning may help towards a balanced appreciation of the New Testament. The gospels, though conventionally printed first in the book, were not the first Christian documents to be written. The first written documents of Christianity which we have are the letters of Paul (some hold the Letter of James to be earlier still). These letters, written to Churches or individuals in response to some need, include here and there short passages, historical traditions, hymns, sayings, about Jesus which were already abroad in the Christian communities. It was, however, only later that the full traditions of what Jesus said and did were collected and put together in the four gospels which we now possess.

This Reader's Edition of *The New Jerusalem Bible* New Testament is based on the much larger Standard Edition of the Bible first published in 1985. While the biblical text remains unchanged, the notes and introductory material have been pared to make the volume more accessible and manageable. There will be questions left unanswered here for which the answer can be found in the Standard Edition. The Index of Persons and the Chronological Table at the end have been simplified. A new help has, however, been added, in the form of a Theological Glossary; this gives succinct notes on nearly 200 key words and concepts of the Bible. Each note ends with half a dozen references to the key passages in the Bible for the concept, thus providing a mini-concordance; a number of these passages are from the Old Testament, since the concept in the New Testament can be fully understood only against its background in the Old Testament.

The work of many devoted scholars has contributed to this Bible: those who produced the parent *Bible de Jérusalem* in 1956, the collaborators on the first English *Jerusalem Bible* (1966), the revisers of the *Bible de Jérusalem* (1973), and those who combined to produce the Standard Edition of *The New Jerusalem Bible* in 1985. The grateful reader might spare a prayer of thanks and blessing on them.

St Benet's Hall, Oxford   HENRY WANSBROUGH
Whitsun 1991

THE
NEW TESTAMENT

INTRODUCTION TO
THE SYNOPTIC GOSPELS

The gospels are not 'lives' or biographies of Jesus, but are four versions of the record of the Good News brought by Jesus. Jesus himself preached the coming of God's rule, the establishment of his sovereignty, breaking through the bonds of evil, sin and death to which all people had been subject. The gospels are full also of wonder at the mystery of Jesus himself, and why a shameful death was the means by which God must triumph in him.

At the heart of the gospel tradition is the first preaching of the Good News of Jesus by the apostles. The tradition was handed down in the community in the form of stories, parables and short sayings remembered for their teaching or the light they threw on the person or message of Jesus. To some extent these stories would be moulded to bring out their lesson, e.g. the fulfilment of Scripture in the life, death and resurrection of Jesus, or their application to Christian behaviour in the world. The tradition was expressed also in hymns and short summaries to be learnt by heart.

Which of the gospels was the first to be written is still in dispute, although it is clear that the three 'synoptic' (i.e. 'with the same eye') gospels are interrelated. The most common view is that Mk was the first, and that this was expanded independently by Mt and Lk, each using a now lost collection of the Sayings of Jesus. The traditional view is that Mt came first and was used by Lk, with Mk finally making a digest of them both. In either view the gospels are the end product of a long process of development in the Christian community under the guidance of the Spirit.

Nor is it possible to establish firmly the date or authorship of these gospels. Tradition from the 2nd century holds that Matthew the apostle stands authority for Mt, that Mk represents the tradition of Peter, and that the author of Lk was a companion of Paul. But the identity of the authors is less important than the guarantee of their material by the tradition of the early community, of which each must have been an authorised interpreter. Of the date, we can only be sure that they all stem from the last forty years of the 1st century.

THE GOSPEL OF
MATTHEW

Mt is the gospel of the Kingdom of Heaven. This points to three principal emphases: (i) While Mk concentrates on the gradual unfolding of the disciples' understanding of Jesus, Mt stresses from the first that Jesus is a king; he is a noble and dignified figure who deserves and receives homage from all around him; already in his earthly life he is seen as the exalted

Christ. (ii) The Kingdom of Heaven, still to be completed, but already strongly associated with the community which Jesus founded, is the fulfilment of God's plan for Israel. So the Church is the true Israel, the recipient of God's promises, which goes out to all nations in the power of Christ. (iii) Mt is the most Semitic of the gospels, constantly touching on Jewish and rabbinic customs and ways of thought and argument, stressing that Jesus fulfils the hopes of the OT both in general and in minute detail. There is a strong and typically Jewish interest in the final retribution, about which Mt is full of warnings.

The main part of the gospel, apart from the infancy stories and the passion narrative, is divided into five sections (each with a narrative and a teaching section) by analogy with the five books of the Jewish Law. Mt is more interested than Mk in Jesus' teaching, which he assembles in five great discourses, each with its own subject: the Sermon on the Mount (5—7), the Missionary Discourse (10—11), Parables (13), the Community (18) and the Last Discourse (24—25). So this Jewish-Christian scribe shows that Jesus is not only the Davidic Messiah but also the Lawgiver or second Moses.

PLAN OF THE BOOK

THE GOSPEL ACCORDING TO
MATTHEW

I: THE BIRTH AND INFANCY OF JESUS

The ancestry of Jesus

1 Roll of the genealogy of Jesus Christ, son of David, son of Abraham:

²Abraham fathered Isaac,
  Isaac fathered Jacob,
  Jacob fathered Judah and his brothers,
³Judah fathered Perez and Zerah,
  whose mother was Tamar,
  Perez fathered Hezron,
  Hezron fathered Ram,

⁴Ram fathered Amminadab,
  Amminadab fathered Nahshon,
  Nahshon fathered Salmon,
⁵Salmon fathered Boaz,
  whose mother was Rahab,
  Boaz fathered Obed,
  whose mother was Ruth,
  Obed fathered Jesse;
⁶and Jesse fathered King David.

David fathered Solomon,
  whose mother had been Uriah's wife,

7Solomon fathered Rehoboam,
Rehoboam fathered Abijah,
Abijah fathered Asa,
8Asa fathered Jehoshaphat,
Jehoshaphat fathered Joram,
Joram fathered Uzziah,
9Uzziah fathered Jotham,
Jotham fathered Ahaz,
Ahaz fathered Hezekiah,
10Hezekiah fathered Manasseh,
Manasseh fathered Amon,
Amon fathered Josiah;
11and Josiah fathered Jechoniah
and his brothers.
Then the deportation to Babylon
took place.

12After the deportation to Babylon:
Jechoniah fathered Shealtiel,
Shealtiel fathered Zerubbabel,
13Zerubbabel fathered Abiud,
Abiud fathered Eliakim,
Eliakim fathered Azor,
14Azor fathered Zadok,
Zadok fathered Achim,
Achim fathered Eliud,
15Eliud fathered Eleazar,
Eleazar fathered Matthan,
Matthan fathered Jacob;
16and Jacob fathered Joseph
the husband of Mary;
of her was born Jesus
who is called Christ.

17The sum of generations is therefore: fourteen from Abraham to David; fourteen from David to the Babylonian deportation; and fourteen from the Babylonian deportation to Christ.

Joseph adopts Jesus as his son

18This is how Jesus Christ came to be born. His mother Mary was betrothed to Joseph; but before they came to live together she was found to be with child through the Holy Spirit. 19Her husband Joseph, being an upright man and wanting to spare her disgrace, decided to divorce her informally. 20He had made up his mind to do this when suddenly the angel of the Lord appeared to him in a dream and said, 'Joseph son of David, do not be afraid to take Mary home as your wife, because she has conceived what is in her by the Holy Spirit. 21She will give birth to a son and you must name him Jesus, because he is the one who is to save his people from their sins.' 22Now all this took place to fulfil what the Lord had spoken through the prophet:

23*Look! the virgin is with child*
and will give birth to a son
whom they will call Immanuel,[a]

a name which means 'God-is-with-us'. 24When Joseph woke up he did what the angel of the Lord had told him to do: he took his wife to his home; 25he had not had intercourse with her when she gave birth to a son; and he named him Jesus.

The visit of the Magi

2 After Jesus had been born at Bethlehem in Judaea during the reign of King Herod, suddenly some wise men came to Jerusalem from the east 2asking, 'Where is the infant king of the Jews? We saw his star as it rose and have come to do him homage.' 3When King Herod heard this he was perturbed, and so was the whole of Jerusalem. 4He called together all the chief priests and the scribes of the people, and enquired of them where the Christ was to be born. 5They told him, 'At Bethlehem in Judaea, for this is what the prophet wrote:

6*And you, Bethlehem,*
in the land of Judah,
you are by no means the *least*
among the leaders of Judah,
for *from you will come a leader*
who will *shepherd* my people Israel.'[a]

7Then Herod summoned the wise men to see him privately. He asked them the exact date on which the star had appeared 8and sent them on to Bethlehem with the words, 'Go and find out all about the child, and when you have found him, let me know, so that I too may go and do him homage.' 9Having listened to what the king had to say, they set out. And suddenly the star they had seen rising went forward and halted over the place where the child was. 10The sight of the star filled them with delight, 11and going into the house they saw the child with his mother Mary, and falling to their knees they did him

1a Is 7:14.
2a Mi 5:1.

homage. Then, opening their treasures, they offered him gifts of gold and frankincense and myrrh. [12]But they were given a warning in a dream not to go back to Herod, and returned to their own country by a different way.

The flight into Egypt
The massacre of the Innocents

[13]After they had left, suddenly the angel of the Lord appeared to Joseph in a dream and said, 'Get up, take the child and his mother with you, and escape into Egypt, and stay there until I tell you, because Herod intends to search for the child and do away with him.' [14]So Joseph got up and, taking the child and his mother with him, left that night for Egypt, [15]where he stayed until Herod was dead. This was to fulfil what the Lord had spoken through the prophet:

I called my son out of Egypt.[b]

[16]Herod was furious on realising that he had been fooled by the wise men, and in Bethlehem and its surrounding district he had all the male children killed who were two years old or less, reckoning by the date he had been careful to ask the wise men. [17]Then were fulfilled the words spoken through the prophet Jeremiah:

[18]*A voice is heard in Ramah,*
lamenting and weeping bitterly:
it is Rachel weeping for her children,
refusing to be comforted
because they are no more.[c]

From Egypt to Nazareth

[19]After Herod's death, suddenly the angel of the Lord appeared in a dream to Joseph in Egypt [20]and said,[d] 'Get up, take the child and his mother with you and go back to the land of Israel, for those who wanted to kill the child are dead.' [21]So Joseph got up and, taking the child and his mother with him, went back to the land of Israel. [22]But when he learnt that Archelaus had succeeded his father Herod as ruler of Judaea he was afraid to go there, and being warned in a dream he withdrew to the region of Galilee. [23]There he settled in a town called Nazareth. In this way the words spoken through the prophets were to be fulfilled:

He will be called a Nazarene.

II: THE KINGDOM OF HEAVEN IS ANNOUNCED

A: NARRATIVE SECTION

The proclamation of John the Baptist

3 In due course John the Baptist appeared; he proclaimed this message in the desert of Judaea, [2]'Repent, for the kingdom of Heaven is close at hand.' [3]This was the man spoken of by the prophet Isaiah when he said:

A voice of one that cries in the desert,
'Prepare a way for the Lord,
make his paths straight.'[a]

[4]This man John wore a garment made of camel-hair with a leather loin-cloth round his waist,[b] and his food was locusts and wild honey. [5]Then Jerusalem and all Judaea and the whole Jordan district made their way to him, [6]and as they were baptised by him in the river Jordan they confessed their sins. [7]But when he saw a number of Pharisees and Sadducees coming for baptism he said to them, 'Brood of vipers, who warned you to flee from the coming retribution? [8]Produce fruit in keeping with repentance, [9]and do not presume to tell yourselves, "We have Abraham as our father," because, I tell you, God can raise children for Abraham from these stones. [10]Even now the axe is being laid to the root of the trees, so that any tree failing to produce good fruit will be cut down and thrown on the fire. [11]I baptise you in water for repentance, but the one who comes after me is more powerful than I, and I am not fit

---

2b Nb 23:22.
2c In Jr 31:15 she weeps for the northern tribes. But traditionally she was buried near Bethlehem.
2d cf. Ex. 4:19–20. There are several parallels with the stories of Moses' infancy.
3a Is 40:3.
3b As Elijah, 2 K 1:8.

to carry his sandals; he will baptise you with the Holy Spirit and fire. [12]His winnowing-fan is in his hand; he will clear his threshing-floor and gather his wheat into his barn; but the chaff he will burn in a fire that will never go out.'

Jesus is baptised

[13]Then Jesus appeared: he came from Galilee to the Jordan to be baptised by John. [14]John tried to dissuade him, with the words, 'It is I who need baptism from you, and yet you come to me!' [15]But Jesus replied, 'Leave it like this for the time being; it is fitting that we should, in this way, do all that uprightness demands.' Then John gave in to him.

[16]And when Jesus had been baptised he at once came up from the water, and suddenly the heavens opened and he saw the Spirit of God descending like a dove and coming down on him. [17]And suddenly there was a voice from heaven, 'This is my Son, the Beloved; my favour rests on him.'[c]

Testing in the desert

4 Then Jesus was led by the Spirit out into the desert to be put to the test by the devil. [2]He fasted for forty days and forty nights, after which he was hungry, [3]and the tester came and said to him, 'If you are Son of God, tell these stones to turn into loaves.' [4]But he replied, 'Scripture says:

Human beings live not on bread alone
but on every word
that comes from the mouth of God.'[a]

[5]The devil then took him to the holy city and set him on the parapet of the Temple. [6]'If you are Son of God,' he said, 'throw yourself down; for scripture says:

He has given his angels orders about you,
and they will carry you in their arms
in case you trip over a stone.'[b]

[7]Jesus said to him, 'Scripture also says:

Do not put the Lord your God to the test.'[c]

[8]Next, taking him to a very high mountain, the devil showed him all the kingdoms of the world and their splendour. [9]And he said to him, 'I will give you all these, if you fall at my feet and do me homage.' [10]Then Jesus replied, 'Away with you, Satan! For scripture says:

The Lord your God is the one
to whom you must do homage,
him alone you must serve.'[d]

[11]Then the devil left him, and suddenly angels appeared and looked after him.

Return to Galilee

[12]Hearing that John had been arrested he withdrew to Galilee, [13]and leaving Nazara he went and settled in Capernaum, beside the lake, on the borders of Zebulun and Naphtali. [14]This was to fulfil what was spoken by the prophet Isaiah:

[15]*Land of Zebulun! Land of Naphtali!*
Way of the sea beyond Jordan.
Galilee of the nations!
[16]*The people that lived in darkness*
have seen a great light;
on those who lived
    in a country of shadow dark as death
a light has dawned.[e]

[17]From then onwards Jesus began his proclamation with the message, 'Repent, for the kingdom of Heaven is close at hand.'

The first four disciples are called

[18]As he was walking by the Lake of Galilee he saw two brothers, Simon, who was called Peter, and his brother Andrew; they were making a cast into the lake with their net, for they were fishermen. [19]And he said to them, 'Come after me and I will make you fishers of people.' [20]And at once they left their nets and followed him.

[21]Going on from there he saw another pair of brothers, James son of Zebedee and his brother John; they were in their boat with their father Zebedee, mending their nets, and he called them. [22]And at once, leaving the boat and their father, they followed him.

3c cf. Is 42:1.
4a Dt 8:3.
4b Ps 91:10–12.
4c Dt 6:16.
4d Dt 6:13.
4e Is 8:23–9:1.

Jesus proclaims the message and heals the sick

²³He went round the whole of Galilee teaching in their synagogues, proclaiming the good news of the kingdom and curing all kinds of disease and illness among the people. ²⁴His fame spread throughout Syria, and those who were suffering from diseases and painful complaints of one kind or another, the possessed, epileptics, the paralysed, were all brought to him, and he cured them. ²⁵Large crowds followed him, coming from Galilee, the Decapolis, Jerusalem, Judaea and Transjordan.

B: THE SERMON ON THE MOUNT

The Beatitudes*a*

5 Seeing the crowds, he went onto the mountain. And when he was seated his disciples came to him. ²Then he began to speak. This is what he taught them:

³How blessed are the poor in spirit:
the kingdom of Heaven is theirs.
⁴Blessed are *the gentle:*b
*they shall have the earth as inheritance.*c
⁵Blessed are those who mourn:
they shall be comforted.
⁶Blessed are those
who hunger and thirst for uprightness:
they shall have their fill.
⁷Blessed are the merciful:
they shall have mercy shown them.
⁸Blessed are the pure in heart:
they shall see God.
⁹Blessed are the peacemakers:
they shall be recognised
as children of God.
¹⁰Blessed are those who are persecuted
in the cause of uprightness:
the kingdom of Heaven is theirs.

¹¹'Blessed are you when people abuse you and persecute you and speak all kinds of calumny against you falsely on my account. ¹²Rejoice and be glad, for your reward will be great in heaven; this is how they persecuted the prophets before you.

Salt for the earth and light for the world

¹³'You are salt for the earth. But if salt loses its taste, what can make it salty again? It is good for nothing, and can only be thrown out to be trampled under people's feet.

¹⁴'You are light for the world. A city built on a hill-top cannot be hidden. ¹⁵No one lights a lamp to put it under a tub; they put it on the lamp-stand where it shines for everyone in the house. ¹⁶In the same way your light must shine in people's sight, so that, seeing your good works, they may give praise to your Father in heaven.

The fulfilment of the Law

¹⁷'Do not imagine that I have come to abolish the Law or the Prophets. I have come not to abolish but to complete them. ¹⁸In truth I tell you, till heaven and earth disappear, not one dot, not one little stroke, is to disappear from the Law until all its purpose is achieved. ¹⁹Therefore, anyone who infringes even one of the least of these commandments and teaches others to do the same will be considered the least in the kingdom of Heaven; but the person who keeps them and teaches them will be considered great in the kingdom of Heaven.

The new standard higher than the old

²⁰'For I tell you, if your uprightness does not surpass that of the scribes and Pharisees, you will never get into the kingdom of Heaven.

²¹'You have heard how it was said to our ancestors, *You shall not kill;*d and if anyone does kill he must answer for it before the court. ²²But I say this to you, anyone who is angry with a brother will answer for it before the court; anyone who calls a brother "Fool" will answer for it before the Sanhedrin; and anyone who calls him "Traitor" will answer for it in hell fire. ²³So then, if you are bringing your offering to the altar and there remember that your brother has something against you, ²⁴leave your offering there before the altar, go and be reconciled with your brother first, and then come back and present your offering. ²⁵Come to terms with your opponent in good time while you are still on

5a Lk 6:20–23.
5b Ps 37:11.
5c Gn 13:15.
5d Ex 20:13.

the way to the court with him, or he may hand you over to the judge and the judge to the officer, and you will be thrown into prison. ²⁶In truth I tell you, you will not get out till you have paid the last penny.

²⁷'You have heard how it was said, *You shall not commit adultery.*[e] ²⁸But I say this to you, if a man looks at a woman lustfully, he has already committed adultery with her in his heart. ²⁹If your right eye should be your downfall, tear it out and throw it away; for it will do you less harm to lose one part of yourself than to have your whole body thrown into hell. ³⁰And if your right hand should be your downfall, cut it off and throw it away; for it will do you less harm to lose one part of yourself than to have your whole body go to hell. ³¹'It has also been said, *Anyone who divorces his wife must give her a writ of dismissal.*[f] ³²But I say this to you, everyone who divorces his wife, except for the case of an illicit marriage,[g] makes her an adulteress; and anyone who marries a divorced woman commits adultery.

³³'Again, you have heard how it was said to our ancestors, *You must not break your oath, but must fulfil your oaths to the Lord.*[h] ³⁴But I say this to you, do not swear at all, either by *heaven*, since that is *God's throne*; ³⁵or by *earth*, since that is *his footstool*; or by Jerusalem, since that is *the city of the great King.*[i] ³⁶Do not swear by your own head either, since you cannot turn a single hair white or black. ³⁷All you need say is "Yes" if you mean yes, "No" if you mean no; anything more than this comes from the Evil One.

³⁸'You have heard how it was said: *Eye for eye and tooth for tooth.*[j] ³⁹But I say this to you: offer no resistance to the wicked. On the contrary, if anyone hits you on the right cheek, offer him the other as well; ⁴⁰if someone wishes to go to law with you to get your tunic, let him have your cloak as well. ⁴¹And if anyone requires you to go one mile, go two miles with him. ⁴²Give to anyone who asks you, and if anyone wants to borrow, do not turn away.

⁴³'You have heard how it was said, *You will love your neighbour*[k] and hate your enemy. ⁴⁴But I say this to you, love your enemies and pray for those who persecute you; ⁴⁵so that you may be children of your Father in heaven, for he causes his sun to rise on the bad as well as the good, and sends down rain to fall on the upright and the wicked alike. ⁴⁶For if you love those who love you, what reward will you get? Do not even the tax collectors do as much? ⁴⁷And if you save your greetings for your brothers, are you doing anything exceptional? ⁴⁸Do not even the gentiles do as much? You must therefore be perfect, just as your heavenly Father is perfect.'

Almsgiving in secret

6 'Be careful not to parade your uprightness in public to attract attention; otherwise you will lose all reward from your Father in heaven. ²So when you give alms, do not have it trumpeted before you; this is what the hypocrites do in the synagogues and in the streets to win human admiration. In truth I tell you, they have had their reward. ³But when you give alms, your left hand must not know what your right is doing; ⁴your almsgiving must be secret, and your Father who sees all that is done in secret will reward you.

Prayer in secret

⁵'And when you pray, do not imitate the hypocrites: they love to say their prayers standing up in the synagogues and at the street corners for people to see them. In truth I tell you, they have had their reward. ⁶But when you pray, *go to your private* room, shut yourself in, and so pray[a] to your Father who is in that secret place, and your Father who sees all that is done in secret will reward you.

How to pray. The Lord's Prayer

⁷'In your prayers do not babble as the gentiles do, for they think that by using many words they will make themselves heard. ⁸Do not be

5e Ex 20:14.
5f Dt 24:1.
5g Marriage within the Jewish forbidden degrees, allowed by the Romans but not in Christianity.
5h Ex 20:7.
5i Ps 48:2.
5j Ex 21:24.
5k Lv 19:18. The rest of the sentence is not from the OT.
6a Is 26:20.

like them; your Father knows what you need before you ask him. ⁹So you should pray like this:

Our Father in heaven,
may your name be held holy,
¹⁰your kingdom come,
your will be done,
on earth as in heaven.
¹¹Give us today our daily bread.
¹²And forgive us our debts,
as we have forgiven those
who are in debt to us.
¹³And do not put us to the test,
but save us from the Evil One.ᵇ

¹⁴'Yes, if you forgive others their failings, your heavenly Father will forgive you yours; ¹⁵but if you do not forgive others, your Father will not forgive your failings either.

Fasting in secret

¹⁶'When you are fasting, do not put on a gloomy look as the hypocrites do: they go about looking unsightly to let people know they are fasting. In truth I tell you, they have had their reward. ¹⁷But when you fast, put scent on your head and wash your face, ¹⁸so that no one will know you are fasting except your Father who sees all that is done in secret; and your Father who sees all that is done in secret will reward you.

True treasures

¹⁹'Do not store up treasures for yourselves on earth, where moth and woodworm destroy them and thieves can break in and steal. ²⁰But store up treasures for yourselves in heaven, where neither moth nor woodworm destroys them and thieves cannot break in and steal. ²¹For wherever your treasure is, there will your heart be too.

The eye, the lamp of the body

²²'The lamp of the body is the eye. It follows that if your eye is clear, your whole body will be filled with light. ²³But if your eye is diseased, your whole body will be darkness. If then, the light inside you is darkened, what darkness that will be!

God and money

²⁴'No one can be the slave of two masters: he will either hate the first and love the second, or be attached to the first and despise the second. You cannot be the slave both of God and of money.

Trust in Providence

²⁵'That is why I am telling you not to worry about your life and what you are to eat, nor about your body and what you are to wear. Surely life is more than food, and the body more than clothing! ²⁶Look at the birds in the sky. They do not sow or reap or gather into barns; yet your heavenly Father feeds them. Are you not worth much more than they are? ²⁷Can any of you, however much you worry, add one single cubit to your span of life? ²⁸And why worry about clothing? Think of the flowers growing in the fields; they never have to work or spin; ²⁹yet I assure you that not even Solomon in all his royal robes was clothed like one of these. ³⁰Now if that is how God clothes the wild flowers growing in the field which are there today and thrown into the furnace tomorrow, will he not much more look after you, you who have so little faith? ³¹So do not worry; do not say, "What are we to eat? What are we to drink? What are we to wear?" ³²It is the gentiles who set their hearts on all these things. Your heavenly Father knows you need them all. ³³Set your hearts on his kingdom first, and on God's saving justice, and all these other things will be given you as well. ³⁴So do not worry about tomorrow: tomorrow will take care of itself. Each day has enough trouble of its own.'

Do not judge

7'Do not judge, and you will not be judged; ²because the judgements you give are the judgements you will get, and the standard you use will be the standard used for you. ³Why do you observe the splinter in your brother's eye and never notice the great log in your own? ⁴And how dare you say to your brother, "Let me take that splinter out of your eye," when, look, there is a great log in your own? ⁵Hypocrite! Take the log out of your own eye first, and then you will see

6b Lk 11:2–4.

clearly enough to take the splinter out of your brother's eye.

Do not profane sacred things

6'Do not give dogs what is holy; and do not throw your pearls in front of pigs, or they may trample them and then turn on you and tear you to pieces.

Effective prayer

7'Ask, and it will be given to you; search, and you will find; knock, and the door will be opened to you. 8Everyone who asks receives; everyone who searches finds; everyone who knocks will have the door opened. 9Is there anyone among you who would hand his son a stone when he asked for bread? 10Or would hand him a snake when he asked for a fish? 11If you, then, evil as you are, know how to give your children what is good, how much more will your Father in heaven give good things to those who ask him!

The golden rule

12'So always treat others as you would like them to treat you; that is the Law and the Prophets.

The two ways

13'Enter by the narrow gate, since the road that leads to destruction is wide and spacious, and many take it; 14but it is a narrow gate and a hard road that leads to life, and only a few find it.

False prophets

15'Beware of false prophets who come to you disguised as sheep but underneath are ravenous wolves. 16You will be able to tell them by their fruits. Can people pick grapes from thorns, or figs from thistles? 17In the same way, a sound tree produces good fruit but a rotten tree bad fruit. 18A sound tree cannot bear bad fruit, nor a rotten tree bear good fruit. 19Any tree that does not produce good fruit is cut down and thrown on the fire. 20I repeat, you will be able to tell them by their fruits.

The true disciple

21'It is not anyone who says to me, "Lord, Lord," who will enter the kingdom of Heaven, but the person who does the will of my Father in heaven. 22When the day comes many will say to me, "Lord, Lord, did we not prophesy in your name, drive out demons in your name, work many miracles in your name?" 23Then I shall tell them to their faces: I have never known you; *away from me, all evil doers!*[a]

24'Therefore, everyone who listens to these words of mine and acts on them will be like a sensible man who built his house on rock. 25Rain came down, floods rose, gales blew and hurled themselves against that house, and it did not fall: it was founded on rock. 26But everyone who listens to these words of mine and does not act on them will be like a stupid man who built his house on sand. 27Rain came down, floods rose, gales blew and struck that house, and it fell; and what a fall it had!'

The amazement of the crowds

28Jesus had now finished what he wanted to say, and his teaching made a deep impression on the people 29because he taught them with authority, unlike their own scribes.

III: THE KINGDOM OF HEAVEN IS PREACHED

A: NARRATIVE SECTION: TEN MIRACLES

Cure of a man with skin-disease

8 After he had come down from the mountain large crowds followed him. 2Suddenly a man with a virulent skin-disease came up and bowed low in front of him, saying, 'Lord, if you are willing, you can cleanse me.' 3Jesus stretched out his hand and touched him saying, 'I am willing. Be cleansed.' And his skin-disease was cleansed at once. 4Then Jesus said to him, 'Mind you tell no one, but

7a Ps 6:8.

go and show yourself to the priest and make the offering prescribed by Moses,[a] as evidence to them.'

Cure of the centurion's servant

[5]When he went into Capernaum a centurion came up and pleaded with him. [6]'Sir,' he said, 'my servant is lying at home paralysed and in great pain.' [7]Jesus said to him, 'I will come myself and cure him.' [8]The centurion replied, 'Sir, I am not worthy to have you under my roof; just give the word and my servant will be cured. [9]For I am under authority myself and have soldiers under me; and I say to one man, "Go," and he goes; to another, "Come here," and he comes; to my servant, "Do this," and he does it.' [10]When Jesus heard this he was astonished and said to those following him, 'In truth I tell you, in no one in Israel have I found faith as great as this. [11]And I tell you that many will come from east and west and sit down with Abraham and Isaac and Jacob at the feast in the kingdom of Heaven; [12]but the children of the kingdom will be thrown out into the darkness outside, where there will be weeping and grinding of teeth.' [13]And to the centurion Jesus said, 'Go back, then; let this be done for you, as your faith demands.' And the servant was cured at that moment.

Cure of Peter's mother-in-law

[14]And going into Peter's house Jesus found Peter's mother-in-law in bed and feverish. [15]He touched her hand and the fever left her, and she got up and began to serve him.

A number of cures

[16]That evening they brought him many who were possessed by devils. He drove out the spirits with a command and cured all who were sick. [17]This was to fulfil what was spoken by the prophet Isaiah:

*He himself bore our sicknesses away
and carried our diseases.*[b]

Unconditional commitment

[18]When Jesus saw the crowd all about him he gave orders to leave for the other side. [19]One of the scribes then came up and said to him, 'Master, I will follow you wherever you go.' [20]Jesus said, 'Foxes have holes and the birds of the air have nests, but the Son of man has nowhere to lay his head.'

[21]Another man, one of the disciples, said to him, 'Lord, let me go and bury my father first.' [22]But Jesus said, 'Follow me, and leave the dead to bury their dead.'

The calming of the storm

[23]Then he got into the boat followed by his disciples. [24]Suddenly a storm broke over the lake, so violent that the boat was being swamped by the waves. But he was asleep. [25]So they went to him and woke him saying, 'Save us, Lord, we are lost!' [26]And he said to them, 'Why are you so frightened, you who have so little faith?' And then he stood up and rebuked the winds and the sea; and there was a great calm. [27]They were astounded and said, 'Whatever kind of man is this, that even the winds and the sea obey him?'

The demoniacs of Gadara

[28]When he reached the territory of the Gadarenes on the other side, two demoniacs came towards him out of the tombs—they were so dangerously violent that nobody could use that path. [29]Suddenly they shouted, 'What do you want with us, Son of God? Have you come here to torture us before the time?' [30]Now some distance away there was a large herd of pigs feeding, [31]and the devils pleaded with Jesus, 'If you drive us out, send us into the herd of pigs.' [32]And he said to them, 'Go then,' and they came out and made for the pigs; and at that the whole herd charged down the cliff into the lake and perished in the water. [33]The herdsmen ran off and made for the city, where they told the whole story, including what had happened to the demoniacs. [34]Suddenly the whole city set out to meet Jesus; and as soon as they saw him they implored him to leave their neighbourhood.

Cure of a paralytic

9 He got back in the boat, crossed the water and came to his home town. [2]And suddenly some people brought him a para-

8a Lv 14:1–32.
8b Is 53:4.

lytic stretched out on a bed. Seeing their faith, Jesus said to the paralytic, 'Take comfort, my child, your sins are forgiven.' [3]And now some scribes said to themselves, 'This man is being blasphemous.' [4]Knowing what was in their minds Jesus said, 'Why do you have such wicked thoughts in your hearts? [5]Now, which of these is easier: to say, "Your sins are forgiven," or to say, "Get up and walk"? [6]But to prove to you that the Son of man has authority on earth to forgive sins,'—then he said to the paralytic—'get up, pick up your bed and go off home.' [7]And the man got up and went home. [8]A feeling of awe came over the crowd when they saw this, and they praised God for having given such authority to human beings.

The call of Matthew

[9]As Jesus was walking on from there he saw a man named Matthew sitting at the tax office, and he said to him, 'Follow me.' And he got up and followed him.

Eating with sinners

[10]Now while he was at table in the house it happened that a number of tax collectors and sinners came to sit at the table with Jesus and his disciples. [11]When the Pharisees saw this, they said to his disciples, 'Why does your master eat with tax collectors and sinners?' [12]When he heard this he replied, 'It is not the healthy who need the doctor, but the sick. [13]Go and learn the meaning of the words: *Mercy is what pleases me, not sacrifice.*[a] And indeed I came to call not the upright, but sinners.'

A discussion on fasting

[14]Then John's disciples came to him and said, 'Why is it that we and the Pharisees fast, but your disciples do not?' [15]Jesus replied, 'Surely the bridegroom's attendants cannot mourn as long as the bridegroom is still with them? But the time will come when the bridegroom is taken away from them, and then they will fast. [16]No one puts a piece of unshrunken cloth onto an old cloak, because the patch pulls away from the cloak and the tear gets worse. [17]Nor do people put new wine into old wineskins; otherwise, the skins burst, the wine runs out, and the skins are lost. No; they put new wine in fresh skins and both are preserved.'

Cure of the woman with a haemorrhage
The official's daughter raised to life

[18]While he was speaking to them, suddenly one of the officials came up, who bowed low in front of him and said, 'My daughter has just died, but come and lay your hand on her and her life will be saved.' [19]Jesus rose and, with his disciples, followed him.

[20]Then suddenly from behind him came a woman, who had been suffering from a haemorrhage for twelve years, and she touched the fringe of his cloak, [21]for she was thinking, 'If only I can touch his cloak I shall be saved.' [22]Jesus turned round and saw her; and he said to her, 'Courage, my daughter, your faith has saved you.' And from that moment the woman was saved.

[23]When Jesus reached the official's house and saw the flute-players, with the crowd making a commotion, he said, [24]'Get out of here; the little girl is not dead; she is asleep.' And they ridiculed him. [25]But when the people had been turned out he went inside and took her by the hand; and she stood up. [26]And the news of this spread all round the countryside.

Cure of two blind men

[27]As Jesus went on his way two blind men followed him shouting, 'Take pity on us, son of David.' [28]And when Jesus reached the house the blind men came up to him and he said to them, 'Do you believe I can do this?' They said, 'Lord, we do.' [29]Then he touched their eyes saying, 'According to your faith, let it be done to you.' [30]And their sight returned. Then Jesus sternly warned them, 'Take care that no one learns about this.' [31]But when they had gone away, they talked about him all over the countryside.

Cure of a dumb demoniac

[32]They had only just left when suddenly a man was brought to him, a dumb demoniac. [33]And when the devil was driven out, the dumb man spoke and the people were amazed and said, 'Nothing like this has ever been

9a Ho 6:6.

seen in Israel.' [34]But the Pharisees said, 'It is through the prince of devils that he drives out devils.'

The distress of the crowds

[35]Jesus made a tour through all the towns and villages, teaching in their synagogues, proclaiming the good news of the kingdom and curing all kinds of disease and all kinds of illness.
[36]And when he saw the crowds he felt sorry for them because they were harassed and dejected, like sheep without a shepherd. [37]Then he said to his disciples, 'The harvest is rich but the labourers are few, so ask the Lord of the harvest to send out labourers to his harvest.'

B: INSTRUCTION FOR APOSTLES

The mission of the Twelve[a]

10He summoned his twelve disciples and gave them authority over unclean spirits with power to drive them out and to cure all kinds of disease and all kinds of illness.
[2]These are the names of the twelve apostles: first, Simon who is known as Peter, and his brother Andrew; James the son of Zebedee, and his brother John; [3]Philip and Bartholomew; Thomas, and Matthew the tax collector; James the son of Alphaeus, and Thaddaeus; [4]Simon the Zealot and Judas Iscariot, who was also his betrayer. [5]These twelve Jesus sent out, instructing them as follows:
'Do not make your way to gentile territory, and do not enter any Samaritan town; [6]go instead to the lost sheep of the House of Israel. [7]And as you go, proclaim that the kingdom of Heaven is close at hand. [8]Cure the sick, raise the dead, cleanse those suffering from virulent skin-diseases, drive out devils. You received without charge, give without charge. [9]Provide yourselves with no gold or silver, not even with coppers for your purses, [10]with no haversack for the journey or spare tunic or footwear or a staff, for the labourer deserves his keep.
[11]'Whatever town or village you go into, seek out someone worthy and stay with him

until you leave. [12]As you enter his house, salute it, [13]and if the house deserves it, may your peace come upon it; if it does not, may your peace come back to you. [14]And if anyone does not welcome you or listen to what you have to say, as you walk out of the house or town shake the dust from your feet. [15]In truth I tell you, on the Day of Judgement it will be more bearable for Sodom and Gomorrah than for that town. [16]Look, I am sending you out like sheep among wolves; so be cunning as snakes and yet innocent as doves.

Missionaries will be persecuted

[17]'Be prepared for people to hand you over to sanhedrins and scourge you in their synagogues. [18]You will be brought before governors and kings for my sake, as evidence to them and to the gentiles. [19]But when you are handed over, do not worry about how to speak or what to say; what you are to say will be given to you when the time comes, [20]because it is not you who will be speaking; the Spirit of your Father will be speaking in you.
[21]'Brother will betray brother to death, and a father his child; children will come forward against their parents and have them put to death. [22]You will be universally hated on account of my name; but anyone who stands firm to the end will be saved. [23]If they persecute you in one town, take refuge in the next; and if they persecute you in that, take refuge in another. In truth I tell you, you will not have gone the round of the towns of Israel before the Son of man comes.
[24]'Disciple is not superior to teacher, nor slave to master. [25]It is enough for disciple to grow to be like teacher, and slave like master. If they have called the master of the house "Beelzebul", how much more the members of his household?

Open and fearless speech

[26]'So do not be afraid of them. Everything now covered up will be uncovered, and everything now hidden will be made clear. [27]What I say to you in the dark, tell in the daylight; what you hear in whispers, proclaim from the housetops.
[28]'Do not be afraid of those who kill the

10a Mk 3:14–19; Lk 6:13–16; the order and even some of the names vary in the different lists.

body but cannot kill the soul; fear him rather who can destroy both body and soul in hell. [29]Can you not buy two sparrows for a penny? And yet not one falls to the ground without your Father knowing. [30]Why, every hair on your head has been counted. [31]So there is no need to be afraid; you are worth more than many sparrows.

[32]'So if anyone declares himself for me in the presence of human beings, I will declare myself for him in the presence of my Father in heaven. [33]But the one who disowns me in the presence of human beings, I will disown in the presence of my Father in heaven.

Jesus, the cause of dissension

[34]'Do not suppose that I have come to bring peace to the earth: it is not peace I have come to bring, but a sword. [35]For I have come to set son against *father, daughter against mother, daughter-in-law against mother-in-law;* [36]*a person's enemies will be the members of his own household.*[b]

Renouncing self to follow Jesus

[37]'No one who prefers father or mother to me is worthy of me. No one who prefers son or daughter to me is worthy of me. [38]Anyone who does not take his cross and follow in my footsteps is not worthy of me. [39]Anyone who finds his life will lose it; anyone who loses his life for my sake will find it.

Conclusion of the Instruction

[40]'Anyone who welcomes you welcomes me; and anyone who welcomes me welcomes the one who sent me. [41]'Anyone who welcomes a prophet because he is a prophet will have a prophet's reward; and anyone who welcomes an upright person because he is upright will have the reward of an upright person. [42]'If anyone gives so much as a cup of cold water to one of these little ones because he is a disciple, then in truth I tell you, he will most certainly not go without his reward.'

IV: THE MYSTERY OF THE KINGDOM OF HEAVEN

A: NARRATIVE SECTION

11 When Jesus had finished instructing his twelve disciples he moved on from there to teach and preach in their towns.

The Baptist's question
Jesus commends him

[2]Now John had heard in prison what Christ was doing and he sent his disciples to ask him, [3]'Are you the one who is to come, or are we to expect someone else?' [4]Jesus answered, 'Go back and tell John what you hear and see; [5]the blind see again, and the lame walk, those suffering from virulent skin-diseases are cleansed, and the deaf hear, the dead are raised to life and the good news is proclaimed to the poor;[a] [6]and blessed is anyone who does not find me a cause of falling.'

[7]As the men were leaving, Jesus began to talk to the people about John, 'What did you go out into the desert to see? A reed swaying in the breeze? No? [8]Then what did you go out to see? A man wearing fine clothes? Look, those who wear fine clothes are to be found in palaces. [9]Then what did you go out for? To see a prophet? Yes, I tell you, and much more than a prophet: [10]he is the one of whom scripture says:

Look, I am going to send my messenger
in front of you
to prepare your way before you.[b]

[11]'In truth I tell you, of all the children born to women, there has never been anyone greater than John the Baptist; yet the least in the kingdom of Heaven is greater than he. [12]Since John the Baptist came, up to this present time, the kingdom of Heaven has been subjected to violence and the violent are taking it by storm. [13]Because it was towards John that all the prophecies of the prophets and of the Law were leading; [14]and he, if you will believe me, is the Elijah who was to return. [15]Anyone who has ears should listen!

10b Mi 7:6.
11a cf. Is 35:5; 61:1.
11b Ml 3:1.

Jesus condemns his contemporaries

[16] 'What comparison can I find for this generation? It is like children shouting to each other as they sit in the market place:

[17] We played the pipes for you,
 and you wouldn't dance;
 we sang dirges,
 and you wouldn't be mourners.

[18] 'For John came, neither eating nor drinking, and they say, "He is possessed." [19] The Son of man came, eating and drinking, and they say, "Look, a glutton and a drunkard, a friend of tax collectors and sinners." Yet wisdom is justified by her deeds.'

Lament over the lake-towns

[20] Then he began to reproach the towns in which most of his miracles had been worked, because they refused to repent.

[21] 'Alas for you, Chorazin! Alas for you, Bethsaida! For if the miracles done in you had been done in Tyre and Sidon, they would have repented long ago in sackcloth and ashes. [22] Still, I tell you that it will be more bearable for Tyre and Sidon on Judgement Day than for you. [23] And as for you, Capernaum, did you want to be *raised as high as heaven? You shall be flung down to hell.*[c] For if the miracles done in you had been done in Sodom, it would have been standing yet. [24] Still, I tell you that it will be more bearable for Sodom on Judgement Day than for you.'

The good news revealed to the simple
The Father and the Son

[25] At that time Jesus exclaimed, 'I bless you, Father, Lord of heaven and of earth, for hiding these things from the learned and the clever and revealing them to little children. [26] Yes, Father, for that is what it pleased you to do. [27] Everything has been entrusted to me by my Father; and no one knows the Son except the Father, just as no one knows the Father except the Son and those to whom the Son chooses to reveal him.

The gentle mastery of Christ

[28] 'Come to me, all you who labour and are overburdened, and I will give you rest. [29] Shoulder my yoke and learn from me, for I am gentle and humble in heart, *and you will find rest for your souls.*[d] [30] Yes, my yoke is easy and my burden light.'

Picking corn on the Sabbath

12 At that time Jesus went through the cornfields one Sabbath day. His disciples were hungry and began to pick ears of corn and eat them. [2] The Pharisees noticed it and said to him, 'Look, your disciples are doing something that is forbidden on the Sabbath.' [3] But he said to them, 'Have you not read what David did when he and his followers were hungry—[4] how he went into the house of God and they ate the loaves of the offering although neither he nor his followers were permitted to eat them, but only the priests? [5] Or again, have you not read in the Law that on the Sabbath day the Temple priests break the Sabbath without committing any fault? [6] Now here, I tell you, is something greater than the Temple. [7] And if you had understood the meaning of the words: *Mercy is what pleases me, not sacrifice,*[a] you would not have condemned the blameless. [8] For the Son of man is master of the Sabbath.'

Cure of the man with a withered hand

[9] He moved on from there and went to their synagogue; [10] now a man was there with a withered hand. They asked him, 'Is it permitted to cure somebody on the Sabbath day?' hoping for something to charge him with. [11] But he said to them, 'If any one of you here had only one sheep and it fell down a hole on the Sabbath day, would he not get hold of it and lift it out? [12] Now a man is far more important than a sheep, so it follows that it is permitted on the Sabbath day to do good.' [13] Then he said to the man, 'Stretch out your hand.' He stretched it out and his hand was restored, as sound as the other one. [14] At this the Pharisees went out and began to plot against him, discussing how to destroy him.

11c Is 14:13, 15.
11d Jr 6:16.
12a Ho 6:6.

Jesus the 'servant of Yahweh'

¹⁵ Jesus knew this and withdrew from the district. Many followed him and he cured them all ¹⁶ but warned them not to make him known. ¹⁷ This was to fulfil what was spoken by the prophet Isaiah:

¹⁸ *Look! My servant whom I have chosen,*
my beloved, in whom my soul delights,
I will send my Spirit upon him,
and he will present judgement
     to the nations;
¹⁹ *he will not brawl or cry out,*
his voice is not heard in the streets,
²⁰ *he will not break the crushed reed,*
or snuff the faltering wick,
²¹ *until he has made judgement victorious;*
in him the nations will put their hope. ᵇ

Jesus and Beelzebul

²² Then they brought to him a blind and dumb demoniac; and he cured him, so that the dumb man could speak and see. ²³ All the people were astounded and said, 'Can this be the son of David?' ²⁴ But when the Pharisees heard this they said, 'The man drives out devils only through Beelzebul, the chief of the devils.'

²⁵ Knowing what was in their minds he said to them, 'Every kingdom divided against itself is heading for ruin; and no town, no household divided against itself can last. ²⁶ Now if Satan drives out Satan, he is divided against himself; so how can his kingdom last? ²⁷ And if it is through Beelzebul that I drive devils out, through whom do your own experts drive them out? They shall be your judges, then. ²⁸ But if it is through the Spirit of God that I drive out devils, then be sure that the kingdom of God has caught you unawares.

²⁹ 'Or again, how can anyone make his way into a strong man's house and plunder his property unless he has first tied up the strong man? Only then can he plunder his house.

³⁰ 'Anyone who is not with me is against me, and anyone who does not gather in with me throws away. ³¹ And so I tell you, every human sin and blasphemy will be forgiven, but blasphemy against the Spirit will not be forgiven; ³² And anyone who says a word against the Son of man will be forgiven; but no one who speaks against the Holy Spirit will be forgiven either in this world or in the next.

Words betray the heart

³³ 'Make a tree sound and its fruit will be sound; make a tree rotten and its fruit will be rotten. For the tree can be told by its fruit. ³⁴ You brood of vipers, how can your speech be good when you are evil? For words flow out of what fills the heart. ³⁵ Good people draw good things from their store of goodness; bad people draw bad things from their store of badness. ³⁶ So I tell you this, that for every unfounded word people utter they will answer on Judgement Day, ³⁷ since it is by your words you will be justified, and by your words condemned.'

The sign of Jonah

³⁸ Then some of the scribes and Pharisees spoke up. 'Master,' they said, 'we should like to see a sign from you.' ³⁹ He replied, 'It is an evil and unfaithful generation that asks for a sign! The only sign it will be given is the sign of the prophet Jonah. ⁴⁰ For as Jonah re-*mained in the belly of the sea-monster for three days and three nights,* ᶜ so will the Son of man be in the heart of the earth for three days and three nights. ⁴¹ On Judgement Day the men of Nineveh will appear against this generation and they will be its condemnation, because when Jonah preached they repented; and look, there is something greater than Jonah here. ⁴² On Judgement Day the Queen of the South will appear against this generation and be its condemnation, because she came from the ends of the earth to hear the wisdom of Solomon; and look, there is something greater than Solomon here.

The return of the unclean spirit

⁴³ 'When an unclean spirit goes out of someone it wanders through waterless country looking for a place to rest, and cannot find one. ⁴⁴ Then it says, "I will return to the home I came from." But on arrival, finding it unoccupied, swept and tidied, ⁴⁵ it then goes off and collects seven other spirits more wicked than itself, and they go in and set up

12b Is 42:1–4.
12c Jon 2:1.

house there, and so that person ends up worse off than before. That is what will happen to this wicked generation.'

The true kinsfolk of Jesus

46He was still speaking to the crowds when suddenly his mother and his brothers*d* were standing outside and were anxious to have a word with him.[47]*e* 48But to the man who told him this Jesus replied, 'Who is my mother? Who are my brothers?' 49And stretching out his hand towards his disciples he said, 'Here are my mother and my brothers. 50Anyone who does the will of my Father in heaven is my brother and sister and mother.'

B: DISCOURSE OF PARABLES

Introduction

13That same day, Jesus left the house and sat by the lakeside, 2but such large crowds gathered round him that he got into a boat and sat there. The people all stood on the shore, 3and he told them many things in parables.

Parable of the sower

He said, 'Listen, a sower went out to sow. 4As he sowed, some seeds fell on the edge of the path, and the birds came and ate them up. 5Others fell on patches of rock where they found little soil and sprang up at once, because there was no depth of earth; 6but as soon as the sun came up they were scorched and, not having any roots, they withered away. 7Others fell among thorns, and the thorns grew up and choked them. 8Others fell on rich soil and produced their crop, some a hundredfold, some sixty, some thirty. 9Anyone who has ears should listen!'

Why Jesus speaks in parables

10Then the disciples went up to him and asked, 'Why do you talk to them in parables?' 11In answer, he said, 'Because to you is granted to understand the mysteries of the kingdom of Heaven, but to them it is not granted. 12Anyone who has will be given more and will have more than enough; but anyone who has not will be deprived even of what he has. 13The reason I talk to them in parables is that they look without seeing and listen without hearing or understanding. 14So in their case what was spoken by the prophet Isaiah is being fulfilled:

Listen and listen, but never understand!
Look and look, but never perceive!
15*This people's heart has grown coarse,*
  their ears dulled,
    they have shut their eyes tight
to avoid using their eyes to see,
    their ears to hear,
their heart to understand,
changing their ways
  and being healed by me.^a

16'But blessed are your eyes because they see, your ears because they hear! 17In truth I tell you, many prophets and upright people longed to see what you see, and never saw it; to hear what you hear, and never heard it.

The parable of the sower explained

18'So pay attention to the parable of the sower. 19When anyone hears the word of the kingdom without understanding, the Evil One comes and carries off what was sown in his heart: this is the seed sown on the edge of the path. 20The seed sown on patches of rock is someone who hears the word and welcomes it at once with joy. 21But such a person has no root deep down and does not last; should some trial come, or some persecution on account of the word, at once he falls away. 22The seed sown in thorns is someone who hears the word, but the worry of the world and the lure of riches choke the word and so it produces nothing. 23And the seed sown in rich soil is someone who hears the word and understands it; this is the one who yields a harvest and produces now a hundredfold, now sixty, now thirty.'

Parable of the darnel

24He put another parable before them, 'The kingdom of Heaven may be compared to a

---

12d   Not necessarily Mary's children. The Hebr. and Aram. word includes cousins and close relations.
12e   v. 47 ('Someone said to him: Your mother and brothers are standing outside and want to speak to you') is omitted by some important textual witnesses. It is probably a restatement of v. 46 modelled on Mk and Lk.
13a   Is 6:9–10.

man who sowed good seed in his field. [25]While everybody was asleep his enemy came, sowed darnel all among the wheat, and made off. [26]When the new wheat sprouted and ripened, then the darnel appeared as well. [27]The owner's labourers went to him and said, "Sir, was it not good seed that you sowed in your field? If so, where does the darnel come from?" [28]He said to them, "Some enemy has done this." And the labourers said, "Do you want us to go and weed it out?" [29]But he said, "No, because when you weed out the darnel you might pull up the wheat with it. [30]Let them both grow till the harvest; and at harvest time I shall say to the reapers: First collect the darnel and tie it in bundles to be burnt, then gather the wheat into my barn." '

Parable of the mustard seed

[31]He put another parable before them, 'The kingdom of Heaven is like a mustard seed which a man took and sowed in his field. [32]It is the smallest of all the seeds, but when it has grown it is the biggest of shrubs and becomes a tree, so that the birds of the air can come and shelter in its branches.'

Parable of the yeast

[33]He told them another parable, 'The kingdom of Heaven is like the yeast a woman took and mixed in with three measures of flour till it was leavened all through.'

The people are taught only in parables

[34]In all this Jesus spoke to the crowds in parables; indeed, he would never speak to them except in parables. [35]This was to fulfil what was spoken by the prophet:

I will speak to you in parables,
unfold what has been hidden
*   since the foundation of the world.*[b]

The parable of the darnel explained

[36]Then, leaving the crowds, he went to the house; and his disciples came to him and said, 'Explain to us the parable about the darnel in the field.' [37]He said in reply, 'The sower of the good seed is the Son of man. [38]The field is the world; the good seed is the subjects of the kingdom; the darnel, the subjects of the Evil One; [39]the enemy who sowed it, the devil; the harvest is the end of the world; the reapers are the angels. [40]Well then, just as the darnel is gathered up and burnt in the fire, so it will be at the end of time. [41]The Son of man will send his angels and they will gather out of his kingdom all causes of falling and all who do evil, [42]and throw them into the blazing furnace, where there will be weeping and grinding of teeth. [43]Then the upright will shine like the sun in the kingdom of their Father. Anyone who has ears should listen!

Parables of the treasure and of the pearl

[44]'The kingdom of Heaven is like treasure hidden in a field which someone has found; he hides it again, goes off in his joy, sells everything he owns and buys the field.

[45]'Again, the kingdom of Heaven is like a merchant looking for fine pearls; [46]when he finds one of great value he goes and sells everything he owns and buys it.

Parable of the dragnet

[47]'Again, the kingdom of Heaven is like a dragnet that is cast in the sea and brings in a haul of all kinds of fish. [48]When it is full, the fishermen bring it ashore; then, sitting down, they collect the good ones in baskets and throw away those that are no use. [49]This is how it will be at the end of time: the angels will appear and separate the wicked from the upright, [50]to throw them into the blazing furnace, where there will be weeping and grinding of teeth.

Conclusion

[51]'Have you understood all these?' They said, 'Yes.' [52]And he said to them, 'Well then, every scribe who becomes a disciple of the kingdom of Heaven is like a householder who brings out from his storeroom new things as well as old.'

13b Ps 78:2.

V: THE CHURCH
FIRST-FRUITS OF THE KINGDOM OF HEAVEN

A: NARRATIVE SECTION

A visit to Nazareth

⁵³When Jesus had finished these parables he left the district; ⁵⁴and, coming to his home town, he taught the people in their synagogue in such a way that they were astonished and said, 'Where did the man get this wisdom and these miraculous powers? ⁵⁵This is the carpenter's son, surely? Is not his mother the woman called Mary, and his brothers James and Joseph and Simon and Jude? ⁵⁶His sisters, too, are they not all here with us? So where did the man get it all?' ⁵⁷And they would not accept him. But Jesus said to them, 'A prophet is despised only in his own country and in his own house,' ⁵⁸and he did not work many miracles there because of their lack of faith.

Herod and Jesus

14 At that time Herod the tetrarch heard about the reputation of Jesus ²and said to his court, 'This is John the Baptist himself; he has risen from the dead, and that is why miraculous powers are at work in him.'

John the Baptist beheaded

³Now it was Herod who had arrested John, chained him up and put him in prison because of Herodias, his brother Philip's wife. ⁴For John had told him, 'It is against the Law for you to have her.' ⁵He had wanted to kill him but was afraid of the people, who regarded John as a prophet. ⁶Then, during the celebrations for Herod's birthday, the daughter of Herodias danced before the company and so delighted Herod ⁷that he promised on oath to give her anything she asked. ⁸Prompted by her mother she said, 'Give me John the Baptist's head, here, on a dish.' ⁹The king was distressed but, thinking of the oaths he had sworn and of his guests, he ordered it to be given her, ¹⁰and sent and had John beheaded in the prison. ¹¹The head was brought in on a dish and given to the girl, who took it to her mother. ¹²John's disciples came and took the body and buried it; then they went off to tell Jesus.

First miracle of the loaves[a]

¹³When Jesus received this news he withdrew by boat to a lonely place where they could be by themselves. But the crowds heard of this and, leaving the towns, went after him on foot. ¹⁴So as he stepped ashore he saw a large crowd; and he took pity on them and healed their sick.

¹⁵When evening came, the disciples went to him and said, 'This is a lonely place, and time has slipped by; so send the people away, and they can go to the villages to buy themselves some food.' ¹⁶Jesus replied, 'There is no need for them to go: give them something to eat yourselves.' ¹⁷But they answered, 'All we have with us is five loaves and two fish.' ¹⁸So he said, 'Bring them here to me.' ¹⁹He gave orders that the people were to sit down on the grass; then he took the five loaves and the two fish, raised his eyes to heaven and said the blessing. And breaking the loaves he handed them to his disciples, who gave them to the crowds. ²⁰They all ate as much as they wanted, and they collected the scraps left over, twelve baskets full. ²¹Now about five thousand men had eaten, to say nothing of women and children.

Jesus walks on the water and, with him, Peter

²²And at once he made the disciples get into the boat and go on ahead to the other side while he sent the crowds away. ²³After sending the crowds away he went up into the hills by himself to pray. When evening came, he was there alone, ²⁴while the boat, by now some furlongs from land, was hard pressed by rough waves, for there was a head-wind. ²⁵In the fourth watch of the night he came towards them, walking on the sea, ²⁶and when the disciples saw him walking on the sea they were terrified. 'It is a ghost,' they said, and cried out in fear. ²⁷But at once Jesus

---

14a This and 15:32–39 are probably varying accounts of the same incident. This one echoes 2 K 4:42.

called out to them, saying, 'Courage! It's me! Don't be afraid.' [28]It was Peter who answered. 'Lord,' he said, 'if it is you, tell me to come to you across the water.' [29]Jesus said, 'Come.' Then Peter got out of the boat and started walking towards Jesus across the water, [30]but then noticing the wind, he took fright and began to sink. 'Lord,' he cried, 'save me!' [31]Jesus put out his hand at once and held him. 'You have so little faith,' he said, 'why did you doubt?' [32]And as they got into the boat the wind dropped. [33]The men in the boat bowed down before him and said, 'Truly, you are the Son of God.'

Cures at Gennesaret

[34]Having made the crossing, they came to land at Gennesaret. [35]When the local people recognised him they spread the news through the whole neighbourhood and took all that were sick to him, [36]begging him just to let them touch the fringe of his cloak. And all those who touched it were saved.

The traditions of the Pharisees

15 Then Pharisees and scribes from Jerusalem came to Jesus and said, [2]'Why do your disciples break away from the tradition of the elders? They eat without washing their hands.' [3]He answered, 'And why do you break away from the commandment of God for the sake of your tradition? [4]For God said, *"Honour your father and your mother"* and *"Anyone who curses his father or mother will be put to death."*[a] [5]But you say, "If anyone says to his father or mother: Anything I might have used to help you is dedicated to God, [6]he is rid of his duty to father or mother." In this way you have made God's word ineffective by means of your tradition. [7]Hypocrites! How rightly Isaiah prophesied about you when he said:

[8]*This people honours me*
  only with lip-service,
while their hearts are far from me.
[9]*Their reverence of me is worthless;*
  the lessons they teach are nothing
  but human commandments.'[b]

On clean and unclean

[10]He called the people to him and said, 'Listen, and understand. [11]What goes into the mouth does not make anyone unclean; it is what comes out of the mouth that makes someone unclean.'

[12]Then the disciples came to him and said, 'Do you know that the Pharisees were shocked when they heard what you said?' [13]He replied, 'Any plant my heavenly Father has not planted will be pulled up by the roots. [14]Leave them alone. They are blind leaders of the blind; and if one blind person leads another, both will fall into a pit.'

[15]At this, Peter said to him, 'Explain the parable for us.' [16]Jesus replied, 'Even you—don't you yet understand? [17]Can't you see that whatever goes into the mouth passes through the stomach and is discharged into the sewer? [18]But whatever comes out of the mouth comes from the heart, and it is this that makes someone unclean. [19]For from the heart come evil intentions: murder, adultery, fornication, theft, perjury, slander. [20]These are the things that make a person unclean. But eating with unwashed hands does not make anyone unclean.'

The daughter of the Canaanite woman healed

[21]Jesus left that place and withdrew to the region of Tyre and Sidon. [22]And suddenly out came a Canaanite woman from that district and started shouting, 'Lord, Son of David, take pity on me. My daughter is tormented by a devil.' [23]But he said not a word in answer to her. And his disciples went and pleaded with him, saying, 'Give her what she wants, because she keeps shouting after us.' [24]He said in reply, 'I was sent only to the lost sheep of the House of Israel.' [25]But the woman had come up and was bowing low before him. 'Lord,' she said, 'help me.' [26]He replied, 'It is not fair to take the children's food and throw it to little dogs.' [27]She retorted, 'Ah yes, Lord; but even little dogs eat the scraps that fall from their masters' table.' [28]Then Jesus answered her, 'Woman, you have great faith. Let your desire be granted.' And from that moment her daughter was well again.

15a Ex 20:12 and 21:17.
15b Is 29:13.

Cures near the lake

[29]Jesus went on from there and reached the shores of the Lake of Galilee, and he went up onto the mountain. He took his seat, [30]and large crowds came to him bringing the lame, the crippled, the blind, the dumb and many others; these they put down at his feet, and he cured them. [31]The crowds were astonished to see the dumb speaking, the cripples whole again, the lame walking and the blind with their sight, and they praised the God of Israel.

Second miracle of the loaves

[32]But Jesus called his disciples to him and said, 'I feel sorry for all these people; they have been with me for three days now and have nothing to eat. I do not want to send them off hungry, or they might collapse on the way.' [33]The disciples said to him, 'Where in a deserted place could we get sufficient bread for such a large crowd to have enough to eat?' [34]Jesus said to them, 'How many loaves have you?' They said, 'Seven, and a few small fish.' [35]Then he instructed the crowd to sit down on the ground, [36]and he took the seven loaves and the fish, and after giving thanks he broke them and began handing them to the disciples, who gave them to the crowds. [37]They all ate as much as they wanted, and they collected what was left of the scraps, seven baskets full. [38]Now four thousand men had eaten, to say nothing of women and children. [39]And when he had sent the crowds away he got into the boat and went to the territory of Magadan.

The Pharisees ask for a sign from heaven

16 The Pharisees and Sadducees came, and to put him to the test they asked if he would show them a sign from heaven. [2]He replied, 'In the evening you say, "It will be fine; there's a red sky," [3]and in the morning, "Stormy weather today; the sky is red and overcast." You know how to read the face of the sky, but you cannot read the signs of the times. [4]It is an evil and unfaithful generation asking for a sign, and the only sign it will be given is the sign of Jonah.' And he left them and went off.

The yeast of the Pharisees and Sadducees

[5]The disciples, having crossed to the other side, had forgotten to take any food. [6]Jesus said to them, 'Keep your eyes open, and be on your guard against the yeast of the Pharisees and Sadducees.' [7]And they said among themselves, 'It is because we have not brought any bread.' [8]Jesus knew it, and he said, 'You have so little faith, why are you talking among yourselves about having no bread? [9]Do you still not understand? Do you not remember the five loaves for the five thousand and the number of baskets you collected? [10]Or the seven loaves for the four thousand and the number of baskets you collected? [11]How could you fail to understand that I was not talking about bread? What I said was: Beware of the yeast of the Pharisees and Sadducees.' [12]Then they understood that he was telling them to be on their guard, not against yeast for making bread, but against the teaching of the Pharisees and Sadducees.

Peter's profession of faith;
his pre-eminence

[13]When Jesus came to the region of Caesarea Philippi he put this question to his disciples, 'Who do people say the Son of man is?' [14]And they said, 'Some say John the Baptist, some Elijah, and others Jeremiah or one of the prophets.' [15]'But you,' he said, 'who do you say I am?' [16]Then Simon Peter spoke up and said, 'You are the Christ, the Son of the living God.' [17]Jesus replied, 'Simon son of Jonah, you are a blessed man! Because it was no human agency that revealed this to you but my Father in heaven. [18]So I now say to you: You are Peter[a] and on this rock I will build my community. And the gates of the underworld can never overpower it. [19]I will give you the keys of the kingdom of Heaven: whatever you bind on earth will be bound in heaven; whatever you loose on earth will be loosed in heaven.' [20]Then he gave the disciples strict orders not to say to anyone that he was the Christ.

First prophecy of the Passion

[21]From then onwards Jesus began to make it clear to his disciples that he was destined to

---

16a The name means 'rock'.

go to Jerusalem and suffer grievously at the hands of the elders and chief priests and scribes and to be put to death and to be raised up on the third day. [22]Then, taking him aside, Peter started to rebuke him. 'Heaven preserve you, Lord,' he said, 'this must not happen to you.' [23]But he turned and said to Peter, 'Get behind me, Satan! You are an obstacle in my path, because you are thinking not as God thinks but as human beings do.'

The condition of following Christ

[24]Then Jesus said to his disciples, 'If anyone wants to be a follower of mine, let him renounce himself and take up his cross and follow me. [25]Anyone who wants to save his life will lose it; but anyone who loses his life for my sake will find it. [26]What, then, will anyone gain by winning the whole world and forfeiting his life? Or what can anyone offer in exchange for his life?

[27]'For the Son of man is going to come in the glory of his Father with his angels, and then he will reward each one according to his behaviour. [28]In truth I tell you, there are some standing here who will not taste death before they see the Son of man coming with his kingdom.'

The transfiguration

17 Six days later, Jesus took with him Peter and James and his brother John and led them up a high mountain by themselves. [2]There in their presence he was transfigured: his face shone like the sun and his clothes became as dazzling as light. [3]And suddenly Moses and Elijah appeared to them; they were talking with him. [4]Then Peter spoke to Jesus. 'Lord,' he said, 'it is wonderful for us to be here; if you want me to, I will make three shelters here, one for you, one for Moses and one for Elijah.' [5]He was still speaking when suddenly a bright cloud[a] covered them with shadow, and suddenly from the cloud there came a voice which said, 'This is my Son, the Beloved; he enjoys my favour. Listen to him.'[b] [6]When they heard this, the disciples fell on their faces, overcome with fear. [7]But Jesus came up and touched them, saying, 'Stand up, do

not be afraid.' [8]And when they raised their eyes they saw no one but Jesus.

The question about Elijah

[9]As they came down from the mountain Jesus gave them this order, 'Tell no one about this vision until the Son of man has risen from the dead.' [10]And the disciples put this question to him, 'Why then do the scribes say that Elijah must come first?' [11]He replied, 'Elijah is indeed coming, and he will set everything right again; [12]however, I tell you that Elijah has come already and they did not recognise him but treated him as they pleased; and the Son of man will suffer similarly at their hands.' [13]Then the disciples understood that he was speaking of John the Baptist.

The epileptic demoniac

[14]As they were rejoining the crowd a man came up to him and went down on his knees before him. [15]'Lord,' he said, 'take pity on my son: he is demented and in a wretched state; he is always falling into fire and into water. [16]I took him to your disciples and they were unable to cure him.' [17]In reply, Jesus said, 'Faithless and perverse generation! How much longer must I be with you? How much longer must I put up with you? Bring him here to me.' [18]And when Jesus rebuked it the devil came out of the boy, who was cured from that moment.

[19]Then the disciples came privately to Jesus. 'Why were we unable to drive it out?' they asked. [20]He answered, 'Because you have so little faith. In truth I tell you, if your faith is the size of a mustard seed you will say to this mountain, "Move from here to there," and it will move; nothing will be impossible for you.'[21]c

Second prophecy of the Passion

[22]When they were together in Galilee, Jesus said to them, 'The Son of man is going to be delivered into the power of men; [23]they will put him to death, and on the third day he will be raised up again.' And a great sadness came over them.

17a cf. Ex 13:22.
17b Dt 18:15, 19; Is 42:1.
17c Some authorities add v. 21, 'As for this kind, it is cast out only by prayer and fasting.' cf. Mk 9:29.

The Temple tax paid by Jesus and Peter

[24]When they reached Capernaum, the collectors of the half-shekel[d] came to Peter and said, 'Does your master not pay the half-shekel?' [25]'Yes,' he replied, and went into the house. But before he could speak, Jesus said, 'Simon, what is your opinion? From whom do earthly kings take toll or tribute? From their sons or from foreigners?' [26]And when he replied, 'From foreigners,' Jesus said, 'Well then, the sons are exempt. [27]However, so that we shall not be the downfall of others, go to the lake and cast a hook; take the first fish that rises, open its mouth and there you will find a shekel; take it and give it to them for me and for yourself.'

B: THE DISCOURSE ON THE CHURCH

Who is the greatest?

18 At this time the disciples came to Jesus and said, 'Who is the greatest in the kingdom of Heaven?' [2]So he called a little child to him whom he set among them. [3]Then he said, 'In truth I tell you, unless you change and become like little children you will never enter the kingdom of Heaven. [4]And so, the one who makes himself as little as this little child is the greatest in the kingdom of Heaven.

On leading others astray

[5]'Anyone who welcomes one little child like this in my name welcomes me. [6]But anyone who is the downfall of one of these little ones who have faith in me would be better drowned in the depths of the sea with a great millstone round his neck. [7]Alas for the world that there should be such causes of falling! Causes of falling indeed there must be, but alas for anyone who provides them!

[8]'If your hand or your foot should be your downfall, cut it off and throw it away: it is better for you to enter into life crippled or lame, than to have two hands or two feet and be thrown into eternal fire. [9]And if your eye should be your downfall, tear it out and throw it away: it is better for you to enter into life

with one eye, than to have two eyes and be thrown into the hell of fire.

[10]'See that you never despise any of these little ones, for I tell you that their angels in heaven are continually in the presence of my Father in heaven.[11][a]

The lost sheep

[12]'Tell me. Suppose a man has a hundred sheep and one of them strays; will he not leave the ninety-nine on the hillside and go in search of the stray? [13]In truth I tell you, if he finds it, it gives him more joy than do the ninety-nine that did not stray at all. [14]Similarly, it is never the will of your Father in heaven that one of these little ones should be lost.

Brotherly correction

[15]'If your brother does something wrong, go and have it out with him alone, between your two selves. If he listens to you, you have won back your brother. [16]If he does not listen, take one or two others along with you: *whatever the misdemeanour, the evidence of two or three witnesses is required to sustain the charge.*[b] [17]But if he refuses to listen to these, report it to the community; and if he refuses to listen to the community, treat him like a gentile or a tax collector.

[18]'In truth I tell you, whatever you bind on earth will be bound in heaven; whatever you loose on earth will be loosed in heaven.

Prayer in common

[19]'In truth I tell you once again, if two of you on earth agree to ask anything at all, it will be granted to you by my Father in heaven. [20]For where two or three meet in my name, I am there among them.'

Forgiveness of injuries

[21]Then Peter went up to him and said, 'Lord, how often must I forgive my brother if he wrongs me? As often as seven times?' [22]Jesus answered, 'Not seven, I tell you, but seventy-seven times.

17d A yearly tax on all Jews for the upkeep of the Temple.
18a Some authorities add v. 11, 'For the Son of man has come to save what was lost.' cf. Lk 19:10.
18b Dt 19:15.

Parable of the unforgiving debtor

[23]'And so the kingdom of Heaven may be compared to a king who decided to settle his accounts with his servants. [24]When the reckoning began, they brought him a man who owed ten thousand talents; [25]he had no means of paying, so his master gave orders that he should be sold, together with his wife and children and all his possessions, to meet the debt. [26]At this, the servant threw himself down at his master's feet, with the words, "Be patient with me and I will pay the whole sum." [27]And the servant's master felt so sorry for him that he let him go and cancelled the debt. [28]Now as this servant went out, he happened to meet a fellow-servant who owed him one hundred denarii;[c] and he seized him by the throat and began to throttle him, saying, "Pay what you owe me." [29]His fellow-servant fell at his feet and appealed to him, saying, "Be patient with me and I will pay you." [30]But the other would not agree; on the contrary, he had him thrown into prison till he should pay the debt. [31]His fellow-servants were deeply distressed when they saw what had happened, and they went to their master and reported the whole affair to him. [32]Then the master sent for the man and said to him, "You wicked servant, I cancelled all that debt of yours when you appealed to me. [33]Were you not bound, then, to have pity on your fellow-servant just as I had pity on you?" [34]And in his anger the master handed him over to the torturers till he should pay all his debt. [35]And that is how my heavenly Father will deal with you unless you each forgive your brother from your heart.'

VI: THE APPROACHING ADVENT
OF THE KINGDOM OF HEAVEN

A: NARRATIVE SECTION

The question about divorce

19 Jesus had now finished what he wanted to say, and he left Galilee and came into the territory of Judaea on the far side of the Jordan. [2]Large crowds followed him and he healed them there.

[3]Some Pharisees approached him, and to put him to the test they said, 'Is it against the Law for a man to divorce his wife on any pretext whatever?' [4]He answered, 'Have you not read that the Creator from the beginning *made them male and female* [5]and that he said: *This is why a man leaves his father and mother and becomes attached to his wife, and the two become one flesh?*[a] [6]They are no longer two, therefore, but one flesh. So then, what God has united, human beings must not divide.'

[7]They said to him, 'Then why did Moses command that a writ of dismissal should be given in cases of divorce?'[b] [8]He said to them, 'It was because you were so hard-hearted, that Moses allowed you to divorce your wives, but it was not like this from the beginning.

[9]Now I say this to you: anyone who divorces his wife—I am not speaking of an illicit marriage—and marries another, is guilty of adultery.'

Continence

[10]The disciples said to him, 'If that is how things are between husband and wife, it is advisable not to marry.' [11]But he replied, 'It is not everyone who can accept what I have said, but only those to whom it is granted. [12]There are eunuchs born so from their mother's womb, there are eunuchs made so by human agency and there are eunuchs who have made themselves so for the sake of the kingdom of Heaven. Let anyone accept this who can.'

Jesus and the children

[13]Then people brought little children to him, for him to lay his hands on them and pray. The disciples scolded them, [14]but Jesus said, 'Let the little children alone, and do not stop them from coming to me; for it is to such as

18c About $200, contrasted with the other debt of over $60 million.
19a Gn 1:17; 2:24.
19b Dt 24:1. On Mt's exception in v. 9, *see* 5:32.

these that the kingdom of Heaven belongs.' ¹⁵Then he laid his hands on them and went on his way.

The rich young man

¹⁶And now a man came to him and asked, 'Master, what good deed must I do to possess eternal life?' ¹⁷Jesus said to him, 'Why do you ask me about what is good? There is one alone who is good. But if you wish to enter into life, keep the commandments.' ¹⁸He said, 'Which ones?' Jesus replied, 'These: *You shall not kill. You shall not commit adultery. You shall not steal. You shall not give false witness. ¹⁹Honour your father and your mother. You shall love your neighbour as yourself.*'ᶜ ²⁰The young man said to him, 'I have kept all these. What more do I need to do?' ²¹Jesus said, 'If you wish to be perfect, go and sell your possessions and give the money to the poor, and you will have treasure in heaven; then come, follow me.' ²²But when the young man heard these words he went away sad, for he was a man of great wealth.

The danger of riches

²³Then Jesus said to his disciples, 'In truth I tell you, it is hard for someone rich to enter the kingdom of Heaven. ²⁴Yes, I tell you again, it is easier for a camel to pass through the eye of a needle than for someone rich to enter the kingdom of Heaven.' ²⁵When the disciples heard this they were astonished. 'Who can be saved, then?' they said. ²⁶Jesus gazed at them. 'By human resources', he told them, 'this is impossible; for God everything is possible.'

The reward of renunciation

²⁷Then Peter answered and said, 'Look, we have left everything and followed you. What are we to have, then?' ²⁸Jesus said to them, 'In truth I tell you, when everything is made new again and the Son of man is seated on his throne of glory, you yourselves will sit on twelve thrones to judge the twelve tribes of Israel. ²⁹And everyone who has left houses, brothers, sisters, father, mother, children or land for the sake of my name will receive a hundred times as much, and also inherit eternal life.

³⁰'Many who are first will be last, and the last, first.'

Parable of the labourers in the vineyard

20'Now the kingdom of Heaven is like a landowner going out at daybreak to hire workers for his vineyard. ²He made an agreement with the workers for one denarius a day and sent them to his vineyard. ³Going out at about the third hour he saw others standing idle in the market place ⁴and said to them, "You go to my vineyard too and I will give you a fair wage." ⁵So they went. At about the sixth hour and again at about the ninth hour, he went out and did the same. ⁶Then at about the eleventh hour he went out and found more men standing around, and he said to them, "Why have you been standing here idle all day?" ⁷"Because no one has hired us," they answered. He said to them, "You go into my vineyard too." ⁸In the evening, the owner of the vineyard said to his bailiff, "Call the workers and pay them their wages, starting with the last arrivals and ending with the first." ⁹So those who were hired at about the eleventh hour came forward and received one denarius each. ¹⁰When the first came, they expected to get more, but they too received one denarius each. ¹¹They took it, but grumbled at the landowner saying, ¹²"The men who came last have done only one hour, and you have treated them the same as us, though we have done a heavy day's work in all the heat." ¹³He answered one of them and said, "My friend, I am not being unjust to you; did we not agree on one denarius? ¹⁴Take your earnings and go. I choose to pay the lastcomer as much as I pay you. ¹⁵Have I no right to do what I like with my own? Why should you be envious because I am generous?" ¹⁶Thus the last will be first, and the first, last.'

Third prophecy of the Passion

¹⁷Jesus was going up to Jerusalem, and on the road he took the Twelve aside by themselves and said to them, ¹⁸'Look, we are going up to Jerusalem, and the Son of man is about to be handed over to the chief priests and scribes. They will condemn him to death ¹⁹and will hand him over to the gentiles to be

---

19c Ex 20:12–16.

mocked and scourged and crucified; and on the third day he will be raised up again.'

The mother of Zebedee's sons makes her request

²⁰Then the mother of Zebedee's sons came with her sons to make a request of him, and bowed low; ²¹and he said to her, 'What is it you want?' She said to him, 'Promise that these two sons of mine may sit one at your right hand and the other at your left in your kingdom.' ²²Jesus answered, 'You do not know what you are asking. Can you drink the cup that I am going to drink?' They replied, 'We can.' ²³He said to them, 'Very well; you shall drink my cup, but as for seats at my right hand and my left, these are not mine to grant; they belong to those to whom they have been allotted by my Father.'

Leadership with service

²⁴When the other ten heard this they were indignant with the two brothers. ²⁵But Jesus called them to him and said, 'You know that among the gentiles the rulers lord it over them, and great men make their authority felt. ²⁶Among you this is not to happen. No; anyone who wants to become great among you must be your servant, ²⁷and anyone who wants to be first among you must be your slave, ²⁸just as the Son of man came not to be served but to serve, and to give his life as a ransom for many.'

The two blind men of Jericho

²⁹As they left Jericho a large crowd followed him. ³⁰And now there were two blind men sitting at the side of the road. When they heard that it was Jesus who was passing by, they shouted, 'Lord! Have pity on us, son of David.' ³¹And the crowd scolded them and told them to keep quiet, but they only shouted the louder, 'Lord! Have pity on us, son of David.' ³²Jesus stopped, called them over and said, 'What do you want me to do for you?' ³³They said to him, 'Lord, let us have our sight back.' ³⁴Jesus felt pity for them and touched their eyes, and at once their sight returned and they followed him.

The Messiah enters Jerusalem

21 When they were near Jerusalem and had come to Bethphage on the Mount of Olives, then Jesus sent two disciples, ²saying to them, 'Go to the village facing you, and you will at once find a tethered donkey and a colt with her. Untie them and bring them to me. ³If anyone says anything to you, you are to say, "The Master needs them and will send them back at once." ' ⁴This was to fulfil what was spoken by the prophet:

⁵*Say to the daughter of Zion:*
Look, your king is approaching,
humble and riding on a donkey
and on a colt,
    the foal of a beast of burden.ᵃ

⁶So the disciples went and did as Jesus had told them. ⁷They brought the donkey and the colt, then they laid their cloaks on their backs and he took his seat on them. ⁸Great crowds of people spread their cloaks on the road, while others were cutting branches from the trees and spreading them in his path. ⁹The crowds who went in front of him and those who followed were all shouting:

Hosanna to the son of David!
Blessed is he
    who is coming in the name of the Lord!ᵇ
Hosanna in the highest heavens!

¹⁰And when he entered Jerusalem, the whole city was in turmoil as people asked, 'Who is this?' ¹¹and the crowds answered, 'This is the prophet Jesus from Nazareth in Galilee.'

The expulsion of the dealers from the Temple

¹²Jesus then went into the Temple and drove out all those who were selling and buying there; he upset the tables of the money-changers and the seats of the dove-sellers. ¹³He said to them, 'According to scripture, *my house will be called a house of prayer*; but you are turning it into a *bandits' den.*ᶜ ¹⁴There were also blind and lame people who came to him in the Temple, and he cured them. ¹⁵At the sight of the wonderful things he did and of the children shouting, 'Hosanna to the son of David' in the Temple, the chief priests and

21a Zc 9:9.
21b Ps 118:26.
21c Is 56:7; Jr 7:11.

the scribes were indignant and said to him, [16]'Do you hear what they are saying?' Jesus answered, 'Yes. Have you never read this:

By the mouths of children, babes in arms,
you have made sure of praise?'[d]

[17]With that he left them and went out of the city to Bethany, where he spent the night.

The barren fig tree withers
Faith and prayer

[18]As he was returning to the city in the early morning, he felt hungry. [19]Seeing a fig tree by the road, he went up to it and found nothing on it but leaves. And he said to it, 'May you never bear fruit again,' and instantly the fig tree withered. [20]The disciples were amazed when they saw it and said, 'How is it that the fig tree withered instantly?' [21]Jesus answered, 'In truth I tell you, if you have faith and do not doubt at all, not only will you do what I have done to the fig tree, but even if you say to this mountain, "Be pulled up and thrown into the sea," it will be done. [22]And if you have faith, everything you ask for in prayer, you will receive.'

The authority of Jesus is questioned

[23]He had gone into the Temple and was teaching, when the chief priests and the elders of the people came to him and said, 'What authority have you for acting like this? And who gave you this authority?' [24]In reply Jesus said to them, 'And I will ask you a question, just one; if you tell me the answer to it, then I will tell you my authority for acting like this. [25]John's baptism: what was its origin, heavenly or human?' And they argued this way among themselves, 'If we say heavenly, he will retort to us, "Then why did you refuse to believe him?"; [26]but if we say human, we have the people to fear, for they all hold that John was a prophet.' [27]So their reply to Jesus was, 'We do not know.' And he retorted to them, 'Nor will I tell you my authority for acting like this.'

Parable of the two sons

[28]'What is your opinion? A man had two sons. He went and said to the first, "My boy, go and work in the vineyard today." [29]He answered, "I will not go," but afterwards thought better of it and went. [30]The man then went and said the same thing to the second who answered, "Certainly, sir," but did not go. [31]Which of the two did the father's will?' They said, 'The first.' Jesus said to them, 'In truth I tell you, tax collectors and prostitutes are making their way into the kingdom of God before you. [32]For John came to you, showing the way of uprightness, but you did not believe him, and yet the tax collectors and prostitutes did. Even after seeing that, you refused to think better of it and believe in him.

Parable of the wicked tenants

[33]'Listen to another parable. There was a man, a landowner, who planted a vineyard; he fenced it round, dug a winepress in it and built a tower; then he leased it to tenants and went abroad. [34]When vintage time drew near he sent his servants to the tenants to collect his produce. [35]But the tenants seized his servants, thrashed one, killed another and stoned a third. [36]Next he sent some more servants, this time a larger number, and they dealt with them in the same way. [37]Finally he sent his son to them thinking, "They will respect my son." [38]But when the tenants saw the son, they said to each other, "This is the heir. Come on, let us kill him and take over his inheritance." [39]So they seized him and threw him out of the vineyard and killed him. [40]Now when the owner of the vineyard comes, what will he do to those tenants?' [41]They answered, 'He will bring those wretches to a wretched end and lease the vineyard to other tenants who will deliver the produce to him at the proper time.' [42]Jesus said to them, 'Have you never read in the scriptures:

The stone which the builders rejected
has become the cornerstone;
this is the Lord's doing
and we marvel at it?[e]

[43]'I tell you, then, that the kingdom of God will be taken from you and given to a people who will produce its fruit.'[[44]f]

[45]When they heard his parables, the chief priests and the scribes realised he was speaking about them, [46]but though they

---

21d Ps 8:2.
21e Ps 118:22–23.
21f Some authorities add v. 44, taken from Lk 20:18.

would have liked to arrest him they were afraid of the crowds, who looked on him as a prophet.

Parable of the wedding feast

22 Jesus began to speak to them in parables once again, [2]'The kingdom of Heaven may be compared to a king who gave a feast for his son's wedding. [3]He sent his servants to call those who had been invited, but they would not come. [4]Next he sent some more servants with the words, "Tell those who have been invited: Look, my banquet is all prepared, my oxen and fattened cattle have been slaughtered, everything is ready. Come to the wedding." [5]But they were not interested: one went off to his farm, another to his business, [6]and the rest seized his servants, maltreated them and killed them. [7]The king was furious. He despatched his troops, destroyed those murderers and burnt their town. [8]Then he said to his servants, "The wedding is ready; but as those who were invited proved to be unworthy, [9]go to the main crossroads and invite everyone you can find to come to the wedding." [10]So these servants went out onto the roads and collected together everyone they could find, bad and good alike; and the wedding hall was filled with guests. [11]When the king came in to look at the guests he noticed one man who was not wearing a wedding garment, [12]and said to him, "How did you get in here, my friend, without a wedding garment?" And the man was silent. [13]Then the king said to the attendants, "Bind him hand and foot and throw him into the darkness outside, where there will be weeping and grinding of teeth." [14]For many are invited but not all are chosen.'

On tribute to Caesar

[15]Then the Pharisees went away to work out between them how to trap him in what he said. [16]And they sent their disciples to him, together with some Herodians, to say, 'Master, we know that you are an honest man and teach the way of God in all honesty, and that you are not afraid of anyone, because human rank means nothing to you. [17]Give us your opinion, then. Is it permissible to pay taxes to Caesar or not?' [18]But Jesus was aware of their malice and replied, 'You hypocrites! Why are you putting me to the test? [19]Show me the money you pay the tax with.' They handed him a denarius, [20]and he said, 'Whose portrait is this? Whose title?' [21]They replied, 'Caesar's.' Then he said to them, 'Very well, pay Caesar what belongs to Caesar—and God what belongs to God.' [22]When they heard this they were amazed; they left him alone and went away.

The resurrection of the dead

[23]That day some Sadducees—who deny that there is a resurrection—approached him and they put this question to him, [24]'Master, Moses said[a] that if a man dies childless, his brother is to marry the widow, his sister-in-law, to raise children for his brother. [25]Now we had a case involving seven brothers; the first married and then died without children, leaving his wife to his brother; [26]the same thing happened with the second and third and so on to the seventh, [27]and then last of all the woman herself died. [28]Now at the resurrection, whose wife among the seven will she be, since she had been married to them all?' [29]Jesus answered them, 'You are wrong, because you understand neither the scriptures nor the power of God. [30]For at the resurrection men and women do not marry; no, they are like the angels in heaven. [31]And as for the resurrection of the dead, have you never read what God himself said to you: [32]I am the God of Abraham, the God of Isaac and the God of Jacob?[b] He is God, not of the dead, but of the living.' [33]And his teaching made a deep impression on the people who heard it.

The greatest commandment of all

[34]But when the Pharisees heard that he had silenced the Sadducees they got together [35]and, to put him to the test, one of them put a further question, [36]'Master, which is the greatest commandment of the Law?' [37]Jesus said to him, 'You must love the Lord your God with all your heart, with all your soul, and with all your mind. [38]This is the greatest and the first commandment. [39]The second resembles it: You must love your neighbour as yourself.[c] [40]On these two commandments hang the whole Law, and the Prophets too.'

22a Dt 25:5–6.
22b Ex 3:6.
22c Dt 6:5 combined with Lv 19:18.

Christ not only son but also Lord of David

[41]While the Pharisees were gathered round, Jesus put to them this question, [42]'What is your opinion about the Christ? Whose son is he?' They told him, 'David's.' [43]He said to them, 'Then how is it that David, moved by the Spirit, calls him Lord, where he says:

[44]*The Lord declared to my Lord,*
take your seat at my right hand,
till I have made your enemies
your footstool?[d]

[45]'If David calls him Lord, how then can he be his son?' [46]No one could think of anything to say in reply, and from that day no one dared to ask him any further questions.

The scribes and Pharisees:
their hypocrisy and vanity

23 Then addressing the crowds and his disciples Jesus said, [2]'The scribes and the Pharisees occupy the chair of Moses. [3]You must therefore do and observe what they tell you; but do not be guided by what they do, since they do not practise what they preach. [4]They tie up heavy burdens and lay them on people's shoulders, but will they lift a finger to move them? Not they! [5]Everything they do is done to attract attention, like wearing broader headbands and longer tassels, [6]like wanting to take the place of honour at banquets and the front seats in the synagogues, [7]being greeted respectfully in the market squares and having people call them Rabbi.

[8]'You, however, must not allow yourselves to be called Rabbi, since you have only one Master, and you are all brothers. [9]You must call no one on earth your father, since you have only one Father, and he is in heaven. [10]Nor must you allow yourselves to be called teachers, for you have only one Teacher, the Christ. [11]The greatest among you must be your servant. [12]Anyone who raises himself up will be humbled, and anyone who humbles himself will be raised up.

The sevenfold indictment
of the scribes and Pharisees

[13]'Alas for you, scribes and Pharisees, you hypocrites! You shut up the kingdom of Heaven in people's faces, neither going in yourselves nor allowing others to go in who want to.[14]a

[15]'Alas for you, scribes and Pharisees, you hypocrites! You travel over sea and land to make a single proselyte, and anyone who becomes one you make twice as fit for hell as you are.

[16]'Alas for you, blind guides! You say, "If anyone swears by the Temple, it has no force; but anyone who swears by the gold of the Temple is bound." [17]Fools and blind! For which is of greater value, the gold or the Temple that makes the gold sacred? [18]Again, "If anyone swears by the altar it has no force; but anyone who swears by the offering on the altar, is bound." [19]You blind men! For which is of greater worth, the offering or the altar that makes the offering sacred? [20]Therefore, someone who swears by the altar is swearing by that and by everything on it. [21]And someone who swears by the Temple is swearing by that and by the One who dwells in it. [22]And someone who swears by heaven is swearing by the throne of God and by the One who is seated there.

[23]'Alas for you, scribes and Pharisees, you hypocrites! You pay your tithe of mint and dill and cummin and have neglected the weightier matters of the Law—justice, mercy, good faith! These you should have practised, those not neglected. [24]You blind guides, straining out gnats and swallowing camels!

[25]'Alas for you, scribes and Pharisees, you hypocrites! You clean the outside of cup and dish and leave the inside full of extortion and intemperance. [26]Blind Pharisee! Clean the inside of cup and dish first so that it and the outside are both clean.

[27]'Alas for you, scribes and Pharisees, you hypocrites! You are like whitewashed tombs that look handsome on the outside, but inside are full of the bones of the dead and every kind of corruption. [28]In just the same way, from the outside you look upright, but inside you are full of hypocrisy and lawlessness.

[29]'Alas for you, scribes and Pharisees, you hypocrites! You build the sepulchres of the prophets and decorate the tombs of the upright, [30]saying, "We would never have joined in shedding the blood of the prophets, had we lived in our ancestors' day." [31]So!

22d Ps 110:1.
23a Some authorities add v. 14, taken from Mk 12:40.

Your own evidence tells against you! You are the children of those who murdered the prophets! ³²Very well then, finish off the work that your ancestors began.

Their crimes
and approaching punishment

³³'You serpents, brood of vipers, how can you escape being condemned to hell? ³⁴This is why—look—I am sending you prophets and wise men and scribes; some you will slaughter and crucify, some you will scourge in your synagogues and hunt from town to town; ³⁵and so you will draw down on yourselves the blood of every upright person that has been shed on earth, from the blood of Abel the holy to the blood of Zechariah son of Barachiah whom you murdered between the sanctuary and the altar. ³⁶In truth I tell you, it will all recoil on this generation.

Jerusalem admonished

³⁷'Jerusalem, Jerusalem, you that kill the prophets and stone those who are sent to you! How often have I longed to gather your children together, as a hen gathers her chicks under her wings, and you refused! ³⁸Look! Your house will be deserted, ³⁹for, I promise, you shall not see me any more until you are saying:

Blessed is he
who is coming in the name of the Lord!'ᵇ

B: THE END
AND THE SECOND COMINGᵃ

Introduction

24 Jesus left the Temple, and as he was going away his disciples came up to draw his attention to the Temple buildings. ²He said to them in reply, 'You see all these? In truth I tell you, not a single stone here will be left on another: everything will be pulled down.' ³And while he was sitting on the Mount of Olives the disciples came and asked him when they were by themselves, 'Tell us, when is this going to happen, and what sign will there be of your coming and of the end of the world?'

The beginning of sorrows

⁴And Jesus answered them, 'Take care that no one deceives you, ⁵because many will come using my name and saying, "I am the Christ," and they will deceive many. ⁶You will hear of wars and rumours of wars; see that you are not alarmed, for this is something that must happen, but the end will not be yet. ⁷For nation will fight against nation, and kingdom against kingdom. There will be famines and earthquakes in various places. ⁸All this is only the beginning of the birthpangs.

⁹'Then you will be handed over to be tortured and put to death; and you will be hated by all nations on account of my name. ¹⁰And then many will fall away; people will betray one another and hate one another. ¹¹Many false prophets will arise; they will deceive many, ¹²and with the increase of lawlessness, love in most people will grow cold; ¹³but anyone who stands firm to the end will be saved.

¹⁴'This good news of the kingdom will be proclaimed to the whole world as evidence to the nations. And then the end will come.

The great tribulation of Jerusalem

¹⁵'So when you see *the appalling abomination,ᵇ* of which the prophet Daniel spoke, set up in the holy place (let the reader understand), ¹⁶then those in Judaea must escape to the mountains; ¹⁷if anyone is on the housetop, he must not come down to collect his belongings from the house; ¹⁸if anyone is in the fields, he must not turn back to fetch his cloak. ¹⁹Alas for those with child, or with babies at the breast, when those days come! ²⁰Pray that you will not have to make your escape in winter or on a Sabbath. ²¹For then there will be *great distress, unparalleled sinceᶜ* the world began, and such as will never be again. ²²And if that time had not been shortened, no human being would have survived; but shor-

---

23b Ps 118:26.
24a In this discourse on the future of Christ's community, Mt links the destruction of Jerusalem in AD 70 to the final coming of Christ.
24b Dn 9:27; 11:31; 12:11.
24c Dn 12:1.

tened that time shall be, for the sake of those who are chosen.

²³'If anyone says to you then, "Look, here is the Christ," or "Over here," do not believe it; ²⁴for false Christs and false prophets will arise and provide great signs and portents, enough to deceive even the elect, if that were possible. ²⁵Look! I have given you warning.

The coming of the Son of man

²⁶'If, then, they say to you, "Look, he is in the desert," do not go there; "Look, he is in some hiding place," do not believe it; ²⁷because the coming of the Son of man will be like lightning striking in the east and flashing far into the west. ²⁸Wherever the corpse is, that is where the vultures will gather.

The universal significance of this coming

²⁹'Immediately after the distress of those days the sun will be darkened,ᵈ the moon will not give its light, the stars will fall from the sky and the powers of the heavens will be shaken. ³⁰And then the sign of the Son of man will appear in heaven; then, too, all the peoples of the earth will beat their breasts; and they will see the *Son of man coming on the clouds of heaven* with power and great glory.ᵉ ³¹And he will send his angels with a loud trumpet to gather his elect from the four winds, from one end of heaven to the other.

The time of this coming

³²'Take the fig tree as a parable: as soon as its twigs grow supple and its leaves come out, you know that summer is near. ³³So with you when you see all these things: know that he is near, right at the gates. ³⁴In truth I tell you, before this generation has passed away, all these things will have taken place. ³⁵Sky and earth will pass away, but my words will never pass away. ³⁶But as for that day and hour, nobody knows it, neither the angels of heaven, nor the Son, no one but the Father alone.

Be on the alert

³⁷'As it was in Noah's day, so will it be when the Son of man comes. ³⁸For in those days

before the Flood people were eating, drinking, taking wives, taking husbands, right up to the day Noah went into the ark,ᶠ ³⁹and they suspected nothing till the Flood came and swept them all away. This is what it will be like when the Son of man comes. ⁴⁰Then of two men in the fields, one is taken, one left; ⁴¹of two women grinding at the mill, one is taken, one left.

⁴²'So stay awake, because you do not know the day when your master is coming. ⁴³You may be quite sure of this, that if the house-holder had known at what time of the night the burglar would come, he would have stayed awake and would not have allowed anyone to break through the wall of his house. ⁴⁴Therefore, you too must stand ready because the Son of man is coming at an hour you do not expect.

Parable of the conscientious steward

⁴⁵'Who, then, is the wise and trustworthy servant whom the master placed over his household to give them their food at the proper time? ⁴⁶Blessed that servant if his master's arrival finds him doing exactly that. ⁴⁷In truth I tell you, he will put him in charge of everything he owns. ⁴⁸But if the servant is dishonest and says to himself, "My master is taking his time," ⁴⁹and sets about beating his fellow-servants and eating and drinking with drunkards, ⁵⁰his master will come on a day he does not expect and at an hour he does not know. ⁵¹The master will cut him off and send him to the same fate as the hypocrites, where there will be weeping and grinding of teeth.'

Parable of the ten wedding attendants

25 'Then the kingdom of Heaven will be like this: Ten wedding attendants took their lamps and went to meet the bridegroom. ²Five of them were foolish and five were sensible: ³the foolish ones, though they took their lamps, took no oil with them, ⁴whereas the sensible ones took flasks of oil as well as their lamps. ⁵The bridegroom was late, and they all grew drowsy and fell asleep. ⁶But at midnight there was a cry, "Look! The bridegroom! Go out and meet him." ⁷Then all those wedding attendants woke up and trimmed their lamps, ⁸and the foolish ones

24d Am 8:9.
24e Dn 7:13–14.
24f Gn 7:11–23.

said to the sensible ones, "Give us some of your oil: our lamps are going out." ⁹But they replied, "There may not be enough for us and for you; you had better go to those who sell it and buy some for yourselves." ¹⁰They had gone off to buy it when the bridegroom arrived. Those who were ready went in with him to the wedding hall and the door was closed. ¹¹The other attendants arrived later. "Lord, Lord," they said, "open the door for us." ¹²But he replied, "In truth I tell you, I do not know you." ¹³So stay awake, because you do not know either the day or the hour.

Parable of the talents

¹⁴"It is like a man about to go abroad who summoned his servants and entrusted his property to them. ¹⁵To one he gave five talents, to another two, to a third one, each in proportion to his ability. Then he set out on his journey. ¹⁶The man who had received the five talents promptly went and traded with them and made five more. ¹⁷The man who had received two made two more in the same way. ¹⁸But the man who had received one went off and dug a hole in the ground and hid his master's money. ¹⁹Now a long time afterwards, the master of those servants came back and went through his accounts with them. ²⁰The man who had received the five talents came forward bringing five more. "Sir," he said, "you entrusted me with five talents; here are five more that I have made." ²¹His master said to him, "Well done, good and trustworthy servant; you have shown you are trustworthy in small things; I will trust you with greater; come and join in your master's happiness." ²²Next the man with the two talents came forward. "Sir," he said, "you entrusted me with two talents; here are two more that I have made." ²³His master said to him, "Well done, good and trustworthy servant; you have shown you are trustworthy in small things; I will trust you with greater; come and join in your master's happiness." ²⁴Last came forward the man who had the single talent. "Sir," said he, "I had heard you were a hard man, reaping where you had not sown and gathering where you had not scattered; ²⁵so I was afraid, and I went off and hid your talent in the ground. Here it is; it was yours, you have it back." ²⁶But his master answered him, "You wicked and lazy servant! So you knew that I reap where I have not sown and gather where I have

not scattered? ²⁷Well then, you should have deposited my money with the bankers, and on my return I would have got my money back with interest. ²⁸So now, take the talent from him and give it to the man who has the ten talents. ²⁹For to everyone who has will be given more, and he will have more than enough; but anyone who has not, will be deprived even of what he has. ³⁰As for this good-for-nothing servant, throw him into the darkness outside, where there will be weeping and grinding of teeth."

The Last Judgement

³¹"When the Son of man comes in his glory, escorted by all the angels, then he will take his seat on his throne of glory. ³²All nations will be assembled before him and he will separate people one from another as the shepherd separates sheep from goats. ³³He will place the sheep on his right hand and the goats on his left. ³⁴Then the King will say to those on his right hand, "Come, you whom my Father has blessed, take as your heritage the kingdom prepared for you since the foundation of the world. ³⁵For I was hungry and you gave me food, I was thirsty and you gave me drink, I was a stranger and you made me welcome, ³⁶lacking clothes and you clothed me, sick and you visited me, in prison and you came to see me." ³⁷Then the upright will say to him in reply, "Lord, when did we see you hungry and feed you, or thirsty and give you drink? ³⁸When did we see you a stranger and make you welcome, lacking clothes and clothe you? ³⁹When did we find you sick or in prison and go to see you?" ⁴⁰And the King will answer, "In truth I tell you, in so far as you did this to one of the least of these brothers of mine, you did it to me." ⁴¹Then he will say to those on his left hand, "Go away from me, with your curse upon you, to the eternal fire prepared for the devil and his angels. ⁴²For I was hungry and you never gave me food, I was thirsty and you never gave me anything to drink, ⁴³I was a stranger and you never made me welcome, lacking clothes and you never clothed me, sick and in prison and you never visited me." ⁴⁴Then it will be their turn to ask, "Lord, when did we see you hungry or thirsty, a stranger or lacking clothes, sick or in prison, and did not come to your help?" ⁴⁵Then he will answer, "In truth I tell you, in so far as you neglected

to do this to one of the least of these, you neglected to do it to me.'" [46]And they will go away to eternal punishment, and the upright to eternal life.'

VII: PASSION AND RESURRECTION

The conspiracy against Jesus

26 Jesus had now finished all he wanted to say, and he told his disciples, [2]'It will be Passover, as you know, in two days' time, and the Son of man will be handed over to be crucified.'

[3]Then the chief priests and the elders of the people assembled in the palace of the high priest, whose name was Caiaphas, [4]and made plans to arrest Jesus by some trick and have him put to death. [5]They said, however, 'It must not be during the festivities; there must be no disturbance among the people.'

The anointing at Bethany

[6]Jesus was at Bethany in the house of Simon, a man who had suffered from a virulent skin-disease, when [7]a woman came to him with an alabaster jar of very expensive ointment, and poured it on his head as he was at table. [8]When they saw this, the disciples said indignantly, 'Why this waste? [9]This could have been sold for a high price and the money given the poor.' [10]But Jesus noticed this and said, 'Why are you upsetting the woman? What she has done for me is indeed a good work! [11]You have the poor with you always, but you will not always have me. [12]When she poured this ointment on my body, she did it to prepare me for burial. [13]In truth I tell you, wherever in all the world this gospel is proclaimed, what she has done will be told as well, in remembrance of her.'

Judas betrays Jesus

[14]Then one of the Twelve, the man called Judas Iscariot, went to the chief priests [15]and said, 'What are you prepared to give me if I hand him over to you?' They paid him thirty silver pieces, [16]and from then onwards he began to look for an opportunity to betray him.

Preparations for the Passover supper

[17]Now on the first day of Unleavened Bread the disciples came to Jesus to say, 'Where do you want us to make the preparations for you to eat the Passover?' [18]He said, 'Go to a certain man in the city and say to him, "The Master says: My time is near. It is at your house that I am keeping Passover with my disciples." ' [19]The disciples did what Jesus told them and prepared the Passover.

The treachery of Judas foretold

[20]When evening came he was at table with the Twelve. [21]And while they were eating he said, 'In truth I tell you, one of you is about to betray me.' [22]They were greatly distressed and started asking him in turn, 'Not me, Lord, surely?' [23]He answered, 'Someone who has dipped his hand into the dish with me will betray me. [24]The Son of man is going to his fate, as the scriptures say he will, but alas for that man by whom the Son of man is betrayed! Better for that man if he had never been born!' [25]Judas, who was to betray him, asked in his turn, 'Not me, Rabbi, surely?' Jesus answered, 'It is you who say it.'

The institution of the Eucharist

[26]Now as they were eating, Jesus took bread, and when he had said the blessing he broke it and gave it to the disciples. 'Take it and eat,' he said, 'this is my body.' [27]Then he took a cup, and when he had given thanks he handed it to them saying, 'Drink from this, all of you, [28]for this is my blood, the blood of the covenant, poured out for many for the forgiveness of sins. [29]From now on, I tell you, I shall never again drink wine until the day I drink the new wine with you in the kingdom of my Father.'

Peter's denial foretold

[30]After the psalms had been sung they left for the Mount of Olives. [31]Then Jesus said to them, 'You will all fall away from me tonight, for the scripture says: *I shall strike the shepherd*

and the sheep of the flock will be scattered,[a]
[32]but after my resurrection I shall go ahead of you to Galilee.' [33]At this, Peter said to him, 'Even if all fall away from you, I will never fall away.' [34]Jesus answered him, 'In truth I tell you, this very night, before the cock crows, you will have disowned me three times.' [35]Peter said to him, 'Even if I have to die with you, I will never disown you.' And all the disciples said the same.

Gethsemane

[36]Then Jesus came with them to a plot of land called Gethsemane; and he said to his disciples, 'Stay here while I go over there to pray.' [37]He took Peter and the two sons of Zebedee with him. And he began to feel sadness and anguish. [38]Then he said to them, 'My soul is sorrowful to the point of death. Wait here and stay awake with me.' [39]And going on a little further he fell on his face and prayed. 'My Father,' he said, 'if it is possible, let this cup pass me by. Nevertheless, let it be as you, not I, would have it.' [40]He came back to the disciples and found them sleeping, and he said to Peter, 'So you had not the strength to stay awake with me for one hour? [41]Stay awake, and pray not to be put to the test. The spirit is willing enough, but human nature is weak.' [42]Again, a second time, he went away and prayed: 'My Father,' he said, 'if this cup cannot pass by, but I must drink it, your will be done!'[b] [43]And he came back again and found them sleeping, their eyes were so heavy. [44]Leaving them there, he went away again and prayed for the third time, repeating the same words. [45]Then he came back to the disciples and said to them, 'You can sleep on now and have your rest. Look, the hour has come when the Son of man is to be betrayed into the hands of sinners. [46]Get up! Let us go! Look, my betrayer is not far away.'

The arrest

[47]And suddenly while he was still speaking, Judas, one of the Twelve, appeared, and with him a large number of men armed with swords and clubs, sent by the chief priests and elders of the people. [48]Now the traitor had arranged a sign with them saying, 'The one I kiss, he is the man. Arrest him.' [49]So he went up to Jesus at once and said, 'Greetings, Rabbi,' and kissed him. [50]Jesus said to him, 'My friend, do what you are here for.' Then they came forward, seized Jesus and arrested him. [51]And suddenly, one of the followers of Jesus grasped his sword and drew it; he struck the high priest's servant and cut off his ear. [52]Jesus then said, 'Put your sword back, for all who draw the sword will die by the sword. [53]Or do you think that I cannot appeal to my Father, who would promptly send more than twelve legions of angels to my defence? [54]But then, how would the scriptures be fulfilled that say this is the way it must be?' [55]It was at this time that Jesus said to the crowds, 'Am I a bandit, that you had to set out to capture me with swords and clubs? I sat teaching in the Temple day after day and you never laid a hand on me.' [56]Now all this happened to fulfil the prophecies in scripture. Then all the disciples deserted him and ran away.

Jesus before the Sanhedrin[c]

[57]The men who had arrested Jesus led him off to the house of Caiaphas the high priest, where the scribes and the elders were assembled. [58]Peter followed him at a distance right to the high priest's palace, and he went in and sat down with the attendants to see what the end would be. [59]The chief priests and the whole Sanhedrin were looking for evidence against Jesus, however false, on which they might have him executed. [60]But they could not find any, though several lying witnesses came forward. Eventually two came forward [61]and made a statement, 'This man said, "I have power to destroy the Temple of God and in three days build it up." ' [62]The high priest then rose and said to him, 'Have you no answer to that? What is this evidence these men are bringing against you?' [63]But Jesus was silent. And the high priest said to him, 'I put you on oath by the living God to tell us if you are the Christ, the Son of God.' [64]Jesus answered him, 'It is you who say it. But, I tell you that from this time onward you will see the *Son of man seated at the right hand of*

26a Zc 13:7.
26b =6:10.
26c The gospels differ: Lk and Jn mention an interrogation at night and a Sanhedrin session in the morning. Mt and Mk place this morning session in the night.

the Power and *coming on the clouds of heaven.'*[d] 65Then the high priest tore his clothes and said, 'He has blasphemed. What need of witnesses have we now? There! You have just heard the blasphemy. 66What is your opinion?' They answered, 'He deserves to die.'

67Then they spat in his face and hit him with their fists; others said as they struck him, 68'Prophesy to us, Christ! Who hit you then?'

Peter's denials

69Meanwhile Peter was sitting outside in the courtyard, and a servant-girl came up to him saying, 'You, too, were with Jesus the Galilean.' 70But he denied it in front of them all. 'I do not know what you are talking about,' he said. 71When he went out to the gateway another servant-girl saw him and said to the people there, 'This man was with Jesus the Nazarene.' 72And again, with an oath, he denied it, 'I do not know the man.' 73A little later the bystanders came up and said to Peter, 'You are certainly one of them too! Why, your accent*[e] gives you away.' 74Then he started cursing and swearing, 'I do not know the man.' And at once the cock crowed, 75and Peter remembered what Jesus had said, 'Before the cock crows you will have disowned me three times.' And he went outside and wept bitterly.

Jesus is taken before Pilate

27When morning came, all the chief priests and the elders of the people met in council to bring about the death of Jesus. 2They had him bound and led him away to hand him over to Pilate, the governor.

The death of Judas

3When he found that Jesus had been condemned, then Judas, his betrayer, was filled with remorse and took the thirty silver pieces back to the chief priests and elders 4saying, 'I have sinned. I have betrayed innocent blood.' They replied, 'What is that to us? That is your concern.' 5And flinging down the silver pieces in the sanctuary he made off, and went and hanged himself. 6The chief priests picked up the silver pieces and said, 'It is against the Law to put this into the treasury; it is blood-money.' 7So they discussed the matter and with it bought the potter's field as a graveyard for foreigners, 8and this is why the field is still called the Field of Blood. 9The word spoken through the prophet Jeremiah was then fulfilled: *And they took the thirty silver pieces, the sum at which the precious One was priced by the children of Israel, 10and they gave them for the potter's field, just as the Lord directed me.*[a]

Jesus before Pilate

11Jesus, then, was brought before the governor, and the governor put to him this question, 'Are you the king of the Jews?' Jesus replied, 'It is you who say it.' 12But when he was accused by the chief priests and the elders he refused to answer at all. 13Pilate then said to him, 'Do you not hear how many charges they have made against you?' 14But to the governor's amazement, he offered not a word in answer to any of the charges.

15At festival time it was the governor's practice to release a prisoner for the people, anyone they chose. 16Now there was then a notorious prisoner whose name was Barabbas. 17So when the crowd gathered, Pilate said to them, 'Which do you want me to release for you: Barabbas, or Jesus who is called Christ?' 18For Pilate knew it was out of jealousy that they had handed him over.

19Now as he was seated in the chair of judgement, his wife sent him a message, 'Have nothing to do with that upright man; I have been extremely upset today by a dream that I had about him.'

20The chief priests and the elders, however, had persuaded the crowd to demand the release of Barabbas and the execution of Jesus. 21So when the governor spoke and asked them, 'Which of the two do you want me to release for you?' they said, 'Barabbas.' 22Pilate said to them, 'But in that case, what am I to do with Jesus who is called Christ?' They all said, 'Let him be crucified!' 23He asked, 'But what harm has he done?' But they shouted all the louder, 'Let him be crucified!' 24Then Pilate saw that he was

---

26d Ps 110:1 and Dn 7:13.
26e Presumably Galileans had a local accent.
27a Zc 11:12–13.

making no impression, that in fact a riot was imminent. So he took some water, washed his hands in front of the crowd and said, 'I am innocent of this man's blood. It is your concern.' ²⁵And the people, every one of them, shouted back, 'Let his blood be on us and on our children!' ²⁶Then he released Barabbas for them. After having Jesus scourged he handed him over to be crucified.

Jesus is crowned with thorns

²⁷Then the governor's soldiers took Jesus with them into the Praetorium and collected the whole cohort round him. ²⁸And they stripped him and put a scarlet cloak round him, ²⁹and having twisted some thorns into a crown they put this on his head and placed a reed in his right hand. To make fun of him they knelt to him saying, 'Hail, king of the Jews!' ³⁰And they spat on him and took the reed and struck him on the head with it. ³¹And when they had finished making fun of him, they took off the cloak and dressed him in his own clothes and led him away to crucifixion.

The crucifixion

³²On their way out, they came across a man from Cyrene, called Simon, and enlisted him to carry his cross. ³³When they had reached a place called Golgotha, that is, the place of the skull, ³⁴they gave him wine to drink mixed with gall,ᵇ which he tasted but refused to drink. ³⁵When they had finished crucifying him they shared out his clothing by casting lots, ³⁶and then sat down and stayed there keeping guard over him.

³⁷Above his head was placed the charge against him; it read: 'This is Jesus, the King of the Jews.' ³⁸Then two bandits were crucified with him, one on the right and one on the left.

The crucified Jesus is mocked

³⁹The passers-by jeered at him; they shook their heads ⁴⁰and said, 'So you would destroy the Temple and in three days rebuild it! Then save yourself if you are God's son and come down from the cross!' ⁴¹The chief priests with the scribes and elders mocked him in the same way, ⁴²with the words, 'He saved others; he cannot save himself. He is the king of Israel; let him come down from the cross now, and we will believe in him. ⁴³He has put his trust in God; now let God rescue him if he wants him. For he did say, "I am God's son."ᶜ ⁴⁴Even the bandits who were crucified with him taunted him in the same way.

The death of Jesus

⁴⁵From the sixth hour there was darkness over all the land until the ninth hour. ⁴⁶And about the ninth hour, Jesus cried out in a loud voice, 'Eli, eli, lama sabachthani?' that is, 'My God, my God, why have you forsaken me?'ᵈ ⁴⁷When some of those who stood there heard this, they said, 'The man is calling on Elijah,' ⁴⁸and one of them quickly ran to get a sponge which he filled with vinegar and, putting it on a reed, gave it him to drink. ⁴⁹But the rest of them said, 'Wait! And see if Elijah will come to save him.' ⁵⁰But Jesus, again crying out in a loud voice, yielded up his spirit.

⁵¹And suddenly, the veil of the Sanctuary was torn in two from top to bottom, the earth quaked, the rocks were split, ⁵²the tombs opened and the bodies of many holy people rose from the dead, ⁵³and these, after his resurrection, came out of the tombs, entered the holy city and appeared to a number of people. ⁵⁴The centurion, together with the others guarding Jesus, had seen the earthquake and all that was taking place, and they were terrified and said, 'In truth this man was son of God.'

⁵⁵And many women were there, watching from a distance, the same women who had followed Jesus from Galilee and looked after him. ⁵⁶Among them were Mary of Magdala, Mary the mother of James and Joseph, and the mother of Zebedee's sons.

The burial

⁵⁷When it was evening, there came a rich man of Arimathaea, called Joseph, who had himself become a disciple of Jesus. ⁵⁸This man went to Pilate and asked for the body of Jesus. Then Pilate ordered it to be handed over. ⁵⁹So Joseph took the body, wrapped it

27b cf. Ps 69:21.
27c cf. Ws 2:18–20.
27d Ps 22:1.

in a clean shroud [60]and put it in his own new tomb which he had hewn out of the rock. He then rolled a large stone across the entrance of the tomb and went away. [61]Now Mary of Magdala and the other Mary were there, sitting opposite the sepulchre.

The guard at the tomb

[62]Next day, that is, when Preparation Day was over, the chief priests and the Pharisees went in a body to Pilate [63]and said to him, 'Your Excellency, we recall that this impostor said, while he was still alive, "After three days I shall rise again." [64]Therefore give the order to have the sepulchre kept secure until the third day, for fear his disciples come and steal him away and tell the people, "He has risen from the dead." This last piece of fraud would be worse than what went before.' [65]Pilate said to them, 'You may have your guard; go and make all as secure as you know how.' [66]So they went and made the sepulchre secure, putting seals on the stone and mounting a guard.

The empty tomb. The angel's message

28 After the Sabbath, and towards dawn on the first day of the week, Mary of Magdala and the other Mary went to visit the sepulchre. [2]And suddenly there was a violent earthquake, for an angel of the Lord, descending from heaven, came and rolled away the stone and sat on it. [3]His face was like lightning, his robe white as snow. [4]The guards were so shaken by fear of him that they were like dead men. [5]But the angel spoke; and he said to the women, 'There is no need for you to be afraid. I know you are looking for Jesus, who was crucified. [6]He is not here, for he has risen, as he said he would. Come and see the place where he lay, [7]then go quickly and tell his disciples, "He has risen from the dead and now he is going ahead of you to Galilee; that is where you will see him." Look! I have told you.' [8]Filled with awe and great joy the women came quickly

away from the tomb and ran to tell his disciples.

Appearance to the women

[9]And suddenly, coming to meet them, was Jesus. 'Greetings,' he said. And the women came up to him and, clasping his feet, they did him homage. [10]Then Jesus said to them, 'Do not be afraid; go and tell my brothers that they must leave for Galilee; there they will see me.'

Precautions taken by the leaders of the people

[11]Now while they were on their way, some of the guards went off into the city to tell the chief priests all that had happened. [12]These held a meeting with the elders and, after some discussion, handed a considerable sum of money to the soldiers [13]with these instructions, 'This is what you must say, "His disciples came during the night and stole him away while we were asleep." [14]And should the governor come to hear of this, we undertake to put things right with him ourselves and to see that you do not get into trouble.' [15]So they took the money and carried out their instructions, and to this day that is the story among the Jews.

Appearance in Galilee
The mission to the world

[16]Meanwhile the eleven disciples set out for Galilee, to the mountain where Jesus had arranged to meet them. [17]When they saw him they fell down before him, though some hesitated. [18]Jesus came up and spoke to them. He said, 'All authority in heaven and on earth has been given to me.[a] [19]Go, therefore, make disciples of all nations; baptise them in the name of the Father and of the Son and of the Holy Spirit, [20]and teach them to observe all the commands I gave you. And look, I am with you always; yes, to the end of time.'

28a cf. Dn 7:14.

THE GOSPEL OF
MARK

Mark is often considered the earliest gospel to have been written. If so, Mark is responsible for evolving a new type of literature, neither history nor biography but the imparting of the Good News (the Old English word is 'Gospel') of the reign of God in Jesus. It is the most compact gospel, concentrating not on Jesus' teaching but on the mystery of his person, the gradual way in which the disciples reach an understanding of him which still remains hidden from the crowds. The paradox is that Jesus is acknowledged as Son of God by the Father and by evil spirits, and yet he is rejected by the leaders of the Jews and is even misunderstood by his own disciples. The gospel has been called a passion narrative with extended introduction; or it may be seen in two halves, the first being the revelation that Jesus is Messiah, the second — after the decisive turning-point at Caesarea Philippi (8:29) — being the revelation of his role of suffering. Mark shows that the rejection was an essential part of God's plan, foretold in the Scriptures, and crowned by Jesus' awesome resurrection.

PLAN OF THE BOOK

THE GOSPEL ACCORDING TO
MARK

I: PRELUDE TO THE PUBLIC MINISTRY OF JESUS

The proclamation of John the Baptist

1 The beginning of the gospel about Jesus Christ, the Son of God. [2] It is written in the prophet Isaiah:

Look, I am going to send my messenger
    in front of you
to prepare your way before you. [a]

[3] A voice of one that cries in the desert:
    Prepare a way for the Lord,
    make his paths straight.

[4] John the Baptist was in the desert, proclaiming a baptism of repentance for the forgiveness of sins. [5] All Judaea and all the people of Jerusalem made their way to him, and as they were baptised by him in the river

---

1a Ml 3:1 followed by Is 40:3.

Jordan they confessed their sins. [6]John wore a garment of camel-skin, and he lived on locusts and wild honey. [7]In the course of his preaching he said, 'After me is coming someone who is more powerful than me, and I am not fit to kneel down and undo the strap of his sandals. [8]I have baptised you with water, but he will baptise you with the Holy Spirit.'

Jesus is baptised

[9]It was at this time that Jesus came from Nazareth in Galilee and was baptised in the Jordan by John. [10]And at once, as he was coming up out of the water, he saw the heavens torn apart and the Spirit, like a dove, descending on him. [11]And a voice came from heaven, 'You are my Son, the Beloved; my favour rests on you.'

Testing in the desert

[12]And at once the Spirit drove him into the desert [13]and he remained there for forty days, and was put to the test by Satan. He was with the wild animals, and the angels looked after him.

II: THE GALILEAN MINISTRY

Jesus begins to proclaim the message

[14]After John had been arrested, Jesus went into Galilee. There he proclaimed the gospel from God saying, [15]'The time is fulfilled, and the kingdom of God is close at hand. Repent, and believe the gospel.'

The first four disciples are called

[16]As he was walking along by the Lake of Galilee he saw Simon and Simon's brother Andrew casting a net in the lake—for they were fishermen. [17]And Jesus said to them, 'Come after me and I will make you into fishers of people.' [18]And at once they left their nets and followed him.

[19]Going on a little further, he saw James son of Zebedee and his brother John; they too were in their boat, mending the nets. [20]At once he called them and, leaving their father Zebedee in the boat with the men he employed, they went after him.

Jesus teaches in Capernaum and cures a demoniac

[21]They went as far as Capernaum, and at once on the Sabbath he went into the synagogue and began to teach. [22]And his teaching made a deep impression on them because, unlike the scribes, he taught them with authority.

[23]And at once in their synagogue there was a man with an unclean spirit, and he shouted, [24]'What do you want with us, Jesus of Naza-reth? Have you come to destroy us? I know who you are: the Holy One of God.' [25]But Jesus rebuked it saying, 'Be quiet! Come out of him!' [26]And the unclean spirit threw the man into convulsions and with a loud cry went out of him. [27]The people were so aston-ished that they started asking one another what it all meant, saying, 'Here is a teaching that is new, and with authority behind it: he gives orders even to unclean spirits and they obey him.' [28]And his reputation at once spread everywhere, through all the surrounding Galilean countryside.

Cure of Simon's mother-in-law

[29]And at once on leaving the synagogue, he went with James and John straight to the house of Simon and Andrew. [30]Now Simon's mother-in-law was in bed and feverish, and at once they told him about her. [31]He went in to her, took her by the hand and helped her up. And the fever left her and she began to serve them.

A number of cures

[32]That evening, after sunset, they brought to him all who were sick and those who were possessed by devils. [33]The whole town came crowding round the door, [34]and he cured many who were sick with diseases of one kind or another; he also drove out many devils, but he would not allow them to speak, because they knew who he was.

Jesus quietly leaves Capernaum and travels through Galilee

[35] In the morning, long before dawn, he got up and left the house and went off to a lonely place and prayed there. [36] Simon and his companions set out in search of him, [37] and when they found him they said, 'Everybody is looking for you.' [38] He answered, 'Let us go elsewhere, to the neighbouring country towns, so that I can proclaim the message there too, because that is why I came.' [39] And he went all through Galilee, preaching in their synagogues and driving out devils.

Cure of a man suffering from a virulent skin-disease

[40] A man suffering from a virulent skin-disease came to him and pleaded on his knees saying, 'If you are willing, you can cleanse me.' [41] Feeling sorry for him, Jesus stretched out his hand, touched him and said to him, 'I am willing. Be cleansed.' [42] And at once the skin-disease left him and he was cleansed. [43] And at once Jesus sternly sent him away and said to him, [44] 'Mind you tell no one anything, but go and show yourself to the priest, and make the offering for your cleansing prescribed by Moses as evidence to them.' [45] The man went away, but then started freely proclaiming and telling the story everywhere, so that Jesus could no longer go openly into any town, but stayed outside in deserted places. Even so, people from all around kept coming to him.

Cure of a paralytic

2 When he returned to Capernaum, some time later word went round that he was in the house; [2] and so many people collected that there was no room left, even in front of the door. He was preaching the word to them [3] when some people came bringing him a paralytic carried by four men, [4] but as they could not get the man to him through the crowd, they stripped the roof over the place where Jesus was; and when they had made an opening, they lowered the stretcher on which the paralytic lay. [5] Seeing their faith, Jesus said to the paralytic, 'My child, your sins are forgiven.' [6] Now some scribes were sitting there, and they thought to themselves, [7] 'How can this man talk like that? He is being blasphemous. Who but God can forgive sins?' [8] And at once, Jesus, inwardly aware that this is what they were thinking, said to them, 'Why do you have these thoughts in your hearts? [9] Which of these is easier: to say to the paralytic, "Your sins are forgiven" or to say, "Get up, pick up your stretcher and walk"? [10] But to prove to you that the Son of man has authority to forgive sins on earth' — [11] he said to the paralytic — 'I order you: get up, pick up your stretcher, and go off home.' [12] And the man got up, and at once picked up his stretcher and walked out in front of everyone, so that they were all astonished and praised God saying, 'We have never seen anything like this.'

The call of Levi

[13] He went out again to the shore of the lake; and all the people came to him, and he taught them. [14] As he was walking along he saw Levi the son of Alphaeus sitting at the tax office, and he said to him, 'Follow me.' And he got up and followed him.

Eating with sinners

[15] When Jesus was at dinner in his house, a number of tax collectors and sinners were also sitting at table with Jesus and his disciples; for there were many of them among his followers. [16] When the scribes of the Pharisee party saw him eating with sinners and tax collectors, they said to his disciples, 'Why does he eat with tax collectors and sinners?' [17] When Jesus heard this he said to them, 'It is not the healthy who need the doctor, but the sick. I came to call not the upright, but sinners.'

A discussion on fasting

[18] John's disciples and the Pharisees were keeping a fast, when some people came to him and said to him, 'Why is it that John's disciples and the disciples of the Pharisees fast, but your disciples do not?' [19] Jesus replied, 'Surely the bridegroom's attendants cannot fast while the bridegroom is still with them? As long as they have the bridegroom with them, they cannot fast. [20] But the time will come when the bridegroom is taken away from them, and then, on that day, they will fast. [21] No one sews a piece of unshrunken cloth on an old cloak; otherwise, the patch pulls away from it, the new from the old, and

the tear gets worse. ²²And nobody puts new wine into old wineskins; otherwise, the wine will burst the skins, and the wine is lost and the skins too. No! New wine into fresh skins!'

Picking corn on the Sabbath

²³It happened that one Sabbath day he was taking a walk through the cornfields, and his disciples began to make a path by plucking ears of corn. ²⁴And the Pharisees said to him, 'Look, why are they doing something on the Sabbath day that is forbidden?' ²⁵And he replied, 'Have you never read what David did in his time of need when he and his followers were hungry—²⁶how he went into the house of God when Abiathar*ᵃ* was high priest, and ate the loaves of the offering which only the priests are allowed to eat, and how he also gave some to the men with him?'

²⁷And he said to them, 'The Sabbath was made for man, not man for the Sabbath; ²⁸so the Son of man is master even of the Sabbath.'

Cure of the man with a withered hand

3 Another time he went into the synagogue, and there was a man present whose hand was withered. ²And they were watching him to see if he would cure him on the Sabbath day, hoping for something to charge him with. ³He said to the man with the withered hand, 'Get up and stand in the middle!' ⁴Then he said to them, 'Is it permitted on the Sabbath day to do good, or to do evil; to save life, or to kill?' But they said nothing. ⁵Then he looked angrily round at them, grieved to find them so obstinate, and said to the man, 'Stretch out your hand.' He stretched it out and his hand was restored. ⁶The Pharisees went out and began at once to plot with the Herodians*ᵃ* against him, discussing how to destroy him.

The crowds follow Jesus

⁷Jesus withdrew with his disciples to the lakeside, and great crowds from Galilee followed him. From Judaea, ⁸and from Jerusalem, and from Idumaea and Transjordan and the region of Tyre and Sidon, great numbers who had heard of all he was doing came to him. ⁹And he asked his disciples to have a boat ready for him because of the crowd, to keep him from being crushed. ¹⁰For he had cured so many that all who were afflicted in any way were crowding forward to touch him. ¹¹And the unclean spirits, whenever they saw him, would fall down before him and shout, 'You are the Son of God!' ¹²But he warned them strongly not to make him known.

The appointment of the Twelve

¹³He now went up onto the mountain and summoned those he wanted. So they came to him ¹⁴and he appointed twelve; they were to be his companions and to be sent out to proclaim the message, ¹⁵with power to drive out devils. ¹⁶And so he appointed the Twelve, Simon to whom he gave the name Peter, ¹⁷James the son of Zebedee and John the brother of James, to whom he gave the name Boanerges or 'Sons of Thunder'; ¹⁸Andrew, Philip, Bartholomew, Matthew, Thomas, James the son of Alphaeus, Thaddaeus, Simon the Zealot ¹⁹and Judas Iscariot, the man who was to betray him.

His family are concerned about Jesus

²⁰He went home again, and once more such a crowd collected that they could not even have a meal. ²¹When his relations heard of this, they set out to take charge of him; they said, 'He is out of his mind.'

Allegations of the scribes

²²The scribes who had come down from Jerusalem were saying, 'Beelzebul is in him,' and, 'It is through the prince of devils that he drives devils out.' ²³So he called them to him and spoke to them in parables, ²⁴'How can Satan drive out Satan? If a kingdom is divided against itself, that kingdom cannot last. ²⁵And if a household is divided against itself, that household can never last. ²⁶Now if Satan has rebelled against himself and is divided, he cannot last either—it is the end of him. ²⁷But no one can make his way into a strong man's house and plunder his property unless he has first tied up the strong man. Only then can he plunder his house. ²⁸'In truth I tell you, all human sins will

---

2a In fact his father, Ahimelech, was high priest, 1 S 21:1–7.
3a Supporters of the Herodian dynasty, campaigning for the return of all Palestine to their rule.

be forgiven, and all the blasphemies ever uttered; [29]but anyone who blasphemes against the Holy Spirit will never be forgiven, but is guilty of an eternal sin.' [30]This was because they were saying, 'There is an unclean spirit in him.'

The true kinsmen of Jesus

[31]Now his mother and his brothers arrived and, standing outside, sent in a message asking for him. [32]A crowd was sitting round him at the time the message was passed to him, 'Look, your mother and brothers and sisters are outside asking for you.' [33]He replied, 'Who are my mother and my brothers?' [34]And looking at those sitting in a circle round him, he said, 'Here are my mother and my brothers. [35]Anyone who does the will of God, that person is my brother and sister and mother.'

Parable of the sower

4 Again he began to teach them by the lakeside, but such a huge crowd gathered round him that he got into a boat on the water and sat there. The whole crowd were at the lakeside on land. [2]He taught them many things in parables, and in the course of his teaching he said to them, [3]'Listen! Imagine a sower going out to sow. [4]Now it happened that, as he sowed, some of the seed fell on the edge of the path, and the birds came and ate it up. [5]Some seed fell on rocky ground where it found little soil and at once sprang up, because there was no depth of earth; [6]and when the sun came up it was scorched and, not having any roots, it withered away. [7]Some seed fell into thorns, and the thorns grew up and choked it, and it produced no crop. [8]And some seeds fell into rich soil, grew tall and strong, and produced a good crop; the yield was thirty, sixty, even a hundredfold.' [9]And he said, 'Anyone who has ears for listening should listen!'

Why Jesus spoke in parables

[10]When he was alone, the Twelve, together with the others who formed his company, asked what the parables meant. [11]He told them, 'To you is granted the secret of the kingdom of God, but to those who are outside everything comes in parables,

[12]so that *they may look and look,*
  but never perceive;
listen and listen, but never understand;
to avoid changing their ways
  and being healed.'[a]

The parable of the sower explained

[13]He said to them, 'Do you not understand this parable? Then how will you understand any of the parables? [14]What the sower is sowing is the word. [15]Those on the edge of the path where the word is sown are people who have no sooner heard it than Satan at once comes and carries away the word that was sown in them. [16]Similarly, those who are sown on patches of rock are people who, when first they hear the word, welcome it at once with joy. [17]But they have no root deep down and do not last; should some trial come, or some persecution on account of the word, at once they fall away. [18]Then there are others who are sown in thorns. These have heard the word, [19]but the worries of the world, the lure of riches and all the other passions come in to choke the word, and so it produces nothing. [20]And there are those who have been sown in rich soil; they hear the word and accept it and yield a harvest, thirty and sixty and a hundredfold.'

Receiving and handing on the teaching of Jesus

[21]He also said to them, 'Is a lamp brought in to be put under a tub or under the bed? Surely to be put on the lamp-stand? [22]For there is nothing hidden, but it must be disclosed, nothing kept secret except to be brought to light. [23]Anyone who has ears for listening should listen!'

Parable of the measure

[24]He also said to them, 'Take notice of what you are hearing. The standard you use will be used for you—and you will receive more besides; [25]anyone who has, will be given more; anyone who has not, will be deprived even of what he has.'

4a Is 6:9–10.

Parable of the seed growing by itself

²⁶He also said, 'This is what the kingdom of God is like. A man scatters seed on the land. ²⁷Night and day, while he sleeps, when he is awake, the seed is sprouting and growing; how, he does not know. ²⁸Of its own accord the land produces first the shoot, then the ear, then the full grain in the ear. ²⁹And when the crop is ready, at once he starts to reap because the harvest has come.'

Parable of the mustard seed

³⁰He also said, 'What can we say that the kingdom is like? What parable can we find for it? ³¹It is like a mustard seed which, at the time of its sowing, is the smallest of all the seeds on earth. ³²Yet once it is sown it grows into the biggest shrub of them all and puts out big branches so that the birds of the air can shelter in its shade.'

The use of parables

³³Using many parables like these, he spoke the word to them, so far as they were capable of understanding it. ³⁴He would not speak to them except in parables, but he explained everything to his disciples when they were by themselves.

The calming of the storm

³⁵With the coming of evening that same day, he said to them, 'Let us cross over to the other side.' ³⁶And leaving the crowd behind they took him, just as he was, in the boat; and there were other boats with him. ³⁷Then it began to blow a great gale and the waves were breaking into the boat so that it was almost swamped. ³⁸But he was in the stern, his head on the cushion, asleep. ³⁹They woke him and said to him, 'Master, do you not care? We are lost!' And he woke up and rebuked the wind and said to the sea, 'Quiet now! Be calm!' And the wind dropped, and there followed a great calm. ⁴⁰Then he said to them, 'Why are you so frightened? Have you still no faith?' ⁴¹They were overcome with awe and said to one another, 'Who can this be? Even the wind and the sea obey him.'

The Gerasene demoniac

5 They reached the territory of the Gerasenes on the other side of the lake, ²and when he disembarked, a man with an unclean spirit at once came out from the tombs towards him. ³The man lived in the tombs and no one could secure him any more, even with a chain, ⁴because he had often been secured with fetters and chains but had snapped the chains and broken the fetters, and no one had the strength to control him. ⁵All night and all day, among the tombs and in the mountains, he would howl and gash himself with stones. ⁶Catching sight of Jesus from a distance, he ran up and fell at his feet ⁷and shouted at the top of his voice, 'What do you want with me, Jesus, son of the Most High God? In God's name do not torture me!' ⁸For Jesus had been saying to him, 'Come out of the man, unclean spirit.' ⁹Then he asked, 'What is your name?' He answered, 'My name is Legion, for there are many of us.' ¹⁰And he begged him earnestly not to send them out of the district. ¹¹Now on the mountainside there was a great herd of pigs feeding, ¹²and the unclean spirits begged him, 'Send us to the pigs, let us go into them.' ¹³So he gave them leave. With that, the unclean spirits came out and went into the pigs, and the herd of about two thousand pigs charged down the cliff into the lake, and there they were drowned. ¹⁴The men looking after them ran off and told their story in the city and in the country round about; and the people came to see what had really happened. ¹⁵They came to Jesus and saw the demoniac sitting there—the man who had had the legion in him—properly dressed and in his full senses, and they were afraid. ¹⁶And those who had witnessed it reported what had happened to the demoniac and what had become of the pigs. ¹⁷Then they began to implore Jesus to leave their neighbourhood. ¹⁸As he was getting into the boat, the man who had been possessed begged to be allowed to stay with him. ¹⁹Jesus would not let him but said to him, 'Go home to your people and tell them all that the Lord in his mercy has done for you.' ²⁰So the man went off and proceeded to proclaim in the Decapolis all that Jesus had done for him. And everyone was amazed.

Cure of the woman with a haemorrhage
The daughter of Jairus raised to life

²¹When Jesus had crossed again in the boat to the other side, a large crowd gathered round him and he stayed by the lake. ²²Then the president of the synagogue came up, named Jairus, and seeing him, fell at his feet ²³and begged him earnestly, saying, 'My little daughter is desperately sick. Do come and lay your hands on her that she may be saved and may live.' ²⁴Jesus went with him and a large crowd followed him; they were pressing all round him.

²⁵Now there was a woman who had suffered from a haemorrhage for twelve years; ²⁶after long and painful treatment under various doctors, she had spent all she had without being any the better for it; in fact, she was getting worse. ²⁷She had heard about Jesus, and she came up through the crowd and touched his cloak from behind, thinking, ²⁸'If I can just touch his clothes, I shall be saved.' ²⁹And at once the source of the bleeding dried up, and she felt in herself that she was cured of her complaint. ³⁰And at once aware of the power that had gone out from him, Jesus turned round in the crowd and said, 'Who touched my clothes?' ³¹His disciples said to him, 'You see how the crowd is pressing round you; how can you ask, "Who touched me?" ' ³²But he continued to look all round to see who had done it. ³³Then the woman came forward, frightened and trembling because she knew what had happened to her, and she fell at his feet and told him the whole truth. ³⁴'My daughter,' he said, 'your faith has restored you to health; go in peace and be free of your complaint.'

³⁵While he was still speaking some people arrived from the house of the president of the synagogue to say, 'Your daughter is dead; why put the Master to any further trouble?' ³⁶But Jesus overheard what they said and he said to the president of the synagogue, 'Do not be afraid; only have faith.' ³⁷And he allowed no one to go with him except Peter and James and John the brother of James. ³⁸So they came to the house of the president of the synagogue, and Jesus noticed all the commotion, with people weeping and wailing unrestrainedly. ³⁹He went in and said to them, 'Why all this commotion and crying? The child is not dead, but asleep.' ⁴⁰But they ridiculed him. So he turned them all out and, taking with him the child's father and mother

and his own companions, he went into the place where the child lay. ⁴¹And taking the child by the hand he said to her, *'Talitha kum!'* which means, 'Little girl, I tell you to get up.' ⁴²The little girl got up at once and began to walk about, for she was twelve years old. At once they were overcome with astonishment, ⁴³and he gave them strict orders not to let anyone know about it, and told them to give her something to eat.

A visit to Nazareth

6 Leaving that district, he went to his home town, and his disciples accompanied him. ²With the coming of the Sabbath he began teaching in the synagogue, and most of them were astonished when they heard him. They said, 'Where did the man get all this? What is this wisdom that has been granted him, and these miracles that are worked through him? ³This is the carpenter, surely, the son of Mary, the brother of James and Joset and Jude and Simon? His sisters, too, are they not here with us?' And they would not accept him. ⁴And Jesus said to them, 'A prophet is despised only in his own country, among his own relations and in his own house'; ⁵and he could work no miracle there, except that he cured a few sick people by laying his hands on them. ⁶He was amazed at their lack of faith.

The mission of the Twelve

He made a tour round the villages, teaching. ⁷Then he summoned the Twelve and began to send them out in pairs, giving them authority over unclean spirits. ⁸And he instructed them to take nothing for the journey except a staff—no bread, no haversack, no coppers for their purses. ⁹They were to wear sandals but, he added, 'Don't take a spare tunic.' ¹⁰And he said to them, 'If you enter a house anywhere, stay there until you leave the district. ¹¹And if any place does not welcome you and people refuse to listen to you, as you walk away shake off the dust under your feet as evidence to them.' ¹²So they set off to proclaim repentance; ¹³and they cast out many devils, and anointed many sick people with oil and cured them.

Herod and Jesus

¹⁴King Herod had heard about him, since by now his name was well known. Some were

saying, 'John the Baptist has risen from the dead, and that is why miraculous powers are at work in him.' [15]Others said, 'He is Elijah,' others again, 'He is a prophet, like the prophets we used to have.' [16]But when Herod heard this he said, 'It is John whose head I cut off; he has risen from the dead.'

John the Baptist beheaded

[17]Now it was this same Herod who had sent to have John arrested, and had had him chained up in prison because of Herodias, his brother Philip's wife whom he had married. [18]For John had told Herod, 'It is against the law for you to have your brother's wife.' [19]As for Herodias, she was furious with him and wanted to kill him, but she was not able to do so, [20]because Herod was in awe of John, knowing him to be a good and upright man, and gave him his protection. When he had heard him speak he was greatly perplexed, and yet he liked to listen to him.

[21]An opportunity came on Herod's birthday when he gave a banquet for the nobles of his court, for his army officers and for the leading figures in Galilee. [22]When the daughter of this same Herodias came in and danced, she delighted Herod and his guests; so the king said to the girl, 'Ask me anything you like and I will give it you.' [23]And he swore her an oath, 'I will give you anything you ask, even half my kingdom.' [24]She went out and said to her mother, 'What shall I ask for?' She replied, 'The head of John the Baptist.' [25]The girl at once rushed back to the king and made her request, 'I want you to give me John the Baptist's head, immediately, on a dish.' [26]The king was deeply distressed but, thinking of the oaths he had sworn and of his guests, he was reluctant to break his word to her. [27]At once the king sent one of the bodyguard with orders to bring John's head. [28]The man went off and beheaded him in the prison; then he brought the head on a dish and gave it to the girl, and the girl gave it to her mother. [29]When John's disciples heard about this, they came and took his body and laid it in a tomb.

First miracle of the loaves

[30]The apostles rejoined Jesus and told him all they had done and taught. [31]And he said to them, 'Come away to some lonely place all by yourselves and rest for a while'; for there were so many coming and going that there was no time for them even to eat. [32]So they went off in the boat to a lonely place where they could be by themselves. [33]But people saw them going, and many recognised them; and from every town they all hurried to the place on foot and reached it before them. [34]So as he stepped ashore he saw a large crowd; and he took pity on them because they were like sheep without a shepherd, and he set himself to teach them at some length. [35]By now it was getting very late, and his disciples came up to him and said, 'This is a lonely place and it is getting very late, [36]so send them away, and they can go to the farms and villages round about, to buy themselves something to eat.' [37]He replied, 'Give them something to eat yourselves.' They answered, 'Are we to go and spend two hundred denarii on bread for them to eat?' [38]He asked, 'How many loaves have you? Go and see.' And when they had found out they said, 'Five, and two fish.' [39]Then he ordered them to get all the people to sit down in groups on the green grass, [40]and they sat down on the ground in squares of hundreds and fifties. [41]Then he took the five loaves and the two fish, raised his eyes to heaven and said the blessing; then he broke the loaves and began handing them to his disciples to distribute among the people. He also shared out the two fish among them all. [42]They all ate as much as they wanted. [43]They collected twelve basketfuls of scraps of bread and pieces of fish. [44]Those who had eaten the loaves numbered five thousand men.

Jesus walks on the water

[45]And at once he made his disciples get into the boat and go on ahead to the other side near Bethsaida, while he himself sent the crowd away. [46]After saying goodbye to them he went off into the hills to pray. [47]When evening came, the boat was far out on the sea, and he was alone on the land. [48]He could see that they were hard pressed in their rowing, for the wind was against them; and about the fourth watch of the night he came towards them, walking on the sea. He was going to pass them by, [49]but when they saw him walking on the sea they thought it was a ghost and cried out; [50]for they had all seen him and were terrified. But at once he spoke to them and said, 'Courage! It's me! Don't

be afraid.' [51]Then he got into the boat with them and the wind dropped. They were utterly and completely dumbfounded, [52]because they had not seen what the miracle of the loaves meant; their minds were closed.

Cures at Gennesaret

[53]Having made the crossing, they came to land at Gennesaret and moored there. [54]When they disembarked people at once recognised him, [55]and started hurrying all through the countryside and brought the sick on stretchers to wherever they heard he was. [56]And wherever he went, to village or town or farm, they laid down the sick in the open spaces, begging him to let them touch even the fringe of his cloak. And all those who touched him were saved.

The traditions of the Pharisees

7 The Pharisees and some of the scribes who had come from Jerusalem gathered round him, [2]and they noticed that some of his disciples were eating with unclean hands, that is, without washing them. [3]For the Pharisees, and all the Jews, keep the tradition of the elders and never eat without washing their arms as far as the elbow; [4]and on returning from the market place they never eat without first sprinkling themselves. There are also many other observances which have been handed down to them to keep, concerning the washing of cups and pots and bronze dishes. [5]So the Pharisees and scribes asked him, 'Why do your disciples not respect the tradition of the elders but eat their food with unclean hands?' [6]He answered, 'How rightly Isaiah prophesied about you hypocrites in the passage of scripture:

> This people honours me
>   only with lip-service,
>   while their hearts are far from me.
> [7]Their reverence of me is worthless;

> the lessons they teach
>   are nothing but human commandments.[a]

[8]You put aside the commandment of God to observe human traditions.' [9]And he said to them, 'How ingeniously you get round the commandment of God in order to preserve your own tradition! [10]For Moses said: Honour your father and your mother, and, Anyone who curses father or mother must be put to death.[b] [11]But you say, "If a man says to his father or mother: Anything I have that I might have used to help you is Korban[c] (that is, dedicated to God)," [12]then he is forbidden from that moment to do anything for his father or mother. [13]In this way you make God's word ineffective for the sake of your tradition which you have handed down. And you do many other things like this.'

On clean and unclean

[14]He called the people to him again and said, 'Listen to me, all of you, and understand. [15]Nothing that goes into someone from outside can make that person unclean; it is the things that come out of someone that make that person unclean. [16]Anyone who has ears for listening should listen!'

[17]When he had gone into the house, away from the crowd, his disciples questioned him about the parable. [18]He said to them, 'Even you—don't you understand? Can't you see that nothing that goes into someone from outside can make that person unclean, [19]because it goes not into the heart but into the stomach and passes into the sewer?' (Thus he pronounced all foods clean.) [20]And he went on, 'It is what comes out of someone that makes that person unclean. [21]For it is from within, from the heart, that evil intentions emerge: fornication, theft, murder, [22]adultery, avarice, malice, deceit, indecency, envy, slander, pride, folly. [23]All these evil things come from within and make a person unclean.'

7a Is 29:13.
7b Ex 20:12; 21:17.
7c Nothing Korban could be used for anyone else – a convenient legal fiction.

III: JOURNEYS OUTSIDE GALILEE

The daughter of
the Syro-Phoenician woman healed

²⁴He left that place and set out for the territory of Tyre. There he went into a house and did not want anyone to know he was there; but he could not pass unrecognised. ²⁵At once a woman whose little daughter had an unclean spirit heard about him and came and fell at his feet. ²⁶Now this woman was a gentile, by birth a Syro-Phoenician, and she begged him to drive the devil out of her daughter. ²⁷And he said to her, 'The children should be fed first, because it is not fair to take the children's food and throw it to little dogs.' ²⁸But she spoke up, 'Ah yes, sir,' she replied, 'but little dogs under the table eat the scraps from the children.' ²⁹And he said to her, 'For saying this you may go home happy; the devil has gone out of your daughter.' ³⁰So she went off home and found the child lying on the bed and the devil gone.

Healing of the deaf man

³¹Returning from the territory of Tyre, he went by way of Sidon towards the Lake of Galilee, right through the Decapolis territory. ³²And they brought him a deaf man who had an impediment in his speech; and they asked him to lay his hand on him. ³³He took him aside to be by themselves, away from the crowd, put his fingers into the man's ears and touched his tongue with spittle. ³⁴Then looking up to heaven he sighed; and he said to him, '*Ephphatha,*' that is, 'Be opened.' ³⁵And his ears were opened, and at once the impediment of his tongue was loosened and he spoke clearly. ³⁶And Jesus ordered them to tell no one about it, but the more he insisted, the more widely they proclaimed it. ³⁷Their admiration was unbounded, and they said, 'Everything he does is good, he makes the deaf hear and the dumb speak.'

Second miracle of the loaves

8 And now once again a great crowd had gathered, and they had nothing to eat. So he called his disciples to him and said to them, ²'I feel sorry for all these people; they

have been with me for three days now and have nothing to eat. ³If I send them off home hungry they will collapse on the way; some have come a great distance.' ⁴His disciples replied, 'Where could anyone get these people enough bread to eat in a deserted place?' ⁵He asked them, 'How many loaves have you?' And they said to him, 'Seven.' ⁶Then he instructed the crowd to sit down on the ground, and he took the seven loaves, and after giving thanks he broke them and began handing them to his disciples to distribute; and they distributed them among the crowd. ⁷They had a few small fishes as well, and over these he said a blessing and ordered them to be distributed too. ⁸They ate as much as they wanted, and they collected seven basketfuls of the scraps left over. ⁹Now there had been about four thousand people. He sent them away ¹⁰and at once, getting into the boat with his disciples, went to the region of Dalmanutha.

The Pharisees ask for a sign from heaven

¹¹The Pharisees came up and started a discussion with him; they demanded of him a sign from heaven, to put him to the test. ¹²And with a profound sigh he said, 'Why does this generation demand a sign? In truth I tell you, no sign shall be given to this generation.' ¹³And, leaving them again, he re-embarked and went away to the other side.

The yeast of the Pharisees and of Herod

¹⁴The disciples had forgotten to take any bread and they had only one loaf with them in the boat. ¹⁵Then he gave them this warning, 'Keep your eyes open; look out for the yeast of the Pharisees and the yeast of Herod.' ¹⁶And they said to one another, 'It is because we have no bread.' ¹⁷And Jesus knew it, and he said to them, 'Why are you talking about having no bread? Do you still not understand, still not realise? Are your minds closed? ¹⁸Have you *eyes and do not see, ears and do not hear?*[a] Or do you not remember? ¹⁹When I broke the five loaves for the five thousand, how many baskets full of scraps did you collect?' They answered, 'Twelve.' ²⁰'And

---

8a Jr 5:21; Ezk 12:2.

when I broke the seven loaves for the four thousand, how many baskets full of scraps did you collect?' And they answered, 'Seven.' ²¹Then he said to them, 'Do you still not realise?'

Cure of a blind man at Bethsaida

²²They came to Bethsaida, and some people brought to him a blind man whom they begged him to touch. ²³He took the blind man by the hand and led him outside the village. Then, putting spittle on his eyes and laying his hands on him, he asked, 'Can you see anything?' ²⁴The man, who was beginning to see, replied, 'I can see people; they look like trees as they walk around.' ²⁵Then he laid his hands on the man's eyes again and he saw clearly; he was cured, and he could see everything plainly and distinctly. ²⁶And Jesus sent him home, saying, 'Do not even go into the village.'

Peter's profession of faith

²⁷Jesus and his disciples left for the villages round Caesarea Philippi. On the way he put this question to his disciples, 'Who do people say I am?' ²⁸And they told him, 'John the Baptist, others Elijah, others again, one of the prophets.' ²⁹'But you,' he asked them, 'who do you say I am?' Peter spoke up and said to him, 'You are the Christ.' ³⁰And he gave them strict orders not to tell anyone about him.

First prophecy of the Passion

³¹Then he began to teach them that the Son of man was destined to suffer grievously, and to be rejected by the elders and the chief priests and the scribes, and to be put to death, and after three days to rise again; ³²and he said all this quite openly. Then, taking him aside, Peter tried to rebuke him. ³³But, turning and seeing his disciples, he rebuked Peter and said to him, 'Get behind me, Satan! You are thinking not as God thinks, but as human beings do.'

The condition of following Christ

³⁴He called the people and his disciples to him and said, 'If anyone wants to be a follower of mine, let him renounce himself and take up his cross and follow me. ³⁵Anyone who wants to save his life will lose it; but anyone who loses his life for my sake, and for the sake of the gospel, will save it. ³⁶What gain, then, is it for anyone to win the whole world and forfeit his life? ³⁷And indeed what can anyone offer in exchange for his life? ³⁸For if anyone in this sinful and adulterous generation is ashamed of me and of my words, the Son of man will also be ashamed of him when he comes in the glory of his Father with the holy angels.'

9And he said to them, 'In truth I tell you, there are some standing here who will not taste death before they see the kingdom of God come with power.'

The Transfiguration

²Six days later, Jesus took with him Peter and James and John and led them up a high mountain on their own by themselves. There in their presence he was transfigured: ³his clothes became brilliantly white, whiter than any earthly bleacher could make them. ⁴Elijah appeared to them with Moses; and they were talking to Jesus. ⁵Then Peter spoke to Jesus, 'Rabbi,' he said, 'it is wonderful for us to be here; so let us make three shelters, one for you, one for Moses and one for Elijah.' ⁶He did not know what to say; they were so frightened. ⁷And a cloud came, covering them in shadow; and from the cloud there came a voice, 'This is my Son, the Beloved. Listen to him.' ⁸Then suddenly, when they looked round, they saw no one with them any more but only Jesus.

The question about Elijah

⁹As they were coming down from the mountain he warned them to tell no one what they had seen, until after the Son of man had risen from the dead. ¹⁰They observed the warning faithfully, though among themselves they discussed what 'rising from the dead' could mean. ¹¹And they put this question to him, 'Why do the scribes say that Elijah must come first?' ¹²He said to them, 'Elijah is indeed first coming to set everything right again; yet how is it that the scriptures say about the Son of man that he must suffer grievously and be treated with contempt? ¹³But I tell you that Elijah has come and they have treated him as they pleased, just as the scriptures say about him.'

The epileptic demoniac

¹⁴As they were rejoining the disciples they saw a large crowd round them and some scribes arguing with them. ¹⁵At once, when they saw him, the whole crowd were struck with amazement and ran to greet him. ¹⁶And he asked them, 'What are you arguing about with them?' ¹⁷A man answered him from the crowd, 'Master, I have brought my son to you; there is a spirit of dumbness in him, ¹⁸and when it takes hold of him it throws him to the ground, and he foams at the mouth and grinds his teeth and goes rigid. And I asked your disciples to drive it out and they were unable to.' ¹⁹In reply he said to them, 'Faithless generation, how much longer must I be among you? How much longer must I put up with you? Bring him to me.' ²⁰They brought the boy to him, and at once the spirit of dumbness threw the boy into convulsions, and he fell to the ground and lay writhing there, foaming at the mouth. ²¹Jesus asked the father, 'How long has this been happening to him?' 'From childhood,' he said, ²²'and it has often thrown him into fire and into water, in order to destroy him. ²³But if you can do anything, have pity on us and help us.' ²⁴'If you can?' retorted Jesus. 'Everything is possible for one who has faith.' At once the father of the boy cried out, 'I have faith. Help my lack of faith!' ²⁵And when Jesus saw that a crowd was gathering, he rebuked the unclean spirit. 'Deaf and dumb spirit,' he said, 'I command you: come out of him and never enter him again.' ²⁶Then it threw the boy into violent convulsions and came out shouting, and the boy lay there so like a corpse that most of them said, 'He is dead.' ²⁷But Jesus took him by the hand and helped him up, and he was able to stand. ²⁸When he had gone indoors, his disciples asked him when they were by themselves, 'Why were we unable to drive it out?' ²⁹He answered, 'This is the kind that can be driven out only by prayer.'

Second prophecy of the Passion

³⁰After leaving that place they made their way through Galilee; and he did not want anyone to know, ³¹because he was instructing his disciples; he was telling them, 'The Son of man will be delivered into the power of men; they will put him to death; and three days after he has been put to death he will rise again.' ³²But they did not understand what he said and were afraid to ask him.

Who is the greatest?

³³They came to Capernaum, and when he got into the house he asked them, 'What were you arguing about on the road?' ³⁴They said nothing, because on the road they had been arguing which of them was the greatest. ³⁵So he sat down, called the Twelve to him and said, 'If anyone wants to be first, he must make himself last of all and servant of all.' ³⁶He then took a little child whom he set among them and embraced, and he said to them, ³⁷'Anyone who welcomes a little child such as this in my name, welcomes me; and anyone who welcomes me, welcomes not me but the one who sent me.'

On using the name of Jesus

³⁸John said to him, 'Master, we saw someone who is not one of us driving out devils in your name, and because he was not one of us we tried to stop him.' ³⁹But Jesus said, 'You must not stop him; no one who works a miracle in my name could soon afterwards speak evil of me. ⁴⁰Anyone who is not against us is for us.

Generosity shown to Christ's disciples

⁴¹'If anyone gives you a cup of water to drink because you belong to Christ, then in truth I tell you, he will most certainly not lose his reward.

On leading others astray

⁴²'But anyone who is the downfall of one of these little ones who have faith, would be better thrown into the sea with a great millstone hung round his neck. ⁴³And if your hand should be your downfall, cut it off; it is better for you to enter into life crippled, than to have two hands and go to hell, into the fire that can never be put out.[⁴⁴]ᵃ ⁴⁵And if your foot should be your downfall, cut it off; it is better for you to enter into life lame, than to have two feet and be thrown into hell.

9a Omitting, with the best MSS, vv. 44 and 46 (Vulg.), as repetitions of v. 48.

[46] b 47 And if your eye should be your downfall, tear it out; it is better for you to enter into the kingdom of God with one eye, than to have two eyes and be thrown into hell 48 where *their worm will never die nor their fire be put out.* c 49 For everyone will be salted with fire. 50 Salt is a good thing, but if salt has become insipid, how can you make it salty again? Have salt in yourselves and be at peace with one another.'

The question about divorce

10 After leaving there, he came into the territory of Judaea and Transjordan. And again crowds gathered round him, and again he taught them, as his custom was. 2 Some Pharisees approached him and asked, 'Is it lawful for a man to divorce his wife?' They were putting him to the test. 3 He answered them, 'What did Moses command you?' 4 They replied, 'Moses allowed us to draw up a writ of dismissal in cases of divorce.' a 5 Then Jesus said to them, 'It was because you were so hard hearted that he wrote this commandment for you. 6 But from the beginning of creation *he made them male and female.* 7 *This is why a man leaves his father and mother,* 8 *and the two become one flesh.* b They are no longer two, therefore, but one flesh. 9 So then, what God has united, human beings must not divide.' 10 Back in the house the disciples questioned him again about this, 11 and he said to them, 'Whoever divorces his wife and marries another is guilty of adultery against her. 12 And if a woman divorces her husband and marries another she is guilty of adultery too.'

Jesus and the children

13 People were bringing little children to him, for him to touch them. The disciples scolded them, 14 but when Jesus saw this he was indignant and said to them, 'Let the little children come to me; do not stop them; for it is to such as these that the kingdom of God belongs. 15 In truth I tell you, anyone who does not welcome the kingdom of God like a little child will never enter it.' 16 Then he embraced them, laid his hands on them and gave them his blessing.

The rich young man

17 He was setting out on a journey when a man ran up, knelt before him and put this question to him, 'Good master, what must I do to inherit eternal life?' 18 Jesus said to him, 'Why do you call me good? No one is good but God alone. 19 You know the commandments: *You shall not kill; You shall not commit adultery; You shall not steal; You shall not give false witness;* You shall not defraud; *Honour your father and mother.'* c 20 And he said to him, 'Master, I have kept all these since my earliest days.' 21 Jesus looked steadily at him and he was filled with love for him, and he said, 'You need to do one thing more. Go and sell what you own and give the money to the poor, and you will have treasure in heaven; then come, follow me.' 22 But his face fell at these words and he went away sad, for he was a man of great wealth.

The danger of riches

23 Jesus looked round and said to his disciples, 'How hard it is for those who have riches to enter the kingdom of God!' 24 The disciples were astounded by these words, but Jesus insisted, 'My children,' he said to them, 'how hard it is to enter the kingdom of God! 25 It is easier for a camel to pass through the eye of a needle than for someone rich to enter the kingdom of God.' 26 They were more astonished than ever, saying to one another, 'In that case, who can be saved?' 27 Jesus gazed at them and said, 'By human resources it is impossible, but not for God: because for God everything is possible.'

The reward of renunciation

28 Peter took this up. 'Look,' he said to him, 'we have left everything and followed you.' 29 Jesus said, 'In truth I tell you, there is no one who has left house, brothers, sisters, mother, father, children or land for my sake and for the sake of the gospel 30 who will not

---

9b See 9a above.
9c Is 66:24. The word for hell is 'Gehenna', the rubbish-dump of Jerusalem, with its perpetual fires.
10a Dt 24:1.
10b Gn 1:27; 2:24.
10c Ex 20:12–16.

receive a hundred times as much, houses, brothers, sisters, mothers, children and land—and persecutions too—now in this present time and, in the world to come, eternal life. [31]Many who are first will be last, and the last, first.'

Third prophecy of the Passion

[32]They were on the road, going up to Jerusalem; Jesus was walking on ahead of them; they were in a daze, and those who followed were apprehensive. Once more taking the Twelve aside he began to tell them what was going to happen to him, [33]'Now we are going up to Jerusalem, and the Son of man is about to be handed over to the chief priests and the scribes. They will condemn him to death and will hand him over to the gentiles, [34]who will mock him and spit at him and scourge him and put him to death; and after three days he will rise again.'

The sons of Zebedee make their request

[35]James and John, the sons of Zebedee, approached him. 'Master,' they said to him, 'We want you to do us a favour.' [36]He said to them, 'What is it you want me to do for you?' [37]They said to him, 'Allow us to sit one at your right hand and the other at your left in your glory.' [38]But Jesus said to them, 'You do not know what you are asking. Can you drink the cup that I shall drink, or be baptised with the baptism with which I shall be baptised?' [39]They replied, 'We can.' Jesus said to them, 'The cup that I shall drink you shall drink, and with the baptism with which I shall be baptised you shall be baptised, [40]but as for seats at my right hand or my left,

these are not mine to grant; they belong to those to whom they have been allotted.'

Leadership with service

[41]When the other ten heard this they began to feel indignant with James and John, [42]so Jesus called them to him and said to them, 'You know that among the gentiles those they call their rulers lord it over them, and their great men make their authority felt. [43]Among you this is not to happen. No; anyone who wants to become great among you must be your servant, [44]and anyone who wants to be first among you must be slave to all. [45]For the Son of man himself came not to be served but to serve, and to give his life as a ransom for many.'

The blind man of Jericho

[46]They reached Jericho; and as he left Jericho with his disciples and a great crowd, Bartimaeus—that is, the son of Timaeus—a blind beggar, was sitting at the side of the road. [47]When he heard that it was Jesus of Nazareth, he began to shout and cry out, 'Son of David, Jesus, have pity on me.' [48]And many of them scolded him and told him to keep quiet, but he only shouted all the louder, 'Son of David, have pity on me.' [49]Jesus stopped and said, 'Call him here.' So they called the blind man over. 'Courage,' they said, 'get up; he is calling you.' [50]So throwing off his cloak, he jumped up and went to Jesus. [51]Then Jesus spoke, 'What do you want me to do for you?' The blind man said to him, 'Rabbuni, let me see again.' [52]Jesus said to him, 'Go; your faith has saved you.' And at once his sight returned and he followed him along the road.

IV: THE JERUSALEM MINISTRY

The Messiah enters Jerusalem

11 When they were approaching Jerusalem, at Bethphage and Bethany, close by the Mount of Olives, he sent two of his disciples [2]and said to them, 'Go to the village facing you, and as you enter it you will at once find a tethered colt that no one has yet ridden. Untie it and bring it here. [3]If anyone says to you, "What are you doing?" say,

"The Master needs it and will send it back here at once." ' [4]They went off and found a colt tethered near a door in the open street. As they untied it, [5]some men standing there said, 'What are you doing, untying that colt?' [6]They gave the answer Jesus had told them, and the men let them go. [7]Then they took the colt to Jesus and threw their cloaks on its back, and he mounted it. [8]Many people spread their cloaks on the road, and others greenery which they had cut in the fields. ⁹And those who went in front and those who followed were all shouting, '*Hosanna! Blessed is he who is coming in the name of the Lord!*ᵃ ¹⁰Blessed is the coming kingdom of David our father!ᵇ *Hosanna* in the highest heavens!' ¹¹He entered Jerusalem and went into the Temple; and when he had surveyed it all, as it was late by now, he went out to Bethany with the Twelve.

The barren fig tree

¹²Next day as they were leaving Bethany, he felt hungry. ¹³Seeing a fig tree in leaf some distance away, he went to see if he could find any fruit on it, but when he came up to it he found nothing but leaves; for it was not the season for figs. ¹⁴And he addressed the fig tree, 'May no one ever eat fruit from you again.' And his disciples heard him say this.

The expulsion of the dealers
from the Temple

¹⁵So they reached Jerusalem and he went into the Temple and began driving out the men selling and buying there; he upset the tables of the money changers and the seats of the dove sellers. ¹⁶Nor would he allow anyone to carry anything through the Temple. ¹⁷And he taught them and said, 'Does not scripture say: *My house will be called a house of prayer for all peoples*? But you have turned it into *a bandits' den.*ᶜ ¹⁸This came to the ears of the chief priests and the scribes, and they tried to find some way of doing away with him; they were afraid of him because the people were carried away by his teaching. ¹⁹And when evening came he went out of the city.

The fig tree withered. Faith and prayer

²⁰Next morning, as they passed by, they saw the fig tree withered to the roots. ²¹Peter remembered. 'Look, Rabbi,' he said to Jesus, 'the fig tree that you cursed has withered away.' ²²Jesus answered, 'Have faith in God. ²³In truth I tell you, if anyone says to this mountain, "Be pulled up and thrown into the sea," with no doubt in his heart, but believing that what he says will happen, it

will be done for him. ²⁴I tell you, therefore, everything you ask and pray for, believe that you have it already, and it will be yours. ²⁵And when you stand in prayer, forgive whatever you have against anybody, so that your Father in heaven may forgive your failings too.'[26]ᵈ

The authority of Jesus is questioned

²⁷They came to Jerusalem again, and as Jesus was walking in the Temple, the chief priests and the scribes and the elders came to him, ²⁸and they said to him, 'What authority have you for acting like this? Or who gave you authority to act like this?' ²⁹Jesus said to them, 'And I will ask you a question, just one; answer me and I will tell you my authority for acting like this. ³⁰John's baptism, what was its origin, heavenly or human? Answer me that.' ³¹And they argued this way among themselves, 'If we say heavenly, he will say, "Then why did you refuse to believe him?" ³²But dare we say human?'—they had the people to fear, for everyone held that John had been a real prophet. ³³So their reply to Jesus was, 'We do not know.' And Jesus said to them, 'Nor will I tell you my authority for acting like this.'

Parable of the wicked tenants

12 He went on to speak to them in parables, 'A man planted a vineyard; he fenced it round, dug out a trough for the winepress and built a tower; then he leased it to tenants and went abroad. ²When the time came, he sent a servant to the tenants to collect from them his share of the produce of the vineyard. ³But they seized the man, thrashed him and sent him away empty handed. ⁴Next he sent another servant to them; him they beat about the head and treated shamefully. ⁵And he sent another and him they killed; then a number of others, and they thrashed some and killed the rest. ⁶He had still someone left: his beloved son. He sent him to them last of all, thinking, "They will respect my son." ⁷But those tenants said to each other, "This is the heir. Come on, let us kill him, and the inheritance will be ours." ⁸So they seized him and killed him and threw

11a Ps 118:25–26.
11b 2 S 7:16.
11c Is 56:7 followed by Jr 7:11.
11d Some authorities add a v. borrowed from Mt 6:15.

him out of the vineyard. ⁹Now what will the owner of the vineyard do? He will come and make an end of the tenants and give the vineyard to others. ¹⁰Have you not read this text of scripture:

> *The stone which the builders rejected*
> *has become the cornerstone;*
> ¹¹ *this is the Lord's doing,*
> *and we marvel at it ?'ᵃ*

¹²And they would have liked to arrest him, because they realised that the parable was aimed at them, but they were afraid of the crowds. So they left him alone and went away.

On tribute to Caesar

¹³Next they sent to him some Pharisees and some Herodians to catch him out in what he said. ¹⁴These came and said to him, 'Master, we know that you are an honest man, that you are not afraid of anyone, because human rank means nothing to you, and that you teach the way of God in all honesty. Is it permissible to pay taxes to Caesar or not? Should we pay or not?' ¹⁵Recognising their hypocrisy he said to them, 'Why are you putting me to the test? Hand me a denarius and let me see it.' ¹⁶They handed him one and he said to them, 'Whose portrait is this? Whose title?' They said to him, 'Caesar's.' ¹⁷Jesus said to them, 'Pay Caesar what belongs to Caesar—and God what belongs to God.' And they were amazed at him.

The resurrection of the dead

¹⁸Then some Sadducees—who deny that there is a resurrection—came to him and they put this question to him, ¹⁹'Master, Moses prescribed for us that if a man's brother dies leaving a wife but no child, the man must marry the widow to raise up children for his brother. ²⁰Now there were seven brothers; the first married a wife and then died leaving no children. ²¹The second married the widow, and he too died leaving no children; with the third it was the same, ²²and none of the seven left any children. Last of all the woman herself died. ²³Now at the resurrec-

tion, when they rise again, whose wife will she be, since she had been married to all seven?'

²⁴Jesus said to them, 'Surely the reason why you are wrong is that you understand neither the scriptures nor the power of God. ²⁵For when they rise from the dead, men and women do not marry; no, they are like the angels in heaven. ²⁶Now about the dead rising again, have you never read in the Book of Moses, in the passage about the bush, how God spoke to him and said: *I am the God of Abraham, the God of Isaac and the God of Jacob?*ᵇ ²⁷He is God, not of the dead, but of the living. You are very much mistaken.'

The greatest commandment of all

²⁸One of the scribes who had listened to them debating appreciated that Jesus had given a good answer and put a further question to him, 'Which is the first of all the commandments?' ²⁹Jesus replied, 'This is the first:ᶜ *Listen, Israel, the Lord our God is the one, only Lord,* ³⁰*and you must love the Lord your God with all your heart, with all your soul,* with all your mind *and with all your strength.* ³¹The second is this:ᵈ *You must love your neighbour as yourself.* There is no commandment greater than these.' ³²The scribe said to him, 'Well spoken, Master; what you have said is true, that *he is one and there is no other.* ³³To *love him with all your heart, with all your understanding and strength,* and to *love your neighbour as yourself,* this is far more important than any burnt offering or sacrifice.' ³⁴Jesus, seeing how wisely he had spoken, said, 'You are not far from the kingdom of God.' And after that no one dared to question him any more.

Jesus not only son but also Lord of David

³⁵While teaching in the Temple, Jesus said, 'How can the scribes maintain that the Christ is the son of David? ³⁶David himself, moved by the Holy Spirit, said:

> *The Lord declared to my Lord,*
> *take your seat at my right hand*

12a Ps 118:22–23.
12b Ex 3:6.
12c Dt 6:4–5.
12d Lv 19:18.

*till I have made your enemies
your footstool.*[e]

[37]David himself calls him Lord; in what way then can he be his son?' And the great crowd listened to him with delight.

The scribes condemned by Jesus

[38]In his teaching he said, 'Beware of the scribes who like to walk about in long robes, to be greeted respectfully in the market squares, [39]to take the front seats in the synagogues and the places of honour at banquets; [40]these are the men who devour the property of widows and for show offer long prayers. The more severe will be the sentence they receive.'

The widow's mite

[41]He sat down opposite the treasury and watched the people putting money into the treasury, and many of the rich put in a great deal. [42]A poor widow came and put in two small coins, the equivalent of a penny. [43]Then he called his disciples and said to them, 'In truth I tell you, this poor widow has put more in than all who have contributed to the treasury; [44]for they have all put in money they could spare, but she in her poverty has put in everything she possessed, all she had to live on.'

The eschatological discourse: Introduction[a]

13 As he was leaving the Temple one of his disciples said to him, 'Master, look at the size of those stones! Look at the size of those buildings!' [2]And Jesus said to him, 'You see these great buildings? Not a single stone will be left on another; everything will be pulled down.'

[3]And while he was sitting on the Mount of Olives, facing the Temple, Peter, James, John and Andrew questioned him when they were by themselves, [4]'Tell us, when is this going to happen, and what sign will there be that it is all about to take place?'

The beginning of sorrows

[5]Then Jesus began to tell them, 'Take care that no one deceives you. [6]Many will come using my name and saying, "I am he," and they will deceive many. [7]When you hear of wars and rumours of wars, do not be alarmed; this is something that must happen, but the end will not be yet. [8]For nation will fight against nation, and kingdom against kingdom. There will be earthquakes in various places; there will be famines. This is the beginning of the birth-pangs.

[9]'Be on your guard: you will be handed over to sanhedrins; you will be beaten in synagogues; and you will be brought before governors and kings for my sake, as evidence to them, [10]since the gospel must first be proclaimed to all nations. [11]'And when you are taken to be handed over, do not worry beforehand about what to say; no, say whatever is given to you when the time comes, because it is not you who will be speaking; it is the Holy Spirit. [12]Brother will betray brother to death, and a father his child; children will come forward against their parents and have them put to death. [13]You will be universally hated on account of my name; but anyone who stands firm to the end will be saved.

The great tribulation of Jerusalem

[14]'When you see *the appalling abomination*[b] set up where it ought not to be (let the reader understand), then those in Judaea must escape to the mountains; [15]if a man is on the housetop, he must not come down or go inside to collect anything from his house; [16]if a man is in the fields, he must not turn back to fetch his cloak. [17]Alas for those with child, or with babies at the breast, when those days come! [18]Pray that this may not be in winter. [19]For in those days there will be *great distress, unparalleled since*[c] God created the world, and such as will never be again. [20]And if the Lord had not shortened that time, no human being would have survived; but he did shorten the time, for the sake of the elect whom he chose.

[21]'And if anyone says to you then, "Look, here is the Christ" or, "Look, he is there,"

12e Ps 110:1.
13a By contrast with Mt 24—25, Mk's discourse concerns only the destruction of Jerusalem as an act of God delivering his people.
13b Dn 9:27; 11:31; 12:11.
13c Dn 12:1.

do not believe it; [22] for false Christs and false prophets will arise and produce signs and portents to deceive the elect, if that were possible. [23] You, therefore, must be on your guard. I have given you full warning.

The coming of the Son of man

[24] 'But in those days, after that time of distress, the sun will be darkened, the moon will not give its light, [25] the stars will come falling out of the sky and the powers in the heavens will be shaken. [26] And then they will see the *Son of man coming in the clouds* with great power and glory.[d] [27] And then he will send the angels to gather his elect from the four winds, from the ends of the world to the ends of the sky.[e]

The time of this coming

[28] 'Take the fig tree as a parable: as soon as its twigs grow supple and its leaves come out, you know that summer is near. [29] So with you when you see these things happening: know that he is near, right at the gates. [30] In truth I tell you, before this generation has passed away all these things will have taken place. [31] Sky and earth will pass away, but my words will not pass away. [32] 'But as for that day or hour, nobody knows it, neither the angels in heaven, nor the Son; no one but the Father.

Be on the alert

[33] 'Be on your guard, stay awake, because you never know when the time will come. [34] It is like a man travelling abroad: he has gone from his home, and left his servants in charge, each with his own work to do; and he has told the doorkeeper to stay awake. [35] So stay awake, because you do not know when the master of the house is coming, evening, midnight, cockcrow or dawn; [36] if he comes unexpectedly, he must not find you asleep. [37] And what I am saying to you I say to all: Stay awake!'

V: PASSION AND RESURRECTION

The conspiracy against Jesus

14 It was two days before the Passover and the feast of Unleavened Bread, and the chief priests and the scribes were looking for a way to arrest Jesus by some trick and have him put to death. [2] For they said, 'It must not be during the festivities, or there will be a disturbance among the people.'

The anointing at Bethany

[3] He was at Bethany in the house of Simon, a man who had suffered from a virulent skin-disease; he was at table when a woman came in with an alabaster jar of very costly ointment, pure nard. She broke the jar and poured the ointment on his head. [4] Some who were there said to one another indignantly, 'Why this waste of ointment? [5] Ointment like this could have been sold for over three hundred denarii and the money given to the poor'; and they were angry with her. [6] But Jesus said, 'Leave her alone. Why are you upsetting her? What she has done for me is a good work. [7] You have the poor with you always, and you can be kind to them whenever you wish, but you will not always have me. [8] She has done what she could: she has anointed my body beforehand for its burial. [9] In truth I tell you, wherever throughout all the world the gospel is proclaimed, what she has done will be told as well, in remembrance of her.'

Judas betrays Jesus

[10] Judas Iscariot, one of the Twelve, approached the chief priests with an offer to hand Jesus over to them. [11] They were delighted to hear it, and promised to give him money; and he began to look for a way of betraying him when the opportunity should occur.

Preparations for the Passover supper

[12] On the first day of Unleavened Bread, when the Passover lamb was sacrificed, his disciples

13d Dn 7:13–14.
13e Dt 30:4.

said to him, 'Where do you want us to go and make the preparations for you to eat the Passover?' ¹³So he sent two of his disciples, saying to them, 'Go into the city and you will meet a man carrying a pitcher of water. Follow him, ¹⁴and say to the owner of the house which he enters, "The Master says: Where is the room for me to eat the Passover with my disciples?" ¹⁵He will show you a large upper room furnished with couches, all prepared. Make the preparations for us there.' ¹⁶The disciples set out and went to the city and found everything as he had told them, and prepared the Passover.

The treachery of Judas foretold

¹⁷When evening came he arrived with the Twelve. ¹⁸And while they were at table eating, Jesus said, 'In truth I tell you, one of you is about to betray me, one of you *eating with me.'ᵃ* ¹⁹They were distressed and said to him, one after another, 'Not me, surely?' ²⁰He said to them, 'It is one of the Twelve, one who is dipping into the same dish with me. ²¹Yes, the Son of man is going to his fate, as the scriptures say he will, but alas for that man by whom the Son of man is betrayed! Better for that man if he had never been born.'

The institution of the Eucharist

²²And as they were eating he took bread, and when he had said the blessing he broke it and gave it to them. 'Take it,' he said, 'this is my body.' ²³Then he took a cup, and when he had given thanks he handed it to them, and all drank from it, ²⁴and he said to them, 'This is my blood, the blood of the covenant, poured out for many. ²⁵In truth I tell you, I shall never drink wine any more until the day I drink the new wine in the kingdom of God.'

Peter's denial foretold

²⁶After the psalms had been sung they left for the Mount of Olives. ²⁷And Jesus said to them, 'You will all fall away, for the scripture says: *I shall strike the shepherd and the sheep will be scattered;ᵇ* ²⁸however, after my resur-

rection I shall go before you into Galilee.' ²⁹Peter said, 'Even if all fall away, I will not.' ³⁰And Jesus said to him, 'In truth I tell you, this day, this very night, before the cock crows twice, you will have disowned me three times.' ³¹But he repeated still more earnestly, 'If I have to die with you, I will never disown you.' And they all said the same.

Gethsemane

³²They came to a plot of land called Gethsemane, and he said to his disciples, 'Stay here while I pray.' ³³Then he took Peter and James and John with him. ³⁴And he began to feel terror and anguish. And he said to them, 'My soul is sorrowful to the point of death. Wait here, and stay awake.' ³⁵And going on a little further he threw himself on the ground and prayed that, if it were possible, this hour might pass him by. ³⁶'*Abba,ᶜ* Father!' he said, 'For you everything is possible. Take this cup away from me. But let it be as you, not I, would have it.' ³⁷He came back and found them sleeping, and he said to Peter, 'Simon, are you asleep? Had you not the strength to stay awake one hour? ³⁸Stay awake and pray not to be put to the test. The spirit is willing enough, but human nature is weak.' ³⁹Again he went away and prayed, saying the same words. ⁴⁰And once more he came back and found them sleeping, their eyes were so heavy; and they could find no answer for him. ⁴¹He came back a third time and said to them, 'You can sleep on now and have your rest. It is all over. The hour has come. Now the Son of man is to be betrayed into the hands of sinners. ⁴²Get up! Let us go! My betrayer is not far away.'

The arrest

⁴³And at once, while he was still speaking, Judas, one of the Twelve, came up and with him a number of men armed with swords and clubs, sent by the chief priests and the scribes and the elders. ⁴⁴Now the traitor had arranged a signal with them saying, 'The one I kiss, he is the man. Arrest him, and see he is well guarded when you lead him away.' ⁴⁵So when the traitor came, he went up to

---

14a Ps 41:9.
14b Zc 13:7.
14c An affectionate Aramaic word, address of child to father.

Jesus at once and said, 'Rabbi!' and kissed him. ⁴⁶The others seized him and arrested him. ⁴⁷Then one of the bystanders drew his sword and struck out at the high priest's servant and cut off his ear. ⁴⁸Then Jesus spoke. 'Am I a bandit,' he said, 'that you had to set out to capture me with swords and clubs? ⁴⁹I was among you teaching in the Temple day after day and you never laid a hand on me. But this is to fulfil the scriptures.' ⁵⁰And they all deserted him and ran away. ⁵¹A young man followed with nothing on but a linen cloth. They caught hold of him, ⁵²but he left the cloth in their hands and ran away naked.

Jesus before the Sanhedrin

⁵³They led Jesus off to the high priest; and all the chief priests and the elders and the scribes assembled there. ⁵⁴Peter had followed him at a distance, right into the high priest's palace, and was sitting with the attendants warming himself at the fire.

⁵⁵The chief priests and the whole Sanhedrin were looking for evidence against Jesus in order to have him executed. But they could not find any. ⁵⁶Several, indeed, brought false witness against him, but their evidence was conflicting. ⁵⁷Some stood up and submitted this false evidence against him, ⁵⁸'We heard him say, "I am going to destroy this Temple made by human hands, and in three days build another, not made by human hands." ' ⁵⁹But even on this point their evidence was conflicting. ⁶⁰The high priest then rose before the whole assembly and put this question to Jesus, 'Have you no answer to that? What is this evidence these men are bringing against you?' ⁶¹But he was silent and made no answer at all. The high priest put a second question to him saying, 'Are you the Christ, the Son of the Blessed One?' ⁶²'I am,' said Jesus, 'and you will see the *Son of man seated at the right hand of the Power and coming with the clouds of heaven.*'ᵈ ⁶³The high priest tore his robes and said, 'What need of witnesses have we now? ⁶⁴You heard the blasphemy. What is your finding?' Their verdict was unanimous: he deserved to die.

⁶⁵Some of them started spitting at his face, hitting him and saying, 'Play the prophet!' And the attendants struck him too.

Peter's denials

⁶⁶While Peter was down below in the courtyard, one of the high priest's servant-girls came up. ⁶⁷She saw Peter warming himself there, looked closely at him and said, 'You too were with Jesus, the man from Nazareth.' ⁶⁸But he denied it. 'I do not know, I do not understand what you are talking about,' he said. And he went out into the forecourt, and a cock crowed. ⁶⁹The servant-girl saw him and again started telling the bystanders, 'This man is one of them.' ⁷⁰But again he denied it. A little later the bystanders themselves said to Peter, 'You are certainly one of them! Why, you are a Galilean.' ⁷¹But he started cursing and swearing, 'I do not know the man you speak of.' ⁷²And at once the cock crowed for the second time, and Peter recalled what Jesus had said to him, 'Before the cock crows twice, you will have disowned me three times.' And he burst into tears.

Jesus before Pilate

15 First thing in the morning, the chief priests, together with the elders and scribes and the rest of the Sanhedrin, had their plan ready. They had Jesus bound and took him away and handed him over to Pilate. ²Pilate put to him this question, 'Are you the king of the Jews?' He replied, 'It is you who say it.' ³And the chief priests brought many accusations against him. ⁴Pilate questioned him again, 'Have you no reply at all? See how many accusations they are bringing against you!' ⁵But, to Pilate's surprise, Jesus made no further reply.

⁶At festival time Pilate used to release a prisoner for them, any one they asked for. ⁷Now a man called Barabbas was then in prison with the rebels who had committed murder during the uprising. ⁸When the crowd went up and began to ask Pilate the customary favour, ⁹Pilate answered them, 'Do you want me to release for you the king of the Jews?' ¹⁰For he realised it was out of jealousy that the chief priests had handed Jesus over. ¹¹The chief priests, however, had incited the crowd to demand that he should release Barabbas for them instead. ¹²Then Pilate spoke again, 'But in that case, what am I to do with the man you call king of the Jews?' ¹³They shouted back, 'Crucify him!'

14d Dn 7:13; Ps 110:1.

[14]Pilate asked them, 'What harm has he done?' But they shouted all the louder, 'Crucify him!' [15]So Pilate, anxious to placate the crowd, released Barabbas for them and, after having Jesus scourged, he handed him over to be crucified.

Jesus crowned with thorns

[16]The soldiers led him away to the inner part of the palace, that is, the Praetorium, and called the whole cohort together. [17]They dressed him up in purple, twisted some thorns into a crown and put it on him. [18]And they began saluting him, 'Hail, king of the Jews!' [19]They struck his head with a reed and spat on him; and they went down on their knees to do him homage. [20]And when they had finished making fun of him, they took off the purple and dressed him in his own clothes.

The way of the cross

They led him out to crucify him. [21]They enlisted a passer-by, Simon of Cyrene, father of Alexander and Rufus,[a] who was coming in from the country, to carry his cross. [22]They brought Jesus to the place called Golgotha, which means the place of the skull.

The crucifixion

[23]They offered him wine mixed with myrrh, but he refused it. [24]Then they crucified him, and shared out his clothing, casting lots to decide what each should get. [25]It was the third hour when they crucified him. [26]The inscription giving the charge against him read, 'The King of the Jews'. [27]And they crucified two bandits with him, one on his right and one on his left.[28][b]

The crucified Jesus is mocked

[29]The passers-by jeered at him; they shook their heads and said, 'Aha! So you would destroy the Temple and rebuild it in three days! [30]Then save yourself; come down from the cross!' [31]The chief priests and the scribes mocked him among themselves in the same way with the words, 'He saved others, he cannot save himself.' [32]Let the Christ, the king of Israel, come down from the cross now, for us to see it and believe.' Even those who were crucified with him taunted him.

The death of Jesus

[33]When the sixth hour came there was darkness over the whole land until the ninth hour. [34]And at the ninth hour Jesus cried out in a loud voice, *'Eloi, eloi,[c] lama sabachthani?'* which means, *'My God, my God, why have you forsaken me?'* [35]When some of those who stood by heard this, they said, 'Listen, he is calling on Elijah.' [36]Someone ran and soaked a sponge in vinegar and, putting it on a reed, gave it to him to drink saying, 'Wait! And see if Elijah will come to take him down.' [37]But Jesus gave a loud cry and breathed his last. [38]And the veil of the Sanctuary was torn in two from top to bottom. [39]The centurion, who was standing in front of him, had seen how he had died, and he said, 'In truth this man was Son of God.'

The women on Calvary

[40]There were some women watching from a distance. Among them were Mary of Magdala, Mary who was the mother of James the younger and Joset, and Salome. [41]These used to follow him and look after him when he was in Galilee. And many other women were there who had come up to Jerusalem with him.

The burial

[42]It was now evening, and since it was Preparation Day—that is, the day before the Sabbath—[43]there came Joseph of Arimathaea, a prominent member of the Council, who himself lived in the hope of seeing the kingdom of God, and he boldly went to Pilate and asked for the body of Jesus. [44]Pilate, astonished that he should have died so soon, summoned the centurion and enquired if he had been dead for some time. [45]Having been assured of this by the centurion, he granted

15a cf. Rm 16:13.
15b Some authorities add a verse similar to Lk 22:37.
15c This Aramaic form cf. Ps 22:1, explains the soldiers' pun about Elijah better than Mt's Hebr form *eli*.

the corpse to Joseph ⁴⁶who bought a shroud, took Jesus down from the cross, wrapped him in the shroud and laid him in a tomb which had been hewn out of the rock. He then rolled a stone against the entrance to the tomb. ⁴⁷Mary of Magdala and Mary the mother of Joset took note of where he was laid.

The empty tomb. The angel's message

16 When the Sabbath was over, Mary of Magdala, Mary the mother of James, and Salome, bought spices with which to go and anoint him. ²And very early in the morning on the first day of the week they went to the tomb when the sun had risen.

³They had been saying to one another, 'Who will roll away the stone for us from the entrance to the tomb?' ⁴But when they looked they saw that the stone—which was very big—had already been rolled back. ⁵On entering the tomb they saw a young man in a white robe seated on the right-hand side, and they were struck with amazement. ⁶But he said to them, 'There is no need to be so amazed. You are looking for Jesus of Nazareth, who was crucified: he has risen, he is not here. See, here is the place where they laid him. ⁷But you must go and tell his disciples and Peter, "He is going ahead of you to Galilee; that is where you will see him, just as he told you." ' ⁸And the women came out and ran away from the tomb because they were frightened out of their wits; and they said nothing to anyone, for they were afraid.ᵃ

Appearances of the risen Christ

⁹Having risen in the morning on the first day of the week, he appeared first to Mary of Magdala from whom he had cast out seven devils. ¹⁰She then went to those who had been his companions, and who were mourning and in tears, and told them. ¹¹But they did not believe her when they heard her say that he was alive and that she had seen him.

¹²After this, he showed himself under another form to two of them as they were on their way into the country. ¹³These went back and told the others, who did not believe them either.

¹⁴Lastly, he showed himself to the Eleven themselves while they were at table. He reproached them for their incredulity and obstinacy, because they had refused to believe those who had seen him after he had risen. ¹⁵And he said to them, 'Go out to the whole world; proclaim the gospel to all creation. ¹⁶Whoever believes and is baptised will be saved; whoever does not believe will be condemned. ¹⁷These are the signs that will be associated with believers: in my name they will cast out devils; they will have the gift of tongues; ¹⁸they will pick up snakes in their hands and be unharmed should they drink deadly poison; they will lay their hands on the sick, who will recover.'

¹⁹And so the Lord Jesus, after he had spoken to them, was taken up into heaven; there at the right hand of God he took his place, ²⁰while they, going out, preached everywhere, the Lord working with them and confirming the word by the signs that accompanied it.

16a Originally Mk probably ended abruptly on this note of awe and wonder. The next 12 vv., missing in some MSS, are a summary of material gathered from other NT writings.

THE GOSPEL OF
LUKE

Luke's gospel is very warm and human, concentrating on Jesus' mercy and forgiveness, his call especially to the poor and underprivileged, inviting both Jew and gentile to salvation. Luke writes a more sophisticated Greek than the other evangelists, giving the impression that he is providing a history for the civilised Greek reader. Perhaps for this reason much of his special material consists of teaching on points of individual morality, especially the danger of material possessions and misuse of wealth. Luke also brings out the importance of individual spiritual qualities, especially prayer, joy and praise of God, and the essential part played by the Holy Spirit in the Chris-

tian life. But in spite of his attention to Greek readers, Luke is very much aware that Jesus is the completion of the OT: the stories of Jesus' infancy, especially, are shot through with reminiscences of the OT.

Many of these emphases occur also in Acts, which once formed the second part of a single two-volume work. The turning-point is Jerusalem, for Luke begins and ends the gospel in Jerusalem, much of Jesus' instruction being brought together in the great final journey up to Jerusalem (section IV); the resurrection appearances are in and around Jerusalem, and it is from Jerusalem that the faith spreads in Acts.

PLAN OF THE BOOK

THE GOSPEL ACCORDING TO
LUKE

Prologue

1 Seeing that many others have undertaken to draw up accounts of the events that have reached their fulfilment among us, [2]as these were handed down to us by those who from the outset were eyewitnesses and ministers of the word, [3]I in my turn, after carefully going over the whole story from the beginning, have decided to write an ordered account for you, Theophilus,[a] [4]so that your Excellency may learn how well founded the teaching is that you have received.

1a Theophilus (='God-lover') may be real or imaginary.

I: THE BIRTH AND HIDDEN LIFE
OF JOHN THE BAPTIST AND OF JESUS

The birth of John the Baptist foretold

[5]In the days of King Herod of Judaea there lived a priest called Zechariah who belonged to the Abijah section of the priesthood, and he had a wife, Elizabeth by name, who was a descendant of Aaron. [6]Both were upright in the sight of God and impeccably carried out all the commandments and observances of the Lord. [7]But they were childless: Elizabeth was barren and they were both advanced in years.

[8]Now it happened that it was the turn of his section to serve, and he was exercising his priestly office before God [9]when it fell to him by lot, as the priestly custom was, to enter the Lord's sanctuary and burn incense there. [10]And at the hour of incense all the people were outside, praying.

[11]Then there appeared to him the angel of the Lord, standing on the right of the altar of incense. [12]The sight disturbed Zechariah and he was overcome with fear. [13]But the angel said to him, 'Zechariah, do not be afraid, for your prayer has been heard. Your wife Elizabeth is to bear you a son and you shall name him John. [14]He will be your joy and delight and many will rejoice at his birth, [15]for he will be great in the sight of the Lord; he must drink no wine, no strong drink;[b] even from his mother's womb he will be filled with the Holy Spirit, [16]and he will bring back many of the Israelites to the Lord their God. [17]With the spirit and power of Elijah, he will go before him *to reconcile fathers to their children*[c] and the disobedient to the good sense of the upright, preparing for the Lord a people fit for him.' [18]Zechariah said to the angel, *'How can I know this?*[d] I am an old man and my wife is getting on in years.' [19]The angel replied, 'I am Gabriel, who stand in God's presence, and I have been sent to speak to you and bring you this good news. [20]Look! Since you did not believe my words, which will come true at their appointed time, you will be silenced and have no power of speech

until this has happened.' [21]Meanwhile the people were waiting for Zechariah and were surprised that he stayed in the sanctuary so long. [22]When he came out he could not speak to them, and they realised that he had seen a vision in the sanctuary. But he could only make signs to them and remained dumb.

[23]When his time of service came to an end he returned home. [24]Some time later his wife Elizabeth conceived and for five months she kept to herself, saying, [25]'The Lord has done this for me, now that it has pleased him to take away the humiliation I suffered in public.'

The annunciation

[26]In the sixth month the angel Gabriel was sent by God to a town in Galilee called Nazareth, [27]to a virgin betrothed to a man named Joseph, of the House of David; and the virgin's name was Mary. [28]He went in and said to her, 'Rejoice, you who enjoy God's favour! The Lord is with you.' [29]She was deeply disturbed by these words and asked herself what this greeting could mean, [30]but the angel said to her, 'Mary, do not be afraid; you have won God's favour. [31]Look! You are to conceive in your womb and bear a son, and you must name him Jesus. [32]He will be great and will be called Son of the Most High. The Lord God will give him the throne of his ancestor David; [33]he will rule over the House of Jacob for ever and his reign will have no end.'[e] [34]Mary said to the angel, 'But how can this come about, since I have no knowledge of man?' [35]The angel answered, 'The Holy Spirit will come upon you, and the power of the Most High will cover you with its shadow. And so the child will be holy and will be called Son of God. [36]And I tell you this too: your cousin Elizabeth also, in her old age, has conceived a son, and she whom people called barren is now in her sixth month, [37]*for nothing is impossible to God.*[f] [38]Mary said, 'You see before you the Lord's

---

1b cf. Nb 6:2–3.
1c Ml 3:23–24.
1d Gn 15:8.
1e cf. 2 S 7:12–16.
1f Gn 18:14.

servant, let it happen to me as you have said.'
And the angel left her.

The visitation

³⁹Mary set out at that time and went as quickly as she could into the hill country to a town in Judah. ⁴⁰She went into Zechariah's house and greeted Elizabeth. ⁴¹Now it happened that as soon as Elizabeth heard Mary's greeting, the child leapt in her womb and Elizabeth was filled with the Holy Spirit. ⁴²She gave a loud cry and said, 'Of all women you are the most blessed, and blessed is the fruit of your womb. ⁴³Why should I be honoured with a visit from the mother of my Lord? ⁴⁴Look, the moment your greeting reached my ears, the child in my womb leapt for joy. ⁴⁵Yes, blessed is she who believed that the promise made her by the Lord would be fulfilled.'

The Magnificat^g

⁴⁶And Mary said:

My soul proclaims
    the greatness of the Lord
⁴⁷and my spirit *rejoices*
    in God my Saviour;
⁴⁸because *he has looked upon*
    the humiliation of his servant.
Yes, from now onwards
    all generations will call me blessed,
⁴⁹for the Almighty
    has done great things for me.
Holy is his name,
⁵⁰and *his faithful love extends age after age*
    to those who fear him.
⁵¹He has used the power of his arm,
    he has routed the arrogant of heart.
⁵²*He has pulled down princes*
    from their thrones
    and raised high the lowly.
⁵³*He has filled the starving with good things,*
    sent the rich away empty.
⁵⁴*He has come to the help*
    of Israel his servant,
    mindful of his faithful love
⁵⁵ —according to the promise
    he made to our ancestors—
of his mercy to Abraham
    and to his descendants for ever.

⁵⁶Mary stayed with her some three months and then went home.

The birth of John the Baptist and visit of the neighbours

⁵⁷The time came for Elizabeth to have her child, and she gave birth to a son; ⁵⁸and when her neighbours and relations heard that the Lord had lavished on her his faithful love, they shared her joy.

The circumcision of John the Baptist

⁵⁹Now it happened that on the eighth day they came to circumcise the child; they were going to call him Zechariah after his father, ⁶⁰but his mother spoke up. 'No,' she said, 'he is to be called John.' ⁶¹They said to her, 'But no one in your family has that name,' ⁶²and made signs to his father to find out what he wanted him called. ⁶³The father asked for a writing-tablet and wrote, 'His name is John.' And they were all astonished. ⁶⁴At that instant his power of speech returned and he spoke and praised God. ⁶⁵All their neighbours were filled with awe and the whole affair was talked about throughout the hill country of Judaea. ⁶⁶All those who heard of it treasured it in their hearts. 'What will this child turn out to be?' they wondered. And indeed the hand of the Lord was with him.

The Benedictus^h

⁶⁷His father Zechariah was filled with the Holy Spirit and spoke this prophecy:

⁶⁸*Blessed be the Lord, the God of Israel,*
    for he has visited his people,
    he has *set them free,*
⁶⁹and he has established for us
    a saving power
    in the House of his servant David,
⁷⁰just as he proclaimed,
    by the mouth of his holy prophets
    from ancient times,
⁷¹that he would save us from our *enemies*
    and *from the hands of all those*
    who hate us,
⁷²and show *faithful love to our ancestors,*
    and so *keep in mind his* holy *covenant.*

1g Mary's canticle echoes Hannah's 1 S 2:1–10, and also 1 S 1:11; Ps 103:17; 111:9; Jb 5:11; 12:19; Ps 98:2; 107:9; Is 41:8–9.
1h The canticle uses Ps 41:13; 111:9; Lv 26:42; Is 9:1.

73This was the oath he swore
to our father Abraham,
74that he would grant us, free from fear,
to be delivered
from the hands of our enemies,
75to serve him in holiness and uprightness
in his presence, all our days.
76And you, little child,
you shall be called
Prophet of the Most High,
for you will go before *the Lord*
to prepare a way for him,
77to give his people knowledge of salvation
through the forgiveness of their sins,
78because of the faithful love of our God
in which the rising Sun
has come from on high to visit us,
79to give light to *those who live*
in darkness and the shadow dark as death,
and to guide our feet
into *the way of peace.*

The hidden life of John the Baptist

80Meanwhile the child grew up and his spirit grew strong. And he lived in the desert until the day he appeared openly to Israel.

The birth of Jesus
and visit of the shepherds

2 Now it happened that at this time Caesar Augustus issued a decree that a census should be made of the whole inhabited world. 2This census—the first—took place while Quirinius was governor of Syria, 3and everyone went to be registered, each to his own town. 4So Joseph set out from the town of Nazareth in Galilee for Judaea, to David's town called Bethlehem, since he was of David's House and line, 5in order to be registered together with Mary, his betrothed, who was with child. 6Now it happened that, while they were there, the time came for her to have her child, 7and she gave birth to a son, her first-born. She wrapped him in swaddling clothes and laid him in a manger because there was no room for them in the living-space. 8In the countryside close by there were shepherds out in the fields keeping guard over their sheep during the watches of the night. 9An angel of the Lord stood over them and the glory of the Lord shone round

them. They were terrified, 10but the angel said, 'Do not be afraid. Look, I bring you news of great joy, a joy to be shared by the whole people. 11Today in the town of David a Saviour has been born to you; he is Christ the Lord. 12And here is a sign for you: you will find a baby wrapped in swaddling clothes and lying in a manger.' 13And all at once with the angel there was a great throng of the hosts of heaven, praising God with the words:

14Glory to God in the highest heaven,
and on earth peace for those he favours.

15Now it happened that when the angels had gone from them into heaven, the shepherds said to one another, 'Let us go to Bethlehem and see this event which the Lord has made known to us.' 16So they hurried away and found Mary and Joseph, and the baby lying in the manger. 17When they saw the child they repeated what they had been told about him, 18and everyone who heard it was astonished at what the shepherds said to them. 19As for Mary, she treasured all these things and pondered them in her heart. 20And the shepherds went back glorifying and praising God for all they had heard and seen, just as they had been told.

The circumcision of Jesus

21When the eighth day came and the child was to be circumcised, they gave him the name Jesus, the name the angel had given him before his conception.

Jesus is presented in the Temple

22And when the day came for them to be purified in keeping with the Law of Moses, they took him up to Jerusalem to present him to the Lord—23observing what is written in the Law of the Lord: *Every first-born male must be consecrated to the Lord—*[a] 24and also to offer in sacrifice, in accordance with what is prescribed in the Law of the Lord, *a pair of turtledoves or two young pigeons.*[b] 25Now in Jerusalem there was a man named Simeon. He was an upright and devout man; he looked forward to the restoration of Israel and the Holy Spirit rested on him. 26It had been revealed to him by the Holy Spirit that he would not see death until he had set eyes on

2a Ex 13:2.
2b Lv 5:7.

the Christ of the Lord. [27]Prompted by the Spirit he came to the Temple; and when the parents brought in the child Jesus to do for him what the Law required, [28]he took him into his arms and blessed God; and he said:

The Nunc Dimittis

[29]Now, Master, you are letting
    your servant go in peace
  as you promised;
[30]for my eyes have seen the salvation
[31]which you have made ready
  in the sight of the nations;
[32]a light of revelation for the gentiles
  and glory for your people Israel.

The prophecy of Simeon

[33]As the child's father and mother were wondering at the things that were being said about him, [34]Simeon blessed them and said to Mary his mother, 'Look, he is destined for the fall and for the rise of many in Israel, destined to be a sign that is opposed — [35]and a sword will pierce your soul too — so that the secret thoughts of many may be laid bare.'

The prophecy of Anna

[36]There was a prophetess, too, Anna the daughter of Phanuel, of the tribe of Asher. She was well on in years. Her days of girlhood over, she had been married for seven years [37]before becoming a widow. She was now eighty-four years old and never left the Temple, serving God night and day with fasting and prayer. [38]She came up just at that moment and began to praise God; and she spoke of the child to all who looked forward to the deliverance of Jerusalem.

The hidden life of Jesus at Nazareth

[39]When they had done everything the Law of the Lord required, they went back to Galilee, to their own town of Nazareth. [40]And as the child grew to maturity, he was filled with wisdom; and God's favour was with him.

Jesus among the doctors of the Law

[41]Every year his parents used to go to Jerusalem for the feast of the Passover. [42]When he was twelve years old, they went up for the feast as usual. [43]When the days of the feast were over and they set off home, the boy Jesus stayed behind in Jerusalem without his parents knowing it. [44]They assumed he was somewhere in the party, and it was only after a day's journey that they went to look for him among their relations and acquaintances. [45]When they failed to find him they went back to Jerusalem looking for him everywhere.

[46]It happened that, three days later, they found him in the Temple, sitting among the teachers, listening to them, and asking them questions; [47]and all those who heard him were astounded at his intelligence and his replies. [48]They were overcome when they saw him, and his mother said to him, 'My child, why have you done this to us? See how worried your father and I have been, looking for you.' [49]He replied, 'Why were you looking for me? Did you not know that I must be in my Father's house?' [50]But they did not understand what he meant.

The hidden life at Nazareth resumed

[51]He went down with them then and came to Nazareth and lived under their authority. His mother stored up all these things in her heart. [52]And Jesus increased in wisdom, in stature, and in favour with God and with people.

II: PRELUDE TO THE PUBLIC MINISTRY OF JESUS

The proclamation of John the Baptist

3 In the fifteenth year of Tiberius Caesar's reign, when Pontius Pilate was governor of Judaea, Herod tetrarch of Galilee, his brother Philip tetrarch of the territories of Ituraea and Trachonitis, Lysanias tetrarch of Abilene, [2]and while the high-priesthood was held by Annas and Caiaphas, the word of God came to John the son of Zechariah, in the desert. [3]He went through the whole Jordan area proclaiming a baptism of repent-

ance for the forgiveness of sins, ⁴as it is written in the book of the sayings of Isaiah the prophet:

> A voice of one that cries in the desert:
> Prepare a way for the Lord,
> make his paths straight!
> ⁵Let every valley be filled in,
> every mountain and hill be levelled,
> winding ways be straightened
> and rough roads made smooth,
> ⁶and all humanity
> will see the salvation of God.ᵃ

⁷He said, therefore, to the crowds who came to be baptised by him, 'Brood of vipers, who warned you to flee from the coming retribution? ⁸Produce fruit in keeping with repentance, and do not start telling yourselves, "We have Abraham as our father," because, I tell you, God can raise children for Abraham from these stones. ⁹Yes, even now the axe is being laid to the root of the trees, so that any tree failing to produce good fruit will be cut down and thrown on the fire.'

¹⁰When all the people asked him, 'What must we do, then?' ¹¹he answered, 'Anyone who has two tunics must share with the one who has none, and anyone with something to eat must do the same.' ¹²There were tax collectors, too, who came for baptism, and these said to him, 'Master, what must we do?' ¹³He said to them, 'Exact no more than the appointed rate.' ¹⁴Some soldiers asked him in their turn, 'What about us? What must we do?' He said to them, 'No intimidation! No extortion! Be content with your pay!'

¹⁵A feeling of expectancy had grown among the people, who were beginning to wonder whether John might be the Christ, ¹⁶so John declared before them all, 'I baptise you with water, but someone is coming, who is more powerful than me, and I am not fit to undo the strap of his sandals; he will baptise you with the Holy Spirit and fire. ¹⁷His winnowing-fan is in his hand, to clear his threshing-floor and to gather the wheat into his barn; but the chaff he will burn in a fire that will never go out.' ¹⁸And he proclaimed the good news to the people with many other exhortations too.

John the Baptist imprisoned

¹⁹But Herod the tetrarch, censured by John for his relations with his brother's wife Herodias and for all the other crimes he had committed, ²⁰added a further crime to all the rest by shutting John up in prison.

Jesus is baptised

²¹Now it happened that when all the people had been baptised and while Jesus after his own baptism was at prayer, heaven opened ²²and the Holy Spirit descended on him in a physical form, like a dove. And a voice came from heaven, 'You are my Son; today have I fathered you.'ᵇ

The ancestry of Jesus

²³When he began, Jesus was about thirty years old, being the son, as it was thought, of Joseph son of Heli, ²⁴son of Matthat, son of Levi, son of Melchi, son of Jannai, son of Joseph, ²⁵son of Mattathias, son of Amos, son of Nahum, son of Esli, son of Naggai, ²⁶son of Maath, son of Mattathias, son of Semein, son of Josech, son of Joda, ²⁷son of Joanan, son of Rhesa, son of Zerubbabel, son of Shealtiel, son of Neri, ²⁸son of Melchi, son of Addi, son of Cosam, son of Elmadam, son of Er, ²⁹son of Jesus, son of Eliezer, son of Jorim, son of Matthat, son of Levi, ³⁰son of Symeon, son of Judah, son of Joseph, son of Jonam, son of Eliakim, ³¹son of Melea, son of Menna, son of Mattatha, son of Nathan, son of David, ³²son of Jesse, son of Obed, son of Boaz, son of Sala, son of Nahshon, ³³son of Amminadab, son of Admin, son of Arni, son of Hezron, son of Perez, son of Judah, ³⁴son of Jacob, son of Isaac, son of Abraham, son of Terah, son of Nahor, ³⁵son of Serug, son of Reu, son of Peleg, son of Eber, son of Shelah, ³⁶son of Cainan, son of Arphaxad, son of Shem, son of Noah, son of Lamech, ³⁷son of Methuselah, son of Enoch, son of Jared, son of Mahalaleel, son of Cainan, ³⁸son of Enos, son of Seth, son of Adam, son of God.

3a Is 40:3–5.
3b Ps 2:7.

Testing in the desert

4 Filled with the Holy Spirit, Jesus left the Jordan and was led by the Spirit into the desert, [2]for forty days being put to the test by the devil. During that time he ate nothing and at the end he was hungry. [3]Then the devil said to him, 'If you are Son of God, tell this stone to turn into a loaf.' [4]But Jesus replied, 'Scripture says:

Human beings live not on bread alone.'[a]

[5]Then leading him to a height, the devil showed him in a moment of time all the kingdoms of the world [6]and said to him, 'I will give you all this power and their splendour, for it has been handed over to me, for me to give it to anyone I choose. [7]Do homage, then, to me, and it shall all be yours.' [8]But Jesus answered him, 'Scripture says:

You must do homage to the Lord your God, him alone you must serve.'[b]

[9]Then he led him to Jerusalem and set him on the parapet of the Temple. 'If you are Son of God,' he said to him, 'throw yourself down from here, [10]for scripture says:

He has given his angels orders about you, to guard you,

and again:

[11]*They will carry you in their arms in case you trip over a stone.'[c]*

[12]But Jesus answered him, 'Scripture says:

Do not put the Lord your God to the test.'[d]

[13]Having exhausted every way of putting him to the test, the devil left him, until the opportune moment.

III: THE GALILEAN MINISTRY

Jesus begins to preach

[14]Jesus, with the power of the Spirit in him, returned to Galilee; and his reputation spread throughout the countryside. [15]He taught in their synagogues and everyone glorified him.

Jesus at Nazareth

[16]He came to Nazara, where he had been brought up, and went into the synagogue on the Sabbath day as he usually did. He stood up to read, [17]and they handed him the scroll of the prophet Isaiah. Unrolling the scroll he found the place where it is written:

[18]*The spirit of the Lord is on me, for he has anointed me to bring the good news to the afflicted. He has sent me to proclaim liberty to captives, sight to the blind, to let the oppressed go free, [19]to proclaim a year of favour from the Lord.[e]*

[20]He then rolled up the scroll, gave it back to the assistant and sat down. And all eyes in the synagogue were fixed on him. [21]Then he began to speak to them, 'This text is being fulfilled today even while you are listening.' [22]And he won the approval of all, and they were astonished by the gracious words that came from his lips.

They said, 'This is Joseph's son, surely?' [23]But he replied, 'No doubt you will quote me the saying, "Physician, heal yourself," and tell me, "We have heard all that happened in Capernaum, do the same here in your own country." ' [24]And he went on, 'In truth I tell you, no prophet is ever accepted in his own country.

[25]'There were many widows in Israel, I can assure you, in Elijah's day, when heaven remained shut for three years and six months and a great famine raged throughout the land, [26]but Elijah was not sent to any one of these: he was sent to a widow at Zarephath, a town in Sidonia.[f] [27]And in the prophet Elisha's time there were many suffering from

4a Dt 8:3.
4b Dt 6:13.
4c Ps 91:11–12.
4d Dt 6:16.
4e Is 61:1–2.
4f 1 K 17:9.

virulent skin-diseases in Israel, but none of these was cured—only Naaman the Syrian.'ᵍ

²⁸When they heard this everyone in the synagogue was enraged. ²⁹They sprang to their feet and hustled him out of the town; and they took him up to the brow of the hill their town was built on, intending to throw him off the cliff, ³⁰but he passed straight through the crowd and walked away.

Jesus teaches in Capernaum and cures a demoniac

³¹He went down to Capernaum, a town in Galilee, and taught them on the Sabbath. ³²And his teaching made a deep impression on them because his word carried authority. ³³In the synagogue there was a man possessed by the spirit of an unclean devil, and he shouted at the top of his voice, ³⁴'Ha! What do you want with us, Jesus of Nazareth? Have you come to destroy us? I know who you are: the Holy One of God.' ³⁵But Jesus rebuked it, saying, 'Be quiet! Come out of him!' And the devil, throwing the man into the middle, went out of him without hurting him at all. ³⁶Astonishment seized them and they were all saying to one another, 'What is it in his words? He gives orders to unclean spirits with authority and power and they come out.' ³⁷And the news of him travelled all through the surrounding countryside.

Cure of Simon's mother-in-law

³⁸Leaving the synagogue he went to Simon's house. Now Simon's mother-in-law was in the grip of a high fever and they asked him to do something for her. ³⁹Standing over her he rebuked the fever and it left her. And she immediately got up and began to serve them.

A number of cures

⁴⁰At sunset all those who had friends suffering from diseases of one kind or another brought them to him, and laying his hands on each he cured them. ⁴¹Devils too came out of many people, shouting, 'You are the Son of God.' But he warned them and would not allow them to speak because they knew that he was the Christ.

Dawn departure from Capernaum and travels through Judaea

⁴²When daylight came he left the house and made his way to a lonely place. The crowds went to look for him, and when they had caught up with him they wanted to prevent him leaving them, ⁴³but he answered, 'I must proclaim the good news of the kingdom of God to the other towns too, because that is what I was sent to do.' ⁴⁴And he continued his proclamation in the synagogues of Judaea.

The first four disciples are called

5 Now it happened that he was standing one day by the Lake of Gennesaret, with the crowd pressing round him listening to the word of God, ²when he caught sight of two boats at the water's edge. The fishermen had got out of them and were washing their nets. ³He got into one of the boats—it was Simon's—and asked him to put out a little from the shore. Then he sat down and taught the crowds from the boat.

⁴When he had finished speaking he said to Simon, 'Put out into deep water and pay out your nets for a catch.' ⁵Simon replied, 'Master, we worked hard all night long and caught nothing, but if you say so, I will pay out the nets.' ⁶And when they had done this they netted such a huge number of fish that their nets began to tear, ⁷so they signalled to their companions in the other boat to come and help them; when these came, they filled both boats to sinking point.

⁸When Simon Peter saw this he fell at the knees of Jesus saying, 'Leave me, Lord; I am a sinful man.' ⁹For he and all his companions were completely awestruck at the catch they had made; ¹⁰so also were James and John, sons of Zebedee, who were Simon's partners. But Jesus said to Simon, 'Do not be afraid; from now on it is people you will be catching.' ¹¹Then, bringing their boats back to land they left everything and followed him.

Cure of a man suffering from a virulent skin-disease

¹²Now it happened that Jesus was in one of the towns when suddenly a man appeared, covered with a skin-disease. Seeing Jesus he fell on his face and implored him saying, 'Sir,

4g 2 K 5:14.

if you are willing you can cleanse me.' ¹³He stretched out his hand, and touched him saying, 'I am willing. Be cleansed.' At once the skin-disease left him. ¹⁴He ordered him to tell no one, 'But go and show yourself to the priest and make the offering for your cleansing just as Moses prescribed, as evidence to them.'

¹⁵But the news of him kept spreading, and large crowds would gather to hear him and to have their illnesses cured, ¹⁶but he would go off to some deserted place and pray.

Cure of a paralytic

¹⁷Now it happened that he was teaching one day, and Pharisees and teachers of the Law, who had come from every village in Galilee, from Judaea and from Jerusalem, were sitting there. And the power of the Lord was there so that he should heal. ¹⁸And now some men appeared, bringing on a bed a paralysed man whom they were trying to bring in and lay down in front of him. ¹⁹But as they could find no way of getting the man through the crowd, they went up onto the top of the house and lowered him and his stretcher down through the tiles into the middle of the gathering, in front of Jesus. ²⁰Seeing their faith he said, 'My friend, your sins are forgiven you.' ²¹The scribes and the Pharisees began to think this over. 'Who is this man, talking blasphemy? Who but God alone can forgive sins?' ²²But Jesus, aware of their thoughts, made them this reply, 'What are these thoughts you have in your hearts? ²³Which of these is easier: to say, "Your sins are forgiven you," or to say, "Get up and walk"? ²⁴But to prove to you that the Son of man has authority on earth to forgive sins,'—he said to the paralysed man—'I order you: get up, and pick up your stretcher and go home.' ²⁵And immediately before their very eyes he got up, picked up what he had been lying on and went home praising God. ²⁶They were all astounded and praised God and were filled with awe, saying, 'We have seen strange things today.'

The call of Levi

²⁷When he went out after this, he noticed a tax collector, Levi by name, sitting at the tax office, and said to him, 'Follow me.' ²⁸And

leaving everything Levi got up and followed him.

Eating with sinners in Levi's house

²⁹In his honour Levi held a great reception in his house, and with them at table was a large gathering of tax collectors and others. ³⁰The Pharisees and their scribes complained to his disciples and said, 'Why do you eat and drink with tax collectors and sinners?' ³¹Jesus said to them in reply, 'It is not those that are well who need the doctor, but the sick. ³²I have come to call not the upright but sinners to repentance.'

Discussion on fasting

³³They then said to him, 'John's disciples are always fasting and saying prayers, and the disciples of the Pharisees, too, but yours go on eating and drinking.' ³⁴Jesus replied, 'Surely you cannot make the bridegroom's attendants fast while the bridegroom is still with them? ³⁵But the time will come when the bridegroom is taken away from them; then, in those days, they will fast.'

³⁶He also told them a parable, 'No one tears a piece from a new cloak to put it on an old cloak; otherwise, not only will the new one be torn, but the piece taken from the new will not match the old.

³⁷'And nobody puts new wine in old wineskins; otherwise, the new wine will burst the skins and run to waste, and the skins will be ruined. ³⁸No; new wine must be put in fresh skins. ³⁹And nobody who has been drinking old wine wants new. "The old is good," he says.'

Picking corn on the Sabbath

6 It happened that one Sabbath he was walking through the cornfields, and his disciples were picking ears of corn, rubbing them in their hands and eating them. ²Some of the Pharisees said, 'Why are you doing something that is forbidden on the Sabbath day?' ³Jesus answered them, 'So you have not read what David did*a* when he and his followers were hungry—⁴how he went into the house of God and took the loaves of the offering and ate them and gave them to his

---

6a 1 S 21:2–7.

followers, loaves which the priests alone are allowed to eat?' ⁵And he said to them, 'The Son of man is master of the Sabbath.'

Cure of the man with a withered hand

⁶Now on another Sabbath he went into the synagogue and began to teach, and a man was present, and his right hand was withered. ⁷The scribes and the Pharisees were watching him to see if he would cure somebody on the Sabbath, hoping to find something to charge him with. ⁸But he knew their thoughts; and he said to the man with the withered hand, 'Get up and stand out in the middle!' And he came forward and stood there. ⁹Then Jesus said to them, 'I put it to you: is it permitted on the Sabbath to do good, or to do evil; to save life, or to destroy it?' ¹⁰Then he looked round at them all and said to the man, 'Stretch out your hand.' He did so, and his hand was restored. ¹¹But they were furious and began to discuss the best way of dealing with Jesus.

The choice of the Twelve

¹²Now it happened in those days that he went onto the mountain to pray; and he spent the whole night in prayer to God. ¹³When day came he summoned his disciples and picked out twelve of them; he called them 'apostles': ¹⁴Simon whom he called Peter, and his brother Andrew, James, John, Philip, Bartholomew, ¹⁵Matthew, Thomas, James son of Alphaeus, Simon called the Zealot, ¹⁶Judas son of James, and Judas Iscariot who became a traitor.

The crowds follow Jesus

¹⁷He then came down with them and stopped at a piece of level ground where there was a large gathering of his disciples, with a great crowd of people from all parts of Judaea and Jerusalem and the coastal region of Tyre and Sidon ¹⁸who had come to hear him and to be cured of their diseases. People tormented by unclean spirits were also cured, ¹⁹and everyone in the crowd was trying to touch him because power came out of him that cured them all.

The first sermon. The Beatitudes[b]

²⁰Then fixing his eyes on his disciples he said:

How blessed are you who are poor:
    the kingdom of God is yours.
²¹Blessed are you who are hungry now:
    you shall have your fill.
Blessed are you who are weeping now:
    you shall laugh.

²²'Blessed are you when people hate you, drive you out, abuse you, denounce your name as criminal, on account of the Son of man. ²³Rejoice when that day comes and dance for joy, look!—your reward will be great in heaven. This was the way their ancestors treated the prophets.

The curses

²⁴But alas for you who are rich:
    you are having your consolation now.
²⁵Alas for you who have plenty to eat now:
    you shall go hungry.
Alas for you who are laughing now:
    you shall mourn and weep.

²⁶'Alas for you when everyone speaks well of you! This was the way their ancestors treated the false prophets.

Love of enemies

²⁷'But I say this to you who are listening: Love your enemies, do good to those who hate you, ²⁸bless those who curse you, pray for those who treat you badly. ²⁹To anyone who slaps you on one cheek, present the other cheek as well; to anyone who takes your cloak from you, do not refuse your tunic. ³⁰Give to everyone who asks you, and do not ask for your property back from someone who takes it. ³¹Treat others as you would like people to treat you. ³²If you love those who love you, what credit can you expect? Even sinners love those who love them. ³³And if you do good to those who do good to you, what credit can you expect? For even sinners do that much. ³⁴And if you lend to those from whom you hope to get money back, what credit can you expect? Even sinners lend to sinners to get back the same amount. ³⁵Instead, love your enemies and do good to them, and lend without any hope of return. You will have a great reward, and you will be children of the

6b Mt 5:1.

Most High, for he himself is kind to the ungrateful and the wicked.

Compassion and generosity

36'Be compassionate just as your Father is compassionate. 37Do not judge, and you will not be judged; do not condemn, and you will not be condemned; forgive, and you will be forgiven. 38Give, and there will be gifts for you: a full measure, pressed down, shaken together, and overflowing, will be poured into your lap; because the standard you use will be the standard used for you.'

Integrity

39He also told them a parable, 'Can one blind person guide another? Surely both will fall into a pit? 40Disciple is not superior to teacher; but fully trained disciple will be like teacher. 41Why do you observe the splinter in your brother's eye and never notice the great log in your own? 42How can you say to your brother, "Brother, let me take out that splinter in your eye," when you cannot see the great log in your own? Hypocrite! Take the log out of your own eye first, and then you will see clearly enough to take out the splinter in your brother's eye.

43'There is no sound tree that produces rotten fruit, nor again a rotten tree that produces sound fruit. 44Every tree can be told by its own fruit: people do not pick figs from thorns, nor gather grapes from brambles. 45Good people draw what is good from the store of goodness in their hearts; bad people draw what is bad from the store of badness. For the words of the mouth flow out of what fills the heart.

The true disciple

46'Why do you call me, "Lord, Lord" and not do what I say?

47'Everyone who comes to me and listens to my words and acts on them—I will show you what such a person is like. 48Such a person is like the man who, when he built a house, dug, and dug deep, and laid the foundations on rock; when the river was in flood it bore down on that house but could not shake it, it was so well built. 49But someone who listens and does nothing is like the man who built a house on soil, with no foundations; as soon as the river bore down on it, it collapsed; and what a ruin that house became!'

Cure of the centurion's servant

7When he had come to the end of all he wanted the people to hear, he went into Capernaum. 2A centurion there had a servant, a favourite of his, who was sick and near death. 3Having heard about Jesus he sent some Jewish elders to him to ask him to come and heal his servant. 4When they came to Jesus they pleaded earnestly with him saying, 'He deserves this of you, 5because he is well disposed towards our people; he built us our synagogue himself.' 6So Jesus went with them, and was not very far from the house when the centurion sent word to him by some friends to say to him, 'Sir, do not put yourself to any trouble because I am not worthy to have you under my roof; 7and that is why I did not presume to come to you myself; let my boy be cured by your giving the word. 8For I am under authority myself, and have soldiers under me; and I say to one man, "Go," and he goes; to another, "Come here," and he comes; to my servant, "Do this," and he does it.' 9When Jesus heard these words he was astonished at him and, turning round, said to the crowd following him, 'I tell you, not even in Israel have I found faith as great as this.' 10And when the messengers got back to the house they found the servant in perfect health.

The son of the widow of Nain restored to life

11It happened that soon afterwards he went to a town called Nain, accompanied by his disciples and a great number of people. 12Now when he was near the gate of the town there was a dead man being carried out, the only son of his mother, and she was a widow. And a considerable number of the towns-people was with her. 13When the Lord saw her he felt sorry for her and said to her, 'Don't cry.' 14Then he went up and touched the bier and the bearers stood still, and he said, 'Young man, I tell you: get up.' 15And the dead man sat up and began to talk, and Jesus *gave him to his mother.*[a] 16Everyone was filled

---

7a 1 K 17:23.

with awe and glorified God saying, 'A great prophet has risen up among us; God has visited his people.' ¹⁷And this view of him spread throughout Judaea and all over the countryside.

The Baptist's question
Jesus commends him

¹⁸The disciples of John gave him all this news, and John, summoning two of his disciples, ¹⁹sent them to the Lord to ask, 'Are you the one who is to come, or are we to expect someone else?' ²⁰When the men reached Jesus they said, 'John the Baptist has sent us to you to ask, "Are you the one who is to come or are we to expect someone else?" ' ²¹At that very time he cured many people of diseases and afflictions and of evil spirits, and gave the gift of sight to many who were blind. ²²Then he gave the messengers their answer, 'Go back and tell John what you have seen and heard: the blind see again, the lame walk, those suffering from virulent skin-diseases are cleansed, and the deaf hear, the dead are raised to life, the good news is proclaimed to the poor; ²³and blessed is anyone who does not find me a cause of falling.'

²⁴When John's messengers had gone he began to talk to the people about John, ²⁵'What did you go out into the desert to see? A reed swaying in the breeze? No! Then what did you go out to see? A man dressed in fine clothes? Look, those who go in magnificent clothes and live luxuriously are to be found at royal courts! ²⁶Then what did you go out to see? A prophet? Yes, I tell you, and much more than a prophet: ²⁷he is the one of whom scripture says:

Look, I am going to send my messenger
in front of you
to prepare your way before you. ᵇ

²⁸'I tell you, of all the children born to women, there is no one greater than John; yet the least in the kingdom of God is greater than he.' ²⁹All the people who heard him, and the tax collectors too, acknowledged God's saving justice by accepting baptism from John; ³⁰but by refusing baptism from him the Pharisees and the lawyers thwarted God's plan for them.

Jesus condemns his contemporaries

³¹'What comparison, then, can I find for the people of this generation? What are they like? ³²They are like children shouting to one another while they sit in the market place:

We played the pipes for you,
and you wouldn't dance;
we sang dirges,
and you wouldn't cry.

³³'For John the Baptist has come, not eating bread, not drinking wine, and you say, "He is possessed." ³⁴The Son of man has come, eating and drinking, and you say, "Look, a glutton and a drunkard, a friend of tax collectors and sinners." ³⁵Yet wisdom is justified by all her children.'

The woman who was a sinner

³⁶One of the Pharisees invited him to a meal. When he arrived at the Pharisee's house and took his place at table, ³⁷suddenly a woman came in, who had a bad name in the town. She had heard he was dining with the Pharisee and had brought with her an alabaster jar of ointment. ³⁸She waited behind him at his feet, weeping, and her tears fell on his feet, and she wiped them away with her hair; then she covered his feet with kisses and anointed them with the ointment.

³⁹When the Pharisee who had invited him saw this, he said to himself, 'If this man were a prophet, he would know who this woman is and what sort of person it is who is touching him and what a bad name she has.' ⁴⁰Then Jesus took him up and said, 'Simon, I have something to say to you.' He replied, 'Say on, Master.' ⁴¹'There was once a creditor who had two men in his debt; one owed him five hundred denarii, the other fifty. ⁴²They were unable to pay, so he let them both off. Which of them will love him more?' ⁴³Simon answered, 'The one who was let off more, I suppose.' Jesus said, 'You are right.'

⁴⁴Then he turned to the woman and said to Simon, 'You see this woman? I came into your house, and you poured no water over my feet, but she has poured out her tears over my feet and wiped them away with her hair. ⁴⁵You gave me no kiss, but she has been covering my feet with kisses ever since I came in. ⁴⁶You did not anoint my head with oil,

7b Ml 3:1.

but she has anointed my feet with ointment. [47]For this reason I tell you that her sins, many as they are, have been forgiven her, because she has shown such great love.[c] It is someone who is forgiven little who shows little love.' [48]Then he said to her, 'Your sins are forgiven.' [49]Those who were with him at table began to say to themselves, 'Who is this man, that even forgives sins?' [50]But he said to the woman, 'Your faith has saved you; go in peace.'

The women accompanying Jesus

8 Now it happened that after this he made his way through towns and villages preaching and proclaiming the good news of the kingdom of God. With him went the Twelve, [2]as well as certain women who had been cured of evil spirits and ailments: Mary surnamed the Magdalene, from whom seven demons had gone out, [3]Joanna the wife of Herod's steward Chuza, Susanna, and many others who provided for them out of their own resources.

Parable of the sower

[4]With a large crowd gathering and people from every town finding their way to him, he told this parable:

[5]'A sower went out to sow his seed. Now as he sowed, some fell on the edge of the path and was trampled on; and the birds of the air ate it up. [6]Some seed fell on rock, and when it came up it withered away, having no moisture. [7]Some seed fell in the middle of thorns and the thorns grew with it and choked it. [8]And some seed fell into good soil and grew and produced its crop a hundredfold.' Saying this he cried, 'Anyone who has ears for listening should listen!'

Why Jesus speaks in parables

[9]His disciples asked him what this parable might mean, [10]and he said, 'To you is granted to understand the secrets of the kingdom of God; for the rest it remains in parables, so that

they may look but not perceive,
listen but not understand.[a]

The parable of the sower explained

[11]'This, then, is what the parable means: the seed is the word of God. [12]Those on the edge of the path are people who have heard it, and then the devil comes and carries away the word from their hearts in case they should believe and be saved. [13]Those on the rock are people who, when they first hear it, welcome the word with joy. But these have no root; they believe for a while, and in time of trial they give up. [14]As for the part that fell into thorns, this is people who have heard, but as they go on their way they are choked by the worries and riches and pleasures of life and never produce any crops. [15]As for the part in the rich soil, this is people with a noble and generous heart who have heard the word and take it to themselves and yield a harvest through their perseverance.

Parable of the lamp

[16]'No one lights a lamp to cover it with a bowl or to put it under a bed. No, it is put on a lamp-stand so that people may see the light when they come in. [17]For nothing is hidden but it will be made clear, nothing secret but it will be made known and brought to light. [18]So take care how you listen; anyone who has, will be given more; anyone who has not, will be deprived even of what he thinks he has.'

The true family of Jesus

[19]His mother and his brothers came looking for him, but they could not get to him because of the crowd. [20]He was told, 'Your mother and brothers are standing outside and want to see you.' [21]But he said in answer, 'My mother and my brothers are those who hear the word of God and put it into practice.'

The calming of the storm

[22]It happened that one day he got into a boat with his disciples and said to them, 'Let us cross over to the other side of the lake.' So they set out, [23]and as they sailed he fell asleep. When a squall of wind came down on the lake the boat started shipping water and they found themselves in danger. [24]So they went

---

7c In most of the story love wins forgiveness, but in vv. 40–43 and 47a, forgiveness nourishes love.
8a Is 6:9.

to rouse him saying, 'Master! Master! We are lost!' Then he woke up and rebuked the wind and the rough water; and they subsided and it was calm again. ²⁵He said to them, 'Where is your faith?' They were awestruck and astounded and said to one another, 'Who can this be, that gives orders even to winds and waves and they obey him?'

The Gerasene demoniac

²⁶They came to land in the territory of the Gerasenes, which is opposite Galilee. ²⁷He was stepping ashore when a man from the city who was possessed by devils came towards him; for a long time the man had been living with no clothes on, not in a house, but in the tombs.

²⁸Catching sight of Jesus he gave a shout, fell at his feet and cried out at the top of his voice, 'What do you want with me, Jesus, son of the Most High God? I implore you, do not torture me.' ²⁹For Jesus had been telling the unclean spirit to come out of the man. It had seized on him a great many times, and then they used to secure him with chains and fetters to restrain him, but he would always break the fastenings, and the devil would drive him out into the wilds. ³⁰Jesus asked him, 'What is your name?' He said, 'Legion'—because many devils had gone into him. ³¹And these begged him not to order them to depart into the Abyss.

³²Now there was a large herd of pigs feeding there on the mountain, and the devils begged him to let them go into these. So he gave them leave. ³³The devils came out of the man and went into the pigs, and the herd charged down the cliff into the lake and was drowned.

³⁴When the swineherds saw what had happened they ran off and told their story in the city and in the country round about; ³⁵and the people went out to see what had happened. When they came to Jesus they found the man from whom the devils had gone out sitting at the feet of Jesus, wearing clothes and in his right mind; and they were afraid. ³⁶Those who had witnessed it told them how the man who had been possessed came to be saved. ³⁷The entire population of the Gerasene territory was in great fear and asked Jesus to leave them. So he got into the boat and went back.

³⁸The man from whom the devils had gone out asked to be allowed to stay with him, but he sent him away saying, ³⁹'Go back home and report all that God has done for you.' So the man went off and proclaimed throughout the city all that Jesus had done for him.

Cure of the woman with a haemorrhage Jairus' daughter raised to life

⁴⁰On his return Jesus was welcomed by the crowd, for they were all there waiting for him. ⁴¹And suddenly there came a man named Jairus, who was president of the synagogue. He fell at Jesus' feet and pleaded with him to come to his house, ⁴²because he had an only daughter about twelve years old, who was dying. And the crowds were almost stifling Jesus as he went.

⁴³Now there was a woman suffering from a haemorrhage for the past twelve years, whom no one had been able to cure. ⁴⁴She came up behind him and touched the fringe of his cloak; and the haemorrhage stopped at that very moment. ⁴⁵Jesus said, 'Who was it that touched me?' When they all denied it, Peter said, 'Master, it is the crowds round you, pushing.' ⁴⁶But Jesus said, 'Somebody touched me. I felt that power had gone out from me.' ⁴⁷Seeing herself discovered, the woman came forward trembling, and falling at his feet explained in front of all the people why she had touched him and how she had been cured at that very moment. ⁴⁸'My daughter,' he said, 'your faith has saved you; go in peace.'

⁴⁹While he was still speaking, someone arrived from the house of the president of the synagogue to say, 'Your daughter has died. Do not trouble the Master any further.' ⁵⁰But Jesus heard this, and he spoke to the man, 'Do not be afraid, only have faith and she will be saved.' ⁵¹When he came to the house he allowed no one to go in with him except Peter and John and James, and the child's father and mother. ⁵²They were all crying and mourning for her, but Jesus said, 'Stop crying; she is not dead, but asleep.' ⁵³But they ridiculed him, knowing she was dead. ⁵⁴But taking her by the hand himself he spoke to her, 'Child, get up.' ⁵⁵And her spirit returned and she got up at that very moment. Then he told them to give her something to eat. ⁵⁶Her parents were astonished, but he ordered them not to tell anyone what had happened.

The mission of the Twelve

9 He called the Twelve together and gave them power and authority over all devils and to cure diseases, ²and he sent them out to proclaim the kingdom of God and to heal. ³He said to them, 'Take nothing for the journey: neither staff, nor haversack, nor bread, nor money; and do not have a spare tunic. ⁴Whatever house you enter, stay there; and when you leave let your departure be from there. ⁵As for those who do not welcome you, when you leave their town shake the dust from your feet as evidence against them.' ⁶So they set out and went from village to village proclaiming the good news and healing everywhere.

Herod and Jesus

⁷Meanwhile Herod the tetrarch had heard about all that was going on; and he was puzzled, because some people were saying that John had risen from the dead, ⁸others that Elijah had reappeared, still others that one of the ancient prophets had come back to life. ⁹But Herod said, 'John? I beheaded him. So who is this I hear such reports about?' And he was anxious to see him.

The return of the apostles
Miracle of the loaves

¹⁰On their return the apostles gave him an account of all they had done. Then he took them with him and withdrew towards a town called Bethsaida where they could be by themselves. ¹¹But the crowds got to know and they went after him. He made them welcome and talked to them about the kingdom of God; and he cured those who were in need of healing.

¹²It was late afternoon when the Twelve came up to him and said, 'Send the people away, and they can go to the villages and farms round about to find lodging and food; for we are in a lonely place here.' ¹³He replied, 'Give them something to eat yourselves.' But they said, 'We have no more than five loaves and two fish, unless we are to go ourselves and buy food for all these people.' ¹⁴For there were about five thousand men. But he said to his disciples, 'Get them to sit down in parties of about fifty.' ¹⁵They did so and made them all sit down. ¹⁶Then he took the five loaves and the two fish, raised his eyes to heaven, and said the blessing over them; then he broke them and handed them to his disciples to distribute among the crowd. ¹⁷They all ate as much as they wanted, and when the scraps left over were collected they filled twelve baskets.

Peter's profession of faith

¹⁸Now it happened that he was praying alone, and his disciples came to him and he put this question to them, 'Who do the crowds say I am?' ¹⁹And they answered, 'Some say John the Baptist; others Elijah; others again one of the ancient prophets come back to life.' ²⁰'But you,' he said to them, 'who do you say I am?' It was Peter who spoke up. 'The Christ of God,' he said. ²¹But he gave them strict orders and charged them not to say this to anyone.

First prophecy of the Passion

²²He said, 'The Son of man is destined to suffer grievously, to be rejected by the elders and chief priests and scribes and to be put to death, and to be raised up on the third day.'

The condition of following Christ

²³Then, speaking to all, he said, 'If anyone wants to be a follower of mine, let him renounce himself and take up his cross every day and follow me. ²⁴Anyone who wants to save his life will lose it; but anyone who loses his life for my sake, will save it. ²⁵What benefit is it to anyone to win the whole world and forfeit or lose his very self? ²⁶For if anyone is ashamed of me and of my words, of him the Son of man will be ashamed when he comes in his own glory and in the glory of the Father and the holy angels.

The kingdom will come soon

²⁷'I tell you truly, there are some standing here who will not taste death before they see the kingdom of God.'

The transfiguration

²⁸Now about eight days after this had been said, he took with him Peter, John and James and went up the mountain to pray. ²⁹And it happened that, as he was praying, the aspect

of his face was changed and his clothing became sparkling white. [30]And suddenly there were two men talking to him; they were Moses and Elijah [31]appearing in glory, and they were speaking of his passing which he was to accomplish in Jerusalem. [32]Peter and his companions were heavy with sleep, but they woke up and saw his glory and the two men standing with him. [33]As these were leaving him, Peter said to Jesus, 'Master, it is wonderful for us to be here; so let us make three shelters, one for you, one for Moses and one for Elijah.' He did not know what he was saying. [34]As he was saying this, a cloud came and covered them with shadow; and when they went into the cloud the disciples were afraid. [35]And a voice came from the cloud saying, 'This is my Son, the Chosen One. Listen to him.'[a] [36]And after the voice had spoken, Jesus was found alone. The disciples kept silence and, at that time, told no one what they had seen.

The epileptic demoniac

[37]Now it happened that on the following day when they were coming down from the mountain a large crowd came to meet him. [38]And suddenly a man in the crowd cried out. 'Master,' he said, 'I implore you to look at my son: he is my only child. [39]A spirit will suddenly take hold of him, and all at once it gives a sudden cry and throws the boy into convulsions with foaming at the mouth; it is slow to leave him, but when it does, it leaves the boy worn out. [40]I begged your disciples to drive it out, and they could not.' [41]In reply Jesus said, 'Faithless and perverse generation! How much longer must I be among you and put up with you? Bring your son

here.' [42]Even while the boy was coming, the devil threw him to the ground in convulsions. But Jesus rebuked the unclean spirit and cured the boy and gave him back to his father, [43]and everyone was awestruck by the greatness of God.

Second prophecy of the Passion

But while everyone was full of admiration for all he did, he said to his disciples, [44]'For your part, you must have these words constantly in mind: The Son of man is going to be delivered into the power of men.' [45]But they did not understand what he said; it was hidden from them so that they should not see the meaning of it, and they were afraid to ask him about it.

Who is the greatest?

[46]An argument started between them about which of them was the greatest. [47]Jesus knew what thoughts were going through their minds, and he took a little child whom he set by his side [48]and then he said to them, 'Anyone who welcomes this little child in my name welcomes me; and anyone who welcomes me, welcomes the one who sent me. The least among you all is the one who is the greatest.'

On using the name of Jesus

[49]John spoke up. 'Master,' he said, 'we saw someone driving out devils in your name, and because he is not with us we tried to stop him.' [50]But Jesus said to him, 'You must not stop him: anyone who is not against you is for you.'

IV: THE JOURNEY TO JERUSALEM

A Samaritan village is inhospitable

[51]Now it happened that as the time drew near for him to be taken up, he resolutely turned his face towards Jerusalem [52]and sent messengers ahead of him. These set out, and they went into a Samaritan village to make preparations for him, [53]but the people would not receive him because he was making for Jerusalem. [54]Seeing this, the disciples James

and John said, 'Lord, do you want us to call down fire from heaven to burn them up?' [55]But he turned and rebuked them, [56]and they went on to another village.

Hardships of the apostolic calling

[57]As they travelled along they met a man on the road who said to him, 'I will follow you wherever you go.' [58]Jesus answered, 'Foxes

---

9a Dt 18:15, 19; Is 42:1.

have holes and the birds of the air have nests, but the Son of man has nowhere to lay his head.'

⁵⁹Another to whom he said, 'Follow me,' replied, 'Let me go and bury my father first.' ⁶⁰But he answered, 'Leave the dead to bury their dead; your duty is to go and spread the news of the kingdom of God.'

⁶¹Another said, 'I will follow you, sir, but first let me go and say good-bye to my people at home.' ⁶²Jesus said to him, 'Once the hand is laid on the plough, no one who looks back is fit for the kingdom of God.'

The mission of the seventy-two disciples

10 After this the Lord appointed seventy-two others and sent them out ahead of him in pairs, to all the towns and places he himself would be visiting. ²And he said to them, 'The harvest is rich but the labourers are few, so ask the Lord of the harvest to send labourers to do his harvesting. ³Start off now, but look, I am sending you out like lambs among wolves. ⁴Take no purse with you, no haversack, no sandals. Salute no one on the road. ⁵Whatever house you enter, let your first words be, "Peace to this house!" ⁶And if a man of peace lives there, your peace will go and rest on him; if not, it will come back to you. ⁷Stay in the same house, taking what food and drink they have to offer, for the labourer deserves his wages; do not move from house to house. ⁸Whenever you go into a town where they make you welcome, eat what is put before you. ⁹Cure those in it who are sick, and say, "The kingdom of God is very near to you." ¹⁰But whenever you enter a town and they do not make you welcome, go out into its streets and say, ¹¹"We wipe off the very dust of your town that clings to our feet, and leave it with you. Yet be sure of this: the kingdom of God is very near." ¹²I tell you, on the great Day it will be more bearable for Sodom than for that town.

¹³'Alas for you, Chorazin! Alas for you, Bethsaida! For if the miracles done in you had been done in Tyre and Sidon, they would have repented long ago, sitting in sackcloth and ashes. ¹⁴And still, it will be more bearable for Tyre and Sidon at the Judgement than for you. ¹⁵And as for you, Capernaum, did

you want to be *raised high as heaven? You shall be flung down to hell.*[a]

¹⁶'Anyone who listens to you listens to me; anyone who rejects you rejects me, and those who reject me reject the one who sent me.'

True cause for the apostles to rejoice

¹⁷The seventy-two came back rejoicing. 'Lord,' they said, 'even the devils submit to us when we use your name.' ¹⁸He said to them, 'I watched Satan fall like lightning from heaven. ¹⁹Look, I have given you power to tread down serpents and scorpions and the whole strength of the enemy; nothing shall ever hurt you. ²⁰Yet do not rejoice that the spirits submit to you; rejoice instead that your names are written in heaven.'

The good news revealed to the simple
The Father and the Son

²¹Just at this time, filled with joy by the Holy Spirit, he said, 'I bless you, Father, Lord of heaven and of earth, for hiding these things from the learned and the clever and revealing them to little children. Yes, Father, for that is what it has pleased you to do. ²²Everything has been entrusted to me by my Father; and no one knows who the Son is except the Father, and who the Father is except the Son and those to whom the Son chooses to reveal him.'

The privilege of the disciples

²³Then turning to his disciples he spoke to them by themselves, 'Blessed are the eyes that see what you see, ²⁴for I tell you that many prophets and kings wanted to see what you see, and never saw it; to hear what you hear, and never heard it.'

The great commandment

²⁵And now a lawyer stood up and, to test him, asked, 'Master, what must I do to inherit eternal life?' ²⁶He said to him, 'What is written in the Law? What is your reading of it?' ²⁷He replied, *'You must love the Lord your God with all your heart, with all your soul, with all your strength, and with all your mind, and your neighbour as yourself.'*[b] ²⁸Jesus said to

---

10a Is 14:13–15.
10b Dt 6:5 and Lv 19:18.

him, 'You have answered right, do this and life is yours.'

Parable of the good Samaritan

²⁹But the man was anxious to justify himself and said to Jesus, 'And who is my neighbour?' ³⁰In answer Jesus said, 'A man was once on his way down from Jerusalem to Jericho and fell into the hands of bandits; they stripped him, beat him and then made off, leaving him half dead. ³¹Now a priest happened to be travelling down the same road, but when he saw the man, he passed by on the other side. ³²In the same way a Levite who came to the place saw him, and passed by on the other side. ³³But a Samaritan traveller who came on him was moved with compassion when he saw him. ³⁴He went up to him and bandaged his wounds, pouring oil and wine on them. He then lifted him onto his own mount and took him to an inn and looked after him. ³⁵Next day, he took out two denarii and handed them to the innkeeper and said, "Look after him, and on my way back I will make good any extra expense you have." ³⁶Which of these three, do you think, proved himself a neighbour to the man who fell into the bandits' hands?' ³⁷He replied, 'The one who showed pity towards him.' Jesus said to him, 'Go, and do the same yourself.'

Martha and Mary

³⁸In the course of their journey he came to a village, and a woman named Martha welcomed him into her house. ³⁹She had a sister called Mary, who sat down at the Lord's feet and listened to him speaking. ⁴⁰Now Martha, who was distracted with all the serving, came to him and said, 'Lord, do you not care that my sister is leaving me to do the serving all by myself? Please tell her to help me.' ⁴¹But the Lord answered, 'Martha, Martha,' he said, 'you worry and fret about so many things, ⁴²and yet few are needed, indeed only one. It is Mary who has chosen the better part, and it is not to be taken from her.'

The Lord's prayer

11 Now it happened that he was in a certain place praying, and when he had

finished, one of his disciples said, 'Lord, teach us to pray, as John taught his disciples.' ²He said to them, 'When you pray, this is what to say:

Father, may your name be held holy,
your kingdom come;
³give us each day our daily bread,
and forgive us our sins,
⁴for we ourselves forgive each one
who is in debt to us.
And do not put us to the test.'ᵃ

The importunate friend

⁵He also said to them, 'Suppose one of you has a friend and goes to him in the middle of the night to say, "My friend, lend me three loaves, ⁶because a friend of mine on his travels has just arrived at my house and I have nothing to offer him;" ⁷and the man answers from inside the house, "Do not bother me. The door is bolted now, and my children are with me in bed; I cannot get up to give it to you." ⁸I tell you, if the man does not get up and give it to him for friendship's sake, persistence will make him get up and give his friend all he wants.

Effective prayer

⁹'So I say to you: Ask, and it will be given to you; search, and you will find; knock, and the door will be opened to you. ¹⁰For everyone who asks receives; everyone who searches finds; everyone who knocks will have the door opened. ¹¹What father among you, if his son asked for a fish, would hand him a snake? ¹²Or if he asked for an egg, hand him a scorpion? ¹³If you then, evil as you are, know how to give your children what is good, how much more will the heavenly Father give the Holy Spirit to those who ask him!'

Jesus and Beelzebul

¹⁴He was driving out a devil and it was dumb; and it happened that when the devil had gone out the dumb man spoke, and the people were amazed. ¹⁵But some of them said, 'It is through Beelzebul, the prince of devils, that he drives devils out.' ¹⁶Others asked him, as a test, for a sign from heaven; ¹⁷but, knowing what they were thinking, he said to them,

11a Mt 6:9–13.

'Any kingdom which is divided against itself is heading for ruin, and house collapses against house. ¹⁸So, too, with Satan: if he is divided against himself, how can his kingdom last?—since you claim that it is through Beelzebul that I drive devils out. ¹⁹Now if it is through Beelzebul that I drive devils out, through whom do your own sons drive them out? They shall be your judges, then. ²⁰But if it is through the finger of God that I drive devils out, then the kingdom of God has indeed caught you unawares. ²¹So long as a strong man fully armed guards his own home, his goods are undisturbed; ²²but when someone stronger than himself attacks and defeats him, the stronger man takes away all the weapons he relied on and shares out his spoil.

No compromise

²³'Anyone who is not with me is against me; and anyone who does not gather in with me throws away.

Return of the unclean spirit

²⁴'When an unclean spirit goes out of someone it wanders through waterless country looking for a place to rest, and not finding one it says, "I will go back to the home I came from." ²⁵But on arrival, finding it swept and tidied, ²⁶it then goes off and brings seven other spirits more wicked than itself, and they go in and set up house there, and so that person ends up worse off than before.'

The truly blessed

²⁷It happened that as he was speaking, a woman in the crowd raised her voice and said, 'Blessed the womb that bore you and the breasts that fed you!' ²⁸But he replied, 'More blessed still are those who hear the word of God and keep it!'

The sign of Jonah

²⁹The crowds got even bigger and he addressed them, 'This is an evil generation; it is asking for a sign. The only sign it will be given is the sign of Jonah. ³⁰For just as Jonah became a sign to the people of Nineveh, so will the Son of man be a sign to this generation. ³¹On Judgement Day the Queen of the South will stand up against the people of this generation and be their condemnation, because she came from the ends of the earth to hear the wisdom of Solomon;ᵇ and, look, there is something greater than Solomon here. ³²On Judgement Day the men of Nineveh will appear against this generation and be its condemnation, because when Jonah preached they repented; and, look, there is something greater than Jonah here.

The parable of the lamp repeated

³³'No one lights a lamp and puts it in some hidden place or under a tub; they put it on the lamp-stand so that people may see the light when they come in. ³⁴The lamp of the body is your eye. When your eye is clear, your whole body, too, is filled with light; but when it is diseased your body, too, will be darkened. ³⁵See to it then that the light inside you is not darkness. ³⁶If, therefore, your whole body is filled with light, and not darkened at all, it will be light entirely, as when the lamp shines on you with its rays.'

The Pharisees and the lawyers attacked

³⁷He had just finished speaking when a Pharisee invited him to dine at his house. He went in and sat down at table. ³⁸The Pharisee saw this and was surprised that he had not first washed before the meal. ³⁹But the Lord said to him, 'You Pharisees! You clean the outside of cup and plate, while inside yourselves you are filled with extortion and wickedness. ⁴⁰Fools! Did not he who made the outside make the inside too? ⁴¹Instead, give alms from what you have and, look, everything will be clean for you. ⁴²But alas for you Pharisees, because you pay your tithe of mint and rue and all sorts of garden herbs and neglect justice and the love of God! These you should have practised, without neglecting the others. ⁴³Alas for you Pharisees, because you like to take the seats of honour in the synagogues and to be greeted respectfully in the market squares! ⁴⁴Alas for you, because you are like the unmarked tombs that people walk on without knowing it!'

⁴⁵A lawyer then spoke up. 'Master,' he

11b 1 K 10:1–10.

said, 'when you speak like this you insult us too.' ⁴⁶But he said, 'Alas for you lawyers as well, because you load on people burdens that are unendurable, burdens that you yourselves do not touch with your fingertips.

⁴⁷'Alas for you because you build tombs for the prophets, the people your ancestors killed! ⁴⁸In this way you both witness to what your ancestors did and approve it; they did the killing, you do the building.

⁴⁹'And that is why the Wisdom of God said, "I will send them prophets and apostles; some they will slaughter and persecute, ⁵⁰so that this generation will have to answer for every prophet's blood that has been shed since the foundation of the world, ⁵¹from the blood of Abel to the blood of Zechariah, who perished between the altar and the Temple." Yes, I tell you, this generation will have to answer for it all.

⁵²'Alas for you lawyers who have taken away the key of knowledge! You have not gone in yourselves and have prevented others from going in who wanted to.'

⁵³When he left there, the scribes and the Pharisees began a furious attack on him and tried to force answers from him on innumerable questions, ⁵⁴lying in wait to catch him out in something he might say.

Open and fearless speech

12 Meanwhile the people had gathered in their thousands so that they were treading on one another. And he began to speak, first of all to his disciples. 'Be on your guard against the yeast of the Pharisees—their hypocrisy. ²Everything now covered up will be uncovered, and everything now hidden will be made clear. ³For this reason, whatever you have said in the dark will be heard in the daylight, and what you have whispered in hidden places will be proclaimed from the housetops.

⁴'To you my friends I say: Do not be afraid of those who kill the body and after that can do no more. ⁵I will tell you whom to fear: fear him who, after he has killed, has the power to cast into hell. Yes, I tell you, he is the one to fear. ⁶Can you not buy five sparrows for two pennies? And yet not one is forgotten in God's sight. ⁷Why, every hair on your head has been counted. There is no need to be afraid: you are worth more than many sparrows.

⁸'I tell you, if anyone openly declares himself for me in the presence of human beings, the Son of man will declare himself for him in the presence of God's angels. ⁹But anyone who disowns me in the presence of human beings will be disowned in the presence of God's angels.

¹⁰'Everyone who says a word against the Son of man will be forgiven, but no one who blasphemes against the Holy Spirit will be forgiven.

¹¹'When they take you before synagogues and magistrates and authorities, do not worry about how to defend yourselves or what to say, ¹²because when the time comes, the Holy Spirit will teach you what you should say.'

On hoarding possessions

¹³A man in the crowd said to him, 'Master, tell my brother to give me a share of our inheritance.' ¹⁴He said to him, 'My friend, who appointed me your judge, or the arbitrator of your claims?' ¹⁵Then he said to them, 'Watch, and be on your guard against avarice of any kind, for life does not consist in possessions, even when someone has more than he needs.'

¹⁶Then he told them a parable, 'There was once a rich man who, having had a good harvest from his land, ¹⁷thought to himself, "What am I to do? I have not enough room to store my crops." ¹⁸Then he said, "This is what I will do: I will pull down my barns and build bigger ones, and store all my grain and my goods in them, ¹⁹and I will say to my soul: My soul, you have plenty of good things laid by for many years to come; take things easy, eat, drink, have a good time." ²⁰But God said to him, "Fool! This very night the demand will be made for your soul; and this hoard of yours, whose will it be then?" ²¹So it is when someone stores up treasure for himself instead of becoming rich in the sight of God.'

Trust in Providence

²²Then he said to his disciples, 'That is why I am telling you not to worry about your life and what you are to eat, nor about your body and how you are to clothe it. ²³For life is more than food, and the body more than clothing. ²⁴Think of the ravens. They do not sow or reap; they have no storehouses and no barns; yet God feeds them. And how much more you are worth than the birds! ²⁵Can any of you, however much you worry, add a single

cubit to your span of life? ²⁶If a very small thing is beyond your powers, why worry about the rest? ²⁷Think how the flowers grow; they never have to spin or weave; yet, I assure you, not even Solomon in all his royal robes was clothed like one of them. ²⁸Now if that is how God clothes a flower which is growing wild today and is thrown into the furnace tomorrow, how much more will he look after you, who have so little faith! ²⁹But you must not set your hearts on things to eat and things to drink; nor must you worry. ³⁰It is the gentiles of this world who set their hearts on all these things. Your Father well knows you need them. ³¹No; set your hearts on his kingdom, and these other things will be given you as well.

³²'There is no need to be afraid, little flock, for it has pleased your Father to give you the kingdom.

On almsgiving

³³'Sell your possessions and give to those in need. Get yourselves purses that do not wear out, treasure that will not fail you, in heaven where no thief can reach it and no moth destroy it. ³⁴For wherever your treasure is, that is where your heart will be too.

On being ready for the Master's return

³⁵'See that you have your belts done up and your lamps lit. ³⁶Be like people waiting for their master to return from the wedding feast, ready to open the door as soon as he comes and knocks. ³⁷Blessed those servants whom the master finds awake when he comes. In truth I tell you, he will do up his belt, sit them down at table and wait on them. ³⁸It may be in the second watch that he comes, or in the third, but blessed are those servants if he finds them ready. ³⁹You may be quite sure of this, that if the householder had known at what time the burglar would come, he would not have let anyone break through the wall of his house. ⁴⁰You too must stand ready, because the Son of man is coming at an hour you do not expect.'

⁴¹Peter said, 'Lord, do you mean this parable for us, or for everyone?' ⁴²The Lord replied, 'Who, then, is the wise and trustworthy steward whom the master will place over his household to give them at the proper time their allowance of food? ⁴³Blessed that servant if his master's arrival finds him doing exactly that. ⁴⁴I tell you truly, he will put him in charge of everything that he owns. ⁴⁵But if the servant says to himself, "My master is taking his time coming," and sets about beating the menservants and the servant-girls, and eating and drinking and getting drunk, ⁴⁶his master will come on a day he does not expect and at an hour he does not know. The master will cut him off and send him to the same fate as the unfaithful.

⁴⁷'The servant who knows what his master wants, but has got nothing ready and done nothing in accord with those wishes, will be given a great many strokes of the lash. ⁴⁸The one who did not know, but has acted in such a way that he deserves a beating, will be given fewer strokes. When someone is given a great deal, a great deal will be demanded of that person; when someone is entrusted with a great deal, of that person even more will be expected.

Jesus and his Passion

⁴⁹'I have come to bring fire to the earth, and how I wish it were blazing already! ⁵⁰There is a baptism I must still receive, and what constraint I am under until it is completed!

Jesus the cause of dissension

⁵¹'Do you suppose that I am here to bring peace on earth? No, I tell you, but rather division. ⁵²For from now on, a household of five will be divided: three against two and two against three; ⁵³*father opposed to son*, son to father, mother to daughter, *daughter to mother*, mother-in-law to daughter-in-law, *daughter-in-law to mother-in-law.*'^a

On reading the signs of the times

⁵⁴He said again to the crowds, 'When you see a cloud looming up in the west you say at once that rain is coming, and so it does. ⁵⁵And when the wind is from the south you say it's going to be hot, and it is. ⁵⁶Hypocrites! You know how to interpret the face of the earth and the sky. How is it you do not know how to interpret these times?

⁵⁷'Why not judge for yourselves what is upright? ⁵⁸For example: when you are going

---

12a Mi 7:6.

to court with your opponent, make an effort to settle with him on the way, or he may drag you before the judge and the judge hand you over to the officer and the officer have you thrown into prison. ⁵⁹I tell you, you will not get out till you have paid the very last penny.'

Examples inviting repentance

13It was just about this time that some people arrived and told him about the Galileans whose blood Pilate had mingled with that of their sacrifices. At this he said to them, ²'Do you suppose that these Galileans were worse sinners than any others, that this should have happened to them? ³They were not, I tell you. No; but unless you repent you will all perish as they did. ⁴Or those eighteen on whom the tower at Siloam fell, killing them all? Do you suppose that they were more guilty than all the other people living in Jerusalem? ⁵They were not, I tell you. No; but unless you repent you will all perish as they did.'

Parable of the barren fig tree

⁶He told this parable, 'A man had a fig tree planted in his vineyard, and he came looking for fruit on it but found none. ⁷He said to his vinedresser, "For three years now I have been coming to look for fruit on this fig tree and finding none. Cut it down: why should it be taking up the ground?" ⁸"Sir," the man replied, "leave it one more year and give me time to dig round it and manure it: ⁹it may bear fruit next year; if not, then you can cut it down." '

Healing of a crippled woman on the Sabbath

¹⁰One Sabbath day he was teaching in one of the synagogues, ¹¹and there before him was a woman who for eighteen years had been possessed by a spirit that crippled her; she was bent double and quite unable to stand upright. ¹²When Jesus saw her he called her over and said, 'Woman, you are freed from your disability,' ¹³and he laid his hands on her. And at once she straightened up, and she glorified God.

¹⁴But the president of the synagogue was indignant because Jesus had healed on the Sabbath, and he addressed all those present saying, 'There are six days when work is to be done. Come and be healed on one of those days and not on the Sabbath.' ¹⁵But the Lord answered him and said, 'Hypocrites! Is there one of you who does not untie his ox or his donkey from the manger on the Sabbath and take it out for watering? ¹⁶And this woman, a daughter of Abraham whom Satan has held bound these eighteen years—was it not right to untie this bond on the Sabbath day?' ¹⁷When he said this, all his adversaries were covered with confusion, and all the people were overjoyed at all the wonders he worked.

Parable of the mustard seed

¹⁸He went on to say, 'What is the kingdom of God like? What shall I compare it with? ¹⁹It is like a mustard seed which a man took and threw into his garden: it grew and became a tree, and the birds of the air sheltered in its branches.'

Parable of the yeast

²⁰Again he said, 'What shall I compare the kingdom of God with? ²¹It is like the yeast a woman took and mixed in with three measures of flour till it was leavened all through.'

The narrow door; rejection of the Jews, call of the gentiles

²²Through towns and villages he went teaching, making his way to Jerusalem. ²³Someone said to him, 'Sir, will there be only a few saved?' He said to them, ²⁴'Try your hardest to enter by the narrow door, because, I tell you, many will try to enter and will not succeed.

²⁵'Once the master of the house has got up and locked the door, you may find yourself standing outside knocking on the door, saying, "Lord, open to us," but he will answer, "I do not know where you come from." ²⁶Then you will start saying, "We once ate and drank in your company; you taught in our streets," ²⁷but he will reply, "I do not know where you come from; *away from me, all evil doers!*"ᵃ

²⁸'Then there will be weeping and grinding of teeth, when you see Abraham and Isaac and Jacob and all the prophets in the kingdom

13a Ps 6:8.

of God, and yourselves thrown out. ²⁹And people from east and west, from north and south, will come and sit down at the feast in the kingdom of God.

³⁰'Look, there are those now last who will be first, and those now first who will be last.'

Herod the fox

³¹Just at this time some Pharisees came up. 'Go away,' they said. 'Leave this place, because Herod*ᵇ* means to kill you.' ³²He replied, 'You may go and give that fox this message: Look! Today and tomorrow I drive out devils and heal, and on the third day I attain my end. ³³But for today and tomorrow and the next day I must go on, since it would not be right for a prophet to die outside Jerusalem.

Jerusalem admonished

³⁴'Jerusalem, Jerusalem, you that kill the prophets and stone those who are sent to you! How often have I longed to gather your children together, as a hen gathers her brood under her wings, and you refused! ³⁵Look! Your house will be left to you. Yes, I promise you, you shall not see me till the time comes when you are saying:

Blessed is he
who is coming in the name of the Lord!'ᶜ

Healing of a dropsical man on the Sabbath

14 Now it happened that on a Sabbath day he had gone to share a meal in the house of one of the leading Pharisees; and they watched him closely. ²Now there in front of him was a man with dropsy, ³and Jesus addressed the lawyers and Pharisees with the words, 'Is it against the law to cure someone on the Sabbath, or not?' ⁴But they remained silent, so he took the man and cured him and sent him away. ⁵Then he said to them, 'Which of you here, if his son falls into a well, or his ox, will not pull him out on a Sabbath day without any hesitation?' ⁶And to this they could find no answer.

On choosing places at table

⁷He then told the guests a parable, because he had noticed how they picked the places of honour. He said this, ⁸'When someone invites you to a wedding feast, do not take your seat in the place of honour. A more distinguished person than you may have been invited, ⁹and the person who invited you both may come and say, "Give up your place to this man." And then, to your embarrassment, you will have to go and take the lowest place. ¹⁰No; when you are a guest, make your way to the lowest place and sit there, so that, when your host comes, he may say, "My friend, move up higher." Then, everyone with you at the table will see you honoured. ¹¹For everyone who raises himself up will be humbled, and the one who humbles himself will be raised up.'

On choosing guests to be invited

¹²Then he said to his host, 'When you give a lunch or a dinner, do not invite your friends or your brothers or your relations or rich neighbours, in case they invite you back and so repay you. ¹³No; when you have a party, invite the poor, the crippled, the lame, the blind; ¹⁴then you will be blessed, for they have no means to repay you and so you will be repaid when the upright rise again.'

The invited guests who made excuses

¹⁵On hearing this, one of those gathered round the table said to him, 'Blessed is anyone who will share the meal in the kingdom of God!' ¹⁶But he said to him, 'There was a man who gave a great banquet, and he invited a large number of people. ¹⁷When the time for the banquet came, he sent his servant to say to those who had been invited, "Come along: everything is ready now." ¹⁸But all alike started to make excuses. The first said, "I have bought a piece of land and must go and see it. Please accept my apologies." ¹⁹Another said, "I have bought five yoke of oxen and am on my way to try them out. Please accept my apologies." ²⁰Yet another said, "I have just got married and so am unable to come." ²¹'The servant returned and reported this to his master. Then the householder, in a rage, said to his servant, "Go out quickly into

---

13b Herod Antipas, son of Herod the Great.
13c Ps 118:26.

the streets and alleys of the town and bring in here the poor, the crippled, the blind and the lame." ²²"Sir," said the servant, "your orders have been carried out and there is still room." ²³Then the master said to his servant, "Go to the open roads and the hedgerows and press people to come in, to make sure my house is full; ²⁴because, I tell you, not one of those who were invited shall have a taste of my banquet." '

Renouncing all that one holds dear

²⁵Great crowds accompanied him on his way and he turned and spoke to them. ²⁶'Anyone who comes to me without hating father, mother, wife, children, brothers, sisters, yes and his own life too, cannot be my disciple. ²⁷No one who does not carry his cross and come after me can be my disciple.

Renouncing possessions

²⁸'And indeed, which of you here, intending to build a tower, would not first sit down and work out the cost to see if he had enough to complete it? ²⁹Otherwise, if he laid the foundation and then found himself unable to finish the work, anyone who saw it would start making fun of him and saying, ³⁰"Here is someone who started to build and was unable to finish." ³¹Or again, what king marching to war against another king would not first sit down and consider whether with ten thousand men he could stand up to the other who was advancing against him with twenty thousand? ³²If not, then while the other king was still a long way off, he would send envoys to sue for peace. ³³So in the same way, none of you can be my disciple without giving up all that he owns.

On loss of enthusiasm in a disciple

³⁴'Salt is a good thing. But if salt itself loses its taste, what can make it salty again? ³⁵It is good for neither soil nor manure heap. People throw it away. Anyone who has ears for listening should listen!'

The three parables of God's mercy

15 The tax collectors and sinners, however, were all crowding round to listen to him, ²and the Pharisees and scribes complained saying, 'This man welcomes sinners and eats with them.' ³So he told them this parable:

The lost sheep

⁴'Which one of you with a hundred sheep, if he lost one, would fail to leave the ninety-nine in the desert and go after the missing one till he found it? ⁵And when he found it, would he not joyfully take it on his shoulders ⁶and then, when he got home, call together his friends and neighbours, saying to them, "Rejoice with me, I have found my sheep that was lost." ⁷In the same way, I tell you, there will be more rejoicing in heaven over one sinner repenting than over ninety-nine upright people who have no need of repentance.

The lost drachma

⁸'Or again, what woman with ten drachmas would not, if she lost one, light a lamp and sweep out the house and search thoroughly till she found it? ⁹And then, when she had found it, call together her friends and neighbours, saying to them, "Rejoice with me, I have found the drachma I lost." ¹⁰In the same way, I tell you, there is rejoicing among the angels of God over one repentant sinner.'

The lost son (the 'prodigal') and the dutiful son

¹¹Then he said, 'There was a man who had two sons. ¹²The younger one said to his father, "Father, let me have the share of the estate that will come to me." So the father divided the property between them. ¹³A few days later, the younger son got together everything he had and left for a distant country where he squandered his money on a life of debauchery.

¹⁴'When he had spent it all, that country experienced a severe famine, and now he began to feel the pinch; ¹⁵so he hired himself out to one of the local inhabitants who put him on his farm to feed the pigs. ¹⁶And he would willingly have filled himself with the husks the pigs were eating but no one would let him have them. ¹⁷Then he came to his senses and said, "How many of my father's hired men have all the food they want and more, and here am I dying of hunger! ¹⁸I will leave this place and go to my father and say: Father, I have sinned against heaven and

against you; [19]I no longer deserve to be called your son; treat me as one of your hired men." [20]So he left the place and went back to his father.

'While he was still a long way off, his father saw him and was moved with pity. He ran to the boy, clasped him in his arms and kissed him. [21]Then his son said, "Father, I have sinned against heaven and against you. I no longer deserve to be called your son." [22]But the father said to his servants, "Quick! Bring out the best robe and put it on him; put a ring on his finger and sandals on his feet. [23]Bring the calf we have been fattening, and kill it; we will celebrate by having a feast, [24]because this son of mine was dead and has come back to life; he was lost and is found." And they began to celebrate.

[25]'Now the elder son was out in the fields, and on his way back, as he drew near the house, he could hear music and dancing. [26]Calling one of the servants he asked what it was all about. [27]The servant told him, "Your brother has come, and your father has killed the calf we had been fattening because he has got him back safe and sound." [28]He was angry then and refused to go in, and his father came out and began to urge him to come in; [29]but he retorted to his father, "All these years I have slaved for you and never once disobeyed any orders of yours, yet you never offered me so much as a kid for me to celebrate with my friends. [30]But, for this son of yours, when he comes back after swallowing up your property—he and his loose women—you kill the calf we had been fattening."

[31]'The father said, "My son, you are with me always and all I have is yours. [32]But it was only right we should celebrate and rejoice, because your brother here was dead and has come to life; he was lost and is found." '

The crafty steward

16 He also said to his disciples, 'There was a rich man and he had a steward who was denounced to him for being wasteful with his property. [2]He called for the man and said, "What is this I hear about you? Draw me up an account of your stewardship because you are not to be my steward any longer." [3]Then the steward said to himself, "Now that my master is taking the stewardship from me, what am I to do? Dig? I am not strong enough. Go begging? I should be

too ashamed. [4]Ah, I know what I will do to make sure that when I am dismissed from office there will be some to welcome me into their homes."

[5]'Then he called his master's debtors one by one. To the first he said, "How much do you owe my master?" [6]"One hundred measures of oil," he said. The steward said, "Here, take your bond; sit down and quickly write fifty." [7]To another he said, "And you, sir, how much do you owe?" "One hundred measures of wheat," he said. The steward said, "Here, take your bond and write eighty."

[8]'The master praised the dishonest steward for his astuteness. For the children of this world are more astute in dealing with their own kind than are the children of light.'

The right use of money

[9]'And so I tell you this: use money, tainted as it is, to win you friends, and thus make sure that when it fails you, they will welcome you into eternal dwellings. [10]Anyone who is trustworthy in little things is trustworthy in great; anyone who is dishonest in little things is dishonest in great. [11]If then you are not trustworthy with money, that tainted thing, who will trust you with genuine riches? [12]And if you are not trustworthy with what is not yours, who will give you what is your very own?

[13]'No servant can be the slave of two masters: he will either hate the first and love the second, or be attached to the first and despise the second. You cannot be the slave both of God and of money.'

Against the Pharisees
and their love of money

[14]The Pharisees, who loved money, heard all this and jeered at him. [15]He said to them, 'You are the very ones who pass yourselves off as upright in people's sight, but God knows your hearts. For what is highly esteemed in human eyes is loathsome in the sight of God.

The kingdom stormed

[16]'Up to the time of John it was the Law and the Prophets; from then onwards, the kingdom of God has been preached, and everyone is forcing their way into it.

The Law remains

17'It is easier for heaven and earth to disappear than for one little stroke to drop out of the Law.

Marriage indissoluble

18'Everyone who divorces his wife and marries another is guilty of adultery, and the man who marries a woman divorced by her husband commits adultery.

The parable of the rich man and Lazarus

19'There was a rich man who used to dress in purple and fine linen and feast magnificently every day. 20And at his gate there used to lie a poor man called Lazarus, covered with sores, 21who longed to fill himself with what fell from the rich man's table. Even dogs came and licked his sores. 22Now it happened that the poor man died and was carried away by the angels into Abraham's embrace. The rich man also died and was buried.

23'In his torment in Hades he looked up and saw Abraham a long way off with Lazarus in his embrace. 24So he cried out, "Father Abraham, pity me and send Lazarus to dip the tip of his finger in water and cool my tongue, for I am in agony in these flames." 25Abraham said, "My son, remember that during your life you had your fill of good things, just as Lazarus his fill of bad. Now he is being comforted here while you are in agony. 26But that is not all: between us and you a great gulf has been fixed, to prevent those who want to cross from our side to yours or from your side to ours."

27'So he said, "Father, I beg you then to send Lazarus to my father's house, 28since I have five brothers, to give them warning so that they do not come to this place of torment too." 29Abraham said, "They have Moses and the prophets, let them listen to them." 30The rich man replied, "Ah no, father Abraham, but if someone comes to them from the dead, they will repent." 31Then Abraham said to him, "If they will not listen either to Moses or to the prophets, they will not be convinced even if someone should rise from the dead." '

On leading others astray

17 He said to his disciples, 'Causes of falling are sure to come, but alas for the one through whom they occur! 2It would be better for such a person to be thrown into the sea with a millstone round the neck than to be the downfall of a single one of these little ones. 3Keep watch on yourselves!

Brotherly correction

'If your brother does something wrong, rebuke him and, if he is sorry, forgive him. 4And if he wrongs you seven times a day and seven times comes back to you and says, "I am sorry," you must forgive him.'

The power of faith

5The apostles said to the Lord, 'Increase our faith.' 6The Lord replied, 'If you had faith like a mustard seed you could say to this mulberry tree, "Be uprooted and planted in the sea," and it would obey you.

Humble service

7'Which of you, with a servant ploughing or minding sheep, would say to him when he returned from the fields, "Come and have your meal at once"? 8Would he not be more likely to say, "Get my supper ready; fasten your belt and wait on me while I eat and drink. You yourself can eat and drink afterwards"? 9Must he be grateful to the servant for doing what he was told? 10So with you: when you have done all you have been told to do, say, "We are useless servants: we have done no more than our duty." '

The ten victims of skin-disease

11Now it happened that on the way to Jerusalem he was travelling in the borderlands of Samaria and Galilee. 12As he entered one of the villages, ten men suffering from a virulent skin-disease came to meet him. They stood some way off 13and called to him, 'Jesus! Master! Take pity on us.' 14When he saw them he said, 'Go and show yourselves to the priests.' Now as they were going away they were cleansed. 15Finding himself cured, one of them turned back praising God at the top of his voice 16and threw himself prostrate at the feet of Jesus and thanked him. The man was a Samaritan. 17This led Jesus to say, 'Were not all ten made clean? The other nine, where are they? 18It seems that no one has come back to give praise to God, except this foreigner.' ¹⁹And he said to the man, 'Stand up and go on your way. Your faith has saved you.'

The coming of the kingdom of God

²⁰Asked by the Pharisees when the kingdom of God was to come, he gave them this answer, 'The coming of the kingdom of God does not admit of observation ²¹and there will be no one to say, "Look, it is here! Look, it is there!" For look, the kingdom of God is among you.'

The Day of the Son of man

²²He said to the disciples, 'A time will come when you will long to see one of the days of the Son of man and will not see it. ²³They will say to you, "Look, it is there!" or, "Look, it is here!" Make no move; do not set off in pursuit; ²⁴for as the lightning flashing from one part of heaven lights up the other, so will be the Son of man when his Day comes. ²⁵But first he is destined to suffer grievously and be rejected by this generation.
²⁶'As it was in Noah's day, so will it also be in the days of the Son of man. ²⁷People were eating and drinking, marrying wives and husbands, right up to the day Noah went into the ark, and the Flood came and destroyed them all. ²⁸It will be the same as it was in Lot's day: people were eating and drinking, buying and selling, planting and building, ²⁹but the day Lot left Sodom, it rained fire and brimstone from heaven and it destroyed them all. ³⁰It will be the same when the day comes for the Son of man to be revealed.
³¹'When that Day comes, no one on the housetop, with his possessions in the house, must come down to collect them, nor must anyone in the fields turn back. ³²Remember Lot's wife. ³³Anyone who tries to preserve his life will lose it; and anyone who loses it will keep it safe. ³⁴I tell you, on that night, when two are in one bed, one will be taken, the other left; ³⁵when two women are grinding corn together, one will be taken, the other left.' [36]ᵃ ³⁷The disciples spoke up and asked, 'Where, Lord?' He said, 'Where the body is, there too will the vultures gather.'

The unscrupulous judge and the importunate widow

18 Then he told them a parable about the need to pray continually and never lose heart. ²'There was a judge in a certain town,' he said, 'who had neither fear of God nor respect for anyone. ³In the same town there was also a widow who kept on coming to him and saying, "I want justice from you against my enemy!" ⁴For a long time he refused, but at last he said to himself, "Even though I have neither fear of God nor respect for any human person, ⁵I must give this widow her just rights since she keeps pestering me, or she will come and slap me in the face." '
⁶And the Lord said, 'You notice what the unjust judge has to say? ⁷Now, will not God see justice done to his elect if they keep calling to him day and night even though he still delays to help them? ⁸I promise you, he will see justice done to them, and done speedily. But when the Son of man comes, will he find any faith on earth?'

The Pharisee and the tax collector

⁹He spoke the following parable to some people who prided themselves on being upright and despised everyone else, ¹⁰'Two men went up to the Temple to pray, one a Pharisee, the other a tax collector. ¹¹The Pharisee stood there and said this prayer to himself, "I thank you, God, that I am not grasping, unjust, adulterous like everyone else, and particularly that I am not like this tax collector here. ¹²I fast twice a week; I pay tithes on all I get." ¹³The tax collector stood some distance away, not daring even to raise his eyes to heaven; but he beat his breast and said, "God, be merciful to me, a sinner." ¹⁴This man, I tell you, went home again justified; the other did not. For everyone who raises himself up will be humbled, but anyone who humbles himself will be raised up.'

Jesus and the children

¹⁵People even brought babies to him, for him to touch them; but when the disciples saw this they scolded them. ¹⁶But Jesus called the children to him and said, 'Let the little children come to me, and do not stop them; for it is to such as these that the kingdom of

---

17a Add. v. 36, 'There will be two men in the fields; one will be taken, the other left,' cf. Mt 24:40.

God belongs. ¹⁷In truth I tell you, anyone who does not welcome the kingdom of God like a little child will never enter it.'

The rich aristocrat

¹⁸One of the rulers put this question to him, 'Good Master, what shall I do to inherit eternal life?' ¹⁹Jesus said to him, 'Why do you call me good? No one is good but God alone. ²⁰You know the commandments: *You shall not commit adultery; You shall not kill; You shall not steal; You shall not give false witness; Honour your father and your mother.*'ᵃ ²¹He replied, 'I have kept all these since my earliest days.' ²²And when Jesus heard this he said, 'There is still one thing you lack. Sell everything you own and distribute the money to the poor, and you will have treasure in heaven; then come, follow me.' ²³But when he heard this he was overcome with sadness, for he was very rich.

The danger of riches

²⁴Jesus looked at him and said, 'How hard it is for those who have riches to make their way into the kingdom of God! ²⁵Yes, it is easier for a camel to pass through the eye of a needle than for someone rich to enter the kingdom of God.' ²⁶Those who were listening said, 'In that case, who can be saved?' ²⁷He replied, 'Things that are impossible by human resources, are possible for God.'

The reward of renunciation

²⁸But Peter said, 'Look, we left all we had to follow you.' ²⁹He said to them, 'In truth I tell you, there is no one who has left house, wife, brothers, parents or children for the sake of the kingdom of God ³⁰who will not receive many times as much in this present age and, in the world to come, eternal life.'

Third prophecy of the Passion

³¹Then taking the Twelve aside he said to them, 'Look, we are going up to Jerusalem, and everything that is written by the prophets about the Son of man is to come true. ³²For he will be handed over to the gentiles and will be mocked, maltreated and spat on, ³³and when they have scourged him they will put him to death; and on the third day he will rise again.' ³⁴But they could make nothing of

this; what he said was quite obscure to them, they did not understand what he was telling them.

Entering Jericho: the blind man

³⁵Now it happened that as he drew near to Jericho there was a blind man sitting at the side of the road begging. ³⁶When he heard the crowd going past he asked what it was all about, ³⁷and they told him that Jesus the Nazarene was passing by. ³⁸So he called out, 'Jesus, Son of David, have pity on me.' ³⁹The people in front scolded him and told him to keep quiet, but he only shouted all the louder, 'Son of David, have pity on me.' ⁴⁰Jesus stopped and ordered them to bring the man to him, and when he came up, asked him, ⁴¹'What do you want me to do for you?' 'Sir,' he replied, 'let me see again.' ⁴²Jesus said to him, 'Receive your sight. Your faith has saved you.' ⁴³And instantly his sight returned and he followed him praising God, and all the people who saw it gave praise to God.

Zacchaeus

19 He entered Jericho and was going through the town ²and suddenly a man whose name was Zacchaeus made his appearance; he was one of the senior tax collectors and a wealthy man. ³He kept trying to see which Jesus was, but he was too short and could not see him for the crowd; ⁴so he ran ahead and climbed a sycamore tree to catch a glimpse of Jesus who was to pass that way. ⁵When Jesus reached the spot he looked up and spoke to him, 'Zacchaeus, come down. Hurry, because I am to stay at your house today.' ⁶And he hurried down and welcomed him joyfully. ⁷They all complained when they saw what was happening. 'He has gone to stay at a sinner's house,' they said. ⁸But Zacchaeus stood his ground and said to the Lord, 'Look, sir, I am going to give half my property to the poor, and if I have cheated anybody I will pay him back four times the amount.' ⁹And Jesus said to him, 'Today salvation has come to this house, because this man too is a son of Abraham; ¹⁰for the Son of man has come to seek out and save what was lost.'

Parable of the pounds

¹¹While the people were listening to this he went on to tell a parable, because he was near

---

18a Ex 20:12–16.

Jerusalem and they thought that the kingdom of God was going to show itself then and there. [12]Accordingly he said, 'A man of noble birth went to a distant country to be appointed king and then return. [13]He summoned ten of his servants and gave them ten pounds, telling them, "Trade with these, until I get back." [14]But his compatriots detested him and sent a delegation to follow him with this message, "We do not want this man to be our king."

[15]'Now it happened that on his return, having received his appointment as king, he sent for those servants to whom he had given the money, to find out what profit each had made by trading. [16]The first came in, "Sir," he said, "your one pound has brought in ten." [17]He replied, "Well done, my good servant! Since you have proved yourself trustworthy in a very small thing, you shall have the government of ten cities." [18]Then came the second, "Sir," he said, "your one pound has made five." [19]To this one also he said, "And you shall be in charge of five cities." [20]Next came the other, "Sir," he said, "here is your pound. I put it away safely wrapped up in a cloth [21]because I was afraid of you; for you are an exacting man: you gather in what you have not laid out and reap what you have not sown." [22]He said to him, "You wicked servant! Out of your own mouth I condemn you. So you knew that I was an exacting man, gathering in what I have not laid out and reaping what I have not sown? [23]Then why did you not put my money in the bank? On my return I could have drawn it out with interest." [24]And he said to those standing by, "Take the pound from him and give it to the man who has ten pounds." [25]And they said to him, "But, sir, he has ten pounds . . ." [26]"I tell you, to everyone who has will be given more; but anyone who has not will be deprived even of what he has.

[27]"As for my enemies who did not want me for their king, bring them here and execute them in my presence." '

V: TEACHING IN JERUSALEM

The Messiah enters Jerusalem

[28]When he had said this he went on ahead, going up to Jerusalem. [29]Now it happened that when he was near Bethphage and Bethany, close by the Mount of Olives as it is called, he sent two of the disciples, saying, [30]'Go to the village opposite, and as you enter it you will find a tethered colt that no one has ever yet ridden. Untie it and bring it here. [31]If anyone asks you, "Why are you untying it?" you are to say this, "The Master needs it." ' [32]The messengers went off and found everything just as he had told them. [33]As they were untying the colt, its owners said, 'Why are you untying it?' [34]and they answered, 'The Master needs it.'

[35]So they took the colt to Jesus and, throwing their cloaks on its back, they lifted Jesus on to it. [36]As he moved off, they spread their cloaks in the road, [37]and now, as he was approaching the downward slope of the Mount of Olives, the whole group of disciples joyfully began to praise God at the top of their voices for all the miracles they had seen. [38]They cried out:

Blessed is he who is coming
as King *in the name of the Lord!*[a]
Peace in heaven
and glory in the highest heavens!

Jesus defends his disciples for acclaiming him

[39]Some Pharisees in the crowd said to him, 'Master, reprove your disciples,' [40]but he answered, 'I tell you, if these keep silence, the stones will cry out.'

Lament for Jerusalem

[41]As he drew near and came in sight of the city he shed tears over it [42]and said, 'If you too had only recognised on this day the way to peace! But in fact it is hidden from your eyes! [43]Yes, a time is coming when your enemies will raise fortifications all round you, when they will encircle you and hem you in

---

19a Ps 118:26.

on every side; [44]they will dash you and the children inside your walls to the ground; they will leave not one stone standing on another within you, because you did not recognise the moment of your visitation.'

The expulsion of the dealers from the Temple

[45]Then he went into the Temple and began driving out those who were busy trading, saying to them, [46]'According to scripture, *my house shall be a house of prayer* but you have turned it into *a bandits' den.'*[b]

Jesus teaches in the Temple

[47]He taught in the Temple every day. The chief priests and the scribes, in company with the leading citizens, tried to do away with him, [48]but they could not find a way to carry this out because the whole people hung on his words.

The Jews question the authority of Jesus

20 Now it happened that one day while he was teaching the people in the Temple and proclaiming the good news, the chief priests and the scribes came up, together with the elders, [2]and spoke to him. 'Tell us,' they said, 'what authority have you for acting like this? Or who gives you this authority?' [3]In reply he said to them, 'And I will ask you a question, just one. Tell me: [4]John's baptism: what was its origin, heavenly or human?' [5]And they debated this way among themselves, 'If we say heavenly, he will retort, "Why did you refuse to believe him?"'; [6]and if we say human, the whole people will stone us, for they are convinced that John was a prophet.' [7]So their reply was that they did not know where it came from. [8]And Jesus said to them, 'Nor will I tell you my authority for acting like this.'

Parable of the wicked tenants

[9]And he went on to tell the people this parable, 'A man planted a vineyard and leased it to tenants, and went abroad for a long while. [10]When the right time came, he sent a servant to the tenants to get his share of the produce of the vineyard. But the tenants thrashed him, and sent him away empty-handed. [11]But he went on to send a second servant; they thrashed him too and treated him shamefully and sent him away empty-handed. [12]He still went on to send a third; they wounded this one too, and threw him out. [13]Then the owner of the vineyard thought, "What am I to do? I will send them my own beloved son. Perhaps they will respect him." [14]But when the tenants saw him they put their heads together saying, "This is the heir, let us kill him so that the inheritance will be ours." [15]So they threw him out of the vineyard and killed him.

'Now what will the owner of the vineyard do to them? [16]He will come and make an end of these tenants and give the vineyard to others.' Hearing this they said, 'God forbid!' [17]But he looked hard at them and said, 'Then what does this text in the scriptures mean:

*The stone which the builders rejected
has become the cornerstone?*[a]

[18]Anyone who falls on that stone will be dashed to pieces; anyone it falls on will be crushed.'

[19]And the scribes and the chief priests would have liked to lay hands on him that very moment, because they realised that this parable was aimed at them, but they were afraid of the people.

On tribute to Caesar

[20]So they awaited their opportunity and sent agents to pose as upright men, and to catch him out in something he might say and so enable them to hand him over to the jurisdiction and authority of the governor. [21]They put to him this question, 'Master, we know that you say and teach what is right; you favour no one, but teach the way of God in all honesty. [22]Is it permissible for us to pay taxes to Caesar or not?' [23]But he was aware of their cunning and said, [24]'Show me a denarius. Whose portrait and title are on it?' They said, 'Caesar's.' [25]He said to them, 'Well then, pay Caesar what belongs to Caesar—and God what belongs to God.' [26]They were unable to catch him out in anything he had to say in public; they were amazed at his answer and were silenced.

19b Is 56:7 and Jr 7:11.
20a Ps 118:22.

The resurrection of the dead

²⁷Some Sadducees—those who argue that there is no resurrection—approached him and they put this question to him, ²⁸'Master, Moses prescribed for us, if a man's married brother dies childless, the man must marry the widow to raise up children for his brother. ²⁹Well then, there were seven brothers; the first, having married a wife, died childless. ³⁰The second ³¹and then the third married the widow. And the same with all seven, they died leaving no children. ³²Finally the woman herself died. ³³Now, at the resurrection, whose wife will she be, since she had been married to all seven?'

³⁴Jesus replied, 'The children of this world take wives and husbands, ³⁵but those who are judged worthy of a place in the other world and in the resurrection from the dead do not marry ³⁶because they can no longer die, for they are the same as the angels, and being children of the resurrection they are children of God. ³⁷And Moses himself implies that the dead rise again, in the passage about the bush where he calls the Lord *the God of Abraham, the God of Isaac and the God of Jacob.*[b] ³⁸Now he is God, not of the dead, but of the living; for to him everyone is alive.'

³⁹Some scribes then spoke up. They said, 'Well put, Master.' ⁴⁰They did not dare to ask him any more questions.

Christ not only son but also Lord of David

⁴¹He then said to them, 'How can people maintain that the Christ is son of David? ⁴²Why, David himself says in the Book of Psalms:

The Lord declared to my Lord,
take your seat at my right hand,
⁴³*till I have made your enemies*
your footstool.[c]

⁴⁴David here calls him Lord; how then can he be his son?'

The scribes condemned by Jesus

⁴⁵While all the people were listening he said to the disciples, ⁴⁶'Beware of the scribes who like to walk about in long robes and love to be greeted respectfully in the market squares, to take the front seats in the synagogues and the places of honour at banquets, ⁴⁷who devour the property of widows, and for show offer long prayers. The more severe will be the sentence they receive.'

The widow's mite

21 Looking up, he saw rich people putting their offerings into the treasury; ²and he noticed a poverty-stricken widow putting in two small coins, ³and he said, 'I tell you truly, this poor widow has put in more than any of them; ⁴for these have all put in money they could spare, but she in her poverty has put in all she had to live on.'

Discourse on the destruction of Jerusalem: Introduction

⁵When some were talking about the Temple, remarking how it was adorned with fine stonework and votive offerings, he said, ⁶'All these things you are staring at now—the time will come when not a single stone will be left on another; everything will be destroyed.' ⁷And they put to him this question, 'Master,' they said, 'when will this happen, then, and what sign will there be that it is about to take place?'

The warning signs

⁸But he said, 'Take care not to be deceived, because many will come using my name and saying, "I am the one" and "The time is near at hand." Refuse to join them. ⁹And when you hear of wars and revolutions, do not be terrified, for this is something that must happen first, but the end will not come at once.' ¹⁰Then he said to them, 'Nation will fight against nation, and kingdom against kingdom. ¹¹There will be great earthquakes and plagues and famines in various places; there will be terrifying events and great signs from heaven.

¹²'But before all this happens, you will be seized and persecuted; you will be handed over to the synagogues and to imprisonment, and brought before kings and governors for the sake of my name ¹³—and that will be your opportunity to bear witness. ¹⁴Make up your

20b Ex 3:6.
20c Ps 110:1.

minds not to prepare your defence, ¹⁵because I myself shall give you an eloquence and a wisdom that none of your opponents will be able to resist or contradict. ¹⁶You will be betrayed even by parents and brothers, relations and friends; and some of you will be put to death. ¹⁷You will be hated universally on account of my name, ¹⁸but not a hair of your head will be lost. ¹⁹Your perseverance will win you your lives.

The siege

²⁰'When you see Jerusalem surrounded by armies, then you must realise that it will soon be laid desolate. ²¹Then those in Judaea must escape to the mountains, those inside the city must leave it, and those in country districts must not take refuge in it. ²²For this is the time of retribution when all that scripture says must be fulfilled. ²³Alas for those with child, or with babies at the breast, when those days come!

The disaster and the age of the gentiles

²⁴'For great misery will descend on the land and retribution on this people. They will fall by the edge of the sword and be led captive to every gentile country; and Jerusalem will be trampled down by the gentiles until their time is complete.

Cosmic disasters and the glorious appearing of the Son of man

²⁵'There will be signs in the sun and moon and stars; on earth nations in agony, bewildered by the turmoil of the ocean and its waves; ²⁶men fainting away with terror and fear at what menaces the world, for the powers of heaven will be shaken. ²⁷And then they will see the *Son of man coming in a cloud with power and great glory.*ᵃ ²⁸When these things begin to take place, stand erect, hold your heads high, because your liberation is near at hand.'

The time of this coming

²⁹And he told them a parable, 'Look at the fig tree and indeed every tree. ³⁰As soon as you see them bud, you can see for yourselves that summer is now near. ³¹So with you when you see these things happening: know that the kingdom of God is near. ³²In truth I tell you, before this generation has passed away all will have taken place. ³³Sky and earth will pass away, but my words will never pass away.

Be on the alert

³⁴'Watch yourselves, or your hearts will be coarsened by debauchery and drunkenness and the cares of life, and that day will come upon you unexpectedly, ³⁵like a trap. For it will come down on all those living on the face of the earth. ³⁶Stay awake, praying at all times for the strength to survive all that is going to happen, and to hold your ground before the Son of man.'

The last days of Jesus

³⁷All day long he would be in the Temple teaching, but would spend the night in the open on the hill called the Mount of Olives. ³⁸And from early morning the people thronged to him in the Temple to listen to him.

VI: THE PASSION*ᵃ*

The conspiracy against Jesus: Judas betrays him

22 The feast of Unleavened Bread, called the Passover, was now drawing near, ²and the chief priests and the scribes were looking for some way of doing away with him, because they were afraid of the people. ³Then Satan entered into Judas, surnamed Iscariot, who was one of the Twelve. ⁴He approached the chief priests and the officers of the guard to discuss some way of handing

---

21a Dn 7:13–14.
22a For this section Lk has a good deal of information which he does not share with Mt and Mk. It is often close to Jn.

Jesus over to them. ⁵They were delighted and agreed to give him money. ⁶He accepted and began to look for an opportunity to betray him to them without people knowing about it.

Preparation for the Passover supper

⁷The day of Unleavened Bread came round, on which the Passover had to be sacrificed, ⁸and he sent Peter and John, saying, 'Go and make the preparations for us to eat the Passover.' ⁹They asked him, 'Where do you want us to prepare it?' ¹⁰He said to them, 'Look, as you go into the city you will meet a man carrying a pitcher of water. Follow him into the house he enters ¹¹and tell the owner of the house, "The Master says this to you: Where is the room for me to eat the Passover with my disciples?" ¹²The man will show you a large upper room furnished with couches. Make the preparations there.' ¹³They set off and found everything as he had told them and prepared the Passover.

The supper

¹⁴When the time came he took his place at table, and the apostles with him. ¹⁵And he said to them, 'I have ardently longed to eat this Passover with you before I suffer; ¹⁶because, I tell you, I shall not eat it until it is fulfilled in the kingdom of God.'

¹⁷Then, taking a cup, he gave thanks and said, 'Take this and share it among you, ¹⁸because from now on, I tell you, I shall never again drink wine until the kingdom of God comes.'

The institution of the Eucharist

¹⁹Then he took bread, and when he had given thanks, he broke it and gave it to them, saying, 'This is my body given for you; do this in remembrance of me.' ²⁰He did the same with the cup after supper, and said, 'This cup is the new covenant in my blood poured out for you.

The treachery of Judas foretold

²¹'But look, here with me on the table is the hand of the man who is betraying me. ²²The Son of man is indeed on the path which was decreed, but alas for that man by whom he is betrayed!' ²³And they began to ask one another which of them it could be who was to do this.

Who is the greatest?

²⁴An argument also began between them about who should be reckoned the greatest; ²⁵but he said to them, 'Among the gentiles it is the kings who lord it over them, and those who have authority over them are given the title Benefactor. ²⁶With you this must not happen. No; the greatest among you must behave as if he were the youngest, the leader as if he were the one who serves. ²⁷For who is the greater: the one at table or the one who serves? The one at table, surely? Yet here am I among you as one who serves!

The reward promised to the apostles

²⁸'You are the men who have stood by me faithfully in my trials; ²⁹and now I confer a kingdom on you, just as my Father conferred one on me: ³⁰you will eat and drink at my table in my kingdom, and you will sit on thrones to judge the twelve tribes of Israel.

Peter's denial and repentance foretold

³¹'Simon, Simon! Look, Satan has got his wish to sift you all like wheat; ³²but I have prayed for you, Simon, that your faith may not fail, and once you have recovered, you in your turn must strengthen your brothers.' ³³'Lord,' he answered, 'I would be ready to go to prison with you, and to death.' ³⁴Jesus replied, 'I tell you, Peter, by the time the cock crows today you will have denied three times that you know me.'

A time of crisis

³⁵He said to them, 'When I sent you out without purse or haversack or sandals, were you short of anything?' ³⁶'No, nothing,' they said. He said to them, 'But now if you have a purse, take it, and the same with a haversack; if you have no sword, sell your cloak and buy one, ³⁷because I tell you these words of scripture are destined to be fulfilled in me: *He was counted as one of the rebellious.*ᵇ Yes, what it says about me is even now

---

22b Is 53:12.

reaching its fulfilment.' [38]They said, 'Lord, here are two swords.' He said to them, 'That is enough!'

The Mount of Olives

[39]He then left to make his way as usual to the Mount of Olives, with the disciples following. [40]When he reached the place he said to them, 'Pray not to be put to the test.'

[41]Then he withdrew from them, about a stone's throw away, and knelt down and prayed. [42]'Father,' he said, 'if you are willing, take this cup away from me. Nevertheless, let your will be done, not mine.' [43]Then an angel appeared to him, coming from heaven to give him strength. [44]In his anguish he prayed even more earnestly, and his sweat fell to the ground like great drops of blood.

[45]When he rose from prayer he went to the disciples and found them sleeping for sheer grief. [46]And he said to them, 'Why are you asleep? Get up and pray not to be put to the test.'

The arrest

[47]Suddenly, while he was still speaking, a number of men appeared, and at the head of them the man called Judas, one of the Twelve, who went up to Jesus to kiss him. [48]Jesus said, 'Judas, are you betraying the Son of man with a kiss?' [49]His followers, seeing what was about to happen, said, 'Lord, shall we use our swords?' [50]And one of them struck the high priest's servant and cut off his right ear. [51]But at this Jesus said, 'That is enough.' And touching the man's ear he healed him.

[52]Then Jesus said to the chief priests and captains of the Temple guard and elders who had come for him, 'Am I a bandit, that you had to set out with swords and clubs? [53]When I was among you in the Temple day after day you never made a move to lay hands on me. But this is your hour; this is the reign of darkness.'

Peter's denials

[54]They seized him then and led him away, and they took him to the high priest's house. Peter followed at a distance. [55]They had lit a fire in the middle of the courtyard and Peter

sat down among them, [56]and as he was sitting there by the blaze a servant-girl saw him, peered at him, and said, 'This man was with him too.' [57]But he denied it. 'Woman, I do not know him,' he said. [58]Shortly afterwards someone else saw him and said, 'You are one of them too.' But Peter replied, 'I am not, my friend.' [59]About an hour later another man insisted, saying, 'This fellow was certainly with him. Why, he is a Galilean.' [60]Peter said, 'My friend, I do not know what you are talking about.' At that instant, while he was still speaking, the cock crowed, [61]and the Lord turned and looked straight at Peter, and Peter remembered the Lord's words when he had said to him, 'Before the cock crows today, you will have disowned me three times.' [62]And he went outside and wept bitterly.

Jesus mocked by the guards

[63]Meanwhile the men who guarded Jesus were mocking and beating him. [64]They blindfolded him and questioned him, saying, 'Prophesy! Who hit you then?' [65]And they heaped many other insults on him.

Jesus before the Sanhedrin

[66]When day broke there was a meeting of the elders of the people, the chief priests and scribes. He was brought before their council, [67]and they said to him, 'If you are the Christ, tell us.' He replied, 'If I tell you, you will not believe, [68]and if I question you, you will not answer. [69]But from now on, the *Son of man* will be *seated at the* right hand of the Power *of God.'*[c] [70]They all said, 'So you are the Son of God then?' He answered, 'It is you who say I am.' [71]Then they said, 'Why do we need any evidence? We have heard it for ourselves from his own lips.'

23 The whole assembly then rose, and they brought him before Pilate.

Jesus before Pilate

[2]They began their accusation by saying, 'We found this man inciting our people to revolt, opposing payment of the tribute to Caesar, and claiming to be Christ, a king.' [3]Pilate put to him this question, 'Are you the king of the Jews?' He replied, 'It is you who say it.'

22c Ps 110:1.

⁴Pilate then said to the chief priests and the crowd, 'I find no case against this man.' ⁵But they persisted, 'He is inflaming the people with his teaching all over Judaea and all the way from Galilee, where he started, down to here.' ⁶When Pilate heard this, he asked if the man were a Galilean; ⁷and finding that he came under Herod's jurisdiction, he passed him over to Herod, who was also in Jerusalem at that time.

Jesus before Herod

⁸Herod was delighted to see Jesus; he had heard about him and had been wanting for a long time to set eyes on him; moreover, he was hoping to see some miracle worked by him. ⁹So he questioned him at some length, but without getting any reply. ¹⁰Meanwhile the chief priests and the scribes were there, vigorously pressing their accusations. ¹¹Then Herod, together with his guards, treated him with contempt and made fun of him; he put a rich cloak on him and sent him back to Pilate. ¹²And though Herod and Pilate had been enemies before, they were reconciled that same day.

Jesus before Pilate again

¹³Pilate then summoned the chief priests and the leading men and the people. ¹⁴He said to them, 'You brought this man before me as a popular agitator. Now I have gone into the matter myself in your presence and found no grounds in the man for any of the charges you bring against him. ¹⁵Nor has Herod either, since he has sent him back to us. As you can see, the man has done nothing that deserves death, ¹⁶so I shall have him flogged and then let him go.'[17]a ¹⁸But as one man they howled, 'Away with him! Give us Barabbas!' ¹⁹(This man had been thrown into prison because of a riot in the city and murder.)

²⁰In his desire to set Jesus free, Pilate addressed them again, ²¹but they shouted back, 'Crucify him! Crucify him!' ²²And for the third time he spoke to them, 'But what harm has this man done? I have found no case against him that deserves death, so I shall have him flogged and then let him go.' ²³But they kept on shouting at the top of their voices, demanding that he should be crucified. And their shouts kept growing louder.

²⁴Pilate then gave his verdict: their demand was to be granted. ²⁵He released the man they asked for, who had been imprisoned because of rioting and murder, and handed Jesus over to them to deal with as they pleased.

The way to Calvary

²⁶As they were leading him away they seized on a man, Simon from Cyrene, who was coming in from the country, and made him shoulder the cross and carry it behind Jesus. ²⁷Large numbers of people followed him, and women too, who mourned and lamented for him. ²⁸But Jesus turned to them and said, 'Daughters of Jerusalem, do not weep for me; weep rather for yourselves and for your children. ²⁹For look, the days are surely coming when people will say, "Blessed are those who are barren, the wombs that have never borne children, the breasts that have never suckled!" ³⁰Then they will begin to *say to the mountains, "Fall on us!"; to the hills, "Cover us!"*[b] ³¹For if this is what is done to green wood, what will be done when the wood is dry?' ³²Now they were also leading out two others, criminals, to be executed with him.

The crucifixion

³³When they reached the place called The Skull, there they crucified him and the two criminals, one on his right, the other on his left. ³⁴Jesus said, 'Father, forgive them; they do not know what they are doing.' Then they cast lots to share out his clothing.

The crucified Christ is mocked

³⁵The people stayed there watching. As for the leaders, they jeered at him with the words, 'He saved others, let him save himself if he is the Christ of God, the Chosen One.' ³⁶The soldiers mocked him too, coming up to him, offering him vinegar, ³⁷and saying, 'If you are the king of the Jews, save yourself.' ³⁸Above him there was an inscription: 'This is the King of the Jews'.

23a Some authorities add v. 17, borrowed from Mt 27:15.
23b Ho 10:8.

The good thief

³⁹One of the criminals hanging there abused him: 'Are you not the Christ? Save yourself and us as well.' ⁴⁰But the other spoke up and rebuked him. 'Have you no fear of God at all?' he said. 'You got the same sentence as he did, ⁴¹but in our case we deserved it: we are paying for what we did. But this man has done nothing wrong.' ⁴²Then he said, 'Jesus, remember me when you come into your kingdom.' ⁴³He answered him, 'In truth I tell you, today you will be with me in paradise.'

The death of Jesus

⁴⁴It was now about the sixth hour and the sun's light failed, so that darkness came over the whole land until the ninth hour. ⁴⁵The veil of the Sanctuary was torn right down the middle. ⁴⁶Jesus cried out in a loud voice saying, 'Father, *into your hands I commit my spirit.*'^c With these words he breathed his last.

After the death

⁴⁷When the centurion saw what had taken place, he gave praise to God and said, 'Truly, this was an upright man.' ⁴⁸And when all the crowds who had gathered for the spectacle saw what had happened, they went home beating their breasts.

⁴⁹All his friends stood at a distance; so also did the women who had accompanied him from Galilee and saw all this happen.

The burial

⁵⁰And now a member of the Council arrived, a good and upright man named Joseph. ⁵¹He had not consented to what the others had planned and carried out. He came from Arimathaea, a Jewish town, and he lived in the hope of seeing the kingdom of God. ⁵²This man went to Pilate and asked for the body of Jesus. ⁵³He then took it down, wrapped it in a shroud and put it in a tomb which was hewn in stone and which had never held a body. ⁵⁴It was Preparation day and the Sabbath was beginning to grow light.

⁵⁵Meanwhile the women who had come from Galilee with Jesus were following behind. They took note of the tomb and how the body had been laid.

⁵⁶Then they returned and prepared spices and ointments. And on the Sabbath day they rested, as the Law required.

VII: AFTER THE RESURRECTION

The empty tomb. The angel's message

24 On the first day of the week, at the first sign of dawn, they went to the tomb with the spices they had prepared. ²They found that the stone had been rolled away from the tomb, ³but on entering they could not find the body of the Lord Jesus. ⁴As they stood there puzzled about this, two men in brilliant clothes suddenly appeared at their side. ⁵Terrified, the women bowed their heads to the ground. But the two said to them, 'Why look among the dead for someone who is alive? ⁶He is not here; he has risen. Remember what he told you when he was still in Galilee: ⁷that the Son of man was destined to be handed over into the power of sinful men and be crucified, and rise again on the third day.' ⁸And they remembered his words.

The apostles refuse to believe the women

⁹And they returned from the tomb and told all this to the Eleven and to all the others. ¹⁰The women were Mary of Magdala, Joanna, and Mary the mother of James. And the other women with them also told the apostles, ¹¹but this story of theirs seemed pure nonsense, and they did not believe them.

Peter at the tomb

¹²Peter, however, went off to the tomb, running. He bent down and looked in and saw the linen cloths but nothing else; he then went back home, amazed at what had happened.

23c   Ps 31:5.

The road to Emmaus

[13]Now that very same day, two of them were on their way to a village called Emmaus, seven miles from Jerusalem, [14]and they were talking together about all that had happened. [15]And it happened that as they were talking together and discussing it, Jesus himself came up and walked by their side; [16]but their eyes were prevented from recognising him. [17]He said to them, 'What are all these things that you are discussing as you walk along?' They stopped, their faces downcast.

[18]Then one of them, called Cleopas, answered him, 'You must be the only person staying in Jerusalem who does not know the things that have been happening there these last few days.' [19]He asked, 'What things?' They answered, 'All about Jesus of Nazareth, who showed himself a prophet powerful in action and speech before God and the whole people; [20]and how our chief priests and our leaders handed him over to be sentenced to death, and had him crucified. [21]Our own hope had been that he would be the one to set Israel free. And this is not all: two whole days have now gone by since it all happened; [22]and some women from our group have astounded us: they went to the tomb in the early morning, [23]and when they could not find the body, they came back to tell us they had seen a vision of angels who declared he was alive. [24]Some of our friends went to the tomb and found everything exactly as the women had reported, but of him they saw nothing.'

[25]Then he said to them, 'You foolish men! So slow to believe all that the prophets have said! [26]Was it not necessary that the Christ should suffer before entering into his glory?' [27]Then, starting with Moses and going through all the prophets, he explained to them the passages throughout the scriptures that were about himself.

[28]When they drew near to the village to which they were going, he made as if to go on; [29]but they pressed him to stay with them saying, 'It is nearly evening, and the day is almost over.' So he went in to stay with them. [30]Now while he was with them at table, he took the bread and said the blessing; then he broke it and handed it to them. [31]And their eyes were opened and they recognised him; but he had vanished from their sight. [32]Then they said to each other, 'Did not our hearts burn within us as he talked to us on the road and explained the scriptures to us?'

[33]They set out that instant and returned to Jerusalem. There they found the Eleven assembled together with their companions, [34]who said to them, 'The Lord has indeed risen and has appeared to Simon.' [35]Then they told their story of what had happened on the road and how they had recognised him at the breaking of bread.

Jesus appears to the apostles

[36]They were still talking about all this when he himself stood among them and said to them, 'Peace be with you!' [37]In a state of alarm and fright, they thought they were seeing a ghost. [38]But he said, 'Why are you so agitated, and why are these doubts stirring in your hearts? [39]See by my hands and my feet that it is I myself. Touch me and see for yourselves; a ghost has no flesh and bones as you can see I have.' [40]And as he said this he showed them his hands and his feet. [41]Their joy was so great that they still could not believe it, as they were dumbfounded; so he said to them, 'Have you anything here to eat?' [42]And they offered him a piece of grilled fish, [43]which he took and ate before their eyes.

Last instructions to the apostles

[44]Then he told them, 'This is what I meant when I said, while I was still with you, that everything written about me in the Law of Moses, in the Prophets and in the Psalms, was destined to be fulfilled.' [45]He then opened their minds to understand the scriptures, [46]and he said to them, 'So it is written that the Christ would suffer and on the third day rise from the dead, [47]and that, in his name, repentance for the forgiveness of sins would be preached to all nations, beginning from Jerusalem. [48]You are witnesses to this.

[49]'And now I am sending upon you what the Father has promised. Stay in the city, then, until you are clothed with the power from on high.'

The ascension

[50]Then he took them out as far as the outskirts of Bethany, and raising his hands he blessed them. [51]Now as he blessed them, he withdrew from them and was carried up to heaven. [52]They worshipped him and then went back to Jerusalem full of joy; [53]and they were continually in the Temple praising God.

THE GOSPEL OF
JOHN

The fourth gospel stands apart from the others in several ways. Instead of the patchwork quilt of little incidents of the Synoptics, this gospel is conceived on broader lines. Episodes are followed by a developed discourse or dialogue which explains the meaning of the signs: Jesus is the revelation of the Father. He replaces in his own person the Temple and the religious institutions of the Jews. All those who encounter Jesus judge themselves by their response to him and to his message. Finally, the Hour of Jesus, his passion and resurrection, is not a disgrace but is the triumph of the King Messiah.

The plan and pattern of the gospel are also different. Instead of a Galilean ministry followed by a final week in Jerusalem, there is a passing backwards and forwards between Galilee and Jerusalem, and the highly significant cleansing of the Temple dramatises Jesus' message not at the end but at the beginning of the ministry. Many of the themes of the gospel are gathered up in the great discourse at the Last Supper (chh. 14—17) when Jesus assures his followers of his continuing presence in his Spirit, who will guide them into all truth. The stress on the Spirit of truth now present brings a new emphasis: many of the blessings of the final coming are seen as already present whereas the first three gospels look for them in the future. The final conflict with the powers of evil is already taking place, and eternal life is already granted to believers.

Ancient tradition associates the gospel with John the Apostle, but modern studies show that a complex process of development occurred, either from a primitive core or from several separate sources. Such a development, through a group of John's disciples in the latter half of the first century, would account for numerous repetitions and overlaps, the result of a determination to lose nothing of the tradition of the teaching of the Beloved Disciple.

PLAN OF THE BOOK

THE GOSPEL ACCORDING TO
JOHN

A: PROLOGUE

1 In the beginning was the Word:[a]
the Word was with God
and the Word was God.
[2]He was with God in the beginning.
[3]Through him all things came into being,
not one thing came into being
except through him.
[4]What has come into being in him was life,
life that was the light of men;
[5]and light shines in darkness,
and darkness could not overpower it.

[6]A man came, sent by God.
His name was John.
[7]He came as a witness,
to bear witness to the light,
so that everyone might believe
through him.
[8]He was not the light,
he was to bear witness to the light.

[9]The Word was the real light
that gives light to everyone;
he was coming into the world.
[10]He was in the world
that had come into being through him,
and the world did not recognise him.
[11]He came to his own
and his own people did not accept him.

[12]But to those who did accept him
he gave power to become children of God,
to those who believed in his name
[13]who were[b] born not from human stock
or human desire
or human will
but from God himself.
[14]The Word became flesh,
he lived among us,
and we saw his glory,
the glory that he has from the Father
as only Son of the Father,
full of grace and truth.

[15]John witnesses to him. He proclaims:
'This is the one of whom I said:
He who comes after me
has passed ahead of me
because he existed before me.'

[16]Indeed, from his fullness
we have, all of us, received—
one gift replacing another,
[17]for the Law was given through Moses,
grace and truth have come
through Jesus Christ.
[18]No one has ever seen God;
it is the only Son,
who is close to the Father's heart,
who has made him known.

1a In the OT the Word or Wisdom of God is present with God before the world existed and reveals God
to the world. Jn sees this Word-Wisdom in the person of Jesus.
1b Some MSS have the singular 'was', which would refer to Jesus' divine origin.

B: JESUS' MINISTRY

I: PROCLAMATION OF THE NEW ORDER:
THE MINISTRY OF JESUS

A: THE OPENING WEEK

The witness of John

¹⁹This was the witness of John, when the Jews sent to him priests and Levites from Jerusalem to ask him, 'Who are you?' ²⁰He declared, he did not deny but declared, 'I am not the Christ.' ²¹So they asked, 'Then are you Elijah?' He replied, 'I am not.' 'Are you the Prophet?' He answered, 'No.' ²²So they said to him, 'Who are you? We must take back an answer to those who sent us. What have you to say about yourself?' ²³So he said, 'I am, as Isaiah prophesied:

A voice of one that cries in the desert:
Prepare a way for the Lord.
Make his paths straight!'ᶜ

²⁴Now those who had been sent were Pharisees, ²⁵and they put this question to him, 'Why are you baptising if you are not the Christ, and not Elijah, and not the Prophet?' ²⁶John answered them, 'I baptise with water; but standing among you — unknown to you — ²⁷is the one who is coming after me; and I am not fit to undo the strap of his sandal.' ²⁸This happened at Bethany, on the far side of the Jordan, where John was baptising.

²⁹The next day, he saw Jesus coming towards him and said, 'Look, there is the lamb of God that takes away the sin of the world.' ³⁰It was of him that I said, "Behind me comes one who has passed ahead of me because he existed before me." ³¹I did not know him myself, and yet my purpose in coming to baptise with water was so that he might be revealed to Israel.' ³²And John declared, 'I saw the Spirit come down on him like a dove from heaven and rest on him. ³³I did not know him myself, but he who sent me to baptise with water had said to me, "The man on whom you see the Spirit come down and rest is the one who is to baptise

with the Holy Spirit." ³⁴I have seen and I testify that he is the Chosen One of God.'

The first disciples

³⁵The next day as John stood there again with two of his disciples, Jesus went past, ³⁶and John looked towards him and said, 'Look, there is the lamb of God.' ³⁷And the two disciples heard what he said and followed Jesus. ³⁸Jesus turned round, saw them following and said, 'What do you want?' They answered, 'Rabbi' — which means Teacher — 'where do you live?' ³⁹He replied, 'Come and see'; so they went and saw where he lived, and stayed with him that day. It was about the tenth hour.

⁴⁰One of these two who became followers of Jesus after hearing what John had said was Andrew, the brother of Simon Peter. ⁴¹The first thing Andrew did was to find his brother and say to him, 'We have found the Messiah' — which means the Christ — ⁴²and he took Simon to Jesus. Jesus looked at him and said, 'You are Simon son of John; you are to be called Cephas' — which means Rock.

⁴³The next day, after Jesus had decided to leave for Galilee, he met Philip and said, 'Follow me.' ⁴⁴Philip came from the same town, Bethsaida, as Andrew and Peter. ⁴⁵Philip found Nathanael and said to him, 'We have found him of whom Moses in the Law and the prophets wrote, Jesus son of Joseph, from Nazareth.' ⁴⁶Nathanael said to him, 'From Nazareth? Can anything good come from that place?' Philip replied, 'Come and see.' ⁴⁷When Jesus saw Nathanael coming he said of him, 'There, truly, is an Israelite in whom there is no deception.' ⁴⁸Nathanael asked, 'How do you know me?' Jesus replied, 'Before Philip came to call you, I saw you under the fig tree.' ⁴⁹Nathanael answered, 'Rabbi, you are the Son of God, you are the king of Israel.' ⁵⁰Jesus replied, 'You believe that just because I said: I

1c Is 40:3.

saw you under the fig tree. You are going to see greater things than that.' ⁵¹And then he added, 'In all truth I tell you, you will see heaven open and the angels of God ascending and descending over the Son of man.'

The wedding at Cana

2 On the third day there was a wedding at Cana in Galilee. The mother of Jesus was there, ²and Jesus and his disciples had also been invited. ³And they ran out of wine, since the wine provided for the feast had all been used, and the mother of Jesus said to him, 'They have no wine.' ⁴Jesus said, 'Woman, what do you want from me? My hour has not come yet.' ⁵His mother said to the servants, '*Do whatever he tells you.*'ᵃ ⁶There were six stone water jars standing there, meant for the ablutions that are customary among the Jews: each could hold twenty or thirty gallons. ⁷Jesus said to the servants, 'Fill the jars with water,' and they filled them to the brim. ⁸Then he said to them, 'Draw some out now and take it to the president of the feast.' ⁹They did this; the president tasted the water, and it had turned into wine. Having no idea where it came from—though the servants who had drawn the water knew—the president of the feast called the bridegroom ¹⁰and said, 'Everyone serves good wine first and the worse wine when the guests are well wined; but you have kept the best wine till now.'

¹¹This was the first of Jesus' signs: it was at Cana in Galilee. He revealed his glory, and his disciples believed in him. ¹²After this he went down to Capernaum with his mother and his brothers and his disciples, but they stayed there only a few days.

B: THE PASSOVER

The cleansing of the Temple

¹³When the time of the Jewish Passover was near Jesus went up to Jerusalem, ¹⁴and in the Temple he found people selling cattle and sheep and doves, and the money changers sitting there. ¹⁵Making a whip out of cord, he drove them all out of the Temple, sheep and cattle as well, scattered the money changers' coins, knocked their tables over ¹⁶and said to the dove sellers, 'Take all this out of here and stop using my Father's house as a market.' ¹⁷Then his disciples remembered the words of scripture: *I am eaten up with zeal for your house.*ᵇ ¹⁸The Jews intervened and said, 'What sign can you show us that you should act like this?' ¹⁹Jesus answered, 'Destroy this Temple, and in three days I will raise it up.' ²⁰The Jews replied, 'It has taken forty-six years to build this Temple:ᶜ are you going to raise it up again in three days?' ²¹But he was speaking of the Temple that was his body, ²²and when Jesus rose from the dead, his disciples remembered that he had said this, and they believed the scripture and what he had said.

Jesus in Jerusalem

²³During his stay in Jerusalem for the feast of the Passover many believed in his name when they saw the signs that he did, ²⁴but Jesus knew all people and did not trust himself to them; ²⁵he never needed evidence about anyone; he could tell what someone had within.

The conversation with Nicodemus

3 There was one of the Pharisees called Nicodemus, a leader of the Jews, ²who came to Jesus by night and said, 'Rabbi, we know that you have come from God as a teacher; for no one could perform the signs that you do unless God were with him.' ³Jesus answered:

In all truth I tell you,
no one can see the kingdom of God
without being born from above.

⁴Nicodemus said, 'How can anyone who is already old be born? Is it possible to go back into the womb again and be born?' ⁵Jesus replied:

In all truth I tell you,
no one can enter the kingdom of God
without being born
through water and the Spirit;
⁶what is born of human nature is human;
what is born of the Spirit is spirit.

2a Gn 41:55.
2b Ps 69:9.
2c Reconstruction work began in 19 BC, so this is Passover AD 28.

⁷Do not be surprised when I say:
You must be born from above.
⁸The wind blows where it pleases;
you can hear its sound,
but you cannot tell where it comes from
or where it is going.
So it is with everyone
who is born of the Spirit.

⁹'How is that possible?' asked Nicodemus.
¹⁰Jesus replied, 'You are the Teacher of
Israel, and you do not know these things!

¹¹'In all truth I tell you,
we speak only about what we know
and witness only to what we have seen
and yet you people reject our evidence.
¹²If you do not believe me
when I speak to you about earthly things,
how will you believe me
when I speak to you about heavenly things?
¹³No one has gone up to heaven
except the one
who came down from heaven,
the Son of man;
¹⁴as Moses lifted up the snake in the desert,
so must the Son of man be lifted up
¹⁵so that everyone who believes
may have eternal life in him.
¹⁶For this is how God loved the world:
he gave his only Son,
so that everyone who believes in him
may not perish
but may have eternal life.
¹⁷For God sent his Son into the world
not to judge the world,
but so that through him
the world might be saved.
¹⁸No one who believes in him
will be judged;
but whoever does not believe
is judged already,
because that person does not believe
in the Name of God's only Son.
¹⁹And the judgement is this:
though the light has come into the world
people have preferred
darkness to the light
because their deeds were evil.
²⁰And indeed, everybody who does wrong
hates the light and avoids it,
to prevent his actions
from being shown up;
²¹but whoever does the truth
comes out into the light,
so that what he is doing
may plainly appear as done in God.'

Jesus' ministry in Judaea
John bears witness for the last time

²²After this, Jesus went with his disciples into
the Judaean countryside and stayed with
them there and baptised. ²³John also was
baptising at Aenon near Salim, where there
was plenty of water, and people were going
there and were being baptised. ²⁴For John
had not yet been put in prison.
²⁵Now a discussion arose between some of
John's disciples and a Jew about purification,
²⁶so they went to John and said, 'Rabbi, the
man who was with you on the far side of the
Jordan, the man to whom you bore witness,
is baptising now, and everyone is going to
him.' ²⁷John replied:

'No one can have anything
except what is given him from heaven.

²⁸'You yourselves can bear me out. I said, "I
am not the Christ; I am the one who has been
sent to go in front of him."

²⁹'It is the bridegroom who has the bride;
and yet the bridegroom's friend,
who stands there and listens to him,
is filled with joy at the bridegroom's voice.
This is the joy I feel, and it is complete.
³⁰He must grow greater,
I must grow less.
³¹He who comes from above
is above all others;
he who is of the earth
is earthly himself
and speaks in an earthly way.
He who comes from heaven
³²bears witness to the things
he has seen and heard,
but his testimony
is not accepted by anybody;
³³though anyone
who does accept his testimony
is attesting that God is true,
³⁴since he whom God has sent
speaks God's own words,
for God gives him the Spirit
without reserve.
³⁵The Father loves the Son
and has entrusted everything to his hands.
³⁶Anyone who believes in the Son
has eternal life,
but anyone who refuses
to believe in the Son
will never see life:
God's retribution hangs over him.'

Jesus among the Samaritans

4 When Jesus heard that the Pharisees had found out that he was making and baptising more disciples than John—²though in fact it was his disciples who baptised, not Jesus himself—³he left Judaea and went back to Galilee. ⁴He had to pass through Samaria. ⁵On the way he came to the Samaritan town called Sychar near the land that Jacob gave to his son Joseph. ⁶Jacob's well was there and Jesus, tired by the journey, sat down by the well. It was about the sixth hour. ⁷When a Samaritan woman came to draw water, Jesus said to her, 'Give me something to drink.' ⁸His disciples had gone into the town to buy food. ⁹The Samaritan woman said to him, 'You are a Jew. How is it that you ask me, a Samaritan, for something to drink?'—Jews, of course, do not associate with Samaritans. ¹⁰Jesus replied to her:

If you only knew what God is offering
and who it is that is saying to you,
'Give me something to drink,'
you would have been the one to ask,
and he would have given you living water.

¹¹'You have no bucket, sir,' she answered, 'and the well is deep: how do you get this living water? ¹²Are you a greater man than our father Jacob, who gave us this well and drank from it himself with his sons and his cattle?' ¹³Jesus replied:

Whoever drinks this water
will be thirsty again;
¹⁴but no one who drinks the water
that I shall give
will ever be thirsty again:
the water that I shall give
will become a spring of water within,
welling up for eternal life.

¹⁵'Sir,' said the woman, 'give me some of that water, so that I may never be thirsty or come here again to draw water.' ¹⁶'Go and call your husband,' said Jesus to her, 'and come back here.' ¹⁷The woman answered, 'I have no husband.' Jesus said to her, 'You are right to say, "I have no husband"; ¹⁸for although you have had five, the one you now have is not your husband. You spoke the truth there.' ¹⁹'I see you are a prophet, sir,' said the woman. ²⁰'Our fathers worshipped on this mountain,ᵃ though you say that Jeru-

salem is the place where one ought to worship.' ²¹Jesus said:

Believe me, woman, the hour is coming
when you will worship the Father
neither on this mountain
nor in Jerusalem.
²²You worship what you do not know;
we worship what we do know;
for salvation comes from the Jews.
²³But the hour is coming—
indeed is already here—
when true worshippers
will worship the Father
in spirit and truth:
that is the kind of worshipper
the Father seeks.
²⁴God is spirit,
and those who worship
must worship in spirit and truth.

²⁵The woman said to him, 'I know that Messiah—that is, Christ—is coming; and when he comes he will explain everything.' ²⁶Jesus said, 'That is who I am, I who speak to you.' ²⁷At this point his disciples returned and were surprised to find him speaking to a woman, though none of them asked, 'What do you want from her?' or, 'What are you talking to her about?' ²⁸The woman put down her water jar and hurried back to the town to tell the people, ²⁹'Come and see a man who has told me everything I have done; could this be the Christ?' ³⁰This brought people out of the town and they made their way towards him.
³¹Meanwhile, the disciples were urging him, 'Rabbi, do have something to eat'; ³²but he said, 'I have food to eat that you do not know about.' ³³So the disciples said to one another, 'Has someone brought him food?' ³⁴But Jesus said:

My food
is to do the will of the one who sent me,
and to complete his work.
³⁵Do you not have a saying:
Four months and then the harvest?
Well, I tell you,
look around you, look at the fields;
already they are white,
ready for harvest!
³⁶Already the reaper
is being paid his wages,

4a Gerizim, where there had been a Temple rivalling Jerusalem's. To Jesus both are provisional.

already he is bringing in the grain
for eternal life,
so that sower and reaper
can rejoice together.
[37]For here the proverb holds true:
one sows, another reaps;
[38]I sent you to reap
a harvest you have not laboured for.
Others have laboured for it;
and you have come
into the rewards of their labour.

[39]Many Samaritans of that town believed in him on the strength of the woman's words of testimony, 'He told me everything I have done.' [40]So, when the Samaritans came up to him, they begged him to stay with them. He stayed for two days, and [41]many more came to believe on the strength of the words he spoke to them; [42]and they said to the woman, 'Now we believe no longer because of what you told us; we have heard him ourselves and we know that he is indeed the Saviour of the world.'

Jesus in Galilee

[43]When the two days were over Jesus left for Galilee. [44]He himself had declared that a prophet is not honoured in his own home town. [45]On his arrival the Galileans received him well, having seen all that he had done at Jerusalem during the festival which they too had attended.

Second sign at Cana
The cure of a royal official's son

[46]He went again to Cana in Galilee, where he had changed the water into wine. And there was a royal official whose son was ill at Capernaum; [47]hearing that Jesus had arrived in Galilee from Judaea, he went and asked him to come and cure his son, as he was at the point of death. [48]Jesus said to him, 'Unless you see signs and portents you will not believe!' [49]'Sir,' answered the official, 'come down before my child dies.' [50]'Go home,' said Jesus, 'your son will live.' The man believed what Jesus had said and went on his way home; [51]and while he was still on the way his servants met him with the news that his boy was alive. [52]He asked them when the boy had begun to recover. They replied, 'The fever left him yesterday at the seventh hour.' [53]The father realised that this was exactly the time when Jesus had said, 'Your son will live'; and he and all his household believed.
[54]This new sign, the second, Jesus performed on his return from Judaea to Galilee.

II: THE SECOND FEAST AT JERUSALEM:
FIRST OPPOSITION TO REVELATION

The cure of a sick man
at the Pool of Bethesda

5 After this there was a Jewish festival, and Jesus went up to Jerusalem. [2]Now in Jerusalem next to the Sheep Pool there is a pool called Bethesda in Hebrew, which has five porticos; [3]and under these were crowds of sick people, blind, lame, paralysed.[a] [5]One man there had an illness which had lasted thirty-eight years, [6]and when Jesus saw him lying there and knew he had been in that condition for a long time, he said, 'Do you want to be well again?' [7]'Sir,' replied the sick man, 'I have no one to put me into the pool when the water is disturbed; and while I am still on the way, someone else gets down there before me.' [8]Jesus said, 'Get up, pick up your sleeping-mat and walk around.' [9]The man was cured at once, and he picked up his mat and started to walk around.

Now that day happened to be the Sabbath, [10]so the Jews said to the man who had been cured, 'It is the Sabbath; you are not allowed to carry your sleeping-mat.' [11]He replied, 'But the man who cured me told me, "Pick up your sleeping-mat and walk around." ' [12]They asked, 'Who is the man who said to you, "Pick up your sleeping-mat and walk around"? ' [13]The man had no idea who it

---

5a Some ancient MSS add: 'waiting for the water to move; [4]for at intervals the angel of the Lord came down into the pool, and the water was disturbed, and the first person to enter the water after this disturbance was cured of any ailment from which he was suffering'.

was, since Jesus had disappeared, as the place was crowded. ¹⁴After a while Jesus met him in the Temple and said, 'Now you are well again, do not sin any more, or something worse may happen to you.' ¹⁵The man went back and told the Jews that it was Jesus who had cured him. ¹⁶It was because he did things like this on the Sabbath that the Jews began to harass Jesus. ¹⁷His answer to them was, 'My Father still goes on working, and I am at work, too.' ¹⁸But that only made the Jews even more intent on killing him, because not only was he breaking the Sabbath, but he spoke of God as his own Father and so made himself God's equal.

¹⁹To this Jesus replied:

In all truth I tell you,
by himself the Son can do nothing;
he can do only
    what he sees the Father doing:
and whatever the Father does
    the Son does too.
²⁰For the Father loves the Son
and shows him everything
    he himself does,
and he will show him
    even greater things than these,
works that will astonish you.
²¹Thus, as the Father raises the dead
    and gives them life,
so the Son gives life to anyone he chooses;
²²for the Father judges no one;
he has entrusted all judgement to the Son,
²³so that all may honour the Son
as they honour the Father.
Whoever refuses honour to the Son
refuses honour to the Father
    who sent him.
²⁴In all truth I tell you,
whoever listens to my words,
and believes in the one who sent me,
has eternal life;
without being brought to judgement
such a person
    has passed from death to life.
²⁵In all truth I tell you,
    the hour is coming—
        indeed it is already here—
when the dead
    will hear the voice of the Son of God,
and all who hear it will live.
²⁶For as the Father has life in himself,
so he has granted the Son also
    to have life in himself;
²⁷and, because he is the Son of man,

has granted him power
    to give judgement.
²⁸Do not be surprised at this,
for the hour is coming
when the dead will leave their graves
at the sound of his voice:
²⁹those who did good
will come forth to life;
and those who did evil
will come forth to judgement.
³⁰By myself I can do nothing;
I can judge only as I am told to judge,
and my judging is just,
because I seek to do not my own will
but the will of him who sent me.
³¹Were I to testify on my own behalf,
my testimony would not be true;
³²but there is another witness
    who speaks on my behalf,
and I know that his testimony is true.
³³You sent messengers to John,
and he gave his testimony to the truth—
³⁴not that I depend on human testimony;
no, it is for your salvation
    that I mention it.
³⁵John was a lamp lit and shining
and for a time you were content
    to enjoy the light that he gave.
³⁶But my testimony is greater than John's:
the deeds my Father has given me
    to perform,
these same deeds of mine
testify that the Father has sent me.
³⁷Besides, the Father who sent me
bears witness to me himself.
You have never heard his voice,
you have never seen his shape,
³⁸and his word finds no home in you
because you do not believe
in the one whom he has sent.

³⁹You pore over the scriptures,
believing that in them
    you can find eternal life;
it is these scriptures that testify to me,
⁴⁰and yet you refuse to come to me
    to receive life!
⁴¹Human glory means nothing to me.
⁴²Besides, I know you too well:
you have no love of God in you.
⁴³I have come in the name of my Father
and you refuse to accept me;
if someone else should come
    in his own name
you would accept him.

44How can you believe,
since you look to each other for glory
and are not concerned
with the glory that comes
from the one God?
45Do not imagine
that I am going to accuse you
before the Father:

you have placed your hopes on Moses,
and Moses will be the one
who accuses you.
46If you really believed him
you would believe me too,
since it was about me that he was writing;
47but if you will not believe what he wrote,
how can you believe what I say?

III: THE PASSOVER OF THE BREAD OF LIFE:
FURTHER OPPOSITION TO REVELATION

The miracle of the loaves

6After this, Jesus crossed the Sea of Galilee—or of Tiberias— 2and a large crowd followed him, impressed by the signs he had done in curing the sick. 3Jesus climbed the hillside and sat down there with his disciples. 4The time of the Jewish Passover was near.

5Looking up, Jesus saw the crowds approaching and said to Philip, 'Where can we buy some bread for these people to eat?' 6He said this only to put Philip to the test; he himself knew exactly what he was going to do. 7Philip answered, 'Two hundred denarii would not buy enough to give them a little piece each.' 8One of his disciples, Andrew, Simon Peter's brother, said, 9'Here is a small boy with five barley loaves and two fish; but what is that among so many?' 10Jesus said to them, 'Make the people sit down.' There was plenty of grass there, and as many as five thousand men sat down. 11Then Jesus took the loaves, gave thanks, and distributed them to those who were sitting there; he then did the same with the fish, distributing as much as they wanted. 12When they had eaten enough he said to the disciples, 'Pick up the pieces left over, so that nothing is wasted.' 13So they picked them up and filled twelve large baskets with scraps left over from the meal of five barley loaves. 14Seeing the sign that he had done, the people said, 'This is indeed the prophet who is to come into the world.' 15Jesus, as he realised they were about to come and take him by force and make him king, fled back to the hills alone.

Jesus comes to his disciples walking on the waters

16That evening the disciples went down to the shore of the sea 17and got into a boat to make for Capernaum on the other side of the sea. It was getting dark by now and Jesus had still not rejoined them. 18The wind was strong, and the sea was getting rough. 19They had rowed three or four miles when they saw Jesus walking on the sea and coming towards the boat. They were afraid, 20but he said, 'It's me. Don't be afraid.' 21They were ready to take him into the boat, and immediately it reached the shore at the place they were making for.

The discourse in the synagogue at Capernaum

22Next day, the crowd that had stayed on the other side saw that only one boat had been there, and that Jesus had not got into the boat with his disciples, but that the disciples had set off by themselves. 23Other boats, however, had put in from Tiberias, near the place where the bread had been eaten. 24When the people saw that neither Jesus nor his disciples were there, they got into those boats and crossed to Capernaum to look for Jesus. 25When they found him on the other side, they said to him, 'Rabbi, when did you come here?' 26Jesus answered:

In all truth I tell you,
you are looking for me
not because you have seen the signs
but because you had all the bread
you wanted to eat.
27Do not work for food that goes bad,
but work for food
that endures for eternal life,
which the Son of man will give you,
for on him the Father, God himself,
has set his seal.

28Then they said to him, 'What must we do if we are to carry out God's work?' 29Jesus gave them this answer, 'This is carrying out God's work: you must believe in the one he has sent.' ³⁰So they said, 'What sign will you yourself do, the sight of which will make us believe in you? What work will you do? ³¹Our fathers ate manna in the desert; as scripture says: *He gave them bread from heaven to eat.*'ᵃ ³²Jesus answered them:

In all truth I tell you,
it was not Moses
    who gave you the bread from heaven,
it is my Father
    who gives you the bread from heaven,
    the true bread;
³³for the bread of God
is the bread
    which comes down from heaven
and gives life to the world.

³⁴'Sir,' they said, 'give us that bread always.' ³⁵Jesus answered them:

I am the bread of life.
No one who comes to me will ever hunger;
no one who believes in me will ever thirst.
³⁶But, as I have told you,
    you can see me and still you do not believe.
³⁷Everyone whom the Father gives me
    will come to me;
I will certainly not reject
    anyone who comes to me,
³⁸because I have come from heaven,
    not to do my own will,
    but to do the will of him who sent me.
³⁹Now the will of him who sent me
    is that I should lose nothing
    of all that he has given to me,
    but that I should raise it up
    on the last day.
⁴⁰It is my Father's will
    that whoever sees the Son
    and believes in him
    should have eternal life,
    and that I should raise that person up
    on the last day.

⁴¹Meanwhile the Jews were complaining to each other about him, because he had said, 'I am the bread that has come down from heaven.' ⁴²They were saying, 'Surely this is Jesus son of Joseph, whose father and mother we know. How can he now say, "I have come down from heaven?" ' ⁴³Jesus said in reply to them, 'Stop complaining to each other.

⁴⁴'No one can come to me
unless drawn by the Father who sent me,
and I will raise that person up
    on the last day.
⁴⁵It is written in the prophets:
*They will all be taught by God;*ᵇ
everyone who has listened to the Father,
and learnt from him,
comes to me.
⁴⁶Not that anybody has seen the Father,
except him who has his being from God:
he has seen the Father.
⁴⁷In all truth I tell you,
everyone who believes has eternal life.
⁴⁸I am the bread of life.
⁴⁹Your fathers ate manna in the desert
and they are dead;
⁵⁰but this is the bread
    which comes down from heaven,
so that a person may eat it and not die.
⁵¹I am the living bread
    which has come down from heaven.
Anyone who eats this bread
    will live for ever;
and the bread that I shall give
is my flesh, for the life of the world.'

⁵²Then the Jews started arguing among themselves, 'How can this man give us his flesh to eat?' ⁵³Jesus replied to them:

In all truth I tell you,
if you do not eat
    the flesh of the Son of man
and drink his blood,
you have no life in you.
⁵⁴Anyone who does eat my flesh
    and drink my blood
    has eternal life,
and I shall raise that person up
    on the last day.
⁵⁵For my flesh is real food
and my blood is real drink.
⁵⁶Whoever eats my flesh
    and drinks my blood
lives in me
and I live in that person.
⁵⁷As the living Father sent me
and I draw life from the Father,
so whoever eats me
    will also draw life from me.
⁵⁸This is the bread
    which has come down from heaven;
    it is not like the bread our ancestors ate:

6a Ps 78:24. 'Bread from heaven' is commented vv. 32–48 and 'to eat' vv. 49–58.
6b Is 54:13.

they are dead,
but anyone who eats this bread
   will live for ever.

⁵⁹This is what he taught at Capernaum in the synagogue. ⁶⁰After hearing it, many of his followers said, 'This is intolerable language. How could anyone accept it?' ⁶¹Jesus was aware that his followers were complaining about it and said, 'Does this disturb you? ⁶²What if you should see the Son of man ascend to where he was before?

⁶³'It is the spirit that gives life,
   the flesh has nothing to offer.
The words I have spoken to you are spirit
   and they are life.

⁶⁴'But there are some of you who do not believe.' For Jesus knew from the outset who did not believe and who was to betray him. ⁶⁵He went on, 'This is why I told you that no one could come to me except by the gift of the Father.' ⁶⁶After this, many of his disciples went away and accompanied him no more.

Peter's profession of faith

⁶⁷Then Jesus said to the Twelve, 'What about you, do you want to go away too?' ⁶⁸Simon Peter answered, 'Lord, to whom shall we go? You have the message of eternal life, ⁶⁹and we believe; we have come to know that you are the Holy One of God.' ⁷⁰Jesus replied to them, 'Did I not choose the Twelve of you? Yet one of you is a devil.' ⁷¹He meant Judas son of Simon Iscariot, since this was the man, one of the Twelve, who was to betray him.

IV: THE FEAST OF SHELTERS:
THE GREAT REJECTION

Jesus goes up to Jerusalem for the feast and teaches there

7 After this Jesus travelled round Galilee; he could not travel round Judaea, because the Jews were seeking to kill him. ²As the Jewish feast of Shelters drew near, ³his brothers said to him, 'Leave this place and go to Judaea, so that your disciples, too, can see the works you are doing; ⁴no one who wants to be publicly known acts in secret; if this is what you are doing, you should reveal yourself to the world.' ⁵Not even his brothers had faith in him. ⁶Jesus answered, 'For me the right time has not come yet, but for you any time is the right time. ⁷The world cannot hate you, but it does hate me, because I give evidence that its ways are evil. ⁸Go up to the festival yourselves: I am not going to this festival, because for me the time is not ripe yet.' ⁹Having said that, he stayed behind in Galilee.

¹⁰However, after his brothers had left for the festival, he went up as well, not publicly but secretly. ¹¹At the festival the Jews were on the look-out for him: 'Where is he?' they said. ¹²There was a great deal of talk about him in the crowds. Some said, 'He is a good man'; others, 'No, he is leading the people astray.' ¹³Yet no one spoke about him openly, for fear of the Jews.

¹⁴When the festival was half over, Jesus went to the Temple and began to teach. ¹⁵The Jews were astonished and said, 'How did he learn to read? He has not been educated.' ¹⁶Jesus answered them:

'My teaching is not from myself:
   it comes from the one who sent me;
¹⁷anyone who is prepared to do his will,
   will know whether my teaching
     is from God
or whether I speak on my own account.
¹⁸When someone speaks
     on his own account,
he is seeking honour for himself;
but when he is seeking
   the honour of the person who sent him,
   then he is true
and altogether without dishonesty.
¹⁹Did not Moses give you the Law?
And yet not one of you keeps the Law!

'Why do you want to kill me?' ²⁰The crowd replied, 'You are mad! Who wants to kill you?' ²¹Jesus answered, 'One work I did, and you are all amazed at it. ²²Moses ordered you to practise circumcision—not that it began with him, it goes back to the patriarchs—and you circumcise on the Sabbath. ²³Now if someone can be circumcised on the Sabbath so that the Law of Moses is not broken, why are you angry with me for making someone completely healthy on a Sabbath? [24]Do not keep judging according to appearances; let your judgement be according to what is right.'

The people discuss the origin of the Messiah

[25]Meanwhile some of the people of Jerusalem were saying, 'Isn't this the man they want to kill? [26]And here he is, speaking openly, and they have nothing to say to him! Can it be true the authorities have recognised that he is the Christ? [27]Yet we all know where he comes from, but when the Christ appears no one will know where he comes from.'

[28]Then, as Jesus was teaching in the Temple, he cried out:

You know me
    and you know where I came from.
Yet I have not come of my own accord:
but he who sent me is true;
You do not know him,
[29]but I know him
because I have my being from him
and it was he who sent me.

[30]They wanted to arrest him then, but because his hour had not yet come no one laid a hand on him.

Jesus foretells his approaching departure

[31]There were many people in the crowds, however, who believed in him; they were saying, 'When the Christ comes, will he give more signs than this man has?' [32]Hearing that talk like this about him was spreading among the people, the Pharisees sent the Temple guards to arrest him.

[33]Then Jesus said:

For a short time I am with you still;
    then I shall go back to the one
      who sent me.
[34]You will look for me
    and will not find me;
where I am
    you cannot come.

[35]So the Jews said to one another, 'Where is he intending to go that we shall not be able to find him? Is he intending to go abroad to the people who are dispersed among the Greeks and to teach the Greeks? [36]What does he mean when he says:

"You will look for me
    and will not find me;
where I am,
    you cannot come?" '

The promise of living water

[37]On the last day, the great day of the festival, Jesus stood and cried out:

'Let anyone who is thirsty come to me!
[38]Let anyone who believes in me
    come and drink!

As scripture says, "From his heart shall flow streams of living water." '

[39]He was speaking of the Spirit which those who believed in him were to receive; for there was no Spirit as yet because Jesus had not yet been glorified.

Fresh discussions on the origin of the Messiah

[40]Some of the crowd who had been listening said, 'He is indeed the prophet,' [41]and some said, 'He is the Christ,' but others said, 'Would the Christ come from Galilee? [42]Does not scripture say that the Christ must be descended from David and come from Bethlehem, the village where David was?' [43]So the people could not agree about him. [44]Some wanted to arrest him, but no one actually laid a hand on him.

[45]The guards went back to the chief priests and Pharisees who said to them, 'Why haven't you brought him?' [46]The guards replied, 'No one has ever spoken like this man.' [47]'So,' the Pharisees answered, 'you, too, have been led astray? [48]Have any of the authorities come to believe in him? Any of the Pharisees? [49]This rabble knows nothing about the Law—they are damned.' [50]One of them, Nicodemus—the same man who had come to Jesus earlier—said to them, [51]'But surely our Law does not allow us to pass judgement on anyone without first giving him a hearing and discovering what he is doing?' [52]To this they answered, 'Are you a Galilean too? Go into the matter, and see for yourself: prophets do not arise in Galilee.'

The adulterous woman[a]

⁵³They all went home,

8 and Jesus went to the Mount of Olives. ²At daybreak he appeared in the Temple again; and as all the people came to him, he sat down and began to teach them.

³The scribes and Pharisees brought a woman along who had been caught committing adultery; and making her stand there in the middle ⁴they said to Jesus, 'Master, this woman was caught in the very act of committing adultery, ⁵and in the Law Moses has ordered us to stone women of this kind. What have you got to say?' ⁶They asked him this as a test, looking for an accusation to use against him. But Jesus bent down and started writing on the ground with his finger. ⁷As they persisted with their question, he straightened up and said, 'Let the one among you who is guiltless be the first to throw a stone at her.' ⁸Then he bent down and continued writing on the ground. ⁹When they heard this they went away one by one, beginning with the eldest, until the last one had gone and Jesus was left alone with the woman, who remained in the middle. ¹⁰Jesus again straightened up and said, 'Woman, where are they? Has no one condemned you?' ¹¹'No one, sir,' she replied. 'Neither do I condemn you,' said Jesus. 'Go away, and from this moment sin no more.'

Jesus, the light of the world

¹²When Jesus spoke to the people again, he said:

I am the light of the world;
anyone who follows me
 will not be walking in the dark,
but will have the light of life.

A discussion on the testimony of Jesus to himself

¹³At this the Pharisees said to him, 'You are testifying on your own behalf; your testimony is not true.' ¹⁴Jesus replied:

Even though I am testifying
 on my own behalf,
my testimony is still true,
because I know

where I have come from
 and where I am going;
but you do not know
where I come from or where I am going.
¹⁵You judge by human standards;
I judge no one,
¹⁶but if I judge,
my judgement will be true,
because I am not alone:
the one who sent me is with me;
¹⁷and in your Law it is written
that the testimony of two witnesses is
 true.
¹⁸I testify on my own behalf,
but the Father who sent me
 testifies on my behalf, too.

¹⁹They asked him, 'Where is your Father then?' Jesus answered:

You do not know me,
 nor do you know my Father;
if you did know me,
 you would know my Father as well.

²⁰He spoke these words in the Treasury, while teaching in the Temple. No one arrested him, because his hour had not yet come.

²¹Again he said to them:

I am going away; you will look for me
and you will die in your sin.
Where I am going, you cannot come.

²²So the Jews said to one another, 'Is he going to kill himself, that he says, "Where I am going, you cannot come?"' ²³Jesus went on:

You are from below;
I am from above.
You are of this world;
I am not of this world.
²⁴I have told you already:
 You will die in your sins.
Yes, if you do not believe that I am He,[a]
you will die in your sins.

²⁵So they said to him, 'Who are you?' Jesus answered:

What I have told you from the outset.
²⁶About you I have much to say
and much to judge;
but the one who sent me is true,
and what I declare to the world
I have learnt from him.

7a Many ancient MSS omit 7:53—8:11.
8a Here and in vv. 28, 58 Jesus appropriates the divine name revealed to Moses in Ex 3:14.

[27]They did not recognise that he was talking to them about the Father. [28]So Jesus said:

When you have lifted up the Son of man,
then you will know that I am He
and that I do nothing of my own accord.
What I say
is what the Father has taught me;
[29]he who sent me is with me,
and has not left me to myself,
for I always do what pleases him.

[30]As he was saying this, many came to believe in him.

Jesus and Abraham

[31]To the Jews who believed in him Jesus said:

If you make my word your home
you will indeed be my disciples;
[32]you will come to know the truth,
and the truth will set you free.

[33]They answered, 'We are descended from Abraham and we have never been the slaves of anyone; what do you mean, "You will be set free?" ' [34]Jesus replied:

In all truth I tell you,
everyone who commits sin is a slave.
[35]Now a slave has no permanent standing
in the household,
but a son belongs to it for ever.
[36]So if the Son sets you free,
you will indeed be free.
[37]I know that you are descended
from Abraham;
but you want to kill me
because my word finds no place in you.
[38]What I speak of
is what I have seen at my Father's side,
and you too put into action
the lessons you have learnt
from your father.

[39]They repeated, 'Our father is Abraham.' Jesus said to them:

If you are Abraham's children,
do as Abraham did.
[40]As it is, you want to kill me,
a man who has told you the truth
as I have learnt it from God;
that is not what Abraham did.
[41]You are doing your father's work.

They replied, 'We were not born illegitimate, the only father we have is God.' [42]Jesus answered:

If God were your father,
you would love me,
since I have my origin in God
and have come from him;
I did not come of my own accord,
but he sent me.
[43]Why do you not understand what I say?
Because you cannot bear to listen
to my words.
[44]You are from your father, the devil,
and you prefer to do
what your father wants.
He was a murderer from the start;
he was never grounded in the truth;
there is no truth in him at all.
When he lies
he is speaking true to his nature,
because he is a liar, and the father of lies.
[45]But it is because I speak the truth
that you do not believe me.
[46]Can any of you convict me of sin?
If I speak the truth,
why do you not believe me?
[47]Whoever comes from God
listens to the words of God;
the reason why you do not listen
is that you are not from God.

[48]The Jews replied, 'Are we not right in saying that you are a Samaritan and possessed by a devil?' Jesus answered:

[49]I am not possessed;
but I honour my Father,
and you deny me honour.
[50]I do not seek my own glory;
there is someone who does seek it
and is the judge of it.
[51]In all truth I tell you,
whoever keeps my word
will never see death.

[52]The Jews said, 'Now we know that you are possessed. Abraham is dead, and the prophets are dead, and yet you say, "Whoever keeps my word will never know the taste of death." [53]Are you greater than our father Abraham, who is dead? The prophets are dead too. Who are you claiming to be?' [54]Jesus answered:

If I were to seek my own glory
my glory would be worth nothing;
in fact, my glory
is conferred by the Father,
by the one of whom you say,
'He is our God,'
[55]although you do not know him.

But I know him,
and if I were to say, 'I do not know him,'
I should be a liar, as you yourselves are.
But I do know him, and I keep his word.
⁵⁶Your father Abraham rejoiced
to think that he would see my Day;
he saw it and was glad.

⁵⁷The Jews then said, 'You are not fifty yet, and you have seen Abraham!' ⁵⁸Jesus replied:

In all truth I tell you,
before Abraham ever was,
I am.

⁵⁹At this they picked up stones to throw at him; but Jesus hid himself and left the Temple.

The cure of the man born blind

9As he went along, he saw a man who had been blind from birth. ²His disciples asked him, 'Rabbi, who sinned, this man or his parents, that he should have been born blind?' ³'Neither he nor his parents sinned,' Jesus answered, 'he was born blind so that the works of God might be revealed in him.

⁴'As long as day lasts
we must carry out the work of the one
who sent me;
the night will soon be here
when no one can work.
⁵As long as I am in the world
I am the light of the world.'

⁶Having said this, he spat on the ground, made a paste with the spittle, put this over the eyes of the blind man, ⁷and said to him, 'Go and wash in the Pool of Siloam' (the name means 'one who has been sent'). So he went off and washed and came back able to see.

⁸His neighbours and the people who used to see him before (for he was a beggar) said, 'Isn't this the man who used to sit and beg?' ⁹Some said, 'Yes, it is the same one.' Others said, 'No, but he looks just like him.' The man himself said, 'Yes, I am the one.' ¹⁰So they said to him, 'Then how is it that your eyes were opened?' ¹¹He answered, 'The man called Jesus made a paste, daubed my eyes with it and said to me, "Go off and wash at Siloam"; so I went, and when I washed I gained my sight.' ¹²They asked, 'Where is he?' He answered, 'I don't know.'

¹³They brought to the Pharisees the man who had been blind. ¹⁴It had been a Sabbath day when Jesus made the paste and opened the man's eyes, ¹⁵so when the Pharisees asked him how he had gained his sight, he said, 'He put a paste on my eyes, and I washed, and I can see.' ¹⁶Then some of the Pharisees said, 'That man cannot be from God: he does not keep the Sabbath.' Others said, 'How can a sinner produce signs like this?' And there was division among them. ¹⁷So they spoke to the blind man again, 'What have you to say about him yourself, now that he has opened your eyes?' The man answered, 'He is a prophet.'

¹⁸However, the Jews would not believe that the man had been blind without first sending for the parents of the man who had gained his sight and ¹⁹asking them, 'Is this man really the son of yours who you say was born blind? If so, how is it that he is now able to see?' ²⁰His parents answered, 'We know he is our son and we know he was born blind, ²¹but how he can see, we don't know, nor who opened his eyes. Ask him. He is old enough: let him speak for himself.' ²²His parents spoke like this out of fear of the Jews, who had already agreed to ban from the synagogue anyone who should acknowledge Jesus as the Christ. ²³This was why his parents said, 'He is old enough; ask him.'

²⁴So the Jews sent for the man again and said to him, 'Give glory to God! We are satisfied that this man is a sinner.' ²⁵The man answered, 'Whether he is a sinner I don't know; all I know is that I was blind and now I can see.' ²⁶They said to him, 'What did he do to you? How did he open your eyes?' ²⁷He replied, 'I have told you once and you wouldn't listen. Why do you want to hear it all again? Do you want to become his disciples yourselves?' ²⁸At this they hurled abuse at him, 'It is you who are his disciple, we are disciples of Moses: ²⁹we know that God spoke to Moses, but as for this man, we don't know where he comes from.' ³⁰The man replied, 'That is just what is so amazing! You don't know where he comes from and he has opened my eyes! ³¹We know that God doesn't listen to sinners, but God does listen to people who are devout and do his will. ³²Ever since the world began it is unheard of for anyone to open the eyes of someone born blind; ³³if this man were not from God, he wouldn't have been able to do anything.' ³⁴They retorted, 'Are you trying to teach us, and you a sinner

through and through ever since you were born!' And they ejected him.

³⁵Jesus heard they had ejected him, and when he found him he said to him, 'Do you believe in the Son of man?' ³⁶'Sir,' the man replied, 'tell me who he is so that I may believe in him.' ³⁷Jesus said, 'You have seen him; he is speaking to you.' ³⁸The man said, 'Lord, I believe,' and worshipped him.

³⁹Jesus said:

It is for judgement
that I have come into this world,
so that those without sight may see
and those with sight may become blind.

⁴⁰Hearing this, some Pharisees who were present said to him, 'So we are blind, are we?' ⁴¹Jesus replied:

If you were blind,
you would not be guilty,
but since you say, 'We can see,'
your guilt remains.

The good shepherd[a]

10 ¹'In all truth I tell you, anyone who does not enter the sheepfold through the gate, but climbs in some other way, is a thief and a bandit. ²He who enters through the gate is the shepherd of the flock; ³the gate-keeper lets him in, the sheep hear his voice, one by one he calls his own sheep and leads them out. ⁴When he has brought out all those that are his, he goes ahead of them, and the sheep follow because they know his voice. ⁵They will never follow a stranger, but will run away from him because they do not recognise the voice of strangers.'

⁶Jesus told them this parable but they failed to understand what he was saying to them.

⁷So Jesus spoke to them again:

In all truth I tell you,
I am the gate of the sheepfold.
⁸All who have come before me
are thieves and bandits,
but the sheep took no notice of them.
⁹I am the gate.

Anyone who enters through me
will be safe:
such a one will go in and out
and will find pasture.
¹⁰The thief comes
only to steal and kill and destroy.
I have come
so that they may have life
and have it to the full.
¹¹I am the good shepherd:
the good shepherd lays down his life
for his sheep.
¹²The hired man,
since he is not the shepherd
and the sheep do not belong to him,
abandons the sheep
as soon as he sees a wolf coming,
and runs away,
and then the wolf attacks
and scatters the sheep;
¹³he runs away
because he is only a hired man
and has no concern for the sheep.
¹⁴I am the good shepherd;
I know my own
and my own know me,
¹⁵just as the Father knows me
and I know the Father;
and I lay down my life for my sheep.
¹⁶And there are other sheep I have
that are not of this fold,
and I must lead these too.
They too will listen to my voice,
and there will be only one flock,
one shepherd.
¹⁷The Father loves me,
because I lay down my life
in order to take it up again.
¹⁸No one takes it from me;
I lay it down of my own free will,
and as I have power to lay it down,
so I have power to take it up again;
and this is the command
I have received from my Father.

¹⁹These words caused a fresh division among the Jews. ²⁰Many said, 'He is possessed, he is raving; why do you listen to him?' ²¹Others said, 'These are not the words of a man possessed by a devil: could a devil open the eyes of the blind?'

10a cf. Jr 23; Ezk 34.

V: THE FEAST OF DEDICATION:
THE DECISION TO KILL JESUS

Jesus claims to be the Son of God

²²It was the time of the feast of Dedication in Jerusalem. It was winter, ²³and Jesus was in the Temple walking up and down in the Portico of Solomon. ²⁴The Jews gathered round him and said, 'How much longer are you going to keep us in suspense? If you are the Christ, tell us openly.' ²⁵Jesus replied:

I have told you, but you do not believe.
The works I do in my Father's name
    are my witness;
²⁶but you do not believe,
    because you are no sheep of mine.
²⁷The sheep that belong to me
    listen to my voice;
I know them and they follow me.
²⁸I give them eternal life;
    they will never be lost
and no one will ever steal them
    from my hand.
²⁹The Father, for what he has given me,
    is greater than anyone,
and no one can steal anything
    from the Father's hand.
³⁰The Father and I are one.

³¹The Jews fetched stones to stone him, ³²so Jesus said to them, 'I have shown you many good works from my Father; for which of these are you stoning me?' ³³The Jews answered him, 'We are stoning you, not for doing a good work, but for blasphemy;

though you are only a man, you claim to be God.' ³⁴Jesus answered:

Is it not written in your Law:
I said, you are gods?[b]
³⁵So it uses the word 'gods'
of those people to whom
    the word of God was addressed
—and scripture cannot be set aside.
³⁶Yet to someone
    whom the Father has consecrated
and sent into the world you say,
    'You are blaspheming'
because I said, 'I am Son of God.'
³⁷If I am not doing my Father's work,
    there is no need to believe me;
³⁸but if I am doing it,
then even if you refuse to believe in me,
    at least believe in the work I do;
then you will know for certain
    that the Father is in me
    and I am in the Father.

³⁹They again wanted to arrest him then, but he eluded their clutches.

Jesus withdraws to the other side of the Jordan

⁴⁰He went back again to the far side of the Jordan to the district where John had been baptising at first and he stayed there. ⁴¹Many people who came to him said, 'John gave no signs, but all he said about this man was true'; ⁴²and many of them believed in him.

VI: JESUS MOVES TOWARDS HIS DEATH

The resurrection of Lazarus

11 There was a man named Lazarus of Bethany, the village of Mary and her sister, Martha, and he was ill. ²It was the same Mary, the sister of the sick man Lazarus, who anointed the Lord with ointment and wiped his feet with her hair. ³The sisters sent this message to Jesus, 'Lord, the man you love is

ill.' ⁴On receiving the message, Jesus said, 'This sickness will not end in death, but it is for God's glory so that through it the Son of God may be glorified.'

⁵Jesus loved Martha and her sister and Lazarus, ⁶yet when he heard that he was ill he stayed where he was for two more days ⁷before saying to the disciples, 'Let us go back to Judaea.' ⁸The disciples said, 'Rabbi,

10b Ps 82:6.

it is not long since the Jews were trying to stone you; are you going back there again?' ⁹Jesus replied:

Are there not twelve hours in the day?
No one who walks in the daytime stumbles,
having the light of this world to see by;
¹⁰anyone who walks around at night stumbles,
having no light as a guide.

¹¹He said that and then added, 'Our friend Lazarus is at rest; I am going to wake him.' ¹²The disciples said to him, 'Lord, if he is at rest he will be saved.' ¹³Jesus was speaking of the death of Lazarus, but they thought that by 'rest' he meant 'sleep'; ¹⁴so Jesus put it plainly, 'Lazarus is dead; ¹⁵and for your sake I am glad I was not there because now you will believe. But let us go to him.' ¹⁶Then Thomas—known as the Twin—said to the other disciples, 'Let us also go to die with him.'

¹⁷On arriving, Jesus found that Lazarus had been in the tomb for four days already. ¹⁸Bethany is only about two miles from Jerusalem, ¹⁹and many Jews had come to Martha and Mary to comfort them about their brother. ²⁰When Martha heard that Jesus was coming she went to meet him. Mary remained sitting in the house. ²¹Martha said to Jesus, 'Lord, if you had been here, my brother would not have died, ²²but even now I know that God will grant whatever you ask of him.' ²³Jesus said to her, 'Your brother will rise again.' ²⁴Martha said, 'I know he will rise again at the resurrection on the last day.' ²⁵Jesus said:

I am the resurrection.
Anyone who believes in me,
even though that person dies, will live,
²⁶and whoever lives and believes in me
will never die.
Do you believe this?

²⁷'Yes, Lord,' she said, 'I believe that you are the Christ, the Son of God, the one who was to come into this world.'
²⁸When she had said this, she went and called her sister Mary, saying in a low voice, 'The Master is here and wants to see you.' ²⁹Hearing this, Mary got up quickly and went to him. ³⁰Jesus had not yet come into the village; he was still at the place where Martha had met him. ³¹When the Jews who were in the house comforting Mary saw her get up

so quickly and go out, they followed her, thinking that she was going to the tomb to weep there.

³²Mary went to Jesus, and as soon as she saw him she threw herself at his feet, saying, 'Lord, if you had been here, my brother would not have died.' ³³At the sight of her tears, and those of the Jews who had come with her, Jesus was greatly distressed, and with a profound sigh he said, ³⁴'Where have you put him?' They said, 'Lord, come and see.' ³⁵Jesus wept; ³⁶and the Jews said, 'See how much he loved him!' ³⁷But there were some who remarked, 'He opened the eyes of the blind man. Could he not have prevented this man's death?' ³⁸Sighing again, Jesus reached the tomb: it was a cave with a stone to close the opening. ³⁹Jesus said, 'Take the stone away.' Martha, the dead man's sister, said to him, 'Lord, by now he will smell; this is the fourth day since he died.' ⁴⁰Jesus replied, 'Have I not told you that if you believe you will see the glory of God?' ⁴¹So they took the stone away. Then Jesus lifted up his eyes and said:

Father, I thank you
for hearing my prayer.
⁴²I myself knew that you hear me always,
but I speak
for the sake of all these
who are standing around me,
so that they may believe
it was you who sent me.

⁴³When he had said this, he cried in a loud voice, 'Lazarus, come out!' ⁴⁴The dead man came out, his feet and hands bound with strips of material, and a cloth over his face. Jesus said to them, 'Unbind him, let him go free.'

The Jewish leaders decide on the death of Jesus

⁴⁵Many of the Jews who had come to visit Mary, and had seen what he did, believed in him, ⁴⁶but some of them went to the Pharisees to tell them what Jesus had done. ⁴⁷Then the chief priests and Pharisees called a meeting. 'Here is this man working all these signs,' they said, 'and what action are we taking? ⁴⁸If we let him go on in this way everybody will believe in him, and the Romans will come and suppress the Holy Place and our nation.' ⁴⁹One of them, Caiaphas, the high priest that year, said, 'You do not seem to

have grasped the situation at all; [50]you fail to see that it is to your advantage that one man should die for the people, rather than that the whole nation should perish.'[51] He did not speak in his own person, but as high priest of that year he was prophesying that Jesus was to die for the nation— [52]and not for the nation only, but also to gather together into one the scattered children of God. [53]From that day onwards they were determined to kill him. [54]So Jesus no longer went about openly among the Jews, but left the district for a town called Ephraim, in the country bordering on the desert, and stayed there with his disciples.

The Passover draws near

[55]The Jewish Passover was drawing near, and many of the country people who had gone up to Jerusalem before the Passover to purify themselves [56]were looking out for Jesus, saying to one another as they stood about in the Temple, 'What do you think? Will he come to the festival or not?' [57]The chief priests and Pharisees had by now given their orders: anyone who knew where he was must inform them so that they could arrest him.

The anointing at Bethany

12 Six days before the Passover, Jesus went to Bethany, where Lazarus was, whom he had raised from the dead. [2]They gave a dinner for him there; Martha waited on them and Lazarus was among those at table. [3]Mary brought in a pound of very costly ointment, pure nard, and with it anointed the feet of Jesus, wiping them with her hair; the house was filled with the scent of the ointment. [4]Then Judas Iscariot—one of his disciples, the man who was to betray him— said, [5]'Why was this ointment not sold for three hundred denarii and the money given to the poor?' [6]He said this, not because he cared about the poor, but because he was a thief; he was in charge of the common fund and used to help himself to the contents. [7]So Jesus said, 'Leave her alone; let her keep it for the day of my burial. [8]You have the poor with you always, you will not always have me.'

[9]Meanwhile a large number of Jews heard that he was there and came not only on account of Jesus but also to see Lazarus whom he had raised from the dead. [10]Then the chief priests decided to kill Lazarus as well, [11]since it was on his account that many of the Jews were leaving them and believing in Jesus.

The Messiah enters Jerusalem

[12]The next day the great crowd of people who had come up for the festival heard that Jesus was on his way to Jerusalem. [13]They took branches of palm and went out to receive him, shouting:

> 'Hosanna!
> Blessed is he
>   who is coming in the name of the Lord,[a]
> the king of Israel.'

[14]Jesus found a young donkey and mounted it—as scripture says:

> [15]Do not be afraid, daughter of Zion;
> look, your king is approaching,
> riding on the foal of a donkey.[b]

[16]At first his disciples did not understand this, but later, after Jesus had been glorified, they remembered that this had been written about him and that this was what had happened to him. [17]The crowd who had been with him when he called Lazarus out of the tomb and raised him from the dead kept bearing witness to it; [18]this was another reason why the crowd came out to receive him: they had heard that he had given this sign. [19]Then the Pharisees said to one another, 'You see, you are making no progress; look, the whole world has gone after him!'

Jesus foretells his death and subsequent glorification

[20]Among those who went up to worship at the festival were some Greeks. [21]These approached Philip, who came from Bethsaida in Galilee, and put this request to him, 'Sir, we should like to see Jesus.' [22]Philip went to tell Andrew, and Andrew and Philip together went to tell Jesus.

[23]Jesus replied to them:

> Now the hour has come
> for the Son of man to be glorified.
> [24]In all truth I tell you,
>   unless a wheat grain falls into the earth
>   and dies,

12a Ps 118:25–26.
12b Zc 9:9–10.

it remains only a single grain;
but if it dies
it yields a rich harvest.
²⁵Anyone who loves his life loses it;
anyone who hates his life in this world
will keep it for eternal life.
²⁶Whoever serves me, must follow me,
and my servant will be with me
wherever I am.
If anyone serves me,
my Father will honour him.
²⁷Now my soul is troubled.
What shall I say:
Father, save me from this hour?ᶜ
But it is for this very reason
that I have come to this hour.
²⁸Father, glorify your name!

A voice came from heaven, 'I have glorified
it, and I will again glorify it.'
²⁹The crowd standing by, who heard this,
said it was a clap of thunder; others said,
'It was an angel speaking to him.' ³⁰Jesus
answered, 'It was not for my sake that this
voice came, but for yours.

³¹'Now sentence is being passed
on this world;
now the prince of this world
is to be driven out.
³²And when I am lifted up from the earth,
I shall draw all people to myself.'

³³By these words he indicated the kind of
death he would die. ³⁴The crowd answered,
'The Law has taught us that the Christ will
remain for ever. So how can you say,
"The Son of man must be lifted up"? Who
is this Son of man?' ³⁵Jesus then said:

The light will be with you
only a little longer now.
Go on your way while you have the light,
or darkness will overtake you,
and nobody who walks in the dark
knows where he is going.
³⁶While you still have the light,
believe in the light
so that you may become children of light.

Having said this, Jesus left them and was
hidden from their sight.

Conclusion: the unbelief of the Jews

³⁷Though they had been present when he
gave so many signs, they did not believe in
him; ³⁸this was to fulfil the words of the
prophet Isaiah:

*Lord, who has given credence
    to what they have heard from us,
and who has seen in it
    a revelation of the Lord's arm?ᵈ*

³⁹Indeed, they were unable to believe
because, as Isaiah says again:

⁴⁰*He has blinded their eyes,
he has hardened their heart,
to prevent them from using their eyes to see,
using their heart to understand,
changing their ways and being healed by me.ᵉ*

⁴¹Isaiah said this because he saw his glory,
and his words referred to Jesus.
⁴²And yet there were many who did believe
in him, even among the leading men, but
they did not admit it, because of the Pharisees
and for fear of being banned from the synagogue: ⁴³they put human glory before God's
glory.
⁴⁴Jesus declared publicly:

Whoever believes in me
believes not in me
but in the one who sent me,
⁴⁵and whoever sees me,
sees the one who sent me.
⁴⁶I have come into the world as light,
to prevent anyone who believes in me
from staying in the dark any more.
⁴⁷If anyone hears my words
and does not keep them faithfully,
it is not I who shall judge such a person,
since I have come not to judge the world,
but to save the world:
⁴⁸anyone who rejects me
and refuses my words
has his judge already:
the word itself that I have spoken
will be his judge on the last day.
⁴⁹For I have not spoken of my own accord;
but the Father who sent me
commanded me what to say
and what to speak,
⁵⁰and I know that his commands
mean eternal life.
And therefore what the Father
has told me
is what I speak.

12c cf. Lk 22:40–46par.
12d Is 53:1.
12e Is 6:10.

C: JESUS' HOUR COMES:
THE PASSION AND THE RESURRECTION

I: JESUS' LAST MEAL WITH HIS DISCIPLES

The washing of feet

13 Before the festival of the Passover, Jesus, knowing that his hour had come to pass from this world to the Father, having loved those who were his in the world, loved them to the end.

²They were at supper, and the devil had already put it into the mind of Judas Iscariot son of Simon, to betray him. ³Jesus knew that the Father had put everything into his hands, and that he had come from God and was returning to God, ⁴and he got up from table, removed his outer garments and, taking a towel, wrapped it round his waist; ⁵he then poured water into a basin and began to wash the disciples' feet and to wipe them with the towel he was wearing.

⁶He came to Simon Peter, who said to him, 'Lord, are you going to wash my feet?' ⁷Jesus answered, 'At the moment you do not know what I am doing, but later you will understand.' ⁸'Never!' said Peter. 'You shall never wash my feet.' Jesus replied, 'If I do not wash you, you can have no share with me.' Simon Peter said, ⁹'Well then, Lord, not only my feet, but my hands and my head as well!' ¹⁰Jesus said, 'No one who has had a bath needs washing, such a person is clean all over. You too are clean, though not all of you are.' ¹¹He knew who was going to betray him, and that was why he said, 'though not all of you are'.

¹²When he had washed their feet and put on his outer garments again he went back to the table. 'Do you understand', he said, 'what I have done to you? ¹³You call me Master and Lord, and rightly; so I am. ¹⁴If I, then, the Lord and Master, have washed your feet, you must wash each other's feet. ¹⁵I have given you an example so that you may copy what I have done to you.

¹⁶'In all truth I tell you,
no servant is greater than his master,
no messenger is greater
than the one who sent him.

¹⁷'Now that you know this, blessed are you if you behave accordingly. ¹⁸I am not speaking about all of you: I know the ones I have chosen; but what scripture says must be fulfilled:

'*He who shares my table
takes advantage of me.*ᵃ

¹⁹I tell you this now, before it happens,
so that when it does happen
you may believe that I am He.
²⁰In all truth I tell you,
whoever welcomes the one I send,
welcomes me,
and whoever welcomes me,
welcomes the one who sent me.'

The treachery of Judas foretold

²¹Having said this, Jesus was deeply disturbed and declared, 'In all truth I tell you, one of you is going to betray me.' ²²The disciples looked at each other, wondering whom he meant. ²³The disciple Jesus loved was reclining next to Jesus; ²⁴Simon Peter signed to him and said, 'Ask who it is he means,' ²⁵so leaning back close to Jesus' chest he said, 'Who is it, Lord?' ²⁶Jesus answered, 'It is the one to whom I give the piece of bread that I dip in the dish.' And when he had dipped the piece of bread he gave it to Judas son of Simon Iscariot. ²⁷At that instant, after Judas had taken the bread, Satan entered him. Jesus then said, 'What you are going to do, do quickly.' ²⁸None of the others at table understood why he said this. ²⁹Since Judas had charge of the common fund, some of them thought Jesus was telling him, 'Buy what we need for the festival,' or telling him to give something to the poor. ³⁰As soon as Judas had taken the piece of bread he went out. It was night.

13a Ps 41:9.

Farewell discourses[b]

³¹When he had gone, Jesus said:

Now has the Son of man been glorified,
and in him God has been glorified.
³²If God has been glorified in him,
God will in turn glorify him in himself,
and will glorify him very soon.
³³Little children,
I shall be with you only a little longer.
You will look for me,
and, as I told the Jews,
where I am going,
you cannot come.
³⁴I give you a new commandment:
love one another;
you must love one another
just as I have loved you.
³⁵It is by your love for one another,
that everyone will recognise you
as my disciples.

³⁶Simon Peter said, 'Lord, where are you going?' Jesus replied, 'Now you cannot follow me where I am going, but later you shall follow me.' ³⁷Peter said to him, 'Why can I not follow you now? I will lay down my life for you.' ³⁸'Lay down your life for me?' answered Jesus. 'In all truth I tell you, before the cock crows you will have disowned me three times.'

14 Do not let your hearts be troubled. You trust in God, trust also in me.
²In my Father's house
there are many places to live in;
otherwise I would have told you.
I am going now to prepare a place for you,
³and after I have gone
and prepared you a place,
I shall return to take you to myself,
so that you may be with me
where I am.
⁴You know the way
to the place where I am going.

⁵Thomas said, 'Lord, we do not know where you are going, so how can we know the way?' ⁶Jesus said:

I am the Way; I am Truth and Life.
No one can come to the Father
except through me.

⁷If you know me,
you will know my Father too.
From this moment you know him
and have seen him.

⁸Philip said, 'Lord, show us the Father and then we shall be satisfied.' Jesus said to him, ⁹'Have I been with you all this time, Philip, and you still do not know me?

'Anyone who has seen me
has seen the Father,
so how can you say,
"Show us the Father"?
¹⁰Do you not believe
that I am in the Father
and the Father is in me?
What I say to you
I do not speak of my own accord:
it is the Father, living in me,
who is doing his works.
¹¹You must believe me when I say
that I am in the Father
and the Father is in me;
or at least believe it
on the evidence of these works.
¹²In all truth I tell you,
whoever believes in me
will perform the same works
as I do myself,
and will perform even greater works,
because I am going to the Father.
¹³Whatever you ask in my name
I will do,
so that the Father may be glorified
in the Son.
¹⁴If you ask me anything in my name,
I will do it.
¹⁵If you love me
you will keep my commandments.
¹⁶I shall ask the Father,
and he will give you another Paraclete[a]
to be with you for ever,
¹⁷the Spirit of truth
whom the world can never accept
since it neither sees nor knows him;
but you know him,
because he is with you, he is in you.
¹⁸I shall not leave you orphans;
I shall come to you.
¹⁹In a short time
the world will no longer see me;

13b These contain teaching given also on other occasions, and perhaps in different versions. Ch. 16 may be another version of ch. 14, and ch. 17 yet another.
14a The Gk word means 'advocate', 'counsellor', 'protector'.

but you will see that I live
and you also will live.
²⁰On that day
you will know that I am in my Father
and you in me and I in you.
²¹Whoever holds to my commandments
    and keeps them
is the one who loves me;
and whoever loves me
    will be loved by my Father,
and I shall love him
    and reveal myself to him.'

²²Judas—not Judas Iscariot—said to him,
'Lord, what has happened, that you intend
to show yourself to us and not to the world?'
²³Jesus replied:

Anyone who loves me will keep my word,
and my Father will love him,
and we shall come to him
and make a home in him.
²⁴Anyone who does not love me
    does not keep my words.
And the word that you hear
    is not my own:
it is the word of the Father who sent me.
²⁵I have said these things to you
    while still with you;
²⁶but the Paraclete, the Holy Spirit,
    whom the Father will send in my name,
will teach you everything
and remind you of all I have said to you.
²⁷Peace I bequeath to you,
    my own peace I give you,
a peace which the world cannot give,
    this is my gift to you.
Do not let your hearts be troubled
    or afraid.
²⁸You heard me say:
I am going away and shall return.
If you loved me you would be glad
    that I am going to the Father,
for the Father is greater than I.
²⁹I have told you this now,
    before it happens,
so that when it does happen
    you may believe.
³⁰I shall not talk to you much longer,
because the prince of this world
    is on his way.
He has no power over me,
³¹but the world must recognise
    that I love the Father

and that I act
    just as the Father commanded.
Come now, let us go.

The true vine[a]

15 I am the true vine,
    and my Father is the vinedresser.
²Every branch in me that bears no fruit
he cuts away,
and every branch that does bear fruit
    he prunes
to make it bear even more.
³You are clean already,
by means of the word
    that I have spoken to you.
⁴Remain in me, as I in you.
As a branch cannot bear fruit all by itself,
unless it remains part of the vine,
neither can you unless you remain in me.
⁵I am the vine,
you are the branches.
Whoever remains in me, with me in him,
bears fruit in plenty;
for cut off from me you can do nothing.
⁶Anyone who does not remain in me
is thrown away like a branch
—and withers;
these branches are collected
    and thrown on the fire
and are burnt.
⁷If you remain in me
and my words remain in you,
you may ask for whatever you please
and you will get it.
⁸It is to the glory of my Father
    that you should bear much fruit
and be my disciples.
⁹I have loved you
just as the Father has loved me.
Remain in my love.
¹⁰If you keep my commandments
you will remain in my love,
just as I have kept
    my Father's commandments
and remain in his love.
¹¹I have told you this
so that my own joy may be in you
and your joy be complete.
¹²This is my commandment:
love one another,
as I have loved you.
¹³No one can have greater love
than to lay down his life for his friends.

15a cf. Is 5:1–7; Mk 12:1–12.

¹⁴You are my friends,
  if you do what I command you.
¹⁵I shall no longer call you servants,
  because a servant does not know
  the master's business;
  I call you friends,
  because I have made known to you
  everything I have learnt from my Father.
¹⁶You did not choose me,
  no, I chose you;
  and I commissioned you
  to go out and to bear fruit,
  fruit that will last;
  so that the Father will give you
  anything you ask him in my name.
¹⁷My command to you
  is to love one another.

The disciples and the world

¹⁸If the world hates you,
  you must realise that it hated me
    before it hated you.
¹⁹If you belonged to the world,
  the world would love you as its own;
  but because you do not belong to the world,
  because my choice of you
    has drawn you out of the world,
  that is why the world hates you.
²⁰Remember the words I said to you:
  A servant is not greater than his master.
  If they persecuted me,
  they will persecute you too;
  if they kept my word,
  they will keep yours as well.
²¹But it will be on my account
  that they will do all this to you,
  because they do not know
    the one who sent me.
²²If I had not come,
  if I had not spoken to them,
  they would have been blameless;
  but as it is they have no excuse
    for their sin.
²³Anyone who hates me hates my Father.
²⁴If I had not performed
    such works among them
  as no one else has ever done,
  they would be blameless;
  but as it is, in spite of what they have seen,
  they hate both me and my Father.
²⁵But all this was only to fulfil
    the words written in their Law:
  *They hated me without reason.*ᵇ

²⁶When the Paraclete comes,
  whom I shall send to you from the Father,
  the Spirit of truth
    who issues from the Father,
  he will be my witness.
²⁷And you too will be witnesses,
  because you have been with me
    from the beginning.

16 I have told you all this
  so that you may not fall away.
²They will expel you
  from the synagogues,
  and indeed the time is coming
  when anyone who kills you
    will think he is doing
      a holy service to God.
³They will do these things
  because they have never known
    either the Father or me.
⁴But I have told you all this,
  so that when the time for it comes
  you may remember that I told you.

The coming of the Paraclete

  I did not tell you this from the beginning,
  because I was with you;
⁵but now I am going to the one
    who sent me.
  Not one of you asks,
    'Where are you going?'
⁶Yet you are sad at heart
    because I have told you this.
⁷Still, I am telling you the truth:
  it is for your own good that I am going,
  because unless I go,
  the Paraclete will not come to you;
  but if I go,
  I will send him to you.
⁸And when he comes,
  he will show the world how wrong it was,
  about sin,
  and about who was in the right,
  and about judgement:
⁹about sin:
  in that they refuse to believe in me;
¹⁰about who was in the right:
  in that I am going to the Father
  and you will see me no more;
¹¹about judgement:
  in that the prince of this world
    is already condemned.
¹²I still have many things to say to you

15b Ps 69:4.

but they would be too much for you
  to bear now.
[13] However, when the Spirit of truth comes
  he will lead you to the complete truth,
  since he will not be speaking
    of his own accord,
  but will say only what he has been told;
  and he will reveal to you
    the things to come.
[14] He will glorify me,
  since all he reveals to you
  will be taken from what is mine.
[15] Everything the Father has is mine;
  that is why I said:
  all he reveals to you
  will be taken from what is mine.

Jesus to return very soon

[16] In a short time you will no longer see me,
  and then a short time later
    you will see me again.

[17] Then some of his disciples said to one another, 'What does he mean, "In a short time you will no longer see me, and then a short time later you will see me again," and, "I am going to the Father"? [18] What is this "short time"? We don't know what he means.' [19] Jesus knew that they wanted to question him, so he said, 'You are asking one another what I meant by saying, "In a short time you will no longer see me, and then a short time later you will see me again."

[20] 'In all truth I tell you,
  you will be weeping and wailing
  while the world will rejoice;
  you will be sorrowful,
  but your sorrow will turn to joy.
[21] A woman in childbirth suffers,
  because her time has come;
  but when she has given birth to the child
    she forgets the suffering
  in her joy that a human being
    has been born into the world.
[22] So it is with you: you are sad now,
  but I shall see you again,
  and your hearts will be full of joy,
  and that joy no one shall take from you.
[23] When that day comes,
  you will not ask me any questions.
  In all truth I tell you,
  anything you ask from the Father
  he will grant in my name.
[24] Until now you have not asked
  anything in my name.

Ask and you will receive,
  and so your joy will be complete.
[25] I have been telling you these things
  in veiled language.
The hour is coming
  when I shall no longer speak to you
  in veiled language
  but tell you about the Father
  in plain words.
[26] When that day comes
  you will ask in my name;
  and I do not say
  that I shall pray to the Father for you,
[27] because the Father himself loves you
  for loving me,
  and believing that I came from God.
[28] I came from the Father
  and have come into the world
  and now I am leaving the world
  to go to the Father.'

[29] His disciples said, 'Now you are speaking plainly and not using veiled language. [30] Now we see that you know everything and need not wait for questions to be put into words; because of this we believe that you came from God.' [31] Jesus answered them:

Do you believe at last?
[32] Listen; the time will come—
  indeed it has come already—
  when you are going to be scattered,
    each going his own way
  and leaving me alone.
  And yet I am not alone,
  because the Father is with me.
[33] I have told you all this
  so that you may find peace in me.
  In the world you will have hardship,
  but be courageous:
  I have conquered the world.

The prayer of Jesus

17 After saying this, Jesus raised his eyes to heaven and said:

Father, the hour has come:
glorify your Son
so that your Son may glorify you;
[2] so that, just as you have given him
  power over all humanity,
  he may give eternal life
    to all those you have entrusted to him.
[3] And eternal life is this:
  to know you,
  the only true God,
  and Jesus Christ whom you have sent.

⁴I have glorified you on earth
by finishing the work
that you gave me to do.
⁵Now, Father, glorify me
with that glory I had with you
before ever the world existed.
⁶I have revealed your name
to those whom you took from the world
to give me.
They were yours
and you gave them to me,
and they have kept your word.
⁷Now at last they have recognised
that all you have given me
comes from you
⁸for I have given them
the teaching you gave to me,
and they have indeed accepted it
and know for certain
that I came from you,
and have believed
that it was you who sent me.
⁹It is for them that I pray.
I am not praying for the world
but for those you have given me,
because they belong to you.
¹⁰All I have is yours
and all you have is mine,
and in them I am glorified.
¹¹I am no longer in the world,
but they are in the world,
and I am coming to you.
Holy Father,
keep those you have given me
true to your name,
so that they may be one like us.
¹²While I was with them,
I kept those you had given me
true to your name.
I have watched over them
and not one is lost
except one who was destined to be lost,
and this was to fulfil the scriptures.
¹³But now I am coming to you
and I say these things in the world
to share my joy with them to the full.
¹⁴I passed your word on to them,
and the world hated them,
because they belong to the world
no more than I belong to the world.

¹⁵I am not asking you
to remove them from the world,
but to protect them from the Evil One.
¹⁶They do not belong to the world
any more than I belong to the world.
¹⁷Consecrate them in the truth;
your word is truth.
¹⁸As you sent me into the world,
I have sent them into the world,
¹⁹and for their sake I consecrate myself
so that they too
may be consecrated in truth.
²⁰I pray not only for these
but also for those
who through their teaching
will come to believe in me.
²¹May they all be one,
just as, Father, you are in me
and I am in you,
so that they also may be in us,
so that the world may believe
it was you who sent me.
²²I have given them the glory
you gave to me,
that they may be one as we are one.
²³With me in them and you in me,
may they be so perfected in unity
that the world will recognise
that it was you who sent me
and that you have loved them
as you have loved me.

²⁴Father,
I want those you have given me
to be with me where I am,
so that they may always see my glory
which you have given me
because you loved me
before the foundation of the world.
²⁵Father, Upright One,
the world has not known you,
but I have known you,
and these have known
that you have sent me.
²⁶I have made your name known to them
and will continue to make it known,
so that the love with which you loved me
may be in them,
and so that I may be in them.

II: THE PASSION

The arrest of Jesus

18 After he had said all this, Jesus left with his disciples and crossed the Kidron valley where there was a garden into which he went with his disciples. ²Judas the traitor knew the place also, since Jesus had often met his disciples there, ³so Judas brought the cohort to this place together with guards sent by the chief priests and the Pharisees, all with lanterns and torches and weapons. ⁴Knowing everything that was to happen to him, Jesus came forward and said, 'Who are you looking for?' ⁵They answered, 'Jesus the Nazarene.' He said, 'I am he.' Now Judas the traitor was standing among them. ⁶When Jesus said to them, 'I am he,' they moved back and fell on the ground. ⁷He asked them a second time, 'Who are you looking for?' They said, 'Jesus the Nazarene.' ⁸Jesus replied, 'I have told you that I am he. If I am the one you are looking for, let these others go.' ⁹This was to fulfil the words he had spoken, 'Not one of those you gave me have I lost.'

¹⁰Simon Peter, who had a sword, drew it and struck the high priest's servant, cutting off his right ear. The servant's name was Malchus. ¹¹Jesus said to Peter, 'Put your sword back in its scabbard; am I not to drink the cup that the Father has given me?'

Jesus before Annas and Caiaphas
Peter disowns him

¹²The cohort and its tribune and the Jewish guards seized Jesus and bound him. ¹³They took him first to Annas, because Annas was the father-in-law of Caiaphas, who was high priest that year. ¹⁴It was Caiaphas who had counselled the Jews, 'It is better for one man to die for the people.'

¹⁵Simon Peter, with another disciple, followed Jesus. This disciple, who was known to the high priest, went with Jesus into the high priest's palace, ¹⁶but Peter stayed outside the door. So the other disciple, the one known to the high priest, went out, spoke to the door-keeper and brought Peter in. ¹⁷The girl on duty at the door said to Peter, 'Aren't you another of that man's disciples?' He answered, 'I am not.' ¹⁸Now it was cold, and the servants and guards had

lit a charcoal fire and were standing there warming themselves; so Peter stood there too, warming himself with the others.

¹⁹The high priest questioned Jesus about his disciples and his teaching. ²⁰Jesus answered, 'I have spoken openly for all the world to hear; I have always taught in the synagogue and in the Temple where all the Jews meet together; I have said nothing in secret. ²¹Why ask me? Ask my hearers what I taught; they know what I said.' ²²At these words, one of the guards standing by gave Jesus a slap in the face, saying, 'Is that the way you answer the high priest?' ²³Jesus replied, 'If there is some offence in what I said, point it out; but if not, why do you strike me?' ²⁴Then Annas sent him, bound, to Caiaphas the high priest.ᵃ

²⁵As Simon Peter stood there warming himself, someone said to him, 'Aren't you another of his disciples?' He denied it saying, 'I am not.' ²⁶One of the high priest's servants, a relation of the man whose ear Peter had cut off, said, 'Didn't I see you in the garden with him?' ²⁷Again Peter denied it; and at once a cock crowed.

Jesus before Pilate

²⁸They then led Jesus from the house of Caiaphas to the Praetorium. It was now morning. They did not go into the Praetorium themselves to avoid becoming defiled and unable to eat the Passover. ²⁹So Pilate came outside to them and said, 'What charge do you bring against this man?' They replied, ³⁰'If he were not a criminal, we should not have handed him over to you.' ³¹Pilate said, 'Take him yourselves, and try him by your own Law.' The Jews answered, 'We are not allowed to put anyone to death.' ³²This was to fulfil the words Jesus had spoken indicating the way he was going to die.

³³So Pilate went back into the Praetorium and called Jesus to him and asked him, 'Are you the king of the Jews?' ³⁴Jesus replied, 'Do you ask this of your own accord, or have others said it to you about me?' ³⁵Pilate answered, 'Am I a Jew? It is your own people and the chief priests who have handed you over to me: what have you done?' ³⁶Jesus replied, 'Mine is not a kingdom of this world;

18a Jn has no Sanhedrin session as the other gospels have, only a private interrogation at night.

if my kingdom were of this world, my men would have fought to prevent my being surrendered to the Jews. As it is, my kingdom does not belong here.' ³⁷Pilate said, 'So, then you are a king?' Jesus answered, 'It is you who say that I am a king. I was born for this, I came into the world for this, to bear witness to the truth; and all who are on the side of truth listen to my voice.' ³⁸'Truth?' said Pilate. 'What is that?' And so saying he went out again to the Jews and said, 'I find no case against him. ³⁹But according to a custom of yours I should release one prisoner at the Passover; would you like me, then, to release for you the king of the Jews?' ⁴⁰At this they shouted, 'Not this man,' they said, 'but Barabbas.' Barabbas was a bandit.

19 Pilate then had Jesus taken away and scourged; ²and after this, the soldiers twisted some thorns into a crown and put it on his head and dressed him in a purple robe. ³They kept coming up to him and saying, 'Hail, king of the Jews!' and slapping him in the face.

⁴Pilate came outside again and said to them, 'Look, I am going to bring him out to you to let you see that I find no case against him.' ⁵Jesus then came out wearing the crown of thorns and the purple robe. Pilate said, 'Here is the man.' ⁶When they saw him, the chief priests and the guards shouted, 'Crucify him! Crucify him!' Pilate said, 'Take him yourselves and crucify him: I find no case against him.' ⁷The Jews replied, 'We have a Law, and according to that Law he ought to be put to death, because he has claimed to be Son of God.'

⁸When Pilate heard them say this his fears increased. ⁹Re-entering the Praetorium, he said to Jesus, 'Where do you come from?' But Jesus made no answer. ¹⁰Pilate then said to him, 'Are you refusing to speak to me? Surely you know I have power to release you and I have power to crucify you?' ¹¹Jesus replied, 'You would have no power over me at all if it had not been given you from above; that is why the man who handed me over to you has the greater guilt.'

Jesus is condemned to death

¹²From that moment Pilate was anxious to set him free, but the Jews shouted, 'If you set him free you are no friend of Caesar's;

anyone who makes himself king is defying Caesar.' ¹³Hearing these words, Pilate had Jesus brought out, and seated him on the chair of judgement at a place called the Pavement, in Hebrew Gabbatha. ¹⁴It was the Day of Preparation, about the sixth hour. 'Here is your king,' said Pilate to the Jews. ¹⁵But they shouted, 'Away with him, away with him, crucify him.' Pilate said, 'Shall I crucify your king?' The chief priests answered, 'We have no king except Caesar.' ¹⁶So at that Pilate handed him over to them to be crucified.

The crucifixion

They then took charge of Jesus, ¹⁷and carrying his own cross he went out to the Place of the Skull or, as it is called in Hebrew, Golgotha, ¹⁸where they crucified him with two others, one on either side, Jesus being in the middle. ¹⁹Pilate wrote out a notice and had it fixed to the cross; it ran: 'Jesus the Nazarene, King of the Jews'. ²⁰This notice was read by many of the Jews, because the place where Jesus was crucified was near the city, and the writing was in Hebrew, Latin and Greek. ²¹So the Jewish chief priests said to Pilate, 'You should not write "King of the Jews", but that the man said, "I am King of the Jews". ' ²²Pilate answered, 'What I have written, I have written.'

Jesus' garments divided

²³When the soldiers had finished crucifying Jesus they took his clothing and divided it into four shares, one for each soldier. His undergarment was seamless, woven in one piece from neck to hem; ²⁴so they said to one another, 'Instead of tearing it, let's throw dice to decide who is to have it.' In this way the words of scripture were fulfilled:

*They divide my garments among them and cast lots for my clothes.*ᵃ

That is what the soldiers did.

Jesus and his mother

²⁵Near the cross of Jesus stood his mother and his mother's sister, Mary the wife of Clopas, and Mary of Magdala. ²⁶Seeing his mother and the disciple whom he loved

---

19a Ps 22:18.

standing near her, Jesus said to his mother, 'Woman, this is your son.' [27]Then to the disciple he said, 'This is your mother.' And from that hour the disciple took her into his home.

The death of Jesus

[28]After this, Jesus knew that everything had now been completed and, so that the scripture should be completely fulfilled, he said:

I am thirsty.[b]

[29]A jar full of sour wine stood there; so, putting a sponge soaked in the wine on a hyssop stick, they held it up to his mouth. [30]After Jesus had taken the wine he said, 'It is fulfilled'; and bowing his head he gave up his spirit.

The pierced Christ

[31]It was the Day of Preparation, and to avoid the bodies' remaining on the cross during the Sabbath—since that Sabbath was a day of special solemnity—the Jews asked Pilate to have the legs broken and the bodies taken away. [32]Consequently the soldiers came and broke the legs of the first man who had been crucified with him and then of the other. [33]When they came to Jesus, they saw he was already dead, and so instead of breaking his legs [34]one of the soldiers pierced his side with a lance; and immediately there came out blood and water. [35]This is the evidence of one who saw it—true evidence, and he knows that what he says is true—and he gives it so that you may believe as well. [36]Because all this happened to fulfil the words of scripture:

Not one bone of his will be broken;[c]

[37]and again, in another place scripture says:

*They will look to the one
whom they have pierced.*[d]

The burial

[38]After this, Joseph of Arimathaea, who was a disciple of Jesus—though a secret one because he was afraid of the Jews—asked Pilate to let him remove the body of Jesus. Pilate gave permission, so they came and took it away. [39]Nicodemus came as well—the same one who had first come to Jesus at night-time—and he brought a mixture of myrrh and aloes, weighing about a hundred pounds. [40]They took the body of Jesus and bound it in linen cloths with the spices, following the Jewish burial custom. [41]At the place where he had been crucified there was a garden, and in this garden a new tomb in which no one had yet been buried. [42]Since it was the Jewish Day of Preparation and the tomb was nearby, they laid Jesus there.

III: THE DAY OF CHRIST'S RESURRECTION

The empty tomb

20 It was very early on the first day of the week and still dark, when Mary of Magdala came to the tomb. She saw that the stone had been moved away from the tomb [2]and came running to Simon Peter and the other disciple, the one whom Jesus loved. 'They have taken the Lord out of the tomb,' she said, 'and we don't know where they have put him.'

[3]So Peter set out with the other disciple to go to the tomb. [4]They ran together, but the other disciple, running faster than Peter, reached the tomb first; [5]he bent down and saw the linen cloths lying on the ground, but did not go in. [6]Simon Peter, following him, also came up, went into the tomb, saw the linen cloths lying on the ground [7]and also the cloth that had been over his head; this was not with the linen cloths but rolled up in a place by itself. [8]Then the other disciple who had reached the tomb first also went in; he saw and he believed. [9]Till this moment they had still not understood the scripture, that he must rise from the dead. [10]The disciples then went back home.

19b Ps 69:21.
19c Ex 12:46 and Ps 34:20.
19d Zc 12:10.

The appearance to Mary of Magdala

[11]But Mary was standing outside near the tomb, weeping. Then, as she wept, she stooped to look inside, [12]and saw two angels in white sitting where the body of Jesus had been, one at the head, the other at the feet. [13]They said, 'Woman, why are you weeping?' 'They have taken my Lord away,' she replied, 'and I don't know where they have put him.' [14]As she said this she turned round and saw Jesus standing there, though she did not realise that it was Jesus. [15]Jesus said to her, 'Woman, why are you weeping? Who are you looking for?' Supposing him to be the gardener, she said, 'Sir, if you have taken him away, tell me where you have put him, and I will go and remove him.' [16]Jesus said, 'Mary!' She turned round then and said to him in Hebrew, 'Rabbuni!'—which means Master. [17]Jesus said to her, 'Do not cling to me, because I have not yet ascended to the Father. But go to the brothers, and tell them: I am ascending to my Father and your Father, to my God and your God.' [18]So Mary of Magdala told the disciples, 'I have seen the Lord,' and that he had said these things to her.

Appearances to the disciples

[19]In the evening of that same day, the first day of the week, the doors were closed in the room where the disciples were, for fear of the Jews. Jesus came and stood among them. He said to them, 'Peace be with you,' [20]and, after saying this, he showed them his hands and his side. The disciples were filled with joy at seeing the Lord, [21]and he said to them again, 'Peace be with you.

'As the Father sent me,
so am I sending you.'

[22]After saying this he breathed on them and said:

Receive the Holy Spirit.
[23]If you forgive anyone's sins,
they are forgiven;
if you retain anyone's sins,
they are retained.

[24]Thomas, called the Twin, who was one of the Twelve, was not with them when Jesus came. [25]So the other disciples said to him, 'We have seen the Lord,' but he answered, 'Unless I can see the holes that the nails made in his hands and can put my finger into the holes they made, and unless I can put my hand into his side, I refuse to believe.' [26]Eight days later the disciples were in the house again and Thomas was with them. The doors were closed, but Jesus came in and stood among them. 'Peace be with you,' he said. [27]Then he spoke to Thomas, 'Put your finger here; look, here are my hands. Give me your hand; put it into my side. Do not be unbelieving any more but believe.' [28]Thomas replied, 'My Lord and my God!' [29]Jesus said to him:

You believe because you can see me.
Blessed are those who have not seen
and yet believe.

IV: FIRST CONCLUSION

[30]There were many other signs that Jesus worked in the sight of the disciples, but they are not recorded in this book. [31]These are recorded so that you may believe that Jesus is the Christ, the Son of God, and that believing this you may have life through his name.

D: EPILOGUE[a]

I: THE APPEARANCE ON THE SHORE OF TIBERIAS

21 Later on, Jesus revealed himself again to the disciples. It was by the Sea of Tiberias, and it happened like this: ²Simon Peter, Thomas called the Twin, Nathanael from Cana in Galilee, the sons of Zebedee and two more of his disciples were together. ³Simon Peter said, 'I'm going fishing.' They replied, 'We'll come with you.' They went out and got into the boat but caught nothing that night.

⁴When it was already light, there stood Jesus on the shore, though the disciples did not realise that it was Jesus. ⁵Jesus called out, 'Haven't you caught anything, friends?' And when they answered, 'No,' ⁶he said, 'Throw the net out to starboard and you'll find something.' So they threw the net out and could not haul it in because of the quantity of fish. ⁷The disciple whom Jesus loved said to Peter, 'It is the Lord.' At these words, 'It is the Lord,' Simon Peter tied his outer garment round him (for he had nothing on) and jumped into the water. ⁸The other disciples came on in the boat, towing the net with the fish; they were only about a hundred yards from land.

⁹As soon as they came ashore they saw that there was some bread there and a charcoal fire with fish cooking on it. ¹⁰Jesus said, 'Bring some of the fish you have just caught.' ¹¹Simon Peter went aboard and dragged the net ashore, full of big fish, one hundred and fifty-three of them; and in spite of there being so many the net was not broken. ¹²Jesus said to them, 'Come and have breakfast.' None of the disciples was bold enough to ask, 'Who are you?'. They knew quite well it was the Lord. ¹³Jesus then stepped forward, took the bread and gave it to them, and the same with the fish. ¹⁴This was the third time that Jesus revealed himself to the disciples after rising from the dead.

¹⁵When they had eaten, Jesus said to Simon Peter, 'Simon son of John, do you love me more than these others do?' He answered, 'Yes, Lord, you know I love you.' Jesus said to him, 'Feed my lambs.' ¹⁶A second time he said to him, 'Simon son of John, do you love me?' He replied, 'Yes, Lord, you know I love you.' Jesus said to him, 'Look after my sheep.' ¹⁷Then he said to him a third time, 'Simon son of John, do you love me?' Peter was hurt that he asked him a third time, 'Do you love me?' and said, 'Lord, you know everything; you know I love you.' Jesus said to him, 'Feed my sheep.

¹⁸In all truth I tell you,
  when you were young
  you put on your own belt
  and walked where you liked;
  but when you grow old
  you will stretch out your hands,
  and somebody else
    will put a belt round you
  and take you
    where you would rather not go.'

¹⁹In these words he indicated the kind of death by which Peter would give glory to God. After this he said, 'Follow me.'

²⁰Peter turned and saw the disciple whom Jesus loved[b] following them—the one who had leant back close to his chest at the supper and had said to him, 'Lord, who is it that will betray you?' ²¹Seeing him, Peter said to Jesus, 'What about him, Lord?' ²²Jesus answered, 'If I want him to stay behind till I come, what does it matter to you? You are to follow me.' ²³The rumour then went out among the brothers that this disciple would not die. Yet Jesus had not said to Peter, 'He will not die,' but, 'If I want him to stay behind till I come.'

21a Added by the evangelist or one of his disciples.
21b The source of Jn's tradition; but his identity is uncertain.

II: SECOND CONCLUSION

²⁴This disciple is the one who vouches for these things and has written them down, and we know that his testimony is true.
²⁵There was much else that Jesus did; if it were written down in detail, I do not suppose the world itself would hold all the books that would be written.

ACTS
OF THE APOSTLES

This is the story of the spread of the Christian faith across the Mediterranean world, first in Judaea, then further in Palestine and finally in the capital of the empire, Rome. The main figures are Peter, leader of the apostles, and Paul, apostle of the gentiles, closely related in their work by similarities in preaching and in miracles.

The whole Christian community is filled with the Spirit of Jesus, whose guidance inspires every new initiative, and who ensures the harmony of the early community in its prayer, joy and praise. Even persecution brings only joy and thanksgiving, for the early Jerusalem community is presented as a model of perseverance, generosity and devotion. But although it is stressed that Christianity is the logical outcome of Judaism and is in full continuity with it, the Jews reject it again and again, even stirring up trouble with the Roman authorities and forcing the missionaries to turn to the gentiles.

The author, like any historian, moulds his material to bring out its message. Paul the Roman citizen, and the other Christians are unfailingly loyal to the authorities, and Christianity is a benign influence. By comparison with Paul's letters and other NT epistles the picture of the early Church seems idealised: there were differences of opinion and even bitter dissensions in the Church, particularly over relationships between gentile and Jewish Christians. Modern historians and archaeologists, however, have confirmed the accuracy of the legal and constitutional information given.

Certain passages in the travel-story are related in the first person, showing that the author of these actually travelled with Paul. Nevertheless considerable divergences from Paul's own account of some events and particularly of his theological views (e.g. on observance of the Jewish Law) raise doubts about how well the author actually knew Paul—unless he adjusted the picture to fit his theme of church harmony. He certainly followed contemporary convention in composing speeches for Peter and Paul: each sermon follows a set pattern (story of Jesus' death and resurrection, his ministry, an appeal to Scripture, a call to commitment to Christ and repentance), and the argumentation from Scripture is highly elaborate, often relying on the Gk text of the Bible, though the speech must originally have been delivered in Hebrew or Aramaic.

Of all the books of the Bible Acts is the one most at home in the classical Roman world: the author is a civilised and urbane hellenistic Jew. Style, vocabulary and theological emphases all combine to show that Acts and Luke issue from the same pen. Acts is the latter part of a two-volume work, split

when the four gospels were gathered together about AD 150. There is no clear evidence of the date of the book. No event later than the early 60s is mentioned, but Paul's arrival in Rome is a natural cut-off point for the story, and no conclusions about the date may be drawn from Acts' failure to narrate later history. It must have been written in the last quarter of the century.

PLAN OF THE BOOK

ACTS
OF THE APOSTLES

Prologue

1 In my earlier work, Theophilus, I dealt with everything Jesus had done and taught from the beginning ²until the day he gave his instructions to the apostles he had chosen through the Holy Spirit, and was taken up to heaven. ³He had shown himself alive to them after his Passion by many demonstrations: for forty days he had continued to appear to them and tell them about the kingdom of God. ⁴While at table with them, he had told them not to leave Jerusalem, but to wait there for what the Father had promised. 'It is', he had said, 'what you have heard me speak about: ⁵John baptised with water but, not many days from now, you are going to be baptised with the Holy Spirit.'

The ascension

⁶Now having met together, they asked him, 'Lord, has the time come for you to restore the kingdom to Israel?' ⁷He replied, 'It is not for you to know times or dates that the Father has decided by his own authority, ⁸but you will receive the power of the Holy Spirit which will come on you, and then you will be my witnesses not only in Jerusalem but throughout Judaea and Samaria, and indeed to earth's remotest end.'

⁹As he said this he was lifted up while they looked on, and a cloud took him from their sight. ¹⁰They were still staring into the sky as he went, when suddenly two men in white were standing beside them, ¹¹and they said, 'Why are you Galileans standing here looking into the sky? This Jesus who has been taken up from you into heaven will come back in the same way as you have seen him go to heaven.'

I: THE CHURCH IN JERUSALEM

The group of apostles

[12]So from the Mount of Olives, as it is called, they went back to Jerusalem, a short distance away, no more than a Sabbath walk; [13]and when they reached the city they went to the upper room where they were staying; there were Peter and John, James and Andrew, Philip and Thomas, Bartholomew and Matthew, James son of Alphaeus and Simon the Zealot, and Jude son of James. [14]With one heart all these joined constantly in prayer, together with some women, including Mary the mother of Jesus, and with his brothers.

Judas is replaced

[15]One day Peter stood up to speak to the brothers—there were about a hundred and twenty people in the congregation, [16]'Brothers,' he said, 'the passage of scripture had to be fulfilled in which the Holy Spirit, speaking through David, foretells the fate of Judas, who acted as guide to the men who arrested Jesus—[17]after being one of our number and sharing our ministry. [18]As you know, he bought a plot of land with the money he was paid for his crime. He fell headlong and burst open, and all his entrails poured out.[a] [19]Everybody in Jerusalem heard about it and the plot came to be called "Bloody Acre", in their language Hakeldama. [20]Now in the Book of Psalms it says:

Reduce his encampment to ruin
and leave his tent unoccupied.

And again:

Let someone else take over his office.

[21]'Out of the men who have been with us the whole time that the Lord Jesus was living with us, [22]from the time when John was baptising until the day when he was taken up from us, one must be appointed to serve with us as a witness to his resurrection.'
[23]Having nominated two candidates, Joseph known as Barsabbas, whose surname was Justus, and Matthias, [24]they prayed, 'Lord, you can read everyone's heart; show us therefore which of these two you have chosen [25]to take over this ministry and

apostolate, which Judas abandoned to go to his proper place.' [26]They then drew lots for them, and as the lot fell to Matthias, he was listed as one of the twelve apostles.

Pentecost

2When Pentecost day came round, they had all met together, [2]when suddenly there came from heaven a sound as of a violent wind which filled the entire house in which they were sitting; [3]and there appeared to them tongues as of fire; these separated and came to rest on the head of each of them. [4]They were all filled with the Holy Spirit and began to speak different languages as the Spirit gave them power to express themselves.

[5]Now there were devout men living in Jerusalem from every nation under heaven, [6]and at this sound they all assembled, and each one was bewildered to hear these men speaking his own language. [7]They were amazed and astonished. 'Surely,' they said, 'all these men speaking are Galileans? [8]How does it happen that each of us hears them in his own native language? [9]Parthians, Medes and Elamites; people from Mesopotamia, Judaea and Cappadocia, Pontus and Asia, [10]Phrygia and Pamphylia, Egypt and the parts of Libya round Cyrene; residents of Rome—[11]Jews and proselytes alike—Cretans and Arabs, we hear them preaching in our own language about the marvels of God.' [12]Everyone was amazed and perplexed; they asked one another what it all meant. [13]Some, however, laughed it off. 'They have been drinking too much new wine,' they said.

Peter's address to the crowd

[14]Then Peter stood up with the Eleven and addressed them in a loud voice:
'Men of Judaea, and all you who live in Jerusalem, make no mistake about this, but listen carefully to what I say. [15]These men are not drunk, as you imagine; why, it is only the third hour of the day. [16]On the contrary, this is what the prophet was saying:

1a cf. Ws 4:19. Ps 69:5; 109:8 are also used.

[17] In the last days—the Lord declares—
I shall pour out my Spirit on all humanity.
Your sons and daughters shall prophesy,
your young people shall see visions,
your old people dream dreams.
[18] *Even on the slaves, men and women,*
shall I pour out my Spirit.
[19] *I will show portents in the sky* above
and signs on the earth below.
[20] *The sun will be turned into darkness*
and the moon into blood
before the day of the Lord comes,
that great and terrible Day.
[21] *And all who call on the name of the Lord*
will be saved. [a]

[22] 'Men of Israel, listen to what I am going to say: Jesus the Nazarene was a man commended to you by God by the miracles and portents and signs that God worked through him when he was among you, as you know. [23] This man, who was put into your power by the deliberate intention and foreknowledge of God, you took and had crucified and killed by men outside the Law. [24] But God raised him to life, freeing him from the pangs of Hades; for it was impossible for him to be held in its power since, [25] as David says of him:

I kept the Lord before my sight always,
for with him at my right hand
nothing can shake me.
[26] *So my heart rejoiced*
my tongue delighted;
my body, too, will rest secure,
[27] *for you will not abandon me to Hades*
or allow your holy one to see corruption.
[28] *You have taught me the way of life,*
you will fill me with joy in your presence. [b]

[29] 'Brothers, no one can deny that the patriarch David himself is dead and buried: his tomb is still with us. [30] But since he was a prophet, and knew that God *had sworn him* an oath *to make one of his descendants succeed him on the throne,* [31] he spoke with foreknowledge about the resurrection of the Christ: he is the one who was *not abandoned to Hades,* and whose body did not *see corruption.* [32] God raised this man Jesus to life, and of that we are all witnesses. [33] Now raised to the heights by God's right hand, he has received from the Father the Holy Spirit, who was prom-

ised, and what you see and hear is the outpouring of that Spirit. [34] For David himself never went up to heaven, but yet he said:

The Lord declared to my Lord,
take your seat at my right hand,
[35] *till I have made your enemies*
your footstool. [c]

[36] 'For this reason the whole House of Israel can be certain that the Lord and Christ whom God has made is this Jesus whom you crucified.'

The first conversions

[37] Hearing this, they were cut to the heart and said to Peter and the other apostles, 'What are we to do, brothers?' [38] 'You must repent,' Peter answered, 'and every one of you must be baptised in the name of Jesus Christ for the forgiveness of your sins, and you will receive the gift of the Holy Spirit. [39] The promise that was made is for you and your children, and for all *those who are far away, for all those whom the Lord* our God *is calling to himself.'* [d] [40] He spoke to them for a long time using many other arguments, and he urged them, 'Save yourselves from this perverse generation.' [41] They accepted what he said and were baptised. That very day about three thousand were added to their number.

The early Christian community

[42] These remained faithful to the teaching of the apostles, to the brotherhood, to the breaking of bread and to the prayers.
[43] And everyone was filled with awe; the apostles worked many signs and miracles.
[44] And all who shared the faith owned everything in common; [45] they sold their goods and possessions and distributed the proceeds among themselves according to what each one needed.
[46] Each day, with one heart, they regularly went to the Temple but met in their houses for the breaking of bread; they shared their food gladly and generously; [47] they praised God and were looked up to by everyone. Day by day the Lord added to their community those destined to be saved.

2a Jl 3:1–5.
2b Ps 16:8–11 LXX.
2c Ps 110:1.
2d Ps 57:19.

The cure of a lame man[a]

3 Once, when Peter and John were going up to the Temple for the prayers at the ninth hour, [2]it happened that there was a man being carried along. He was a cripple from birth; and they used to put him down every day near the Temple entrance called the Beautiful Gate so that he could beg from the people going in. [3]When this man saw Peter and John on their way into the Temple he begged from them. [4]Peter, and John too, looked straight at him and said, 'Look at us.' [5]He turned to them expectantly, hoping to get something from them, [6]but Peter said, 'I have neither silver nor gold, but I will give you what I have: in the name of Jesus Christ the Nazarene, walk!' [7]Then he took him by the right hand and helped him to stand up. Instantly his feet and ankles became firm, [8]he jumped up, stood, and began to walk, and he went with them into the Temple, walking and jumping and praising God. [9]Everyone could see him walking and praising God, [10]and they recognised him as the man who used to sit begging at the Beautiful Gate of the Temple. They were all astonished and perplexed at what had happened to him.

Peter's address to the people

[11]Everyone came running towards them in great excitement, to the Portico of Solomon, as it is called, where the man was still clinging to Peter and John. [12]When Peter saw the people he addressed them, 'Men of Israel, why are you so surprised at this? Why are you staring at us as though we had made this man walk by our own power or holiness? [13]It is *the God of Abraham, Isaac and Jacob, the God of our ancestors, who has glorified his servant*[b] Jesus whom you handed over and then disowned in the presence of Pilate after he had given his verdict to release him. [14]It was you who accused the Holy and Upright One, you who demanded that a murderer should be released to you [15]while you killed the prince of life. God, however, raised him from the dead, and to that fact we are witnesses; [16]and it is the name of Jesus which, through faith in him, has brought back the strength of this man whom you see here and who is well known to you. It is faith in him that has restored this man to health, as you can all see.

[17]'Now I know, brothers, that neither you nor your leaders had any idea what you were really doing; [18]but this was the way God carried out what he had foretold, when he said through all his prophets that his Christ would suffer. [19]Now you must repent and turn to God, so that your sins may be wiped out, [20]and so that the Lord may send the time of comfort. Then he will send you the Christ he has predestined, that is Jesus, [21]whom heaven must keep till the universal restoration comes which God proclaimed, speaking through his holy prophets. [22]Moses, for example, said, *"From among your brothers the Lord God will raise up for you a prophet like me; you will listen to whatever he tells you.* [23]*Anyone who refuses to listen to that prophet shall be cut off from the people."*[c] [24]In fact, all the prophets that have ever spoken, from Samuel onwards, have predicted these days. [25]'You are the heirs of the prophets, the heirs of the covenant God made with your ancestors when he told Abraham, *"All the nations of the earth will be blessed in your descendants"*.[d] [26]It was for you in the first place that God raised up his servant and sent him to bless you as every one of you turns from his wicked ways.'

Peter and John before the Sanhedrin

4 While they were still talking to the people the priests came up to them, accompanied by the captain of the Temple and the Sadducees. [2]They were extremely annoyed at their teaching the people the resurrection from the dead by proclaiming the resurrection of Jesus. [3]They arrested them, and, as it was already late, they kept them in prison till the next day. [4]But many of those who had listened to their message became believers; the total number of men had now risen to something like five thousand.

[5]It happened that the next day the rulers, elders and scribes held a meeting in Jerusalem [6]with Annas the high priest, Caiaphas, Jonathan, Alexander and all the members of the high-priestly families. [7]They made the

---

3a cf. Ac 14:8–10; Lk 8:51.
3b Ex 3:6 with Is 52:13.
3c Dt 18:15, 19.
3d Gn 22:18.

prisoners stand in the middle and began to interrogate them, 'By what power, and by whose name have you men done this?' [8]Then Peter, filled with the Holy Spirit, addressed them, 'Rulers of the people, and elders! [9]If you are questioning us today about an act of kindness to a cripple and asking us how he was healed, [10]you must know, all of you, and the whole people of Israel, that it is by the name of Jesus Christ the Nazarene, whom you crucified, and God raised from the dead, by this name and by no other that this man stands before you cured. [11]This is *the stone which* you, *the builders, rejected* but which *has become the cornerstone.*[a] Only in him is there salvation; [12]for of all the names in the world given to men, this is the only one by which we can be saved.'

[13]They were astonished at the fearlessness shown by Peter and John, considering that they were uneducated laymen; and they recognised them as associates of Jesus; [14]but when they saw the man who had been cured standing by their side, they could find no answer. [15]So they ordered them to stand outside while the Sanhedrin had a private discussion. [16]'What are we going to do with these men?' they asked. 'It is obvious to everybody in Jerusalem that a notable miracle has been worked through them, and we cannot deny it. [17]But to stop the whole thing spreading any further among the people, let us threaten them against ever speaking to anyone in this name again.'

[18]So they called them in and gave them a warning on no account to make statements or to teach in the name of Jesus. [19]But Peter and John retorted, 'You must judge whether in God's eyes it is right to listen to you and not to God. [20]We cannot stop proclaiming what we have seen and heard.' [21]The court repeated the threats and then released them; they could not think of any way to punish them, since all the people were giving glory to God for what had happened. [22]The man who had been miraculously cured was over forty years old.

The apostles' prayer under persecution

[23]As soon as they were released they went to the community and told them everything the chief priests and elders had said to them.

[24]When they heard it they lifted up their voice to God with one heart. 'Master,' they prayed, 'it is you who made sky and earth and sea, and everything in them; [25]it is you who said through the Holy Spirit and speaking through our ancestor David, your servant:

Why this uproar among the nations,
this impotent muttering of the peoples?
[26]*Kings on earth take up position,*
princes plot together
against the Lord and his Anointed.[b]

[27]'This is what has come true: in this very city Herod and Pontius Pilate *plotted together* with the gentile *nations* and the *peoples* of Israel, against your holy servant Jesus whom you *anointed,* [28]to bring about the very thing that you in your strength and your wisdom had predetermined should happen. [29]And now, Lord, take note of their threats and help your servants to proclaim your message with all fearlessness, [30]by stretching out your hand to heal and to work miracles and marvels through the name of your holy servant Jesus.' [31]As they prayed, the house where they were assembled rocked. From this time they were all filled with the Holy Spirit and began to proclaim the word of God fearlessly.

The early Christian community

[32]The whole group of believers was united, heart and soul; no one claimed private ownership of any possessions, as everything they owned was held in common. [33]The apostles continued to testify to the resurrection of the Lord Jesus with great power, and they were all accorded great respect. [34]None of their members was ever in want, as all those who owned land or houses would sell them, and bring the money from the sale of them, [35]to present it to the apostles; it was then distributed to any who might be in need.

The generosity of Barnabas

[36]There was a Levite of Cypriot origin called Joseph whom the apostles surnamed Barnabas (which means 'son of encouragement'). [37]He owned a piece of land and he sold it and brought the money and presented it to the apostles.

4a Ps 118:22.
4b Ps 2:1–2.

The fraud of Ananias and Sapphira

5 There was also a man called Ananias. He and his wife, Sapphira, agreed to sell a property; ²but with his wife's connivance he kept back part of the price and brought the rest and presented it to the apostles. ³Peter said, 'Ananias, how can Satan have so possessed you that you should lie to the Holy Spirit and keep back part of the price of the land? ⁴While you still owned the land, wasn't it yours to keep, and after you had sold it wasn't the money yours to do with as you liked? What put this scheme into your mind? You have been lying not to men, but to God.' ⁵When he heard this Ananias fell down dead. And a great fear came upon everyone present. ⁶The younger men got up, wrapped up the body, carried it out and buried it.

⁷About three hours later his wife came in, not knowing what had taken place. ⁸Peter challenged her, 'Tell me, was this the price you sold the land for?' 'Yes,' she said, 'that was the price.' ⁹Peter then said, 'Why did you and your husband agree to put the Spirit of the Lord to the test? Listen! At the door are the footsteps of those who have buried your husband; they will carry you out, too.' ¹⁰Instantly she dropped dead at his feet. When the young men came in they found she was dead, and they carried her out and buried her by the side of her husband. ¹¹And a great fear came upon the whole church and on all who heard it.

The general situation

¹²The apostles worked many signs and miracles among the people. One in heart, they all used to meet in the Portico of Solomon. ¹³No one else dared to join them, but the people were loud in their praise ¹⁴and the numbers of men and women who came to believe in the Lord increased steadily. Many signs and wonders were worked among the people at the hands of the apostles ¹⁵so that the sick were even taken out into the streets and laid on beds and sleeping-mats in the hope that at least the shadow of Peter might fall across some of them as he went past. ¹⁶People even came crowding in from the towns round about Jerusalem, bringing with them their sick and those tormented by unclean spirits, and all of them were cured.

The apostles' arrest and miraculous deliverance[a]

¹⁷Then the high priest intervened with all his supporters from the party of the Sadducees. Filled with jealousy, ¹⁸they arrested the apostles and had them put in the public gaol.

¹⁹But at night the angel of the Lord opened the prison gates and said as he led them out, ²⁰'Go and take up position in the Temple, and tell the people all about this new Life.' ²¹They did as they were told; they went into the Temple at dawn and began to preach.

A summons to appear before the Sanhedrin

When the high priest arrived, he and his supporters convened the Sanhedrin—this was the full Senate of Israel—and sent to the gaol for them to be brought. ²²But when the officials arrived at the prison they found they were not inside, so they went back and reported, ²³'We found the gaol securely locked and the warders on duty at the gates, but when we unlocked the door we found no one inside.' ²⁴When the captain of the Temple and the chief priests heard this news they wondered what could be happening. ²⁵Then a man arrived with fresh news. 'Look!' he said, 'the men you imprisoned are in the Temple. They are standing there preaching to the people.' ²⁶The captain went with his men and fetched them—though not by force, for they were afraid that the people might stone them.

²⁷When they had brought them in to face the Sanhedrin, the high priest demanded an explanation. ²⁸'We gave you a strong warning', he said, 'not to preach in this name, and what have you done? You have filled Jerusalem with your teaching, and seem determined to fix the guilt for this man's death on us.' ²⁹In reply Peter and the apostles said, 'Obedience to God comes before obedience to men; ³⁰it was the God of our ancestors who raised up Jesus, whom you executed by hanging on a tree. ³¹By his own right hand God has now raised him up to be leader and Saviour, to give repentance and forgiveness of sins through him to Israel. ³²We are witnesses to this, we and the Holy Spirit whom God has given to those who obey him.'

5a cf. 12:6–11; 16:26–27.

³³This so infuriated them that they wanted to put them to death.

Gamaliel's intervention

³⁴One member of the Sanhedrin, however, a Pharisee called Gamaliel, who was a teacher of the Law respected by the whole people, stood up and asked to have the men taken outside for a time. ³⁵Then he addressed the Sanhedrin, 'Men of Israel, be careful how you deal with these people. ³⁶Some time ago there arose Theudas. He claimed to be someone important, and collected about four hundred followers; but when he was killed, all his followers scattered and that was the end of them. ³⁷And then there was Judas the Galilean, at the time of the census, who attracted crowds of supporters; but he was killed too, and all his followers dispersed. ³⁸What I suggest, therefore, is that you leave these men alone and let them go. If this enterprise, this movement of theirs, is of human origin it will break up of its own accord; ³⁹but if it does in fact come from God you will be unable to destroy them. Take care not to find yourselves fighting against God.'

His advice was accepted; ⁴⁰and they had the apostles called in, gave orders for them to be flogged, warned them not to speak in the name of Jesus and released them. ⁴¹And so they left the presence of the Sanhedrin, glad to have had the honour of suffering humiliation for the sake of the name.

⁴²Every day they went on ceaselessly teaching and proclaiming the good news of Christ Jesus, both in the temple and in private houses.

II: THE EARLIEST MISSIONS

The institution of the Seven

6 About this time, when the number of disciples was increasing, the Hellenists^a made a complaint against the Hebrews: in the daily distribution their own widows were being overlooked. ²So the Twelve called a full meeting of the disciples and addressed them, 'It would not be right for us to neglect the word of God so as to give out food; ³you, brothers, must select from among yourselves seven men of good reputation, filled with the Spirit and with wisdom, to whom we can hand over this duty. ⁴We ourselves will continue to devote ourselves to prayer and to the service of the word.' ⁵The whole assembly approved of this proposal and elected Stephen, a man full of faith and of the Holy Spirit, together with Philip, Prochorus, Nicanor, Timon, Parmenas, and Nicolaus of Antioch, a convert to Judaism. ⁶They presented these to the apostles, and after prayer they laid their hands on them.

⁷The word of the Lord continued to spread: the number of disciples in Jerusalem was greatly increased, and a large group of priests made their submission to the faith.

Stephen's arrest

⁸Stephen was filled with grace and power and began to work miracles and great signs among the people. ⁹Then certain people came forward to debate with Stephen, some from Cyrene and Alexandria who were members of the synagogue called the Synagogue of Freedmen, and others from Cilicia and Asia. ¹⁰They found they could not stand up against him because of his wisdom, and the Spirit that prompted what he said. ¹¹So they procured some men to say, 'We heard him using blasphemous language against Moses and against God.' ¹²Having turned the people against him as well as the elders and scribes, they took Stephen by surprise, and arrested him and brought him before the Sanhedrin. ¹³There they put up false witnesses to say, 'This man is always making speeches against this Holy Place and the Law. ¹⁴We have heard him say that Jesus, this Nazarene, is going to destroy this Place and alter the traditions that Moses handed down to us.' ¹⁵The members of the Sanhedrin all looked intently at Stephen, and his face appeared to them like the face of an angel.

6a Jews from outside Palestine, or Gk-speakers.

Stephen's speech[a]

7 The high priest asked, 'Is this true?' [2]He replied, 'My brothers, my fathers, listen to what I have to say. The God of glory appeared to our ancestor Abraham, while he was in Mesopotamia before settling in Haran, [3]and *said to* him, *"Leave your country, your kindred and your father's house for this country which I shall show you."* [4]So he left Chaldaea and settled in Haran; and after his father died God made him leave that place and come to this land where you are living today. [5]God did not give him any property in this land or even a foothold, yet he promised to *give it to him and after him to his descendants, childless* though he was. [6]The actual words God used when he spoke to him are that *his descendants would be exiles in a land not their own, where they would be enslaved and oppressed for four hundred years.* [7]*"But I will bring judgement on the nation that enslaves them,"* God said, *"and after this they will leave, and worship me in this place."* [8]Then he made the *covenant of circumcision* with him: and so when his son Isaac was born Abraham *circumcised him on the eighth day*; similarly Isaac circumcised Jacob, and Jacob the twelve patriarchs.

[9]'The patriarchs were *jealous of Joseph and sold him into slavery in Egypt.* But *God was with him,* [10]and rescued him from all his miseries by making him so wise that he *won the favour* of Pharaoh king of Egypt, who *made him governor of Egypt* and *put him in charge of his household.* [11]*Then a famine set in* that caused much suffering *throughout Egypt and Canaan,* and our ancestors could find nothing to eat. [12]When Jacob *heard that there were supplies in Egypt,* he sent our ancestors there on a first visit; [13]and on the second *Joseph made himself known to his brothers,* and Pharaoh came to know his origin. [14]Joseph then sent for his father Jacob and his whole family, a total of *seventy-five people.* [15]Jacob went down into Egypt and after he and our ancestors had died there, [16]their bodies were brought back to Shechem and buried in the tomb that Abraham had bought for money from the sons of Hamor, the father of Shechem.

[17]'As the time drew near for God to fulfil the promise he had solemnly made to Abraham, our nation in Egypt *became very powerful and numerous,* [18]there came to power in Egypt a new king who had never heard of *Joseph.* [19]*He took precautions and wore down* our race, forcing our ancestors to expose their babies rather than *letting them live.* [20]It was at this time that Moses was born, *a fine child* before God. He was looked after for *three months* in his father's house, [21]and after he had been exposed, *Pharaoh's daughter* adopted him and brought him up *like a son.* [22]So Moses was taught all the wisdom of the Egyptians and became a man with power both in his speech and in his actions.

[23]'At the age of forty he decided to visit *his kinsmen, the Israelites.* [24]When he saw one of them being ill-treated he went to his defence and rescued the man by *killing the Egyptian.* [25]He thought his brothers would realise that through him God would liberate them, but they did not. [26]The next day, when he came across some of them fighting, he tried to reconcile them, and said, "Friends, you are brothers; why are you hurting each other?" [27]But *the man who was attacking his kinsman* pushed him aside, saying, *"And who appointed you to be prince over us and judge? [28]Do you intend to kill me as you killed the Egyptian yesterday?"* [29]Moses fled when he heard this and *he went to dwell in the land of Midian,* where he fathered two sons.

[30]'When forty years were fulfilled, *in the desert near Mount Sinai, an angel appeared to him in a flame blazing from a bush* that was on fire. [31]Moses was amazed by what he saw. *As he went nearer to look at it, the voice of the Lord was* heard, [32]"I am the God of your ancestors, the God of Abraham, Isaac and Jacob." Moses trembled and *was afraid to look.* [33]The Lord said to him, *"Take off your sandals,* for the place where you are standing is holy ground. [34]*I have seen the misery of my people in Egypt, I have heard them crying for help, and I have come down to rescue them. So come here; I am sending you into Egypt."*

[35]'It was the same Moses that they had disowned when they said, *"Who appointed you to be our leader and judge?"* whom God sent to be both leader and redeemer through the angel who had appeared to him in the bush. [36]It was this man who led them out, after performing *miracles and signs in Egypt* and at the Red Sea and *in the desert for forty years.* [37]It was this Moses who told the sons of Israel, *"From among your own brothers God will raise up a prophet like me."* [38]When they

---

7a A survey using chiefly Gn and Ex.

held the assembly in the desert it was he who was with our ancestors and the angel who had spoken to him on Mount Sinai; it was he who was entrusted with words of life to hand on to us. ³⁹This is the man that our ancestors refused to listen to; they pushed him aside, *went back to Egypt* in their thoughts, ⁴⁰*and said to Aaron, "Make us a god to go at our head; for that Moses, the man who brought us here from Egypt, we do not know what has become of him."* ⁴¹It was then that *they made the statue of a calf and offered sacrifice* to the idol. They were perfectly happy with something they had made for themselves. ⁴²God turned away from them and abandoned them to the worship of the army of heaven, as scripture says in the book of the prophets:

*Did you bring me sacrifices and oblations
those forty years in the desert,
　House of Israel?*
⁴³*No, you carried the tent of Moloch
　on your shoulders
and the star of the god Rephan,
the idols you made
　for yourselves to adore,
and so now I am about to drive you
into captivity beyond* Babylon.*ᵇ*

⁴⁴'While they were in the desert our ancestors possessed the Tent of Testimony that had been constructed according to the instructions God gave Moses, telling him to *work to the design* he had been shown. ⁴⁵It was handed down from one ancestor of ours to another until Joshua brought it into the country that had belonged to the nations which were driven out by God before us. Here it stayed until the time of David. ⁴⁶He won God's favour and asked permission *to find a dwelling for* the House of *Jacob*, ⁴⁷though it was *Solomon* who actually *built a house for God*. ⁴⁸Even so the Most High does not live in a house that human hands have built: for as the prophet says:

⁴⁹*With heaven my throne
and earth my footstool,
what house could you build me,
　says the Lord,
what place for me to rest,*
⁵⁰*when all these things were made by me?ᶜ*

⁵¹'You stubborn people, with uncircumcised hearts and ears. You are always resisting the Holy Spirit, just as your ancestors used to do. ⁵²Can you name a single prophet your ancestors never persecuted? They killed those who foretold the coming of the Upright One, and now you have become his betrayers, his murderers. ⁵³In spite of being given the Law through angels, you have not kept it.'

⁵⁴They were infuriated when they heard this, and ground their teeth at him.

The stoning of Stephen
Saul as persecutor

⁵⁵But Stephen, filled with the Holy Spirit, gazed into heaven and saw the glory of God, and Jesus standing at God's right hand. ⁵⁶'Look! I can see heaven thrown open,' he said, 'and the Son of man standing at the right hand of God.' ⁵⁷All the members of the council shouted out and stopped their ears with their hands; then they made a concerted rush at him, ⁵⁸thrust him out of the city and stoned him. The witnesses put down their clothes at the feet of a young man called Saul. ⁵⁹As they were stoning him, Stephen said in invocation, 'Lord Jesus, receive my spirit.' ⁶⁰Then he knelt down and said aloud, 'Lord, do not hold this sin against them.' And with these words he fell asleep.

8 Saul approved of the killing.
That day a bitter persecution started against the church in Jerusalem, and everyone except the apostles scattered to the country districts of Judaea and Samaria. ²There were some devout people, however, who buried Stephen and made great mourning for him.

³Saul then began doing great harm to the church; he went from house to house arresting both men and women and sending them to prison.

Philip in Samaria

⁴Once they had scattered, they went from place to place preaching the good news. ⁵And Philip went to a Samaritan town and proclaimed the Christ to them. ⁶The people unanimously welcomed the message Philip preached, because they had heard of the miracles he worked and because they saw them for themselves. ⁷For unclean spirits

7b Am 5:25–27.
7c Is 66:1–2.

came shrieking out of many who were possessed, and several paralytics and cripples were cured. [8]As a result there was great rejoicing in that town.

Simon the magician

[9]Now a man called Simon had for some time been practising magic arts in the town and astounded the Samaritan people. He had given it out that he was someone momentous, [10]and everyone believed in him; eminent citizens and ordinary people alike had declared, 'He is the divine power that is called Great.' [11]He had this following because for a considerable period they had been astounded by his wizardry. [12]But when they came to accept Philip's preaching of the good news about the kingdom of God and the name of Jesus Christ, they were baptised, both men and women, [13]and even Simon himself became a believer. After his baptism Simon went round constantly with Philip and was astonished when he saw the wonders and great miracles that took place.

[14]When the apostles in Jerusalem heard that Samaria had accepted the word of God, they sent Peter and John to them, [15]and they went down there and prayed for them to receive the Holy Spirit, [16]for as yet he had not come down on any of them: they had only been baptised in the name of the Lord Jesus. [17]Then they laid hands on them, and they received the Holy Spirit.

[18]When Simon saw that the Spirit was given through the laying on of the apostles' hands, he offered them money, [19]with the words, 'Give me the same power so that anyone I lay my hands on will receive the Holy Spirit.' [20]Peter answered, 'May your silver be lost for ever, and you with it, for thinking that money could buy what God has given for nothing! [21]You have no share, no part, in this: God can see how your heart is warped. [22]Repent of this wickedness of yours, and pray to the Lord that this scheme of yours may be forgiven; [23]it is plain to me that you are held in the bitterness of gall and the chains of sin.' [24]Simon replied, 'Pray to the Lord for me yourselves so that none of the things you have spoken about may happen to me.'

[25]Having given their testimony and proclaimed the word of the Lord, they went back to Jerusalem, preaching the good news to a number of Samaritan villages.

Philip baptises a eunuch

[26]The angel of the Lord spoke to Philip saying, 'Set out at noon and go along the road that leads from Jerusalem down to Gaza, the desert road.' [27]So he set off on his journey. Now an Ethiopian had been on pilgrimage to Jerusalem; he was a eunuch and an officer at the court of the kandake, or queen, of Ethiopia; he was her chief treasurer. [28]He was now on his way home; and as he sat in his chariot he was reading the prophet Isaiah. [29]The Spirit said to Philip, 'Go up and join that chariot.' [30]When Philip ran up, he heard him reading Isaiah the prophet and asked, 'Do you understand what you are reading?' [31]He replied, 'How could I, unless I have someone to guide me?' So he urged Philip to get in and sit by his side. [32]Now the passage of scripture he was reading was this:

Like a lamb led to the slaughter-house,
like a sheep dumb in front of its shearers,
he never opens his mouth.
[33]*In his humiliation*
    fair judgement was denied him.
Who will ever talk about his descendants,
since his life on earth has been cut short?[a]

[34]The eunuch addressed Philip and said, 'Tell me, is the prophet referring to himself or someone else?' [35]Starting, therefore, with this text of scripture Philip proceeded to explain the good news of Jesus to him. [36]Further along the road they came to some water, and the eunuch said, 'Look, here is some water; is there anything to prevent my being baptised?'[37][b] [38]He ordered the chariot to stop, then Philip and the eunuch both went down into the water and he baptised him. [39]But after they had come up out of the water again Philip was taken away by the Spirit of the Lord, and the eunuch never saw him again but went on his way rejoicing. [40]Philip appeared in Azotus and continued his journey, proclaiming the good news in every town as far as Caesarea.

8a Is 53:7–8.
8b v. 37, omitted here, is a very ancient gloss: 'And Philip said, "If you believe with all your heart, you may." And he replied, "I believe that Jesus is the Son of God." '

The conversion of Saul[a]

9 Meanwhile Saul was still breathing threats to slaughter the Lord's disciples. He went to the high priest [2]and asked for letters addressed to the synagogues in Damascus, that would authorise him to arrest and take to Jerusalem any followers of the Way, men or women, that he might find.

[3]It happened that while he was travelling to Damascus and approaching the city, suddenly a light from heaven shone all round him. [4]He fell to the ground, and then he heard a voice saying, 'Saul, Saul, why are you persecuting me?' [5]'Who are you, Lord?' he asked, and the answer came, 'I am Jesus, whom you are persecuting. [6]Get up and go into the city, and you will be told what you are to do.' [7]The men travelling with Saul stood there speechless, for though they heard the voice they could see no one. [8]Saul got up from the ground, but when he opened his eyes he could see nothing at all, and they had to lead him into Damascus by the hand. [9]For three days he was without his sight and took neither food nor drink.

[10]There was a disciple in Damascus called Ananias, and he had a vision in which the Lord said to him, 'Ananias!' When he replied, 'Here I am, Lord,' [11]the Lord said, 'Get up and go to Straight Street and ask at the house of Judas for someone called Saul, who comes from Tarsus. At this moment he is praying, [12]and has seen a man called Ananias coming in and laying hands on him to give him back his sight.'

[13]But in response, Ananias said, 'Lord, I have heard from many people about this man and all the harm he has been doing to your holy people in Jerusalem. [14]He has come here with a warrant from the chief priests to arrest everybody who invokes your name.' [15]The Lord replied, 'Go, for this man is my chosen instrument to bring my name before gentiles and kings and before the people of Israel; [16]I myself will show him how much he must suffer for my name.' [17]Then Ananias went. He entered the house, and laid his hands on Saul and said, 'Brother Saul, I have been sent by the Lord Jesus, who appeared to you on your way here, so that you may recover your sight and be filled with the Holy Spirit.' [18]It was as though scales fell away from his eyes and immediately he was able to see again. So he got up and was baptised, [19]and after taking some food he regained his strength.

Saul's preaching at Damascus

After he had spent only a few days with the disciples in Damascus, [20]he began preaching in the synagogues, 'Jesus is the Son of God.' [21]All his hearers were amazed, and said, 'Surely, this is the man who did such damage in Jerusalem to the people who invoke this name, and who came here for the sole purpose of arresting them to have them tried by the chief priests?' [22]Saul's power increased steadily, and he was able to throw the Jewish colony at Damascus into complete confusion by the way he demonstrated that Jesus was the Christ.

[23]Some time passed, and the Jews worked out a plot to kill him, [24]but news of it reached Saul. They were keeping watch at the gates day and night in order to kill him, [25]but the disciples took him by night and let him down from the wall, lowering him in a basket.

Saul's visit to Jerusalem[b]

[26]When he got to Jerusalem he tried to join the disciples, but they were all afraid of him: they could not believe he was really a disciple. [27]Barnabas, however, took charge of him, introduced him to the apostles, and explained how the Lord had appeared to him and spoken to him on his journey, and how he had preached fearlessly at Damascus in the name of Jesus. [28]Saul now started to go round with them in Jerusalem, preaching fearlessly in the name of the Lord. [29]But after he had spoken to the Hellenists and argued with them, they became determined to kill him. [30]When the brothers got to know of this, they took him to Caesarea and sent him off from there to Tarsus.

A lull

[31]The churches throughout Judaea, Galilee and Samaria were now left in peace, building themselves up and living in the fear of the Lord; encouraged by the Holy Spirit, they continued to grow.

9a =22; 26; cf. 2 M 3.
9b ‖ Ga 1:18–19?

Peter cures a paralytic at Lydda

³²It happened that Peter visited one place after another and eventually came to God's holy people living down in Lydda. ³³There he found a man called Aeneas, a paralytic who had been bedridden for eight years. ³⁴Peter said to him, 'Aeneas, Jesus Christ cures you: get up and make your bed.' Aeneas got up immediately; ³⁵everybody who lived in Lydda and Sharon saw him, and they were converted to the Lord.

Peter raises a woman to life at Jaffa

³⁶At Jaffa there was a disciple called Tabitha, or in Greek, Dorcas, who never tired of doing good or giving to those in need. ³⁷But it happened that at this time she became ill and died, and they washed her and laid her out in an upper room. ³⁸Lydda is not far from Jaffa, so when the disciples heard that Peter was there, they sent two men to urge him, 'Come to us without delay.'

³⁹Peter went back with them immediately, and on his arrival they took him to the upper room, where all the widows stood round him in tears, showing him tunics and other clothes Dorcas had made when she was with them. ⁴⁰Peter sent everyone out of the room and knelt down and prayed. Then he turned to the dead woman and said, 'Tabitha, stand up.' She opened her eyes, looked at Peter and sat up. ⁴¹Peter helped her to her feet, then he called in the members of the congregation and widows and showed them she was alive. ⁴²The whole of Jaffa heard about it and many believed in the Lord.

⁴³Peter stayed on some time in Jaffa, lodging with a leather-tanner called Simon.

Peter visits a Roman centurion

10One of the centurions of the Italica cohort stationed in Caesarea was called Cornelius. ²He and the whole of his household were devout and God-fearing, and he gave generously to Jewish causes and prayed constantly to God. ³One day at about the ninth hour he had a vision in which he distinctly saw the angel of God come into his house and call out to him, 'Cornelius!' ⁴He stared at the vision in terror and exclaimed, 'What is it, Lord?' The angel answered, 'Your prayers and charitable gifts have been accepted by God. ⁵Now you must

send some men to Jaffa and fetch a man called Simon, known as Peter, ⁶who is lodging with Simon the tanner whose house is by the sea.' ⁷When the angel who said this had gone, Cornelius called two of the slaves and a devout soldier of his staff, ⁸told them all that had happened, and sent them off to Jaffa.

⁹Next day, while they were still on their journey and had only a short distance to go before reaching the town, Peter went to the housetop at about the sixth hour to say his prayers. ¹⁰He felt hungry and was looking forward to his meal, but before it was ready he fell into a trance ¹¹and saw heaven thrown open and something like a big sheet being let down to earth by its four corners; ¹²it contained every kind of animal, reptile and bird. ¹³A voice then said to him, 'Now, Peter, kill and eat!' ¹⁴But Peter answered, 'Certainly not, Lord; I have never yet eaten anything profane or unclean.' ¹⁵Again, a second time, the voice spoke to him, 'What God has made clean, you have no right to call profane.' ¹⁶This was repeated three times, and then suddenly the container was drawn up to heaven again.

¹⁷Peter was still at a loss over the meaning of the vision he had seen, when the men sent by Cornelius arrived. They had asked where Simon's house was and they were now standing at the door, ¹⁸calling out to know if the Simon known as Peter was lodging there. ¹⁹While Peter's mind was still on the vision, the Spirit told him, 'Look! Some men have come to see you. ²⁰Hurry down, and do not hesitate to return with them; it was I who told them to come.' ²¹Peter went down and said to them, 'I am the man you are looking for; why have you come?' ²²They said, 'The centurion Cornelius, who is an upright and God-fearing man, highly regarded by the entire Jewish people, was told by God through a holy angel to send for you and bring you to his house and to listen to what you have to say.' ²³So Peter asked them in and gave them lodging.

Next day, he was ready to go off with them, accompanied by some of the brothers from Jaffa. ²⁴They reached Caesarea the following day, and Cornelius was waiting for them. He had asked his relations and close friends to be there, ²⁵and as Peter reached the house Cornelius went out to meet him, fell at his feet and did him reverence. ²⁶But Peter helped him up. 'Stand up,' he said, ' after all, I am only a man!' ²⁷Talking together they went in to meet all the people assembled there, [28]and Peter said to them, 'You know it is forbidden for Jews to mix with people of another race and visit them; but God has made it clear to me that I must not call anyone profane or unclean. [29]That is why I made no objection to coming when I was sent for; but I should like to know exactly why you sent for me.' [30]Cornelius replied, 'At this time three days ago I was in my house saying the prayers for the ninth hour, when I suddenly saw a man in front of me in shining robes. [31]He said, "Cornelius, your prayer has been heard and your charitable gifts have not been forgotten by God; [32]so now you must send to Jaffa and fetch Simon known as Peter who is lodging in the house of Simon the tanner, by the sea." [33]So I sent for you at once, and you have been kind enough to come. Here we all are, assembled in front of you to hear all the instructions God has given you.'

Peter's address in the house of Cornelius

[34]Then Peter addressed them, 'I now really understand', he said, 'that God has no favourites, [35]but that anybody of any nationality who fears him and does what is right is acceptable to him.

[36]'God sent his word to the people of Israel, and it was to them that *the good news of peace was brought*[a] by Jesus Christ—he is the Lord of all. [37]You know what happened all over Judaea, how Jesus of Nazareth began in Galilee, after John had been preaching baptism. [38]*God had anointed him with the Holy Spirit* and with power, and because God was with him, Jesus went about doing good and curing all who had fallen into the power of the devil. [39]Now we are witnesses to everything he did throughout the countryside of Judaea and in Jerusalem itself: and they killed him by hanging him on a tree, [40]yet on the third day God raised him to life and allowed him to be seen, [41]not by the whole people but only by certain witnesses that God had chosen beforehand. Now we are those witnesses—we have eaten and drunk with him after his resurrection from the dead— [42]and he has ordered us to proclaim this to his people and to bear witness that God has appointed him to judge everyone, alive or dead. [43]It is to him that all the prophets bear this witness: that all who believe in Jesus

will have their sins forgiven through his name.'

Baptism of the first gentiles

[44]While Peter was still speaking the Holy Spirit came down[b] on all the listeners. [45]Jewish believers who had accompanied Peter were all astonished that the gift of the Holy Spirit should be poured out on gentiles too, [46]since they could hear them speaking strange languages and proclaiming the greatness of God. Peter himself then said, [47]'Could anyone refuse the water of baptism to these people, now they have received the Holy Spirit just as we have?' [48]He then gave orders for them to be baptised in the name of Jesus Christ. Afterwards they begged him to stay on for some days.

Jerusalem: Peter justifies his conduct

11 The apostles and the brothers in Judaea heard that gentiles too had accepted the word of God, [2]and when Peter came up to Jerusalem the circumcised believers protested to him [3]and said, 'So you have been visiting the uncircumcised and eating with them!' [4]Peter in reply gave them the details point by point, [5]'One day, when I was in the town of Jaffa,' he began, 'I fell into a trance as I was praying and had a vision of something like a big sheet being let down from heaven by its four corners. This sheet came right down beside me. [6]I looked carefully into it and saw four-footed animals of the earth, wild beasts, reptiles, and birds of heaven. [7]Then I heard a voice that said to me, "Now, Peter, kill and eat!" [8]But I answered, "Certainly not, Lord; nothing profane or unclean has ever crossed my lips." [9]And a second time the voice spoke from heaven, "What God has made clean, you have no right to call profane." [10]This was repeated three times, before the whole of it was drawn up to heaven again.

[11]'Just at that moment, three men stopped outside the house where we were staying; they had been sent from Caesarea to fetch me, [12]and the Spirit told me to have no hesitation about going back with them. The six brothers here came with me as well, and we entered the man's house. [13]He told us he had seen an angel standing in his house who

---

10a Is 52:7 and in v. 38 Is 61:1.
10b cf. 2:3–4.

said, "Send to Jaffa and fetch Simon known as Peter; [14]he has a message for you that will save you and your entire household."

[15]'I had scarcely begun to speak when the Holy Spirit came down on them in the same way as it came on us at the beginning, [16]and I remembered that the Lord had said, "John baptised with water, but you will be baptised with the Holy Spirit." [17]I realised then that God was giving them the identical gift he gave to us when we believed in the Lord Jesus Christ; and who was I to stand in God's way?' [18]This account satisfied them, and they gave glory to God, saying, 'God has clearly granted to the gentiles too the repentance that leads to life.'

Foundation of the church of Antioch

[19]Those who had scattered because of the persecution that arose over Stephen travelled as far as Phoenicia and Cyprus and Antioch, but they proclaimed the message only to Jews. [20]Some of them, however, who came from Cyprus and Cyrene, went to Antioch where they started preaching also to the Greeks, proclaiming the good news of the Lord Jesus to them. [21]The Lord helped them, and a great number believed and were converted to the Lord.

[22]The news of them came to the ears of the church in Jerusalem and they sent Barnabas out to Antioch. [23]There he was glad to see for himself that God had given grace, and he urged them all to remain faithful to the Lord with heartfelt devotion; [24]for he was a good man, filled with the Holy Spirit and with faith. And a large number of people were won over to the Lord.

[25]Barnabas then left for Tarsus to look for Saul, [26]and when he found him he brought him to Antioch. And it happened that they stayed together in that church a whole year, instructing a large number of people. It was at Antioch that the disciples were first called 'Christians'.

Barnabas and Saul
sent as deputies to Jerusalem

[27]While they were there some prophets came down to Antioch from Jerusalem, [28]and one of them whose name was Agabus, seized by the Spirit, stood up and predicted that a severe and universal famine was going to happen. This in fact happened while Clau-

dius was emperor. [29]The disciples decided to send relief, each to contribute what he could afford, to the brothers living in Judaea. [30]They did this and delivered their contributions to the elders through the agency of Barnabas and Saul.

Peter's arrest and miraculous deliverance

12 It was about this time that King Herod started persecuting certain members of the church. [2]He had James the brother of John beheaded, [3]and when he saw that this pleased the Jews he went on to arrest Peter as well. [4]As it was during the days of Unleavened Bread that he had arrested him, he put him in prison, assigning four sections of four soldiers each to guard him, meaning to try him in public after the Passover. [5]All the time Peter was under guard the church prayed to God for him unremittingly.

[6]On the night before Herod was to try him, Peter was sleeping between two soldiers, fastened with two chains, while guards kept watch at the main entrance to the prison. [7]Then suddenly an angel of the Lord stood there, and the cell was filled with light. He tapped Peter on the side and woke him. 'Get up!' he said, 'Hurry!'—and the chains fell from his hands. [8]The angel then said, 'Put on your belt and sandals.' After he had done this, the angel next said, 'Wrap your cloak round you and follow me.' [9]He followed him out, but had no idea that what the angel did was all happening in reality; he thought he was seeing a vision. [10]They passed through the first guard post and then the second and reached the iron gate leading to the city. This opened of its own accord; they went through it and had walked the whole length of one street when suddenly the angel left him. [11]It was only then that Peter came to himself. And he said, 'Now I know it is all true. The Lord really did send his angel and save me from Herod and from all that the Jewish people were expecting.'

[12]As soon as he realised this he went straight to the house of Mary the mother of John Mark, where a number of people had assembled and were praying. [13]He knocked at the outside door and a servant called Rhoda came to answer it. [14]She recognised Peter's voice and was so overcome with joy that, instead of opening the door, she ran inside with the news that Peter was standing at the main entrance. [15]They said to her, 'You are

out of your mind,' but she insisted that it was true. Then they said, 'It must be his angel!' [16]Peter, meanwhile, was still knocking. When they opened the door, they were amazed to see that it really was Peter himself. [17]He raised his hand for silence and described to them how the Lord had led him out of prison. He added, 'Tell James and the brothers.' Then he left and went elsewhere.

[18]When daylight came there was a great commotion among the soldiers, who could not imagine what had become of Peter. [19]Herod put out an unsuccessful search for him; he had the guards questioned, and before leaving Judaea to take up residence in Caesarea he gave orders for their execution.

The death of the persecutor[a]

[20]Now Herod was on bad terms with the Tyrians and Sidonians. Yet they sent a joint deputation which managed to enlist the support of Blastus, the king's chamberlain, and through him negotiated a treaty, since their country depended for its food supply on the king's territory. [21]A day was fixed, and Herod, wearing his robes of state and seated on a throne, began to make a speech to them. [22]The people acclaimed him with, 'It is a god speaking, not a man!' [23]and at that moment the angel of the Lord struck him down, because he had not given the glory to God. He was eaten away by worms and died.

Barnabas and Saul return to Antioch

[24]The word of God continued to spread and to gain followers.

[25]Barnabas and Saul completed their task at Jerusalem and came back, bringing John Mark with them.

III: THE MISSION OF BARNABAS AND PAUL
THE COUNCIL OF JERUSALEM

The mission sent out

13 In the church at Antioch the following were prophets and teachers: Barnabas, Simeon called Niger, and Lucius of Cyrene, Manaen, who had been brought up with Herod the tetrarch, and Saul. [2]One day while they were offering worship to the Lord and keeping a fast, the Holy Spirit said, 'I want Barnabas and Saul set apart for the work to which I have called them.' [3]So it was that after fasting and prayer they laid their hands on them and sent them off.

Cyprus: the magician Elymas

[4]So these two, sent on their mission by the Holy Spirit, went down to Seleucia and from there set sail for Cyprus. [5]They landed at Salamis and proclaimed the word of God in the synagogues of the Jews; John acted as their assistant.

[6]They travelled the whole length of the island, and at Paphos they came in contact with a Jewish magician and false prophet called Bar-Jesus. [7]He was one of the attend-ants of the proconsul Sergius Paulus, who was an extremely intelligent man. The proconsul summoned Barnabas and Saul and asked to hear the word of God, [8]but Elymas the magician (this is what his name means in Greek) tried to stop them so as to prevent the proconsul's conversion to the faith. [9]Then Saul, whose other name is Paul, filled with the Holy Spirit, looked at him intently [10]and said, 'You utter fraud, you impostor, you son of the devil, you enemy of all uprightness, will you not stop twisting the straightforward ways of the Lord? [11]Now watch how the hand of the Lord will strike you: you will be blind, and for a time you will not see the sun.' That instant, everything went misty and dark for him, and he groped about to find someone to lead him by the hand. [12]The proconsul, who had watched everything, became a believer, being much struck by what he had learnt about the Lord.

They arrive at Antioch in Pisidia

[13]Paul and his companions went by sea from Paphos to Perga in Pamphylia where John

12a cf. 2 M 9:5–28.

left them to go back to Jerusalem. [14]The others carried on from Perga till they reached Antioch in Pisidia. Here they went to synagogue on the Sabbath and took their seats. [15]After the passages from the Law and the Prophets had been read, the presidents of the synagogue sent them a message, 'Brothers, if you would like to address some words of encouragement to the congregation, please do so.' [16]Paul stood up, raised his hand for silence and began to speak:

Paul's preaching before the Jews[a]

'Men of Israel, and fearers of God, listen! [17]The God of our nation Israel chose our ancestors and made our people great when they were living in Egypt, a land not their own; then by divine power he led them out [18]and for about forty years *took care of* them in the desert. [19]*When he had destroyed seven nations in Canaan, he put them in possession of* their land [20]for about four hundred and fifty years. After this he gave them judges, down to the prophet Samuel. [21]Then they demanded a king, and God gave them Saul son of Kish, a man of the tribe of Benjamin. After forty years, [22]he deposed him and raised up David to be king, whom he attested in these words, "*I have found David* son of Jesse, *a man after my own heart, who will perform my entire will.*" [23]To keep his promise, God has raised up for Israel one of David's descendants, Jesus, as Saviour, [24]whose coming was heralded by John when he proclaimed a baptism of repentance for the whole people of Israel. [25]Before John ended his course he said, "I am not the one you imagine me to be; there is someone coming after me whose sandal I am not fit to undo."

[26]'My brothers, sons of Abraham's race, and all you godfearers, this message of salvation is meant for you. [27]What the people of Jerusalem and their rulers did, though they did not realise it, was in fact to fulfil the prophecies read on every Sabbath. [28]Though they found nothing to justify his execution, they condemned him and asked Pilate to have him put to death. [29]When they had carried out everything that scripture foretells about him they took him down from the tree and buried him in a tomb. [30]But God raised him from the dead, [31]and for many days he appeared to those who had accompanied him from Galilee to Jerusalem: and it is these same companions of his who are now his witnesses before our people.

[32]'We have come here to tell you the good news that the promise made to our ancestors has come about. [33]God has fulfilled it to their children by raising Jesus from the dead. As scripture says in the psalms: *You are my son: today I have fathered you.* [34]The fact that God raised him from the dead, never to return to corruption, is no more than what he had declared: *To you I shall give the holy things promised to David which can be relied upon.* [35]This is also why it says in another text: *You will not allow your Holy One to see corruption.* [36]Now when David in his own time had served God's purposes he died; he was buried with his ancestors and has certainly *seen corruption.* [37]The one whom God has raised up, however, has not *seen corruption.*

[38]'My brothers, I want you to realise that it is through him that forgiveness of sins is being proclaimed to you. Through him justification from all sins from which the Law of Moses was unable to justify [39]is being offered to every believer.

[40]'So be careful—or what the prophets say will happen to you.

[41]*Cast your eyes around you, mockers;*
be amazed, and perish!
For I am doing something in your own days
that you would never believe
   if you were told of it.'

[42]As they left they were urged to continue this preaching the following Sabbath. [43]When the meeting broke up many Jews and devout converts followed Paul and Barnabas, and in their talks with them Paul and Barnabas urged them to remain faithful to the grace God had given them.

Paul and Barnabas preach to the gentiles

[44]The next Sabbath almost the whole town assembled to hear the word of God. [45]When they saw the crowds, the Jews, filled with jealousy, used blasphemies to contradict everything Paul said. [46]Then Paul and Barnabas spoke out fearlessly. 'We had to proclaim the word of God to you first, but since you have rejected it, since you do not think yourselves worthy of eternal life, here and now we turn to the gentiles. [47]For this is

---

13a Paul uses Dt 1:31; 7:1; Ps 89:14; 2:7; Is 55:3; Ps 16:9; Hab 1:5.

what the Lord commanded us to do when he said:

I have made you a light to the nations,
so that my salvation may reach
the remotest parts of the earth.' [b]

⁴⁸It made the gentiles very happy to hear this and they gave thanks to the Lord for his message; all who were destined for eternal life became believers. ⁴⁹Thus the word of the Lord spread through the whole countryside. ⁵⁰But the Jews worked on some of the devout women of the upper classes and the leading men of the city; they stirred up a persecution against Paul and Barnabas and expelled them from their territory. ⁵¹So they shook the dust from their feet in protest against them and went off to Iconium; but the converts were filled with joy and the Holy Spirit.

Iconium evangelised

14 It happened that at Iconium they went to the Jewish synagogue, in the same way, and they spoke so effectively that a great many Jews and Greeks became believers.

²(However, the Jews who refused to believe stirred up the gentiles against the brothers and set them in opposition.) ³Accordingly Paul and Barnabas stayed on for some time, preaching fearlessly in the Lord; and he attested all they said about his gift of grace, allowing signs and wonders to be performed by them. ⁴The people in the city were divided; some supported the Jews, others the apostles, ⁵but eventually with the connivance of the authorities a move was made by gentiles as well as Jews to make attacks on them and to stone them. ⁶When they came to hear of this, they went off for safety to Lycaonia where, in the towns of Lystra and Derbe and in the surrounding country, ⁷they preached the good news.

Healing of a cripple

⁸There was a man sitting there who had never walked in his life, because his feet were crippled from birth; ⁹he was listening to Paul preaching, and Paul looked at him intently and saw that he had the faith to be cured. ¹⁰Paul said in a loud voice, 'Get to your feet —

stand up,' and the cripple jumped up and began to walk.

¹¹When the crowds saw what Paul had done they shouted in the language of Lycaonia, 'The gods have come down to us in human form.' ¹²They addressed Barnabas as Zeus, and since Paul was the principal speaker they called him Hermes. ¹³The priests of Zeus-outside-the-Gate, proposing that all the people should offer sacrifice with them, brought garlanded oxen to the gates. ¹⁴When the apostles Barnabas and Paul heard what was happening they tore their clothes, and rushed into the crowd, shouting, ¹⁵'Friends, what do you think you are doing? We are only human beings, mortal like yourselves. We have come with good news to make you turn from these empty idols to the living God who made sky and earth and the sea and all that these hold. ¹⁶In the past he allowed all the nations to go their own way; ¹⁷but even then he did not leave you without evidence of himself in the good things he does for you: he sends you rain from heaven and seasons of fruitfulness; he fills you with food and your hearts with merriment.' ¹⁸With this speech they just managed to prevent the crowd from offering them sacrifice.

End of the mission

¹⁹Then some Jews arrived from Antioch and Iconium and turned the people against them. They stoned Paul and dragged him outside the town, thinking he was dead. ²⁰The disciples came crowding round him but, as they did so, he stood up and went back to the town. The next day he and Barnabas left for Derbe.

²¹Having preached the good news in that town and made a considerable number of disciples, they went back through Lystra, Iconium and Antioch. ²²They put fresh heart into the disciples, encouraging them to persevere in the faith, saying, 'We must all experience many hardships before we enter the kingdom of God.' ²³In each of these churches they appointed elders, and with prayer and fasting they commended them to the Lord in whom they had come to believe.

²⁴They passed through Pisidia and reached Pamphylia. ²⁵Then after proclaiming the word at Perga they went down to Attalia ²⁶and from there sailed for Antioch, where

13b Is 49:6; cf. 18:6; 28:25.

they had originally been commended to the grace of God for the work they had now completed.

²⁷On their arrival they assembled the church and gave an account of all that God had done with them, and how he had opened the door of faith to the gentiles. ²⁸They stayed there with the disciples for some time.

Controversy at Antioch

15 Then some men came down from Judaea and taught the brothers, 'Unless you have yourselves circumcised in the tradition of Moses you cannot be saved.' ²This led to disagreement, and after Paul and Barnabas had had a long argument with these men it was decided that Paul and Barnabas and others of the church should go up to Jerusalem and discuss the question with the apostles and elders.

³The members of the church saw them off, and as they passed through Phoenicia and Samaria they told how the gentiles had been converted, and this news was received with the greatest satisfaction by all the brothers. ⁴When they arrived in Jerusalem they were welcomed by the church and by the apostles and elders, and gave an account of all that God had done through them.

Controversy at Jerusalem

⁵But certain members of the Pharisees' party who had become believers objected, insisting that gentiles should be circumcised and instructed to keep the Law of Moses. ⁶The apostles and elders met*ᵃ* to look into the matter, ⁷and after a long discussion, Peter stood up and addressed them.

Peter's speech

'My brothers,' he said, 'you know perfectly well that in the early days God made his choice among you: the gentiles were to learn the good news from me and so become believers. ⁸And God, who can read everyone's heart, showed his approval of them by giving the Holy Spirit to them just as he had to us. ⁹God made no distinction between them and us, since he purified their hearts by faith. ¹⁰Why do you put God to the test now by imposing on the disciples the very burden that neither our ancestors nor we ourselves were strong enough to support? ¹¹But we believe that we are saved in the same way as they are: through the grace of the Lord Jesus.'

¹²The entire assembly fell silent, and they listened to Barnabas and Paul describing all the signs and wonders God had worked through them among the gentiles.

James' speech

¹³When they had finished it was James who spoke. 'My brothers,' he said, 'listen to me. ¹⁴Simeon has described how God first arranged to enlist a people for his name out of the gentiles. ¹⁵This is entirely in harmony with the words of the prophets, since the scriptures say:

¹⁶*After that I shall return*
and rebuild the fallen hut of David;
I shall make good the gaps in it
and restore it.
¹⁷*Then the rest of humanity,*
and of all the nations once called mine,
will look for the Lord,
says the Lord who made this ¹⁸known
so long ago.*ᵇ*

¹⁹'My verdict is, then, that instead of making things more difficult for gentiles who turn to God, ²⁰we should send them a letter telling them merely to abstain from anything polluted by idols, from illicit marriages, from the meat of strangled animals and from blood. ²¹For Moses has always had his preachers in every town and is read aloud in the synagogues every Sabbath.'

The apostolic letter

²²Then the apostles and elders, with the whole church, decided to choose delegates from among themselves to send to Antioch with Paul and Barnabas. They chose Judas, known as Barsabbas, and Silas, both leading men in the brotherhood, ²³and gave them this letter to take with them:

'The apostles and elders, your brothers,

15a Two disputes are combined: Peter's speech concerns obligations of gentiles to keep the Jewish Law, James' concerns social contact.
15b Am 9:11–12.

send greetings to the brothers of gentile birth in Antioch, Syria and Cilicia. ²⁴We hear that some people coming from here, but acting without any authority from ourselves, have disturbed you with their demands and have unsettled your minds; ²⁵and so we have decided unanimously to elect delegates and to send them to you with our well-beloved Barnabas and Paul, ²⁶who have committed their lives to the name of our Lord Jesus Christ. ²⁷Accordingly we are sending you Judas and Silas, who will confirm by word of mouth what we have written. ²⁸It has been decided by the Holy Spirit and by ourselves not to impose on you any burden beyond these essentials: ²⁹you are to abstain from food sacrificed to idols, from blood, from the meat of strangled animals and from illicit marriages. Avoid these, and you will do what is right. Farewell.'

The delegates at Antioch

³⁰The party left and went down to Antioch, where they summoned the whole community and delivered the letter. ³¹The community read it and were delighted with the encouragement it gave them. ³²Judas and Silas, being themselves prophets, spoke for a long time, encouraging and strengthening the brothers. ³³These two spent some time there, and then the brothers wished them peace and they went back to those who had sent them.^{[34]c} ³⁵Paul and Barnabas, however, stayed on in Antioch, and there with many others they taught and proclaimed the good news, the word of the Lord.

IV: PAUL'S MISSIONS

Paul separates from Barnabas and recruits Silas

³⁶On a later occasion Paul said to Barnabas, 'Let us go back and visit the brothers in all the towns where we preached the word of the Lord, so that we can see how they are doing.' ³⁷Barnabas suggested taking John Mark, ³⁸but Paul was not in favour of taking along the man who had deserted them in Pamphylia and had refused to share in their work. ³⁹There was sharp disagreement so that they parted company, and Barnabas sailed off with Mark to Cyprus. ⁴⁰Before Paul left, he chose Silas to accompany him and was commended by the brothers to the grace of God.

Lycaonia: Paul recruits Timothy

⁴¹He travelled through Syria and Cilicia, consolidating the churches.

16 From there he went to Derbe, and then on to Lystra, where there was a disciple called Timothy, whose mother was Jewish and had become a believer; but his father was a Greek. ²The brothers at Lystra and Iconium spoke well of him, ³and Paul, who wanted to have him as a travelling companion, had him circumcised. This was on account of the Jews in the locality where everyone knew his father was a Greek.

⁴As they visited one town after another, they passed on the decisions reached by the apostles and elders in Jerusalem, with instructions to observe them.

⁵So the churches grew strong in the faith, as well as growing daily in numbers.

The crossing into Asia Minor

⁶They travelled through Phrygia and the Galatian country, because they had been told by the Holy Spirit not to preach the word in Asia. ⁷When they reached the frontier of Mysia they tried to go into Bithynia, but as the Spirit of Jesus would not allow them, ⁸they went through Mysia and came down to Troas.

⁹One night Paul had a vision: a Macedonian appeared and kept urging him in these words, 'Come across to Macedonia and help us.' ¹⁰Once he had seen this vision we lost no time in arranging a passage to Macedonia, convinced that God had called us to bring them the good news.

15c Some MSS add v. 34 'But Silas decided to stay there'.

Arrival at Philippi

[11]Sailing from Troas we made a straight run for Samothrace; the next day for Neapolis, [12]and from there for Philippi, a Roman colony and the principal city of that district of Macedonia. [13]After a few days in this city we went outside the gates beside a river as it was the Sabbath and this was a customary place for prayer. We sat down and preached to the women who had come to the meeting. [14]One of these women was called Lydia, a woman from the town of Thyatira who was in the purple-dye trade, and who revered God. She listened to us, and the Lord opened her heart to accept what Paul was saying. [15]After she and her household had been baptised she kept urging us, 'If you judge me a true believer in the Lord,' she said, 'come and stay with us.' And she would take no refusal.

Imprisonment of Paul and Silas

[16]It happened one day that as we were going to prayer, we were met by a slave-girl who was a soothsayer and made a lot of money for her masters by foretelling the future. [17]This girl started following Paul and the rest of us and shouting, 'Here are the servants of the Most High God; they have come to tell you how to be saved!' [18]She did this day after day until Paul was exasperated and turned round and said to the spirit, 'I order you in the name of Jesus Christ to leave that woman.' The spirit went out of her then and there.

[19]When her masters saw that there was no hope of making any more money out of her, they seized Paul and Silas and dragged them into the market place before the authorities. [20]Taking them before the magistrates they said, 'These people are causing a disturbance in our city. They are Jews [21]and are advocating practices which it is unlawful for us as Romans to accept or follow.' [22]The crowd joined in and showed its hostility to them, so the magistrates had them stripped and ordered them to be flogged. [23]They were given many lashes and then thrown into prison, and the gaoler was told to keep a close watch on them. [24]So, following such instructions, he threw them into the inner prison and fastened their feet in the stocks.

The miraculous deliverance of Paul and Silas

[25]In the middle of the night Paul and Silas were praying and singing God's praises, while the other prisoners listened. [26]Suddenly there was an earthquake that shook the prison to its foundations. All the doors flew open and the chains fell from all the prisoners. [27]When the gaoler woke and saw the doors wide open he drew his sword and was about to commit suicide, presuming that the prisoners had escaped. [28]But Paul shouted at the top of his voice, 'Do yourself no harm; we are all here.'

[29]He called for lights, then rushed in, threw himself trembling at the feet of Paul and Silas, [30]and escorted them out, saying, 'Sirs, what must I do to be saved?' [31]They told him, 'Become a believer in the Lord Jesus, and you will be saved, and your household too.' [32]Then they preached the word of the Lord to him and to all his household. [33]Late as it was, he took them to wash their wounds, and was baptised then and there with all his household. [34]Afterwards he took them into his house and gave them a meal, and the whole household celebrated their conversion to belief in God.

[35]When it was daylight the magistrates sent the lictors with the order: 'Release those men.' [36]The gaoler reported the message to Paul, 'The magistrates have sent an order for your release; you can go now and be on your way.' [37]'What!' Paul replied. 'Without trial they gave us a public flogging, though we are Roman citizens, and threw us into prison, and now they want to send us away on the quiet! Oh no! They must come and escort us out themselves.'

[38]The lictors reported this to the magistrates, who were terrified when they heard they were Roman citizens. [39]They came and urged them to leave the town. [40]From the prison they went to Lydia's house where they saw all the brothers and gave them some encouragement; then they left.

Thessalonica: difficulties with the Jews

17 Passing through Amphipolis and Apollonia, they eventually reached Thessalonica, where there was a Jewish synagogue. [2]Paul as usual went in and for three consecutive Sabbaths developed the arguments from scripture for them, [3]explaining and proving how it was ordained that the

Christ should suffer and rise from the dead. 'And the Christ', he said, 'is this Jesus whom I am proclaiming to you.' [4]Some of them were convinced and joined Paul and Silas, and so did a great many godfearing people and Greeks, as well as a number of the leading women.

[5]The Jews, full of resentment, enlisted the help of a gang from the market place, stirred up a crowd, and soon had the whole city in an uproar. They made for Jason's house, hoping to bring them before the People's Assembly; [6]however, they found only Jason and some of the brothers, and these they dragged before the city council, shouting, 'The people who have been turning the whole world upside down have come here now; [7]they have been staying at Jason's. They have broken Caesar's edicts by claiming that there is another king, Jesus.' [8]Hearing this, the citizens and the city councillors were alarmed, [9]and they made Jason and the rest give security before setting them free.

Fresh difficulties at Beroea

[10]When it was dark the brothers immediately sent Paul and Silas away to Beroea, where they went to the Jewish synagogue as soon as they arrived. [11]Here the Jews were more noble-minded than those in Thessalonica, and they welcomed the word very readily; every day they studied the scriptures to check whether it was true. [12]Many of them became believers, and so did many Greek women of high standing and a number of the men.

[13]When the Jews of Thessalonica came to learn that the word of God was being preached by Paul in Beroea as well, they went there to make trouble and stir up the people. [14]So the brothers arranged for Paul to go immediately as far as the coast, leaving Silas and Timothy behind. [15]Paul's escort took him as far as Athens, and went back with instructions for Silas and Timothy to rejoin Paul as soon as they could.

Paul in Athens

[16]Paul waited for them in Athens and there his whole soul was revolted at the sight of a city given over to idolatry. [17]In the synagogue he debated with the Jews and the godfearing,

and in the market place he debated every day with anyone whom he met. [18]Even a few Epicurean and Stoic philosophers argued with him. Some said, 'What can this parrot mean?' And, because he was preaching about Jesus and Resurrection, others said, 'He seems to be a propagandist for some outlandish gods.'

[19]They got him to accompany them to the Areopagus, where they said to him, 'Can we know what this new doctrine is that you are teaching? [20]Some of the things you say seemed startling to us and we would like to find out what they mean.' [21]The one amusement the Athenians and the foreigners living there seem to have is to discuss and listen to the latest ideas.

[22]So Paul stood before the whole council of the Areopagus and made this speech:

Paul's speech
before the council of the Areopagus

'Men of Athens, I have seen for myself how extremely scrupulous you are in all religious matters, [23]because, as I strolled round looking at your sacred monuments, I noticed among other things an altar inscribed: To An Unknown God. In fact, the unknown God you revere is the one I proclaim to you.

[24]'Since the God who made the world and everything in it is himself Lord of heaven and earth, he does not make his home in shrines made by human hands. [25]Nor is he in need of anything, that he should be served by human hands; on the contrary, it is he who gives everything—including life and breath—to everyone. [26]From one single principle he not only created the whole human race so that they could occupy the entire earth, but he decreed the times and limits of their habitation. [27]And he did this so that they might seek the deity and, by feeling their way towards him, succeed in finding him; and indeed he is not far from any of us, [28]since it is in him that we live, and move, and exist,[a] as indeed some of your own writers have said:

We are all his children.[b]

[29]'Since we are the children of God, we have no excuse for thinking that the deity looks like anything in gold, silver or stone

17a From the Gk poet Epimenides.
17b The Gk philosopher Aratus.

that has been carved and designed by a man.

[30]'But now, overlooking the times of ignorance, God is telling everyone everywhere that they must repent, [31]because he has fixed a day when the whole world will be judged in uprightness by a man he has appointed. And God has publicly proved this by raising him from the dead.'

[32]At this mention of rising from the dead, some of them burst out laughing; others said, 'We would like to hear you talk about this another time.' [33]After that Paul left them, [34]but there were some who attached themselves to him and became believers, among them Dionysius the Areopagite and a woman called Damaris, and others besides.

Foundation of the church of Corinth

18 After this Paul left Athens and went to Corinth, [2]where he met a Jew called Aquila whose family came from Pontus. He and his wife Priscilla had recently left Italy because an edict of Claudius had expelled all the Jews from Rome. Paul went to visit them, [3]and when he found they were tentmakers, of the same trade as himself, he lodged with them, and they worked together. [4]Every Sabbath he used to hold debates in the synagogues, trying to convert Jews as well as Greeks.

[5]After Silas and Timothy had arrived from Macedonia, Paul devoted all his time to preaching, declaring to the Jews that Jesus was the Christ. [6]When they turned against him and started to insult him, he took his cloak and shook it out in front of them,[a] saying, 'Your blood be on your own heads; from now on I will go to the gentiles with a clear conscience.' [7]Then he left the synagogue and moved to the house next door that belonged to a worshipper of God called Justus. [8]Crispus, president of the synagogue, and his whole household, all became believers in the Lord. Many Corinthians when they heard this became believers and were baptised. [9]One night the Lord spoke to Paul in a vision, 'Be fearless; speak out and do not keep silence: [10]I am with you. I have so many people that belong to me in this city that no one will attempt to hurt you.'

[11]So Paul stayed there preaching the word of God among them for eighteen months.

The Jews take Paul to court

[12]But while Gallio was proconsul of Achaia, the Jews made a concerted attack on Paul and brought him before the tribunal, saying, [13]'We accuse this man of persuading people to worship God in a way that breaks the Law.' [14]Before Paul could open his mouth, Gallio said to the Jews, 'Listen, you Jews. If this were a misdemeanour or a crime, it would be in order for me to listen to your plea; [15]but if it is only quibbles about words and names, and about your own Law, then you must deal with it yourselves—I have no intention of making legal decisions about these things.' [16]Then he began to hustle them out of the court, [17]and at once they all turned on Sosthenes, the synagogue president, and beat him in front of the tribunal. Gallio refused to take any notice at all.

Return to Antioch and departure for the third journey

[18]After staying on for some time, Paul took leave of the brothers and sailed for Syria, accompanied by Priscilla and Aquila. At Cenchreae he had his hair cut off, because of a vow he had made. [19]When they reached Ephesus, he left them, but first he went alone to the synagogue to debate with the Jews. [20]They asked him to stay longer, but he declined, [21]though when he took his leave he said, 'I will come back another time, God willing.' Then he sailed from Ephesus.

[22]He landed at Caesarea and went up to greet the church. Then he came down to Antioch [23]where he spent a short time before continuing his journey through the Galatian country and then through Phrygia, encouraging all the followers.

Apollos

[24]An Alexandrian Jew named Apollos[b] now arrived in Ephesus. He was an eloquent man, with a sound knowledge of the scriptures, and yet, [25]though he had been given instruction in the Way of the Lord and preached with great

18a cf. 13:47; 28:25.
18b cf. 1 Co 1:12; 3:4–11.

spiritual fervour and was accurate in all the details he taught about Jesus, he had experienced only the baptism of John. ²⁶He began to teach fearlessly in the synagogue and, when Priscilla and Aquila heard him, they attached themselves to him and gave him more detailed instruction about the Way.

²⁷When Apollos thought of crossing over to Achaia, the brothers encouraged him and wrote asking the disciples to welcome him. When he arrived there he was able by God's grace to help the believers considerably ²⁸by the energetic way he refuted the Jews in public, demonstrating from the scriptures that Jesus was the Christ.

The disciples of John at Ephesus

19 It happened that while Apollos was in Corinth, Paul made his way overland as far as Ephesus, where he found a number of disciples. ²When he asked, 'Did you receive the Holy Spirit when you became believers?' they answered, 'No, we were never even told there was such a thing as a Holy Spirit.' ³He asked, 'Then how were you baptised?' They replied, 'With John's baptism.' ⁴Paul said, 'John's baptism was a baptism of repentance; but he insisted that the people should believe in the one who was to come after him—namely Jesus.' ⁵When they heard this, they were baptised in the name of the Lord Jesus, ⁶and the moment Paul had laid hands on them the Holy Spirit came down on them, and they began to speak with tongues and to prophesy. ⁷There were about twelve of these men in all.

Foundation of the church of Ephesus

⁸He began by going to the synagogue, where he spoke out fearlessly and argued persuasively about the kingdom of God. He did this for three months, ⁹till the attitude of some of the congregation hardened into unbelief. As soon as they began attacking the Way in public, he broke with them and took his disciples apart to hold daily discussions in the lecture room of Tyrannus. ¹⁰This went on for two years, with the result that all the inhabitants of Asia, both Jews and Greeks, were able to hear the word of the Lord.

The Jewish exorcists

¹¹So remarkable were the miracles worked by God at Paul's hands ¹²that handkerchiefs or aprons which had touched him were taken to the sick, and they were cured of their illnesses, and the evil spirits came out of them. ¹³But some itinerant Jewish exorcists too tried pronouncing the name of the Lord Jesus over people who were possessed by evil spirits; they used to say, 'I adjure you by the Jesus whose spokesman is Paul.' ¹⁴Among those who did this were seven sons of Sceva, a Jewish chief priest. ¹⁵The evil spirit replied, 'Jesus I recognise, and Paul I know, but who are you?' ¹⁶and the man with the evil spirit hurled himself at them and overpowered first one and then another, and handled them so violently that they fled from that house stripped of clothing and badly mauled. ¹⁷Everybody in Ephesus, both Jews and Greeks, heard about this episode; everyone was filled with awe, and the name of the Lord Jesus came to be held in great honour.

¹⁸Some believers, too, came forward to admit in detail how they had used spells ¹⁹and a number of them who had practised magic collected their books and made a bonfire of them in public. The value of these was calculated to be fifty thousand silver pieces.

²⁰In this powerful way the word of the Lord spread more and more widely and successfully.

V: THE END OF PAUL'S MISSIONARY JOURNEYS
A PRISONER FOR CHRIST

Paul's plans

²¹When all this was over Paul made up his mind to go back to Jerusalem through Macedonia and Achaia. 'After I have been there,' he said, 'I must go on to see Rome as well.' ²²So he sent two of his helpers, Timothy and Erastus, ahead of him to Macedonia, while he remained for a time in Asia.

Ephesus: the silversmiths' riot

²³It was during this time that a serious disturbance broke out in connection with the Way. ²⁴A silversmith called Demetrius, who provided work for a large number of craftsmen making silver shrines of Diana, ²⁵called a general meeting of them with others in the same trade. 'As you know,' he said, 'it is on this industry that we depend for our prosperity. ²⁶Now you must have seen and heard how, not just in Ephesus but nearly everywhere in Asia, this man Paul has persuaded and converted a great number of people with his argument that gods made by hand are not gods at all. ²⁷This threatens not only to discredit our trade, but also to reduce the sanctuary of the great goddess Diana to unimportance. It could end up by taking away the prestige of a goddess venerated all over Asia, and indeed all over the world.' ²⁸This speech roused them to fury, and they started to shout, 'Great is Diana of the Ephesians!' ²⁹The whole town was filled with the uproar and the mob made a concerted rush to the theatre, dragging along two of Paul's Macedonian travelling companions, Gaius and Aristarchus. ³⁰Paul wanted to make an appeal to the people, but the disciples refused to let him; ³¹in fact, some of the Asiarchs, who were friends of his, sent messages urging him not to take the risk of going into the theatre.

³²By now everybody was shouting different things, till the assembly itself had no idea what was going on; most of them did not even know why they had gathered together. ³³Some of the crowd prevailed upon Alexander, whom the Jews pushed forward; he raised his hand for silence with the intention of explaining things to the people. ³⁴As soon as they realised he was a Jew, they all started shouting in unison, 'Great is Diana of the Ephesians!' and they kept this up for two hours. ³⁵When the town clerk eventually succeeded in calming the crowd, he said, 'Citizens of Ephesus! Is there anybody who does not know that the city of the Ephesians is the guardian of the temple of great Diana and of her statue that fell from heaven? ³⁶Nobody can contradict this and there is no need for you to get excited or do anything rash. ³⁷These men you have brought here are not guilty of any sacrilege or blasphemy against our goddess. ³⁸If Demetrius and the craftsmen he has with him want to complain about anyone, there are the assizes and the proconsuls; let them take the case to court. ³⁹And if you want to ask any more questions you must raise them in the regular assembly. ⁴⁰We could easily be charged with rioting for today's happenings: there is no ground for it all, and we can give no justification for this gathering.' When he had finished this speech he dismissed the assembly.

Paul leaves Ephesus

20 When the disturbance was over, Paul sent for the disciples and, after speaking words of encouragement to them, said good-bye and set out for Macedonia. ²On his way through those areas he said many words of encouragement to them and then made his way into Greece, ³where he spent three months. He was leaving by ship for Syria when a plot organised against him by the Jews made him decide to go back by way of Macedonia. ⁴He was accompanied by Sopater, son of Pyrrhus, who came from Beroea; Aristarchus and Secundus who came from Thessalonica; Gaius from Derbe, and Timothy, as well as Tychicus and Trophimus who were from Asia. ⁵They all went on to Troas where they waited for us. ⁶We ourselves left Philippi by ship after the days of Unleavened Bread and joined them five days later at Troas, where we stayed for a week.

Troas: Paul raises a dead man to life

⁷On the first day of the week we met for the breaking of bread. Paul was due to leave the next day, and he preached a sermon that went on till the middle of the night. ⁸A number of lamps were lit in the upstairs room where we were assembled, ⁹and as Paul went on and on, a young man called Eutychus who was sitting on the window-sill grew drowsy and was overcome by sleep and fell to the ground three floors below. He was picked up dead. ¹⁰Paul went down and stooped to clasp the boy to him, saying, 'There is no need to worry, there is still life in him.' ¹¹Then he went back upstairs where he broke the bread and ate and carried on talking till he left at daybreak. ¹²They took the boy away alive, and were greatly encouraged.

From Troas to Miletus

[13]We were now to go on ahead by sea, so we set sail for Assos, where we were to take Paul on board; this was what he had arranged, for he wanted to go overland. [14]When he rejoined us at Assos we took him aboard and went on to Mitylene. [15]The next day we sailed from there and arrived opposite Chios. The second day we touched at Samos and, after stopping at Trogyllium, made Miletus the next day. [16]Paul had decided to pass wide of Ephesus so as to avoid spending time in Asia, since he was anxious to be in Jerusalem, if possible, for the day of Pentecost.

Farewell to the elders of Ephesus

[17]From Miletus he sent for the elders of the church of Ephesus. [18]When they arrived he addressed these words to them:

'You know what my way of life has been ever since the first day I set foot among you in Asia, [19]how I have served the Lord in all humility, with all the sorrows and trials that came to me through the plots of the Jews. [20]I have not hesitated to do anything that would be helpful to you; I have preached to you and instructed you both in public and in your homes, [21]urging both Jews and Greeks to turn to God and to believe in our Lord Jesus.

[22]'And now you see me on my way to Jerusalem in captivity to the Spirit; I have no idea what will happen to me there, [23]except that the Holy Spirit, in town after town, has made it clear to me that imprisonment and persecution await me. [24]But I do not place any value on my own life, provided that I complete the mission the Lord Jesus gave me—to bear witness to the good news of God's grace.

[25]'I now feel sure that none of you among whom I have gone about proclaiming the kingdom will ever see my face again. [26]And so on this very day I swear that my conscience is clear as far as all of you are concerned, [27]for I have without faltering put before you the whole of God's purpose.

[28]'Be on your guard for yourselves and for all the flock of which the Holy Spirit has made you the guardians, to feed the Church of God which he bought with the blood of his own Son.

[29]'I know quite well that when I have gone fierce wolves will invade you and will have no mercy on the flock. [30]Even from your own ranks there will be men coming forward with a travesty of the truth on their lips to induce the disciples to follow them. [31]So be on your guard, remembering how night and day for three years I never slackened in counselling each one of you with tears. [32]And now I commend you to God and to the word of his grace that has power to build you up and to give you your inheritance among all the sanctified.

[33]'I have never asked anyone for money or clothes; [34]you know for yourselves that these hands of mine earned enough to meet my needs and those of my companions. [35]By every means I have shown you that we must exert ourselves in this way to support the weak, remembering the words of the Lord Jesus, who himself said, "There is more happiness in giving than in receiving." '[a]

[36]When he had finished speaking he knelt down with them all and prayed. [37]By now they were all in tears; they put their arms round Paul's neck and kissed him; [38]what saddened them most was his saying they would never see his face again. Then they escorted him to the ship.

The journey to Jerusalem

21 When we had at last torn ourselves away from them and put to sea, we set a straight course and arrived at Cos; the next day we reached Rhodes, and from there went on to Patara. [2]Here we found a ship bound for Phoenicia, so we went on board and sailed in her. [3]After sighting Cyprus and leaving it to port, we sailed to Syria and put in at Tyre, since the ship was to unload her cargo there. [4]We sought out the disciples and stayed there a week. Speaking in the Spirit, they kept telling Paul not to go on to Jerusalem, [5]but when our time was up we set off. Together with the women and children they all escorted us on our way till we were out of the town. When we reached the beach, we knelt down and prayed; [6]then, after saying good-bye to each other, we went aboard and they returned home.

[7]The end of our voyage from Tyre came when we landed at Ptolemais, where we greeted the brothers and stayed one day with them. [8]The next day we left and came to

---

20a This saying does not occur in the gospels.

Caesarea. Here we called on Philip the evangelist, one of the Seven, and stayed with him. [9]He had four unmarried daughters who were prophets. [10]When we had been there several days a prophet called Agabus arrived from Judaea. [11]He came up to us, took Paul's belt and tied up his own feet and hands, and said, 'This is what the Holy Spirit says, "The man to whom this girdle belongs will be tied up like this by the Jews in Jerusalem and handed over to the gentiles." ' [12]When we heard this, we and all the local people urged Paul not to go on to Jerusalem. [13]To this he replied, 'What are you doing, weeping and breaking my heart? For my part, I am ready not only to be bound but even to die in Jerusalem for the name of the Lord Jesus.' [14]And so, as he would not be persuaded, we gave up the attempt, saying, 'The Lord's will be done.'

Paul's arrival in Jerusalem

[15]After this we made our preparations and went on up to Jerusalem. [16]Some of the disciples from Caesarea accompanied us and took us to the house of a Cypriot with whom we were to lodge; he was called Mnason and had been one of the earliest disciples.

[17]On our arrival in Jerusalem the brothers gave us a very warm welcome. [18]The next day Paul went with us to visit James, and all the elders were present. [19]After greeting them he gave a detailed account of all that God had done among the gentiles through his ministry. [20]They gave glory to God when they heard this. Then they said, 'You see, brother, how thousands of Jews have now become believers, all of them staunch upholders of the Law; [21]and what they have heard about you is that you instruct all Jews living among the gentiles to break away from Moses, authorising them not to circumcise their children or to follow the customary practices. [22]What is to be done? A crowd is sure to gather, for they will hear that you have come. [23]So this is what we suggest that you should do; we have four men here who are under a vow; [24]take these men along and be purified with them and pay all the expenses connected with the shaving of their heads. This will let everyone know there is no truth in the reports they have heard about you, and that you too observe the Law by your way of life. [25]About the gentiles who have become believers, we have written giving them our decision that they must abstain from things

sacrificed to idols, from blood, from the meat of strangled animals and from illicit marriages.'

[26]So the next day Paul took the men along and was purified with them, and he visited the Temple to give notice of the time when the period of purification would be over and the offering would have to be presented on behalf of each of them.

Paul's arrest

[27]The seven days were nearly over when some Jews from Asia caught sight of him in the Temple and stirred up the crowd and seized him, [28]shouting, 'Men of Israel, help! This is the man who preaches to everyone everywhere against our people, against the Law and against this place. He has even profaned this Holy Place by bringing Greeks into the Temple.' [29]They had, in fact, previously seen Trophimus the Ephesian in the city with him and thought that Paul had brought him into the Temple.

[30]This roused the whole city; people came running from all sides; they seized Paul and dragged him out of the Temple, and the gates were closed behind them. [31]While they were setting about killing him, word reached the tribune of the cohort that there was tumult all over Jerusalem. [32]He immediately called out soldiers and centurions and charged down on the crowd, who stopped beating Paul when they saw the tribune and the soldiers. [33]When the tribune came up he took Paul into custody, had him bound with two chains and enquired who he was and what he had done. [34]People in the crowd called out different things, and since the noise made it impossible for him to get any positive information, the tribune ordered Paul to be taken into the fortress. [35]When Paul reached the steps, the crowd became so violent that he had to be carried by the soldiers; [36]and indeed the whole mob was after them, shouting, 'Do away with him!'

[37]Just as Paul was being taken into the fortress, he asked the tribune if he could have a word with him. The tribune said, 'You speak Greek, then? [38]Aren't you the Egyptian who started the recent revolt and led those four thousand cut-throats out into the desert?' [39]'I?' said Paul, 'I am a Jew and a citizen of the well-known city of Tarsus in Cilicia. Please give me permission to speak to the people.' [40]The man gave his consent

and Paul, standing at the top of the steps, raised his hand to the people for silence. A profound silence followed, and he started speaking to them in Hebrew.

Paul's address to the Jews of Jerusalem

22 'My brothers, my fathers, listen to what I have to say to you in my defence.' ²When they realised he was speaking in Hebrew, the silence was even greater than before. ³'I am a Jew', Paul said, 'and was born at Tarsus in Cilicia. I was brought up here in this city. It was under Gamaliel that I studied and was taught the exact observance of the Law of our ancestors. In fact, I was as full of duty towards God as you all are today. ⁴I even persecuted this Way to the death and sent women as well as men to prison in chains ⁵as the high priest and the whole council of elders can testify. I even received letters from them to the brothers in Damascus, which I took with me when I set off to bring prisoners back from there to Jerusalem for punishment.

⁶'It happened*a* that I was on that journey and nearly at Damascus when in the middle of the day a bright light from heaven suddenly shone round me. ⁷I fell to the ground and heard a voice saying, "Saul, Saul, why are you persecuting me?" ⁸I answered, "Who are you, Lord?" and he said to me, "I am Jesus the Nazarene, whom you are persecuting." ⁹The people with me saw the light but did not hear the voice which spoke to me. ¹⁰I said, "What am I to do, Lord?" The Lord answered, "Get up and go into Damascus, and there you will be told what you have been appointed to do." ¹¹Since the light had been so dazzling that I was blind, I got to Damascus only because my companions led me by the hand.

¹²'Someone called Ananias, a devout follower of the Law and highly thought of by all the Jews living there, ¹³came to see me; he stood beside me and said, "Brother Saul, receive your sight." Instantly my sight came back and I was able to see him. ¹⁴Then he said, "The God of our ancestors has chosen you to know his will, to see the Upright One and hear his own voice speaking, ¹⁵because you are to be his witness before all humanity, testifying to what you have seen and heard. ¹⁶And now why delay? Hurry and be baptised

and wash away your sins, calling on his name."

¹⁷'It happened that, when I got back to Jerusalem, and was praying in the Temple, I fell into a trance ¹⁸and then I saw him. "Hurry," he said, "leave Jerusalem at once; they will not accept the testimony you are giving about me." ¹⁹"Lord," I answered, "they know that I used to go from synagogue to synagogue, imprisoning and flogging those who believed in you; ²⁰and that when the blood of your witness Stephen was being shed, I, too, was standing by, in full agreement with his murderers, and in charge of their clothes." ²¹Then he said to me, "Go! I am sending you out to the gentiles far away." '

Paul the Roman citizen

²²So far they had listened to him, but at these words they began to shout, 'Rid the earth of the man! He is not fit to live!' ²³They were yelling, waving their cloaks and throwing dust into the air, ²⁴and so the tribune had him brought into the fortress and ordered him to be examined under the lash, to find out the reason for the outcry against him. ²⁵But when they had strapped him down Paul said to the centurion on duty, 'Is it legal for you to flog a man who is a Roman citizen and has not been brought to trial?' ²⁶When he heard this the centurion went and told the tribune; 'Do you realise what you are doing?' he said. 'This man is a Roman citizen.' ²⁷So the tribune came and asked him, 'Tell me, are you a Roman citizen?' Paul answered 'Yes'. ²⁸To this the tribune replied, 'It cost me a large sum to acquire this citizenship.' 'But I was born to it,' said Paul. ²⁹Then those who were about to examine him hurriedly withdrew, and the tribune himself was alarmed when he realised that he had put a Roman citizen in chains.

His appearance before the Sanhedrin

³⁰The next day, since he wanted to know for sure what charge the Jews were bringing, he freed Paul and gave orders for a meeting of the chief priests and the entire Sanhedrin; then he brought Paul down and set him in front of them.

22a =9; 26.

23 Paul looked steadily at the Sanhedrin and began to speak, 'My brothers, to this day I have conducted myself before God with a perfectly clear conscience.' ²At this the high priest Ananias ordered his attendants to strike him on the mouth. ³Then Paul said to him, 'God will surely strike you, you whitewashed wall! How can you sit there to judge me according to the Law, and then break the Law by ordering a man to strike me?' ⁴The attendants said, 'Are you insulting the high priest of God? ⁵Paul answered, 'Brothers, I did not realise it was the high priest; certainly scripture says, "*You will not curse your people's leader.*" ʼᵃ

⁶Now Paul was well aware that one party was made up of Sadducees and the other of Pharisees, so he called out in the Sanhedrin, 'Brothers, I am a Pharisee and the son of Pharisees. It is for our hope in the resurrection of the dead that I am on trial.' ⁷As soon as he said this, a dispute broke out between the Pharisees and Sadducees, and the assembly was split between the two parties. ⁸For the Sadducees say there is neither resurrection, nor angel, nor spirit, while the Pharisees accept all three. ⁹The shouting grew louder, and some of the scribes from the Pharisees' party stood up and protested strongly, 'We find nothing wrong with this man. Suppose a spirit has spoken to him, or an angel?' ¹⁰Feeling was running high, and the tribune, afraid that they would tear Paul to pieces, ordered his troops to go down and haul him out and bring him into the fortress.

¹¹Next night, the Lord appeared to him and said, 'Courage! You have borne witness for me in Jerusalem, now you must do the same in Rome.'

The conspiracy of the Jews against Paul

¹²When it was day, the Jews held a secret meeting at which they made a vow not to eat or drink until they had killed Paul. ¹³More than forty of them entered this pact, ¹⁴and they went to the chief priests and elders and told them, 'We have made a solemn vow to let nothing pass our lips until we have killed Paul. ¹⁵Now it is up to you and the Sanhedrin together to apply to the tribune to bring him down to you, as though you meant to examine his case more closely; we, on our side, are prepared to dispose of him before he reaches you.'

¹⁶But the son of Paul's sister heard of the ambush they were laying and made his way into the fortress and told Paul, ¹⁷who called one of the centurions and said, 'Take this young man to the tribune; he has something to tell him.' ¹⁸So the man took him to the tribune, and reported, 'The prisoner Paul summoned me and requested me to bring this young man to you; he has something to tell you.' ¹⁹Then the tribune took him by the hand and drew him aside and questioned him in private, 'What is it you have to tell me?' ²⁰He replied, 'The Jews have made a plan to ask you to take Paul down to the Sanhedrin tomorrow, as though they meant to enquire more closely into his case. ²¹Do not believe them. There are more than forty of them lying in wait for him, and they have vowed not to eat or drink until they have got rid of him. They are ready now and only waiting for your order to be given.' ²²The tribune let the young man go with this order, 'Tell no one that you have given me this information.'

Paul transferred to Caesarea

²³Then he summoned two of the centurions and said, 'Get two hundred soldiers ready to leave for Caesarea by the third hour of the night with seventy cavalry and two hundred auxiliaries; ²⁴provide horses for Paul, and deliver him unharmed to Felix the governor.' ²⁵He also wrote a letter in these terms:

²⁶'Claudius Lysias to his Excellency the governor Felix, greetings. ²⁷This man had been seized by the Jews and would have been murdered by them; but I came on the scene with my troops and got him away, having discovered that he was a Roman citizen. ²⁸Wanting to find out what charge they were making against him, I brought him before their Sanhedrin. ²⁹I found that the accusation concerned disputed points of their Law, but that there was no charge deserving death or imprisonment. ³⁰Acting on information that there was a conspiracy against the man, I hasten to send him to you, and have notified his accusers that they must state their case against him in your presence.'

³¹The soldiers carried out their orders;

23a Ex 22:27. Ananias became high priest in AD 47.

they took Paul and escorted him by night to Antipatris. [32]Next day they left the mounted escort to go on with him and returned to the fortress. [33]On arriving at Caesarea the escort delivered the letter to the governor and handed Paul over to him. [34]When he had read it, he asked Paul what province he came from. Learning that he was from Cilicia he said, [35]'I will hear your case as soon as your accusers are here too.' Then he ordered him to be held in Herod's praetorium.

The case before Felix

24 Five days later the high priest Ananias came down with some of the elders and an advocate named Tertullus, and they laid information against Paul before the governor. [2]Paul was called, and Tertullus opened for the prosecution, 'Your Excellency, Felix, the unbroken peace we enjoy and the reforms this nation owes to your foresight [3]are matters we accept, always and everywhere, with all gratitude. [4]I do not want to take up too much of your time, but I urge you in your graciousness to give us a brief hearing. [5]We have found this man a perfect pest; he stirs up trouble among Jews the world over and is a ringleader of the Nazarene sect. [6]He has even attempted to profane the Temple. We placed him under arrest.[a] [7] [8]If you ask him you can find out for yourself the truth of all our accusations against this man.' [9]The Jews supported him, asserting that these were the facts.

[10]When the governor motioned him to speak, Paul answered:

Paul's speech before the Roman governor

'I know that you have administered justice over this nation for many years, and I can therefore speak with confidence in my defence. [11]As you can verify for yourself, it is no more than twelve days since I went up to Jerusalem on pilgrimage, [12]and it is not true that they ever found me arguing with anyone or stirring up the mob, either in the Temple, in the synagogues, or about the town; [13]neither can they give you any proof of the accusations they are making against me now.

[14]'What I do admit to you is this: it is according to the Way, which they describe as a sect, that I worship the God of my ancestors, retaining my belief in all points of the Law and in what is written in the prophets; [15]and I hold the same hope in God as they do that there will be a resurrection of the upright and the wicked alike. [16]In these things, I, as much as they, do my best to keep a clear conscience at all times before God and everyone.

[17]'After several years I came to bring relief-money to my nation[b] and to make offerings; [18]it was in connection with these that they found me in the Temple; I had been purified, and there was no crowd involved, and no disturbance. [19]But some Jews from Asia—these are the ones who should have appeared before you and accused me of whatever they had against me. [20]At least let those who are present say what crime they held against me when I stood before the Sanhedrin, [21]unless it were to do with this single claim, when I stood up among them and called out, "It is about the resurrection of the dead that I am on trial before you today." '

Paul's captivity at Caesarea

[22]At this, Felix, who was fairly well informed about the Way, adjourned the case, saying, 'When Lysias the tribune comes down I will give judgement about your case.' [23]He then gave orders to the centurion that Paul should be kept under arrest but free from restriction, and that none of his own people should be prevented from seeing to his needs.

[24]Some days later Felix came with his wife Drusilla who was a Jewess. He sent for Paul and gave him a hearing on the subject of faith in Christ Jesus. [25]But when Paul began to treat of uprightness, self-control and the coming Judgement, Felix took fright and said, 'You may go for the present; I will send for you when I find it convenient.' [26]At the same time he had hopes of receiving money from Paul, and for this reason he sent for him frequently and had talks with him.

[27]When two years came to an end, Felix was succeeded by Porcius Festus and, being anxious to gain favour with the Jews, Felix left Paul in custody.

24a Several witnesses add 'intending to judge him according to our Law, [7] but the tribune Lysias intervened and took him out of our hands by force,[8] ordering the accusers to appear before you'.
24b cf. 1 Co 16:1.

Paul appeals to Caesar

25 Three days after his arrival in the province, Festus went up to Jerusalem from Caesarea. ²The chief priests and leaders of the Jews informed him of the case against Paul, ³urgently asking him to support them against him, and to have him transferred to Jerusalem. They were preparing an ambush to murder him on the way. ⁴But Festus replied that Paul was in custody in Caesarea, and that he would be going back there shortly himself. ⁵He said, 'Let your authorities come down with me, and if there is anything wrong about the man, they can bring a charge against him.'

⁶After staying with them for eight or ten days at the most, he went down to Caesarea and the next day he took his seat on the tribunal and had Paul brought in. ⁷As soon as Paul appeared, the Jews who had come down from Jerusalem surrounded him, making many serious accusations which they were unable to substantiate. ⁸Paul's defence was this, 'I have committed no offence whatever against either Jewish law, or the Temple, or Caesar.' ⁹Festus was anxious to gain favour with the Jews, so he said to Paul, 'Are you willing to go up to Jerusalem and be tried on these charges before me there?' ¹⁰But Paul replied, 'I am standing before the tribunal of Caesar and this is where I should be tried. I have done the Jews no wrong, as you very well know. ¹¹If I am guilty of committing any capital crime, I do not ask to be spared the death penalty. But if there is no substance in the accusations these persons bring against me, no one has a right to surrender me to them. I appeal to Caesar.' ¹²Then Festus conferred with his advisers and replied, 'You have appealed to Caesar; to Caesar you shall go.'

Paul appears before King Agrippa

¹³Some days later King Agrippa and Bernice arrived in Caesarea and paid their respects to Festus. ¹⁴Their visit lasted several days, and Festus put Paul's case before the king, saying, 'There is a man here whom Felix left behind in custody, ¹⁵and while I was in Jerusalem the chief priests and elders of the Jews laid information against him, demanding his condemnation. ¹⁶But I told them that Romans are not in the habit of surrendering any man, until the accused confronts his accusers and is given an opportunity to defend himself against the charge. ¹⁷So they came here with me, and I wasted no time but took my seat on the tribunal the very next day and had the man brought in. ¹⁸When confronted with him, his accusers did not charge him with any of the crimes I had expected; ¹⁹but they had some argument or other with him about their own religion and about a dead man called Jesus whom Paul alleged to be alive. ²⁰Not feeling qualified to deal with questions of this sort, I asked him if he would be willing to go to Jerusalem to be tried there on this issue. ²¹But Paul put in an appeal for his case to be reserved for the judgement of the emperor, so I ordered him to be remanded until I could send him to Caesar.' ²²Agrippa said to Festus, 'I should like to hear the man myself.' He answered, 'Tomorrow you shall hear him.'

²³So the next day Agrippa and Bernice arrived in great state and entered the audience chamber attended by the tribunes and the city notables; and Festus ordered Paul to be brought in. ²⁴Then Festus said, 'King Agrippa, and all here present with us, you see before you the man about whom the whole Jewish community has petitioned me, both in Jerusalem and here, loudly protesting that he ought not to be allowed to remain alive. ²⁵For my own part I am satisfied that he has committed no capital crime, but when he himself appealed to the emperor I decided to send him. ²⁶But I have nothing definite that I can write to his Imperial Majesty about him; that is why I have produced him before you all, and before you in particular, King Agrippa, so that after the examination I may have something to write. ²⁷It seems to me pointless to send a prisoner without indicating the charges against him.'

26 Then Agrippa said to Paul, 'You have leave to speak on your own behalf.' And Paul held up his hand and began his defence:

Paul's speech before King Agrippa

²'I consider myself fortunate, King Agrippa, in that it is before you I am to answer today all the charges made against me by the Jews, ³the more so because you are an expert in matters of custom and controversy among the Jews. So I beg you to listen to me patiently.

⁴'My manner of life from my youth, a life spent from the beginning among my own

people and in Jerusalem, is common knowledge among the Jews. [5]They have known me for a long time and could testify, if they would, that I followed the strictest party in our religion and lived as a Pharisee. [6]And now it is for my hope in the promise made by God to our ancestors that I am on trial, [7]the promise that our twelve tribes, constant in worship night and day, hope to attain. For that hope, Your Majesty, I am actually put on trial by Jews! [8]Why does it seem incredible to you that God should raise the dead?

[9]'As for me, I once thought it was my duty to use every means to oppose the name of Jesus the Nazarene. [10]This I did in Jerusalem; I myself threw many of God's holy people into prison, acting on authority from the chief priests, and when they were being sentenced to death I cast my vote against them. [11]I often went round the synagogues inflicting penalties, trying in this way to force them to renounce their faith; my fury against them was so extreme that I even pursued them into foreign cities.

[12]'On such an expedition I was going to Damascus, armed with full powers and a commission from the chief priests,[a] [13]and in the middle of the day as I was on my way, Your Majesty, I saw a light from heaven shining more brilliantly than the sun round me and my fellow-travellers. [14]We all fell to the ground, and I heard a voice saying to me in Hebrew, "Saul, Saul, why are you persecuting me? It is hard for you, kicking against the goad. " [15]Then I said, "Who are you, Lord?" And the Lord answered, "I am Jesus, whom you are persecuting. [16]But get up and stand on your feet, for I have appeared to you for this reason: to appoint you as my servant and as witness of this vision in which you have seen me, and of others in which I shall appear to you. [17]*I shall rescue you* from the people and from *the nations to whom I send you* [18]*to open their eyes*, so that they may turn *from darkness to light*,[b] from the dominion of Satan to God, and receive, through faith in me, forgiveness of their sins and a share in the inheritance of the sanctified."

[19]'After that, King Agrippa, I could not disobey the heavenly vision. [20]On the contrary I started preaching, first to the people of Damascus, then to those of Jerusalem and all Judaean territory, and also to the gentiles, urging them to repent and turn to God, proving their change of heart by their deeds. [21]This was why the Jews laid hands on me in the Temple and tried to do away with me. [22]But I was blessed with God's help, and so I have stood firm to this day, testifying to great and small alike, saying nothing more than what the prophets and Moses himself said would happen: [23]that the Christ was to suffer and that, as the first to rise from the dead, he was to proclaim a light for our people and for the gentiles.'

His hearers' reactions

[24]He had reached this point in his defence when Festus shouted out, 'Paul, you are out of your mind; all that learning of yours is driving you mad.' [25]But Paul answered, 'Festus, your Excellency, I am not mad: I am speaking words of sober truth and good sense. [26]The king understands these matters, and to him I now speak fearlessly. I am confident that nothing of all this comes as a surprise to him; after all, these things were not done in a corner. [27]King Agrippa, do you believe in the prophets? I know you do.' [28]At this Agrippa said to Paul, 'A little more, and your arguments would make a Christian of me.' [29]Paul replied, 'Little or much, I wish before God that not only you but all who are listening to me today would come to be as I am—except for these chains.'

[30]At this the king rose to his feet, with the governor and Bernice and those who sat there with them. [31]When they had retired they talked together and agreed, 'This man is doing nothing that deserves death or imprisonment.' [32]And Agrippa remarked to Festus, 'The man could have been set free if he had not appealed to Caesar.'

The departure for Rome

27 When it had been decided that we should sail to Italy, Paul and some other prisoners were handed over to a centurion called Julius, of the Augustan cohort. [2]We boarded a vessel from Adramyttium bound for ports on the Asiatic coast and put to sea; we had Aristarchus with us, a Macedonian of Thessalonica. [3]Next day we put in at Sidon, and Julius was considerate enough to

---

26a =9; 22
26b Jr 1:5–8 followed by Is 42:16.

allow Paul to go to his friends to be looked after.

⁴From there we put to sea again, but as the winds were against us we sailed under the lee of Cyprus, ⁵then across the open sea off Cilicia and Pamphylia, taking a fortnight to reach Myra in Lycia. ⁶There the centurion found an Alexandrian ship leaving for Italy and put us aboard.

⁷For some days we made little headway, and we had difficulty in making Cnidus. The wind would not allow us to touch there, so we sailed under the lee of Crete off Cape Salmone ⁸and struggled along the coast until we came to a place called Fair Havens, near the town of Lasea.

Storm and shipwreck

⁹A great deal of time had been lost, and navigation was already hazardous, since it was now well after the time of the Fast, so Paul gave them this warning, ¹⁰'Friends, I can see this voyage will be dangerous and that we will run considerable risk of losing not only the cargo and the ship but also our lives as well.' ¹¹But the centurion took more notice of the captain and the ship's owner than of what Paul was saying; ¹²and since the harbour was unsuitable for wintering, the majority were for putting out from there in the hope of wintering at Phoenix—a harbour in Crete, facing south-west and north-west.

¹³A southerly breeze sprang up and, thinking their objective as good as reached, they weighed anchor and began to sail past Crete, close inshore. ¹⁴But it was not long before a hurricane, the 'north-easter' as they call it, burst on them from across the island. ¹⁵The ship was caught and could not keep head to wind, so we had to give way to the wind and let ourselves be driven. ¹⁶We ran under the lee of a small island called Cauda and managed with some difficulty to bring the ship's boat under control. ¹⁷Having hauled it up they used it to undergird the ship; then, afraid of running aground on the Syrtis banks, they floated out the sea-anchor and so let themselves drift. ¹⁸As we were thoroughly storm-bound, the next day they began to jettison the cargo, ¹⁹and the third day they threw the ship's gear overboard with their own hands. ²⁰For a number of days both the sun and the stars were invisible and the storm raged unabated until at last we gave up all hope of surviving.

²¹Then, when they had been without food for a long time, Paul stood up among the men. 'Friends,' he said, 'you should have listened to me and not put out from Crete. You would have spared yourselves all this damage and loss. ²²But now I ask you not to give way to despair. There will be no loss of life at all, only of the ship. ²³Last night there appeared beside me an angel of the God to whom I belong and whom I serve, ²⁴and he said, "Do not be afraid, Paul. You are destined to appear before Caesar, and God grants you the safety of all who are sailing with you." ²⁵So take courage, friends; I trust in God that things will turn out just as I was told; ²⁶but we are to be stranded on some island.'

²⁷On the fourteenth night we were being driven one way and another in the Adriatic, when about midnight the crew sensed that land of some sort was near. ²⁸They took soundings and found twenty fathoms; after a short interval they sounded again and found fifteen fathoms. ²⁹Then, afraid that we might run aground somewhere on a reef, they dropped four anchors from the stern and prayed for daylight. ³⁰When the crew tried to escape from the ship and lowered the ship's boat into the sea as though they meant to lay out anchors from the bows, Paul said to the centurion and his men, ³¹'Unless those men stay on board you cannot hope to be saved.' ³²So the soldiers cut the boat's ropes and let it drop away.

³³Just before daybreak Paul urged them all to have something to eat. 'For fourteen days', he said, 'you have been in suspense, going hungry and eating nothing. ³⁴I urge you to have something to eat; your safety depends on it. Not a hair of any of your heads will be lost.' ³⁵With these words he took some bread, gave thanks to God in view of them all, broke it and began to eat. ³⁶They all plucked up courage and took something to eat themselves. ³⁷In all we were two hundred and seventy-six souls on board that ship. ³⁸When they had eaten what they wanted they lightened the ship by throwing the corn overboard into the sea.

³⁹When day came they did not recognise the land, but they could make out a bay with a beach; they planned to run the ship aground on this if they could. ⁴⁰They slipped the anchors and let them fall into the sea, and at the same time loosened the lashings of

the rudders; then, hoisting the foresail to the wind, they headed for the beach. ⁴¹But the cross-currents carried them into a shoal and the vessel ran aground. The bows were wedged in and stuck fast, while the stern began to break up with the pounding of the waves.

⁴²The soldiers planned to kill the prisoners for fear that any should swim off and escape. ⁴³But the centurion was determined to bring Paul safely through and would not let them carry out their plan. He gave orders that those who could swim should jump overboard first and so get ashore, ⁴⁴and the rest follow either on planks or on pieces of wreckage. In this way it happened that all came safe and sound to land.

Waiting in Malta

28 Once we had come safely through, we discovered that the island was called Malta. ²The inhabitants treated us with unusual kindness. They made us all welcome by lighting a huge fire because it had started to rain and the weather was cold. ³Paul had collected a bundle of sticks and was putting them on the fire when a viper brought out by the heat attached itself to his hand. ⁴When the inhabitants saw the creature hanging from his hand they said to one another, 'That man must be a murderer; he may have escaped the sea, but divine justice would not let him live.' ⁵However, he shook the creature off into the fire and came to no harm, ⁶although they were expecting him at any moment to swell up or drop dead on the spot. After they had waited a long time without seeing anything out of the ordinary happen to him, they changed their minds and began to say he was a god.

⁷In that neighbourhood there were estates belonging to the chief man of the island, whose name was Publius. He received us and entertained us hospitably for three days. ⁸It happened that Publius' father was in bed, suffering from fever and dysentery. Paul went in to see him, and after a prayer he laid his hands on the man and healed him. ⁹When this happened, the other sick people on the island also came and were cured; ¹⁰they honoured us with many marks of respect, and when we sailed they put on board the provisions we needed.

From Malta to Rome

¹¹At the end of three months we set sail in a ship that had wintered in the island; she came from Alexandria and her figurehead was the Twins. ¹²We put in at Syracuse and spent three days there; ¹³from there we followed the coast up to Rhegium. After one day there a south wind sprang up and on the second day we made Puteoli, ¹⁴where we found some brothers and had the great encouragement of staying a week with them. And so we came to Rome. ¹⁵When the brothers there heard about us they came to meet us, as far as the Forum of Appius and the Three Taverns. When Paul saw them he thanked God and took courage. ¹⁶On our arrival in Rome Paul was allowed to stay in lodgings of his own with the soldier who guarded him.

Paul makes contact with the Roman Jews

¹⁷After three days he called together the leading Jews. When they had assembled, he said to them, 'Brothers, although I have done nothing against our people or the customs of our ancestors, I was arrested in Jerusalem and handed over to the Romans. ¹⁸They examined me and would have set me free, since they found me guilty of nothing involving the death penalty; ¹⁹but the Jews lodged an objection, and I was forced to appeal to Caesar, though not because I had any accusation to make against my own nation. ²⁰That is why I have urged you to see me and have a discussion with me, for it is on account of the hope of Israel that I wear this chain.'

²¹They answered, 'We have received no letters from Judaea about you, nor has any of the brothers arrived here with any report or story of anything to your discredit. ²²We think it would be as well to hear your own account of your position; all we know about this sect is that it encounters opposition everywhere.'

Paul's declaration to the Roman Jews

²³So they arranged a day with him and a large number of them visited him at his lodgings. He put his case to them, testifying to the kingdom of God and trying to persuade them about Jesus, arguing from the Law of Moses

and the prophets from early morning until evening; [24]and some were convinced by what he said, while the rest were sceptical. [25]So they disagreed among themselves and, as they went away, Paul had one last thing to say to them, 'How aptly the Holy Spirit spoke when he told your ancestors through the prophet Isaiah:

[26]*Go and say to this people:*
Listen and listen but never understand!
Look and look but never perceive!
[27]*This people's heart is torpid,*
their ears dulled,
   they have shut their eyes tight,
to avoid using their eyes to see,
   their ears to hear,

using their heart to understand,
changing their ways
   and being healed by me. [a]

[28]'You must realise, then, that this salvation of God has been sent to the gentiles; and they will listen to it.'[29] [b]

Epilogue

[30]He spent the whole of the two years in his own rented lodging. He welcomed all who came to visit him, [31]proclaiming the kingdom of God and teaching the truth about the Lord Jesus Christ with complete fearlessness and without any hindrance from anyone.

INTRODUCTION TO
THE LETTERS OF PAUL

The general lines of Paul's life as a Christian missionary are clear enough from Acts, though there are some inconsistencies between that picture and the information from Paul's own letters. In the last decade of his apostolate he wrote to the churches he had founded, in response to questions, worries and difficulties they were experiencing. With these as his starting-point he ranges widely over the vital issues of Christian theology and life, discussing often very local issues in the light of basic principles. The letters also provide a fascinating portrait of Paul, capable of affection and anger, working passionately and selflessly for Christ and the churches he loved. Bearing suffering and persecution in unison with his Master, Paul is inspired always by his knowledge of sharing Christ's life as servant of God.

The letters are traditionally printed in decreasing order of length, first letters to communities, then those to individuals. The most probable chronological order is:

1 EARLY EPISTLES   1–2 Thessalonians

2 THE GREAT EPISTLES   1–2 Corinthians, Galatians, Romans, possibly Philippians

---

28a Is 6:9–10; cf. 13:47; 18:6.
28b Some MSS add v. 29 'And when he had said this, the Jews left, arguing hotly among themselves.'

| 3 CAPTIVITY EPISTLES | Colossians, Ephesians (authorship disputed), Philemon |
| 4 PASTORAL EPISTLES | (authorship doubtful) 1–2 Timothy, Titus |

THE LETTER TO THE
ROMANS

As well as being the longest of Paul's letters (and so printed first) Rm is a noble synthesis of his teaching on the Law and faith, a theme already treated in Ga. Writing to the mixed community of Jewish and gentile origin at Rome, Paul wants partly to introduce himself before a proposed visit and partly to give help on the problems which caused friction between the two sections in the community. It is a calmer treatment than Ga, and Paul is less negative towards the Law.

The main point of the letter is that the Law is powerless to save, and gives only knowledge of sin, not strength. Salvation is offered to all humanity through faith in Christ, who delivers from the retribution of God. This faith is expressed in baptism, by which Christians are buried with Christ and rise with Christ to new life as adopted sons and members of Christ, sharing his life and his experiences. Among the most striking of all Pauline passages are chh. 9—11: by reflection on Scripture, Paul explores the agonising problem of the mystery of the refusal of his brothers the Jews to recognise Christ.

PLAN OF THE LETTER

Salvation by Faith   1:16—11
I   Justification   1:16—4
   A   The Retribution of God against Gentile and Jew   1:18—3:20
   B   Faith and the Judgement of God   3:21–31
   C   The Example of Abraham   4
II   Salvation   5—11
   A   Deliverance from Sin, Death and Law   5:12—7
   B   The Christian's Spiritual Life   8
   C   The Place of Israel   9—11
Exhortation   12:1—15:13
Epilogue   15:14—16:27

ROMANS
THE LETTER OF PAUL
TO THE CHURCH IN ROME

Address

1 From Paul, a servant of Christ Jesus, called to be an apostle, ²set apart for the service of the gospel that God promised long ago through his prophets in the holy scriptures.

³This is the gospel concerning his Son who, in terms of human nature ⁴was born a descendant of David and who, in terms of the Spirit and of holiness, was designated Son of God in power by resurrection from the dead: Jesus Christ, our Lord, ⁵through whom we have received grace and our apostolic mission of winning the obedience of faith among all the nations for the honour of his name. ⁶You are among these, and by his call you belong to Jesus Christ. ⁷To you all, God's beloved in Rome, called to be his holy people. Grace and peace from God our Father and the Lord Jesus Christ.

Thanksgiving and prayer

⁸First I give thanks to my God through Jesus Christ for all of you because your faith is talked of all over the world. ⁹God, whom I serve with my spirit in preaching the gospel of his Son, is my witness that I continually mention you in my prayers, ¹⁰asking always that by some means I may at long last be enabled to visit you, if it is God's will. ¹¹For I am longing to see you so that I can convey to you some spiritual gift that will be a lasting strength, ¹²or rather that we may be strengthened together through our mutual faith, yours and mine. ¹³I want you to be quite certain too, brothers, that I have often planned to visit you—though up to the present I have always been prevented—in the hope that I might work as fruitfully among you as I have among the gentiles elsewhere. ¹⁴I have an obligation to Greeks as well as barbarians, to the educated as well as the ignorant, ¹⁵and hence the eagerness on my part to preach the gospel to you in Rome too.

SALVATION BY FAITH

I: JUSTIFICATION

The theme stated

¹⁶For I see no reason to be ashamed of the gospel; it is God's power for the salvation of everyone who has faith—Jews first, but Greeks as well—¹⁷for in it is revealed the saving justice of God: a justice based on faith and addressed to faith. As it says in scripture: *Anyone who is upright through faith will live.* ᵃ

A: THE RETRIBUTION OF GOD AGAINST GENTILE AND JEW

God's retribution against the gentiles

¹⁸The retribution of God from heaven is being revealed against the ungodliness and injustice of human beings who in their injustice hold back the truth. ¹⁹For what can be known

---

1a Hab 2:4 LXX.

about God is perfectly plain to them, since God has made it plain to them: [20]ever since the creation of the world, the invisible existence of God and his everlasting power have been clearly seen by the mind's understanding of created things. And so these people have no excuse: [21]they knew God and yet they did not honour him as God or give thanks to him, but their arguments became futile and their uncomprehending minds were darkened. [22]While they claimed to be wise, in fact they were growing so stupid [23]that *they exchanged the glory* of the immortal God *for an imitation,*[b] for the image of a mortal human being, or of birds, or animals, or crawling things.

[24]That is why God abandoned them in their inmost cravings to filthy practices of dishonouring their own bodies—[25]because they *exchanged God's truth* for a lie and have worshipped and served the creature instead of the Creator, who is blessed for ever. Amen.

[26]That is why God abandoned them to degrading passions: [27]why their women have exchanged natural intercourse for unnatural practices; and the men, in a similar fashion, too, giving up normal relations with women, are consumed with passion for each other, men doing shameful things with men and receiving in themselves due reward for their perversion.

[28]In other words, since they would not consent to acknowledge God, God abandoned them to their unacceptable thoughts and indecent behaviour. [29]And so now they are steeped in all sorts of injustice, rottenness, greed and malice; full of envy, murder, wrangling, treachery and spite, [30]libellers, slanderers, enemies of God, rude, arrogant and boastful, enterprising in evil, rebellious to parents, [31]without brains, honour, love or pity. [32]They are well aware of God's ordinance: that those who behave like this deserve to die—yet they not only do it, but even applaud others who do the same.

The Jews are not exempt from the retribution of God

2 So no matter who you are, if you pass judgement you have no excuse. It is yourself that you condemn when you judge others, since you behave in the same way as those you are condemning. [2]We are well aware that people who behave like that are justly condemned by God. [3]But you—when you judge those who behave like this while you are doing the same yourself—do you think you will escape God's condemnation? [4]Or are you not disregarding his abundant goodness, tolerance and patience, failing to realise that this generosity of God is meant to bring you to repentance? [5]Your stubborn refusal to repent is only storing up retribution for yourself on that Day of retribution when God's just verdicts will be made known. [6]*He will repay everyone as their deeds deserve.*[a] [7]For those who aimed for glory and honour and immortality by persevering in doing good, there will be eternal life; [8]but for those who out of jealousy have taken for their guide not truth but injustice, there will be the fury of retribution. [9]Trouble and distress will come to every human being who does evil—Jews first, but Greeks as well; [10]glory and honour and peace will come to everyone who does good—Jews first, but Greeks as well. [11]*There is no favouritism with God.*[b]

The Law will not save them

[12]All those who have sinned without the Law will perish without the Law; and those under the Law who have sinned will be judged by the Law. [13]For the ones that God will justify are not those who have heard the Law but those who have kept the Law. [14]So, when gentiles, not having the Law, still through their own innate sense behave as the Law commands, then, even though they have no Law, they are a law for themselves. [15]They can demonstrate the effect of the Law engraved on their hearts, to which their own conscience bears witness; since they are aware of various considerations, some of which accuse them, while others provide them with a defence . . . on the day when, [16]according to the gospel that I preach, God, through Jesus Christ, judges all human secrets.

[17]If you can call yourself a Jew, and you really trust in the Law, and are proud of your God, [18]and know his will, and tell right from wrong because you have been taught by the

---

1b Jr 2:11.
2a Ps 62:12.
2b Dt 10:17.

Law; [19]if you are confident that you are a guide to the blind and a beacon to those in the dark, [20]that you can teach the ignorant and instruct the unlearned because the Law embodies all knowledge and all truth—[21]so then, in teaching others, do you teach yourself as well? You preach that there is to be no stealing, but do you steal? [22]You say that adultery is forbidden, but do you commit adultery? You detest the worship of objects, but do you desecrate holy things yourself? [23]If, while you are boasting of the Law, you disobey it, then you are bringing God into contempt. [24]As scripture says: *It is your fault that the name of God is held in contempt among the nations.*[c]

Circumcision will not save them

[25]Circumcision has its value if you keep the Law; but if you go on breaking the Law, you are no more circumcised than the uncircumcised. [26]And if an uncircumcised man keeps the commands of the Law, will not his uncircumcised state count as circumcision? [27]More, the man who, in his native uncircumcised state, keeps the Law, is a condemnation of you, who, by your concentration on the letter and on circumcision, actually break the Law. [28]Being a Jew is not only having the outward appearance of a Jew, and circumcision is not only a visible physical operation. [29]The real Jew is the one who is inwardly a Jew, and real circumcision is in the heart, a thing not of the letter but of the spirit. He may not be praised by any human being, but he will be praised by God.

God's promises will not save them

3 Is there any benefit, then, in being a Jew? Is there any advantage in being circumcised? [2]A great deal, in every way. First of all, it was to the Jews that the message of God was entrusted. [3]What if some of them were unfaithful? Do you think their lack of faith could cancel God's faithfulness? [4]Out of the question! God will always be true even if *no human being can be relied on.*[a] As scripture says: *That you may show your saving justice when you pass sentence and your victory may appear when you give judgement.* [5]But if our injustice serves to bring God's saving justice

into view, can we say that God is unjust when—to use human terms—he brings his retribution down on us? [6]Out of the question! It would mean that God could not be the judge of the world. [7]You might as well say that if my untruthfulness makes God demonstrate his truthfulness, to his greater glory, then I should not be judged to be a sinner at all. [8]In this case, the slanderous report some people are spreading would be true, that we teach that one should do evil that good may come of it. In fact such people are justly condemned.

All are guilty

[9]Well: are we any better off? Not at all: we have already indicted Jews and Greeks as being all alike under the dominion of sin. [10]As scripture says:

Not one of them is upright, not a single one,
[11]*not a single one is wise,*
    not a single one seeks God.
[12]*All have turned away, all alike turned sour,*
    not one of them does right, not a single one.
[13]*Their throats are wide-open graves,*
    their tongues seductive.
Viper's venom behind their lips;
[14]*their speech is full of cursing and bitterness.*
[15]*Their feet quick to shed innocent blood,*
[16]*wherever they go there is havoc and ruin.*
[17]*They do not know the way of peace,*
[18]*there is no fear of God before their eyes.*

[19]Now we are well aware that whatever the Law says is said for those who are subject to the Law, so that every mouth may be silenced, and the whole world brought under the judgement of God. [20]So then, *no human being can be found upright at the tribunal* of God by keeping the Law; all that the Law does is to tell us what is sinful.

B: FAITH AND THE JUDGEMENT OF GOD

The revelation of God's judgement

[21]God's saving justice was witnessed by the Law and the Prophets, but now it has been revealed altogether apart from law: [22]God's saving justice given through faith in Jesus

---

2c Ezk 36:20.
3a In vv. 4–20 Paul uses numerous quotations from the Pss and Is 59:7–8.

Christ to all who believe. [23]No distinction is made: all have sinned and lack God's glory, [24]and all are justified by the free gift of his grace through being set free in Christ Jesus. [25]God appointed him as a sacrifice for reconciliation, through faith, by the shedding of his blood, and so showed his justness; first for the past, when sins went unpunished because he held his hand; [26]and now again for the present age, to show how he is just and justifies everyone who has faith in Jesus.

What faith does

[27]So what becomes of our boasts? There is no room for them. On what principle— that only actions count? No; that faith is what counts, [28]since, as we see it, a person is justified by faith and not by doing what the Law tells him to do. [29]Do you think God is the God only of the Jews, and not of gentiles too? Most certainly of gentiles too, [30]since there is only one God; he will justify the circumcised by their faith, and he will justify the uncircumcised through their faith. [31]Are we saying that the Law has been made pointless by faith? Out of the question; we are placing the Law on its true footing.

C: THE EXAMPLE OF ABRAHAM

Abraham justified by faith

4 Then what do we say about Abraham, the ancestor from whom we are descended physically? [2]If Abraham had been justified because of what he had done, then he would have had something to boast about. But not before God: [3]does not scripture say: *Abraham put his faith in God and this was reckoned to him as uprightness?*[a] [4]Now, when someone works, the wages for this are not considered as a favour but as due; [5]however, when someone, without working, puts faith in the one who justifies the godless, it is this faith that is reckoned as uprightness. [6]David, too, says the same: he calls someone blessed if God attributes uprightness to that person, apart from any action undertaken:

[7]*How blessed are those*
    whose offence is forgiven,
    whose sin is blotted out.

[8]*How blessed are those*
    to whom the Lord imputes no guilt.[b]

Justified before circumcision

[9]Is this blessing only for the circumcised, or is it said of the uncircumcised as well? Well, we said of Abraham that *his faith was reckoned to him as uprightness.* [10]Now how did this come about? When he was already circumcised, or before he had been circumcised? Not when he had been circumcised, but while he was still uncircumcised; [11]and *circumcision*[c] was given to him later, *as a sign* and a guarantee that the faith which he had while still uncircumcised was reckoned to him as uprightness. In this way, Abraham was to be the ancestor of all believers who are uncircumcised, so that they might be reckoned as upright; [12]as well as the ancestor of those of the circumcision who not only have their circumcision but who also follow our ancestor Abraham along the path of faith that he trod before he was circumcised.

Not justified by obedience to the Law

[13]For the promise to Abraham and his descendants that he should inherit the world was not through the Law, but through the uprightness of faith. [14]For if it is those who live by the Law who will gain the inheritance, faith is worthless and the promise is without force; [15]for the Law produces nothing but God's retribution, and it is only where there is no Law that it is possible to live without breaking the Law. [16]That is why the promise is to faith, so that it comes as a free gift and is secure for all the descendants, not only those who rely on the Law but all those others who rely on the faith of Abraham, the ancestor of us all [17](as scripture says: *I have made you the father of many nations*). Abraham is our father in the eyes of God, in whom he put his faith, and who brings the dead to life and calls into existence what does not yet exist.

Abraham's faith a model of Christian faith

[18]Though there seemed no hope, he hoped and believed that he was to become *father of*

4a Gn 15:6.
4b Ps 32:1–2.
4c Quotations about Abraham from Gn (17:10; 17:5; 15:5; 17:17).

many nations in fulfilment of the promise: *Just so will your descendants be.* [19]Even the thought that his body was as good as dead—he was about a hundred years old—and that Sarah's womb was dead too did not shake his faith. [20]Counting on the promise of God, he did not doubt or disbelieve, but drew strength from faith and gave glory to God, [21]fully convinced that whatever God promised he has the power to perform. [22]This is the faith that was *reckoned to him as uprightness.* [23]And the word 'reckoned' in scripture applies not only to him; [24]it is there for our sake too—our faith, too, will be 'reckoned' [25]because we believe in him who raised from the dead our Lord Jesus who was *handed over to death for our sins*[d] and raised to life for our justification.

II: SALVATION

Faith guarantees salvation

5 So then, now that we have been justified by faith, we are at peace with God through our Lord Jesus Christ; [2]it is through him, by faith, that we have been admitted into God's favour in which we are living, and look forward exultantly to God's glory. [3]Not only that; let us exult, too, in our hardships, understanding that hardship develops perseverance, [4]and perseverance develops a tested character, something that gives us hope, [5]and a hope which will not let us down, because the love of God has been poured into our hearts by the Holy Spirit which has been given to us. [6]When we were still helpless, at the appointed time, Christ died for the godless. [7]You could hardly find anyone ready to die even for someone upright; though it is just possible that, for a really good person, someone might undertake to die. [8]So it is proof of God's own love for us, that Christ died for us while we were still sinners. [9]How much more can we be sure, therefore, that, now that we have been justified by his death, we shall be saved through him from the retribution of God. [10]For if, while we were enemies, we were reconciled to God through the death of his Son, how much more can we be sure that, being now reconciled, we shall be saved by his life. [11]What is more, we are filled with exultant trust in God, through our Lord Jesus Christ, through whom we have already gained our reconciliation.

A: DELIVERANCE FROM SIN, DEATH AND LAW

Adam and Jesus Christ

[12]Well then; it was through one man that sin *came into the world,*[a] and through sin death, and thus death has spread through the whole human race because everyone has sinned. [13]Sin already existed in the world before there was any law, even though sin is not reckoned when there is no law. [14]Nonetheless death reigned over all from Adam to Moses, even over those whose sin was not the breaking of a commandment, as Adam's was. He prefigured the One who was to come . . .

[15]There is no comparison between the free gift and the offence. If death came to many through the offence of one man, how much greater an effect the grace of God has had, coming to so many and so plentifully as a free gift through the one man Jesus Christ! [16]Again, there is no comparison between the gift and the offence of one man. One single offence brought condemnation, but now, after many offences, have come the free gift and so acquittal! [17]It was by one man's offence that death came to reign over all, but how much greater the reign in life of those who receive the fullness of grace and the gift of saving justice, through the one man, Jesus Christ. [18]One man's offence brought condemnation on all humanity; and one man's good act has brought justification and life to all humanity. [19]Just as by one man's disobedience many were made sinners, so by one man's obedience are many to be made upright. [20]When law came on the scene, it was to multiply the offences. But however

4d Is 53:6.
5a Ws 2:24.

much sin increased, grace was always greater; [21]so that as sin's reign brought death, so grace was to rule through saving justice that leads to eternal life through Jesus Christ our Lord.

Baptism

6 What should we say then? Should we remain in sin so that grace may be given the more fully? [2]Out of the question! We have died to sin; how could we go on living in it? [3]You cannot have forgotten that all of us, when we were baptised into Christ Jesus, were baptised into his death. [4]So by our baptism into his death we were buried with him, so that as Christ was raised from the dead by the Father's glorious power, we too should begin living a new life. [5]If we have been joined to him by dying a death like his, so we shall be by a resurrection like his; [6]realising that our former self was crucified with him, so that the self which belonged to sin should be destroyed and we should be freed from the slavery of sin. [7]Someone who has died, of course, no longer has to answer for sin.

[8]But we believe that, if we died with Christ, then we shall live with him too. [9]We know that Christ has been raised from the dead and will never die again. Death has no power over him any more. [10]For by dying, he is dead to sin once and for all, and now the life that he lives is life with God. [11]In the same way, you must see yourselves as being dead to sin but alive for God in Christ Jesus.

Holiness, not sin, to be the master

[12]That is why you must not allow sin to reign over your mortal bodies and make you obey their desires; [13]or give any parts of your bodies over to sin to be used as instruments of evil. Instead, give yourselves to God, as people brought to life from the dead, and give every part of your bodies to God to be instruments of uprightness; [14]and then sin will no longer have any power over you — you are living not under law, but under grace.

The Christian is freed
from the slavery of sin

[15]What is the implication? That we are free to sin, now that we are not under law but under grace? Out of the question! [16]You know well that if you undertake to be some-

body's slave and obey him, you are the slave of him you obey: you can be the slave either of sin which leads to death, or of obedience which leads to saving justice. [17]Once you were slaves of sin, but thank God you have given whole-hearted obedience to the pattern of teaching to which you were introduced; [18]and so, being freed from serving sin, you took uprightness as your master. [19]I am putting it in human terms because you are still weak human beings: as once you surrendered yourselves as servants to immorality and to a lawlessness which results in more lawlessness, now you have to surrender yourselves to uprightness which is to result in sanctification.

The reward of sin
and the reward of uprightness

[20]When you were the servants of sin, you felt no obligation to uprightness, [21]and what did you gain from living like that? Experiences of which you are now ashamed, for that sort of behaviour ends in death. [22]But, now you are set free from sin and bound to the service of God, your gain will be sanctification and the end will be eternal life. [23]For the wage paid by sin is death; the gift freely given by God is eternal life in Christ Jesus our Lord.

The Christian is freed
from slavery to the Law

7 As people who are familiar with the Law, brothers, you cannot have forgotten that the law can control a person only during that person's lifetime. [2]A married woman, for instance, is bound to her husband by law, as long as he lives, but when her husband dies all her legal obligation to him as husband is ended. [3]So if she were to have relations with another man while her husband was still alive, she would be termed an adulteress; but if her husband dies, her legal obligation comes to an end and if she then has relations with another man, that does not make her an adulteress. [4]In the same way you, my brothers, through the body of Christ have become dead to the Law and so you are able to belong to someone else, that is, to him who was raised from the dead to make us live fruitfully for God. [5]While we were still living by our natural inclinations, the sinful passions aroused by the Law were working in all parts of our bodies to make us live lives

which were fruitful only for death. [6]But now we are released from the Law, having died to what was binding us, and so we are in a new service, that of the spirit, and not in the old service of a written code.

The function of the Law

[7]What should we say, then? That the Law itself is sin? Out of the question! All the same, if it had not been for the Law, I should not have known what sin was; for instance, I should not have known what it meant to covet if the Law had not said: *You are not to covet.*[a] [8]But, once it found the opportunity through that commandment, sin produced in me all kinds of covetousness; as long as there is no Law, sin is dead.

[9]Once, when there was no Law, I used to be alive; but when the commandment came, sin came to life [10]and I died. The commandment was meant to bring life but I found it brought death, [11]because sin, finding its opportunity by means of the commandment, *beguiled*[b] me and, by means of it, killed me. [12]So then, the Law is holy, and what it commands is holy and upright and good. [13]Does that mean that something good resulted in my dying? Out of the question! But sin, in order to be identified as sin, caused my death through that good thing, and so it is by means of the commandment that sin shows its unbounded sinful power.

The inward struggle

[14]We are well aware that the Law is spiritual: but I am a creature of flesh and blood sold as a slave to sin. [15]I do not understand my own behaviour; I do not act as I mean to, but I do things that I hate. [16]While I am acting as I do not want to, I still acknowledge the Law as good, [17]so it is not myself acting, but the sin which lives in me. [18]And really, I know of nothing good living in me—in my natural self, that is—for though the will to do what is good is in me, the power to do it is not: [19]the good thing I want to do, I never do; the evil thing which I do not want—that is what I do. [20]But every time I do what I do not want to, then it is not myself acting, but the sin that lives in me.

[21]So I find this rule: that for me, where I want to do nothing but good, evil is close at my side. [22]In my inmost self I dearly love God's law, [23]but I see that acting on my body there is a different law which battles against the law in my mind. So I am brought to be a prisoner of that law of sin which lives inside my body.

[24]What a wretched man I am! Who will rescue me from this body doomed to death? [25]God—thanks be to him—through Jesus Christ our Lord.

So it is that I myself with my mind obey the law of God, but in my disordered nature I obey the law of sin.

B: THE CHRISTIAN'S SPIRITUAL LIFE

The life of the spirit

8 Thus, condemnation will never come to those who are in Christ Jesus, [2]because the law of the Spirit which gives life in Christ Jesus has set you free from the law of sin and death. [3]What the Law could not do because of the weakness of human nature, God did, sending his own Son in the same human nature as any sinner to be a sacrifice for sin, and condemning sin in that human nature. [4]This was so that the Law's requirements might be fully satisfied in us as we direct our lives not by our natural inclinations but by the Spirit. [5]Those who are living by their natural inclinations have their minds on the things human nature desires; those who live in the Spirit have their minds on spiritual things. [6]And human nature has nothing to look forward to but death, while the Spirit looks forward to life and peace, [7]because the outlook of disordered human nature is opposed to God, since it does not submit to God's Law, and indeed it cannot, [8]and those who live by their natural inclinations can never be pleasing to God. [9]You, however, live not by your natural inclinations, but by the Spirit, since the Spirit of God has made a home in you. Indeed, anyone who does not have the Spirit of Christ does not belong to him. [10]But when Christ is in you, the body is dead because of sin but the spirit is alive because you have been justified; [11]and if the Spirit of him who raised Jesus from the dead

7a Ex 20:17.
7b Gn 3:13.

has made his home in you, then he who raised Christ Jesus from the dead will give life to your own mortal bodies through his Spirit living in you.

¹²So then, my brothers, we have no obligation to human nature to be dominated by it. ¹³If you do live in that way, you are doomed to die; but if by the Spirit you put to death the habits originating in the body, you will have life.

Children of God

¹⁴All who are guided by the Spirit of God are sons of God; ¹⁵for what you received was not the spirit of slavery to bring you back into fear; you received the Spirit of adoption, enabling us to cry out, '*Abba*, Father!' ¹⁶The Spirit himself joins with our spirit to bear witness that we are children of God. ¹⁷And if we are children, then we are heirs, heirs of God and joint-heirs with Christ, provided that we share his suffering, so as to share his glory.

Glory as our destiny

¹⁸In my estimation, all that we suffer in the present time is nothing in comparison with the glory which is destined to be disclosed for us, ¹⁹for the whole creation is waiting with eagerness for the children of God to be revealed. ²⁰It was not for its own purposes that creation had frustration imposed on it, but for the purposes of him who imposed it — ²¹with the intention that the whole creation itself might be freed from its slavery to corruption and brought into the same glorious freedom as the children of God. ²²We are well aware that the whole creation, until this time, has been groaning in labour pains. ²³And not only that: we too, who have the first-fruits of the Spirit, even we are groaning inside ourselves, waiting with eagerness for our bodies to be set free. ²⁴In hope, we already have salvation; in hope, not visibly present, or we should not be hoping — nobody goes on hoping for something which is already visible. ²⁵But having this hope for what we cannot yet see, we are able to wait for it with persevering confidence.

²⁶And as well as this, the Spirit too comes to help us in our weakness, for, when we do not know how to pray properly, then the Spirit personally makes our petitions for us in groans that cannot be put into words; ²⁷and he who can see into all hearts knows what the Spirit means because the prayers that the Spirit makes for God's holy people are always in accordance with the mind of God.

God has called us to share his glory

²⁸We are well aware that God works with those who love him, those who have been called in accordance with his purpose, and turns everything to their good. ²⁹He decided beforehand who were the ones destined to be moulded to the pattern of his Son, so that he should be the eldest of many brothers; ³⁰it was those so destined that he called; those that he called, he justified, and those that he has justified he has brought into glory.

A hymn to God's love

³¹After saying this, what can we add? If God is for us, who can be against us? ³²Since he did not spare his own Son, but gave him up for the sake of all of us, then can we not expect that with him he will freely give us all his gifts? ³³Who can bring any accusation against those that God has chosen? *When God grants saving justice* ³⁴*who can condemn?*[a] Are we not sure that it is Christ Jesus, who died — yes and more, who was raised from the dead and is at God's right hand — and who is adding his plea for us? ³⁵Can anything cut us off from the love of Christ — can hardships or distress, or persecution, or lack of food and clothing, or threats or violence; ³⁶as scripture says:

For your sake we are being massacred
    all day long,
treated as sheep to be slaughtered?[b]

³⁷No; we come through all these things triumphantly victorious, by the power of him who loved us. ³⁸For I am certain of this: neither death nor life, nor angels, nor principalities, nothing already in existence and nothing still to come, nor any power, ³⁹nor the heights nor the depths, nor any created thing whatever, will be able to come between us and the love of God, known to us in Christ Jesus our Lord.

8a Is 50:8.
8b Ps 44:22.

C: THE PLACE OF ISRAEL[a]

The privileges of Israel

9 This is the truth and I am speaking in Christ, without pretence, as my conscience testifies for me in the Holy Spirit; [2]there is great sorrow and unremitting agony in my heart: [3]I could pray that I myself might be accursed and cut off from Christ, if this could benefit the brothers who are my own flesh and blood. [4]They are Israelites; it was they who were adopted as children, the glory was theirs and the covenants; to them were given the Law and the worship of God and the promises. [5]To them belong the fathers and out of them, so far as physical descent is concerned, came Christ who is above all, God, blessed for ever. Amen.

God has kept his promise

[6]It is not that God's promise has failed. Not all born Israelites belong to Israel, [7]and not all the descendants of Abraham count as his children, for

Isaac is the one through whom
your Name will be carried on.

[8]That is, it is not by being children through physical descent that people become children of God; it is the children of the promise that are counted as the heirs. [9]The actual words of the promise were: *I shall come back to you at this season, and Sarah will have a son.* [10]Even more to the point is what was said to Rebecca when she was pregnant by our ancestor, Isaac, [11]before her children were born, so that neither had yet done anything either good or bad, but in order that it should be God's choice which prevailed [12]—not human merit, but his call—she was told: *the elder one will serve the younger.* [13]Or as scripture says elsewhere: *I loved Jacob but hated Esau.*

God is not unjust

[14]What should we say, then? That God is unjust? Out of the question! [15]For speaking to Moses, he said: *I am gracious to those to whom I am gracious and I take pity on those on whom I take pity.* [16]So it is not a matter of what any person wants or what any person does, but only of God having mercy.

[17]Scripture says to Pharaoh: *I raised you up for this reason,* to display my power in you and to have my name talked of throughout the world. [18]In other words, if God wants to show mercy on someone, he does so, and if he wants to harden someone's heart, he does so.

[19]Then you will ask me, 'How then can he ever blame anyone, since no one can oppose his will?' [20]But you—who do you think you, a human being, are, to answer back to God? *Something that was made, can it say to its maker: why did you make me* this shape? [21]A potter surely has the right over his clay to make out of the same lump either a pot for special use or one for ordinary use.

[22]But suppose that God, although all the time he wanted to reveal his retribution and demonstrate his power, has with great patience gone on putting up with those who are the instruments of his retribution and designed to be destroyed; [23]so that he may make known the glorious riches ready for the people who are the instruments of his faithful love and were long ago prepared for that glory. [24]We are that people, called by him not only out of the Jews but out of the gentiles too.

All has been foretold in the Old Testament

[25]Just as he says in the book of Hosea: *I shall tell those who were not my people, 'You are my people,' and I shall take pity on those on whom I had no pity.* [26]And in the very place where they were told, 'You are not my people,' they will be told that they are 'children of the living God'.* [27]And about Israel, this is what Isaiah cried out: *Though the people of Israel are like the sand of the sea, only a remnant will be saved;* [28]*for without hesitation or delay the Lord will execute his sentence on the earth.* [29]As Isaiah foretold: *Had the Lord Sabaoth not left us a few survivors, we should be like Sodom, we should be the same as Gomorrah.*

[30]What should we say, then? That the gentiles, although they were not looking for saving justice, found it, and this was the saving justice that comes of faith; [31]while Israel, looking for saving justice by lawkeeping, did not succeed in fulfilling the Law. [32]And why? Because they were trying to find it in actions and not in faith, and so they stumbled over the *stumbling-stone*—[33]as

---

9a The quotations in chh. 9—11 are too frequent to be placed.

it says in scripture: *Now I am laying in Zion a stumbling-stone, a rock to trip people up; but he who relies on this will not be brought to disgrace.*

Israel fails to see that it is God who makes us holy

10 Brothers, my dearest wish and my prayer to God is for them, that they may be saved. [2]I readily testify to their fervour for God, but it is misguided. [3]Not recognising God's saving justice they have tried to establish their own, instead of submitting to the saving justice of God. [4]But the Law has found its fulfilment in Christ so that all who have faith will be justified.

The testimony of Moses

[5]Moses writes of the saving justice that comes by the Law and says that *whoever complies with it will find life in it.* [6]But the saving justice of faith says this: *Do not think in your heart, 'Who will go up to heaven?'* — [7]that is to bring Christ down; or *'Who will go down to the depths?'*—that is to bring Christ back from the dead. [8]What does it say, then? *The word is very near to you; it is in your mouth and in your heart,* that is, the word of faith, the faith which we preach, [9] that if you declare with your mouth that Jesus is Lord, and if you believe with your heart that God raised him from the dead, then you will be saved. [10]It is by believing with the heart that you are justified, and by making the declaration with your lips that you are saved. [11]When scripture says: *No one who relies on this will be brought to disgrace,* [12]it makes no distinction between Jew and Greek: the same Lord is the Lord of all, and his generosity is offered to all who appeal to him, [13]for *all who call on the name of the Lord will be saved.*

Israel has no excuse

[14]How then are they to call on him if they have not come to believe in him? And how can they believe in him if they have never heard of him? And how will they hear of him unless there is a preacher for them? [15]And how will there be preachers if they are not sent? As scripture says: *How beautiful are the feet of the messenger of good news.* [16]But in fact they have not all responded to the good news. As Isaiah says: *Lord, who has given credence to what they have heard from us?* [17]But it is in that way faith comes, from hearing, and that means hearing the word of Christ.

[18]Well then, I say, is it possible that they have not heard? Indeed they have: *in the entire earth their voice stands out, their message reaches the whole world.* [19]Well, another question, then: is it possible that Israel did not understand? In the first place Moses said: *I shall rouse you to jealousy with a non-people, I shall exasperate you with a stupid nation.* [20]And Isaiah is even bold enough to say: *I have let myself be found by those who did not seek me; I have let myself be seen by those who did not consult me;* [21]and referring to Israel, he says: *All day long I have been stretching out my hands to a disobedient and rebellious people.*

The remnant of Israel

11 What I am saying is this: is it possible that *God abandoned his people?* Out of the question! I too am an Israelite, descended from Abraham, of the tribe of Benjamin. [2]God never abandoned his own people to whom, ages ago, he had given recognition. Do you not remember what scripture says about Elijah and how he made a complaint to God against Israel: [3]*Lord, they have put your prophets to the sword, torn down your altars. I am the only one left, and now they want to kill me?* [4]And what was the prophetic answer given? *I have spared for myself seven thousand men that have not bent the knee to Baal.* [5]In the same way, then, in our own time, there is a remnant, set aside by grace. [6]And since it is by grace, it cannot now be by good actions, or grace would not be grace at all!

[7]What follows? Israel failed to find what it was seeking; only those who were chosen found it and the rest had their minds hardened; [8]just as it says in scripture: *God has infused them with a spirit of lethargy; until today they have not eyes to see or ears to hear.* [9]David too says: *May their own table prove a trap for them,* a pitfall and *a snare; let that be their retribution.* [10]*May their eyes grow so dim they cannot see, and their backs be bent for ever.*

The Jews to be restored in the future

[11]What I am saying is this: Was this stumbling to lead to their final downfall? Out of the question! On the contrary, their failure has

brought salvation for the gentiles, in order to stir them to envy. [12]And if their fall has proved a great gain to the world, and their loss has proved a great gain to the gentiles—how much greater a gain will come when all is restored to them!

[13]Let me say then to you gentiles that, as far as I am an apostle to the gentiles, I take pride in this work of service; [14]and I want it to be the means of rousing to envy the people who are my own blood-relations and so of saving some of them. [15]Since their rejection meant the reconciliation of the world, do you know what their re-acceptance will mean? Nothing less than life from the dead!

The Jews are still the chosen people

[16]When the first-fruits are made holy, so is the whole batch; and if the root is holy, so are the branches. [17]Now suppose that some branches were broken off, and you are wild olive, grafted among the rest to share with the others the rich sap of the olive tree; [18]then it is not for you to consider yourself superior to the other branches; and if you start feeling proud, think: it is not you that sustain the root, but the root that sustains you. [19]You will say, 'Branches were broken off on purpose for me to be grafted in.' True; [20]they through their unbelief were broken off, and you are established through your faith. So it is not pride that you should have, but fear: [21]if God did not spare the natural branches, he might not spare you either. [22]Remember God's severity as well as his goodness: his severity to those who fell, and his goodness to you as long as you persevere in it; if not, you too will be cut off. [23]And they, if they do not persevere in their unbelief, will be grafted in; for it is within the power of God to graft them back again. [24]After all, if you, cut off from what was by nature a wild olive, could then be grafted unnaturally on to a cultivated

olive, how much easier will it be for them, the branches that naturally belong there, to be grafted on to the olive tree which is their own.

The conversion of the Jews

[25]I want you to be quite certain, brothers, of this mystery, to save you from *congratulating yourselves on your own good sense*: part of Israel had its mind hardened, but only until the gentiles have wholly come in; [26]and this is how all Israel will be saved. As scripture says:

> *From Zion will come the Redeemer,*
> *he will remove godlessness from Jacob.*
> [27]*And this will be my covenant with them,*
> *when I take their sins away.*

[28]As regards the gospel, they are enemies, but for your sake; but as regards those who are God's choice, they are still well loved for the sake of their ancestors. [29]There is no change of mind on God's part about the gifts he has made or of his choice.

[30]Just as you were in the past disobedient to God but now you have been shown mercy, through their disobedience; [31]so in the same way they are disobedient now, so that through the mercy shown to you they too will receive mercy. [32]God has imprisoned all human beings in their own disobedience only to show mercy to them all.

A hymn to God's mercy and wisdom

[33]How rich and deep are the wisdom and the knowledge of God! We cannot reach to the root of his decisions or his ways. [34]*Who has ever known the mind of the Lord? Who has ever been his adviser?* [35]*Who has given anything to him, so that his presents come only as a debt returned?* [36]Everything there is comes from him and is caused by him and exists for him. To him be glory for ever! Amen.

EXHORTATION

Spiritual worship

12I urge you, then, brothers, remembering the mercies of God, to offer your bodies as a living sacrifice, dedicated and acceptable to God; that is the kind of worship

for you, as sensible people. [2]Do not model your behaviour on the contemporary world, but let the renewing of your minds transform you, so that you may discern for yourselves what is the will of God—what is good and acceptable and mature.

Humility and charity

[3]And through the grace that I have been given, I say this to every one of you: never pride yourself on being better than you really are, but think of yourself dispassionately, recognising that God has given to each one his measure of faith. [4]Just as each of us has various parts in one body, and the parts do not all have the same function: [5]in the same way, all of us, though there are so many of us, make up one body in Christ, and as different parts we are all joined to one another. [6]Then since the gifts that we have differ according to the grace that was given to each of us: if it is a gift of prophecy, we should prophesy as much as our faith tells us; [7]if it is a gift of practical service, let us devote ourselves to serving; if it is teaching, to teaching; [8]if it is encouraging, to encouraging. When you give, you should give generously from the heart; if you are put in charge, you must be conscientious; if you do works of mercy, let it be because you enjoy doing them. [9]Let love be without any pretence. Avoid what is evil; stick to what is good. [10]In brotherly love let your feelings of deep affection for one another come to expression and regard others as more important than yourself. [11]In the service of the Lord, work not halfheartedly but with conscientiousness and an eager spirit. [12]Be joyful in hope, persevere in hardship; keep praying regularly; [13]share with any of God's holy people who are in need; look for opportunities to be hospitable.

Charity to everyone, including enemies

[14]Bless your persecutors; never curse them, bless them. [15]Rejoice with others when they rejoice, and be sad with those in sorrow. [16]Give the same consideration to all others alike. Pay no regard to social standing, but meet humble people on their own terms. *Do not congratulate yourself on your own wisdom.*[a] [17]Never pay back evil with evil, but *bear in mind the ideals that all regard with respect.* [18]As much as possible, and to the utmost of your ability, be at peace with everyone. [19]Never try to get revenge: leave that, my dear friends, to the Retribution. As scripture says: *Vengeance is mine—I will pay them back*, the

Lord promises. [20]And more: *If your enemy is hungry, give him something to eat; if thirsty, something to drink. By this, you will be heaping red-hot coals on his head.* [21]Do not be mastered by evil, but master evil with good.

Submission to civil authority

13 Everyone is to obey the governing authorities, because there is no authority except from God and so whatever authorities exist have been appointed by God. [2]So anyone who disobeys an authority is rebelling against God's ordinance; and rebels must expect to receive the condemnation they deserve. [3]Magistrates bring fear not to those who do good, but to those who do evil. So if you want to live with no fear of authority, live honestly and you will have its approval; [4]it is there to serve God for you and for your good. But if you do wrong, then you may well be afraid; because it is not for nothing that the symbol of authority is the sword: it is there to serve God, too, as his avenger, to bring retribution to wrongdoers. [5]You must be obedient, therefore, not only because of this retribution, but also for conscience's sake. [6]And this is why you should pay taxes, too, because the authorities are all serving God as his agents, even while they are busily occupied with that particular task. [7]Pay to each one what is due to each: taxes to the one to whom tax is due, tolls to the one to whom tolls are due, respect to the one to whom respect is due, honour to the one to whom honour is due.

Love and Law

[8]The only thing you should owe to anyone is love for one another, for to love the other person is to fulfil the law. [9]All these: *You shall not commit adultery, You shall not kill, You shall not steal, You shall not covet*, and all the other commandments that there are, are summed up in this single phrase: *You must love your neighbour as yourself.*[a] [10]Love can cause no harm to your neighbour, and so love is the fulfilment of the Law.

Children of the light

[11]Besides, you know the time has come; the moment is here for you to stop sleeping and

---

12a Pr 3:7, followed by Lv 19:18; Pr 25:21–22.
13a Ex 20:13–17 summed up in Lv 19:18.

wake up, because by now our salvation is nearer than when we first began to believe. [12]The night is nearly over, daylight is on the way; so let us throw off everything that belongs to the darkness and equip ourselves for the light. [13]Let us live decently, as in the light of day; with no orgies or drunkenness, no promiscuity or licentiousness, and no wrangling or jealousy. [14]Let your armour be the Lord Jesus Christ, and stop worrying about how your disordered natural inclinations may be fulfilled.

Charity towards the scrupulous

14 Give a welcome to anyone whose faith is not strong, but do not get into arguments about doubtful points. [2]One person may have faith enough to eat any kind of food; another, less strong, will eat only vegetables. [3]Those who feel free to eat freely are not to condemn those who are unwilling to eat freely; nor must the person who does not eat freely pass judgement on the one who does — because God has welcomed him. [4]And who are you, to sit in judgement over somebody else's servant? Whether he deserves to be upheld or to fall is for his own master to decide; and he shall be upheld, for the Lord has power to uphold him. [5]One person thinks that some days are holier than others, and another thinks them all equal. Let each of them be fully convinced in his own mind. [6]The one who makes special observance of a particular day observes it in honour of the Lord. So the one who eats freely, eats in honour of the Lord, making his thanksgiving to God; and the one who does not, abstains from eating in honour of the Lord and makes his thanksgiving to God. [7]For none of us lives for himself and none of us dies for himself; [8]while we are alive, we are living for the Lord, and when we die, we die for the Lord: and so, alive or dead, we belong to the Lord. [9]It was for this purpose that Christ both died and came to life again: so that he might be Lord of both the dead and the living. [10]Why, then, does one of you make himself judge over his brother, and why does another among you despise his brother? All of us will have to stand in front of the judgement-seat of God: [11]as scripture says: *By my own life* says the Lord, *every knee shall bow before me, every*

tongue shall give glory to God. [a] [12]It is to God, then, that each of us will have to give an account of himself.

[13]Let us each stop passing judgement, therefore, on one another and decide instead that none of us will place obstacles in any brother's way, or anything that can bring him down. [14]I am sure, and quite convinced in the Lord Jesus, that no food is unclean in itself; it is only if someone classifies any kind of food as unclean, then for him it is unclean. [15]And indeed, if through any kind of food you are causing offence to a brother, then you are no longer being guided by love. You are not to let the food that you eat cause the ruin of anyone for whom Christ died. [16]A privilege of yours must not be allowed to give rise to harmful talk; [17]for it is not eating and drinking that make the kingdom of God, but the saving justice, the peace and the joy brought by the Holy Spirit. [18]It is the person who serves Christ in these things that will be approved by God and respected by everyone. [19]So then, let us be always seeking the ways which lead to peace and the ways in which we can support one another. [20]Do not wreck God's work for the sake of food. Certainly all foods are clean; but all the same, any kind can be evil for someone to whom it is an offence to eat it. [21]It is best to abstain from eating any meat, or drinking any wine, or from any other activity which might cause a brother to fall away, or to be scandalised, or to weaken.

[22]Within yourself, before God, hold on to what you already believe. Blessed is the person whose principles do not condemn his practice. [23]But anyone who eats with qualms of conscience is condemned, because this eating does not spring from faith — and every action which does not spring from faith is sin.

15 It is for us who are strong to bear with the susceptibilities of the weaker ones, and not please ourselves. [2]Each of us must consider his neighbour's good, so that we support one another. [3]Christ did not indulge his own feelings, either; indeed, as scripture says: *The insults of those who insult you fall on me.* [a] [4]And all these things which were written so long ago were written so that we, learning perseverance and the encouragement which the scriptures give, should have hope. [5]Now

14a Is 45:23.
15a Ps 69:9.

the God of perseverance and encouragement give you all the same purpose, following the example of Christ Jesus, [6]so that you may together give glory to the God and Father of our Lord Jesus Christ with one heart.

[7]Accept one another, then, for the sake of God's glory, as Christ accepted you. [8]I tell you that Christ's work was to serve the circumcised, fulfilling the truthfulness of God by carrying out the promises made to the fathers, [9]and his work was also for the gentiles, so that they should give glory to God for his faithful love; as scripture says: *For this I shall praise you among the nations and sing praise to your name.*[b] [10]And in another place it says: *Nations, rejoice, with his people,* [11]and in another place again: *Praise the Lord, all nations, extol him, all peoples.* [12]And in Isaiah, it says: *The root of Jesse will appear, he who rises up to rule the nations, and in him the nations will put their hope.*

[13]May the God of hope fill you with all joy and peace in your faith, so that in the power of the Holy Spirit you may be rich in hope.

EPILOGUE

Paul's ministry

[14]My brothers, I am quite sure that you, in particular, are full of goodness, fully instructed and capable of correcting each other. [15]But I have special confidence in writing on some points to you, to refresh your memories, because of the grace that was given to me by God. [16]I was given grace to be a minister of Christ Jesus to the gentiles, dedicated to offer them the gospel of God, so that gentiles might become an acceptable offering, sanctified by the Holy Spirit.

[17]So I can be proud, in Christ Jesus, of what I have done for God. [18]Of course I can dare to speak only of the things which Christ has done through me to win the allegiance of the gentiles, using what I have said and done, [19]by the power of signs and wonders, by the power of the Spirit of God. In this way, from Jerusalem and all round, even as far as Illyricum, I have fully carried out the preaching of the gospel of Christ; [20]and what is more, it has been my rule to preach the gospel only where the name of Christ has not already been heard, for I do not build on another's foundations; [21]in accordance with scripture: *Those who have never been told about him will see him, and those who have never heard about him will understand.*[c]

Paul's plans[d]

[22]That is why I have been so often prevented from coming to see you; [23]now, however, as there is nothing more to keep me in these parts, I hope, after longing for many years past to visit you, to see you when I am on the way to Spain — [24]and after enjoying at least something of your company, to be sent on my way with your support. [25]But now I have undertaken to go to Jerusalem in the service of the holy people of God there, [26]since Macedonia and Achaia have chosen to make a generous contribution to the poor among God's holy people at Jerusalem.

[27]Yes, they chose to; not that they did not owe it to them. For if the gentiles have been given a share in their spiritual possessions, then in return to give them help with material possessions is repaying a debt to them. [28]So when I have done this, and given this harvest into their possession, I shall visit you on the way to Spain. [29]I am sure that, when I do come to you, I shall come with the fullest blessing of Christ.

[30]Meanwhile I urge you, brothers, by our Lord Jesus Christ and by the love of the Spirit, that in your prayers to God for me you exert yourselves to help me; [31]praying that I may escape the unbelievers in Judaea, and that the aid I am carrying to Jerusalem will be acceptable to God's holy people. [32]Then I shall come to you, if God wills, for a happy time of relaxation in your company. [33]The God of peace be with you all. Amen.

15b Ps 18:49, followed by Dt 32:43; Ps 117:1; Is 11:10.
15c Is 52:15.
15d We do not know whether Paul completed this journey.

Greetings and good wishes[a]

16 I commend to you our sister Phoebe, a deaconess of the church at Cenchreae; [2]give her, in the Lord, a welcome worthy of God's holy people, and help her with whatever she needs from you—she herself has come to the help of many people, including myself.

[3]My greetings to Prisca and Aquila, my fellow-workers in Christ Jesus, [4]who risked their own necks to save my life; to them, thanks not only from me, but from all the churches among the gentiles; [5]and my greetings to the church at their house.

Greetings to my dear friend Epaenetus, the first of Asia's offerings to Christ. [6]Greetings to Mary, who worked so hard for you. [7]Greetings to those outstanding apostles, Andronicus and Junias, my kinsmen and fellow-prisoners, who were in Christ before me. [8]Greetings to Ampliatus, my dear friend in the Lord. [9]Greetings to Urban, my fellow-worker in Christ, and to my dear friend Stachys. [10]Greetings to Apelles, proved servant of Christ. Greetings to all the household of Aristobulus. [11]Greetings to my kinsman, Herodion, and greetings to those who belong to the Lord in the household of Narcissus. [12]Greetings to Tryphaena and Tryphosa who work hard in the Lord; greetings to my dear friend Persis, also a very hard worker in the Lord. [13]Greetings to Rufus, chosen servant of the Lord, and to his mother—a mother to me too. [14]Greetings to Asyncritus, Phlegon, Hermes, Patrobas, Hermas, and the brothers who are with them. [15]Greetings to Philologus and Julia, Nereus and his sister, and Olympas and all God's holy people who are with them. [16]Greet each other with the holy kiss. All the churches of Christ send their greetings.

A warning and first postscript

[17]I urge you, brothers, be on your guard against the people who are out to stir up disagreements and bring up difficulties against the teaching which you learnt. Avoid them. [18]People of that sort are servants not of our Lord Christ, but of their own greed; and with talk that sounds smooth and reasonable they deceive the minds of the unwary. [19]Your obedience has become known to everyone, and I am very pleased with you for it; but I should want you to be learned only in what is good, and unsophisticated about all that is evil. [20]The God of peace will soon crush Satan under your feet. The grace of our Lord Jesus Christ be with you.

Last greetings and second postscript

[21]Timothy, who is working with me, sends greetings to you, and so do my kinsmen Lucius, Jason and Sosipater. [22]I, Tertius, who am writing this letter, greet you in the Lord. [23]Greetings to you from Gaius, my host here, and host of the whole church. Erastus, the city treasurer, sends greetings to you, and our brother Quartus.[24] [b]

Doxology[c]

[25]And now to him
     who can make you strong
in accordance with the gospel that I preach
and the proclamation of Jesus Christ,
in accordance with that mystery
which for endless ages was kept secret
[26]but now (as the prophets wrote)
     is revealed,
as the eternal God commanded,
to be made known to all the nations,
so that they obey in faith:
[27]to him, the only wise God,
give glory through Jesus Christ
for ever and ever. Amen.

16a vv. 1–23 possibly formed no part of the original letter.
16b Some authorities add v. 24, 'The grace . . . with you' as in v. 20.
16c A solemn summary, placed by some authorities after 15:33.

FIRST CORINTHIANS

The busy port of Corinth had a lively and turbulent Christian community. Their first surviving letter from Paul treats difficulties in the community reported to Paul (at Ephesus, probably in AD 57) by their envoys, then answers various questions they brought to him. Finally Paul teaches about the resurrection. In dealing with these moral and practical issues Paul imparts invaluable teaching about Christ as the Wisdom of God, the Church as his Body, and the gifts of the Spirit in the Christian community. He stresses the primacy of conscience and the independent value of every Christian, for each has a particular part to play as a unique member of the Body of Christ. The gifts of the Spirit, no matter how spectacular, are to be assessed only by their contribution towards building up the Body of Christ.

PLAN OF THE LETTER

1 CORINTHIANS

THE FIRST LETTER OF PAUL TO THE CHURCH AT CORINTH

INTRODUCTION

Address and greetings. Thanksgiving

1 Paul, called by the will of God to be an apostle of Christ Jesus, and Sosthenes, our brother, ²to the church of God in Corinth, to those who have been consecrated in Christ Jesus and called to be God's holy people, with all those everywhere who call on the name of our Lord Jesus Christ, their Lord as well as ours. ³Grace to you and peace from God our Father and the Lord Jesus Christ.

⁴I am continually thanking God about you,

for the grace of God which you have been given in Christ Jesus; [5]in him you have been richly endowed in every kind of utterance and knowledge; [6]so firmly has witness to Christ taken root in you. [7]And so you are not lacking in any gift as you wait for our Lord Jesus Christ to be revealed; [8]he will continue to give you strength till the very end, so that you will be irreproachable on the Day of our Lord Jesus Christ. [9]You can rely on God, who has called you to be partners with his Son Jesus Christ our Lord.

I: DIVISIONS AND SCANDALS

A: FACTIONS IN THE CORINTHIAN CHURCH

Dissensions among the faithful

[10]Brothers, I urge you, in the name of our Lord Jesus Christ, not to have factions among yourselves but all to be in agreement in what you profess; so that you are perfectly united in your beliefs and judgements. [11]From what Chloe's people have been telling me about you, brothers, it is clear that there are serious differences among you. [12]What I mean is this: every one of you is declaring, 'I belong to Paul,' or 'I belong to Apollos,' or 'I belong to Cephas,'[a] or 'I belong to Christ.' [13]Has Christ been split up? Was it Paul that was crucified for you, or was it in Paul's name that you were baptised? [14]I am thankful I did not baptise any of you, except Crispus and Gaius, [15]so that no one can say that you were baptised in my name. [16]Yes, I did baptise the family of Stephanas, too; but besides these I do not think I baptised anyone.

The true wisdom and the false

[17]After all, Christ sent me not to baptise, but to preach the gospel; and not by means of wisdom of language, wise words which would make the cross of Christ pointless. [18]The message of the cross is folly for those who are on the way to ruin, but for those of us who are on the road to salvation it is the power of God. [19]As scripture says: *I am going to destroy the wisdom of the wise and bring to nothing the understanding of any who understand.* [20]*Where are the philosophers? Where are the experts?*[b] And where are the debaters of this age? Do you not see how God has shown up human wisdom as folly? [21]Since in the wisdom of God the world was unable to recognise God through wisdom, it was God's own pleasure to save believers through the folly of the gospel. [22]While the Jews demand miracles and the Greeks look for wisdom, [23]we are preaching a crucified Christ: to the Jews an obstacle they cannot get over, to the gentiles foolishness, [24]but to those who have been called, whether they are Jews or Greeks, a Christ who is both the power of God and the wisdom of God. [25]God's folly is wiser than human wisdom, and God's weakness is stronger than human strength. [26]Consider, brothers, how you were called; not many of you are wise by human standards, not many influential, not many from noble families. [27]No, God chose those who by human standards are fools to shame the wise; he chose those who by human standards are weak to shame the strong, [28]those who by human standards are common and contemptible—indeed those who count for nothing—to reduce to nothing all those that do count for something, [29]so that no human being might feel boastful before God. [30]It is by him that you exist in Christ Jesus, who for us was made wisdom from God, and saving justice and holiness and redemption. [31]As scripture says: *If anyone wants to boast, let him boast of the Lord.*[c]

2 Now when I came to you, brothers, I did not come with any brilliance of oratory or wise argument to announce to you the mystery of God. [2]I was resolved that the only knowledge I would have while I was with you was knowledge of Jesus, and of him as the crucified Christ. [3]I came among you in weakness, in fear and great trembling [4]and what I spoke and proclaimed was not meant to

1a *Cephas* is the Aramaic word for 'Peter'. For Apollos *see* Ac 18:24.
1b Is 29:14; 19:12.
1c cf. Jr 9:22–23.

convince by philosophical argument, but to demonstrate the convincing power of the Spirit, [5]so that your faith should depend not on human wisdom but on the power of God.

[6]But still, to those who have reached maturity, we do talk of a wisdom, not, it is true, a philosophy of this age or of the rulers of this age, who will not last long now. [7]It is of the mysterious wisdom of God that we talk, the wisdom that was hidden, which God predestined to be for our glory before the ages began. [8]None of the rulers of the age recognised it; for if they had recognised it, they would not have crucified the Lord of glory; [9]but it is as scripture says: *What no eye has seen and no ear has heard, what the mind of man cannot visualise; all that God has prepared for those who love him;[a]* [10]to us, though, God has given revelation through the Spirit, for the Spirit explores the depths of everything, even the depths of God. [11]After all, is there anyone who knows the qualities of anyone except his own spirit, within him; and in the same way, nobody knows the qualities of God except the Spirit of God. [12]Now, the Spirit we have received is not the spirit of the world but God's own Spirit, so that we may understand the lavish gifts God has given us. [13]And these are what we speak of, not in the terms learnt from human philosophy, but in terms learnt from the Spirit, fitting spiritual language to spiritual things. [14]The natural person has no room for the gifts of God's Spirit; to him they are folly; he cannot recognise them, because their value can be assessed only in the Spirit. [15]The spiritual person, on the other hand, can assess the value of everything, and that person's value cannot be assessed by anybody else. [16]For: *who has ever known the mind of the Lord? Who has ever been his adviser?[b]* But we are those who have the mind of Christ.

3 And so, brothers, I was not able to talk to you as spiritual people; I had to talk to you as people still living by your natural inclinations, still infants in Christ; [2]I fed you with milk and not solid food, for you were not yet able to take it—and even now, you are still not able to, [3]for you are still living by your natural inclinations. As long as there are jealousy and rivalry among you, that surely means that you are still living by your natural inclinations and by merely human

principles. [4]While there is one that says, 'I belong to Paul' and another that says, 'I belong to Apollos' are you not being only too human?

The place of the Christian preacher

[5]For what is Apollos and what is Paul? The servants through whom you came to believe, and each has only what the Lord has given him. [6]I did the planting, Apollos did the watering, but God gave growth. [7]In this, neither the planter nor the waterer counts for anything; only God, who gives growth. [8]It is all one who does the planting and who does the watering, and each will have the proper pay for the work that he has done. [9]After all, we do share in God's work; you are God's farm, God's building.

[10]By the grace of God which was given to me, I laid the foundations like a trained master-builder, and someone else is building on them. Now each one must be careful how he does the building. [11]For nobody can lay down any other foundation than the one which is there already, namely Jesus Christ. [12]On this foundation, different people may build in gold, silver, jewels, wood, hay or straw [13]but each person's handiwork will be shown for what it is. The Day which dawns in fire will make it clear and the fire itself will test the quality of each person's work. [14]The one whose work stands up to it will be given his wages; [15]the one whose work is burnt down will suffer the loss of it, though he himself will be saved; he will be saved as someone might expect to be saved from a fire.

[16]Do you not realise that you are a temple of God with the Spirit of God living in you? [17]If anybody should destroy the temple of God, God will destroy that person, because God's temple is holy; and you are that temple.

Conclusions

[18]There is no room for self-delusion. Any one of you who thinks he is wise by worldly standards must learn to be a fool in order to be really wise. [19]For the wisdom of the world is folly to God. As scripture says: *He traps the crafty in the snare of their own cunning* [20]and again: *The Lord knows the plans of the wise*

2a A free combination of Is 64:3 and Jr 3:16.
2b Is 40:13.

and how insipid they are.[a] [21]So there is to be no boasting about human beings: everything belongs to you, [22]whether it is Paul, or Apollos, or Cephas, the world, life or death, the present or the future—all belong to you; [23]but you belong to Christ and Christ belongs to God.

4 People should think of us as Christ's servants, stewards entrusted with the mysteries of God. [2]In such a matter, what is expected of stewards is that each one should be found trustworthy. [3]It is of no importance to me how you or any other human court may judge me: I will not even be the judge of my own self. [4]It is true that my conscience does not reproach me, but that is not enough to justify me: it is the Lord who is my judge. [5]For that reason, do not judge anything before the due time, until the Lord comes; he will bring to light everything that is hidden in darkness and reveal the designs of all hearts. Then everyone will receive from God the appropriate commendation.

[6]I have applied all this to myself and Apollos for your sakes, so that you can learn how the saying, 'Nothing beyond what is written' is true of us: no individual among you must become filled with his own importance and make comparisons, to another's detriment. [7]Who made you so important? What have you got that was not given to you? And if it was given to you, why are you boasting as though it were your own? [8]You already have everything—you are rich already—you have come into your kingdom, without any help from us! Well, I wish you were kings and we could be kings with you! [9]For it seems to me that God has put us apostles on show right at the end, like men condemned to death: we have been exhibited as a spectacle to the whole universe, both angelic and human. [10]Here we are, fools for Christ's sake, while you are the clever ones in Christ; we are weak, while you are strong; you are honoured, while we are disgraced. [11]To this day, we go short of food and drink and clothes, we are beaten up and we have no homes; [12]we earn our living by labouring with our own hands; when we are cursed, we answer with a blessing; when we are hounded, we endure it passively; [13]when we are insulted, we give a courteous answer. We

are treated even now as the dregs of the world, the very lowest scum.

An appeal

[14]I am writing all this not to make you ashamed but simply to remind you, as my dear children; [15]for even though you might have ten thousand slaves to look after you in Christ, you still have no more than one father, and it was I who fathered you in Christ Jesus, by the gospel. [16]That is why I urge you to take me as your pattern [17]and why I have sent you Timothy, a dear and faithful son to me in the Lord, who will remind you of my principles of conduct in Christ, as I teach them everywhere in every church.

[18]On the assumption that I was not coming to you, some of you have become filled with your own self-importance; [19]but I shall be coming to you soon, the Lord willing, and then I shall find out not what these self-important people say, but what power they have. [20]For the kingdom of God consists not in spoken words but in power. [21]What do you want then? Am I to come to you with a stick in my hand or in love, and with a spirit of gentleness?

B: INCEST IN CORINTH

5 It is widely reported that there is sexual immorality among you, immorality of a kind that is not found even among gentiles: that one of you is living with his stepmother.[a] [2]And you so filled with your own self-importance! It would have been better if you had been grieving bitterly, so that the man who has done this thing were turned out of the community. [3]For my part, however distant I am physically, I am present in spirit and have already condemned the man who behaved in this way, just as though I were present in person. [4]When you have gathered together in the name of our Lord Jesus, with the presence of my spirit, and in the power of our Lord Jesus, [5]hand such a man over to Satan, to be destroyed as far as natural life is concerned, so that on the Day of the Lord his spirit may be saved.

[6]Your self-satisfaction is ill founded. Do

3a Jb 5:13 followed by Ps 94:11.
5a Against OT and Roman law, but seemingly not Corinthian law, it was forbidden by the Jerusalem decision (Ac 15:20).

you not realise that only a little yeast leavens the whole batch of dough? [7]Throw out the old yeast so that you can be the fresh dough, unleavened as you are. For our Passover has been sacrificed, that is, Christ; [8]let us keep the feast, then, with none of the old yeast and no leavening of evil and wickedness, but only the unleavened bread of sincerity and truth.

[9]In my letter, I wrote to you that you should have nothing to do with people living immoral lives. [10]I was not including everybody in this present world who is sexually immoral, or everybody who is greedy, or dishonest or worships false gods — that would mean you would have to cut yourselves off completely from the world. [11]In fact what I meant was that you were not to have anything to do with anyone going by the name of brother who is sexually immoral, or is greedy, or worships false gods, or is a slanderer or a drunkard or dishonest; never even have a meal with anybody of that kind. [12]It is no concern of mine to judge outsiders. It is for you to judge those who are inside, is it not? [13]But outsiders are for God to judge.

You must banish this evil-doer from among you.[b]

C: RECOURSE TO THE GENTILE COURTS

6 Is one of you with a complaint against another so brazen as to seek judgement from sinners and not from God's holy people? [2]Do you not realise that the holy people of God are to be the judges of the world? And if the world is to be judged by you, are you not competent for petty cases? [3]Do you not realise that we shall be the judges of angels? — then quite certainly over matters of this life. [4]But when you have matters of this life to be judged, you bring them before those who are of no account in the Church! [5]I say this to make you ashamed of yourselves. Can it really be that it is impossible to find in the community one sensible person capable of deciding questions between brothers, [6]and that this is why brother goes to law against brother, and that before unbelievers? [7]No; it

is a fault in you, by itself, that one of you should go to law against another at all: why do you not prefer to suffer injustice, why not prefer to be defrauded? [8]And here you are, doing the injustice and the defrauding, and to your own brothers.

[9]Do you not realise that people who do evil will never inherit the kingdom of God? Make no mistake — the sexually immoral, idolaters, adulterers, the self-indulgent, sodomites, [10]thieves, misers, drunkards, slanderers and swindlers, none of these will inherit the kingdom of God. [11]Some of you used to be of that kind: but you have been washed clean, you have been sanctified, and you have been justified in the name of the Lord Jesus Christ and through the Spirit of our God.

D: SEXUAL IMMORALITY

[12]'For me everything is permissible';[a] maybe, but not everything does good. True, for me everything is permissible, but I am determined not to be dominated by anything. [13]Foods are for the stomach, and the stomach is for foods; and God will destroy them both. But the body is not for sexual immorality; [14]it is for the Lord, and the Lord is for the body. God raised up the Lord and he will raise us up too by his power. [15]Do you not realise that your bodies are members of Christ's body; do you think one can take parts of Christ's body and join them to the body of a prostitute? Out of the question! [16]Or do you not realise that anyone who attaches himself to a prostitute is one body with her, since *the two*, as it is said, *become one flesh.*[b] [17]But anyone who attaches himself to the Lord is one spirit with him.

[18]Keep away from sexual immorality. All other sins that people may commit are done outside the body; but the sexually immoral person sins against his own body. [19]Do you not realise that your body is the temple of the Holy Spirit, who is in you and whom you received from God? [20]You are not your own property, then; you have been bought at a price. So use your body for the glory of God.

5b Dt 13:6.
6a Perhaps a saying of Paul now (and 10:23) quoted against him.
6b Gn 2:24.

II: ANSWERS TO VARIOUS QUESTIONS

A: MARRIAGE AND VIRGINITY

7 Now for the questions about which you wrote. Yes, it is a good thing for a man not to touch a woman; ² yet to avoid immorality every man should have his own wife and every woman her own husband. ³The husband must give to his wife what she has a right to expect, and so too the wife to her husband. ⁴The wife does not have authority over her own body, but the husband does; and in the same way, the husband does not have authority over his own body, but the wife does. ⁵You must not deprive each other, except by mutual consent for a limited time, to leave yourselves free for prayer, and to come together again afterwards; otherwise Satan may take advantage of any lack of self-control to put you to the test. ⁶I am telling you this as a concession, not an order. ⁷I should still like everyone to be as I am myself; but everyone has his own gift from God, one this kind and the next something different.

⁸To the unmarried and to widows I say: it is good for them to stay as they are, like me. ⁹But if they cannot exercise self-control, let them marry, since it is better to be married than to be burnt up.

¹⁰To the married I give this ruling, and this is not mine but the Lord's: a wife must not be separated from her husband — ¹¹or if she has already left him, she must remain unmarried or else be reconciled to her husband — and a husband must not divorce his wife.

¹²For other cases these instructions are my own, not the Lord's. If one of the brothers has a wife who is not a believer, and she is willing to stay with him, he should not divorce her; ¹³and if a woman has a husband who is not a believer and he is willing to stay with her, she should not divorce her husband. ¹⁴You see, the unbelieving husband is sanctified through his wife and the unbelieving wife is sanctified through the brother. If this were not so, your children would be unclean, whereas in fact they are holy. ¹⁵But if the unbeliever chooses to leave, then let the separation take place: in these circumstances, the brother or sister is no longer tied. But God has called you to live in peace: ¹⁶as a wife, how can you tell whether you are to be the salvation of your husband; as a husband, how can you tell whether you are to be the salvation of your wife?

¹⁷Anyway let everyone continue in the part which the Lord has allotted to him, as he was when God called him. This is the rule that I give to all the churches. ¹⁸If a man who is called has already been circumcised, then he must stay circumcised; when an uncircumcised man is called, he may not be circumcised. ¹⁹To be circumcised is of no importance, and to be uncircumcised is of no importance; what is important is the keeping of God's commandments. ²⁰Everyone should stay in whatever state he was in when he was called. ²¹So, if when you were called, you were a slave, do not think it matters — even if you have a chance of freedom, you should prefer to make full use of your condition as a slave. ²²You see, anyone who was called in the Lord while a slave, is a freeman of the Lord; and in the same way, anyone who was free when called, is a slave of Christ. ²³You have been bought at a price; do not be slaves now to any human being. ²⁴Each one of you, brothers, is to stay before God in the state in which you were called.

²⁵About people remaining virgin, I have no directions from the Lord, but I give my own opinion as a person who has been granted the Lord's mercy to be faithful. ²⁶Well then, because of the stress which is weighing upon us, the right thing seems to be this: it is good for people to stay as they are. ²⁷If you are joined to a wife, do not seek to be released; if you are freed of a wife, do not look for a wife. ²⁸However, if you do get married, that is not a sin, and it is not sinful for a virgin to enter upon marriage. But such people will have the hardships consequent on human nature, and I would like you to be without that.

²⁹What I mean, brothers, is that the time has become limited, and from now on, those who have spouses should live as though they had none; ³⁰and those who mourn as though they were not mourning; those who enjoy life as though they did not enjoy it; those who have been buying property as though they had no possessions; ³¹and those who are involved with the world as though they were people not engrossed in it. Because this world as we know it is passing away.

³²I should like you to have your minds free from all worry. The unmarried man gives his mind to the Lord's affairs and to how he can please the Lord; ³³but the man who is married gives his mind to the affairs of this world and to how he can please his wife, and he is divided in mind. ³⁴So, too, the unmarried woman, and the virgin, gives her mind to the Lord's affairs and to being holy in body and spirit; but the married woman gives her mind to the affairs of this world and to how she can please her husband. ³⁵I am saying this only to help you, not to put a bridle on you, but so that everything is as it should be, and you are able to give your undivided attention to the Lord.

³⁶If someone with strong passions thinks that he is behaving badly towards his fiancée and that things should take their due course, he should follow his desires. There is no sin in it; they should marry. ³⁷But if he stands firm in his resolution, without any compulsion but with full control of his own will, and decides to let her remain as his fiancée, then he is acting well. ³⁸In other words, he who marries his fiancée is doing well, and he who does not, better still.

³⁹A wife is tied as long as her husband is alive. But if the husband dies, she is free to marry anybody she likes, only it must be in the Lord. ⁴⁰She would be happier if she stayed as she is, to my way of thinking—and I believe that I too have the Spirit of God.

B: FOOD OFFERED TO FALSE GODS

General principles

8 Now about food which has been dedicated to false gods.ᵃ We are well aware that all of us have knowledge; but while knowledge puffs up, love is what builds up. ²Someone may think that he has full knowledge of something and yet not know it as well as he should; ³but someone who loves God is known by God. ⁴On the subject of eating foods dedicated to false gods, we are well aware that none of the false gods exists in reality and that there is no God other than the One. ⁵Though there are so-called gods, in the heavens or on earth—and there are plenty of gods and plenty of lords—⁶yet for us there is only one God, the Father from whom all things come and for whom we exist, and one Lord, Jesus Christ, through whom all things come and through whom we exist.

The claims of knowledge

⁷However, not everybody has this knowledge. There are some in whose consciences false gods still play such a part that they take the food as though it had been dedicated to a god; then their conscience, being vulnerable, is defiled, ⁸But of course food cannot make us acceptable to God; we lose nothing by not eating it, we gain nothing by eating it. ⁹Only be careful that this freedom of yours does not in any way turn into an obstacle to trip those who are vulnerable. ¹⁰Suppose someone sees you, who have the knowledge, sitting eating in the temple of some false god, do you not think that his conscience, vulnerable as it is, may be encouraged to eat foods dedicated to false gods? ¹¹And then it would be through your knowledge that this brother for whom Christ died, vulnerable as he is, has been lost. ¹²So, sinning against your brothers and wounding their vulnerable consciences, you would be sinning against Christ. ¹³That is why, if food can be the cause of a brother's downfall, I will never eat meat any more, rather than cause my brother's downfall.

Paul invokes his own example

9 Am I not free? Am I not an apostle? Have I not seen Jesus our Lord? Are you not my work in the Lord? ²Even if to others I am not an apostle, to you at any rate I am, for you are the seal of my apostolate in the Lord. ³To those who want to interrogate me, this is my answer. ⁴Have we not every right to eat and drink? ⁵And every right to be accompanied by a Christian wife, like the other apostles, like the brothers of the Lord, and like Cephas? ⁶Are Barnabas and I the only ones who have no right to stop working? ⁷What soldier would ever serve in the army at his own expense? And who is there who would plant a vineyard and never eat the fruit from it; or would keep a flock and not feed on the milk from his flock? ⁸Do not think that this is merely worldly wisdom. Does not the Law say exactly the same? It is written in

---

8a Food, especially meat, left over from sacrifices, was offered for sale cheap in the markets.

the Law of Moses: [9]*You must not muzzle an ox when it is treading out the corn.*[a] Is it about oxen that God is concerned here, [10]or is it not said entirely for our sake? Clearly it was written for our sake, because it is right that whoever ploughs should plough with the expectation of having his share, and whoever threshes should thresh with the expectation of having his share. [11]If we have sown the seed of spiritual things in you, is it too much to ask that we should receive from you a crop of material things? [12]Others have been given such rights over you and do we not deserve more? In fact, we have never exercised this right; on the contrary, we have put up with anything rather than obstruct the gospel of Christ in any way. [13]Do you not realise that the ministers in the Temple get their food from the Temple, and those who serve at the altar can claim their share from the altar? [14]In the same way, the Lord gave the instruction that those who preach the gospel should get their living from the gospel.

[15]However, I have never availed myself of any rights of this kind; and I have not written this to secure such treatment for myself; I would rather die than that . . . No one shall take from me this ground of boasting. [16]In fact, preaching the gospel gives me nothing to boast of, for I am under compulsion and I should be in trouble if I failed to do it. [17]If I did it on my own initiative I would deserve a reward; but if I do it under compulsion I am simply accepting a task entrusted to me. [18]What reward do I have, then? That in my preaching I offer the gospel free of charge to avoid using the rights which the gospel allows me.

[19]So though I was not a slave to any human being, I put myself in slavery to all people, to win as many as I could. [20]To the Jews I made myself as a Jew, to win the Jews; to those under the Law as one under the Law (though I am not), in order to win those under the Law; [21]to those outside the Law as one outside the Law, though I am not outside the Law but under Christ's law, to win those outside the Law. [22]To the weak, I made myself weak, to win the weak. I accommodated myself to people in all kinds of different situations, so that by all possible means I might bring some to salvation. [23]All this I do

for the sake of the gospel, that I may share its benefits with others.

[24]Do you not realise that, though all the runners in the stadium take part in the race, only one of them gets the prize? Run like that—to win. [25]Every athlete concentrates completely on training, and this is to win a wreath that will wither, whereas ours will never wither. [26]So that is how I run, not without a clear goal; and how I box, not wasting blows on air. [27]I punish my body and bring it under control, to avoid any risk that, having acted as herald for others, I myself may be disqualified.

A warning and the lessons of Israel's history

10 I want you to be quite certain, brothers, that our ancestors all had the cloud over them and all passed through the sea. [2]In the cloud and in the sea they were all baptised into Moses; [3]all ate the same spiritual food [4]and all drank the same spiritual drink, since they drank from the spiritual rock which followed them,[a] and that rock was Christ. [5]In spite of this, God was not pleased with most of them, and their corpses *were scattered over the desert.*[b] [6]Now these happenings were examples, for our benefit, so that we should never set our hearts, as they did, on evil things; [7]nor are you to worship false gods, as some of them did, as it says in scripture: *The people sat down to eat and drink, and afterwards got up to amuse themselves.*[c] [8]Nor, again, are we to fall into sexual immorality; some of them did this, and twenty-three thousand met their downfall in one day. [9]And we are not to put the Lord to the test; some of them put him to the test, and they were killed by snakes. [10]Never complain; some of them complained, and they were killed by the Destroyer. [11]Now all these things happened to them by way of example, and they were described in writing to be a lesson for us, to whom it has fallen to live in the last days of the ages. [12]Everyone, no matter how firmly he thinks he is standing, must be careful he does not fall. [13]None of the trials which have come upon you is more than a human being can stand. You can trust that God will not let you be put to the test beyond your strength,

---

9a Dt 25:4.
10a In rabbinic tradition the rock of Nb 20:8 followed them.
10b Nb 14:16.
10c Ex 32:6.

but with any trial will also provide a way out by enabling you to put up with it.

Sacrificial feasts
No compromise with idolatry

¹⁴For that reason, my dear friends, have nothing to do with the worship of false gods. ¹⁵I am talking to you as sensible people; weigh up for yourselves what I have to say. ¹⁶The blessing-cup, which we bless, is it not a sharing in the blood of Christ; and the loaf of bread which we break, is it not a sharing in the body of Christ? ¹⁷And as there is one loaf, so we, although there are many of us, are one single body, for we all share in the one loaf. ¹⁸Now compare the natural people of Israel: is it not true that those who eat the sacrifices share the altar? ¹⁹What does this mean? That the dedication of food to false gods amounts to anything? Or that false gods themselves amount to anything? ²⁰No, it does not; simply that when pagans sacrifice, *what is sacrificed by them is sacrificed to demons who are not God.*^d I do not want you to share with demons. ²¹You cannot drink the cup of the Lord and the cup of demons as well; you cannot have a share at the Lord's table and the demons' table as well. ²²Do we really want to arouse the Lord's jealousy; are we stronger than he is?

Food sacrificed to idols
Practical solutions

²³'Everything is permissible'; maybe so, but not everything does good. True, everything is permissible, but not everything builds people up. ²⁴Nobody should be looking for selfish advantage, but everybody for someone else's. ²⁵Eat anything that is sold in butchers' shops; there is no need to ask questions for conscience' sake, ²⁶since *To the Lord belong the earth and all it contains.*^e ²⁷If an unbeliever invites you to a meal, go if you want to, and eat whatever is put before you; you need not ask questions of conscience first. ²⁸But if someone says to you, 'This food has been offered in sacrifice,' do not eat it, out of consideration for the person that told you, for conscience's sake—²⁹not your own conscience, I mean, but the other person's. Why should my freedom be governed by somebody else's conscience? ³⁰Provided that I accept it with gratitude, why should I be blamed for eating food for which I give thanks? ³¹Whatever you eat, then, or drink, and whatever else you do, do it all for the glory of God. ³²Never be a cause of offence, either to Jews or to Greeks or to the Church of God, ³³just as I try to accommodate everybody in everything, not looking for my own advantage, but for the advantage of everybody else, so that they may be saved.

11 Take me as your pattern, just as I take Christ for mine.

C: DECORUM IN PUBLIC WORSHIP

Women's behaviour at services

²I congratulate you for remembering me so consistently and for maintaining the traditions exactly as I passed them on to you. ³But I should like you to understand that the head of every man is Christ, the head of woman is man, and the head of Christ is God. ⁴For any man to pray or to prophesy with his head covered shows disrespect for his head. ⁵And for a woman to pray or prophesy with her head uncovered shows disrespect for her head; it is exactly the same as if she had her hair shaved off. ⁶Indeed, if a woman does go without a veil, she should have her hair cut off too; but if it is a shameful thing for a woman to have her hair cut off or shaved off, then she should wear a veil.

⁷But for a man it is not right to have his head covered, since he is the image of God and reflects God's glory; but woman is the reflection of man's glory. ⁸For man did not come from woman; no, woman came from man; ⁹nor was man created for the sake of woman, but woman for the sake of man: ¹⁰and this is why it is right for a woman to wear on her head a sign of the authority over her, because of the angels. ¹¹However, in the Lord, though woman is nothing without man, man is nothing without woman; ¹²and though woman came from man, so does every man come from a woman, and everything comes from God.

¹³Decide for yourselves: does it seem fitting that a woman should pray to God without a veil? ¹⁴Does not nature itself teach you that

if a man has long hair, it is a disgrace to him, [15]but when a woman has long hair, it is her glory? After all, her hair was given to her to be a covering.

[16]If anyone wants to be contentious, I say that we have no such custom, nor do any of the churches of God.

The Lord's Supper

[17]Now that I am on the subject of instructions, I cannot congratulate you on the meetings you hold; they do more harm than good. [18]In the first place, I hear that when you all come together in your assembly, there are separate factions among you, and to some extent I believe it. [19]It is no bad thing, either, that there should be differing groups among you so that those who are to be trusted among you can be clearly recognised. [20]So, when you meet together, it is not the Lord's Supper that you eat; [21]for when the eating begins, each one of you has his own supper first, and there is one going hungry while another is getting drunk. [22]Surely you have homes for doing your eating and drinking in? Or have you such disregard for God's assembly that you can put to shame those who have nothing? What am I to say to you? Congratulate you? On this I cannot congratulate you.

[23]For the tradition I received[a] from the Lord and also handed on to you is that on the night he was betrayed, the Lord Jesus took some bread, [24]and after he had given thanks, he broke it, and he said, 'This is my body, which is for you; do this in remembrance of me.' [25]And in the same way, with the cup after supper, saying, 'This cup is the new covenant in my blood. Whenever you drink it, do this as a memorial of me.' [26]Whenever you eat this bread, then, and drink this cup, you are proclaiming the Lord's death until he comes. [27]Therefore anyone who eats the bread or drinks the cup of the Lord unworthily is answerable for the body and blood of the Lord.

[28]Everyone is to examine himself and only then eat of the bread or drink from the cup; [29]because a person who eats and drinks without recognising the body is eating and drinking his own condemnation. [30]That is why many of you are weak and ill and a good number have died. [31]If we were critical of ourselves we would not be condemned, [32]but when we are judged by the Lord, we are corrected by the Lord to save us from being condemned along with the world.

[33]So then, my brothers, when you meet for the Meal, wait for each other; [34]anyone who is hungry should eat at home. Then your meeting will not bring your condemnation. The other matters I shall arrange when I come.

Spiritual gifts

12 About the gifts of the Spirit, brothers, I want you to be quite certain. [2]You remember that, when you were pagans, you were irresistibly drawn to inarticulate heathen gods. [3]Because of that, I want to make it quite clear to you that no one who says 'A curse on Jesus' can be speaking in the Spirit of God, and nobody is able to say, 'Jesus is Lord' except in the Holy Spirit.

The variety and the unity of gifts

[4]There are many different gifts, but it is always the same Spirit; [5]there are many different ways of serving, but it is always the same Lord. [6]There are many different forms of activity, but in everybody it is the same God who is at work in them all. [7]The particular manifestation of the Spirit granted to each one is to be used for the general good. [8]To one is given from the Spirit the gift of utterance expressing wisdom; to another the gift of utterance expressing knowledge, in accordance with the same Spirit; [9]to another, faith, from the same Spirit; and to another, the gifts of healing, through this one Spirit; [10]to another, the working of miracles; to another, prophecy; to another, the power of distinguishing spirits; to one, the gift of different tongues and to another, the interpretation of tongues. [11]But at work in all these is one and the same Spirit, distributing them at will to each individual.

The analogy of the body

[12]For as with the human body which is a unity although it has many parts—all the parts of the body, though many, still making up one single body—so it is with Christ. [13]We were baptised into one body in a single Spirit,

---

[11]a cf. 15:3.

Jews as well as Greeks, slaves as well as free men, and we were all given the same Spirit to drink. [14]And indeed the body consists not of one member but of many. [15]If the foot were to say, 'I am not a hand and so I do not belong to the body,' it does not belong to the body any the less for that. [16]Or if the ear were to say, 'I am not an eye, and so I do not belong to the body,' that would not stop its belonging to the body. [17]If the whole body were just an eye, how would there be any hearing? If the whole body were hearing, how would there be any smelling? [18]As it is, God has put all the separate parts into the body as he chose. [19]If they were all the same part, how could it be a body? [20]As it is, the parts are many but the body is one. [21]The eye cannot say to the hand, 'I have no need of you,' and nor can the head say to the feet, 'I have no need of you.'

[22]What is more, it is precisely the parts of the body that seem to be the weakest which are the indispensable ones. [23]It is the parts of the body which we consider least dignified that we surround with the greatest dignity; and our less presentable parts are given greater presentability [24]which our presentable parts do not need. God has composed the body so that greater dignity is given to the parts which were without it, [25]and so that there may not be disagreements inside the body but each part may be equally concerned for all the others. [26]If one part is hurt, all the parts share its pain. And if one part is honoured, all the parts share its joy.

[27]Now Christ's body is yourselves, each of you with a part to play in the whole. [28]And those whom God has appointed in the Church are, first apostles, secondly prophets, thirdly teachers; after them, miraculous powers, then gifts of healing, helpful acts, guidance, various kinds of tongues. [29]Are all of them apostles? Or all prophets? Or all teachers? Or all miracle-workers? [30]Do all have the gifts of healing? Do all of them speak in tongues and all interpret them?

The order of importance in spiritual gifts
Hymn to Love

[31]Set your mind on the higher gifts. And now I am going to put before you the best way of all.

13 Though I command languages both human and angelic—if I speak without love, I am no more than a gong booming or a cymbal clashing. [2]And though I have the power of prophecy, to penetrate all mysteries and knowledge, and though I have all the faith necessary to move mountains—if I am without love, I am nothing. [3]Though I should give away to the poor all that I possess, and even give up my body to be burned—if I am without love, it will do me no good whatever.

[4]Love is always patient and kind; love is never jealous; love is not boastful or conceited, [5]it is never rude and never seeks its own advantage, it does not take offence or store up grievances. [6]Love does not rejoice at wrongdoing, but finds its joy in the truth. [7]It is always ready to make allowances, to trust, to hope and to endure whatever comes.

[8]Love never comes to an end. But if there are prophecies, they will be done away with; if tongues, they will fall silent; and if knowledge, it will be done away with. [9]For we know only imperfectly, and we prophesy imperfectly; [10]but once perfection comes, all imperfect things will be done away with. [11]When I was a child, I used to talk like a child, and see things as a child does, and think like a child; but now that I have become an adult, I have finished with all childish ways. [12]Now we see only reflections in a mirror, mere riddles, but then we shall be seeing face to face. Now I can know only imperfectly; but then I shall know just as fully as I am myself known.

[13]As it is, these remain: faith, hope and love, the three of them; and the greatest of them is love.

Spiritual gifts:
their respective importance
in the community

14 Make love your aim; but be eager, too, for spiritual gifts, and especially for prophesying. [2]Those who speak in a tongue speak to God, but not to other people, because nobody understands them; they are speaking in the Spirit and the meaning is hidden. [3]On the other hand, someone who prophesies speaks to other people, building them up and giving them encouragement and reassurance. [4]Those who speak in a tongue may build themselves up, but those who prophesy build up the community. [5]While I should like you all to speak in tongues, I would much rather you could prophesy; since those who prophesy are of greater importance than those who speak in tongues, unless they

can interpret what they say so that the church is built up by it.

⁶Now suppose, brothers, I come to you and speak in tongues, what good shall I do you if my speaking provides no revelation or knowledge or prophecy or instruction? ⁷It is the same with an inanimate musical instrument. If it does not make any distinction between notes, how can one recognise what is being played on flute or lyre? ⁸If the trumpet sounds a call which is unrecognisable, who is going to get ready for the attack? ⁹It is the same with you: if you do not use your tongue to produce speech that can be readily understood, how can anyone know what you are saying? You will be talking to the air. ¹⁰However many the languages used in the world, all of them use sound; ¹¹but if I do not understand the meaning of the sound, I am a barbarian*a* to the person who is speaking, and the speaker is a barbarian to me. ¹²So with you, as you are eager to have spiritual powers, aim to be rich in those which build up the community.

¹³That is why anybody who speaks in a tongue must pray that he may be given the interpretation. ¹⁴For if I pray in a tongue, my spirit may be praying but my mind derives no fruit from it. ¹⁵What then? I shall pray with the spirit, but I shall pray with the mind as well: I shall sing praises with the spirit and I shall sing praises with the mind as well. ¹⁶Otherwise, if you say your blessing only with the spirit, how is the uninitiated person going to answer 'Amen' to your thanksgiving, without understanding what you are saying? ¹⁷You may be making your thanksgiving well, but the other person is not built up at all. ¹⁸I thank God that I speak with tongues more than any of you; ¹⁹all the same, when I am in the assembly I would rather say five words with my mind, to instruct others as well, than ten thousand words in a tongue.

²⁰Brothers, do not remain children in your thinking; infants in wickedness — agreed, but in your thinking grown-ups. ²¹It says in the written Law: *In strange tongues and in a foreign language I will talk to this nation, and* even so *they will refuse to listen,ᵇ* says the Lord. ²²So then, strange languages are significant not for believers, but for unbelievers; whereas on the other hand, prophesying is not for unbelievers, but for believers. ²³Suppose that, if the whole congregation were meeting and all of them speaking in tongues, and some uninitiated people or unbelievers were to come in, don't you think they would say that you were all raving? ²⁴But if you were all prophesying when an unbeliever or someone uninitiated came in, he would find himself put to the test by all and judged by all ²⁵and the secrets of his heart revealed; and so he would fall down on his face and worship God, declaring that *God is indeed among you.ᶜ*

Regulating spiritual gifts

²⁶Then what should it be like, brothers? When you come together each of you brings a psalm or some instruction or a revelation, or speaks in a tongue or gives an interpretation. Let all these things be done in a way that will build up the community. ²⁷If there are to be any people speaking in a tongue, then let there be only two, or at the most three, and those one at a time, and let one of these interpret. ²⁸If there is no interpreter, then let each of them be quiet in the assembly, and speak only internally and to God. ²⁹Let two prophets, or three, speak while the rest weigh their words; ³⁰and if a revelation comes to someone else who is sitting by, the speaker should stop speaking. ³¹You can all prophesy, but one at a time, then all will learn something and all receive encouragement. ³²The prophetic spirit is to be under the prophets' control, ³³for God is a God not of disorder but of peace.

As in all the churches of God's holy people, ³⁴women are to remain quiet in the assemblies, since they have no permission to speak: theirs is a subordinate part, as the Law itself says. ³⁵If there is anything they want to know, they should ask their husbands at home: it is shameful for a woman to speak in the assembly.

³⁶Do you really think that you are the source of the word of God? Or that you are the only people to whom it has come? ³⁷Anyone who claims to be a prophet, or to have any spiritual powers must recognise that what I am writing to you is a commandment from the Lord. ³⁸If anyone does not recognise

14a i.e. someone who does not understand Gk.
14b Is 28:11–12.
14c Is 45:14.

this, it is because that person is not recognised himself.

[39]So, my brothers, be eager to prophesy, and do not suppress the gift of speaking in tongues. [40]But make sure that everything is done in a proper and orderly fashion.

III: THE RESURRECTION OF THE DEAD

The fact of the resurrection

15 [1]I want to make quite clear to you, brothers, what the message of the gospel that I preached to you is; you accepted it and took your stand on it, [2]and you are saved by it, if you keep to the message I preached to you; otherwise your coming to believe was in vain. [3]The tradition I handed on to you in the first place, a tradition which I had myself received,[a] was that Christ died for our sins, in accordance with the scriptures, [4]and that he was buried; and that on the third day, he was raised to life, in accordance with the scriptures; [5]and that he appeared to Cephas; and later to the Twelve; [6]and next he appeared to more than five hundred of the brothers at the same time, most of whom are still with us, though some have fallen asleep; [7]then he appeared to James, and then to all the apostles. [8]Last of all he appeared to me too, as though I was a child born abnormally.

[9]For I am the least of the apostles and am not really fit to be called an apostle, because I had been persecuting the Church of God; [10]but what I am now, I am through the grace of God, and the grace which was given to me has not been wasted. Indeed, I have worked harder than all the others—not I, but the grace of God which is with me. [11]Anyway, whether it was they or I, this is what we preach and what you believed.

[12]Now if Christ is proclaimed as raised from the dead, how can some of you be saying that there is no resurrection of the dead? [13]If there is no resurrection of the dead, then Christ cannot have been raised either, [14]and if Christ has not been raised, then our preaching is without substance, and so is your faith. [15]What is more, we have proved to be false witnesses to God, for testifying against God that he raised Christ to life when he did not raise him—if it is true that the dead are not raised. [16]For, if the dead are not raised, neither is Christ; [17]and if Christ has not been raised, your faith is pointless and you have not, after all, been released from your sins. [18]In addition, those who have fallen asleep in Christ are utterly lost. [19]If our hope in Christ has been for this life only, we are of all people the most pitiable.

[20]In fact, however, Christ has been raised from the dead, as the first-fruits of all who have fallen asleep. [21]As it was by one man that death came, so through one man has come the resurrection of the dead. [22]Just as all die in Adam, so in Christ all will be brought to life; [23]but all of them in their proper order: Christ the first-fruits, and next, at his coming, those who belong to him. [24]After that will come the end, when he will hand over the kingdom to God the Father, having abolished every principality, every ruling force and power. [25]For he is to be king *until he has made* his enemies his footstool, [26]and the last of the enemies to be done away with is death, for *he has put all things under his feet.*[b] [27]But when it is said everything is subjected, this obviously cannot include the One who subjected everything to him. [28]When everything has been subjected to him, then the Son himself will be subjected to the One who subjected everything to him, so that God may be all in all.

[29]Otherwise, what are people up to who have themselves baptised on behalf of the dead? If the dead are not raised at all, what is the point of being baptised on their behalf? [30]And what about us? Why should we endanger ourselves every hour of our lives? [31]I swear by the pride that I take in you, in Christ Jesus our Lord, that I face death every day. [32]If I fought wild animals at Ephesus in a purely human perspective, what had I to gain by it? [33]If the dead are not going to be raised, then *Let us eat and drink, for tomorrow we shall be dead.*[c] [34]So do not let anyone lead

---

15a cf. 11:23.
15b Ps 110:1.
15c Is 22:13.

you astray, 'Bad company corrupts good ways.'*d* Wake up from your stupor as you should and leave sin alone; some of you have no understanding of God; I tell you this to instil some shame in you.

The manner of the resurrection

³⁵Someone may ask: How are dead people raised, and what sort of body do they have when they come? ³⁶How foolish! What you sow must die before it is given new life; ³⁷and what you sow is not the body that is to be, but only a bare grain, of wheat I dare say, or some other kind; ³⁸it is God who gives it the sort of body that he has chosen for it, and for each kind of seed its own kind of body.

³⁹Not all flesh is the same flesh: there is human flesh; animals have another kind of flesh, birds another and fish yet another. ⁴⁰Then there are heavenly bodies and earthly bodies; the heavenly have a splendour of their own, and the earthly a different splendour. ⁴¹The sun has its own splendour, the moon another splendour, and the stars yet another splendour; and the stars differ among themselves in splendour. ⁴²It is the same too with the resurrection of the dead: what is sown is perishable, but what is raised is imperishable; ⁴³what is sown is contemptible but what is raised is glorious; what is sown is weak, but what is raised is powerful; ⁴⁴what is sown is a natural body, and what is raised is a spiritual body.

If there is a natural body, there is a spiritual body too. ⁴⁵So the first *man*, Adam, as scripture says, *became a living soul;*ᵉ and the last Adam has become a life-giving spirit. ⁴⁶But first came the natural body, not the spiritual one; that came only afterwards. ⁴⁷The first man, being made of earth, is earthly by nature; the second man is from heaven. ⁴⁸The earthly man is the pattern for earthly people, the heavenly man for heavenly ones. ⁴⁹And as we have borne the likeness of the earthly man, so we shall bear the likeness of the heavenly one.

⁵⁰What I am saying, brothers, is that mere human nature cannot inherit the kingdom of God: what is perishable cannot inherit what is imperishable. ⁵¹Now I am going to tell you a mystery: we are not all going to fall asleep, ⁵²but we are all going to be changed, instantly, in the twinkling of an eye, when the last trumpet sounds. The trumpet is going to sound, and then the dead will be raised imperishable, and we shall be changed, ⁵³because this perishable nature of ours must put on imperishability, this mortal nature must put on immortality.

A hymn of triumph. Conclusion

⁵⁴And after this perishable nature has put on imperishability and this mortal nature has put on immortality, then will the words of scripture come true: *Death is swallowed up in victory.* ⁵⁵*Death, where is your victory? Death, where is your sting?*ᶠ ⁵⁶The sting of death is sin, and the power of sin comes from the Law. ⁵⁷Thank God, then, for giving us the victory through Jesus Christ our Lord.

⁵⁸So, my dear brothers, keep firm and immovable, always abounding in energy for the Lord's work, being sure that in the Lord none of your labours is wasted.

CONCLUSION

Commendations. Greetings

16 Now about the collection for God's holy people;ᵃ you are to do the same as I prescribed for the churches in Galatia. ²On the first day of the week, each of you should put aside and reserve as much as each can spare; do not delay the collection till I arrive.

³When I come, I will send to Jerusalem with letters of introduction those people you approve to deliver your gift; ⁴if it is worth my going too, they can travel with me.

⁵In any case, I shall be coming to you after I have passed through Macedonia, as I have to go through Macedonia; ⁶and I may be staying some time with you, perhaps

15d A proverb found also in Menander's *Thais*.
15e Gn 2:7.
15f A free version of Is 25:8 and Hos 13:14.
16a cf. Ac 24:17; 2 Co 8–9.

wintering, so that you can start me on my next journey, wherever I may be going. [7]I do not want to make only a passing visit to you, and I am hoping to spend quite a time with you, the Lord permitting. [8]But I shall remain at Ephesus until Pentecost, [9]for a very promising door is standing wide open to me and there are many against us.

[10]If Timothy comes, make sure that he has nothing to fear from you; he is doing the Lord's work, just as I am, [11]and nobody is to underrate him. Start him off in peace on his journey to come on to me: the brothers and I are waiting for him. [12]As for our brother Apollos, I urged him earnestly to come to you with the brothers, but he was quite firm that he did not want to go yet, and he will come when he finds an opportunity.

[13]Be vigilant, stay firm in the faith, be brave and strong. [14]Let everything you do be done in love.

[15]There is something else I must urge you to do, brothers. You know how Stephanas' family have been the first-fruits of Achaia and have devoted themselves to the service of God's holy people; [16]I ask you in turn to put yourselves at the service of people like this and all that work with them in this arduous task. [17]I am delighted that Stephanas and Fortunatus and Achaicus have arrived; they have made up for your not being here. [18]They have set my mind at rest, just as they did yours; you should appreciate people like them.

[19]The churches of Asia send their greetings. Aquila and Prisca send their best wishes in the Lord, together with the church that meets in their house. [20]All the brothers send their greetings. Greet one another with the holy kiss.

[21]This greeting is in my own hand—PAUL. [22]If there is anyone who does not love the Lord, a curse on such a one. *Maran atha.* [b] [23]The grace of the Lord Jesus Christ be with you. [24]My love is with you all in Christ Jesus.

SECOND CORINTHIANS

Between 1 Co and 2 Co frequent and stormy interchanges with Corinth intervene, *see* 1[a] note. Paul is still anxious to improve his relations with the community. This gives rise to his reflections on the apostolate, the spreading of the glorious light of Christ, by which we are transformed into the image we reflect. The collection for the Jerusalem community (section II) was close to Paul's heart; he mentions it several times in his letters as a means to unity, showing the devotion of the new communities to the mother church; here he urges especially the example of Christ's generosity. The final section is the fullest piece of Paul's autobiographical writing we possess, giving a fascinating picture of the opposition and difficulties which he met by means of his love of Christ.

It is possible that 2 Co is not a single letter but a collection of separate notes; each of the three sections below may be distinct, and there may be divisions even within these, *see* notes at 6[b] and 9[a].

PLAN OF THE LETTER

16b Aram. 'The Lord is coming' (or perhaps 'Lord, come').

2 CORINTHIANS
THE SECOND LETTER OF PAUL
TO THE CHURCH AT CORINTH

INTRODUCTION

Address and greetings. Thanksgiving

1 Paul, by the will of God an apostle of Christ Jesus, and Timothy, our brother, to the church of God in Corinth and to all God's holy people in the whole of Achaia. ²Grace to you and peace from God our Father and the Lord Jesus Christ.

³Blessed be the God and Father of our Lord Jesus Christ, the merciful Father and the God who gives every possible encouragement; ⁴he supports us in every hardship, so that we are able to come to the support of others, in every hardship of theirs because of the encouragement that we ourselves receive from God. ⁵For just as the sufferings of Christ overflow into our lives; so too does the encouragement we receive through Christ. ⁶So if we have hardships to undergo, this will contribute to your encouragement and your salvation; if we receive encouragement, this is to gain for you the encouragement which enables you to bear with perseverance the same sufferings as we do. ⁷So our hope for you is secure in the knowledge that you share the encouragement we receive, no less than the sufferings we bear.

⁸So in the hardships we underwent in Asia, we want you to be quite certain, brothers, that we were under extraordinary pressure, beyond our powers of endurance, so that we gave up all hope even of surviving. ⁹In fact we were carrying the sentence of death within our own selves, so that we should be forced to trust not in ourselves but in God, who raises the dead. ¹⁰He did save us from such a death and will save us—we are relying on him to do so. ¹¹Your prayer for us will contribute to this, so that, for God's favour shown to us as the result of the prayers of so many, thanks too may be given by many on our behalf.

I: SOME RECENT EVENTS REVIEWED

Why Paul changed his plans

¹²There is one thing that we are proud of, namely our conscientious conviction that we have always behaved towards everyone, and especially towards you, with that unalloyed holiness that comes from God, relying not on human reasoning but on the grace of God. ¹³In our writing, there is nothing that you cannot read clearly and understand; ¹⁴and it is my hope that, just as you have already understood us partially, so you will understand fully that you can be as proud of us as we shall be of you when the Day of our Lord Jesus comes.

¹⁵It was with this assurance that I had been meaning to come to you first, so that you would benefit doubly; ¹⁶both to visit you on my way to Macedonia, and then to return to you again from Macedonia, so that you could set me on my way to Judaea. ¹⁷Since that was my purpose, do you think I lightly changed

my mind? Or that my plans are based on ordinary human promptings and I have in my mind Yes, yes[a] at the same time as No, no? [18]As surely as God is trustworthy, what we say to you is not both Yes and No. [19]The Son of God, Jesus Christ, who was proclaimed to you by us, that is, by me and by Silvanus and Timothy, was never Yes-and-No; his nature is all Yes. [20]For in him is found the Yes to all God's promises and therefore it is 'through him' that we answer 'Amen' to give praise to God. [21]It is God who gives us, with you, a sure place in Christ [22]and has both anointed us and marked us with his seal, giving us as pledge the Spirit in our hearts.

[23]By my life I call on God to be my witness that it was only to spare you that I did not come to Corinth again.[b] [24]We have no wish to lord it over your faith, but to work with you for your joy; for your stand in the faith is firm.

2 I made up my mind, then, that my next visit to you would not be a painful one, [2]for if I cause you distress I am causing distress to my only possible source of joy. [3]Indeed, I wrote as I did precisely to spare myself distress when I visited you, from the very people who should have given me joy, in the conviction that for all of you my joy was yours too. [4]I wrote to you in agony of mind, not meaning to cause you distress but to show you how very much love I have for you.

[5]If anyone did cause distress, he caused it not to me, but—not to exaggerate—in some degree to all of you. [6]The punishment already imposed by the majority was quite enough for such a person; [7]and now by contrast you should forgive and encourage him all the more, or he may be overwhelmed by the extent of his distress. [8]That is why I urge you to give your love towards him definite expression. [9]This was in fact my reason for writing, to test your quality and whether you are completely obedient. [10]But if you forgive anybody, then I too forgive that person; and whatever I have forgiven, if there is anything I have forgiven, I have done it for your sake in Christ's presence, [11]to avoid being outwitted by Satan, whose scheming we know only too well.

From Troas to Macedonia
The apostolate: its importance

[12]When I came to Troas for the sake of the gospel of Christ and a door was opened for me there in the Lord, [13]I had no relief from anxiety, not finding my brother Titus there, and I said goodbye to them and went on to Macedonia. [14]But, thanks be to God who always gives us in Christ a part in his triumphal procession, and through us is spreading everywhere the fragrance of the knowledge of himself. [15]To God we are the fragrance of Christ, both among those who are being saved and among those who are on the way to destruction; [16]for these last, the smell of death leading to death, but for the first, the smell of life leading to life. Who is equal to such a task? [17]At least we do not adulterate the word of God, as so many do, but it is in all purity, as envoys of God and in God's presence, that we speak in Christ.

3 Are we beginning to commend ourselves to you afresh—as though we needed, like some others, to have letters of commendation either to you or from you? [2]You yourselves are our letter, written in our hearts, that everyone can read and understand; [3]and it is plain that you are a letter from Christ, entrusted to our care, written not with ink but with the Spirit of the living God; not on stone tablets but on the tablets of human hearts.

[4]Such is the confidence we have through Christ in facing God; [5]it is not that we are so competent that we can claim any credit for ourselves; all our competence comes from God. [6]He has given us the competence to be ministers of a new covenant, a covenant which is not of written letters, but of the Spirit; for the written letters kill, but the Spirit gives life. [7]Now if the administering of death, engraved in letters on stone, occurred in such glory that the Israelites could not look Moses steadily in the face,[a] because of its glory, transitory though this glory was, [8]how much more will the ministry of the Spirit occur in glory! [9]For if it is glorious to administer condemnation, to administer saving

---

1a The argument is based on the Hebr. word *Amen* = Yes. The root meaning is 'faithful', 'solid'.
1b After writing 1 Co Paul *1* paid a brief, stern visit to Corinth and promised to return, *2* sent a messenger who was insulted, *3* sent a severe reprimand which was effective, and *4* wrote this letter.
3a cf. Ex 34:29–35.

justice is far richer in glory. ¹⁰Indeed, what was once considered glorious has lost all claim to glory, by contrast with the glory which transcends it. ¹¹For if what was transitory had any glory, how much greater is the glory of that which lasts for ever.

¹²With a hope like this, we can speak with complete fearlessness; ¹³not like Moses who put a veil over his face so that the Israelites should not watch the end of what was transitory. ¹⁴But their minds were closed; indeed, until this very day, the same veil remains over the reading of the Old Testament: it is not lifted, for only in Christ is it done away with. ¹⁵As it is, to this day, whenever Moses is read, their hearts are covered with a veil, ¹⁶and this veil will not be taken away till they turn to the Lord. ¹⁷Now this Lord is the Spirit and where the Spirit of the Lord is, there is freedom. ¹⁸And all of us, with our unveiled faces like mirrors reflecting the glory of the Lord, are being transformed into the image that we reflect in brighter and brighter glory; this is the working of the Lord who is the Spirit.

4 Such by God's mercy is our ministry, and therefore we do not waver ²but have renounced all shameful secrecy. It is not our way to be devious, or to falsify the word of God; instead, in God's sight we commend ourselves to every human being with a conscience by showing the truth openly. ³If our gospel seems to be veiled at all, it is so to those who are on the way to destruction, ⁴the unbelievers whose minds have been blinded by the god of this world, so that they cannot see shining the light of the gospel of the glory of Christ, who is the image of God. ⁵It is not ourselves that we are proclaiming, but Christ Jesus as the Lord, and ourselves as your servants for Jesus' sake. ⁶It is God who said, 'Let light shine out of darkness,' that has shone into our hearts to enlighten them with the knowledge of God's glory, the glory on the face of Christ.

The hardships and hopes of the apostolate

⁷But we hold this treasure in pots of earthenware, so that the immensity of the power is God's and not our own. ⁸We are subjected to every kind of hardship, but never distressed; we see no way out but we never despair; ⁹we are pursued but never cut off; knocked down,

but still have some life in us; ¹⁰always we carry with us in our body the death of Jesus so that the life of Jesus, too, may be visible in our body. ¹¹Indeed, while we are still alive, we are continually being handed over to death, for the sake of Jesus, so that the life of Jesus, too, may be visible in our mortal flesh. ¹²In us, then, death is at work; in you, life.

¹³But as we have the same spirit of faith as is described in scripture—*I believed and therefore I spoke*ᵃ—we, too, believe and therefore we, too, speak, ¹⁴realising that he who raised up the Lord Jesus will raise us up with Jesus in our turn, and bring us to himself—and you as well. ¹⁵You see, everything is for your benefit, so that as grace spreads, so, to the glory of God, thanksgiving may also overflow among more and more people.

¹⁶That is why we do not waver; indeed, though this outer human nature of ours may be falling into decay, at the same time our inner human nature is renewed day by day. ¹⁷The temporary, light burden of our hardships is earning us for ever an utterly incomparable, eternal weight of glory, ¹⁸since what we aim for is not visible but invisible. Visible things are transitory, but invisible things eternal.

5 For we are well aware that when the tent that houses us on earth is folded up, there is a house for us from God, not made by human hands but everlasting, in the heavens. ²And in this earthly state we do indeed groan, ³longing to put on our heavenly home over the present one; if indeed we are to be found clothed rather than stripped bare. ⁴Yes, indeed, in this present tent, we groan under the burden, not that we want to be stripped of our covering, but because we want to be covered with a second garment on top, so that what is mortal in us may be swallowed up by life. ⁵It is God who designed us for this very purpose, and he has given us the Spirit as a pledge.

⁶We are always full of confidence, then, realising that as long as we are at home in the body we are exiled from the Lord, ⁷guided by faith and not yet by sight; ⁸we are full of confidence, then, and long instead to be exiled from the body and to be at home with the Lord. ⁹And so whether at home or exiled, we make it our ambition to please him. ¹⁰For at the judgement seat of Christ we are all to

---

4a Ps 116:10.

be seen for what we are, so that each of us may receive what he has deserved in the body, matched to whatever he has done, good or bad.

The apostolate in action

[11] And so it is with the fear of the Lord always in mind that we try to win people over. But God sees us for what we are, and I hope your consciences do too. [12] Again we are saying this not to commend ourselves to you, but simply to give you the opportunity to take pride in us, so that you may have an answer for those who take pride in appearances and not inner reality. [13] If we have been unreasonable, it was for God; if reasonable, for you. [14] For the love of Christ overwhelms us when we consider that if one man died for all, then all have died; [15] his purpose in dying for all humanity was that those who live should live not any more for themselves, but for him who died and was raised to life.

[16] From now onwards, then, we will not consider anyone by human standards: even if we were once familiar with Christ according to human standards, we do not know him in that way any longer. [17] So for anyone who is in Christ, there is a new creation: the old order is gone and a new being is there to see. [18] It is all God's work; he reconciled us to himself through Christ and he gave us the ministry of reconciliation. [19] I mean, God was in Christ reconciling the world to himself, not holding anyone's faults against them, but entrusting to us the message of reconciliation.

[20] So we are ambassadors for Christ; it is as though God were urging you through us, and in the name of Christ we appeal to you to be reconciled to God. [21] For our sake he made the sinless one a victim for sin, so that in him we might become the uprightness of God.

6 As his fellow-workers, we urge you not to let your acceptance of his grace come to nothing. [2] As he said, '*At the time of my favour I have answered you; on the day of salvation I have helped you*';[a] well, now is the real time of favour, now the day of salvation is here. [3] We avoid putting obstacles in anyone's way, so that no blame may attach to our work of service; [4] but in everything we prove ourselves authentic servants of God; by

resolute perseverance in times of hardships, difficulties and distress; [5] when we are flogged or sent to prison or mobbed; labouring, sleepless, starving; [6] in purity, in knowledge, in patience, in kindness; in the Holy Spirit, in a love free of affectation; [7] in the word of truth and in the power of God; by using the weapons of uprightness for attack and for defence: [8] in times of honour or disgrace, blame or praise; taken for impostors and yet we are genuine; [9] unknown and yet we are acknowledged; dying, and yet here we are, alive; scourged but not executed; [10] in pain yet always full of joy; poor and yet making many people rich; having nothing, and yet owning everything.

A warning

[11] People of Corinth, we have spoken frankly and opened our heart to you. [12] Any distress you feel is not on our side; the distress is in your own selves. [13] In fair exchange—I speak as though to children of mine—you must open your hearts too.

[14] Do[b] not harness yourselves in an uneven team with unbelievers; how can uprightness and law-breaking be partners, or what can light and darkness have in common? [15] How can Christ come to an agreement with Beliar and what sharing can there be between a believer and an unbeliever? [16] The temple of God cannot compromise with false gods, and that is what we are—the temple of the living God. We have God's word for it: *I shall fix my home among them and live among them; I will be their God and they will be my people.* [17] *Get away from them, purify yourselves,* says the Lord. *Do not touch anything unclean, and then I shall welcome you.* [18] *I shall be father to you, and* you *will be sons* and daughters *to me,*[c] says the almighty Lord.

7 Since these promises have been made to us, my dear friends, we should wash ourselves clean of everything that pollutes either body or spirit, bringing our sanctification to completion in the fear of God.

[2] Keep a place for us in your hearts. We have not injured anyone, or ruined anyone, or taken advantage of anyone. [3] I am not saying this to condemn anybody; as I have already told you, you are in our hearts—so

6a Is 49:8.
6b 6:14—7:1 may be a fragment on its own, a warning against infiltration of gentile ways.
6c Lv 26:11—12; Is 52:11; 2 S 7:14.

that together we live and together we die. [4]I can speak with the greatest frankness to you; and I can speak with the greatest pride about you: in all our hardship, I am filled with encouragement and overflowing with joy.

Paul in Macedonia; he is joined by Titus

[5]Even after we had come to Macedonia, there was no rest for this body of ours. Far from it; we were beset by hardship on all sides, there were quarrels all around us and misgivings within us. [6]But God, who encourages all those who are distressed, encouraged us through the arrival of Titus; [7]and not simply by his arrival only, but also by means of the encouragement that you had given him, as he told us of your desire to see us, how sorry you were and how concerned for us; so that I was all the more joyful.

[8]So now, though I did distress you with my letter, I do not regret it. Even if I did regret it—and I realise that the letter distressed you, even though not for long—[9]I am glad now, not because you were made to feel distress, but because the distress that you were caused led to repentance; your distress was the kind that God approves and so you have come to no kind of harm through us. [10]For to be distressed in a way that God approves leads to repentance and then to salvation with no regrets; it is the world's kind of distress that ends in death. [11]Just look at this present case: at what the result has been of your being made to feel distress in the way that God approves—what concern, what defence, what indignation and what alarm; what yearning, and what enthusiasm, and what justice done. In every way you have cleared yourselves of blame in this matter. [12]So although I wrote a letter to you, it was not for the sake of the offender, nor for the one offended, but only so that you yourselves should fully realise in the sight of God what concern you have for us. [13]That is what I have found encouraging.

In addition to all this to encourage us, we were made all the more joyful by Titus' joy, now that his spirit has been refreshed by you all. [14]And if I boasted about you to him in any way, then I have not been made to look foolish; indeed, our boast to Titus has been proved to be as true as anything we said to you. [15]His personal affection for you is all the stronger when he remembers how obedient you have all been, and how you welcomed him with fear and trembling. [16]I am glad that I have every confidence in you.

II: ORGANISATION OF THE COLLECTION

Why the Corinthians should be generous

8 Next, brothers, we will tell you of the grace of God which has been granted to the churches of Macedonia, [2]and how, throughout continual ordeals of hardship, their unfailing joy and their intense poverty have overflowed in a wealth of generosity on their part. [3]I can testify that it was of their own accord that they made their gift, which was not merely as far as their resources would allow, but well beyond their resources; [4]and they had kept imploring us most insistently for the privilege of a share in the fellowship of service to God's holy people—[5]it was not something that we expected of them, but it began by their offering themselves to the Lord and to us at the prompting of the will of God. [6]In the end we urged Titus, since he had already made a beginning, also to bring this work of generosity to completion among you. [7]More, as you are rich in everything—faith, eloquence, understanding, concern for everything, and love for us too—then make sure that you excel in this work of generosity too. [8]I am not saying this as an order, but testing the genuineness of your love against the concern of others. [9]You are well aware of the generosity which our Lord Jesus Christ had, that, although he was rich, he became poor for your sake, so that you should become rich through his poverty. [10]I will give you my considered opinion in the matter; this will be the right course for you as you were the first, a year ago, not only to take any action but also even to conceive the project. [11]Now, then, complete the action as well, so that the fulfilment may—so far as your resources permit—be proportionate to your enthusiasm for the project. [12]As long as the enthusiasm is there, the basis on which it is acceptable is what someone has, not what

someone does not have. [13]It is not that you ought to relieve other people's needs and leave yourselves in hardship; but there should be a fair balance—[14]your surplus at present may fill their deficit, and another time their surplus may fill your deficit. So there may be a fair balance; [15]as scripture says: *No one who had collected more had too much, no one who collected less had too little.*[a]

The delegates recommended to the Corinthians

[16]Thank God for putting into Titus' heart the same sincere concern for you. [17]He certainly took our urging to heart; but greater still was his own enthusiasm, and he went off to you of his own accord. [18]We have sent with him the brother who is praised as an evangelist in all the churches [19]and who, what is more, was elected by the churches to be our travelling companion in this work of generosity, a work to be administered by us for the glory of the Lord and our complete satisfaction. [20]We arranged it this way so that no one should be able to make any accusation against us about this large sum we are administering. [21]And so *we have been careful to do right* not only *in the sight of the Lord* but also *in the sight of people.*[b] [22]Along with these, we have sent a brother of ours whose eagerness we have tested over and over again in many ways and who is now all the more eager because he has so much faith in you. [23]If Titus is in question—he is my own partner and fellow-worker in your interests; and if our brothers—they are the emissaries of the churches and the glory of Christ. [24]So then, in full view of all the churches, give proof that you love them, and that we were right to boast of you to them.

9 About the help to God's holy people, there is really no need for me to write to you;[a] [2]for I am well aware of your enthusiasm, and I have been boasting of it to the Macedonians that 'Achaia has been ready for a year'; your enthusiasm has been a spur to many others. [3]All the same, I have sent the brothers, to make sure that our boast about you may not prove hollow in this respect and that you may be ready, as I said you would be; [4]so that if by chance some of the Macedonians came with me and found you unprepared we—to say nothing of yourselves—would not be put to shame by our confidence in you. [5]So I have thought it necessary to encourage the brothers to go to you ahead of us and make sure in advance of the gift that you have already promised, so that it is all at hand as a real gift and not an imposition.

Blessings to be expected from the collection

[6]But remember: anyone who sows sparsely will reap sparsely as well—and anyone who sows generously will reap generously as well. [7]Each one should give as much as he has decided on his own initiative, not reluctantly or under compulsion, for *God loves a cheerful giver.*[b] [8]God is perfectly able to enrich you with every grace, so that you always have enough for every conceivable need, and your resources overflow in all kinds of good work. [9]As scripture says: *To the needy he gave without stint, his uprightness stands firm for ever.*[c] [10]The one who so freely provides *seed for the sower and food to eat*[d] will provide you with ample store of seed for sowing and make *the harvest of your uprightness*[e] a bigger one: [11]you will be rich enough in every way for every kind of generosity that makes people thank God for what we have done. [12]For the help provided by this contribution not only satisfies the needs of God's holy people, but also overflows into widespread thanksgiving to God; [13]because when you have proved your quality by this help, they will give glory to God for the obedience which you show in professing the gospel of Christ, as well as for the generosity of your fellowship towards them and towards all. [14]At the same time, their prayer for you will express the affection they feel for you because of the unbounded grace God has given you. [15]Thanks be to God for his gift that is beyond all telling!

8a Ex 16:18.
8b Pr 3:4 LXX.
9a As he has just done so, this chapter may be a separate note.
9b Pr 22:8 LXX.
9c Ps 112:9.
9d Is 55:10.
9e Ho 12:12.

III: PAUL'S APOLOGIA

Paul's reply to accusations of weakness

10 I urge you by the gentleness and forbearance of Christ—this is Paul now speaking personally—I, the one who is so humble when he is facing you but full of boldness at a distance. ²Yes, my appeal to you is that I should not have to be bold when I am actually with you, or show the same self-assurance as I reckon to use when I am challenging those who reckon that we are guided by human motives. ³For although we are human, it is not by human methods that we do battle. ⁴The weapons with which we do battle are not those of human nature, but they have the power, in God's cause, to demolish fortresses. It is ideas that we demolish, ⁵every presumptuous notion that is set up against the knowledge of God, and we bring every thought into captivity and obedience to Christ; ⁶once you have given your complete obedience, we are prepared to punish any disobedience. ⁷Look at the evidence of your eyes. Anybody who is convinced that he belongs to Christ should go on to reflect that we belong to Christ no less than he does. ⁸Maybe I have taken rather too much pride in our authority, but the Lord gave us that for building you up, not for knocking you down, and I am not going to be shamed ⁹into letting you think that I can put fear into you only by letter. ¹⁰Someone said, 'His letters are weighty enough, and full of strength, but when you see him in person, he makes no impression and his powers of speaking are negligible.' ¹¹I should like that sort of person to take note that our deeds when we are present will show the same qualities as our letters when we were at a distance.

His reply to the accusation of ambition

¹²We are not venturing to rank ourselves, or even to compare ourselves with certain people who provide their own commendations. By measuring themselves by themselves and comparing themselves with themselves, they only show their folly. ¹³By contrast we do not intend to boast beyond measure, but will measure ourselves by the standard which God laid down for us, namely that of having come all the way to you. ¹⁴We are not overreaching ourselves as we would be if we had not come all the way to you; in fact we were the first to come as far as you with the good news of Christ. ¹⁵So we are not boasting beyond measure, about other men's work; in fact, we hope, as your faith increases, to grow greater and greater by this standard of ours, ¹⁶by preaching the gospel to regions beyond you, rather than boasting about work already done in someone else's province. ¹⁷*Let anyone who wants to boast, boast of the Lord.*ᵃ ¹⁸For it is not through self-commendation that recognition is won, but through commendation.

Paul is driven to sound his own praises

11 I wish you would put up with a little foolishness from me—not that you don't do this already. ²The jealousy that I feel for you is, you see, God's own jealousy: I gave you all in marriage to a single husband, a virgin pure for presentation to Christ. ³But I am afraid that, just as the snake with his cunning seduced Eve, your minds may be led astray from single-minded devotion to Christ. ⁴Because any chance comer has only to preach a Jesus other than the one we preached, or you have only to receive a spirit different from the one you received, or a gospel different from the one you accepted—and you put up with that only too willingly. ⁵Now, I consider that I am not in the least inferior to the super-apostles. ⁶Even if there is something lacking in my public speaking, this is not the case with my knowledge, as we have openly shown to you at all times and before everyone.

⁷Have I done wrong, then, humbling myself so that you might be raised up, by preaching the gospel of God to you for nothing? ⁸I was robbing other churches, taking wages from them in order to work for you. ⁹When I was with you and needed money, I was no burden to anybody, for the brothers from Macedonia brought me as much as I needed when they came; I have

---

10a Jr 9:22–23.

always been careful not to let myself be a burden to you in any way, and I shall continue to be so. [10]And as Christ's truth is in me, this boast of mine is not going to be silenced in the regions of Achaia. [11]Why should it be? Because I do not love you? God knows that I do. [12]I will go on acting as I do at present, to cut the ground from under the feet of those who are looking for a chance to be proved my equals in grounds for boasting. [13]These people are counterfeit apostles, dishonest workers disguising themselves as apostles of Christ. [14]There is nothing astonishing in this; even Satan disguises himself as an angel of light. [15]It is nothing extraordinary, then, when his servants disguise themselves as the servants of uprightness. They will come to the end appropriate to what they have done.

[16]To repeat: let no one take me for a fool, but if you do, then treat me as a fool, so that I, too, can do a little boasting. [17]I shall not be following the Lord's way in what I say now, but will be speaking out of foolishness in the conviction that I have something to boast about. [18]So many people boast on merely human grounds that I shall too. [19]I know how happy you are to put up with fools, being so wise yourselves; [20]and how you will still go on putting up with a man who enslaves you, eats up all you possess, keeps you under his orders and sets himself above you, or even slaps you in the face. [21]I say it to your shame; perhaps we have been too weak.

Whatever bold claims anyone makes—now I am talking as a fool—I can make them too. [22]Are they Hebrews? So am I. Are they Israelites? So am I. Are they descendants of Abraham? So am I. [23]Are they servants of Christ? I speak in utter folly—I am too, and more than they are: I have done more work, I have been in prison more, I have been flogged more severely, many times exposed to death. [24]Five times I have been given the thirty-nine lashes by the Jews; [25]three times I have been beaten with sticks; once I was stoned; three times I have been shipwrecked, and once I have been in the open sea for a night and a day; [26]continually travelling, I have been in danger from rivers, in danger from brigands, in danger from my own people and in danger from the gentiles, in danger in the towns and in danger in the open country, in danger at sea and in danger from people masquerading as brothers; [27]I have worked with unsparing energy, for many nights without sleep; I have been hungry and

thirsty, and often altogether without food or drink; I have been cold and lacked clothing. [28]And, besides all the external things, there is, day in day out, the pressure on me of my anxiety for all the churches. [29]If anyone weakens, I am weakened as well; and when anyone is made to fall, I burn in agony myself. [30]If I have to boast, I will boast of all the ways in which I am weak. [31]The God and Father of the Lord Jesus—who is for ever to be blessed—knows that I am not lying. [32]When I was in Damascus, the governor who was under King Aretas put guards round Damascus city to catch me, [33]and I was let down in a basket through a window in the wall, and that was how I escaped from his hands.

12 I am boasting because I have to. Not that it does any good, but I will move on to visions and revelations from the Lord. [2]I know a man in Christ who fourteen years ago—still in the body? I do not know; or out of the body? I do not know: God knows—was caught up right into the third heaven. [3]And I know that this man—still in the body? or outside the body? I do not know, God knows—[4]was caught up into Paradise and heard words said that cannot and may not be spoken by any human being. [5]On behalf of someone like that I am willing to boast, but I am not going to boast on my own behalf except of my weaknesses; [6]and then, if I do choose to boast I shall not be talking like a fool because I shall be speaking the truth. But I will not go on in case anybody should rate me higher than he sees and hears me to be, because of the exceptional greatness of the revelations.

[7]Wherefore, so that I should not get above myself, I was given a thorn in the flesh, a messenger from Satan to batter me and prevent me from getting above myself. [8]About this, I have three times pleaded with the Lord that it might leave me; [9]but he has answered me, 'My grace is enough for you: for power is at full stretch in weakness.' It is, then, about my weaknesses that I am happiest of all to boast, so that the power of Christ may rest upon me; [10]and that is why I am glad of weaknesses, insults, constraints, persecutions and distress for Christ's sake. For it is when I am weak that I am strong.

[11]I have turned into a fool, but you forced me to it. It is you that should have been commending me; those super-apostles had no advantage over me, even if I am nothing

at all. [12]All the marks characteristic of a true apostle have been at work among you: complete perseverance, signs, marvels, demonstrations of power. [13]Is there any way in which you have been given less than the rest of the churches, except that I did not make myself a burden to you? Forgive me for this unfairness!

[14]Here I am, ready to come to you for the third time and I am not going to be a burden on you: it is not your possessions that I want, but yourselves. Children are not expected to save up for their parents, but parents for their children, [15]and I am more than glad to spend what I have and to be spent for the sake of your souls. Is it because I love you so much more, that I am loved the less?

[16]All right, then; I did not make myself a burden to you, but, trickster that I am, I caught you by trickery. [17]Have I taken advantage of you through any of the people I have sent to you? [18]Titus came at my urging, and I sent his companion with him. Did Titus take advantage of you? Can you deny that he and I were following the guidance of the same Spirit and were on the same tracks?

Paul's fears and anxieties

[19]All this time you have been thinking that we have been pleading our own cause before you; no, we have been speaking in Christ and in the presence of God—and all, dear friends, to build you up. [20]I am afraid that in one way or another, when I come, I may find you different from what I should like you to be, and you may find me what you would not like me to be; so that in one way or the other there will be rivalry, jealousy, bad temper, quarrels, slander, gossip, arrogance and disorders; [21]and when I come again, my God may humiliate me in front of you and I shall be grieved by all those who sinned in the past and have still not repented of the impurities and sexual immorality and debauchery that they have committed.

13This will be the third time I have confronted you. *Whatever the misdemeanour, the evidence of two or three witnesses is required to sustain a charge.*[a] [2]I gave you notice once, and now, though I am not with you, I give notice again, just as when I was with you for a second time, to those who sinned before, and to all others; and it is to this effect, that when I do come next time, I shall have no mercy. [3]Since you are asking for a proof that it is Christ who speaks in me; he is not weak with you but his power is at work among you; [4]for, though it was out of weakness that he was crucified, he is alive now with the power of God. We, too, are weak in him, but with regard to you we shall live with him by the power of God.

[5]Put yourselves to the test to make sure you are in the faith. Examine yourselves. Do you not recognise yourselves as people in whom Jesus Christ is present?—unless, that is, you fail the test. [6]But we, as I hope you will come to recognise, do not fail the test. [7]It is our prayer to God that you may do nothing wrong—not so that we have the credit of passing a test, but because you will be doing what is right, even if we do not pass the test. [8]We have no power to resist the truth; only to further the truth; [9]and we are delighted to be weak if only you are strong. What we ask in our prayers is that you should be made perfect. [10]That is why I am writing this while still far away, so that when I am with you I shall not have to be harsh, with the authority that the Lord has given me, an authority that is for building up and not for breaking down.

CONCLUSION

Recommendations, greetings, final good wishes

[11]To end then, brothers, we wish you joy; try to grow perfect; encourage one another; have a common mind and live in peace, and the God of love and peace will be with you.

[12]Greet one another with the holy kiss. All God's holy people send you their greetings.
[13]The grace of the Lord Jesus Christ, the love of God and the fellowship of the Holy Spirit be with you all.

13a Dt 19:15.

THE LETTER TO THE
GALATIANS

A burning problem in the early Church was the attitude to Judaism, and the new Christians of Galatia had been persuaded of the need to keep to Jewish observance. Here is Paul's answer, written with all his characteristic vigour: he points out his own special call and special authority from God, and insists that the cross and faith set aside the Law, for the Law brings only a curse. Using rabbinic arguments especially appealing to the Jews, he shows that true sons of God are sons through faith and God's promise to Abraham, not through physical descent from Abraham.

PLAN OF THE LETTER

GALATIANS
THE LETTER OF PAUL
TO THE CHURCH IN GALATIA

Address*a*

1 From Paul, an apostle appointed not by human beings nor through any human being but by Jesus Christ and God the Father who raised him from the dead, ²and all the brothers who are with me, to the churches of Galatia. ³Grace and peace from God the Father and our Lord Jesus Christ ⁴who gave himself for our sins to liberate us from this present wicked world, in accordance with the will of our God and Father, ⁵to whom be glory for ever and ever. Amen.

A warning

⁶I am astonished that you are so promptly turning away from the one who called you in the grace of Christ and are going over to a different gospel—⁷not that it is another gospel; except that there are trouble-makers among you who are seeking to pervert the gospel of Christ. ⁸But even if we ourselves or an angel from heaven preaches to you a gospel other than the one we preached to you, let God's curse be on him. ⁹I repeat again what we declared before: anyone who preaches to you a gospel other than the one you were first given is to be under God's curse. ¹⁰Whom am I trying to convince now, human beings or God? Am I trying to please human beings? If I were still doing that I should not be a servant of Christ.

1a Unusually, this contains no thanks or praise.

I: PAUL'S APOLOGIA

God's call

[11]Now I want to make it quite clear to you, brothers, about the gospel that was preached by me, that it was no human message. [12]It was not from any human being that I received it, and I was not taught it, but it came to me through a revelation of Jesus Christ. [13]You have surely heard how I lived in the past, within Judaism, and how there was simply no limit to the way I persecuted the Church of God in my attempts to destroy it; [14]and how, in Judaism, I outstripped most of my Jewish contemporaries in my limitless enthusiasm for the traditions of my ancestors. [15]But when God, who had set me apart from the time when I was *in my mother's womb, called*[b] me through his grace and chose [16]to reveal his Son in me, so that I should preach him to the gentiles, I was in no hurry to confer with any human being, [17]or to go up to Jerusalem to see those who were already apostles before me. Instead, I went off to Arabia, and later I came back to Damascus. [18]Only after three years did I go up to Jerusalem to meet Cephas. I stayed fifteen days with him [19]but did not set eyes on any of the rest of the apostles, only James, the Lord's brother. [20]I swear before God that what I have written is the truth. [21]After that I went to places in Syria and Cilicia; [22]and was still unknown by sight to the churches of Judaea which are in Christ, [23]they simply kept hearing it said, 'The man once so eager to persecute us is now preaching the faith that he used to try to destroy,' [24]and they gave glory to God for me.

The meeting at Jerusalem

2 It was not until fourteen years had gone by that I travelled up to Jerusalem again, with Barnabas, and I took Titus with me too. [2]My journey was inspired by a revelation and there, in a private session with the recognised leaders, I expounded the whole gospel that I preach to the gentiles, to make quite sure that the efforts I was making and had already made should not be fruitless.

[3]Even then, and although Titus, a Greek, was with me, there was no demand that he should be circumcised; [4]but because of some false brothers who had secretly insinuated themselves to spy on the freedom that we have in Christ Jesus, intending to reduce us to slavery—[5]people we did not defer to for one moment, or the truth of the gospel preached to you might have been compromised. . .[6]but those who were recognised as important people—whether they actually were important or not: *There is no favouritism with God*[a]—those recognised leaders, I am saying, had nothing to add to my message. [7]On the contrary, once they saw that the gospel for the uncircumcised had been entrusted to me, just as to Peter the gospel for the circumcised [8](for he who empowered Peter's apostolate to the circumcision also empowered mine to the gentiles), [9]and when they acknowledged the grace that had been given to me, then James and Cephas and John, who were the ones recognised as pillars, offered their right hands to Barnabas and to me as a sign of partnership: we were to go to the gentiles and they to the circumcised. [10]They asked nothing more than that we should remember to help the poor, as indeed I was anxious to do in any case.

Peter and Paul at Antioch[b]

[11]However, when Cephas came to Antioch, then I did oppose him to his face since he was manifestly in the wrong. [12]Before certain people from James came, he used to eat with gentiles; but as soon as these came, he backed out and kept apart from them, out of fear of the circumcised. [13]And the rest of the Jews put on the same act as he did, so that even Barnabas was carried away by their insincerity.

[14]When I saw, though, that their behaviour was not true to the gospel, I said to Cephas in front of all of them, 'Since you, though you are a Jew, live like the gentiles and not like the Jews, how can you compel the gentiles to live like the Jews?'

1b Jr 1:5.
2a Dt 10:17.
2b cf. Ac 15:19–29.

The gospel as preached by Paul

[15]We who were born Jews and not gentile sinners [16]have nevertheless learnt that someone is reckoned as upright not by practising the Law but by faith in Jesus Christ; and we too came to believe in Christ Jesus so as to be reckoned as upright by faith in Christ and not by practising the Law: since no human being *can be found upright*[c] by keeping the Law. [17]Now if we too are found to be sinners on the grounds that we seek our justification in Christ, it would surely follow that Christ was at the service of sin. Out of the question! [18]If I now rebuild everything I once demolished, I prove that I was wrong before. [19]In fact, through the Law I am dead to the Law so that I can be alive to God. I have been crucified with Christ [20]and yet I am alive; yet it is no longer I, but Christ living in me. The life that I am now living, subject to the limitation of human nature, I am living in faith, faith in the Son of God who loved me and gave himself for me. [21]I am not setting aside God's grace as of no value; it is merely that if saving justice comes through the Law, Christ died needlessly.

II: DOCTRINAL MATTERS

The Christian experience

3 You stupid people in Galatia! After you have had a clear picture of Jesus Christ crucified, right in front of your eyes, who has put a spell on you? [2]There is only one thing I should like you to tell me: How was it that you received the Spirit — was it by the practice of the Law, or by believing in the message you heard? [3]Having begun in the Spirit, can you be so stupid as to end in the flesh? [4]Can all the favours you have received have had no effect at all — if there really has been no effect? [5]Would you say, then, that he who so lavishly sends the Spirit to you, and causes the miracles among you, is doing this through your practice of the Law or because you believed the message you heard?

Witness of scripture: faith and the Law

[6]*Abraham*, you remember, *put his faith in God*,[a] and this was reckoned to him as uprightness. [7]Be sure, then, that it is people of faith who are the children of Abraham. [8]And it was because scripture foresaw that God would give saving justice to the gentiles through faith, that it announced the future gospel to Abraham in the words: *All nations will be blessed in you.*[b] [9]So it is people of faith who receive the same blessing as Abraham, the man of faith.

The curse brought by the Law

[10]On the other hand, all those who depend on the works of the Law are under a curse, since scripture says: *Accursed be he who does not make what is written in the book of the Law effective, by putting it into practice.*[c] [11]Now it is obvious that nobody is reckoned as upright in God's sight by the Law, since *the upright will live through faith*; [12]and the Law is based not on faith but on the principle, *whoever complies with it will find life in it.* [13]Christ redeemed us from the curse of the Law by being cursed for our sake since scripture says: *Anyone hanged is accursed,* [14]so that the blessing of Abraham might come to the gentiles in Christ Jesus, and so that we might receive the promised Spirit through faith.

The Law did not cancel the promise

[15]To put it in human terms, my brothers: even when a will is only a human one, once it has been ratified nobody can cancel it or add more provisions to it. [16]Now the promises were addressed to Abraham *and to his progeny*. The words were not *and to his progenies* in the plural, but in the singular; *and to your progeny*, which means Christ. [17]What I am saying is this: once a will had been long ago ratified by God, the Law, coming four hundred and thirty years later, could not abolish it and so nullify its promise. [18]You see, if the inherit-

2c Ps 143:2.
3a Gn 15:6.
3b Gn 12:3.
3c Dt 27:26; Hab 2:4; Lv 18:5; Dt 21:23.

ance comes by the Law, it no longer comes through a promise; but it was by a promise that God made his gift to Abraham.

The purpose of the Law

[19] Then what is the purpose of the Law? It was added to deal with crimes until the 'progeny' to whom the promise had been made should come; and it was promulgated through angels,[d] by the agency of an intermediary. [20] Now there can be an intermediary only between two parties, yet God is one. [21] Is the Law contrary, then, to God's promises? Out of the question! If the Law that was given had been capable of giving life, then certainly saving justice would have come from the Law. [22] As it is, scripture makes no exception when it says that sin is master everywhere; so the promise can be given only by faith in Jesus Christ to those who have this faith.

The coming of faith

[23] But before faith came, we were kept under guard by the Law, locked up to wait for the faith which would eventually be revealed to us. [24] So the Law was serving as a slave to look after us, to lead us to Christ, so that we could be justified by faith. [25] But now that faith has come we are no longer under a slave looking after us; [26] for all of you are the children of God, through faith, in Christ Jesus, [27] since every one of you that has been baptised have been clothed in Christ. [28] There can be neither Jew nor Greek, there can be neither slave nor freeman, there can be neither male nor female—for you are all one in Christ Jesus. [29] And simply by being Christ's, you are that progeny of Abraham, the heirs named in the promise.

Sons of God

4 What I am saying is this: an heir, during the time while he is still under age, is no different from a slave, even though he is the owner of all the property; [2] he is under the control of guardians and administrators until the time fixed by his father. [3] So too with us, as long as we were still under age, we were enslaved to the elemental principles of this world; [4] but when the completion of the time came, God sent his Son, born of a woman, born a subject of the Law, [5] to redeem the subjects of the Law, so that we could receive adoption as sons. [6] As you are sons, God has sent into our hearts the Spirit of his Son crying, 'Abba, Father';[a] [7] and so you are no longer a slave, but a son; and if a son, then an heir, by God's own act.

[8] But formerly when you did not know God, you were kept in slavery to things which are not really gods at all, [9] whereas now that you have come to recognise God—or rather, be recognised by God— how can you now turn back again to those powerless and bankrupt elements whose slaves you now want to be all over again? [10] You are keeping special days, and months, and seasons and years— [11] I am beginning to be afraid that I may, after all, have wasted my efforts on you.

A personal appeal

[12] I urge you, brothers,—be like me, as I have become like you. You have never been unfair to me; [13] indeed you remember that it was an illness that first gave me the opportunity to preach the gospel to you, [14] but though my illness was a trial to you, you did not show any distaste or revulsion; instead, you welcomed me as a messenger of God, as if I were Christ Jesus himself. [15] What has happened to the utter contentment you had then? For I can testify to you that you would have plucked your eyes out, were that possible, and given them to me. [16] Then have I turned into your enemy simply by being truthful with you? [17] Their devotion to you has no praiseworthy motive; they simply want to cut you off from me, so that you may centre your devotion on them. [18] Devotion to a praiseworthy cause is praiseworthy at any time, not only when I am there with you. [19] My children, I am going through the pain of giving birth to you all over again, until Christ is formed in you; [20] and how I wish I could be there with you at this moment and find the right way of talking to you: I am quite at a loss with you.

The two covenants: Hagar and Sarah

[21] Tell me then, you are so eager to be subject to the Law, have you listened to what the

---

3d A rabbinic tradition. The intermediary is Moses.
4a cf. Rom 8:15.

Law says? [22]Scripture says that Abraham had two sons, one by the slave girl and one by the freewoman. [23]The son of the slave girl came to be born in the way of human nature; but the son of the freewoman came to be born through a promise. [24]There is an allegory here: these women stand for the two covenants. The one given on Mount Sinai—that is Hagar, whose children are born into slavery; [25]now Sinai is a mountain in Arabia and represents Jerusalem in its present state, for she is in slavery together with her children. [26]But the Jerusalem above is free, and that is the one that is our mother; [27]as scripture says:

Shout for joy, you barren woman who has borne no children! Break into shouts of joy, you who were never in labour. For the sons of the forsaken one are more in number than the sons of the wedded wife.[b] [28]Now you, brothers, are like Isaac, children of the promise; [29]just as at that time, the child born in the way of human nature persecuted the child born through the Spirit, so now. [30]But what is it that scripture says? *Drive away that slave girl and her son; the slave girl's son is not to share the inheritance with the son*[c] of the freewoman. [31]So, brothers, we are the children not of the slave girl but of the freewoman.

III: EXHORTATION

Christian liberty

5 Christ set us free, so that we should remain free. Stand firm, then, and do not let yourselves be fastened again to the yoke of slavery.

[2]I, Paul, give you my word that if you accept circumcision, Christ will be of no benefit to you at all. [3]I give my assurance once again to every man who accepts circumcision that he is under obligation to keep the whole Law; [4]once you seek to be reckoned as upright through the Law, then you have separated yourself from Christ, you have fallen away from grace. [5]We are led by the Spirit to wait in the confident hope of saving justice through faith, [6]since in Christ Jesus it is not being circumcised or being uncircumcised that can effect anything—only faith working through love.

[7]You began your race well; who came to obstruct you and stop you obeying the truth? [8]It was certainly not any prompting from him who called you! [9]A pinch of yeast ferments the whole batch. [10]But I feel sure that, united in the Lord, you will not be led astray, and that anyone who makes trouble with you will be condemned, no matter who he is. [11]And I, brothers—if I were still preaching circumcision, why should I still be persecuted? For then the obstacle which is the cross would have no point any more. [12]I

could wish that those who are unsettling you would go further and mutilate themselves.[a]

Liberty and love

[13]After all, brothers, you were called to be free; do not use your freedom as an opening for self-indulgence, but be servants to one another in love, [14]since the whole of the Law is summarised in the one commandment: *You must love your neighbour as yourself.*[b] [15]If you go snapping at one another and tearing one another to pieces, take care: you will be eaten up by one another.

[16]Instead, I tell you, be guided by the Spirit, and you will no longer yield to self-indulgence. [17]The desires of self-indulgence are always in opposition to the Spirit, and the desires of the Spirit are in opposition to self-indulgence: they are opposites, one against the other; that is how you are prevented from doing the things that you want to. [18]But when you are led by the Spirit, you are not under the Law. [19]When self-indulgence is at work the results are obvious: sexual vice, impurity, and sensuality, [20]the worship of false gods and sorcery; antagonisms and rivalry, jealousy, bad temper and quarrels, disagreements, [21]factions and malice, drunkenness, orgies and all such things. And about these, I tell you now as I have told you in the past, that people who behave in these ways will not

4b Is 54:1.
4c Gn 21:10.
5a Perhaps a reference to the castration practised by the priests of Cybele.
5b Lv 19:18.

inherit the kingdom of God. [22]On the other hand the fruit of the Spirit is love, joy, peace, patience, kindness, goodness, trustfulness, [23]gentleness and self-control; no law can touch such things as these. [24]All who belong to Christ Jesus have crucified self with all its passions and its desires.

[25]Since we are living by the Spirit, let our behaviour be guided by the Spirit [26]and let us not be conceited or provocative and envious of one another.

On kindness and perseverance

6 Brothers, even if one of you is caught doing something wrong, those of you who are spiritual should set that person right in a spirit of gentleness; and watch yourselves that you are not put to the test in the same way. [2]Carry each other's burdens; that is how to keep the law of Christ. [3] Someone who thinks himself important, when he is not, only deceives himself; [4]but everyone is to examine his own achievements, and then he will confine his boasting to his own achievements, not comparing them with anybody else's. [5]Each one has his own load to carry.

[6]When someone is under instruction in doctrine, he should give his teacher a share in all his possessions. [7]Don't delude yourself: God is not to be fooled; whatever someone sows, that is what he will reap. [8]If his sowing is in the field of self-indulgence, then his harvest from it will be corruption; if his sowing is in the Spirit, then his harvest from the Spirit will be eternal life. [9]And let us never slacken in doing good; for if we do not give up, we shall have our harvest in due time. [10]So then, as long as we have the opportunity let all our actions be for the good of everybody, and especially of those who belong to the household of the faith.

Postscript

[11]Notice what large letters I have used in writing to you with my own hand. [12]It is those who want to cut a figure by human standards who force circumcision on you, simply so that they will not be persecuted for the cross of Christ. [13]Even though they are circumcised they still do not keep the Law themselves; they want you to be circumcised only so that they can boast of your outward appearance. [14]But as for me, it is out of the question that I should boast at all, except of the cross of our Lord Jesus Christ, through whom the world has been crucified to me, and I to the world. [15]It is not being circumcised or uncircumcised that matters; but what matters is a new creation. [16]Peace and mercy to all who follow this as their rule and to the Israel of God.

[17]After this, let no one trouble me; I carry branded on my body the marks of Jesus.

[18]The grace of our Lord Jesus Christ be with your spirit, my brothers. Amen.

THE LETTER TO THE
EPHESIANS

A high point in the Pauline tradition. Because of controversy over cosmic forces who were held to control the universe, Paul presents Christ's position as one of universal supremacy. **1** He is supreme over all cosmic forces and is the principle which makes sense of all creation, the head and fullness which was the goal of creation. As the new Adam he is the model and the power which binds renewed humanity, both Jew and gentile, into one. **2** The Church is the Body of Christ in a new way; Christ is the Head, the supreme authority and source of life, and the Church is his completion, filled by him with divine life. The letter makes three separate presentations of this theme:

1:3–14, a hymn in praise of God's plan; 1:15 – 2:10, concentrating on Christ's position; and 2:11–22 concentrating on the unity of all in the New Man.

There is some doubt whether Paul is the actual author of this letter. Besides the development in thought, the style has changed, and Ep is written in a full, florid and almost liturgical language. It is closely related to Col, sometimes reusing phrases from that letter.

PLAN OF THE LETTER

EPHESIANS
THE LETTER OF PAUL
TO THE CHURCH AT EPHESUS

Address and greetings

1 Paul, by the will of God an apostle of Christ Jesus, to God's holy people,*a* faithful in Christ Jesus. ²Grace and peace to you from God our Father and from the Lord Jesus Christ.

I: THE MYSTERY OF SALVATION AND OF THE CHURCH

God's plan of salvation

³Blessed be God
  the Father of our Lord Jesus Christ,
who has blessed us
  with all the spiritual blessings of heaven
    in Christ.
⁴Thus he chose us in Christ
  before the world was made
to be holy and faultless
  before him in love,
⁵marking us out for himself beforehand,
  to be adopted sons,
    through Jesus Christ.
Such was his purpose and good pleasure,
⁶to the praise of the glory of his grace,
  his free gift to us in the Beloved,
⁷in whom, through his blood,
  we gain our freedom,
    the forgiveness of our sins.

Such is the richness of the grace
⁸which he has showered on us
  in all wisdom and insight.
⁹He has let us know
  the mystery of his purpose,
according to his good pleasure
  which he determined beforehand
    in Christ,
¹⁰for him to act upon
  when the times had run their course:
that he would bring everything together
  under Christ, as head,
everything in the heavens
  and everything on earth.
¹¹And it is in him
  that we have received our heritage,
marked out beforehand as we were,
  under the plan of the One
    who guides all things
as he decides by his own will,

1a Some authorities add 'who are at Ephesus' or 'who are . . .', leaving a gap for a place-name to be filled in.

12chosen to be,
for the praise of his glory,
the people who
would put their hopes in Christ
before he came.
13Now you too, in him,
have heard the message of the truth
and the gospel of your salvation,
and having put your trust in it
you have been stamped with the seal
of the Holy Spirit of the Promise,
14who is the pledge of our inheritance,
for the freedom of the people
whom God has taken for his own,
for the praise of his glory.

The triumph and the supremacy of Christ

15That is why I, having once heard about your faith in the Lord Jesus, and your love for all God's holy people, 16have never failed to thank God for you and to remember you in my prayers. 17May the God of our Lord Jesus Christ, the Father of glory, give you a spirit of wisdom and perception of what is revealed, to bring you to full knowledge of him. 18May he enlighten the eyes of your mind so that you can see what hope his call holds for you, how rich is the glory of the heritage he offers among his holy people, 19and how extraordinarily great is the power that he has exercised for us believers; this accords with the strength of his power 20at work in Christ, the power which he exercised in raising him from the dead and enthroning him at his right hand, in heaven, 21far above every principality, ruling force, power or sovereignty,*b* or any other name that can be named, not only in this age but also in the age to come. 22*He has put all things under his feet,*c* and made him, as he is above all things, the head of the Church; 23which is his Body, the fullness of him who is filled, all in all.

Salvation in Christ a free gift

2 And you were dead, through the crimes and the sins 2which used to make up your way of life when you were living by the principles of this world, obeying the ruler who dominates the air, the spirit who is at work in those who rebel. 3We too were all among them once, living only by our natural inclinations, obeying the demands of human self-indulgence and our own whim; our nature made us no less liable to God's retribution than the rest of the world. 4But God, being rich in faithful love, through the great love with which he loved us, 5even when we were dead in our sins, brought us to life with Christ—it is through grace that you have been saved—6and raised us up with him and gave us a place with him in heaven, in Christ Jesus.

7This was to show for all ages to come, through his goodness towards us in Christ Jesus, how extraordinarily rich he is in grace. 8Because it is by grace that you have been saved, through faith; not by anything of your own, but by a gift from God; 9not by anything that you have done, so that nobody can claim the credit. 10We are God's work of art, created in Christ Jesus for the good works which God has already designated to make up our way of life.

Reconciliation of the Jews and the gentiles with each other and with God

11Do not forget, then, that there was a time when you who were gentiles by physical descent, termed the uncircumcised by those who speak of themselves as the circumcised by reason of a physical operation, 12do not forget, I say, that you were at that time separate from Christ and excluded from membership of Israel, aliens with no part in the covenants of the Promise, limited to this world, without hope and without God. 13But now in Christ Jesus, you that used to be so far off have been brought close, by the blood of Christ. 14For he is the peace between us, and has made the two into one entity and broken down the barrier which used to keep them apart, by destroying in his own person the hostility, 15that is, the Law of commandments with its decrees. His purpose in this was, by restoring peace, to create a single New Man out of the two of them, 16and through the cross, to reconcile them both to God in one Body; in his own person he killed the hostility. 17He came to bring the good news of *peace to you who were far off and peace*

1b Names for cosmic powers.
1c Ps 8:6.

to those who were near.[a] [18]Through him, then, we both in the one Spirit have free access to the Father.

[19]So you are no longer aliens or foreign visitors; you are fellow-citizens with the holy people of God and part of God's household. [20]You are built upon the foundations of the apostles and prophets, and Christ Jesus himself is the cornerstone. [21]Every structure knit together in him grows into a holy temple in the Lord; [22]and you too, in him, are being built up into a dwelling-place of God in the Spirit.

Paul, a servant of the mystery

3 It is because of this that I, Paul, a prisoner of the Lord Jesus on behalf of you gentiles. . . [2]You have surely heard the way in which God entrusted me with the grace he gave me for your sake; [3]he made known to me by a revelation the mystery I have just described briefly — [4]a reading of it will enable you to perceive my understanding of the mystery of Christ. [5]This mystery, as it is now revealed in the Spirit to his holy apostles and prophets, was unknown to humanity in previous generations: [6]that the gentiles now have the same inheritance and form the same Body and enjoy the same promise in Christ Jesus through the gospel. [7]I have been made the servant of that gospel by a gift of grace from God who gave it to me by the workings of his power. [8]I, who am less than the least of all God's holy people, have been entrusted with this special grace, of proclaiming to the gentiles the unfathomable treasure of Christ [9]and of throwing light on the inner workings of the mystery kept hidden through all the ages in God, the Creator of everything. [10]The purpose of this was, that now, through the Church, the principalities and ruling forces should learn how many-sided God's wisdom is, [11]according to the plan which he had formed from all eternity in Christ Jesus our Lord. [12]In him we are bold enough to approach God in complete confidence, through our faith in him; [13]so, I beg you, do not let the hardships I go through on your account make you waver; they are your glory.

Paul's prayer

[14]This, then, is what I pray, kneeling before the Father, [15]from whom every fatherhood, in heaven or on earth, takes its name. [16]In the abundance of his glory may he, through his Spirit, enable you to grow firm in power with regard to your inner self, [17]so that Christ may live in your hearts through faith, and then, planted in love and built on love, [18]with all God's holy people you will have the strength to grasp the breadth and the length, the height and the depth; [19]so that, knowing the love of Christ, which is beyond knowledge, you may be filled with the utter fullness of God.

[20]Glory be to him whose power, working in us, can do infinitely more than we can ask or imagine; [21]glory be to him from generation to generation in the Church and in Christ Jesus for ever and ever. Amen.

II: EXHORTATION

A call to unity

4 I, the prisoner in the Lord, urge you therefore to lead a life worthy of the vocation to which you were called. [2]With all humility and gentleness, and with patience, support each other in love. [3]Take every care to preserve the unity of the Spirit by the peace that binds you together. [4]There is one Body, one Spirit, just as one hope is the goal of your calling by God. [5]There is one Lord, one faith, one baptism, [6]and one God and Father of all, over all, through all and within all.

[7]On each one of us God's favour has been bestowed in whatever way Christ allotted it. [8]That is why it says:

He went up to the heights, took captives,
he gave gifts to humanity.[a]

[9]When it says, 'he went up', it must mean that he had gone down to the deepest levels of the earth. [10]The one who went down is none other than the one who went up above

---

2a　Is 57:19.
4a　Ps 68:18.

all the heavens to fill all things. [11]And to some, his 'gift' was that they should be apostles; to some prophets; to some, evangelists; to some, pastors and teachers; [12]to knit God's holy people together for the work of service to build up the Body of Christ, [13]until we all reach unity in faith and knowledge of the Son of God and form the perfect Man, fully mature with the fullness of Christ himself.

[14]Then we shall no longer be children, or tossed one way and another, and carried hither and thither by every new gust of teaching, at the mercy of all the tricks people play and their unscrupulousness in deliberate deception. [15]If we live by the truth and in love, we shall grow completely into Christ, who is the head [16]by whom the whole Body is fitted and joined together, every joint adding its own strength, for each individual part to work according to its function. So the body grows until it has built itself up in love.

The new life in Christ

[17]So this I say to you and attest to you in the Lord, do not go on living the empty-headed life that the gentiles live. [18]Intellectually they are in the dark, and they are estranged from the life of God, because of the ignorance which is the consequence of closed minds. [19]Their sense of right and wrong once dulled, they have abandoned all self-control and pursue to excess every kind of uncleanness. [20]Now that is hardly the way you have learnt Christ, [21]unless you failed to hear him properly when you were taught what the truth is in Jesus. [22]You were to put aside your old self, which belongs to your old way of life and is corrupted by following illusory desires. [23]Your mind was to be renewed in spirit [24]so that you could put on the New Man that has been created on God's principles, in the uprightness and holiness of the truth.

[25]So from now on, there must be no more lies. *Speak the truth to one another,[b]* since we are all parts of one another. [26]*Even if you are angry, do not sin:[c]* never let the sun set on your anger [27]or else you will give the devil a foothold. [28]Anyone who was a thief must stop stealing; instead he should exert himself at some honest job with his own hands so that

he may have something to share with those in need. [29]No foul word should ever cross your lips; let your words be for the improvement of others, as occasion offers, and do good to your listeners; [30]do not grieve the Holy Spirit of God who has marked you with his seal, ready for the day when we shall be set free. [31]Any bitterness or bad temper or anger or shouting or abuse must be far removed from you—as must every kind of malice. [32]Be generous to one another, sympathetic, forgiving each other as readily as God forgave you in Christ.

5 As God's dear children, then, take him as your pattern, [2]and follow Christ by loving as he loved you, giving himself up for us *as an offering and a sweet-smelling sacrifice to God.[a]* [3]Among you there must be not even a mention of sexual vice or impurity in any of its forms, or greed: this would scarcely become the holy people of God! [4]There must be no foul or salacious talk or coarse jokes—all this is wrong for you; there should rather be thanksgiving. [5]For you can be quite certain that nobody who indulges in sexual immorality or impurity or greed—which is worshipping a false god—can inherit the kingdom of God. [6]Do not let anyone deceive you with empty arguments: it is such behaviour that draws down God's retribution on those who rebel against him. [7]Make sure that you do not throw in your lot with them. [8]You were darkness once, but now you are light in the Lord; behave as children of light, [9]for the effects of the light are seen in complete goodness and uprightness and truth. [10]Try to discover what the Lord wants of you, [11]take no part in the futile works of darkness but, on the contrary, show them up for what they are. [12]The things which are done in secret are shameful even to speak of; [13]but anything shown up by the light will be illuminated [14]and anything illuminated is itself a light. That is why it is said:

Wake up, sleeper,
rise from the dead,
and Christ will shine on you.

[15]So be very careful about the sort of lives you lead, like intelligent and not like senseless people. [16]Make the best of the present time, for it is a wicked age. [17]This is why you must

4b Zc 8:16.
4c Ps 4:4.
5a Ex 29:18.

not be thoughtless but must recognise what is the will of the Lord. [18]*Do not get drunk with wine;*[b] this is simply dissipation; be filled with the Spirit. [19]Sing psalms and hymns and inspired songs among yourselves, singing and chanting to the Lord in your hearts, [20]always and everywhere giving thanks to God who is our Father in the name of our Lord Jesus Christ.

The morals of the home

[21]Be subject to one another out of reverence for Christ. [22]Wives should be subject to their husbands as to the Lord, [23]since, as Christ is head of the Church and saves the whole body, so is a husband the head of his wife; [24]and as the Church is subject to Christ, so should wives be to their husbands, in everything. [25]Husbands should love their wives, just as Christ loved the Church and sacrificed himself for her [26]to make her holy by washing her in cleansing water with a form of words, [27]so that when he took the Church to himself she would be glorious, with no speck or wrinkle or anything like that, but holy and faultless. [28]In the same way, husbands must love their wives as they love their own bodies; for a man to love his wife is for him to love himself. [29]A man never hates his own body, but he feeds it and looks after it; and that is the way Christ treats the Church, [30]because we are parts of his Body. [31]*This is why a man leaves his father and mother and becomes attached to his wife, and the two become one flesh.*[c] [32]This mystery has great significance, but I am applying it to Christ and the Church. [33]To sum up: you also, each one of you, must love his wife as he loves himself; and let every wife respect her husband.

6 Children, be obedient to your parents in the Lord—that is what uprightness demands. [2]The first commandment that has a promise attached to it is: *Honour your father and your mother*, [3]and the promise is: *so that you may have long life and prosper in the land.*[a] [4]And parents, never drive your children to resentment but bring them up with correction and advice inspired by the Lord.

[5]Slaves, be obedient to those who are, according to human reckoning, your masters, with deep respect and sincere loyalty, as you are obedient to Christ: [6]not only when you are under their eye, as if you had only to please human beings, but as slaves of Christ who wholeheartedly do the will of God. [7]Work willingly for the sake of the Lord and not for the sake of human beings. [8]Never forget that everyone, whether a slave or a free man, will be rewarded by the Lord for whatever work he has done well. [9]And those of you who are employers, treat your slaves in the same spirit; do without threats, and never forget that they and you have the same Master in heaven and there is no favouritism with him.

The spiritual war

[10]Finally, grow strong in the Lord, with the strength of his power. [11]Put on the full armour of God so as to be able to resist the devil's tactics. [12]For it is not against human enemies that we have to struggle, but against the principalities and the ruling forces who are masters of the darkness in this world, the spirits of evil in the heavens. [13]That is why you must take up all God's armour, or you will not be able to put up any resistance on the evil day, or stand your ground even though you exert yourselves to the full.

[14]So stand your ground, with *truth a belt round your waist*, and *uprightness a breastplate*, [15]wearing for shoes on your feet *the eagerness to spread the gospel of peace*[b] [16]and always carrying the shield of faith so that you can use it to quench the burning arrows of the Evil One. [17]And then you must take *salvation as your helmet* and the sword of the Spirit, that is, the word of God.

[18]In all your prayer and entreaty keep praying in the Spirit on every possible occasion. Never get tired of staying awake to pray for all God's holy people, [19]and pray for me to be given an opportunity to open my mouth and fearlessly make known the mystery of the gospel [20]of which I am an ambassador in chains; pray that in proclaiming it I may speak as fearlessly as I ought to.

5b Pr 23:31.
5c Gn 2:24.
6a Ex 20:12.
6b Is 59:17; 40:9.

Personal news and final salutation

²¹So that you know, as well, what is happening to me and what I am doing, my dear friend Tychicus, my trustworthy helper in the Lord, will tell you everything. ²²I am sending him to you precisely for this purpose, to give you news about us and encourage you thoroughly.

²³May God the Father and the Lord Jesus Christ grant peace, love and faith to all the brothers. ²⁴May grace be with all who love our Lord Jesus Christ, in life imperishable.

THE LETTER TO THE
PHILIPPIANS

Philippians is a joyful piece of writing, containing news and messages of friendship; the Philippians were the only church from whom Paul would accept gifts. It also has some valuable reflections on Paul's vital union with Christ in his sufferings. A most important fragment is the early hymn of Christ's exaltation quoted by Paul (2:6–11); it contrasts Christ's obedience and elevation with Adam's pride and fall. Dating is difficult, and indeed it may be a collection of three short letters: A = 4:10–20; B = 1:1–3 + 4:2–9; C = 3:2—4:1.

PHILIPPIANS
THE LETTER OF PAUL
TO THE CHURCH AT PHILIPPI

Address

1 Paul and Timothy, servants of Christ Jesus, to all God's holy people in Christ Jesus at Philippi, together with their presiding elders and the deacons. ²Grace and peace to you from God our Father and the Lord Jesus Christ.

Thanksgiving and prayer

³I thank my God whenever I think of you, ⁴and every time I pray for you all, I always pray with joy ⁵for your partnership in the gospel from the very first day up to the present. ⁶I am quite confident that the One who began a good work in you will go on completing it until the Day of Jesus Christ comes. ⁷It is only right that I should feel like this towards you all, because you have a place in my heart, since you have all shared together in the grace that has been mine, both my chains and my work defending and establishing the gospel. ⁸For God will testify for me how much I long for you all with the warm longing of Christ Jesus; ⁹it is my prayer that your love for one another may grow more and more with the knowledge and complete understanding ¹⁰that will help you to come to true discernment, so that you will be

innocent and free of any trace of guilt when the Day of Christ comes, [11]entirely filled with the fruits of uprightness through Jesus Christ, for the glory and praise of God.

Paul's own circumstances

[12]Now I want you to realise, brothers, that the circumstances of my present life are helping rather than hindering the advance of the gospel. [13]My chains in Christ have become well known not only to all the Praetorium,[a] but to everybody else, [14]and so most of the brothers in the Lord have gained confidence from my chains and are getting more and more daring in announcing the Message without any fear. [15]It is true that some of them are preaching Christ out of malice and rivalry; but there are many as well whose intentions are good; [16]some are doing it out of love, knowing that I remain firm in my defence of the gospel. [17]There are others who are proclaiming Christ out of jealousy, not in sincerity but meaning to add to the weight of my chains. [18]But what does it matter? Only that in both ways, whether with false motives or true, Christ is proclaimed, and for that I am happy; [19]and I shall go on being happy, too, because I know that *this is what will save me*,[b] with your prayers and with the support of the Spirit of Jesus Christ; [20]all in accordance with my most confident hope and trust that I shall never have to admit defeat, but with complete fearlessness I shall go on, so that now, as always, Christ will be glorified in my body, whether by my life or my death. [21]Life to me, of course, is Christ, but then death would be a positive gain. [22]On the other hand again, if to be alive in the body gives me an opportunity for fruitful work, I do not know which I should choose. [23]I am caught in this dilemma: I want to be gone and to be with Christ, and this is by far the stronger desire—[24]and yet for your sake to stay alive in this body is a more urgent need. [25]This much I know for certain, that I shall stay and stand by you all, to encourage your advance and your joy in the faith, [26]so that my return to be among you may increase to overflowing your pride in Jesus Christ on my account.

Fight for the faith

[27]But you must always behave in a way that is worthy of the gospel of Christ, so that whether I come to you and see for myself or whether I only hear all about you from a distance, I shall find that you are standing firm and united in spirit, battling, as a team with a single aim, for the faith of the gospel, [28]undismayed by any of your opponents. This will be a clear sign, for them that they are to be lost, and for you that you are to be saved. [29]This comes from God, for you have been granted the privilege for Christ's sake not only of believing in him but of suffering for him as well; [30]you are fighting the same battle which you saw me fighting for him and which you hear I am fighting still.

Preserve unity in humility

2 So if in Christ there is anything that will move you, any incentive in love, any fellowship in the Spirit, any warmth or sympathy—I appeal to you, [2]make my joy complete by being of a single mind, one in love, one in heart and one in mind. [3]Nothing is to be done out of jealousy or vanity; instead, out of humility of mind everyone should give preference to others, [4]everyone pursuing not selfish interests but those of others. [5]Make your own the mind of Christ Jesus:

[6]Who, being in the form of God,
did not count equality with God
something to be grasped.

[7]But he emptied himself,
taking the form of a slave,
becoming as human beings are;
and being in every way
like a human being,
[8]he was humbler yet,
even to accepting death,
death on a cross.

[9]And for this God raised him high,
and gave him the name
which is above all other names;

[10]so that *all beings*
in the heavens, on earth
and in the underworld,
should bend the knee at the name of Jesus

1a The headquarters of the Praetorian guard wherever Paul is captive (Ephesus, Caesarea, Rome?).
1b Jb 13:16.

[11] and that *every tongue should acknowledge*[a] Jesus Christ as Lord, to the glory of God the Father.

Work for salvation

[12] So, my dear friends, you have always been obedient; your obedience must not be limited to times when I am present. Now that I am absent it must be more in evidence, so work out your salvation in fear and trembling. [13] It is God who, for his own generous purpose, gives you the intention and the powers to act. [14] Let your behaviour be free of murmuring and complaining [15] so that you remain faultless and pure, *unspoilt children of God* surrounded by *a deceitful and underhand brood*,[b] shining out among them like bright stars in the world, [16] proffering to it the Word of life. Then I shall have reason to be proud on the Day of Christ, for it will not be for nothing that I have run the race and toiled so hard. [17] Indeed, even if my blood has to be poured as a libation over your sacrifice and the offering of your faith, then I shall be glad and join in your rejoicing — [18] and in the same way, you must be glad and join in my rejoicing.

The mission of Timothy and Epaphroditus

[19] I hope, in the Lord Jesus, to send Timothy to you soon, so that my mind may be set at rest when I hear how you are. [20] There is nobody else that I can send who is like him and cares as sincerely for your well-being; [21] they all want to work for themselves, not for Jesus Christ. [22] But you know what sort of person he has proved himself, working with me for the sake of the gospel like a son with his father. [23] That is the man, then, that I am hoping to send to you immediately I can make out what is going to happen to me; [24] but I am confident in the Lord that I shall come myself, too, before long. [25] Nevertheless I thought it essential to send to you Epaphroditus, my brother and fellow-worker and companion-in-arms since he came as your representative to look after my needs; [26] because he was missing you all and was worrying because you had heard that he was ill. [27] Indeed he was seriously ill and nearly died; but God took pity on him — and

not only on him but also on me, to spare me one grief on top of another. [28] So I am sending him back as promptly as I can so that you will have the joy of seeing him again, and that will be some comfort to me in my distress. [29] Welcome him in the Lord, then, with all joy; hold people like him in honour, [30] because it was for Christ's work that he came so near to dying, risking his life to do the duty to me which you could not do yourselves.

3 Finally, brothers, I wish you joy in the Lord.

The true way of Christian salvation

To write to you what I have already written before is no trouble to me and to you will be a protection. [2] Beware of dogs! Beware of evil workmen! Beware of self-mutilators! [3] We are the true people of the circumcision since we worship by the Spirit of God and make Christ Jesus our only boast, not relying on physical qualifications, [4] although, I myself could rely on these too. If anyone does claim to rely on them, my claim is better. [5] Circumcised on the eighth day of my life, I was born of the race of Israel, of the tribe of Benjamin, a Hebrew born of Hebrew parents. In the matter of the Law, I was a Pharisee; [6] as for religious fervour, I was a persecutor of the Church; as for the uprightness embodied in the Law, I was faultless. [7] But what were once my assets I now through Christ Jesus count as losses. [8] Yes, I will go further: because of the supreme advantage of knowing Christ Jesus my Lord, I count everything else as loss. For him I have accepted the loss of all other things, and look on them all as filth if only I can gain Christ [9] and be given a place in him, with the uprightness I have gained not from the Law, but through faith in Christ, an uprightness from God, based on faith, [10] that I may come to know him and the power of his resurrection, and partake of his sufferings by being moulded to the pattern of his death, [11] striving towards the goal of resurrection from the dead. [12] Not that I have secured it already, nor yet reached my goal, but I am still pursuing it in the attempt to take hold of the prize for which Christ Jesus took hold of me. [13] Brothers, I do not reckon myself as having taken hold of it; I can only say that forgetting all that lies behind me,

2a Is 45:23.
2b Dt 32:5.

and straining forward to what lies in front, [14]I am racing towards the finishing-point to win the prize of God's heavenly call in Christ Jesus. [15]So this is the way in which all of us who are mature should be thinking, and if you are still thinking differently in any way, then God has yet to make this matter clear to you. [16]Meanwhile, let us go forward from the point we have each attained.

[17]Brothers, be united in imitating me. Keep your eyes fixed on those who act according to the example you have from me. [18]For there are so many people of whom I have often warned you, and now I warn you again with tears in my eyes, who behave like the enemies of Christ's cross. [19]They are destined to be lost; their god is the stomach; they glory in what they should think shameful, since their minds are set on earthly things. [20]But our homeland is in heaven and it is from there that we are expecting a Saviour, the Lord Jesus Christ, [21]who will transfigure the wretched body of ours into the mould of his glorious body, through the working of the power which he has, even to bring all things under his mastery.

4 So then, my brothers and dear friends whom I miss so much, my joy and my crown, hold firm in the Lord, dear friends.

Last advice

[2]I urge Euodia, and I urge Syntyche to come to agreement with each other in the Lord; [3]and I ask you, Syzygus, really to be a 'partner'*a* and help them. These women have struggled hard for the gospel with me, along with Clement and all my other fellow-workers, whose names are written in the book of life.

[4]Always be joyful, then, in the Lord; I repeat, be joyful. [5]Let your good sense be obvious to everybody. The Lord is near. [6]Never worry about anything; but tell God all your desires of every kind in prayer and petition shot through with gratitude, [7]and the peace of God which is beyond our understanding will guard your hearts and your thoughts in Christ Jesus. [8]Finally, brothers, let your minds be filled with everything that is true, everything that is honourable, every-

thing that is upright and pure, everything that we love and admire—with whatever is good and praiseworthy. [9]Keep doing everything you learnt from me and were told by me and have heard or seen me doing. Then the God of peace will be with you.

Thanks for help received

[10]As for me, I am full of joy in the Lord, now that at last your consideration for me has blossomed again; though I recognise that you really did have consideration before, but had no opportunity to show it. [11]I do not say this because I have lacked anything; I have learnt to manage with whatever I have. [12]I know how to live modestly, and I know how to live luxuriously too: in every way now I have mastered the secret of all conditions: full stomach and empty stomach, plenty and poverty. [13]There is nothing I cannot do in the One who strengthens me. [14]All the same, it was good of you to share with me in my hardships. [15]In the early days of the gospel, as you of Philippi well know, when I left Macedonia, no church other than yourselves made common account with me in the matter of expenditure and receipts. You were the only ones; [16]and what is more, you have twice sent me what I needed in Thessalonica. [17]It is not the gift that I value most; what I value is the interest that is mounting up in your account. [18]I have all that I need and more: I am fully provided, now that I have received from Epaphroditus the offering that you sent, *a pleasing smell,*b the sacrifice which is acceptable and pleasing to God. [19]And my God will fulfil all your needs out of the riches of his glory in Christ Jesus. [20]And so glory be to God our Father, for ever and ever. Amen.

Greetings and final wish

[21]My greetings to every one of God's holy people in Christ Jesus. The brothers who are with me send you their greetings. [22]All God's holy people send you their greetings, especially those of Caesar's household.

[23]May the grace of the Lord Jesus Christ be with your spirit.

4a Syzygus means 'yoke-fellow' or 'partner'.
4b Gn 8:21.

THE LETTER TO THE
COLOSSIANS

A new synthesis on Christ's position. The Jewish Christians of Colossae were drawn to reverence angels and various cosmic powers, and this led Paul to rethink Christ's place with regard to them. He is the Lord of these powers, and God's Wisdom, in whom the fullness of divinity dwells. Many of the old doctrines of Rm about belonging to Christ are repeated, with a new depth of experience of what it means to share in Christ's sufferings and be part of the Body of which he is the Head.

The letter is closely related to Ep; some doubt its Pauline authorship, but the balance of argument is in favour of it.

PLAN OF THE LETTER

Preface 1:1–14
I   Formal Instruction 1:15—2:5
II   A Warning Against Some Errors 2:6—3:4
III Encouragement 3:5—4:18

COLOSSIANS
THE LETTER OF PAUL
TO THE CHURCH AT COLOSSAE

PREFACE

Address

1 From Paul, by the will of God an apostle of Christ Jesus, and from our brother Timothy ²to God's holy people in Colossae, our faithful brothers in Christ. Grace and peace to you from God our Father.

Thanksgiving and prayer

³We give thanks for you to God, the Father of our Lord Jesus Christ, continually in our prayers, ⁴ever since we heard about your faith in Christ Jesus and the love that you show towards all God's holy people ⁵because of the hope which is stored up for you in heaven. News of this hope reached you not long ago through the word of truth, the gospel ⁶that came to you in the same way as it is bearing fruit and growing throughout the world. It has had the same effect among you, ever since you heard about the grace of God and recognised it for what it truly is. ⁷This you learnt from Epaphras, our very dear fellow-worker and a trustworthy deputy for us as Christ's servant, ⁸and it was he who also told us all about your love in the Spirit.

⁹That is why, ever since the day he told us, we have never failed to remember you in our prayers and ask that through perfect wisdom and spiritual understanding you should reach the fullest knowledge of his will ¹⁰and so be able to lead a life worthy of the Lord, a life

acceptable to him in all its aspects, bearing fruit in every kind of good work and growing in knowledge of God, [11]fortified, in accordance with his glorious strength, with all power always to persevere and endure, [12]giving thanks with joy to the Father who has made you able to share the lot of God's holy people and with them to inherit the light.

[13]Because that is what he has done. It is he who has rescued us from the ruling force of darkness and transferred us to the kingdom of the Son that he loves, [14]and in him we enjoy our freedom, the forgiveness of sin.

I: FORMAL INSTRUCTION

Christ is the head of all creation[a]

[15]He is the image of the unseen God,
　the first-born of all creation,
[16]for in him were created all things
　in heaven and on earth:
　everything visible
　　and everything invisible,
　thrones, ruling forces,
　　sovereignties, powers—
　all things were created through him
　　and for him.
[17]He exists before all things
　and in him all things hold together,
[18]and he is the Head of the Body,
　that is, the Church.

He is the Beginning,
　the first-born from the dead,
so that he should be supreme in every way;
[19]because God wanted all fullness
　to be found in him
[20]and through him
　to reconcile all things to him,
　everything in heaven
　　and everything on earth,
　by making peace through his death
　　on the cross.

The Colossians have their share in salvation

[21]You were once estranged and of hostile intent through your evil behaviour; [22]now he has reconciled you, by his death and in that mortal body, to bring you before himself holy, faultless and irreproachable—[23]as long as you persevere and stand firm on the solid base of the faith, never letting yourselves drift away from the hope promised by the gospel, which you have heard, which has been preached to every creature under heaven, and of which I, Paul, have become the servant.

Paul's labours in the service of the gentiles

[24]It makes me happy to be suffering for you now, and in my own body to make up all the hardships that still have to be undergone by Christ for the sake of his body, the Church, [25]of which I was made a servant with the responsibility towards you that God gave to me, that of completing God's message, [26]the message which was a mystery hidden for generations and centuries and has now been revealed to his holy people. [27]It was God's purpose to reveal to them how rich is the glory of this mystery among the gentiles; it is Christ among you, your hope of glory: [28]this is the Christ we are proclaiming, admonishing and instructing everyone in all wisdom, to make everyone perfect in Christ. [29]And it is for this reason that I labour, striving with his energy which works in me mightily.

Paul's concern for the Colossians' faith

2 I want you to know, then, what a struggle I am having on your behalf and on behalf of those in Laodicea, and on behalf of so many others who have never seen me face to face. [2]It is all to bind them together in love and to encourage their resolution until they are rich in the assurance of their complete understanding and have knowledge of the mystery of God [3]in which all the jewels of wisdom and knowledge are hidden.

[4]I say this to make sure that no one deceives you with specious arguments. [5]I may be absent in body, but in spirit I am there among you, delighted to find how well-ordered you are and to see how firm your faith in Christ is.

1a cf. Ws 7:26.

II: A WARNING AGAINST SOME ERRORS

Live according to the true faith in Christ, not according to false teaching

[6]So then, as you received Jesus as Lord and Christ, now live your lives in him, [7]be rooted in him and built up on him, held firm by the faith you have been taught, and overflowing with thanksgiving.

[8]Make sure that no one captivates you with the empty lure of a 'philosophy' of the kind that human beings hand on, based on the principles of this world and not on Christ.

Christ alone is the true head of all humanity and the angels

[9]In him, in bodily form, lives divinity in all its fullness, [10]and in him you too find your own fulfilment, in the one who is the head of every sovereignty and ruling force.

[11]In him you have been circumcised, with a circumcision performed, not by human hand, but by the complete stripping of your natural self. This is circumcision according to Christ. [12]You have been buried with him by your baptism; by which, too, you have been raised up with him through your belief in the power of God who raised him from the dead. [13]You were dead, because you were sinners and uncircumcised in body: he has brought you to life with him, he has forgiven us every one of our sins.

[14]He has wiped out the record of our debt to the Law, which stood against us; he has destroyed it by nailing it to the cross; [15]and he has stripped the sovereignties and the ruling forces, and paraded them in public, behind him in his triumphal procession.

Against the false asceticism based on the 'principles of this world'

[16]Then never let anyone criticise you for what you eat or drink, or about observance of annual festivals, New Moons or Sabbaths. [17]These are only a shadow of what was coming: the reality is the body of Christ. [18]Do not be cheated of your prize by anyone who chooses to grovel to angels and worship them, pinning every hope on visions received, vainly puffed up by a human way of thinking; [19]such a person has no connection to the Head, by which the whole body, given all that it needs and held together by its joints and sinews, grows with the growth given by God.

[20]If you have really died with Christ to the principles of this world, why do you still let rules dictate to you, as though you were still living in the world? [21] — 'Do not pick up this, do not eat that, do not touch the other,' [22]and all about things which perish even while they are being used — according to merely *human commandments and doctrines!*[a] [23]In these rules you can indeed find what seems to be good sense — the cultivation of the will, and a humility which takes no account of the body; but in fact they have no value against self-indulgence.

Life-giving union with the glorified Christ

3 Since you have been raised up to be with Christ, you must look for the things that are above, where Christ is, sitting at God's right hand. [2]Let your thoughts be on things above, not on the things that are on the earth, [3]because you have died, and now the life you have is hidden with Christ in God. [4]But when Christ is revealed — and he is your life — you, too, will be revealed with him in glory.

III: ENCOURAGEMENT

General rules of Christian behaviour

[5]That is why you must kill everything in you that is earthly: sexual vice, impurity, uncontrolled passion, evil desires and especially greed, which is the same thing as worshipping a false god; [6]it is precisely these things which draw God's retribution upon those who resist. [7]And these things made up your way of life when you were living among

2a Is 29:13.

such people, [8]but now you also must give up all these things: human anger, hot temper, malice, abusive language and dirty talk; [9]and do not lie to each other. You have stripped off your old behaviour with your old self, [10]and you have put on a new self which will progress towards true knowledge the more it is renewed in the image of its Creator; [11]and in that image there is no room for distinction between Greek and Jew, between the circumcised and uncircumcised, or between barbarian and Scythian, slave and free. There is only Christ: he is everything and he is in everything.

[12]As the chosen of God, then, the holy people whom he loves, you are to be clothed in heartfelt compassion, in generosity and humility, gentleness and patience. [13]Bear with one another; forgive each other if one of you has a complaint against another. The Lord has forgiven you; now you must do the same. [14]Over all these clothes, put on love, the perfect bond. [15]And may the peace of Christ reign in your hearts, because it is for this that you were called together in one body. Always be thankful.

[16]Let the Word of Christ, in all its richness, find a home with you. Teach each other, and advise each other, in all wisdom. With gratitude in your hearts sing psalms and hymns and inspired songs to God; [17]and whatever you say or do, let it be in the name of the Lord Jesus, in thanksgiving to God the Father through him.

The morals of the home and household

[18]Wives, be subject to your husbands, as you should in the Lord. [19]Husbands, love your wives and do not be sharp with them. [20]Children, be obedient to your parents always, because that is what will please the Lord. [21]Parents, do not irritate your children or they will lose heart.

[22]Slaves, be obedient in every way to the people who, according to human reckoning, are your masters; not only when you are under their eye, as if you had only to please human beings, but wholeheartedly, out of respect for the Master. [23]Whatever your work is, put your heart into it as done for the Lord and not for human beings, [24]knowing that the Lord will repay you by making you his heirs. It is Christ the Lord that you are

serving. [25]Anyone who does wrong will be repaid in kind. For there is no favouritism.

4 Masters, make sure that your slaves are given what is upright and fair, knowing that you too have a Master in heaven.

The apostolic spirit

[2]Be persevering in your prayers and be thankful as you stay awake to pray. [3]Pray for us especially, asking God to throw open a door for us to announce the message and proclaim the mystery of Christ, for the sake of which I am in chains; [4]pray that I may proclaim it as clearly as I ought.

[5]Act wisely with outsiders, making the best of the present time. [6]Always talk pleasantly and with a flavour of wit but be sensitive to the kind of answer each one requires.

Personal news

[7]Tychicus will tell you all the news about me. He is a very dear brother, and a trustworthy helper and companion in the service of the Lord. [8]I am sending him to you precisely for this purpose: to give you news about us and to encourage you thoroughly. [9]With him I am sending Onesimus,[a] that dear and trustworthy brother who is a fellow-citizen of yours. They will tell you everything that is happening here.

Greetings and final wishes

[10]Aristarchus, who is here in prison with me, sends his greetings, and so does Mark, the cousin of Barnabas—you were sent some instructions about him; if he comes to you, give him a warm welcome—[11]and Jesus Justus adds his greetings. Of all those who have come over from the circumcision, these are the only ones actually working with me for the kingdom of God. They have been a great comfort to me. [12]Epaphras, your fellow-citizen, sends his greetings; this servant of Christ Jesus never stops battling for you, praying that you will never lapse but always hold perfectly and securely to the will of God. [13]I can testify for him that he works hard for you, as well as for those at Laodicea and Hierapolis. [14]Greetings from my dear friend Luke, the doctor, and also from Demas.

4a cf. Phm 10.

[15]Please give my greetings to the brothers at Laodicea and to Nympha and the church which meets in her house. [16]After this letter has been read among you, send it on to be read in the church of the Laodiceans; and get the letter from Laodicea[b] for you to read yourselves. [17]Give Archippus this message, 'Remember the service that the Lord assigned to you, and try to carry it out.'

[18]This greeting is in my own hand—PAUL. Remember the chains I wear. Grace be with you.

THE LETTERS TO THE
THESSALONIANS

First Thessalonians is probably the earliest letter of Paul that we have, written in AD 50. It begins with affectionate praise for the community and their example of faith. Its main single topic is the imminence of the Second Coming of Christ. Paul describes this by means of rich biblical imagery, the conventional symbols of God's judgement. He stresses especially the suddenness with which God's judgement will come. So strong was his emphasis that he found that he needed to quieten their excitement with the explanation in Second Thessalonians that the time was not yet ripe.

1 THESSALONIANS
THE FIRST LETTER OF PAUL
TO THE CHURCH IN THESSALONICA

Address

1 Paul, Silvanus and Timothy, to the Church in Thessalonica which is in God the Father and the Lord Jesus Christ. Grace to you and peace.

Thanksgiving and congratulations

[2]We always thank God for you all, mentioning you in our prayers continually. [3]We remember before our God and Father how active is the faith, how unsparing the love, how persevering the hope which you have from our Lord Jesus Christ.

[4]We know, brothers loved by God, that you have been chosen, [5]because our gospel came to you not only in words, but also in power and in the Holy Spirit and with great effect. And you observed the sort of life we lived when we were with you, which was for your sake. [6]You took us and the Lord as your model, welcoming the word with the joy of the Holy Spirit in spite of great hardship. [7]And so you became an example to all believers in Macedonia and Achaia [8]since it was from you that the word of the Lord rang out—and not only throughout Macedonia and Achaia, for your faith in God has spread everywhere. We do not need to tell other

4b Possibly this letter is Ep.

people about it: [9]other people tell us how we started the work among you, how you broke with the worship of false gods when you were converted to God and became servants of the living and true God; [10]and how you are now waiting for Jesus, his Son, whom he raised from the dead, to come from heaven. It is he who saves us from the Retribution which is coming.

Paul's example in Thessalonica

2 You know yourselves, my brothers, that our visit to you has not been pointless. [2]Although, as you know, we had received rough treatment and insults at Philippi, God gave us the courage to speak his gospel to you fearlessly, in spite of great opposition. [3]Our encouragement to you does not come from any delusion or impure motives or trickery. [4]No, God has approved us to be entrusted with the gospel, and this is how we preach, seeking to please not human beings but God who *tests* our *hearts.*[a] [5]Indeed, we have never acted with the thought of flattering anyone, as you know, nor as an excuse for greed, God is our witness; [6]nor have we ever looked for honour from human beings, either from you or anybody else, [7]when we could have imposed ourselves on you with full weight, as apostles of Christ.

Instead, we lived unassumingly among you. Like a mother feeding and looking after her children, [8]we felt so devoted to you, that we would have been happy to share with you not only the gospel of God, but also our own lives, so dear had you become. [9]You remember, brothers, with what unsparing energy we used to work, slaving night and day so as not to be a burden on any one of you while we were proclaiming the gospel of God to you. [10]You are witnesses, and so is God, that our treatment of you, since you believed, has been impeccably fair and upright. [11]As you know, we treated every one of you as a father treats his children, [12]urging you, encouraging you and appealing to you to live a life worthy of God, who calls you into his kingdom and his glory.

The faith and the patience of the Thessalonians

[13]Another reason why we continually thank God for you is that as soon as you heard the word that we brought you as God's message, you welcomed it for what it really is, not the word of any human being, but God's word, a power that is working among you believers. [14]For you, my brothers, have modelled yourselves on the churches of God in Christ Jesus which are in Judaea, in that you have suffered the same treatment from your own countrymen as they have had from the Jews, [15]who put the Lord Jesus to death, and the prophets too, and persecuted us also. Their conduct does not please God, and makes them the enemies of the whole human race, [16]because they are hindering us from preaching to gentiles to save them. Thus all the time they are *reaching the full extent of* their *iniquity,*[b] but retribution has finally overtaken them.

Paul's anxiety

[17]Although we had been deprived of you for only a short time in body but never in affection, brothers, we had an especially strong desire and longing to see you face to face again, [18]and we tried hard to come and visit you; I, Paul, tried more than once, but Satan prevented us. [19]What do you think is our hope and our joy, and what *our crown of honour*[c] in the presence of our Lord Jesus when he comes? [20]You are, for you are our pride and joy.

Timothy's mission to Thessalonica

3 When we could not bear it any longer, we decided it would be best to be left without a companion at Athens, [2]and sent our brother Timothy, who is God's helper in spreading the gospel of Christ, to keep you firm and encourage you about your faith [3]and prevent any of you from being unsettled by the present hardships. As you know, these are bound to come our way: [4]indeed, when we were with you, we warned you that we are certain to have hardships to bear, and that is what has happened now, as you have found out. [5]That is why, when I could not bear it any longer, I sent to assure myself of your

---

2a Jr 11:20.
2b Gn 15:16.
2c Pr 16:31.

faith: I was afraid the Tester might have put you to the test, and all our work might have been pointless.

Paul thanks God for good reports of the Thessalonians

[6]However, Timothy has returned from you and has given us good news of your faith and your love, telling us that you always remember us with pleasure and want to see us quite as much as we want to see you. [7]And so, brothers, your faith has been a great encouragement to us in the middle of our own distress and hardship; [8]now we can breathe again, as you are holding firm in the Lord. [9]How can we thank God enough for you, for all the joy we feel before our God on your account? [10]We are earnestly praying night and day to be able to see you face to face again and make up any shortcomings in your faith.

[11]May God our Father himself, and our Lord Jesus, ease our path to you. [12]May the Lord increase and enrich your love for each other and for all, so that it matches ours for you. [13]And may he so confirm your hearts in holiness that you may be blameless in the sight of our God and Father when our Lord Jesus comes *with all his holy ones.*[a]

Live in holiness and charity

4 Finally, brothers, we urge you and appeal to you in the Lord Jesus; we instructed you how to live in the way that pleases God, and you are so living; but make more progress still. [2]You are well aware of the instructions we gave you on the authority of the Lord Jesus.

[3]God wills you all to be holy. He wants you to keep away from sexual immorality, [4]and each one of you to know how to control his body in a way that is holy and honourable, [5]not giving way to selfish lust like *the nations who do not acknowledge God.*[a] [6]He wants nobody at all ever to sin by taking advantage of a brother in these matters; the Lord always *pays back*[b] sins of that sort, as we told you before emphatically. [7]God called us to be holy, not to be immoral; [8]in other words, anyone who rejects this is rejecting not

human authority, but God, *who gives you his Holy Spirit.*[c]

[9]As for brotherly love, there is no need to write to you about that, since you have yourselves learnt from God to love one another, [10]and in fact this is how you treat all the brothers throughout the whole of Macedonia. However, we do urge you, brothers, to go on making even greater progress [11]and to make a point of living quietly, attending to your own business and earning your living, just as we told you to, [12]so that you may earn the respect of outsiders and not be dependent on anyone.

The dead and the living at the time of the Lord's coming

[13]We want you to be quite certain, brothers, about those who have fallen asleep, to make sure that you do not grieve for them, as others do who have no hope. [14]We believe that Jesus died and rose again, and that in the same way God will bring with him those who have fallen asleep in Jesus. [15]We can tell you this from the Lord's own teaching, that we who are still alive for the Lord's coming will not have any advantage over those who have fallen asleep. [16]At the signal given by the voice of the Archangel and the trumpet of God, the Lord himself will come down from heaven; those who have died in Christ will be the first to rise, [17]and only after that shall we who remain alive be taken up in the clouds, together with them, to meet the Lord in the air. This is the way we shall be with the Lord for ever. [18]With such thoughts as these, then, you should encourage one another.

Watchfulness while awaiting the coming of the Lord

5 About times and dates, brothers, there is no need to write to you [2]for you are well aware in any case that the Day of the Lord is going to come like a thief in the night. [3]It is when people are saying, 'How quiet and peaceful it is' that sudden destruction falls on them, as suddenly as labour pains come on a pregnant woman; and there is no escape. [4]But you, brothers, do not live in the dark,

3a Zc 14:5.
4a Ps 79:6.
4b Dt 32:35.
4c Ezk 37:14.

that the Day should take you unawares like a thief. [5]No, you are all children of light and children of the day: we do not belong to the night or to darkness, [6]so we should not go on sleeping, as everyone else does, but stay wide awake and sober. [7]Night is the time for sleepers to sleep and night the time for drunkards to be drunk, [8]but we belong to the day and we should be sober; let us put on faith and love for a *breastplate*, and the hope of *salvation* for a *helmet*.[a] [9]God destined us not for his retribution, but to win salvation through our Lord Jesus Christ, [10]who died for us so that, awake or asleep, we should still live united to him. [11]So give encouragement to each other, and keep strengthening one another, as you do already.

[12]We appeal to you, my brothers, to be considerate to those who work so hard among you as your leaders in the Lord and those who admonish you. [13]Have the greatest respect and affection for them because of their work.

Be at peace among yourselves. [14]We urge you, brothers, to admonish those who are undisciplined, encourage the apprehensive, support the weak and be patient with everyone. [15]Make sure that people do not try to repay evil for evil; always aim at what is best for each other and for everyone. [16]Always be joyful; [17]pray constantly; [18]and for all things give thanks; this is the will of God for you in Christ Jesus.

[19]Do not stifle the Spirit [20]or despise the gift of prophecy with contempt; [21]test everything and hold on to what is good [22]and *shun every form of evil*.[b]

Closing prayer and farewell

[23]May the God of peace make you perfect and holy; and may your spirit, life and body be kept blameless for the coming of our Lord Jesus Christ. [24]He who has called you is trustworthy and will carry it out.

[25]Pray for us, my brothers.

[26]Greet all the brothers with a holy kiss. [27]My orders, in the Lord's name, are that this letter is to be read to all the brothers.

[28]The grace of our Lord Jesus Christ be with you.

2 THESSALONIANS
THE SECOND LETTER OF PAUL
TO THE CHURCH IN THESSALONICA

Address

1 Paul, Silvanus and Timothy, to the Church in Thessalonica which is in God our Father and the Lord Jesus Christ [2]Grace to you and peace from God the Father and the Lord Jesus Christ.

Thanksgiving and encouragement
The Last Judgement

[3]We must always thank God for you, brothers; quite rightly, because your faith is growing so wonderfully and the mutual love that each one of you has for all never stops increasing. [4]Among the churches of God we take special pride in you for your perseverance and faith under all the persecutions and hardships you have to bear. [5]It all shows that God's judgement is just, so that you may be found worthy of the kingdom of God; it is for the sake of this that you are suffering now.

[6]For God's justice will surely mean hardship being inflicted on those who are now inflicting hardship on you, [7]and for you who are now suffering hardship, relief with us, when the Lord Jesus appears from heaven

5a Is 59:17.
5b Jb 1:8.

with the angels of his power. [8]He will come *amid flaming fire; he will impose a penalty[a]* on those who *do not acknowledge God* and *refuse to accept* the gospel of our Lord Jesus. [9]Their punishment is to be lost eternally, excluded *from the presence of the Lord and from the glory of his strength* [10]*on that day* when he comes *to be glorified among his holy ones* and *marvelled at* by all who believe in him; and you are among those who believed our witness.

[11]In view of this we also pray continually that our God will make you worthy of his call, and by his power fulfil all your desires for goodness, and complete all that you have been doing through faith; [12]so that the *name* of our Lord Jesus Christ *may be glorified* in you and you in him, by the grace of our God and the Lord Jesus Christ.

The coming of the Lord and the prelude to it

2 About the coming of our Lord Jesus Christ, brothers, and our being gathered to him: [2]please do not be too easily thrown into confusion or alarmed by any manifestation of the Spirit or any statement or any letter claiming to come from us, suggesting that the Day of the Lord has already arrived. [3]Never let anyone deceive you in any way.

It cannot happen until the Great Revolt[a] has taken place and there has appeared the wicked One, the lost One, [4]the Enemy, who *raises himself above every* so-called *God* or object of worship to *enthrone himself in God's* sanctuary and flaunts the claim that he is God. [5]Surely you remember my telling you about this when I was with you? [6]And you know, too, what is still holding him back from appearing before his appointed time. [7]The mystery of wickedness is already at work, but let him who is restraining it once be removed, [8]and the wicked One will appear openly. The Lord *will destroy him with the breath of his mouth* and will annihilate him with his glorious appearance at his coming. [9]But the coming of the wicked One will be marked by Satan being at work in all kinds of counterfeit miracles and signs and wonders, [10]and every wicked deception aimed at those who are on the way to destruction because they would not accept the love of the truth and so be saved. [11]And therefore God sends

on them a power that deludes people so that they believe what is false, [12]and so that those who do not believe the truth and take their pleasure in wickedness may all be condemned.

Encouragement to persevere

[13]But we must always thank God for you, brothers whom the Lord loves, because God chose you from the beginning to be saved by the Spirit who makes us holy and by faith in the truth. [14]Through our gospel he called you to this so that you should claim as your own the glory of our Lord Jesus Christ. [15]Stand firm, then, brothers, and keep the traditions that we taught you, whether by word of mouth or by letter. [16]May our Lord Jesus Christ himself, and God our Father who has given us his love and, through his grace, such ceaseless encouragement and such sure hope, [17]encourage you and strengthen you in every good word and deed.

3 Finally, brothers, pray for us that the Lord's message may spread quickly, and be received with honour as it was among you; [2]and pray that we may be preserved from bigoted and evil people, for not everyone has faith. [3]You can rely on the Lord, who will give you strength and guard you from the evil One, [4]and we, in the Lord, have every confidence in you, that you are doing and will go on doing all that we tell you. [5]May the Lord turn your hearts towards the love of God and the perseverance of Christ.

Against idleness and disunity

[6]In the name of the Lord Jesus Christ, we urge you, brothers, to keep away from any of the brothers who lives an undisciplined life, not in accordance with the tradition you received from us. [7]You know how you should take us as your model: we were not undisciplined when we were with you, [8]nor did we ever accept food from anyone without paying for it; no, we worked with unsparing energy, night and day, so as not to be a burden on any of you. [9]This was not because we had no right to be, but in order to make ourselves a model for you to imitate. [10]We urged you when we were with you not to let anyone eat who refused to work.

1a This threatening imagery of the Day of the Lord uses Is 66:15; Jr 10:25; Is 2:10–17; 49:3; 66:5.
2a Paul uses biblical symbolism: Is 11:4; 14:13; Ezk 28:2; Ps 33:6.

[11]Now we hear that there are some of you who are living lives without any discipline, doing no work themselves but interfering with other people's. [12]In the Lord Jesus Christ, we urge and call on people of this kind to go on quietly working and earning the food that they eat.

[13]My brothers, never slacken in doing what is right. [14]If anyone refuses to obey what I have written in this letter, take note of him and have nothing to do with him, so that he will be ashamed of himself, [15]though you are not to treat him as an enemy, but to correct him as a brother.

Prayer and farewell wishes

[16]May the Lord of peace himself give you peace at all times and in every way. The Lord be with you all.

[17]This greeting is in my own hand—PAUL. It is the mark of genuineness in every letter; this is my own writing. [18]May the grace of our Lord Jesus Christ be with you all.

THE PASTORAL EPISTLES

The letters to Timothy and Titus or 'Pastoral Epistles' form a group, giving advice to disciples of Paul on the pastoral care of his communities. They give a valuable insight into those communities as they move into the second generation of Christians, especially of the structures of the churches and of the qualities needed by Christian ministers. They also show the Church adapting to the hellenistic environment in the last years of the century. The hymns quoted may well be taken from the liturgy.

The absence of characteristic Pauline doctrines and a certain timidity of outlook combine with a change of literary style and vocabulary to suggest either that the apostle is old and tired, or that the letters spring from another pen. The historical data are not easy to join together, and certainly do not fit the period in Paul's life known from other sources. It may be, therefore, that these letters were not written by Paul but were simply attributed to him as a great authority—a practice not uncommon at the time.

1 TIMOTHY
THE FIRST LETTER
FROM PAUL TO TIMOTHY

Address

1 Paul, apostle of Christ Jesus appointed by the command of God our Saviour and of Christ Jesus our hope, [2]to Timothy, true child of mine in the faith. Grace, mercy and peace from God the Father and from Christ Jesus our Lord.

Suppress the false teachers

[3]When I was setting out for Macedonia I urged you to stay on in Ephesus to instruct certain people not to spread wrong teaching [4]or to give attention to myths and unending genealogies; these things only foster doubts instead of furthering God's plan which is

founded on faith. [5]The final goal at which this instruction aims is love, issuing from a pure heart, a clear conscience and a sincere faith. [6]Some people have missed the way to these things and turned to empty speculation, [7]trying to be teachers of the Law; but they understand neither the words they use nor the matters about which they make such strong assertions.

The purpose of the Law

[8]We are well aware that the Law is good, but only provided it is used legitimately, [9]on the understanding that laws are not framed for people who are upright. On the contrary, they are for criminals and the insubordinate, for the irreligious and the wicked, for the sacrilegious and the godless; they are for people who kill their fathers or mothers and for murderers, [10]for the promiscuous, homosexuals, kidnappers, for liars and for perjurers—and for everything else that is contrary to the sound teaching [11]that accords with the gospel of the glory of the blessed God, the gospel that was entrusted to me.

Paul on his own calling

[12]I thank Christ Jesus our Lord, who has given me strength. By calling me into his service he has judged me trustworthy, [13]even though I used to be a blasphemer and a persecutor and contemptuous. Mercy, however, was shown me, because while I lacked faith I acted in ignorance; [14]but the grace of our Lord filled me with faith and with the love that is in Christ Jesus. [15]Here is a saying that you can rely on and nobody should doubt: that Christ Jesus came into the world to save sinners. I myself am the greatest of them; [16]and if mercy has been shown to me, it is because Jesus Christ meant to make me the leading example of his inexhaustible patience for all the other people who were later to trust in him for eternal life. [17]To the eternal King, the undying, invisible and only God, be honour and glory for ever and ever. Amen.

Timothy's responsibility

[18]Timothy, my son, these are the instructions that I am giving you, in accordance with the words once spoken over you by the prophets, so that in their light you may fight like a good soldier [19]with faith and a good conscience for your weapons. Some people have put conscience aside and wrecked their faith in consequence. [20]I mean men like Hymenaeus and Alexander, whom I have handed over to Satan so that they may learn not to be blasphemous.

Liturgical prayer

2 [1]I urge then, first of all that petitions, prayers, intercessions and thanksgiving should be offered for everyone, [2]for kings and others in authority, so that we may be able to live peaceful and quiet lives with all devotion and propriety. [3]To do this is right, and acceptable to God our Saviour: [4]he wants everyone to be saved and reach full knowledge of the truth. [5]For there is only one God, and there is only one mediator between God and humanity, himself a human being, Christ Jesus, [6]who offered himself as a ransom for all. This was the witness given at the appointed time, [7]of which I was appointed herald and apostle and—I am telling the truth and no lie—a teacher of the gentiles in faith and truth.

[8]In every place, then, I want the men to lift their hands up reverently in prayer, with no anger or argument.

Women in the assembly

[9]Similarly, women are to wear suitable clothes and to be dressed quietly and modestly, without braided hair or gold and jewellery or expensive clothes; [10]their adornment is to do the good works that are proper for women who claim to be religious. [11]During instruction, a woman should be quiet and respectful. [12]I give no permission for a woman to teach or to have authority over a man. A woman ought to be quiet, [13]because Adam was formed first and Eve afterwards, [14]and it was not Adam who was led astray but the woman who was led astray and fell into sin. [15]Nevertheless, she will be saved by child-bearing, provided she lives a sensible life and is constant in faith and love and holiness.

The elder-in-charge

3 Here is a saying that you can rely on: to want to be a presiding elder is to desire a

noble task. [2]That is why the presiding elder must have an impeccable character. Husband of one wife, he must be temperate, discreet and courteous, hospitable and a good teacher; [3]not a heavy drinker, nor hot-tempered, but gentle and peaceable, not avaricious, [4]a man who manages his own household well and brings his children up to obey him and be well-behaved: [5]how can any man who does not understand how to manage his own household take care of the Church of God? [6]He should not be a new convert, in case pride should turn his head and he incur the same condemnation as the devil. [7]It is also necessary that he be held in good repute by outsiders, so that he never falls into disrepute and into the devil's trap.

Deacons

[8]Similarly, deacons must be respectable, not double-tongued, moderate in the amount of wine they drink and with no squalid greed for money. [9]They must hold to the mystery of the faith with a clear conscience. [10]They are first to be examined, and admitted to serve as deacons only if there is nothing against them. [11]Similarly, women must be respectable, not gossips, but sober and wholly reliable. [12]Deacons must be husbands of one wife and must be people who manage their children and households well. [13]Those of them who carry out their duties well as deacons will earn a high standing for themselves and an authoritative voice in matters concerning faith in Christ Jesus.

The Church and the mystery of the spiritual life

[14]I write this to you in the hope that I may be able to come to you soon; [15]but in case I should be delayed, I want you to know how people ought to behave in God's household — that is, in the Church of the living God, pillar and support of the truth. [16]Without any doubt, the mystery of our religion is very deep indeed:

He was made visible in the flesh,
justified in the Spirit,
seen by angels,
proclaimed to the gentiles,
believed in throughout the world,
taken up in glory.

False teachers

4 The Spirit has explicitly said that during the last times some will desert the faith and pay attention to deceitful spirits and doctrines that come from devils, [2]seduced by the hypocrisy of liars whose consciences are branded as though with a red-hot iron: [3]they forbid marriage and prohibit foods which God created to be accepted with thanksgiving by all who believe and who know the truth. [4]Everything God has created is good, and no food is to be rejected, provided it is received with thanksgiving: [5]the word of God and prayer make it holy. [6]If you put all this to the brothers, you will be a good servant of Christ Jesus and show that you have really digested the teaching of the faith and the good doctrine which you have always followed. [7]Have nothing to do with godless myths and old wives' tales. Train yourself for religion. [8]Physical exercise is useful enough, but the usefulness of religion is unlimited, since it holds out promise both for life here and now and for the life to come; [9]that is a saying that you can rely on and nobody should doubt it. [10]I mean that the point of all our toiling and battling is that we have put our trust in the living God and he is the Saviour of the whole human race but particularly of all believers. [11]This is what you are to instruct and teach.

[12]Let no one disregard you because you are young, but be an example to all the believers in the way you speak and behave, and in your love, your faith and your purity. [13]Until I arrive, devote yourself to reading to the people, encouraging and teaching. [14]You have in you a spiritual gift which was given to you when the prophets spoke and the body of elders laid their hands on you; do not neglect it. [15]Let this be your care and your occupation, and everyone will be able to see your progress. [16]Be conscientious about what you do and what you teach; persevere in this, and in this way you will save both yourself and those who listen to you.

Pastoral practice

5 Never speak sharply to a man older than yourself, but appeal to him as you would to your own father; treat younger men as brothers, [2]older women as mothers and young women as sisters with all propriety.

Widows

[3]Be considerate to widows—if they really are widowed. [4]If a widow has children or grandchildren, they are to learn first of all to do their duty to their own families and repay their debt to their parents, because this is what pleases God. [5]But a woman who is really widowed and left on her own has set her hope on God and perseveres night and day in petitions and prayer. [6]The one who thinks only of pleasure is already dead while she is still alive: [7]instruct them in this, too, so that their lives may be blameless. [8]Anyone who does not look after his own relations, especially if they are living with him, has rejected the faith and is worse than an unbeliever.

[9]Enrolment as a widow is permissible only for a woman at least sixty years old who has had only one husband. [10]She must be a woman known for her good works—whether she has brought up her children, been hospitable to strangers and washed the feet of God's holy people, helped people in hardship or been active in all kinds of good work. [11]Do not accept young widows because if their natural desires distract them from Christ, they want to marry again, [12]and then people condemn them for being unfaithful to their original promise. [13]Besides, they learn how to be idle and go round from house to house; and then, not merely idle, they learn to be gossips and meddlers in other people's affairs and to say what should remain unsaid. [14]I think it is best for young widows to marry again and have children and a household to look after, and not give the enemy any chance to raise a scandal about them; [15]there are already some who have turned aside to follow Satan. [16]If a woman believer has widowed relatives, she should support them and not make the Church bear the expense but enable it to support those who are really widowed.

The elders

[17]Elders who do their work well while they are in charge earn double reward, especially those who work hard at preaching and teaching. [18]As scripture says: *You must not muzzle an ox when it is treading out the corn;*[a] and again: *The worker deserves his wages.*

[19]Never accept any accusation brought against an elder unless it is supported *by two or three witnesses*. [20]If anyone is at fault, reprimand him publicly, as a warning to the rest. [21]Before God, and before Jesus Christ and the angels he has chosen, I charge you to keep these rules impartially and never to be influenced by favouritism. [22]Do not be too quick to lay hands on anyone, and never make yourself an accomplice in anybody else's sin; keep yourself pure.

[23]You should give up drinking only water and have a little wine for the sake of your digestion and the frequent bouts of illness that you have.

[24]The faults of some people are obvious long before they come to the reckoning, while others have faults that are not discovered until later. [25]Similarly, the good that people do can be obvious; but even when it is not, it cannot remain hidden.

Slaves

[6]All those under the yoke of slavery must have unqualified respect for their masters, so that the name of God and our teaching are not brought into disrepute. [2]Those whose masters are believers are not to respect them less because they are brothers; on the contrary, they should serve them all the better, since those who have the benefit of their services are believers and dear to God.

The true teacher and the false teacher

This is what you are to teach and urge. [3]Anyone who teaches anything different and does not keep to the sound teaching which is that of our Lord Jesus Christ, the doctrine which is in accordance with true religion, [4]is proud and has no understanding, but rather a weakness for questioning everything and arguing about words. All that can come of this is jealousy, contention, abuse and evil mistrust; [5]and unending disputes by people who are depraved in mind and deprived of truth, and imagine that religion is a way of making a profit. [6]Religion, of course, does bring large profits, but only to those who are content with what they have. [7]We brought nothing into the world, and we can take nothing out of it; [8]but as long as we have food and clothing, we shall be content with that.

5a Dt 25:4 followed by Lk 10:7; Dt 19:15.

⁹People who long to be rich are a prey to trial; they get trapped into all sorts of foolish and harmful ambitions which plunge people into ruin and destruction. ¹⁰'The love of money is the root of all evils' and there are some who, pursuing it, have wandered away from the faith and so given their souls any number of fatal wounds.

Timothy's vocation recalled

¹¹But, as someone dedicated to God, avoid all that. You must aim to be upright and religious, filled with faith and love, perseverance and gentleness. ¹²Fight the good fight of faith and win the eternal life to which you were called and for which you made your noble profession of faith before many witnesses. ¹³Now, before God, the source of all life, and before Jesus Christ, who witnessed to his noble profession of faith before Pontius Pilate, I charge you ¹⁴to do all that you have been told, with no faults or failures, until the appearing of our Lord Jesus Christ,

¹⁵who at the due time will be revealed
　by God, the blessed and only Ruler of all,
　the King of kings and the Lord of lords,

¹⁶who alone is immortal,
　whose home is in inaccessible light,
　whom no human being has seen
　　or is able to see:
　to him be honour and everlasting power.
　Amen.

Rich Christians

¹⁷Instruct those who are rich in this world's goods that they should not be proud and should set their hopes not on money, which is untrustworthy, but on God who gives us richly all that we need for our happiness. ¹⁸They are to do good and be rich in good works, generous in giving and always ready to share— ¹⁹this is the way they can amass a good capital sum for the future if they want to possess the only life that is real.

Final warning and conclusion

²⁰My dear Timothy, take great care of all that has been entrusted to you. Turn away from godless philosophical discussions and the contradictions of the 'knowledge' which is not knowledge at all; ²¹by adopting this, some have missed the goal of faith. Grace be with you.

2 TIMOTHY
THE SECOND LETTER
FROM PAUL TO TIMOTHY

Greeting and thanksgiving

1 From Paul, apostle of Christ Jesus through the will of God in accordance with his promise of life in Christ Jesus, ²to Timothy, dear son of mine. Grace, mercy and peace from God the Father and from Christ Jesus our Lord.

³Night and day I thank God whom I serve with a pure conscience as my ancestors did. I remember you in my prayers constantly night and day; ⁴I remember your tears and long to see you again to complete my joy. ⁵I also remember your sincere faith, a faith which first dwelt in your grandmother Lois, and your mother Eunice, and I am sure dwells also in you.

The gifts that Timothy has received

[6]That is why I am reminding you now to fan into a flame the gift of God that you possess through the laying on of my hands. [7]God did not give us a spirit of timidity, but the Spirit of power and love and self-control. [8]So you are never to be ashamed of witnessing to our Lord, or ashamed of me for being his prisoner; but share in my hardships for the sake of the gospel, relying on the power of God [9]who has saved us and called us to be holy—not because of anything we ourselves had done but for his own purpose and by his own grace. This grace had already been granted to us, in Christ Jesus, before the beginning of time, [10]but it has been revealed only by the appearing of our Saviour Christ Jesus. He has abolished death, and he has brought to light immortality and life through the gospel, [11]in whose service I have been made herald, apostle and teacher.

[12]That is why I am experiencing my present sufferings; but I am not ashamed, because I know in whom I have put my trust, and I have no doubt at all that he is able to safeguard until that Day what I have entrusted to him. [13]Keep as your pattern the sound teaching you have heard from me, in the faith and love that are in Christ Jesus. [14]With the help of the Holy Spirit who dwells in us, look after that precious thing given in trust.

[15]As you know, Phygelus and Hermogenes and all the others in Asia have deserted me. [16]I hope the Lord will be kind to all the family of Onesiphorus, because he has often been a comfort to me and has never been ashamed of my chains. [17]On the contrary, as soon as he reached Rome, he searched hard for me and found me. [18]May the Lord grant him to find the Lord's mercy on that Day. You know better than anyone else how much he helped me at Ephesus.

How Timothy should face hardships

2 As for you, my dear son, take strength from the grace which is in Christ Jesus. [2]Pass on to reliable people what you heard from me through many witnesses so that they in turn will be able to teach others.

[3]Bear with your share of difficulties, like a good soldier of Christ Jesus. [4]No one on active service involves himself in the affairs of civilian life, because he must win the approval of the man who enlisted him; [5]or again someone who enters an athletic contest wins only by competing in the sports—a prize can be won only by competing according to the rules; [6]and again, it is the farmer who works hard that has the first claim on any crop that is harvested. [7]Think over what I have said, and the Lord will give you full understanding.

[8]Remember the gospel that I carry, 'Jesus Christ risen from the dead, sprung from the race of David'; [9]it is on account of this that I have to put up with suffering, even to being chained like a criminal. But God's message cannot be chained up. [10]So I persevere for the sake of those who are chosen, so that they, too, may obtain the salvation that is in Christ Jesus with eternal glory. [11]Here is a saying that you can rely on:

If we have died with him,
  then we shall live with him.
[12]If we persevere,
  then we shall reign with him.
If we disown him, then he will disown us.
[13]If we are faithless, he is faithful still,
  for he cannot disown his own self.

The struggle against the immediate danger from false teachers

[14]Remind them of this; and tell them in the name of God that there must be no wrangling about words: all that this ever achieves is the destruction of those who are listening. [15]Make every effort to present yourself before God as a proven worker who has no need to be ashamed, but who keeps the message of truth on a straight path. [16]Have nothing to do with godless philosophical discussions—they only lead further and further away from true religion. [17]Talk of this kind spreads corruption like gangrene, as in the case of Hymenaeus and Philetus, [18]the men who have gone astray from the truth, claiming that the resurrection has already taken place. They are upsetting some people's faith. [19]However, God's solid foundation-stone stands firm, and this is the seal on it: 'The Lord knows those who are his own' and 'All who call on the name of the Lord[a] must avoid evil.'

[20]Not all the dishes in a large house are

2a Nb 16:5; Is 26:13.

made of gold and silver; some are made of wood or earthenware: the former are held in honour, the latter held cheap. [21]If someone holds himself aloof from these faults I speak of, he will be a vessel held in honour, dedicated and fit for the Master, ready for any good work.

[22]Turn away from the passions of youth, concentrate on uprightness, faith, love and peace, in union with all those who call on the Lord with a pure heart. [23]Avoid these foolish and undisciplined speculations, understanding that they only give rise to quarrels; [24]and a servant of the Lord must not engage in quarrels, but must be kind to everyone, a good teacher, and patient. [25]He must be gentle when he corrects people who oppose him, in the hope that God may give them a change of mind so that they recognise the truth [26]and come to their senses, escaping the trap of the devil who made them his captives and subjected them to his will.

The dangers of the last days

3 You may be quite sure that in the last days there will be some difficult times. [2]People will be self-centred and avaricious, boastful, arrogant and rude; disobedient to their parents, ungrateful, irreligious; [3]heartless and intractable; they will be slanderers, profligates, savages and enemies of everything that is good; [4]they will be treacherous and reckless and demented by pride, preferring their own pleasure to God. [5]They will keep up the outward appearance of religion but will have rejected the inner power of it. Keep away from people like that.

[6]Of the same kind, too, are those men who insinuate themselves into families in order to get influence over silly women who are obsessed with their sins and follow one craze after another, [7]always seeking learning, but unable ever to come to knowledge of the truth. [8]Just as Jannes and Jambres defied Moses,*a* so these men defy the truth, their minds corrupt and their faith spurious. [9]But they will not be able to go on much longer: their folly, like that of the other two, must become obvious to everybody.

[10]You, though, have followed my teaching, my way of life, my aims, my faith, my patience and my love, my perseverance [11]and the persecutions and sufferings that came to me in places like Antioch, Iconium and Lystra—all the persecutions I have endured; and the Lord has rescued me from every one of them. [12]But anybody who tries to live in devotion to Christ is certain to be persecuted; [13]while these wicked impostors will go from bad to worse, deceiving others, and themselves deceived.

[14]You must keep to what you have been taught and know to be true; remember who your teachers were, [15]and how, ever since you were a child, you have known the holy scriptures*b*—from these you can learn the wisdom that leads to salvation through faith in Christ Jesus. [16]All scripture is inspired by God and useful for refuting error, for guiding people's lives and teaching them to be upright. [17]This is how someone who is dedicated to God becomes fully equipped and ready for any good work.

A solemn charge

4 Before God and before Christ Jesus who is to be judge of the living and the dead, I charge you, in the name of his appearing and of his kingdom: [2]proclaim the message and, welcome or unwelcome, insist on it. Refute falsehood, correct error, give encouragement—but do all with patience and with care to instruct. [3]The time is sure to come when people will not accept sound teaching, but their ears will be itching for anything new and they will collect themselves a whole series of teachers according to their own tastes; [4]and then they will shut their ears to the truth and will turn to myths. [5]But you must keep steady all the time; put up with suffering; do the work of preaching the gospel; fulfil the service asked of you.

Paul in the evening of his life

[6]As for me, my life is already being poured away as a libation, and the time has come for me to depart. [7]I have fought the good fight to the end; I have run the race to the finish; I have kept the faith; [8]all there is to come for me now is the crown of uprightness which the Lord, the upright judge, will give to me on that Day; and not only to me but to all those who have longed for his appearing.

3a In Jewish tradition (but not the Bible) the leaders of the Egyptian magicians, cf. Ex 7:11.
3b Probably the OT. There is no sign that the NT writings were yet set on the same level.

Final advice

[9]Make every effort to come and see me as soon as you can. [10]As it is, Demas has deserted me for love of this life and gone to Thessalonica, Crescens has gone to Galatia and Titus to Dalmatia; [11]only Luke is with me. Bring Mark with you; I find him a useful helper in my work. [12]I have sent Tychicus to Ephesus. [13]When you come, bring the cloak I left with Carpus in Troas, and the scrolls, especially the parchment ones. [14]Alexander the coppersmith has done me a lot of harm; *the Lord will repay him as his deeds deserve.*[a] [15]Be on your guard against him yourself, because he has been bitterly contesting everything that we say.

[16]The first time I had to present my defence, no one came into court to support me. Every one of them deserted me—may they not be held accountable for it. [17]But the Lord stood by me and gave me power, so that through me the message might be fully proclaimed for all the gentiles to hear; and so I was *saved from the lion's mouth.*[b] [18]The Lord will rescue me from all evil attempts on me, and bring me safely to his heavenly kingdom. To him be glory for ever and ever. Amen.

Farewells and final good wishes

[19]Greetings to Prisca and Aquila, and the family of Onesiphorus. [20]Erastus stayed behind at Corinth, and I left Trophimus ill at Miletus. [21]Make every effort to come before the winter.

Greetings to you from Eubulus, Pudens, Linus, Claudia and all the brothers.

[22]The Lord be with your spirit. Grace be with you.

TITUS

THE LETTER FROM PAUL
TO TITUS

Address

1 From Paul, servant of God, an apostle of Jesus Christ to bring those whom God has chosen to faith and to the knowledge of the truth that leads to true religion, [2]and to give them the hope of the eternal life that was promised so long ago by God. He does not lie [3]and so, in due time, he made known his message by a proclamation which was entrusted to me by the command of God our Saviour. [4]To Titus, true child of mine in the faith that we share. Grace and peace from God the Father and from Christ Jesus our Saviour.

The appointment of elders

[5]The reason I left you behind in Crete was for you to organise everything that still had to be done and appoint elders in every town, in the way that I told you, [6]that is, each of them must be a man of irreproachable character, husband of one wife, and his children must be believers and not liable to be charged with disorderly conduct or insubordination. [7]The presiding elder has to be irreproachable since he is God's representative: never arrogant or hot-tempered, nor a heavy drinker or violent, nor avaricious; [8]but hospitable and a lover of goodness; sensible,

---

4a Ps 28:4.
4b Ps 22:21.

upright, devout and self-controlled; [9]and he must have a firm grasp of the unchanging message of the tradition, so that he can be counted on both for giving encouragement in sound doctrine and for refuting those who argue against it.

Opposing the false teachers

[10]And in fact there are many people who are insubordinate, who talk nonsense and try to make others believe it, particularly among those of the circumcision. [11]They must be silenced: people of this kind upset whole families, by teaching things that they ought not to, and doing it for the sake of sordid gain. [12]It was one of themselves, one of their own prophets, who said,[a] 'Cretans were never anything but liars, dangerous animals, all greed and laziness'; [13]and that is a true statement. So be severe in correcting them, and make them sound in the faith [14]so that they stop taking notice of Jewish myths and the orders of people who turn away from the truth. [15]To those who are pure themselves, everything is pure; but to those who have been corrupted and lack faith, nothing can be pure — the corruption is both in their minds and in their consciences. [16]They claim to know God but by their works they deny him; they are outrageously rebellious and quite untrustworthy for any good work.

Some specific moral instruction

2 It is for you, then, to preach the behaviour which goes with healthy doctrine. [2]Older men should be reserved, dignified, moderate, sound in faith and love and perseverance. [3]Similarly, older women should behave as befits religious people, with no scandal-mongering and no addiction to wine — they must be the teachers of right behaviour [4]and show younger women how they should love their husbands and love their children, [5]how they must be sensible and chaste, and how to work in their homes, and be gentle, and obey their husbands, so that the message of God is not disgraced. [6]Similarly, urge younger men to be moderate in everything that they do, [7]and you yourself set an example of good works, by sincerity and earnestness, when

you are teaching, and by a message sound and irreproachable [8]so that any opponent will be at a loss, with no accusation to make against us. [9]Slaves must be obedient to their masters in everything, and do what is wanted without argument; [10]and there must be no pilfering — they must show complete honesty at all times, so that they are in every way a credit to the teaching of God our Saviour.

The basis of the Christian moral life

[11]You see, God's grace has been revealed to save the whole human race; [12]it has taught us that we should give up everything contrary to true religion and all our worldly passions; we must be self-restrained and live upright and religious lives in this present world, [13]waiting in hope for the blessing which will come with the appearing of the glory of our great God and Saviour Christ Jesus. [14]He offered himself for us in order to ransom us from all our *faults* and *to purify a people to be his very own*[a] and eager to do good.

[15]This is what you must say, encouraging or arguing with full authority; no one should despise you.

General instruction for believers

3 Remind them to be obedient to the officials in authority; to be ready to do good at every opportunity; [2]not to go slandering other people but to be peaceable and gentle, and always polite to people of all kinds. [3]There was a time when we too were ignorant, disobedient and misled and enslaved by different passions and dissipations; we lived then in wickedness and malice, hating each other and hateful ourselves.

[4]But when the kindness and love of God our Saviour for humanity were revealed, [5]it was not because of any upright actions we had done ourselves; it was for no reason except his own faithful love that he saved us, by means of the cleansing water of rebirth and renewal in the Holy Spirit [6]which he has so generously poured over us through Jesus Christ our Saviour; [7]so that, justified by his grace, we should become heirs in hope of eternal life. [8]This is doctrine that you can rely on.

1a Attributed to the Cretan poet Epimenides.
2a Ex 19:5.

Personal advice to Titus

I want you to be quite uncompromising in teaching all this, so that those who now believe in God may keep their minds constantly occupied in doing good works. All this is good, and useful for everybody. [9]But avoid foolish speculations, and those genealogies, and the quibbles and disputes about the Law—they are useless and futile. [10]If someone disputes what you teach, then after a first and a second warning, have no more to do with him: [11]you will know that anyone of that sort is warped and is self-condemned as a sinner.

Practical recommendations, farewells and good wishes

[12]As soon as I have sent Artemas or Tychicus to you, do your best to join me at Nicopolis, where I have decided to spend the winter. [13]Help eagerly on their way Zenas the lawyer and Apollos, and make sure they have everything they need. [14]All our people must also learn to occupy themselves in doing good works for their practical needs, and not to be unproductive.

[15]All those who are with me send their greetings. Greetings to those who love us in the faith. Grace be with you all.

THE LETTER TO
PHILEMON

A note from Paul carried back to his master by a runaway slave who has become a Christian and one of Paul's helpers. It is an affectionate expression of Christian fellowship and humanity.

PHILEMON
THE LETTER FROM PAUL
TO PHILEMON

Address

From Paul, a prisoner of Christ Jesus and from our brother Timothy; to our dear fellow worker Philemon, [2]our sister Apphia, our fellow soldier Archippus and the church that meets in your house. [3]Grace and the peace of God our Father and the Lord Jesus Christ.

Thanksgiving and prayer

[4]I always thank my God, mentioning you in my prayers, [5]because I hear of the love and the faith which you have for the Lord Jesus and for all God's holy people. [6]I pray that your fellowship in faith may come to expression in full knowledge of all the good we can do for Christ. [7]I have received much joy and encouragement by your love; you have set the hearts of God's holy people at rest.

The request about Onesimus

[8]Therefore, although in Christ I have no hesitations about telling you what your duty is, [9]I am rather appealing to your love, being what I am, Paul, an old man, and now also a prisoner of Christ Jesus. [10]I am appealing to

you for a child of mine, whose father I became while wearing these chains: I mean Onesimus.[a] [11]He was of no use to you before, but now he is useful both to you and to me. [12]I am sending him back to you—that is to say, sending you my own heart. [13]I should have liked to keep him with me; he could have been a substitute for you, to help me while I am in the chains that the gospel has brought me. [14]However, I did not want to do anything without your consent; it would have been forcing your act of kindness, which should be spontaneous. [15]I suppose you have been deprived of Onesimus for a time, merely so that you could have him back for ever, [16]no longer as a slave, but something much better than a slave, a dear brother; especially dear to me, but how much more to you, both on the natural plane and in the Lord. [17]So if you grant me any fellowship with yourself, welcome him as you would me; [18]if he has wronged you in any way or owes you anything, put it down to my account. [19]I am writing this in my own hand: I, Paul, shall pay it back—I make no mention of a further debt, that you owe your very self to me! [20]Well then, brother, I am counting on you, in the Lord; set my heart at rest, in Christ. [21]I am writing with complete confidence in your compliance, sure that you will do even more than I ask.

A personal request. Good wishes

[22]There is another thing: will you get a place ready for me to stay in? I am hoping through your prayers to be restored to you.

[23]Epaphras, a prisoner with me in Christ Jesus, sends his greetings; [24]so do my fellow-workers Mark, Aristarchus, Demas and Luke.

[25]May the grace of our Lord Jesus Christ be with your spirit.

THE LETTER TO THE
HEBREWS

This anonymous letter, joined on to the letters of Paul, was aptly entitled (in the 2nd century) 'To the Hebrews'. It uses scriptural passages throughout to show that the sacrifice and covenant of Christ fulfil God's promises, and bring the faithful to perfection, where the old dispensation failed. It contains a rich theology not only of Christ's effective priesthood but of his human and divine nature. The letter's emphasis on ceremonial suggests that it was addressed to Jewish priests who hankered after the splendour of the Temple worship and its ineffectual sacrifices. The author stresses that the pilgrimage of the Israelites through the desert was only an image of the Christian pilgrimage to the final place of rest, and that the faith of the great patriarchs was a model for Christian faith and perseverance.

It is unclear whether the letter was written before or after the destruction of the Temple in AD 70, and its authorship is similarly unknown. Italy is mentioned as the place of origin (13:24).

a A pun: Onesimus means 'useful'.

PLAN OF THE LETTER

THE LETTER TO THE
HEBREWS

PROLOGUE

The greatness of the incarnate Son of God

1 At many moments in the past and by many means, God spoke to our ancestors through the prophets; but ²in our time, the final days, he has spoken to us in the person of his Son, whom he appointed heir of all things and through whom he made the ages. ³He is the reflection of God's glory and bears the impress of God's own being,ᵃ sustaining all things by his powerful command; and now that he has purged sins away, he has taken his seat at the right hand of the divine Majesty on high. ⁴So he is now as far above the angels as the title which he has inherited is higher than their own name.

I: THE SON IS GREATER THAN THE ANGELS

Proof from the scripturesᵇ

⁵To which of the angels, then, has God ever said:

You are my Son, today I have fathered you,

or:

I shall be a father to him and he a son to me?

⁶Again, when he brings the First-born into the world, he says:

Let all the angels of God pay him homage.

⁷To the angels, he says:

*appointing the winds his messengers
  and flames of fire his servants,*

⁸but to the Son he says:

Your throne, God, is for ever and ever;

and:

*the sceptre of his kingdom
  is a sceptre of justice*;

1a cf. Ws 7:25–26.
1b Texts used: Ps 2:7; 2 S 7:14; Ps 97:7; 104:4; 45:6–7; 102:25–27; 110:1.

⁹*you love uprightness and detest evil.*
This is why God,
> *your God, has anointed you*
> *with the oil of gladness,*
> *as none of your rivals.*

¹⁰And again:

> *Long ago, Lord,*
> *you laid earth's foundations,*
> *the heavens are the work of your hands.*
¹¹*They pass away but you remain,*
> *they all wear out like a garment,*
¹²*Like a cloak you will roll them up,*
> *like a garment,*
> *and they will be changed.*
> *But you never alter*
> *and your years are unending.*

¹³To which of the angels has God ever said:

> *Take your seat at my right hand*
> *till I have made your enemies your footstool?*

¹⁴Are they not all ministering spirits, sent to serve for the sake of those who are to inherit salvation?

An exhortation

2 We ought, then, to turn our minds more attentively than before to what we have been taught, so that we do not drift away. ²If a message that was spoken through angels proved to be so reliable that every infringement and disobedience brought its own proper punishment, ³then we shall certainly not go unpunished if we neglect such a great salvation. It was first announced by the Lord himself, and is guaranteed to us by those who heard him; ⁴God himself confirmed their witness with signs and marvels and miracles of all kinds, and by distributing the gifts of the Holy Spirit in the various ways he wills.

Redemption brought by Christ, not by angels

⁵It was not under angels that he put the world to come, about which we are speaking.

⁶Someone witnesses to this somewhere with the words:

> *What are human beings*
> *that you spare a thought for them,*
> *a child of Adam that you care for him?*
⁷*For a short while you have made him*
> *less than the angels;*
> *you have crowned him*
> *with glory and honour,*
⁸*put all things under his feet.*ᵃ

For in *putting all things under* him he made no exceptions. At present, it is true, we are not able to see that *all things are under him*, ⁹but we do see Jesus, who was *for a short while made less than the angels*, now *crowned with glory and honour* because he submitted to death; so that by God's grace his experience of death should benefit all humanity.

¹⁰It was fitting that God, for whom and through whom everything exists, should, in bringing many sons to glory, make perfect through suffering the leader of their salvation. ¹¹For consecrator and consecrated are all of the same stock; that is why he is not ashamed to call them *brothers* ¹²in the text: *I shall proclaim your name to my brothers, praise you in full assembly*; or in the text:¹³ *I shall put my hope in him*; followed by *Look, I and the children whom God has given me.*ᵇ

¹⁴Since all the *children* share the same human nature, he too shared equally in it, so that by his death he could set aside him who held the power of death, namely the devil, ¹⁵and set free all those who had been held in slavery all their lives by the fear of death. ¹⁶For it was not the angels that he took to himself; he took to himself *the line of Abraham.* ¹⁷It was essential that he should in this way be made completely like his brothers so that he could become a compassionate and trustworthy high priest for their relationship to God, able to expiate the sins of the people. ¹⁸For the suffering he himself passed through while being put to the test enables him to help others when they are being put to the test.

2a Ps 8:4–6.
2b Ps 22:22; Is 8:17, 18.

II: JESUS THE FAITHFUL AND MERCIFUL HIGH PRIEST

Christ higher than Moses

3 That is why all you who are holy brothers and share the same heavenly call should turn your minds to Jesus, the apostle and the high priest of our profession of faith. [2]He was *trustworthy* to the one who appointed him, just like *Moses*, who remained trustworthy *in all his household;*[a] [3]but he deserves a greater glory than Moses, just as the builder of a house is more honoured than the house itself. [4]Every house is built by someone, of course; but God built everything that exists. [5]It is true that Moses was *trustworthy in the household* of God, as a *servant* is, acting as witness to the things which were yet to be revealed, [6]but Christ is trustworthy as a son is, over his household. And we are his household, as long as we fearlessly maintain the hope in which we glory.

How to reach God's land of rest[b]

[7]That is why, as the Holy Spirit says:

If only you would listen to him today!
[8]*Do not harden your hearts,*
  as at the rebellion,
as at the time of testing in the desert,
[9]*when your ancestors challenged me,*
and put me to the test,
  and saw what I could do
[10]*for forty years.*

  That was why

that generation sickened me
and I said, 'Always fickle hearts,
that cannot grasp my ways!'
[11]*And then in my anger I swore*
that they would never enter my place of rest.

[12]Take care, brothers, that none of you ever has a wicked heart, so unbelieving as to turn away from the living God. [13]Every day, as long as this *today* lasts, keep encouraging one another so that none of you is *hardened* by the lure of sin, [14]because we have been granted a share with Christ only if we keep the grasp of our first confidence firm to the end. [15]In this saying: *If only you would listen to him today; do not harden your hearts, as at the Rebellion,* [16]who was it who *listened* and then

rebelled? Surely all those whom Moses led out of Egypt. [17]And with whom was he *angry for forty years?* Surely with those who sinned and whose *dead bodies fell in the desert.* [18]To whom did he *swear they would never enter his place of rest?* Surely those who would not believe. [19]So we see that it was their refusal to believe which prevented them from entering.

4 Let us beware, then: since the promise never lapses, none of you must think that he has come too late for the promise of *entering his place of rest.* [2]We received the gospel exactly as they did; but hearing the message did them no good because they did not share the faith of those who did listen. [3]We, however, who have faith, are *entering a place of rest,* as in the text: *And then in my anger I swore that they would never enter my place of rest.* Now God's work was all finished at the beginning of the world; [4]as one text says, referring to the seventh day: *And God rested on the seventh day after all the work he had been doing.* [5]And, again, the passage above says: *They will never reach my place of rest.* [6]It remains the case, then, that there would be some people who would reach it, and since those who first heard the good news were prevented from entering by their refusal to believe, [7]God fixed another day, a *Today,* when he said through David in the text already quoted: *If only you would listen to him today; do not harden your hearts.* [8]If Joshua had led them into this place of rest, God would not later have spoken of another day. [9]There must still be, therefore, a seventh-day rest reserved for God's people, [10]since to *enter the place of rest* is to *rest after your work,* as God did after his. [11]Let us, then, press forward to *enter this place of rest,* or some of you might copy this example of refusal to believe and be lost.

[12]The word of God is something alive and active: it cuts more incisively than any two-edged sword: it can seek out the place where soul is divided from spirit, or joints from marrow; it can pass judgement on secret emotions and thoughts. [13]No created thing is hidden from him; everything is uncovered and stretched fully open to the eyes of the one to whom we must give account of ourselves.

3a Nb 12:7.
3b An elaboration on Ps 95:7–11.

Jesus the compassionate high priest

[14]Since in Jesus, the Son of God, we have the supreme high priest who has gone through to the highest heaven, we must hold firm to our profession of faith. [15]For the high priest we have is not incapable of feeling our weaknesses with us, but has been put to the test in exactly the same way as ourselves, apart from sin. [16]Let us, then, have no fear in approaching the throne of grace to receive mercy and to find grace when we are in need of help.

5 Every high priest is taken from among human beings and is appointed to act on their behalf in relationships with God, to offer gifts and sacrifices for sins; [2]he can sympathise with those who are ignorant or who have gone astray, because he too is subject to the limitations of weakness. [3]That is why he has to make sin offerings for himself as well as for the people. [4]No one takes this honour on himself; it needs a call from God, as in Aaron's case. [5]And so it was not Christ who gave himself the glory of becoming high priest, but the one who said to him: *You are my Son, today I have fathered you,*[a] [6]and in another text: *You are a priest for ever, of the order of Melchizedek.* [7]During his life on earth, he offered up prayer and entreaty, with loud cries and with tears, to the one who had the power to save him from death, and, winning a hearing by his reverence, [8]he learnt obedience, Son though he was, through his sufferings; [9]when he had been perfected, he became for all who obey him the source of eternal salvation [10]and was acclaimed by God with the title of high *priest of the order of Melchizedek.*

III: THE AUTHENTIC PRIESTHOOD OF JESUS CHRIST

Christian life and theology

[11]On this subject we have many things to say, and they are difficult to explain because you have grown so slow at understanding. [12]Indeed, when you should by this time have become masters, you need someone to teach you all over again the elements of the principles of God's sayings; you have gone back to needing milk, and not solid food. [13]Truly, no one who is still living on milk can digest the doctrine of saving justice, being still a baby. [14]Solid food is for adults with minds trained by practice to distinguish between good and bad.

The author explains his intention

6 Let us leave behind us then all the elementary teaching about Christ and go on to its completion, without going over the fundamental doctrines again: the turning away from dead actions, faith in God, [2]the teaching about baptisms and the laying-on of hands, about the resurrection of the dead and eternal judgement. [3]This, God willing, is what we propose to do.

[4]As for those people who were once brought into the light, and tasted the gift from heaven, and received a share of the Holy Spirit, [5]and tasted the goodness of God's message and the powers of the world to come [6]and yet in spite of this have fallen away—it is impossible for them to be brought to the freshness of repentance a second time, since they are crucifying the Son of God again for themselves, and making a public exhibition of him. [7]A field that drinks up the rain that has fallen frequently on it, and yields the crops that are wanted by the owners who grew them, receives God's blessing; [8]but one that grows brambles and thistles is worthless, and near to being cursed. It will end by being burnt.

Words of hope and encouragement

[9]But you, my dear friends—in spite of what we have just said, we are sure you are in a better state and on the way to salvation. [10]God would not be so unjust as to forget all you have done, the love that you have for his name or the services you have done, and are still doing, for the holy people of God. [11]Our desire is that every one of you should go on showing the same enthusiasm till the ultimate fulfilment of your hope, [12]never growing careless, but taking as your model those who

---

5a Ps 2:7 followed by Ps 110:4.

by their faith and perseverance are heirs of the promises.

¹³When God made the promise to Abraham, he *swore by his own self*, since there was no one greater he could swear by: ¹⁴*I will shower blessings on you and give you many descendants.*[a] ¹⁵Because of that, Abraham persevered and received fulfilment of the promise. ¹⁶Human beings, of course, swear an oath by something greater than themselves, and between them, confirmation by an oath puts an end to all dispute. ¹⁷In the same way, when God wanted to show the heirs of the promise even more clearly how unalterable his plan was, he conveyed it by an oath ¹⁸so that through two unalterable factors in which God could not be lying, we who have fled to him might have a vigorous encouragement to grasp the hope held out to us. ¹⁹This is the anchor our souls have, as sure as it is firm, reaching right through *inside the curtain* ²⁰where Jesus has entered as a forerunner on our behalf, having become a high *priest for ever, of the order of Melchizedek*.

A: CHRIST'S PRIESTHOOD HIGHER THAN LEVITICAL PRIESTHOOD

Melchizedek[a]

7 Melchizedek, *king of Salem, a priest of God Most High, came to meet Abraham when he returned from defeating the kings*, and *blessed him*; ²and Abraham gave him *a tenth of everything*. By the interpretation of his name, he is, first, 'king of saving justice' and also *king of Salem*, that is, 'king of peace'; ³he has no father, mother or ancestry, and his life has no beginning or ending; he is like the Son of God. He remains a priest for ever.

Melchizedek accepted tithes from Abraham

⁴Now think how great this man must have been, if the patriarch *Abraham gave him a tenth* of the finest plunder. ⁵We know that any of the descendants of Levi who are admitted to the priesthood are obliged by the Law to take tithes from the people, that is, from their own brothers although they too are descended from Abraham. ⁶But this man, who was not of the same descent, took his tithe from Abraham, and he gave his blessing to the holder of the promises. ⁷Now it is indisputable that a blessing is given by a superior to an inferior. ⁸Further, in the normal case it is ordinary mortal men who receive the tithes, whereas in that case it was one who is attested as being alive. ⁹It could be said that Levi himself, who receives tithes, actually paid tithes, in the person of Abraham, ¹⁰because he was still in the loins of his ancestor when *Melchizedek came to meet him*.

From levitical priesthood to the priesthood of Melchizedek

¹¹Now if perfection had been reached through the levitical priesthood—and this was the basis of the Law given to the people—why was it necessary for a different kind of priest to arise, spoken of as being *of the order of Melchizedek* rather than of the order of Aaron? ¹²Any change in the priesthood must mean a change in the Law as well.

¹³So our Lord, of whom these things were said, belonged to a different tribe, the members of which have never done service at the altar; ¹⁴everyone knows he came from Judah, a tribe which Moses did not mention at all when dealing with priests.

The abrogation of the old law

¹⁵This becomes even more clearly evident if another priest, of the type of Melchizedek, arises who is a priest ¹⁶not in virtue of a law of physical descent, but in virtue of the power of an indestructible life. ¹⁷For he is attested by the prophecy: *You are a priest for ever of the order of Melchizedek.* ¹⁸The earlier commandment is thus abolished, because of its weakness and ineffectiveness ¹⁹since the Law could not make anything perfect; but now this commandment is replaced by something better—the hope that brings us close to God.

Christ's priesthood is unchanging

²⁰Now the former priests became priests without any oath being sworn, ²¹but this one with the swearing of an oath by him who said

---

6a Gn 22:16.
7a A commentary on Gn 14:17–20.

to him, *The Lord has sworn an oath he will never retract: you are a priest for ever*; ²²the very fact that it occurred with the swearing of an oath makes the covenant of which Jesus is the guarantee all the greater. ²³Further, the former priests were many in number, because death put an end to each one of them; ²⁴but this one, because he remains *for ever*, has a perpetual priesthood. ²⁵It follows, then, that his power to save those who come to God through him is absolute, since he lives for ever to intercede for them.

The perfection of the heavenly high priest

²⁶Such is the high priest that met our need, holy, innocent and uncontaminated, set apart from sinners, and raised up above the heavens; ²⁷he has no need to offer sacrifices every day, as the high priests do, first for their own sins and only then for those of the people; this he did once and for all by offering himself. ²⁸The Law appoints high priests who are men subject to weakness; but the promise on oath, which came after the Law, appointed the Son who is made perfect *for ever*.

B: SUPERIORITY OF THE WORSHIP, SANCTUARY AND MEDIATION OF CHRIST

The new priesthood and the new sanctuary

8 The principal point of all that we have said is that we have a high priest of exactly this kind. He *has taken his seat at the right*[a] of the throne of divine Majesty in the heavens, ²and he is the minister of the sanctuary and of the true *Tent* which *the Lord*, and not any man, *set up*.[b] ³Every high priest is constituted to offer gifts and sacrifices, and so this one too must have something to offer. ⁴In fact, if he were on earth, he would not be a priest at all, since there are others who make the offerings laid down by the Law, ⁵though these maintain the service only of a model or a reflection of the heavenly realities; just as Moses, when he had the Tent to build, was warned by God who said: *See that you work to the design that was shown you on the mountain.*[c]

Christ is the mediator of a greater covenant

⁶As it is, he has been given a ministry as far superior as is the covenant of which he is the mediator, which is founded on better promises. ⁷If that first covenant had been faultless, there would have been no room for a second one to replace it. ⁸And in fact God does find fault with them; he says:

Look, the days are coming, the Lord
    declares,
when I will make a new covenant
    with the House of Israel
    and the House of Judah,
⁹*but not a covenant*
    like the one I made with their ancestors,
the day I took them by the hand
    to bring them out of Egypt,
which covenant of mine they broke,
and I too abandoned them,
    the Lord declares.
¹⁰*No, this is the covenant*
I will make with the House of Israel,
when those days have come,
    the Lord declares:
In their minds I shall plant my laws
writing them on their hearts.
Then I shall be their God,
and they shall be my people.
¹¹*There will be no further need*
    for each to teach his neighbour,
and each his brother,
    saying 'Learn to know the Lord!'
No, they will all know me,
    from the least to the greatest,
¹²*since I shall forgive their guilt*
and never more call their sins to mind.[d]

¹³By speaking of a *new* covenant, he implies that the first one is old. And anything old and ageing is ready to disappear.

Christ enters the heavenly sanctuary

9 The first covenant also had its laws governing worship and its sanctuary, a sanctuary on this earth. ²There was a tent which comprised two compartments: the first, in which the lamp-stand, the table and the loaves of permanent offering were kept, was called the Holy Place; ³then beyond the second veil, a second compartment which

8a Ps 110:1.
8b Nb 24:6.
8c Ex 25:40.
8d Jr 31:31–34.

was called the Holy of Holies [4]to which belonged the gold altar of incense, and the ark of the covenant, plated all over with gold. In this were kept the gold jar containing the manna, Aaron's branch that grew the buds, and the tables of the covenant. [5]On top of it were the glorious winged creatures, overshadowing the throne of mercy. This is not the time to go into detail about this.

[6]Under these provisions, priests go regularly into the outer tent to carry out their acts of worship, [7]but the second tent is entered only once a year, and then only by the high priest who takes in the blood to make an offering for his own and the people's faults of inadvertence. [8]By this, the Holy Spirit means us to see that as long as the old tent stands, the way into the holy place is not opened up; [9]it is a symbol for this present time. None of the gifts and sacrifices offered under these regulations can possibly bring any worshipper to perfection in his conscience; [10]they are rules about outward life, connected with food and drink and washing at various times, which are in force only until the time comes to set things right.

[11]But now Christ has come, as the high priest of all the blessings which were to come. He has passed through the greater, the more perfect tent, not made by human hands, that is, not of this created order; [12]and he has entered the sanctuary once and for all, taking with him not the blood of goats and bull calves, but his own blood, having won an eternal redemption. [13]The blood of goats and bulls and the ashes of a heifer, sprinkled on those who have incurred defilement, may restore their bodily purity. [14]How much more will the blood of Christ, who offered himself, blameless as he was, to God through the eternal Spirit, purify our conscience from dead actions so that we can worship the living God.

Christ seals the new covenant with his blood

[15]This makes him the mediator of a new covenant, so that, now that a death has occurred to redeem the sins committed under an earlier covenant, those who have been called to an eternal inheritance may receive the promise. [16]Now wherever a will is in question, the death of the testator must be established; [17]a testament comes into effect only after a death, since it has no force while the testator is still alive. [18]That is why even the earlier covenant was inaugurated with blood, [19]and why, after Moses had promulgated all the commandments of the Law to the people, he took the calves' blood, the goats' blood and some water, and with these he sprinkled the book itself and all the people, using scarlet wool and hyssop; [20]saying as he did so: *This is the blood of the covenant that God has made with you.*[a] [21]And he sprinkled both the tent and all the liturgical vessels with blood in the same way. [22]In fact, according to the Law, practically every purification takes place by means of blood; and if there is no shedding of blood, there is no remission. [23]Only the copies of heavenly things are purified in this way; the heavenly things themselves have to be purified by a higher sort of sacrifice than this. [24]It is not as though Christ had entered a man-made sanctuary which was merely a model of the real one; he entered heaven itself, so that he now appears in the presence of God on our behalf. [25]And he does not have to offer himself again and again, as the high priest goes into the sanctuary year after year with the blood that is not his own, [26]or else he would have had to suffer over and over again since the world began. As it is, he has made his appearance once and for all, at the end of the last age, to do away with sin by sacrificing himself. [27]Since human beings die only once, after which comes judgement, [28]so Christ too, having offered himself only once *to bear the sin of many,*[b] will manifest himself a second time, sin being no more, to those who are waiting for him, to bring them salvation.

SUMMARY: CHRIST'S SACRIFICE SUPERIOR TO THE SACRIFICES OF THE MOSAIC LAW

The old sacrifices ineffective

10 So, since the Law contains no more than a reflection of the good things which were still to come, and no true image of them, it is quite incapable of bringing the worshippers to perfection, by means of the

9a Ex 24:8.
9b Is 53:12.

same sacrifices repeatedly offered year after year. [2]Otherwise, surely the offering of them would have stopped, because the worshippers, when they had been purified once, would have no awareness of sins. [3]But in fact the sins are recalled year after year in the sacrifices. [4]Bulls' blood and goats' blood are incapable of taking away sins, [5]and that is why he said, on coming into the world:

You wanted no sacrifice or cereal offering,
but you gave me a body.
[6]*You took no pleasure in burnt offering*
or sacrifice for sin;
[7]*then I said, 'Here I am, I am coming,'*
in the scroll of the book it is written of me,
to do your will, God.[a]

[8]He says first *You did not want* what the Law lays down as the things to be offered, that is: *the sacrifices, the cereal offerings, the burnt offerings and the sacrifices for sin,* and *you took no pleasure* in them; [9]and then he says: *Here I am! I am coming to do your will.* He is abolishing the first sort to establish the second. [10]And this *will* was for us to be made holy by the *offering* of the *body* of Jesus Christ made once and for all.

The efficacy of Christ's sacrifice

[11]Every priest stands at his duties every day, offering over and over again the same sacrifices which are quite incapable of taking away sins. [12]He, on the other hand, has offered one single sacrifice for sins, and then *taken his seat for ever, at the right hand of God,* [13]where he is now waiting *till his enemies are made his footstool.*[b] [14]By virtue of that one single offering, he has achieved the eternal perfection of all who are sanctified. [15]The Holy Spirit attests this to us, for after saying:

[16]*No, this is the covenant*
I will make with them,
when those days have come.

the Lord says:

In their minds I will plant my Laws
writing them on their hearts,
[17]*and I shall never more*
call their sins to mind,[c]
or their offences.

[18]When these have been forgiven, there can be no more sin offerings.

IV: PERSEVERING FAITH

The Christian opportunity

[19]We have then, brothers, complete confidence through the blood of Jesus in entering the sanctuary, [20]by a new way which he has opened for us, a living opening through the curtain, that is to say, his flesh. [21]And we have the *high priest* over all *the sanctuary of God.*[d] [22]So as we go in, let us be sincere in heart and filled with faith, our hearts sprinkled and free from any trace of bad conscience, and our bodies washed with pure water. [23]Let us keep firm in the hope we profess, because the one who made the promise is trustworthy. [24]Let us be concerned for each other, to stir a response in love and good works. [25]Do not absent yourself from your own assemblies, as some do, but encourage each other; the more so as you see the Day drawing near.

The danger of apostasy

[26]If, after we have been given knowledge of the truth, we should deliberately commit any sins, then there is no longer any sacrifice for them. [27]There is left only the dreadful prospect of judgement and of *the fiery wrath* that is to *devour your enemies.*[e] [28]Anyone who disregards the Law of Moses is ruthlessly *put to death on the word of two witnesses or three;*[f] [29]and you may be sure that anyone who tramples on the Son of God, and who treats *the blood of the covenant* which sanctified him as if it were not holy, and who insults the Spirit of grace, will be condemned to a far

10a Ps 40:6–8.
10b Ps 110:1.
10c Jr 31:33–34.
10d Zc 6:11–12.
10e Is 26:11.
10f Dt 17:6.

severer punishment. [30]We are all aware who it was that said: *Vengeance is mine; I will pay them back.*[g] And again: *The Lord will vindicate his people.* [31]It is a dreadful thing to fall into the hands of the living God.

Motives for perseverance

[32]Remember the great challenge of the sufferings that you had to meet after you received the light, in earlier days; [33]sometimes by being yourselves publicly exposed to humiliations and violence, and sometimes as associates of others who were treated in the same way. [34]For you not only shared in the sufferings of those who were in prison, but you accepted with joy being stripped of your belongings, knowing that you owned something that was better and lasting. [35]Do not lose your fearlessness now, then, since the reward is so great. [36]You will need perseverance if you are to do God's will and gain what he has promised.

[37]Only *a little while now, a very little while, for come he certainly will before too long.*[h]
[38]*My upright person will live through faith but if he draws back, my soul will take no pleasure in him.*[i]

[39]We are not the sort of people who *draw back*, and are lost by it; we are the sort who keep *faith* until our souls are saved.

The exemplary faith of our ancestors

11 Only faith can guarantee the blessings that we hope for, or prove the existence of realities that are unseen. [2]It is for their faith that our ancestors are acknowledged. [3]It is by faith that we understand that the ages were created by a word from God, so that from the invisible the visible world came to be.

[4]It was because of his faith that Abel offered God a better sacrifice than Cain, and for that he was acknowledged as upright when *God* himself made acknowledgement of *his offerings.* Though he is dead, he still speaks by faith.

[5]It was because of his faith that Enoch was taken up and did not experience death: *he was no more, because God took him;*[a] because before his assumption he was acknowledged to *have pleased God.* [6]Now it is impossible to please God without faith, since anyone who comes to him must believe that he exists and rewards those who seek him.

[7]It was through his faith that Noah, when he had been warned by God of something that had never been seen before, took care to build an ark to save his family. His faith was a judgement on the world, and he was able to claim the uprightness which comes from faith.

[8]It was by faith that Abraham obeyed the call to *set out* for a country that was the inheritance given to him and his descendants, and that *he set out* without knowing where he was going. [9]By faith he *sojourned* in the Promised Land as though it were not his, living in tents with Isaac and Jacob, who were heirs with him of the same promise. [10]He looked forward to the well-founded city, designed and built by God.

[11]It was equally by faith that Sarah, in spite of being past the age, was made able to conceive, because she believed that he who had made the promise was faithful to it. [12]Because of this, there came from one man, and one who already had the mark of death on him, descendants *as numerous as the stars of heaven and the grains of sand on the seashore which cannot be counted.*[b]

[13]All these died in faith, before receiving any of the things that had been promised, but they saw them in the far distance and welcomed them, recognising that they were only *strangers and nomads on earth.* [14]People who use such terms about themselves make it quite plain that they are in search of a homeland. [15]If they had meant the country they came from, they would have had the opportunity to return to it; [16]but in fact they were longing for a better homeland, their heavenly homeland. That is why God is not ashamed to be called their God, since he has founded the city for them.

[17]It was by faith that Abraham, *when put to the test, offered up Isaac.*[c] He offered to sacrifice *his only son* even though he had yet

---

10g Dt 32:35–36.
10h Is 26:20.
10i Hab 2:3–4.
11a Gn 5:24.
11b Gn 22:17.
11c Gn 22:1–14.

to receive what had been promised, ¹⁸and he had been told: *Isaac is the one through whom your name will be carried on.*ᵈ ¹⁹He was confident that God had the power even to raise the dead; and so, figuratively speaking, he was given back Isaac from the dead.

²⁰It was by faith that this same Isaac gave his blessing to Jacob and Esau for the still distant future. ²¹By faith Jacob, when he was dying, blessed each of Joseph's sons, *bowed in reverence, as he leant on his staff.*ᵉ ²²It was by faith that, when he was about to die, Joseph mentioned the Exodus of the Israelites and gave instructions about his own remains.

²³It was by faith that Moses, when he was born, *was kept hidden by his parents for three months;*ᶠ because they *saw* that he was a *fine* child; they were not afraid of the royal edict. ²⁴It was by faith that, *when he was grown up,* Moses refused to be known as the son of Pharaoh's daughter ²⁵and chose to be ill-treated in company with God's people rather than to enjoy the transitory pleasures of sin. ²⁶He considered that the humiliations offered to the Anointed were something more precious than all the treasures of Egypt, because he had his eyes fixed on the reward. ²⁷It was by faith that he left Egypt without fear of the king's anger; he held to his purpose like someone who could see the Invisible. ²⁸It was by faith that he kept *the Passover* and sprinkled *the blood* to prevent the Destroyer from touching any of their first-born sons. ²⁹It was by faith they crossed the Red Sea as easily as dry land, while the Egyptians, trying to do the same, were drowned.

³⁰It was through faith that the walls of Jericho fell down when the people had marched round them for seven days. ³¹It was by faith that Rahab the prostitute welcomed the spies and so was not killed with the unbelievers.

³²What more shall I say? There is not time for me to give an account of Gideon, Barak, Samson, Jephthah, or of David, Samuel and the prophets. ³³These were men who through faith conquered kingdoms, did what was upright and earned the promises. They could keep a lion's mouth shut, ³⁴put out blazing fires and emerge unscathed from battle. They were weak people who were given strength to be brave in war and drive back foreign invaders. ³⁵Some returned to their wives from the dead by resurrection; and others submitted to torture, refusing release so that they would rise again to a better life. ³⁶Some had to bear being pilloried and flogged, or even chained up in prison. ³⁷They were stoned, or sawn in half,ᵍ or killed by the sword; they were homeless, and wore only the skins of sheep and goats; they were in want and hardship, and maltreated. ³⁸They were too good for the world and they wandered in deserts and mountains and in caves and ravines. ³⁹These all won acknowledgement through their faith, but they did not receive what was promised, ⁴⁰since God had made provision for us to have something better, and they were not to reach perfection except with us.

The example of Jesus Christ

12 With so many witnesses in a great cloud all around us, we too, then, should throw off everything that weighs us down and the sin that clings so closely, and with perseverance keep running in the race which lies ahead of us. ²Let us keep our eyes fixed on Jesus, who leads us in our faith and brings it to perfection: for the sake of the joy which lay ahead of him, he endured the cross, disregarding the shame of it, and *has taken his seat at the right* of God's throne. ³Think of the way he persevered against such opposition from sinners and then you will not lose heart and come to grief. ⁴In the fight against sin, you have not yet had to keep fighting to the point of bloodshed.

God's fatherly instruction

⁵Have you forgotten that encouraging text in which you are addressed as sons?

My son, do not scorn correction
　from the Lord,
do not resent his training,
⁶*for the Lord trains those he loves,*
　*and chastises every son he accepts.*ᵃ

11d Gn 21:12.
11e Gn 47:31.
11f Ex 2:2, 11.
11g Some apocryphal texts say that Isaiah was executed in this way by King Manasseh.
12a Pr 3:11–12.

[7]Perseverance is part of your *training*; God is treating you as his *sons*. Has there ever been any *son* whose father did not *train* him? [8]If you were not getting this training, as all of you are, then you would be not *sons* but bastards. [9]Besides, we have all had our human fathers who punished us, and we respected them for it; all the more readily ought we to submit to the Father of spirits, and so earn life. [10]Our human fathers were training us for a short life and according to their own lights; but he does it all for our own good, so that we may share his own holiness. [11]Of course, any discipline is at the time a matter for grief, not joy; but later, in those who have undergone it, it bears fruit in peace and uprightness. [12]So *steady all weary hands and trembling knees*[b] [13]and make your crooked paths straight; then the injured limb will not be maimed, it will get better instead.

Unfaithfulness is punished

[14]*Seek peace*[c] with all people, and the holiness without which no one can ever see the Lord. [15]Be careful that no one is deprived of the grace of God and that no *root of bitterness should begin to grow and make trouble*;[d] this can poison a large number. [16]And be careful that there is no immoral person, or anyone worldly minded like Esau, *who sold his birthright*[e] for one single meal. [17]As you know, when he wanted to obtain the blessing afterwards, he was rejected and, though he pleaded for it with tears, he could find no way of reversing the decision.

The two covenants

[18]What you have come to is nothing known to the senses: not a *blazing fire*,[f] or *gloom* or *total darkness*, or a *storm*; [19]or *trumpet-blast* or the *sound of a voice speaking* which made everyone that heard it beg that no more should be said to them. [20]They could not bear the order that was given: *If even a beast touches the mountain, it must be stoned.*[g] [21]The whole scene was so terrible that Moses said, 'I am afraid and trembling.' [22]But what you have come to is Mount Zion and the city of the living God, the heavenly Jerusalem where the millions of angels have gathered for the festival, [23]with the whole Church of first-born sons, enrolled as citizens of heaven. You have come to God himself, the supreme Judge, and to the spirits of the upright who have been made perfect; [24]and to Jesus, the mediator of a new covenant, and to purifying blood which pleads more insistently than Abel's. [25]Make sure that you never refuse to listen when he speaks. If the people who on earth refused to listen to a warning could not escape their punishment, how shall we possibly escape if we turn away from a voice that warns us from heaven? [26]That time his voice made the earth shake, but now he has given us this promise: *I am going to shake the earth once more and* not only the earth but *heaven as well.*[h] [27]The words *once more* indicate the removal of what is shaken, since these are created things, so that what is not shaken remains. [28]We have been given possession of an unshakeable kingdom. Let us therefore be grateful and use our gratitude to worship God in the way that pleases him, in reverence and fear. [29]For our *God* is a *consuming fire.*[i]

APPENDIX

Final recommendations

13 Continue to love each other like brothers, [2]and remember always to welcome strangers, for by doing this, some people have entertained angels without knowing it. [3]Keep in mind those who are in prison, as though you were in prison with

---

12b Is 35:3.
12c Ps 34:14.
12d Dt 29:17.
12e Gn 25:33.
12f Ex 19—20, followed by Dt 9:19; Hg 2:6; Dt 4:24.
12g Ex 19:12seq.
12h Hg 2:6.
12i Dt 4:24.

them; and those who are being badly treated, since you too are in the body. [4]Marriage must be honoured by all, and marriages must be kept undefiled, because the sexually immoral and adulterers will come under God's judgement. [5]Put avarice out of your lives and be content with whatever you have; God himself has said: *I shall not fail you or desert you,*[a] [6]and so we can say with confidence: *With the Lord on my side, I fear nothing: what can human beings do to me?*[b]

Faithfulness

[7]Remember your leaders, who preached the word of God to you, and as you reflect on the outcome of their lives, take their faith as your model. [8]Jesus Christ is the same today as he was yesterday and as he will be for ever. [9]Do not be led astray by all sorts of strange doctrines: it is better to rely on grace for inner strength than on food, which has done no good to those who concentrate on it. [10]We have our own altar from which those who serve the Tent have no right to eat. [11]The bodies of the animals *whose blood is taken into the sanctuary* by the high priest *for the rite of expiation are burnt outside the camp,*[c] [12]and so Jesus too suffered outside the gate to sanctify the people with his own blood. [13]Let us go to him, then, *outside the camp,* and bear his humiliation. [14]There is no permanent city for us here; we are looking for the one which is yet to be. [15]Through him, *let us offer God* an unending *sacrifice* of praise, the fruit of the lips of those who acknowledge his name. [16]Keep doing good works and sharing your resources, for these are the kinds of sacrifice that please God.

Obedience to religious leaders

[17]Obey your leaders and give way to them; they watch over your souls because they must give an account of them; make this a joy for them to do, and not a grief—you yourselves would be the losers. [18]Pray for us; we are sure that our own conscience is clear and we are certainly determined to behave honourably in everything we do. [19]I ask you very particularly to pray that I may come back to you all the sooner.

EPILOGUE

News, good wishes and greetings

[20]I pray that the God of peace, *who brought back* from the dead our Lord Jesus, the great *Shepherd of the sheep, by the blood that sealed an eternal covenant,*[d] [21]may prepare you to do his will in every kind of good action; effecting in us all whatever is acceptable to himself through Jesus Christ, to whom be glory for ever and ever. Amen.

[22]I urge you, brothers, to take these words of encouragement kindly; that is why I have written to you briefly.

[23]I want you to know that our brother Timothy has been set free. If he arrives in time, he will be with me when I see you. [24]Greetings to all your leaders and to all God's holy people. God's holy people in Italy send you greetings. [25]Grace be with you all.

13a Dt 31:6.
13b Ps 118:6 .
13c Lv 16:27.
13d A combination of Is 63:11 with Ezk 34:23; 37:26.

INTRODUCTION TO
THE LETTERS TO ALL CHRISTIANS

Most of these seven letters are addressed to Christians in general rather than any particular community, and they are often called the 'Catholic' or 'Universal Epistles'. In some cases their authorship is disputed: they claim to stem from the apostles, and they have been accepted by Christians as truly representing the apostolic tradition. They reflect a world towards the end of the 1st century when the spreading Christian communities are at grips with their first difficulties both from within and from outside.

THE LETTER OF
JAMES

More a sermon than a letter, Jm blends OT and gospel tradition with Gk elegance. The author insists that Christian faith must issue in good works: a faith not expressed in good works is no faith at all. In the Wisdom tradition of the OT he gives sharp and sensible advice on many practical points of conduct, especially stressing the danger and transitoriness of wealth.

Some scholars consider Jm the earliest writing of the NT; others place it at the end of the century and deny that it was written by James, brother of the Lord and leader of the Jewish–Christian party in the Jerusalem church.

THE LETTER OF
JAMES

Address and greetings

1 From James, servant of God and of the Lord Jesus Christ. Greetings to the twelve tribes of the Dispersion.[a]

Trials a privilege

[2]My brothers, consider it a great joy when trials of many kinds come upon you, [3]for you well know that the testing of your faith produces perseverance, and [4]perseverance must complete its work so that you will become fully developed, complete, not deficient in any way.

Prayer with confidence

[5]Any of you who lacks wisdom must ask God, who gives to all generously and without scolding; it will be given. [6]But the prayer must be made with faith, and no trace of

---

1a Properly, Jews scattered in the gentile world, successors of the twelve tribes.

doubt, because a person who has doubts is like the waves thrown up in the sea by the buffeting of the wind. [7]That sort of person, in two minds, [8]inconsistent in every activity, must not expect to receive anything from the Lord.

The lot of the rich

[9]It is right that the brother in humble circumstances should glory in being lifted up, [10]and the rich in being brought low. For the rich will last no longer than *the wild flower*; [11]the scorching sun comes up, and the *grass withers*, its *flower falls*,[b] its beauty is lost. It is the same with the rich: in the middle of a busy life, the rich will wither.

Temptation

[12]*Blessed is anyone who perseveres*[c] when trials come. Such a person is of proven worth and will win the prize of life, the crown that the Lord has promised to those who love him. [13]Never, when you are being put to the test, say, 'God is tempting me'; God cannot be tempted by evil, and he does not put anybody to the test . [14]Everyone is put to the test by being attracted and seduced by that person's own wrong desire. [15]Then the desire conceives and gives birth to sin, and when sin reaches full growth, it gives birth to death.

Receiving the Word
and putting it into practice

[16]Make no mistake about this, my dear brothers: [17]all that is good, all that is perfect, is given us from above; it comes down from the Father of all light; with him there is no such thing as alteration, no shadow caused by change. [18]By his own choice he gave birth to us by the message of the truth so that we should be a sort of first-fruits of all his creation.

True religion

[19]Remember this, my dear brothers: everyone should be *quick to listen*[d] but *slow* to speak and slow to human anger; [20]God's saving justice is never served by human anger; [21]so do away with all impurities and remnants of evil. Humbly welcome the Word which has been planted in you and can save your souls.

[22]But you must do what the Word tells you and not just listen to it and deceive yourselves. [23]Anyone who listens to the Word and takes no action is like someone who looks at his own features in a mirror and, [24]once he has seen what he looks like, goes off and immediately forgets it. [25]But anyone who looks steadily at the perfect law of freedom and keeps to it—not listening and forgetting, but putting it into practice—will be blessed in every undertaking.

[26]Nobody who fails to keep a tight rein on the tongue can claim to be religious; this is mere self-deception; that person's religion is worthless. [27]Pure, unspoilt religion, in the eyes of God our Father, is this: coming to the help of orphans and widows in their hardships, and keeping oneself uncontaminated by the world.

Respect for the poor

2 My brothers, do not let class distinction enter into your faith in Jesus Christ, our glorified Lord. [2]Now suppose a man comes into your synagogue, well-dressed and with a gold ring on, and at the same time a poor man comes in, in shabby clothes, [3]and you take notice of the well-dressed man, and say, 'Come this way to the best seats'; then you tell the poor man, 'Stand over there' or 'You can sit on the floor by my foot-rest.' [4]In making this distinction among yourselves have you not used a corrupt standard?

[5]Listen, my dear brothers: it was those who were poor according to the world that God chose, to be rich in faith and to be the heirs to the kingdom which he promised to those who love him. [6]You, on the other hand, have dishonoured the poor. Is it not the rich who lord it over you? [7]Are not they the ones who drag you into court, who insult the honourable name which has been pronounced over you? [8]Well, the right thing to do is to keep the supreme Law of scripture: *you will love your neighbour as yourself;*[a] [9]but as soon as you make class distinctions, you

---

1b Is 40:6–7.
1c Dn 12:2.
1d Si 5:11.
2a Lv 19:18.

are committing sin and under condemnation for breaking the Law.

[10] You see, anyone who keeps the whole of the Law but trips up on a single point, is still guilty of breaking it all. [11] He who said, '*You must not commit adultery*' said also, '*You must not kill.*'[b] Now if you commit murder, you need not commit adultery as well to become a breaker of the Law. [12] Talk and behave like people who are going to be judged by the law of freedom. [13] Whoever acts without mercy will be judged without mercy but mercy can afford to laugh at judgement.

Faith and good deeds

[14] How does it help, my brothers, when someone who has never done a single good act claims to have faith? Will that faith bring salvation? [15] If one of the brothers or one of the sisters is in need of clothes and has not enough food to live on, [16] and one of you says to them, 'I wish you well; keep yourself warm and eat plenty,' without giving them these bare necessities of life, then what good is that? [17] In the same way faith, if good deeds do not go with it, is quite dead.

[18] But someone may say: So you have faith and I have good deeds? Show me this faith of yours without deeds, then! It is by my deeds that I will show you my faith. [19] You believe in the one God—that is creditable enough, but even the demons have the same belief, and they tremble with fear. [20] Fool! Would you not like to know that faith without deeds is useless? [21] Was not Abraham our father justified by his deed, because he *offered his son Isaac on the altar?*[c] [22] So you can see that his faith was working together with his deeds; his faith became perfect by what he did. [23] In this way the scripture was fulfilled: *Abraham put his faith in God, and this was considered as making him upright;*[d] and he received the name 'friend of God'.

[24] You see now that it is by deeds, and not only by believing, that someone is justified. [25] There is another example of the same kind: Rahab the prostitute,[e] was she not justified by her deeds because she welcomed the messengers and showed them a different way to leave? [26] As a body without a spirit is dead, so is faith without deeds.

Uncontrolled language

3 Only a few of you, my brothers, should be teachers, bearing in mind that we shall receive a stricter judgement. [2] For we all trip up in many ways.

Someone who does not trip up in speech has reached perfection and is able to keep the whole body on a tight rein. [3] Once we put a bit in the horse's mouth, to make it do what we want, we have the whole animal under our control. [4] Or think of ships: no matter how big they are, even if a gale is driving them, they are directed by a tiny rudder wherever the whim of the helmsman decides. [5] So the tongue is only a tiny part of the body, but its boasts are great. Think how small a flame can set fire to a huge forest; [6] The tongue is a flame too. Among all the parts of the body, the tongue is a whole wicked world: it infects the whole body; catching fire itself from hell, it sets fire to the whole wheel of creation. [7] Wild animals and birds, reptiles and fish of every kind can all be tamed, and have been tamed, by humans; [8] but nobody can tame the tongue—it is a pest that will not keep still, full of deadly poison. [9] We use it to bless the Lord and Father, but we also use it to curse people who are made in God's image: [10] the blessing and curse come out of the same mouth. My brothers, this must be wrong— [11] does any water supply give a flow of fresh water and salt water out of the same pipe? [12] Can a fig tree yield olives, my brothers, or a vine yield figs? No more can sea water yield fresh water.

Real wisdom and its opposite

[13] Anyone who is wise or understanding among you should from a good life give evidence of deeds done in the gentleness of wisdom. [14] But if at heart you have the bitterness of jealousy, or selfish ambition, do not be boastful or hide the truth with lies; [15] this is not the wisdom that comes from above, but earthly, human and devilish. [16] Wherever there are jealousy and ambition, there are also disharmony and wickedness of every kind; [17] whereas the wisdom that comes down from above is essentially something pure; it is also peaceable, kindly and

2b Ex 20:3, 14.
2c Gn 22:9.
2d Gn 15:6.
2e Jos 2:1seq.

considerate; it is full of mercy and shows itself by doing good; nor is there any trace of partiality or hypocrisy in it. [18]The peace sown by peacemakers brings a harvest of justice.

Disunity among Christians

4 Where do these wars and battles between yourselves first start? Is it not precisely in the desires fighting inside your own selves? [2]You want something and you lack it; so you kill. You have an ambition that you cannot satisfy; so you fight to get your way by force. It is because you do not pray that you do not receive; [3]when you do pray and do not receive, it is because you prayed wrongly, wanting to indulge your passions.

[4]Adulterers! Do you not realise that love for the world is hatred for God? Anyone who chooses the world for a friend is constituted an enemy of God. [5]Can you not see the point of the saying in scripture, 'The longing of the spirit he sent to dwell in us is a jealous longing.'? [6]But he has given us an even greater grace, as scripture says:[a] *God opposes the proud but he accords his favour to the humble.* [7]Give in to God, then; resist the devil, and he will run away from you. [8]The nearer you go to God, the nearer God will come to you. Clean your hands, you sinners, and clear your minds, you waverers. [9]Appreciate your wretchedness, and weep for it in misery. Your laughter must be turned to grief, your happiness to gloom. [10]Humble yourselves before the Lord and he will lift you up.

[11]Brothers, do not slander one another. Anyone who slanders a brother, or condemns one, is speaking against the Law and condemning the Law. But if you condemn the Law, you have ceased to be subject to it and become a judge over it. [12]There is only one lawgiver and he is the only judge and has the power to save or to destroy. Who are you to give a verdict on your neighbour?

A warning for the rich and self-confident

[13]Well now, you who say, 'Today or tomorrow, we are off to this or that town; we are going to spend a year there, trading, and make some money.' [14]You never know what will happen tomorrow: you are no more than

a mist that appears for a little while and then disappears. [15]Instead of this, you should say, 'If it is the Lord's will, we shall still be alive to do this or that.' [16]But as it is, how boastful and loud-mouthed you are! Boasting of this kind is always wrong. [17]Everyone who knows what is the right thing to do and does not do it commits a sin.

5 Well now, you rich! Lament, weep for the miseries that are coming to you. [2]Your wealth is rotting, your clothes are all moth-eaten. [3]All your gold and your silver are corroding away, and the same corrosion will be a witness against you and eat into your body. It is like a fire which you have stored up for the final days. [4]Can you hear crying out against you the wages which you kept back from the labourers mowing your fields? The cries of the reapers have reached the ears of the Lord Sabaoth. [5]On earth you have had a life of comfort and luxury; in the time of slaughter you went on eating to your heart's content. [6]It was you who condemned the upright and killed them; they offered you no resistance.

The coming of the Lord

[7]Now be patient, brothers, until the Lord's coming. Think of a farmer: how patiently he waits for the precious fruit of the ground until it has had the autumn rains and the spring rains! [8]You too must be patient; do not lose heart, because the Lord's coming will be soon. [9]Do not make complaints against one another, brothers, so as not to be brought to judgement yourselves; the Judge is already to be seen waiting at the gates. [10]For your example, brothers, in patiently putting up with persecution, take the prophets who spoke in the Lord's name; [11]remember it is those who had perseverance that we say are the blessed ones. You have heard of the perseverance of Job and understood the Lord's purpose, realising that *the Lord is kind and compassionate.*[a]

[12]Above all, my brothers, do not swear by heaven or by the earth or use any oaths at all. If you mean 'yes', you must say 'yes'; if you mean 'no', say 'no'. Otherwise you make yourselves liable to judgement.

[13]Any one of you who is in trouble should pray; anyone in good spirits should sing a

---

4a Pr 3:34. The saying in v. 5 is not in the OT.
5a Ps 103:8.

psalm. [14]Any one of you who is ill should send for the elders of the church, and they must anoint the sick person with oil in the name of the Lord and pray over him. [15]The prayer of faith will save the sick person and the Lord will raise him up again; and if he has committed any sins, he will be forgiven. [16]So confess your sins to one another, and pray for one another to be cured; the heartfelt prayer of someone upright works very powerfully. [17]Elijah was a human being as frail as ourselves— he prayed earnestly for it not to rain, and no rain fell for three and a half years; [18]then he prayed again and the sky gave rain and the earth gave crops.

[19]My brothers, if one of you strays away from the truth, and another brings him back to it, [20]he may be sure that anyone who can bring back a sinner from his erring ways will be saving his soul from death and *covering over many a sin.*[b]

THE FIRST LETTER OF
PETER

First Peter is written to Christians of Asia Minor to encourage them in time of trial or persecution. The Christian must prove true worth by sharing in Christ's sufferings. The letter is full of practical advice, and the constant return to the idea of the new life of baptism suggests that the letter was written for the newly baptised.

The letter has always been accepted by tradition as Peter's own. If the standard of Gk is too high for a Galilean fisherman, this may be due to the secretary Silvanus.

1 PETER
THE FIRST LETTER OF PETER

Address. Greetings

[1] Peter, apostle of Jesus Christ, to all those living as aliens in the Dispersion[a] of Pontus, Galatia, Cappadocia, Asia and Bithynia, who have been chosen, [2]in the foresight of God the Father, to be made holy by the Spirit, obedient to Jesus Christ and sprinkled with his blood: Grace and peace be yours in abundance.

Introduction
The inheritance of Christians

[3]Blessed be God the Father of our Lord Jesus Christ, who in his great mercy has given us a new birth into a living hope through the resurrection of Jesus Christ from the dead [4]and into a heritage that can never be spoilt or soiled and never fade away. It is reserved in heaven for you [5]who are being kept safe

5b Pr 10:12; Tb 12:9.
1a *See* Jm 1*a* note.

by God's power through faith until the salvation which has been prepared is revealed at the final point of time.

Faithfulness to Christ and love of Christ

[6] This is a great joy to you, even though for a short time yet you must bear all sorts of trials; [7] so that the worth of your faith, more valuable than gold, which is perishable even if it has been tested by fire, may be proved — to your praise and honour when Jesus Christ is revealed. [8] You have not seen him, yet you love him; and still without seeing him you believe in him and so are already filled with a joy so glorious that it cannot be described; [9] and you are sure of the goal of your faith, that is, the salvation of your souls.

The hope of the prophets

[10] This salvation was the subject of the search and investigation of the prophets who spoke of the grace you were to receive, [11] searching out the time and circumstances for which the Spirit of Christ, bearing witness in them, was revealing the sufferings of Christ and the glories to follow them. [12] It was revealed to them that it was for your sake and not their own that they were acting as servants delivering the message which has now been announced to you by those who preached to you the gospel through the Holy Spirit sent from heaven. Even the angels long to catch a glimpse of these things.

The demands of the new life
Holiness of the newly baptised

[13] Your minds, then, must be sober and ready for action; put all your hope in the grace brought to you by the revelation of Jesus Christ. [14] Do not allow yourselves to be shaped by the passions of your old ignorance, [15] but as obedient children, be yourselves holy in all your activity, after the model of the Holy One who calls us, [16] since scripture says, 'Be holy, for I am holy.'[b] [17] And if you address as Father him who judges without favouritism according to each individual's deeds,

live out the time of your exile here in reverent awe. [18] For you know that the price of your ransom from the futile way of life handed down from your ancestors was paid, not in anything perishable like silver or gold,[c] [19] but in precious blood as of a blameless and spotless lamb, Christ. [20] He was marked out before the world was made, and was revealed at the final point of time for your sake. [21] Through him you now have faith in God, who raised him from the dead and gave him glory for this very purpose — that your faith and hope should be in God.

Regeneration by the Word

[22] Since by your obedience to the truth you have purified yourselves so that you can experience the genuine love of brothers, love each other intensely from the heart; [23] for your new birth was not from any perishable seed but from imperishable seed, the living and enduring Word of God. [24] For *all humanity is grass, and all its beauty like the wild flower's. As grass withers, the flower fades,* [25] *but the Word of the Lord remains for ever.*[d] And this Word is the Good News that has been brought to you.

2 Rid yourselves, then, of all spite, deceit, hypocrisy, envy and carping criticism. [2] Like new-born babies all your longing should be for milk — the unadulterated spiritual milk — which will help you to grow up to salvation, [3] at any rate if *you have tasted that the Lord is good*[a].

The new priesthood

[4] He is the living stone, rejected by human beings but chosen by God and precious to him; set yourselves close to him [5] so that you, too, may be living stones making a spiritual house as a holy priesthood to offer the spiritual sacrifices made acceptable to God through Jesus Christ. [6] As scripture says: *Now I am laying a stone in Zion, a chosen, precious cornerstone* and *no one who relies on this will be brought to disgrace.*[b] [7] To you believers it brings honour. But for unbelievers, it is rather a *stone which the builders*

1b Lv 19:2.
1c Is 52:3.
1d Is 40:6–8.
2a Ps 34:8.
2b Is 28:16.

rejected that became a cornerstone,[c] [8]a stumbling stone, a rock to trip people up.[d] They stumble over it because they do not believe in the Word; it was the fate in store for them.

[9]But you are a chosen race, a kingdom of priests, a holy nation, a people to be a personal possession[e] to sing the praises of God who called you out of the darkness into his wonderful light. [10]Once you were a non-people and now you are the People of God; once you were outside his pity; now you have received pity.[f]

The obligations of Christians: towards unbelievers

[11]I urge you, my dear friends, as strangers and nomads,[g] to keep yourselves free from the disordered natural inclinations that attack the soul. [12]Always behave honourably among gentiles so that they can see for themselves what moral lives you lead, and when the day of reckoning comes, give thanks to God for the things which now make them denounce you as criminals.

Towards civil authority

[13]For the sake of the Lord, accept the authority of every human institution: the emperor, as the supreme authority, [14]and the governors as commissioned by him to punish criminals and praise those who do good. [15]It is God's will that by your good deeds you should silence the ignorant talk of fools. [16]You are slaves of no one except God, so behave like free people, and never use your freedom as a cover for wickedness. [17]Have respect for everyone and love for your fellow-believers; fear God and honour the emperor.

Towards masters

[18]Slaves, you should obey your masters respectfully, not only those who are kind and reasonable but also those who are difficult to please. [19]You see, there is merit if, in awareness of God, you put up with the pains of undeserved punishment; [20]but what glory is there in putting up with a beating after you have done something wrong? The merit in the sight of God is in putting up with it patiently when you are punished for doing your duty.

[21]This, in fact, is what you were called to do, because Christ suffered for you and left an example for you to follow in his steps. [22]He had done nothing wrong, and had spoken no deceit.[h] [23]He was insulted and did not retaliate with insults; when he was suffering he made no threats but put his trust in the upright judge. [24]He was bearing our sins in his own body on the cross, so that we might die to our sins and live for uprightness; through his bruises you have been healed. [25]You had gone astray like sheep but now you have returned to the shepherd and guardian of your souls.

In marriage

3 In the same way, you wives should be obedient to your husbands. Then if there are some husbands who do not believe the Word, they may find themselves won over, without a word spoken, by the way their wives behave, [2]when they see the reverence and purity of your way of life. [3]Your adornment should be not an exterior one, consisting of braided hair or gold jewellery or fine clothing, [4]but the interior disposition of the heart, consisting in the imperishable quality of a gentle and peaceful spirit, so precious in the sight of God. [5]That was how the holy women of the past dressed themselves attractively—they hoped in God and were submissive to their husbands; [6]like Sarah, who was obedient to Abraham, and called him her lord.[a] You are now her children, as long as you live good lives free from fear and worry.

[7]In the same way, husbands must always treat their wives with consideration in their life together, respecting a woman as one who, though she may be the weaker partner, is equally an heir to the generous gift of life. This will prevent anything from coming in the way of your prayers.

2c Ps 118:22.
2d Is 8:14.
2e Is 43:20–21.
2f Ho 1:9 and allusions to Ho 2.
2g Ps 39:12.
2h Several quotations from Is 53:5–9.
3a Gn 18:12.

Love the brothers

⁸Finally: you should all agree among yourselves and be sympathetic; love the brothers, have compassion and be self-effacing. ⁹Never repay one wrong with another, or one abusive word with another; instead, repay with a blessing. That is what you are called to do, so that you inherit a blessing. ¹⁰For

> *Who among you delights in life,*
> *longs for time to enjoy prosperity?*
> *Guard your tongue from evil,*
> *your lips from any breath of deceit.*
> ¹¹*Turn away from evil and do good,*
> *seek peace and pursue it.*
> ¹²*For the eyes of the Lord are on the upright,*
> *his ear turned to their cry.*
> *But the Lord's face is set*
> *against those who do evil.*ᵇ

In persecution

¹³No one can hurt you if you are determined to do only what is right; ¹⁴and blessed are you if you have to suffer for being upright. *Have no dread of them; have no fear.*ᶜ ¹⁵Simply *proclaim the Lord* Christ *holy* in your hearts, and always have your answer ready for people who ask you the reason for the hope that you have. ¹⁶But give it with courtesy and respect and with a clear conscience, so that those who slander your good behaviour in Christ may be ashamed of their accusations. ¹⁷And if it is the will of God that you should suffer, it is better to suffer for doing right than for doing wrong.

The resurrection and the descent into hell

¹⁸Christ himself died once and for all for sins, the upright for the sake of the guilty, to lead us to God. In the body he was put to death, in the spirit he was raised to life, ¹⁹and, in the spirit, he went to preach to the spirits in prison. ²⁰They refused to believe long ago, while God patiently waited to receive them, in Noah's time when the ark was being built. In it only a few, that is eight souls, were saved through water. ²¹It is the baptism corresponding to this water which saves you now — not the washing off of physical dirt but the pledge of a good conscience given to God through the resurrection of Jesus Christ,

²²who has entered heaven and is at God's right hand, with angels, ruling forces and powers subject to him.

The break with sin

4 As Christ has undergone bodily suffering, you too should arm yourselves with the same conviction, that anyone who has undergone bodily suffering has broken with sin, ²because for the rest of life on earth that person is ruled not by human passions but only by the will of God. ³You spent quite long enough in the past living the sort of life that gentiles choose to live, behaving in a debauched way, giving way to your passions, drinking to excess, having wild parties and drunken orgies and sacrilegiously worshipping false gods. ⁴So people are taken aback that you no longer hurry off with them to join this flood which is rushing down to ruin, and then abuse you for it. ⁵They will have to answer for it before the judge who is to judge the living and the dead. ⁶And this was why the gospel was brought to the dead as well, so that, though in their bodies they had undergone the judgement that faces all humanity, in their spirit they might enjoy the life of God.

The revelation of Christ is close

⁷The end of all things is near, so keep your minds calm and sober for prayer. ⁸Above all preserve an intense love for each other, since *love covers over many a sin.*ᵃ ⁹Welcome each other into your houses without grumbling. ¹⁰Each one of you has received a special grace, so, like good stewards responsible for all these varied graces of God, put it at the service of others. ¹¹If anyone is a speaker, let it be as the words of God, if anyone serves, let it be as in strength granted by God; so that in everything God may receive the glory, through Jesus Christ, since to him alone belong all glory and power for ever and ever. Amen.

Suffering for Christ

¹²My dear friends, do not be taken aback at the testing by fire which is taking place among you, as though something strange were happening to you; ¹³but in so far as you share

3b Ps 34:12–16.
3c Is 8:12–13.
4a Pr 10:12; Tb 12:9.

in the sufferings of Christ, be glad, so that you may enjoy a much greater gladness when his glory is revealed. [14]If you are insulted for bearing Christ's name, blessed are you, for *on* you *rests the Spirit of God*,[b] the Spirit of glory. [15]None of you should ever deserve to suffer for being a murderer, a thief, a criminal or an informer; [16]but if any one of you should suffer for being a Christian, then there must be no shame but thanksgiving to God for bearing this name. [17]The time has come for the judgement to begin at the household of God; and if it begins with us, what will be the end for those who refuse to believe God's gospel? [18]*If it is hard for the upright to be saved, what will happen to the wicked and to sinners?*[c] [19]So even those whom God allows to suffer should commit themselves to a Creator who is trustworthy, and go on doing good.

Instructions: to the elders

5 I urge the elders among you, as a fellow-elder myself and a witness to the sufferings of Christ, and as one who is to have a share in the glory that is to be revealed: [2]give a shepherd's care to the flock of God that is entrusted to you: watch over it, not simply as a duty but gladly, as God wants; not for sordid money, but because you are eager to do it. [3]Do not lord it over the group which is in your charge, but be an example for the flock. [4]When the chief shepherd appears, you will be given the unfading crown of glory.

To the faithful

[5]In the same way, younger people, be subject to the elders. Humility towards one another must be the garment you all wear constantly, because *God opposes the proud but accords his favour to the humble.*[a] [6]Bow down, then, before the power of God now, so that he may raise you up in due time; [7]*unload all your burden on to him*,[b] since he is concerned about you. [8]Keep sober and alert, because your enemy the devil is on the prowl like a *roaring lion*,[c] looking for someone to devour. [9]Stand up to him, strong in faith and in the knowledge that it is the same kind of suffering that the community of your brothers throughout the world is undergoing. [10]You will have to suffer only for a little while: the God of all grace who called you to eternal glory in Christ will restore you, he will confirm, strengthen and support you. [11]His power lasts for ever and ever. Amen.

Last words. Greetings

[12]I write these few words to you through Silvanus, who is a trustworthy brother, to encourage you and attest that this is the true grace of God. Stand firm in it!
[13]Your sister in Babylon, who is with you among the chosen, sends you greetings; so does my son, Mark.
[14]Greet one another with a kiss of love.
　　Peace to you all who are in Christ.

THE SECOND LETTER OF
PETER

Second Peter encourages its readers to wait for the Day of the Lord Jesus Christ with patience and alert perseverance. It warns against false teachers, and especially ones who value only knowledge at the expense of generosity and self-control. A large section, 2:1—3:3, coincides closely with the Letter of Jude and is probably dependent on it.

4b Is 11:2.
4c Pr 11:31 LXX.
5a Pr 3:34 LXX.
5b Ps 55:22.
5c Ps 22:13.

The letter may well be the latest writing of the NT, and is widely accepted as dating from the 2nd century, well after Peter's death. It is given the authority of Peter by a literary convention.

2 PETER
THE SECOND LETTER OF PETER

Greetings

1 Simon Peter, servant and apostle of Jesus Christ, to those who have received a faith as precious as our own, given through the saving justice of our God and Saviour Jesus Christ. [2]Grace and peace be yours in abundance through the knowledge of our Lord.

The generosity of God

[3]By his divine power, he has lavished on us all the things we need for life and for true devotion, through the knowledge of him who has called us by his own glory and goodness. [4]Through these, the greatest and priceless promises have been lavished on us, that through them you should share the divine nature and escape the corruption rife in the world through disordered passion. [5]With this in view, do your utmost to support your faith with goodness, goodness with understanding, [6]understanding with self-control, self-control with perseverance, perseverance with devotion, [7]devotion with kindness to the brothers, and kindness to the brothers with love. [8]The possession and growth of these qualities will prevent your knowledge of our Lord Jesus Christ from being ineffectual or unproductive. [9]But without them, a person is blind or short-sighted, forgetting how the sins of the past were washed away. [10]Instead of this, brothers, never allow your choice or calling to waver; then there will be no danger of your stumbling, [11]for in this way you will be given the generous gift of entry to the eternal kingdom of our Lord and Saviour Jesus Christ.

The apostolic witness

[12]That is why I will always go on recalling the same truths to you, even though you already know them and are firmly fixed in these truths. [13]I am sure it is my duty, as long as I am in this tent, to keep stirring you up with reminders, [14]since I know the time for me to lay aside this tent is coming soon, as our Lord Jesus Christ made clear to me. [15]And I shall take great care that after my own departure you will still have a means to recall these things to mind.

[16]When we told you about the power and the coming of our Lord Jesus Christ, we were not slavishly repeating cleverly invented myths; no, we had seen his majesty with our own eyes. [17]He was honoured and glorified by God the Father, when a voice came to him from the transcendent Glory, *This is my Son, the Beloved; he enjoys my favour.*[a] [18]We ourselves heard this voice from heaven, when we were with him on the holy mountain.

The value of prophecy

[19]So we have confirmation of the words of the prophets; and you will be right to pay attention to it as to a lamp for lighting a way through the dark, until the dawn comes and the morning star rises in your minds. [20]At the same time, we must recognise that the interpretation of scriptural prophecy is never a matter for the individual. [21]For no prophecy ever came from human initiative. When people spoke for God it was the Holy Spirit that moved them.

1a Mt 17:5par.

False teachers

2 As there were false prophets in the past history of our people, so you too will have your false teachers, who will insinuate their own disruptive views and, by disowning the Lord who bought them freedom, will bring upon themselves speedy destruction. [2]Many will copy their debauched behaviour, and the Way of Truth will be brought into disrepute on their account. [3]In their greed they will try to make a profit out of you with untrue tales. But the judgement made upon them long ago is not idle, and the destruction awaiting them is for ever on the watch.

Lessons of the past

[4]When angels sinned, God did not spare them: he sent them down into the underworld and consigned them to the dark abyss to be held there until the Judgement. [5]He did not spare the world in ancient times: he saved only Noah, the preacher of uprightness, along with seven others, when he sent the Flood over a world of sinners. [6]He condemned the cities of Sodom and Gomorrah by reducing them to ashes as a warning to future sinners; [7]but rescued Lot, an upright man who had been sickened by the debauched way in which these vile people behaved—[8]for that upright man, living among them, was outraged in his upright soul by the crimes that he saw and heard every day. [9]All this shows that the Lord is well able to rescue the good from their trials, and hold the wicked for their punishment until the Day of Judgement, [10]especially those who follow the desires of their corrupt human nature and have no respect for the Lord's authority.

The punishment to come

Such self-willed people with no reverence are not afraid of offending against the glorious ones, [11]but the angels in their greater strength and power make no complaint or accusation against them in the Lord's presence. [12]But these people speak evil of what they do not understand; they are like brute beasts, born only to be caught and killed, and like beasts they will be destroyed, being injured in return for the injuries they have inflicted.

[13]Debauchery even by day they make their pleasure; they are unsightly blots, and amuse themselves by their trickery even when they are sharing your table; [14]with their eyes always looking for adultery, people with an insatiable capacity for sinning, they will seduce any but the most stable soul. Where greed is concerned they are at their peak of fitness. They are under a curse. [15]They have left the right path and wandered off to follow the path of Balaam son of Bosor, who set his heart on a dishonest reward, but soon had his fault pointed out to him: [16]a dumb beast of burden, speaking with a human voice, put a stop to the madness of the prophet.

[17]People like this are dried-up springs, fogs swirling in the wind, and the gloom of darkness is stored up for them. [18]With their high-sounding but empty talk they tempt back people who have scarcely escaped from those who live in error, by playing on the disordered desires of their human nature and by debaucheries. [19]They may promise freedom but are themselves slaves to corruption; because if anyone lets himself be dominated by anything, then he is a slave to it; [20]and anyone who has escaped the pollution of the world by coming to know our Lord and Saviour Jesus Christ, and who then allows himself to be entangled and mastered by it a second time, ends up by being worse than he was before. [21]It would have been better for them never to have learnt the way of uprightness, than to learn it and then desert the holy commandment that was entrusted to them. [22]What they have done is exactly as the proverb rightly says: *The dog goes back to its vomit*[a] and: As soon as the sow has been washed, it wallows in the mud.

The Day of the Lord;
the prophets and the apostles

3 My dear friends, this is the second letter I have written to you, trying to awaken in you by my reminders an unclouded understanding. [2]Remember what was said in the past by the holy prophets and the command of the Lord and Saviour given by your apostles.

False teachers

[3]First of all, do not forget that in the final days there will come sarcastic scoffers whose

---

2a Pr 26:11.

life is ruled by their passions. ⁴'What has happened to the promise of his coming?' they will say, 'Since our Fathers died everything has gone on just as it has since the beginning of creation!' ⁵They deliberately ignore the fact that long ago there were the heavens and the earth, formed out of water and through water by the Word of God, ⁶and that it was through these same factors that the world of those days was destroyed by the floodwaters. ⁷It is the same Word which is reserving the present heavens and earth for fire, keeping them till the Day of Judgement and of the destruction of sinners.

⁸But there is one thing, my dear friends, that you must never forget: that with the Lord, a day is like a thousand years, and *a thousand years are like a day.*ᵃ ⁹The Lord is not being slow in carrying out his promises, as some people think he is; rather is he being patient with you, wanting nobody to be lost and everybody to be brought to repentance. ¹⁰The Day of the Lord will come like a thief, and then with a roar the sky will vanish, the elements will catch fire and melt away, the earth and all that it contains will be burned up.

Fresh call to holiness. Doxology

¹¹Since everything is coming to an end like this, what holy and saintly lives you should be living ¹²while you wait for the Day of God to come, and try to hasten its coming: on that Day the sky will dissolve in flames and the elements melt in the heat. ¹³What we are waiting for, relying on his promises, is the new heavens and new earth, where uprightness will be at home. ¹⁴So then, my dear friends, while you are waiting, do your best to live blameless and unsullied lives so that he will find you at peace. ¹⁵Think of our Lord's patience as your opportunity to be saved; our brother Paul, who is so dear to us, told you this when he wrote to you with the wisdom that he was given. ¹⁶He makes this point too in his letters as a whole wherever he touches on these things. In all his letters there are of course some passages which are hard to understand, and these are the ones that uneducated and unbalanced people distort, in the same way as they distort the rest of scriptureᵇ—to their own destruction. ¹⁷Since you have been forewarned about this, my dear friends, be careful that you do not come to the point of losing the firm ground that you are standing on, carried away by the errors of unprincipled people. ¹⁸Instead, continue to grow in the grace and in the knowledge of our Lord and Saviour Jesus Christ. To him be glory, in time and eternity. Amen.

THE LETTERS OF
JOHN

First John dwells on many of the themes of John's Gospel. It reflects on the position of Christ: he is the revelation of the Father, the source of light, love and truth. The Christian's life must be centred on the twin commandments of faith in Jesus Christ as Son of God, and of love of the brethren. So the Christian will share with Christ the life which he himself shares with the Father.

The letter is addressed to communities threatened by false teaching, and warns Christians to be on guard against an Antichrist who is to be part of the final crisis of the world. It seems to envisage a definite group, who once formed part of the community but who

---

3a Ps 90:4.
3b Paul's letters seemingly already exist as a collection, and are put on the same level as the OT.

have embraced false teaching on Christ.

The other two letters are mere notes, 2 Jn warning against those who deny the reality of the incarnation, and 3 Jn dealing with an unruly church leader who is causing dissension.

PLAN OF THE LETTER

1 JOHN
THE FIRST LETTER OF JOHN

INTRODUCTION

**The Incarnate Word
and sharing with the Father and the Son**

1 Something which has existed
   since the beginning,
which we have heard,
which we have seen with our own eyes,
which we have watched
and touched with our own hands,
the Word of life—
this is our theme.

² That life was made visible;
we saw it and are giving our testimony,
declaring to you the eternal life,
which was present to the Father
and has been revealed to us.
³ We are declaring to you
what we have seen and heard,
so that you too may share our life.
Our life is shared with the Father
and with his Son Jesus Christ.
⁴ We are writing this to you
so that our joy may be complete.

I: TO WALK IN THE LIGHT

⁵ This is what we have heard from him
and are declaring to you:
God is light,
   and there is no darkness in him at all.
⁶ If we say that we share in God's life
while we are living in darkness,
we are lying,
   because we are not living the truth.
⁷ But if we live in light,
as he is in light,
we have a share in one another's life,
and the blood of Jesus, his Son,
cleanses us from all sin.

First condition: to break with sin

⁸ If we say, 'We have no sin,'
we are deceiving ourselves,
and truth has no place in us;
⁹ if we acknowledge our sins,
he is trustworthy and upright,
so that he will forgive our sins
and will cleanse us from all evil.
¹⁰ If we say, 'We have never sinned,'
we make him a liar,
and his word has no place in us.

2 My children, I am writing this
to prevent you from sinning;
but if anyone does sin,
we have an advocate with the Father,
Jesus Christ, the upright.
²He is the sacrifice to expiate our sins,
and not only ours,
but also those of the whole world.

Second condition:
to keep the commandments,
especially that of love

³In this way we know
that we have come to know him,
if we keep his commandments.
⁴Whoever says, 'I know him'
without keeping his commandments,
is a liar,
and truth has no place in him.
⁵But anyone who does keep his word,
in such a one
God's love truly reaches its perfection.
This is the proof
that we are in God.
⁶Whoever claims
to remain in him
must act as he acted.
⁷My dear friends,
this is not a new commandment
I am writing for you,
but an old commandment
that you have had from the beginning;
the old commandment
is the message you have heard.
⁸Yet in another way, I am writing
a new commandment for you
—and this is true for you,
just as much as for him—
for darkness is passing away
and the true light is already shining.
⁹Whoever claims to be in light
but hates his brother
is still in darkness.
¹⁰Anyone who loves his brother
remains in light
and there is in him
nothing to make him fall away.
¹¹But whoever hates his brother
is in darkness
and is walking about in darkness
not knowing where he is going,
because darkness has blinded him.

Third condition:
detachment from the world

¹²I am writing to you, children,
because your sins have been forgiven
through his name.
¹³I am writing to you, fathers,
because you have come to know
the One who has existed
since the beginning.
I am writing to you, young people,
because you have overcome the Evil One.
¹⁴I have written to you, children,
because you have come to know
the Father.
I have written to you, parents,
because you have come to know
the One who has existed
since the beginning.
I have written to you, young people,
because you are strong,
and God's word remains in you,
and you have overcome the Evil One.
¹⁵Do not love the world
or what is in the world.
If anyone does love the world,
the love of the Father
finds no place in him,
¹⁶because everything there is
in the world—
disordered bodily desires,
disordered desires of the eyes,
pride in possession—
is not from the Father
but is from the world.
¹⁷And the world,
with all its disordered desires,
is passing away.
But whoever does the will of God
remains for ever.

Fourth condition:
to be on guard against Antichrists

¹⁸Children, this is the final hour;
you have heard
that the Antichrist*a* is coming,
and now many Antichrists
have already come;
from this we know
that it is the final hour.
¹⁹They have gone from among us,
but they never really belonged to us;

2a cf. 2 Th 2:3–4.

if they had belonged to us,
   they would have stayed with us.
But this was to prove
that not one of them belonged to us.
[20]But you have been anointed
   by the Holy One,
and have all received knowledge.
[21]I have written to you
   not because you are ignorant of the truth,
but because you are well aware of it,
and because no lie
   can come from the truth.
[22]Who is the liar,
   if not one who claims
      that Jesus is not the Christ?
This is the Antichrist,
who denies both the Father and the Son.
[23]Whoever denies the Son
   cannot have the Father either;
whoever acknowledges the Son
   has the Father too.
[24]Let what you heard in the beginning
   remain in you;

as long as
   what you heard in the beginning
      remains in you,
you will remain in the Son
and in the Father.
[25]And the promise he made you himself
is eternal life.
[26]So much have I written to you
   about those
      who are trying to lead you astray.
[27]But as for you,
   the anointing you received from him
remains in you,
and you do not need anyone to teach you;
since the anointing he gave you
   teaches you everything,
and since it is true, not false,
remain in him just as he has taught you.
[28]Therefore remain in him now, children,
so that when he appears
   we may be fearless,
and not shrink from him in shame
at his coming.

II: TO LIVE AS GOD'S CHILDREN

[29]If you know that he is upright
   you must recognise that everyone
      whose life is upright
   is a child of his.

3 You must see what great love
   the Father has lavished on us
by letting us be called God's children —
which is what we are!
The reason why the world
   does not acknowledge us
is that it did not acknowledge him.
[2]My dear friends,
   we are already God's children,
but what we shall be in the future
   has not yet been revealed.
We are well aware that when he appears
we shall be like him,
because we shall see him as he really is.

First condition: to break with sin

[3]Whoever treasures this hope of him
   purifies himself, to be as pure as he is.
[4]Whoever sins, acts wickedly,
   because all sin is wickedness.

[5]Now you are well aware
   that he has appeared
      in order to take sins away,
and that in him there is no sin.
[6]No one who remains in him sins,
   and whoever sins
has neither seen him nor recognised him.
[7]Children, do not let anyone
   lead you astray.
Whoever acts uprightly is upright,
just as he is upright.
[8]Whoever lives sinfully
   belongs to the devil,
since the devil has been a sinner
   from the beginning.
This was the purpose
   of the appearing of the Son of God,
to undo the work of the devil.
[9]No one who is a child of God sins
because God's seed remains in him.
Nor can he sin,
   because he is a child of God.
[10]This is what distinguishes
   the children of God
      from the children of the devil:
whoever does not live uprightly

and does not love his brother
is not from God.

Second condition:
to keep the commandments,
especially that of love

¹¹This is the message
which you heard from the beginning,
that we must love one another,
¹²not to be like Cain,
who was from the Evil One
and murdered his brother.
And why did he murder his brother?
Because his own actions were evil
and his brother's upright.
¹³Do not be surprised, brothers,
if the world hates you.
¹⁴We are well aware
that we have passed over
from death to life
because we love our brothers.
Whoever does not love, remains in death.
¹⁵Anyone who hates his brother
is a murderer,
and you are well aware that no murderer
has eternal life remaining in him.
¹⁶This is the proof of love,
that he laid down his life for us,
and we too ought to lay down our lives
for our brothers.
¹⁷If anyone is well-off
in worldly possessions
and sees his brother in need
but closes his heart to him,
how can the love of God
be remaining in him?
¹⁸Children,
our love must be not just words
or mere talk,
but something active and genuine.
¹⁹This will be the proof
that we belong to the truth,
and it will convince us in his presence,
²⁰even if our own feelings condemn us,
that God is greater than our feelings
and knows all things.
²¹My dear friends,
if our own feelings do not condemn us,
we can be fearless before God,

²²and whatever we ask
we shall receive from him,
because we keep his commandments
and do what is acceptable to him.
²³His commandment is this,
that we should believe
in the name of his Son Jesus Christ
and that we should love one another
as he commanded us.
²⁴Whoever keeps his commandments
remains in God, and God in him.
And this is the proof
that he remains in us:
the Spirit that he has given us.

Third condition:
to be on guard against Antichrists
and against the world

4 My dear friends,
not every spirit is to be trusted,
but test the spirits
to see whether they are from God,
for many false prophets
are at large in the world.
²This is the proof of the spirit of God:
any spirit
which acknowledges Jesus Christ,
come in human nature,
is from God,
³and no spirit
which fails to acknowledge Jesus
is from God;
it is the spirit of Antichrist,
whose coming you have heard of;
he is already at large in the world.
⁴Children, you are from God
and have overcome them,
because he who is in you
is greater than he who is in the world.
⁵They are from the world,
and therefore the world
inspires what they say,
and listens to them.
⁶We are from God;
whoever recognises God listens to us;
anyone who is not from God
refuses to listen to us.
This is how we can distinguish
the spirit of truth
from the spirit of falsehood.

III: THE SOURCE OF LOVE AND FAITH

The source of love

[7] My dear friends,
let us love one another,
since love is from God
and everyone who loves
is a child of God and knows God.
[8] Whoever fails to love does not know God,
because God is love.
[9] This is the revelation
of God's love for us,
that God sent his only Son into the world
that we might have life through him.
[10] Love consists in this:
it is not we who loved God,
but God loved us and sent his Son
to expiate our sins.
[11] My dear friends,
if God loved us so much,
we too should love one another.
[12] No one has ever seen God,
but as long as we love one another
God remains in us
and his love comes to its perfection in us.
[13] This is the proof that we remain in him
and he in us,
that he has given us a share in his Spirit.
[14] We ourselves have seen and testify
that the Father sent his Son
as Saviour of the world.
[15] Anyone who acknowledges
that Jesus is the Son of God,
God remains in him and he in God.
[16] We have recognised for ourselves,
and put our faith in,
the love God has for us.
God is love,
and whoever remains in love
remains in God
and God in him.
[17] Love comes to its perfection in us
when we can face
the Day of Judgement fearlessly,
because even in this world
we have become as he is.
[18] In love there is no room for fear,
but perfect love drives out fear,
because fear implies punishment
and no one who is afraid
has come to perfection in love.

[19] Let us love, then,
because he first loved us.
[20] Anyone who says 'I love God'
and hates his brother,
is a liar,
since no one who fails to love the
brother whom he can see
can love God whom he has not seen.
[21] Indeed this is the commandment
we have received from him,
that whoever loves God,
must also love his brother.

5 Whoever believes that Jesus is the Christ
is a child of God,
and whoever loves the father
loves the son.
[2] In this way we know
that we love God's children,
when we love God
and keep his commandments.
[3] This is what the love of God is:
keeping his commandments.
Nor are his commandments
burdensome,
[4] because every child of God
overcomes the world.
And this is the victory
that has overcome the world —
our faith.

The source of faith

[5] Who can overcome the world
but the one who believes
that Jesus is the Son of God?
[6] He it is who came by water and blood,[a]
Jesus Christ,
not with water alone
but with water and blood,
and it is the Spirit that bears witness,
for the Spirit is Truth.
[7] So there are three witnesses,
[8] the Spirit, water and blood;
and the three of them coincide.
[9] If we accept
the testimony of human witnesses,
God's testimony is greater,
for this is God's testimony
which he gave about his Son.
[10] Whoever believes in the Son of God
has this testimony within him,

5a cf. Jn 19:34.

and whoever does not believe
is making God a liar,
because he has not believed
the testimony
God has given about his Son.
¹¹This is the testimony:
God has given us eternal life,
and this life is in his Son.

¹²Whoever has the Son has life,
and whoever has not the Son of God
has not life.
¹³I have written this to you
who believe
in the name of the Son of God
so that you may know
that you have eternal life.

SUPPLEMENTS

Prayer for sinners

¹⁴Our fearlessness towards him
consists in this,
that if we ask anything
in accordance with his will
he hears us.
¹⁵And if we know
that he listens to whatever we ask him,
we know that we already possess
whatever we have asked of him.
¹⁶If anyone sees his brother commit a sin
that is not a deadly sin,
he has only to pray,
and God will give life to this brother
—provided that it is not a deadly sin.
There is sin that leads to death
and I am not saying
you must pray about that.
¹⁷Every kind of wickedness is sin,
but not all sin leads to death.

Summary of the letter

¹⁸We are well aware
that no one who is a child of God sins,
because he who was born from God
protects him,
and the Evil One has no hold over him.
¹⁹We are well aware that we are from God,
and the whole world
is in the power of the Evil One.
²⁰We are well aware also
that the Son of God has come,
and has given us understanding
so that we may know
the One who is true.
We are in the One who is true
as we are in his Son, Jesus Christ.
He is the true God
and this is eternal life.
Children, be on your guard
against false gods.

2 JOHN

THE SECOND LETTER OF JOHN

From the Elder:^a my greetings to the Lady,
the chosen one,^b and to her children, whom
I love in truth—and I am not the only one,
for so do all who have come to know the
Truth—²because of the truth that remains
in us and will be with us for ever. ³In our
life of truth and love, we shall have grace,
faithful love and peace from God the Father
and from Jesus Christ, the Son of the
Father.

---

a The elders were the leaders in each community; '*the* Elder' must indicate a special leadership.
b i.e. one of the local churches.

The law of love

[4]It has given me great joy to find that children of yours have been living the life of truth as we were commanded by the Father. [5]And now I am asking you—dear lady, not as though I were writing you a new commandment, but only the one which we have had from the beginning—that we should love one another.

[6]To love is to live according to his commandments: this is the commandment which you have heard since the beginning, to live a life of love.

The enemies of Christ

[7]There are many deceivers at large in the world, refusing to acknowledge Jesus Christ as coming in human nature. They are the Deceiver; they are the Antichrist. [8]Watch yourselves, or all our work will be lost and you will forfeit your full reward. [9]If anybody does not remain in the teaching of Christ but goes beyond it, he does not have God with him: only those who remain in what he taught can have the Father and the Son with them. [10]If anyone comes to you bringing a different doctrine, you must not receive him into your house or even give him a greeting. [11]Whoever greets him has a share in his wicked activities.

[12]There are several things I have to tell you, but I have thought it best not to trust them to paper and ink. I hope instead to visit you and talk to you in person, so that our joy may be complete.

[13]Greetings to you from the children of your sister,[c] the chosen one.

3 JOHN

THE THIRD LETTER OF JOHN

From the Elder: greetings to my dear friend Gaius, whom I love in truth. [2]My dear friend, I hope everything is going happily with you and that you are as well physically as you are spiritually. [3]It was a great joy to me when some brothers came and told of your faithfulness to the truth, and of your life in the truth. [4]It is always my greatest joy to hear that my children are living according to the truth.

[5]My dear friend, you have done loyal work in helping these brothers, even though they were strangers to you. [6]They are a proof to the whole Church of your love and it would be a kindness if you could help them on their journey as God would approve. [7]It was entirely for the sake of the name that they set out, without depending on the non-believers for anything: [8]it is our duty to welcome people of this sort and contribute our share to their work for the truth.

Beware of the example of Diotrephes

[9]I have written a note for the members of the church, but Diotrephes, who enjoys being in charge of it, refuses to accept us. [10]So if I come, I shall tell everyone how he has behaved, and about the wicked accusations he has been circulating against us. As if that were not enough, he not only refuses to welcome our brothers, but prevents from doing so other people who would have liked to, and expels them from the church. [11]My dear friend, never follow a bad example, but keep following the good one; whoever does what is right is from God, but no one who does what is wrong has ever seen God.

Commendation of Demetrius

[12]Demetrius has been approved by everyone, and indeed by Truth itself. We too will vouch for him and you know that our testimony is true.

c A neighbouring church.

Epilogue

¹³There were several things I had to tell you but I would rather not trust them to pen and ink. ¹⁴However, I hope to see you soon and talk to you in person. ¹⁵Peace be with you; greetings from your friends; greet each of our friends by name.

THE LETTER OF JUDE

A short letter warning against certain false teachers and their evil way of life, it also encourages its readers to entrust themselves to Christ's mercy and protection. The author claims to be Jude, brother of the Lord; he stands firmly within the Jewish tradition, using both OT and other Jewish writings to express and illustrate his message, but it is equally a fully Christian work. The Second Letter of Peter draws freely upon the letter, which probably stems from the end of the 1st century.

THE LETTER OF JUDE

Address

From Jude, servant of Jesus Christ and brother of James; to those who are called, to those who are dear to God the Father and kept safe for Jesus Christ, ²mercy, peace and love be yours in abundance.

The reason for this letter

³My dear friends, at a time when I was eagerly looking forward to writing to you about the salvation that we all share, I felt that I must write to you encouraging you to fight hard for the faith which has been once and for all entrusted to God's holy people. ⁴Certain people have infiltrated among you, who were long ago marked down for condemnation on this account; without any reverence they pervert the grace of our God to debauchery and deny all religion, rejecting our only Master and Lord, Jesus Christ.

**The false teachers:
the certainty of punishment**

⁵I should like to remind you—though you have already learnt it once and for all— that the Lord rescued the nation from Egypt, but afterwards he still destroyed the people who refused to believe him; ⁶and the angels who did not keep to the authority they had, but left their appointed sphere,ᵃ he has kept in darkness in eternal bonds until the judgement of the great Day. ⁷Sodom and Gomorrah, too, and the neighbouring towns, who with the same sexual immorality pursued unnatural lusts,ᵇ are put before us

---

a Gn 6:1–2, elaborated in *The Book of Enoch*.
b Gn 19:1–11, elaborated in *The Testament of the Twelve Patriarchs*.

as an example since they are paying the penalty of eternal fire.

Their violent language

[8]Nevertheless, these people are doing the same: in their delusions they not only defile their bodies and disregard Authority, but abuse the Glories as well. [9]Not even the archangel Michael, when he was engaged in argument with the devil about the corpse of Moses,[c] dared to denounce him in the language of abuse; all he said was, *'May the Lord rebuke you.'*[d] [10]But these people abuse anything they do not understand; and the only things they do understand—merely by nature like unreasoning animals—will turn out to be fatal to them.

Their vicious behaviour

[11]Alas for them, because they have followed Cain;[e] they have thrown themselves into the same delusion as Balaam[f] for a reward; they have been ruined by the same rebellion as Korah[g]—and share the same fate. [12]They are a dangerous hazard at your community meals, coming for the food and quite shamelessly only looking after themselves. They are like the clouds blown about by the winds and bringing no rain, or like autumn trees, barren and uprooted and so twice dead; [13]like wild sea waves with their own shame for foam; or like wandering stars for whom the gloom of darkness is stored up for ever. [14]It was with them in mind that Enoch, the seventh patriarch from Adam, made his prophecy when he said, 'I tell you, the Lord will come with his holy ones in their tens of thousands, [15]to pronounce judgement on all humanity and to sentence the godless for all the godless things they have done, and for all the defiant things said against him by godless sinners.'[h] [16]They are mischief-makers, grumblers governed only by their own desires, with *mouths full of boastful talk,*[i] ready to flatter others for gain.

A warning

[17]But remember, my dear friends, what the apostles of our Lord Jesus Christ foretold. [18]'At the final point of time', they told you, 'there will be mockers who follow nothing but their own godless desires.' [19]It is they who cause division, who live according to nature and do not possess the Spirit.

The duties of love

[20]But you, my dear friends, must build yourselves up on the foundation of your most holy faith, praying in the Holy Spirit; [21]keep yourselves within the love of God and wait for the mercy of our Lord Jesus Christ to give you eternal life. [22]To some you must be compassionate because they are wavering; [23]others you must save by snatching them from the fire; to others again you must be compassionate but wary, hating even the tunic stained by their bodies.

Doxology

[24]To him who can keep you from falling and bring you safe to his glorious presence, innocent and joyful, [25]to the only God, our Saviour, through Jesus Christ our Lord, be glory, majesty, authority and power, before all ages, now and for ever. Amen.

---

c *See* the apocryphal *Assumption of Moses.*
d Zc 3:2.
e Gn 4:8.
f Nb 22:2.
g Nb 16.
h *Enoch* 1:9.
i Lv 19:15.

THE REVELATION TO JOHN

The Bible is summed up in the message of hope and the rich symbolism of this book. It is a vision of rescue from the trials which beset God's people, and a promise of a glorious future. The message is expressed by means of imagery which draws on the whole of the Bible, so that every feature, animals, colours, numbers, is evocative and full of overtones to a reader familiar with the OT. In this way it is a secret and allusive revelation of what is to come, though the natural symbolism of the great acts of worship and the final vision of the messianic splendour of the new Holy City are clear enough. There was a tradition of such writing in Judaism from Dn onwards, to strengthen God's people in persecution with assurance of eventual deliverance and triumph.

Written to encourage Christians in a time of persecution by the Roman empire, perhaps under Nero, c. AD 68, or more probably under Domitian, c. AD 55, it has wider reference than any particular persecution and provides a promise of eventual deliverance for Christians under any circumstances of trial and oppression.

Much of the imagery is strikingly similar to that of John's Gospel, though some of the theological ideas (e.g. on the Second Coming) are very different. The book probably issues from the Johannine tradition rather than from the same pen. Furthermore, the frequent repetitions suggest that two apocalypses by the same author may have been combined. The initial letters to the seven churches form a preface to the visions.

PLAN OF THE BOOK

THE REVELATION TO JOHN

Prologue

1 A revelation of Jesus Christ, which God gave him so that he could tell his servants *what is* now *to take place*[a] very soon; he sent his angel to make it known to his servant John, [2]and John has borne witness to the Word of God and to the witness of Jesus Christ, everything that he saw. [3]Blessed is anyone who reads the words of this prophecy, and blessed those who hear them, if they treasure the content, because the Time is near.

1a Dn 2:28.

I: THE LETTERS TO THE CHURCHES OF ASIA

Address and greeting[b]

[4]John, to the seven churches of Asia: grace and peace to you from him who is, who was, and who is to come, from the seven spirits who are before his throne, [5]and from Jesus Christ, *the faithful witness, the First-born* from the dead, *the highest of earthly kings.* He loves us and has washed away our sins with his blood, [6]and made us a *Kingdom of Priests* to serve his God and Father; to him, then, be glory and power for ever and ever. Amen. [7]*Look, he is coming on the clouds*; everyone will see him, even *those who pierced him,* and *all the races of the earth will mourn over him.* Indeed this shall be so. Amen. [8]'I am the Alpha and the Omega,' says the Lord God, who is, who was, and who is to come, the Almighty.

Preliminary vision

[9]I, John, your brother and partner in hardships, in the kingdom and in perseverance in Jesus, was on the island of Patmos on account of the Word of God and of witness to Jesus; [10]it was the Lord's Day and I was in ecstasy, and I heard a loud voice behind me, like the sound of a trumpet, saying, [11]'Write down in a book all that you see, and send it to the seven churches of Ephesus, Smyrna, Pergamum, Thyatira, Sardis, Philadelphia and Laodicea.' [12]I turned round to see who was speaking to me, and when I turned I saw seven golden lamp-stands [13]and, in the middle of them, one *like a Son of man,*[c] dressed in a long robe tied at the waist with a *belt of gold.* [14]*His head and his hair were white with the whiteness of wool, like snow, his eyes* like a *burning* flame, [15]*his feet like burnished bronze* when it has been refined in a furnace, and *his voice like the sound of the ocean.* [16]In his right hand he was holding seven stars, out of his mouth came a sharp sword, double-edged, and his face was like the sun shining with all its force.

[17]When I saw him, I fell at his feet as though dead, but he laid his right hand on me and said, 'Do not be afraid; it is I, *the First* and *the Last*; I am the Living One, [18]I was dead and look—I am alive for ever and ever, and I hold the keys of death and of Hades. [19]Now write down all that you see of present happenings and *what is still to come.*[d] [20]The secret of the seven stars you have seen in my right hand, and of the seven golden lamp-stands, is this: the seven stars are the angels of the seven churches, and the seven lamp-stands are the seven churches themselves.'

1 Ephesus

2 'Write to the angel of the church in Ephesus and say, "Here is the message of the one who holds the seven stars in his right hand and who lives among the seven golden lamp-stands: [2]I know your activities, your hard work and your perseverance. I know you cannot stand wicked people, and how you put to the test those who were self-styled apostles, and found them false. [3]I know too that you have perseverance, and have suffered for my name without growing tired. [4]Nevertheless, I have this complaint to make: you have less love now than formerly. [5]Think where you were before you fell; repent, and behave as you did at first, or else, if you will not repent, I shall come to you and take your lamp-stand from its place. [6]It is in your favour, nevertheless, that you loathe as I do the way the Nicolaitans are behaving. [7]Let anyone who can hear, listen to what the Spirit is saying to the churches: those who prove victorious I will feed *from the tree of life* set *in* God's *paradise.*"[a]

2 Smyrna

[8]'Write to the angel of the church in Smyrna and say, "Here is the message of *the First* and *the Last,* who was dead and has come to life again: [9]I know your hardships and your poverty, and—though you are rich—the slander of the people who falsely claim to be Jews but are really members of the synagogue

1b The quotations point to the glorious Messiah: Ps 89:37, 27; Is 55:4; Ex 19:6; Dn 7:13; Zc 12:10, 44.
1c Allusions to Dn 7 and 10 and Ezk 43:2.
1d Dn 2:28.
2a Gn 2:9.

of Satan. [10]Do not be afraid of the sufferings that are coming to you. Look, the devil will send some of you to prison *to put you to the test*, and you must face hardship for *ten days*.[b] Even if you have to die, keep faithful, and I will give you the crown of life for your prize. [11]Let anyone who can hear, listen to what the Spirit is saying to the churches: for those who prove victorious will come to no harm from the second death."

3 Pergamum

[12]'Write to the angel of the church in Pergamum and say, "Here is the message of the one who has the sharp sword, double-edged: [13]I know where you live, in the place where Satan is enthroned, and that you still hold firmly to my name, and did not disown your faith in me even when my faithful witness, Antipas, was killed among you, where Satan lives.

[14]'"Nevertheless, I have one or two charges against you: some of you are followers of Balaam, who taught Balak to set a trap for the Israelites so that they committed adultery by eating food that had been sacrificed to idols; [15]and among you too there are some also who follow the teaching of the Nicolaitans. [16]So repent, or I shall soon come to you and attack these people with the sword out of my mouth. [17]Let anyone who can hear, listen to what the Spirit is saying to the churches: to those who prove victorious I will give some hidden manna and a white stone, with *a new name* written on it, known only to the person who receives it."

4 Thyatira

[18]'Write to the angel of the church in Thyatira and say, "Here is the message of the Son of God who has eyes like a burning flame and feet like burnished bronze: [19]I know your activities, your love, your faith, your service and your perseverance, and I know how you are still making progress. [20]Nevertheless, I have a complaint to make: you tolerate the woman Jezebel[c] who claims to be a prophetess, and by her teaching she is luring my servants away to commit the adultery of eating food which has been sacrificed to idols. [21]I have given her time to repent but she is

not willing to repent of her adulterous life. [22]Look, I am consigning her to a bed of pain, and all her partners in adultery to great hardship, unless they repent of their practices; [23]and I will see that her children die, so that all the churches realise that it is I who *test motives and thoughts and repay* you *as your deeds deserve*.[d] [24]But on the rest of you in Thyatira, all of you who have not accepted this teaching or learnt the deep secrets of Satan, as they are called, I am not laying any other burden; [25]but hold on firmly to what you already have until I come. [26]To anyone who proves victorious, and keeps working for me until the end, *I will give* the authority over *the nations* [27]which I myself have been given by my Father, *to rule them with an iron sceptre and shatter them like so many pots*.[e] [28]And I will give such a person the Morning Star. [29]Let anyone who can hear, listen to what the Spirit is saying to the churches."

5 Sardis

3 'Write to the angel of the church in Sardis and say, "Here is the message of the one who holds the seven spirits of God and the seven stars: I know about your behaviour: how you are reputed to be alive and yet are dead. [2]Wake up; put some resolve into what little vigour you have left: it is dying fast. So far I have failed to notice anything in your behaviour that my God could possibly call perfect; [3]remember how you first heard the message. Hold on to that. Repent! If you do not wake up, I shall come to you like a thief, and you will have no idea at what hour I shall come upon you. [4]There are a few in Sardis, it is true, who have kept their robes unstained, and they are fit to come with me, dressed in white. [5]Anyone who proves victorious will be dressed, like these, in white robes; I shall not blot that name out of the book of life, but acknowledge it in the presence of my Father and his angels. [6]Let anyone who can hear, listen to what the Spirit is saying to the churches."

6 Philadelphia

[7]'Write to the angel of the church in Philadelphia and say, "Here is the message of the

2b Dn 1:12.
2c cf. 2 K 9:22.
2d Jr 11:20; 17:10.
2e Ps 2:8–9.

holy and true one who *has the key of David*, so that *when he opens, no one will close, and when he closes, no one will open:*[a] [8]I know about your activities. Look, I have opened in front of you a door that no one will be able to close—and I know that though you are not very strong, you have kept my commandments and not disowned my name. [9]Look, I am going to make the synagogue of Satan—those who falsely claim to be Jews, but are liars, because they are no such thing—I will make them *come and fall at your feet* and recognize that *I have loved you.*[b] [10]Because you have kept my commandment to persevere, I will keep you safe in the time of trial which is coming for the whole world, to put the people of the world to the test. [11]I am coming soon: hold firmly to what you already have, and let no one take your victor's crown away from you. [12]Anyone who proves victorious I will make into a pillar in the sanctuary of my God, and it will stay there for ever; I will inscribe on it the name of my God and the name of the city of my God, the new Jerusalem which is coming down from my God in heaven, and my own new name as well. [13]Let anyone who can hear, listen to what the Spirit is saying to the churches."

7 Laodicea

[14]'Write to the angel of the church in Laodicea and say, "Here is the message of the Amen,[c] the trustworthy, the true witness, the Principle of God's creation: [15]I know about your activities: how you are neither cold nor hot. I wish you were one or the other, [16]but since you are neither hot nor cold, but only lukewarm, I will spit you out of my mouth. [17]You say to yourself: I am rich, I have made a fortune and have everything I want, never realising that you are wretchedly and pitiably poor, and blind and naked too. [18]I warn you, buy from me the gold that has been tested in the fire to make you truly rich, and white robes to clothe you and hide your shameful nakedness, and ointment to put on your eyes to enable you to see. [19]I *reprove* and *train those whom I love:*[d] so repent in real earnest. [20]Look, I am standing at the door, knocking. If one of you hears me calling and opens the door, I will come in to share a meal at that person's side. [21]Anyone who proves victorious I will allow to share my throne, just as I have myself overcome and have taken my seat with my Father on his throne. [22]Let anyone who can hear, listen to what the Spirit is saying to the churches." '

II: THE PROPHETIC VISIONS

A: THE PRELUDE
TO THE GREAT DAY OF GOD

God entrusts the future of the world to the Lamb[a]

4 Then, in my vision, I saw a door open in heaven and heard the same voice speaking to me, the voice like a trumpet, saying, 'Come up here: I will show you *what is to take place in the future.*' [2]With that, I fell into ecstasy and I saw a throne standing in heaven, and the *One* who was *sitting on the throne*, [3]and the One sitting there looked like a diamond and a ruby. There was a rainbow encircling the throne, and this looked like an emerald.

[4]Round the throne in a circle were twenty-four thrones, and on them twenty-four elders sitting, dressed in white robes with golden crowns on their heads. [5]Flashes of lightning were coming from the throne, and the sound of peals of thunder, and in front of the throne there were seven flaming lamps burning, the seven Spirits of God. [6]In front of the throne was a sea as transparent as crystal. *In the middle* of the throne and around it, were *four living creatures all studded with eyes*, in front and behind. [7]*The first* living creature was like *a lion, the second* like *a bull, the third* living creature had a *human face, and the fourth* living creature was like a *flying eagle.* [8]*Each* of the four living creatures had *six wings* and

---

3a Is 22:22.
3b Is 43:3.
3c *Amen* is Hebr. for truth, firmness.
3d Pr 3:12.
4a The scene draws on Ezk 1; 10 and Is 6.

was studded with eyes all the way round as well as inside; and day and night they never stopped singing:

> *Holy, Holy, Holy*
> *is the Lord God, the Almighty*;
> who was, and is and is to come.'

[9]Every time the living creatures glorified and honoured and gave thanks to the One sitting on the throne, *who lives for ever and ever*, [10]the twenty-four elders prostrated themselves before him to worship the One *who lives for ever and ever*, and threw down their crowns in front of the throne, saying:

> [11]You are worthy, our Lord and God,
> to receive glory and honour and power,
> for you made the whole universe;
> by your will, when it did not exist,
> it was created.

5 I saw that in the right hand of the One sitting on the throne there was *a scroll that was written on back and front*[a] and was sealed with seven seals. [2]Then I saw a powerful angel who called with a loud voice, 'Who is worthy to open the scroll and break its seals?' [3]But there was no one, in heaven or on the earth or under the earth, who was able to open the scroll and read it. [4]I wept bitterly because nobody could be found to open the scroll and read it, [5]but one of the elders said to me, 'Do not weep. Look, *the Lion* of the tribe *of Judah, the Root*[b] of David, has triumphed, and so he will open the scroll and its seven seals.'

[6]Then I saw, in the middle of the throne with its four living creatures and the circle of the elders, a Lamb standing that seemed to have been sacrificed; it had seven horns, and it had seven eyes, which are the seven Spirits that God has *sent out over the whole world*.[c] [7]The Lamb came forward to take the scroll from the right hand of the One sitting on the throne, [8]and when he took it, the four living creatures prostrated themselves before him and with them the twenty-four elders; each one of them was holding a harp and had a golden bowl full of incense which are the prayers of the saints. [9]They sang a new hymn:

> You are worthy to take the scroll
> and to break its seals,
> because you were sacrificed,
> and with your blood
> you bought people for God
> of every race, language, people and nation
> [10]and made them
> *a line of kings and priests*[d] for God,
> to rule the world.

[11]In my vision, I heard the sound of an immense number of angels gathered round the throne and the living creatures and the elders; there were *ten thousand times ten thousand of them* and *thousands upon thousands*,[e] [12]loudly chanting:

> Worthy is the Lamb that was sacrificed
> to receive power, riches, wisdom,
> strength, honour, glory and blessing.

[13]Then I heard all the living things in creation—everything that lives in heaven, and on earth, and under the earth, and in the sea, crying:

> To the One seated on the throne
> and to the Lamb,
> be all praise, honour, glory and power,
> for ever and ever.

[14]And the four living creatures said, 'Amen'; and the elders prostrated themselves to worship.

The Lamb breaks the seven seals

6 Then, in my vision, I saw the Lamb break one of the seven seals, and I heard one of the four living creatures shout in a voice like thunder, 'Come!' [2]Immediately I saw a white horse[a] appear, and its rider was holding a bow; he was given a victor's crown and he went away, to go from victory to victory.

[3]When he broke the second seal, I heard the second living creature shout, 'Come!' [4]And out came another horse, bright red, and its rider was given this duty: to take away peace from the earth and set people killing each other. He was given a huge sword.

[5]When he broke the third seal, I heard the third living creature shout, 'Come!' Immedi-

5a Ezk 2:9.
5b Gn 49:9; Is 11:10.
5c Zc 4:10.
5d Is 61:6.
5e Dn 7:10.
6a The horsemen echo Zc 1:8–10; 6:1–3.

ately I saw a black horse appear, and its rider was holding a pair of scales; [6]and I seemed to hear a voice shout from among the four living creatures and say, 'A day's wages for a quart of corn, and a day's wages for three quarts of barley, but do not tamper with the oil or the wine.'

[7]When he broke the fourth seal, I heard the voice of the fourth living creature shout, 'Come!' [8]Immediately I saw another horse appear, deathly pale, and its rider was called Death, and Hades followed at its heels.

They were given authority over a quarter of the earth, *to kill by the sword, by famine, by plague and through wild beasts.*[b]

[9]When he broke the fifth seal, I saw underneath the altar the souls of all the people who had been killed on account of the Word of God, for witnessing to it. [10]They shouted in a loud voice, 'Holy, true Master, how much longer will you wait before you pass sentence and take vengeance for our death on the inhabitants of the earth?' [11]Each of them was given a white robe, and they were told to be patient a little longer, until the roll was completed of their fellow-servants and brothers who were still to be killed as they had been.

[12]In my vision, when he broke the sixth seal, there was a violent earthquake, and the sun went as black as coarse sackcloth; the moon turned red as blood all over, [13]and *the stars of the sky fell*[c] onto the earth *like figs* dropping from a fig tree when a high wind shakes it; [14]the *sky disappeared like a scroll rolling up* and all the mountains and islands were shaken from their places. [15]Then all the kings of the earth, the governors and the commanders, the rich people and the men of influence, the whole population, slaves and citizens, *hid in caverns and among the rocks of the mountains.*[d] [16]*They said to the mountains*[e] and the rocks, '*Fall on us* and hide us away from the One who sits on the throne and from the retribution of the Lamb. [17]For *the Great Day of his retribution* has come, *and who can face it?*'[f]

God's servants will be preserved[a]

7 Next I saw four angels, standing at *the four corners of the earth,*[b] holding back the four winds of the world to keep them from blowing over the land or the sea or any tree. [2]Then I saw another angel rising where the sun rises, carrying the seal of the living God; he called in a powerful voice to the four angels whose duty was to devastate land and sea, [3]'Wait before you do any damage on land or at sea or to the trees, until we have put the *seal on the foreheads*[c] of the servants of our God.' [4]And I heard how many had been sealed: a hundred and forty-four thousand,[d] out of all the tribes of Israel.

[5]From the tribe of Judah, twelve thousand had been sealed;
from the tribe of Reuben, twelve thousand;
from the tribe of Gad, twelve thousand;
[6]from the tribe of Asher, twelve thousand;
from the tribe of Naphtali, twelve thousand;
from the tribe of Manasseh, twelve thousand;
[7]from the tribe of Simeon, twelve thousand;
from the tribe of Levi, twelve thousand;
from the tribe of Issachar, twelve thousand;
[8]from the tribe of Zebulun, twelve thousand;
from the tribe of Joseph, twelve thousand;
and from the tribe of Benjamin, twelve thousand had been sealed.

The rewarding of the saints[e]

[9]After that I saw that there was a huge number, impossible for anyone to count, of people from every nation, race, tribe and language; they were standing in front of the throne and in front of the Lamb, dressed in white robes and holding palms in their hands. They shouted in a loud voice, [10]'Salvation to our God, who sits on the throne, and to the Lamb!' [11]And all the angels who were standing in a circle round the throne,

6b Ezk 14:21.
6c Is 34:4.
6d Ho 10:8.
6e Is 2:10, 18, 19.
6f Jl 2:11; 3:4.
7a =14:1–5.
7b Ezk 7:2.
7c Ezk 9:4.
7d The sacred number 12 squared and multiplied by 1000 indicates the totality of the saved.
7e =15:2–5.

surrounding the elders and the four living creatures, prostrated themselves before the throne, and touched the ground with their foreheads, worshipping God [12]with these words:

Amen. Praise and glory and wisdom,
thanksgiving and honour
  and power and strength
to our God for ever and ever. Amen.

[13]One of the elders then spoke and asked me, 'Who are these people, dressed in white robes, and where have they come from?' [14]I answered him, 'You can tell me, sir.' Then he said, 'These are the people who have been through the great trial; they have washed their robes white again in the blood of the Lamb. [15]That is why they are standing in front of God's throne and serving him day and night in his sanctuary; and the One who sits on the throne will spread his tent over them. [16]*They will never hunger or thirst again; sun and scorching wind will never plague them,* [17]because the Lamb who is at the heart of the throne *will be their shepherd and will guide them to springs of living water;*[f] and God *will wipe away all tears from their eyes.'*[g]

The seventh seal

8 The Lamb then broke the seventh seal, and there was silence in heaven for about half an hour.

The prayers of the saints bring the coming of the Great Day nearer

[2]Next I saw seven trumpets being given to the seven angels who stand in the presence of God. [3]Another angel, who had a golden censer, came and stood at the altar. A large quantity of incense was given to him to offer with the prayers of all the saints on the golden altar that stood in front of the throne; [4]and so from the angel's hand the smoke of the incense went up in the presence of God and with the prayers of the saints. [5]Then the angel took the censer and *filled it from the fire of the altar,*[a] which he then hurled down onto the earth; immediately there came peals of

thunder and flashes of lightning, and the earth shook.

The first four trumpets[b]

[6]The seven angels that had the seven trumpets now made ready to sound them. [7]The first blew his trumpet and, with that, hail and fire, mixed with blood, were hurled on the earth: a third of the earth was burnt up, and a third of all trees, and every blade of grass was burnt. [8]The second angel blew his trumpet, and it was as though a great mountain blazing with fire was hurled into the sea: a third of the sea turned into blood, [9]a third of all the living things in the sea were killed, and a third of all ships were destroyed. [10]The third angel blew his trumpet, and a huge star fell from the sky, burning like a ball of fire, and it fell on a third of all rivers and on the springs of water; [11]this was the star called Wormwood, and a third of all water turned to wormwood, so that many people died; the water had become so bitter. [12]The fourth angel blew his trumpet, and a third of the sun and a third of the moon and a third of the stars were blasted, so that the light went out of a third of them and the day lost a third of its illumination, and likewise the night.

[13]In my vision, I heard an eagle, calling aloud as it flew high overhead, 'Disaster, disaster, disaster, on all the people on earth at the sound of the other three trumpets which the three angels have yet to blow!'

The fifth trumpet

9 Then the fifth angel blew his trumpet, and I saw a star that had fallen from heaven onto the earth, and the angel was given the key to the shaft leading down to the Abyss. [2]When he unlocked the shaft of the Abyss, *smoke rose* out of the Abyss *like the smoke from a* huge *furnace*[a] so that the sun and the sky were darkened by the smoke from the Abyss, [3]and out of the smoke dropped locusts onto the earth: they were given the powers that scorpions have on the earth: [4]they were forbidden to harm any fields or crops or trees and told to attack only those people who were without God's seal on their

---

7f   Is 49:10.
7g   =21:4; Is 25:8.
8a   Lv 16:12; Ezk 10:2.
8b   =16:1–9.
9a   Ex 19:18.

foreheads. ⁵They were not to kill them, but to give them anguish for five months, and the anguish was to be the anguish of a scorpion's sting. ⁶When this happens, *people will long for death and not find it anywhere;*[b] they will want to die and death will evade them.

⁷These locusts *looked like horses*[c] armoured *for battle*; they had what looked like gold crowns on their heads, and their faces looked human, ⁸and their hair was like women's hair, and *teeth like lion's teeth.* ⁹They had body-armour like iron breastplates, and the noise of their wings sounded like *the racket of chariots with many horses charging.* ¹⁰Their tails were like scorpions' tails, with stings, and with their tails they were able to torture people for five months. ¹¹As their leader they had their emperor, the angel of the Abyss, whose name in Hebrew is Abaddon, and in Greek Apollyon.[d]

¹²That was the first of the disasters; there are still two more to come.

The sixth trumpet

¹³The sixth angel blew his trumpet, and I heard a single voice issuing from the four horns of the golden altar in God's presence. ¹⁴It spoke to the sixth angel with the trumpet, and said, 'Release the four angels that are chained up at the great river Euphrates.' ¹⁵These four angels had been ready for this hour of this day of this month of this year, and ready to destroy a third of the human race. ¹⁶I learnt how many there were in their army: twice ten thousand times ten thousand mounted men. ¹⁷In my vision I saw the horses, and the riders with their breastplates of flame colour, hyacinth-blue and sulphur-yellow; the horses had lions' heads, and fire, smoke and sulphur were coming from their mouths. ¹⁸It was by these three plagues, the fire, the smoke and the sulphur coming from their mouths, that the one third of the human race was killed. ¹⁹All the horses' power was in their mouths and their tails: their tails were like snakes, and had heads which inflicted wounds. ²⁰But the rest of the human race,

who escaped death by these plagues, refused either to abandon *their own handiwork*[e] or to stop worshipping devils, the *idols made of gold, silver, bronze, stone and wood*[f] that can neither see nor hear nor move. ²¹Nor did they give up their murdering, or witchcraft, or fornication or stealing.

The imminence of the last punishment

10 Then I saw another powerful angel coming down from heaven, wrapped in cloud, with a rainbow over his head; his face was like the sun, and his legs were pillars of fire. ²In his hand he had a small scroll, unrolled; he put his right foot in the sea and his left foot on the land ³and he shouted so loud, it was *like a lion roaring.*[a] At this, the seven claps of thunder made themselves heard ⁴and when the seven thunderclaps had sounded, I was preparing to write, when I heard a voice from heaven say to me, 'Keep the words of the seven thunderclaps secret and do not write them down.' ⁵Then the angel that I had seen, standing on the sea and the land, *raised his right hand to heaven,*[b] ⁶and *swore by him who lives for ever* and ever, *and made heaven and all that it contains,*[c] and *earth and all it contains,* and *the sea and all it contains,* 'The time of waiting is over; ⁷at the time when the seventh angel is heard sounding his trumpet, the mystery of God will be fulfilled, just as he announced in the gospel to *his servants the prophets.'*

The seer eats the small scroll

⁸Then I heard the voice I had heard from heaven speaking to me again. 'Go', it said, 'and take that open scroll from the hand of the angel standing on sea and land.' ⁹I went to the angel and asked him to give me the small scroll, and he said, 'Take it and eat it; it will turn your stomach sour, but it will taste as sweet as honey.' ¹⁰So I took it out of the angel's hand, and *I ate it and it tasted sweet as honey,*[d] but when I had eaten it my stomach turned sour. ¹¹Then I was told, 'You are

---

9b Jb 3:21.
9c The details of vv. 7–9 echo Jl 1 and 2.
9d Both names mean 'Destroyer'.
9e Is 17:8.
9f Dn 5:4.
10a Am 1:2; 3:8.
10b Dt 32:40.
10c Ne 9:6.
10d Ezk 3:1–13.

to prophesy again, this time against many different nations and countries and languages and kings.'

The two witnesses

11 Then I was given a long cane like a measuring rod, and I was told, 'Get up and measure God's sanctuary, and the altar, and the people who worship there; ²but exclude the outer court and do not measure it, because it has been handed over to gentiles— they will trample on the holy city for forty-two months.ᵃ ³But I shall send my two witnesses to prophesy for twelve hundred and sixty days, wearing sackcloth. ⁴These are the *two olive trees*ᵇ and the two lamps *in attendance on the Lord of the world.*ᶜ ⁵Fire comes from their mouths and consumes their enemies if anyone tries to harm them; and anyone who tries to harm them will certainly be killed in this way. ⁶They have the power to lock up the sky so that it does not rain as long as they are prophesying; they have the power to turn water into blood and strike the whole world with any plague as often as they like. ⁷When they have completed their witnessing, the beast that comes out of the Abyss *is going to make war on them and overcome them*ᵈ and kill them. ⁸Their corpses lie in the main street of the great city*ᵉ* known by the symbolic names Sodom and Egypt, in which their Lord was crucified. ⁹People of every race, tribe, language and nation stare at their corpses, for three-and-a-half days, not letting them be buried, ¹⁰and the people of the world are glad about it and celebrate the event by giving presents to each other, because these two prophets have been a plague to the people of the world.'

¹¹After the three-and-a-half days, *God breathed life into them and they stood up on their feet,*ᶠ and everybody who saw it happen was terrified; ¹²then I heard a loud voice from heaven say to them, 'Come up here,' and while their enemies were watching, they went up to heaven in a cloud. ¹³Immediately, there was a violent earthquake, and a tenth of the city collapsed; seven thousand persons were killed in the earthquake, and the survivors, overcome with fear, could only praise the God of heaven.

¹⁴That was the second of the disasters; the third is to come quickly after it.

The seventh trumpet

¹⁵Then the seventh angel blew his trumpet, and voices could be heard shouting in heaven, calling, 'The kingdom of the world has become the kingdom of our Lord and his Christ, and he will reign for ever and ever.' ¹⁶The twenty-four elders, enthroned in the presence of God, prostrated themselves and touched the ground with their foreheads worshipping God ¹⁷with these words, 'We give thanks to you, Almighty Lord God, He who is, He who was, for assuming your great power and beginning your reign. ¹⁸*The nations were in uproar*ᵍ and now the time has come for your retribution, and for the dead to be judged, and for *your servants the prophets*, for the saints and for *those who fear* your name, *small and great alike*, to be rewarded. The time has come to destroy those who are destroying the earth.'

¹⁹Then the sanctuary of God in heaven opened, and the ark of the covenant could be seen inside it. Then came flashes of lightning, peals of thunder and an earthquake and violent hail.

The vision of the woman and the dragon

12 Now a great sign appeared in heaven: a woman, robed with the sun, standing on the moon, and on her head a crown of twelve stars. ²She was pregnant, and in labour, crying aloud in the pangs of childbirth. ³Then a second sign appeared in the sky: there was a huge red dragon with seven heads and ten horns, and each of the seven heads crowned with a coronet. ⁴Its tail swept a third of *the stars from the sky and hurled them to the ground,*ᵃ and the dragon

11a Cf. Dn 7:25. Half seven years, so the opposite of completion, a short and incomplete time of persecution.
11b Zc 4:3, 14.
11c 2 K 1:10.
11d Dn 7:21.
11e Also called Babylon. It is the centre of evil and persecution, possibly Rome.
11f Ezk 37:5, 10.
11g Ps 2:1, 5, followed by Am 3:7; Ps 115:13.
12a Dn 8:10.

stopped in front of the woman as she was at the point of giving birth, so that it could eat the child as soon as it was born. ⁵The woman *was delivered of a boy,ᵇ* the son who was *to rule all the nations with an iron sceptre,* and the child was taken straight up to God and to his throne, ⁶while the woman escaped into the desert, where God had prepared a place for her to be looked after for twelve hundred and sixty days.

⁷And now war broke out in heaven, when *Michaelᶜ* with his angels attacked the dragon. The dragon fought back with his angels, ⁸but they were defeated and driven out of heaven. ⁹The great dragon, the primeval serpent, known as the devil or Satan, who had led all the world astray, was hurled down to the earth and his angels were hurled down with him. ¹⁰Then I heard a voice shout from heaven, 'Salvation and power and empire for ever have been won by our God, and all authority for his Christ, now that the accuser, who accused our brothers day and night before our God, has been brought down. ¹¹They have triumphed over him by the blood of the Lamb and by the word to which they bore witness, because even in the face of death they did not cling to life. ¹²So let the heavens rejoice and all who live there; but for you, earth and sea, disaster is coming— because the devil has gone down to you in a rage, knowing that he has little time left.'

¹³As soon as the dragon found himself hurled down to the earth, he sprang in pursuit of the woman, the mother of the male child, ¹⁴but she was given a pair of the great eagle's wings to fly away from the serpent into the desert, to the place where she was to be looked after for *a time, two times and half a time.ᵈ* ¹⁵So the serpent vomited water from his mouth, like a river, after the woman, to sweep her away in the current, ¹⁶but the earth came to her rescue; it opened its mouth and swallowed the river spewed from the dragon's mouth. ¹⁷Then the dragon was enraged with the woman and went away to make war on the rest of her children, who obey God's commandments and have in themselves the witness of Jesus.

The dragon delegates his power to the beast

¹⁸And I took my stand on the seashore.
13Then I saw *a beastᵃ emerge from the sea:* it had seven heads and ten horns, with a coronet on each of its ten horns, and its heads were marked with blasphemous titles. ²I saw that the beast *was like a leopard,* with paws like *a bear* and a mouth like *a lion;* the dragon had handed over to it his own power and his throne and his immense authority. ³I saw that one of its heads seemed to have had a fatal wound but that this deadly injury had healed and the whole world had marvelled and followed the beast. ⁴They prostrated themselves in front of the dragon because he had given the beast his authority; and they prostrated themselves in front of the beast, saying, 'Who can compare with the beast? Who can fight against it?' ⁵The beast was allowed *to mouth its boasts* and blasphemies and to be active for forty-two months; ⁶and it mouthed its blasphemies against God, against his name, his heavenly Tent and all those who are sheltered there. ⁷It was allowed *to make war against the saints and conquer them, and given power* over every race, people, language and nation; ⁸and all people of the world will worship it, that is, everybody whose name has not been written down since the foundation of the world in the sacrificial Lamb's book of life. ⁹Let anyone who can hear, listen: ¹⁰*Those for captivity to captivity; those for* death by *the sword to* death by *the sword.ᵇ* This is why the saints must have perseverance and faith.

The false prophet as the slave of the beast

¹¹Then I saw a second beast, emerging from the ground; it had two horns like a lamb, but made a noise like a dragon. ¹²This second beast exercised all the power of the first beast, on its behalf making the world and all its people worship the first beast, whose deadly injury had healed. ¹³And it worked great miracles, even to calling down fire from heaven onto the earth while people watched. ¹⁴Through the miracles which it was allowed to do on behalf of the first beast, it was able

12b Is 66:7, followed by Ps 2:9. The woman is the people of God, and the boy is the Messiah.
12c God's champion in Dn 10:13; 12:1.
12d *See* 11a note.
13a The vision draws on Dn 7.
13b Jr 15:2.

to lead astray the people of the world and persuade them to put up a statue in honour of the beast that had been wounded by the sword and still lived. ¹⁵It was allowed to breathe life into this statue, so that the statue of the beast was able to speak, and to have *anyone who refused to worship the statue^c* of the beast put to death. ¹⁶It compelled everyone — small and great alike, rich and poor, slave and citizen — to be branded on the right hand or on the forehead, ¹⁷and made it illegal for anyone to buy or sell anything unless he had been branded with the name of the beast or with the number of its name.

¹⁸There is need for shrewdness here: anyone clever may interpret the number of the beast: it is the number of a human being, the number 666.^d

The companions of the Lamb^a

14 Next in my vision I saw Mount Zion, and standing on it the Lamb who had with him a hundred and forty-four thousand people, all with his name and his Father's name written on their foreheads. ²I heard a sound coming out of heaven like the sound of the ocean or the roar of thunder; it was like the sound of harpists playing their harps. ³There before the throne they were singing a new hymn in the presence of the four living creatures and the elders, a hymn that could be learnt only by the hundred and forty-four thousand who had been redeemed from the world. ⁴These are the sons who have kept their virginity and not been defiled with women; they *follow* the Lamb wherever he goes; they, out of all people, have been redeemed to be *the first-fruits for God^b* and for the Lamb. ⁵*No lie^c* was found in their mouths and no fault can be found in them.

Angels announce the Day of Judgement

⁶Then I saw another angel, flying high overhead, sent to announce the gospel of eternity to all who live on the earth, every nation, race, language and tribe. ⁷He was calling, 'Fear God and glorify him, because the time has come for him to sit in judgement; worship *the maker of heaven and earth and sea^d* and the springs of water.'

⁸A second angel followed him, calling, '*Babylon has fallen, Babylon the Great has fallen,* Babylon which gave the whole world *the wine of retribution* to drink.'^e

⁹A third angel followed, shouting aloud, 'All those who worship the beast and his statue, or have had themselves branded on the hand or forehead, ¹⁰will be made to drink the wine of God's fury which is ready, undiluted, in his cup of retribution; in *fire and brimstone^f* they will be tortured in the presence of the holy angels and the Lamb ¹¹and *the smoke* of their torture will *rise for ever and ever.^g* There will be no respite, *night or day*, for those who worship the beast or its statue or accept branding with its name.' ¹²This is why there must be perseverance in the saints who keep the commandments of God and faith in Jesus. ¹³Then I heard a voice from heaven say to me, 'Write down: Blessed are those who die in the Lord! Blessed indeed, the Spirit says; now they can rest for ever after their work, since their good deeds go with them.'

The harvest and vintage of the gentiles^h

¹⁴Now in my vision I saw a white *cloud* and, *sitting on it, one like a son of man* with a gold crown on his head and a sharp sickle in his hand. ¹⁵Then another angel came out of the sanctuary and shouted at the top of his voice to the one sitting on the cloud, '*Ply* your *sickle* and reap: harvest time has come and *the harvest* of the earth *is ripe.*' ¹⁶Then the one sitting on the cloud set his sickle to work on the earth, and the harvest of earth was reaped.

¹⁷Another angel, who also carried a sharp sickle, came out of the temple in heaven, ¹⁸and the angel in charge of the fire left the altar and shouted at the top of his voice to the one with the sharp sickle, 'Put your sickle in,

13c Dn 3:5–7, 15.
13d 6=7–1, so 666=triple imperfection. It may also symbolise a name.
14a = 7:1–8.
14b Jr 2:2–3.
14c Zp 3:13.
14d Ex 20:11.
14e =18:2–3; cf. Is 21:9; 51:17.
14f Gn 19:24.
14g Is 34:9–10.
14h Dn 7:13; Jl 4:12–13.

and harvest the bunches from the vine of the earth; all its grapes are ripe.' [19]So the angel set his sickle to work on the earth and harvested the whole vintage of the earth and put it into a huge winepress, the winepress of God's anger, [20]outside the city, where it was trodden until the blood that came out of the winepress was up to the horses' bridles as far away as sixteen hundred furlongs.

The hymn of Moses and the Lamb[a]

15And I saw in heaven another sign, great and wonderful: seven angels were bringing the seven plagues that are the last of all, because they exhaust the anger of God. [2]I seemed to be looking at a sea of crystal suffused with fire, and standing by the lake of glass, those who had fought against the beast and won, and against his statue and the number which is his name. They all had harps from God, [3]and they were singing the hymn of Moses,[b] the servant of God, and the hymn of the Lamb:

How great and wonderful
 are all your works,
Lord God Almighty;
upright and true are all your ways,
King of nations.
[4]*Who does not revere*
 and *glorify your name, O Lord?*
For you alone are holy,
and all nations will come and adore you
for the many acts of saving justice
 you have shown.

The seven bowls of plagues

[5]After this, in my vision, the sanctuary, the tent of the Testimony, opened in heaven, [6]and out came the seven angels with the seven plagues, wearing pure white linen, fastened round their waists with belts of gold. [7]One of the four living creatures gave the seven angels seven golden bowls filled with the anger of God who lives for ever and ever. [8]*The smoke from the glory* and the power *of God filled* the temple[c] so that no one could go into it until the seven plagues of the seven angels were completed.

16Then I heard a loud voice[a] from the sanctuary calling to the seven angels, 'Go, and empty the seven bowls of God's anger over the earth.'

[2]The first angel went and emptied his bowl over the earth; at once, on all the people who had been branded with the mark of the beast and had worshipped its statue, there came disgusting and virulent sores.

[3]The second angel emptied his bowl over the sea, and it turned to blood, like the blood of a corpse, and every living creature in the sea died.

[4]The third angel emptied his bowl into the rivers and springs of water and they turned into blood. [5]Then I heard the angel of water say, 'You are the Upright One, He who is, He who was, the Holy One, for giving this verdict: [6]they spilt the blood of the saints and the prophets, and blood is what you have given them to drink; it is what they deserve.' [7]And I heard the altar itself say, 'Truly, Lord God Almighty, the punishments you give are true and just.'

[8]The fourth angel emptied his bowl over the sun and it was made to scorch people with its flames; [9]but though people were scorched by the fierce heat of it, they cursed the name of God who had the power to cause such plagues, and they would not repent and glorify him.

[10]The fifth angel emptied his bowl over the throne of the beast and its whole empire was plunged into darkness. People were biting their tongues for pain, [11]but instead of repenting for what they had done, they cursed the God of heaven because of their pains and sores.

[12]The sixth angel emptied his bowl over the great river Euphrates; all the water dried up so that a way was made for the kings of the East to come in. [13]Then from the jaws of dragon and beast and false prophet I saw three foul spirits come; they looked like frogs [14]and in fact were demon spirits, able to work miracles, going out to all the kings of the world to call them together for the war of the Great Day of God the Almighty. — [15]Look, I shall come like a thief. Blessed is anyone who has kept watch, and has kept his clothes on, so that he does not go out naked and expose

15a = 7:1–8.
15b Ex 15; in fact the hymn uses Jr 10:7; Ps 86:9.
15c 1 K 8:10.
16a = 8:6–12.

his shame. — ¹⁶They called the kings together at the place called, in Hebrew, Armageddon.ᵇ

¹⁷The seventh angel emptied his bowl into the air, and a great voice boomed out from the sanctuary, 'The end has come.' ¹⁸Then there were flashes of lightning and peals of thunder and a violent earthquake, *unparalleled since* humanity *first came into existence.*ᶜ ¹⁹The Great City was split into three parts and the cities of the world collapsed; Babylon the Great was not forgotten: God made her drink the full winecup of his retribution. ²⁰Every island vanished and the mountains disappeared; ²¹and hail, with great hailstones weighing a talent each, fell from the sky on the people. They cursed God for sending a plague of hail; it was the most terrible plague.

B: THE PUNISHMENT OF BABYLON

The great prostitute

17 One of the seven angels that had the seven bowls came to speak to me, and said, 'Come here and I will show you the punishment of the great prostitute *who is enthroned beside abundant waters,*ᵃ ²with whom all the kings of the earth have prostituted themselves, and who has made all the population of the world drunk with the wine of her adultery.' ³He took me in spirit to a desert, and there I saw a woman riding a scarlet beast which had seven heads and ten horns and had blasphemous titles written all over it. ⁴The woman was dressed in purple and scarlet and glittered with gold and jewels and pearls, and she was holding a gold winecup filled with the disgusting filth of her prostitution; ⁵on her forehead was written a name, a cryptic name: 'Babylon the Great, the mother of all the prostitutes and of the filthy practices on the earth.' ⁶I saw that she was drunk, drunk with the blood of the saints, and the blood of the martyrs of Jesus; and when I saw her, I was completely mystified. ⁷The angel said to me, 'Do you not understand? I will tell you the meaning of this woman, and of the beast she is riding, with the seven heads and the ten horns.

The symbolism of the beast and the prostitute

⁸'The beast you have seen was once alive and is alive no longer; it is yet to come up from the Abyss, but only to go to its destruction. And the people of the world, whose names have not been written since the beginning of the world in the book of life, will be astonished when they see how the beast was once alive and is alive no longer, and is still to come.

⁹'This calls for shrewdness. The seven heads are the seven hills, on which the woman is sitting. ¹⁰The seven heads are also seven emperors. Five of them have already gone, one is here now, and one is yet to come; once here, he must stay for a short while. ¹¹The beast, who was alive and is alive no longer, is at the same time the eighth and one of the seven, and he is going to his destruction.

¹²'*The ten horns* which you saw *are ten kings*ᵇ who have not yet been given their royal power but will have royal authority only for a single hour and in association with the beast. ¹³They are all of one mind in putting their strength and their powers at the beast's disposal, ¹⁴and they will go to war against the Lamb; but because the Lamb is *Lord of lords* and *King of kings,*ᶜ he will defeat them, he and his followers, the called, the chosen, the trustworthy.'

¹⁵The angel continued, 'The waters you saw, beside which the prostitute was sitting, are all the peoples, the populations, the nations and the languages. ¹⁶But the ten horns and the beast will turn against the prostitute, and *tear off* her *clothes* and leave her stark naked;ᵈ then they will eat her flesh and burn the remains in the fire. ¹⁷In fact, God has influenced their minds to do what he intends, to agree together to put their royal powers at the beast's disposal until the time when God's words shall be fulfilled. ¹⁸The woman you saw is the great city which has authority over all the rulers on earth.'

16b i.e. the mountains of Megiddo, symbol of disaster since King Josiah was killed there, 2 K 23:29.
16c Dn 12:1.
17a Jr 51:13. The seven heads are the seven hills of Rome.
17b Dn 7:24.
17c Dn 10:17.
17d Ezk 16:39.

An angel announces the fall of Babylon[a]

18 After this, I saw another angel come down from heaven, with great authority given to him; *the earth shone with his glory.* [2] At the top of his voice he shouted,[b] '*Babylon has fallen, Babylon the Great has fallen*, and has become *the haunt of devils* and a lodging for every foul spirit and dirty, loathsome bird. [3] All the nations have drunk deep of the wine of her prostitution; every king on the earth has prostituted himself with her, and every merchant grown rich through her debauchery.'

The people of God summoned to flee

[4] Another voice spoke from heaven; I heard it say, 'Come out, my people, away from her, so that you do not share in her crimes and have the same plagues to bear. [5] *Her sins have reached up to the sky*, and God has her crimes in mind: *treat her as she has treated others.* [6] She must be paid double the amount she exacted. She is to have a doubly strong cup of her own mixture. [7] Every one of her pomps and orgies is to be matched by a torture or an agony. *I am enthroned as queen, she thinks; I am no widow and will never know bereavement.* [8] For that, *in one day*, the plagues will fall on her: disease and mourning and famine. She will be burned to the ground. The Lord God who has condemned her is mighty.'

The people of the world mourn for Babylon.

[9] 'There will be mourning and weeping for her by the kings of the earth who have prostituted themselves with her and held orgies with her. They see the smoke as she burns, [10] while they keep at a safe distance through fear of her anguish. They will say:

Mourn, mourn for this great city,
Babylon, so powerful a city,
in one short hour
  your doom has come upon you.

[11] 'There will be weeping and distress over her among all the traders of the earth when no one is left to buy their cargoes of goods; [12] their stocks of gold and silver, jewels and pearls, linen and purple and silks and scarlet; all the sandalwood, every piece in ivory or fine wood, in bronze or iron or marble; [13] the cinnamon and spices, the myrrh and ointment and incense; wine, oil, flour and corn; their stocks of cattle, sheep, horses and chariots, their slaves and their human cargo.

[14] 'All the fruits you had set your hearts on have failed you; gone for ever, never to return again, is your life of magnificence and ease.

[15] 'The traders who had made a fortune out of her will be standing at a safe distance through fear of her anguish, mourning and weeping. [16] They will be saying:

Mourn, mourn for this great city;
for all the linen and purple and scarlet
  that you wore,
for all your finery of gold and jewels
  and pearls;
[17] your huge riches are all destroyed
  within a single hour.'

All the captains and seafaring men, sailors and all those who make a living from the sea kept a safe distance, [18] watching the smoke as she burned, and crying out, 'Has there ever been a city as great as this!' [19] They threw dust on their heads and said, with tears and groans:

'Mourn, mourn for this great city
whose lavish living has made a fortune
for every owner of a sea-going ship,
ruined within a single hour.

[20] 'Now heaven, celebrate her downfall, and all you saints, apostles and prophets: God has given judgement for you against her.'

[21] Then a powerful angel picked up a boulder like a great millstone, and as he hurled it into the sea, he said, 'That is how the great city of Babylon is going to be hurled down, never to be seen again.

[22] Never again in you
will be heard
  the song of harpists and minstrels,
the music of flute and trumpet;
never again will craftsmen of every skill
  be found in you
or *the sound of the handmill*[c] be heard;

18a These songs of doom draw on OT threats to a proud city, especially Jr 50—51; Ezk 26—28; Is 47.
18b =14:8.
18c Jr 25:10, followed by Jr 7:34; Is 23:8.

[23] never again
  will shine *the light of the lamp* in you,
  never again will be heard in you
  the voices of bridegroom and bride.
  Your traders were the princes
    of the earth,
  all the nations were led astray
    by your sorcery.

[24] In her was found the blood of prophets and saints, and all the blood that was ever shed on earth.'

Songs of victory in heaven

19 After this I heard what seemed to be the great sound of a huge crowd in heaven, singing, 'Alleluia! Salvation and glory and power to our God! [2] He judges fairly, he punishes justly, and he has condemned the great prostitute who corrupted the earth with her prostitution; he has avenged the blood of his servants which she shed.' [3] And again they sang, 'Alleluia! *The smoke* of her *will rise for ever and ever.*'[a] [4] Then the twenty-four elders and the four living creatures threw themselves down and worshipped God seated on his throne, and they cried, 'Amen, Alleluia.'
[5] Then a voice came from the throne; it said, 'Praise our God, you servants of his and *those who fear him, small and great alike.*'[b] [6] And I heard what seemed to be the voices of a huge crowd, like the sound of the ocean or the great roar of thunder, answering, 'Alleluia! The reign of the Lord our God Almighty has begun; [7] let us be glad and joyful and give glory to God, because this is the time for the marriage of the Lamb. [8] His bride is ready, and she has been able to dress herself in dazzling white linen, because her linen is made of the good deeds of the saints.' [9] The angel said, 'Write this, "Blessed are those who are invited to the wedding feast of the Lamb," ' and he added, 'These words of God are true.' [10] Then I knelt at his feet to worship him, but he said to me, 'Never do that: I am your fellow-servant and the fellow-servant of all your brothers who have in themselves the witness of Jesus. God alone you must worship.' The witness of Jesus is the spirit of prophecy.

C: THE DESTRUCTION OF THE UNBELIEVERS

The first eschatological battle[c]

[11] And now I saw heaven open, and a white horse appear; its rider was called Trustworthy and True; *in uprightness he judges* and makes war. [12] His eyes were flames of fire, and he was crowned with many coronets; the name written on him was known only to himself, [13] *his cloak was soaked in blood.* He is known by the name, The Word of God. [14] Behind him, dressed in linen of dazzling white, rode the armies of heaven on white horses. [15] From his mouth came a sharp sword with which to strike the unbelievers; he is the one *who will rule them with an iron sceptre*, and tread out the wine of Almighty God's fierce retribution. [16] On his cloak and on his thigh a name was written: *King of kings* and *Lord of lords.*
[17] I saw an angel standing in the sun, and he shouted aloud to all the birds that were flying high overhead in the sky, 'Come here. *Gather together at* God's *great feast.* [18] *You will eat the flesh of kings*, and the flesh of great generals and heroes, the flesh of horses and their riders and of all kinds of people, citizens and slaves, small and great alike.'
[19] Then I saw the beast, with all the kings of the earth and their armies, gathered together to fight the Rider and his army. [20] But the beast was taken prisoner, together with the false prophet who had worked miracles on the beast's behalf and by them had deceived those who had accepted branding with the mark of the beast and those who had worshipped his statue. These two were hurled alive into the fiery lake of burning sulphur. [21] All the rest were killed by the sword of the Rider, which came out of his mouth, and *all the birds glutted themselves with their flesh.*

The reign of a thousand years

20 Then I saw an angel come down from heaven with the key of the Abyss in his hand and an enormous chain. [2] He overpowered the dragon, that primeval serpent which is the devil and Satan, and chained

---

19a Is 34:10.
19b Ps 115:13.
19c =20:7–10. The OT allusions show this avenger to be the Messiah: Is 11:4; 63:1; Ps 2:9; Ezk 39:17, 20.

him up for a thousand years. ³He hurled him into the Abyss and shut the entrance and sealed it over him, to make sure he would not lead the nations astray again until the thousand years had passed. At the end of that time he must be released, but only for a short while.

⁴Then I saw thrones, where they took their seats, and *on them was conferred the power to give judgement.ᵃ* I saw the souls of all who had been beheaded for having witnessed for Jesus and for having preached God's word, and those who refused to worship the beast or his statue and would not accept the brand-mark on their foreheads or hands; they came to life, and reigned with Christ for a thousand years.ᵇ ⁵The rest of the dead did not come to life until the thousand years were over; this is the first resurrection. ⁶Blessed and holy are those who share in the first resurrection; the second death has no power over them but they will be priests of God and of Christ and reign with him for a thousand years.

⁷When the thousand years are over,ᶜ Satan will be released from his prison ⁸and will come out to lead astray all the nations in the four quarters of the earth, *Gog and Magog,ᵈ* and mobilise them for war, his armies being as many as the sands of the sea. ⁹They came swarming over the entire country and besieged the camp of the saints, which is the beloved City. *But fire rained down on them from heavenᵉ* and consumed them. ¹⁰Then the devil, who led them astray, was hurled into the lake of fire and sulphur, where the beast and the false prophet are, and their torture will not come to an end, day or night, for ever and ever.

The Last Judgement

¹¹Then I saw a great white throne and the One who was sitting on it. In his presence, earth and sky vanished, leaving no trace. ¹²I saw the dead, great and small alike, standing in front of his throne while *the books lay open.ᶠ* And another book was opened, which is the book of life, and the dead were judged from what was written in the books, as their deeds deserved.

¹³The sea gave up all the dead who were in it; ¹⁴Death and Hades were emptied of the dead that were in them; and every one was judged as his deeds deserved. Then Death and Hades were hurled into the burning lake. This burning lake is the second death; ¹⁵and anybody whose name could not be found written in the book of life was hurled into the burning lake.

D: THE JERUSALEM OF THE FUTURE

The heavenly Jerusalem

21 Then I saw *a new heaven and a new earth;ᵃ* the first heaven and the first earth had disappeared now, and there was no longer any sea. ²I saw the holy city, the new Jerusalem, coming down out of heaven from God, prepared as a bride dressed for her husband. ³Then I heard a loud voice call from the throne, 'Look, here God lives among human beings. He will make *his home among them; they will be his people,ᵇ* and he will be their God, *God-with-them.* ⁴*He will wipe* away all *tears from their eyes;ᶜ* there will be no more death, and no more mourning or sadness or pain. The world of the past has gone.'

⁵Then the One sitting on the throne spoke. 'Look, I am making the whole of creation new. Write this, "What I am saying is trustworthy and will come true." ' ⁶Then he said to me, 'It has already happened. I am the Alpha and the Omega, the Beginning and the End. I will give water from the well of life free to anybody who is thirsty; ⁷anyone who proves victorious will inherit these things; and *I will be his* God and *he will be my son.ᵈ* ⁸But the legacy for cowards, for those who break their word, or worship obscenities, for murderers and the sexually immoral, and for sorcerers, worshippers of false gods or any

---

20a Dn 7:22.
20b The time of the Church after the end of the persecution, not a reign of a returned Christ.
20c =19:11–21.
20d Ezk 38:2.
20e Ezk 38:22.
20f Dn 7:10. A register of human deeds and a list of the predestined.
21a Is 65:17.
21b Ezk 37:27.
21c Is 8:8; 25:8.
21d 2 S 7:14.

other sort of liars, is the second death in the burning lake of sulphur.'

The messianic Jerusalem

[9]One of the seven angels that had the seven bowls full of the seven final plagues came to speak to me and said, 'Come here and I will show you the bride that the Lamb has married.' [10]*In the spirit, he carried me to the top of a very high mountain,*[e] and showed me Jerusalem, the holy city, coming down out of heaven from God. [11]It had *all the glory of God*[f] and glittered like some precious jewel of crystal-clear diamond. [12]Its wall was of a great height and had twelve gates; at each of the twelve gates there was an angel, and over the gates were written the names *of the twelve tribes of Israel;* [13]*on the east there were three gates, on the north three gates, on the south three gates, and on the west three gates.*[g] [14]The city walls stood on twelve foundation stones, each one of which bore the name of one of the twelve apostles of the Lamb.

[15]The angel that was speaking to me was carrying a gold measuring rod to measure the city and its gates and wall. [16]The plan of the city is perfectly square, its length the same as its breadth. He measured the city with his rod and it was twelve thousand furlongs, equal in length and in breadth, and equal in height. [17]He measured its wall, and this was a hundred and forty-four cubits high—by human measurements. [18]The wall was built of diamond, and the city of pure gold, like clear glass. [19]The foundations of the city wall were faced with all kinds of precious stone: the first with diamond, the second lapis lazuli, the third turquoise, the fourth crystal, [20]the fifth agate, the sixth ruby, the seventh gold quartz, the eighth malachite, the ninth topaz, the tenth emerald, the eleventh sapphire and the twelfth amethyst. [21]The twelve gates were twelve pearls, each gate being made of a single pearl, and the main street of the city was pure gold, transparent as glass. [22]I could not see any temple in the city since the Lord God Almighty and the Lamb were themselves the temple, [23]and the city did not need the sun or the moon for

light, since it was lit by the radiant glory of God, and the Lamb was a lighted torch for it. [24]*The nations will come to its light*[h] and the kings of the earth will bring it their treasures. [25]Its *gates will never be closed by day*—and there will be no night there— [26]and *the nations will come, bringing their treasure* and their wealth. [27]Nothing unclean may come into it: no one who does what is loathsome or false, but only those who are listed in the Lamb's book of life.

22 Then the angel showed me the river of life, rising from the throne of God and of the Lamb and flowing crystal-clear. [2]Down the middle of the city street, *on either bank of the river were the trees of life, which bear twelve crops of fruit in a year, one in each month, and the leaves of which are the cure for the nations.*[a]

[3]*The curse of destruction will be abolished.*[b] The throne of God and of the Lamb will be in the city; his servants will worship him, [4]they will see him face to face, and his name will be written on their foreheads. [5]And night will be abolished; they will not need lamplight or sunlight, because the Lord God will be shining on them. They will reign for ever and ever.

[6]The angel said to me, 'All that you have written is sure and will come true: the Lord God who inspires the prophets has sent his angel to reveal to his servants *what is soon to take place.* [7]I am coming soon!' Blessed are those who keep the prophetic message of this book.

[8]I, John, am the one who heard and saw these things. When I had heard and seen them all, I knelt at the feet of the angel who had shown them to me, to worship him; [9]but he said, 'Do no such thing: I am your fellow-servant and the fellow-servant of your brothers the prophets and those who keep the message of this book. God alone you must worship.'

[10]This, too, he said to me, 'Do not keep the prophecies in this book a secret, because the Time is close. [11]Meanwhile let the sinner continue sinning, and the unclean continue to be unclean; let the upright continue in his uprightness, and those who are holy continue

---

21e Ezk 40:2.
21f Is 60:1–2.
21g Ezk 48:31–35.
21h Is 60:3.
22a Ezk 47:12.
22b Zc 14:11.

to be holy. [12]*Look, I am coming* soon, and my *reward is with* me, *to repay everyone as their deeds deserve.*[c] [13]I am the Alpha and the Omega, *the First and the Last*, the Beginning and the End. [14]Blessed are those who will have washed their robes clean, so that they will have the right to feed on the tree of life and can come through the gates into the city. [15]Others must stay outside: dogs, fortune-tellers, and the sexually immoral, murderers, idolaters, and everyone of false speech and false life.'

EPILOGUE

[16]I, Jesus, have sent my angel to attest these things to you for the sake of the churches. I am the sprig from the root of David and the bright star of the morning.

[17]The Spirit and the Bride say, 'Come!' Let everyone who listens answer, 'Come!' Then *let all who are thirsty come:*[d] all who want it may *have the water* of life, and have it *free.*

[18]This is my solemn attestation to all who hear the prophecies in this book: if anyone adds anything to them, God will add to him every plague mentioned in the book; [19]if anyone cuts anything out of the prophecies in this book, God will cut off his share of the tree of life and of the holy city, which are described in the book.

[20]The one who attests these things says: I am indeed coming soon.

Amen; come, Lord Jesus.

[21]May the grace of the Lord Jesus be with you all. Amen

22c Ps 62:12.
22d Is 55:1.

SUPPLEMENTS

THEOLOGICAL GLOSSARY

Old Testament passages indicated clarify the New Testament use of a term.
*refers the reader for further information to another entry in this glossary.

abba An Aramaic word, an affectionate term of endearment used by children to their father. It was used by Jesus to his Father, and became for Christians a guarantee, almost a talisman, of their close relationship with the Father as children of God. Mk 14:36; Rm 8:15; Ga 4:6.

Adam See 'Second Adam'.

almsgiving With prayer and fasting one of the three principal good works in Judaism. Jesus warns against hypocrisy in their exercise, but Lk especially stresses the importance of generosity to the poor. Paul lays down guidelines for it. Mt 6:2–4; Mk 12:41–44; Lk 18:22; 1 Co 8:7–15.

amen From the Hebr root 'truth', it expresses acceptance or confirmation by the speaker of a statement, prayer or oath of another. Jesus is the 'Amen' of the Father as the fulfilment of his promises. Jesus himself uses the expression, in a unique way, to give emphasis to certain claims. Neh 8:6; Ps 41:13; Jn 3:3, 11; 2 Co 1:20; Rv 3:14.

angels Members of the heavenly court, God's retinue, they are depicted as sent to protect God's friends and deliver messages ('angel' = 'messenger') or interpret events. Some are called cherubim or seraphim. Some of the messengers are named, Gabriel etc. 1 K 22:19; Jb 1:6; Tob 5:4; Mt 28:2; Lk 1–2.

anger of God An aspect of God's awesome holiness and his absolute demand for loyalty, it manifests itself, often unpredictably, in fearful natural phenomena (storm, lightning, etc) and the punishment of offenders. It is to be fully expressed in the great judgement of the Day of the Lord. Nb 11:1; 1 K 14:15; Is 9:11–10:4; Na 1; Rv 16:1.

anointing In ancient Israel the king was made a sacred person by anointing with oil; God's chosen king in the renewal of all things was to be 'the anointed', *Messiah** or *Christ*. Later the high priest also was anointed, and after the Exile, all priests*. Ex 29:7; 1 S 10:1; 16:1; 2 S 19:22; Ps 132:10; Ac 2:36.

antichrist This figure, diametrically opposed to Christ, is the symbolic personification of all evil, also represented as Gog, the Enemy, the Beast. Ezk 38; 2 Th 2:3–12; 1 Jn 2:18, 22; Rv 11:7; 13:1.

apocalyptic A form of literature promising, normally in coded imagery, release from present misery and a glorious future for God's people. It is first seen in Ezk 38–39, is popular in Judaism from 200 BC onwards, and occurs in the NT in Mk 13par and Rv.

apostle Literally an 'envoy', it is used in the Christian sense to refer to those sent to preach the gospel. More narrowly it designates the Twelve chosen by Jesus to be his witnesses*. In the power of the Spirit*, they are the leaders of the young community and continue the ministry of Jesus. After the model of the 12 sons of Jacob, they are the foundation stones of the new Jerusalem. Mk 3:16–19; Mt 28:16; Ac 1:21; 6:2; Rv 21:14.

atonement See 'expiation'.

authority Authority derives from God, who will scrutinise the holder on how it has been exercised. The risen Christ enjoys all authority in heaven and on earth, but authority to make binding decisions is granted also to Peter and to the community itself. Christian authority is linked to service rather than domination. Ws 6:3; Mt 16:19; 18:18; 28:18; Mk 10:42–43.

baptism A rite of immersion used by John the Baptist to signify entry into a community of repentance awaiting the Messiah. Later, as the rite of entry into the Christian community, it purifies and makes the initiate a new person by incorporation into Christ, and especially into his death and resurrection, and by the gift of his Spirit. Mt 3:6, 15; Ac 2:38; Rm 6:4; Ep 5:26.

blessing God blesses by imparting life, success, fertility, happiness. God's representative also may pronounce this gift by an effective word; once it is spoken it cannot be withdrawn. When others bless God it is an acknowledgement of and thanks for these gifts and a prayer for their continuance. Gn 12:2; 27; Ps 66:20; 67:6–7; Ep 1:3.

blood Blood, which signifies life, belongs to God; it may not be eaten. Because of this mysterious significance it is used in solemn oaths, covenants and purification. Particularly the covenant⋆ with Israel is solemnised in blood, and the New Covenant in the blood of Christ, which also cleanses from sin. Christ's blood was also the price by which humanity is redeemed. Gn 9:6; Lv 1:5; Ex 24:8; Mt 26:28; Ep 1:7; Heb 9:12–15.

body In Hebr thought not normally opposed to the soul, the body is conceived as the material aspect of a living person. In Paul the Christian is incorporated into the body of Christ, becoming a member of his body at baptism; the Christian members make up the body of Christ, or later, form the body of which Christ is the head⋆. The eucharistic body of Christ is shared by his members who partake of it. Finally it is the body transformed in Christ which will rise again. Dn 12:3; Rm 7:24; 1 Co 12:12; 15:44; Ep 1:23; Col 2:10.

breath See 'spirit'.

bride Following Ho, Israel is conceived as the bride of Yahweh, temporarily unfaithful to him and flirting with other partners, but finally united with him. So Jesus likens his coming to the marriage feast and himself to the bridegroom. The image is used to teach Christ's self-sacrifice for his bride. Ho 1:2; Ezk 16; Mt 9:15; 22:1; Jn 3:29; Ep 5:22.

canon of scripture The books regarded by the Jews as holy were being distinguished in the 2nd century BC, the collection reaching its final form soon after the sack of Jerusalem in 70 AD. The books and parts of books originally written in Gk were not included. Christian books began to be considered as equally sacred in the 2nd century, and the present canon of the New Testament was virtually standard by the 4th century. One tradition within the Church excluded the Gk books, and this tradition was taken up by the 15th century Reformers, who relegated these books to the Apocrypha. 1 Mc 12:9.

Christos See 'Messiah'.

church The Gk word *ekklesia*, originally designating the Israelite religious assembly, was applied to local Jewish communities, then to their Christian equivalents (Ac, Paul), finally to the Christian community as a whole (Ep, Col). In the gospels it occurs only at Mt 16:18; 18:17. The Pauline churches were organised after the model of Jewish communities, with elders⋆ and a president, but the Spirit inspired many other ministries⋆ in them, contributing to the building up of Christ's body⋆. Other NT images of the Church are God's bride⋆, a flock, a building, a vine⋆, the New Jerusalem. Jn 10:1; 15:1; Ac 15:4; 20:17; Ga 1:2; Ep 2:19; Rv 21–22.

circumcision Originally a rite preparatory to marriage, removal of the foreskin of the penis becomes a reminder of the covenant between God and his people. It gains its full importance as an identifying sign only after the Exile. In the face of hypocrisy the prophets teach circumcision of the heart. Gn 34:15; Ex 12:44; Jr 4:4; 1 M 1:60.

coming See 'Day of the Lord'.

commandments The Ten Commandments, existing in several different versions in the OT, are the basis of the Law⋆, and were treasured in Judaism as words of life. Jesus taught that the chief commandments were not only to love God but also to love one's neighbour. Especially in Jn love⋆ is the basis of all obedience to God's commands. Ex 20; Dt 8:3; Mk 12:28–34; Jn 13:34; 1 Jn 2:8.

conscience The concept as such enters the Bible only through Gk philosophy; the word occurs in the OT only in Ws 17:11, but frequently in Paul. He speaks mostly of a good and clear conscience, founded on faith. But conscience can also show gentiles that they are at fault. Weak consciences must not be hurt by the more robust. Rm 2:8; 1 Co 4:4; 8:7–12; 1 Tm 1:5, 19.

conversion Literally 'turning back', entry upon a new way of life after a renunciation of sin, a necessary condition for entry into the Baptist's or Jesus' community. Christian conversion entails acknowledging Jesus as Lord and the gift of the holy Spirit*. Mt 3:2; Ac 3:19; 9:35; 1P 2:25.

covenant A treaty or alliance on certain conditions, made between equal or unequal parties, sealed by oaths and usually by blood*. The terms to which God bound himself by the covenant with Abraham are the basis of all Israel's hopes, and made Israel God's special people. This covenant was likened to a marriage-bond. But Israel broke the terms of allegiance to God, and when the institutions of Israel are accordingly being destroyed, the prophets look forward to a new covenant of the heart*, expressing individual loyalty. Jesus seals this new covenant in his blood. Gn 15:1; Ex 19:5; Jr 31:31; Ezk 36:27; Mk 14:24; Heb 8:6.

creation In Gn creation is described by means of seemingly historical myths to stress God's sovereign power and the superiority of the human race in God's plan for the world. Elsewhere God's continuous care is stressed, without which everything would lapse into nothingness, and his absolute right, like a potter, to make what he will. In the later OT God is seen to create through his Wisdom* or his Word*. Christ is this Word, and is the exemplar of creation. Gn 1–2; Ps 104; Jr 18:6; Prov 8:22; Jn 1:3; Col 1:15–18.

cross The humiliating and agonizing death of Jesus by crucifixion completed once and for all what the demands of the Law* could not achieve. His obedience there undid the disobedience of Adam. By 'taking up the cross' Christians can share in this sacrifice. Mk 8:34; Rm 5:8–18; Ga 6:14; Heb 7:27.

cup A metaphor for the destiny of individuals or nations, more often unfavourable than favourable. The cup of God's anger* is to be handed to the nations who oppress Israel. In the NT it becomes an image of sharing in Jesus' suffering. Ps 11:6; 16:5; Jr 25:15; Mk 10:38.

darkness See 'light'.

day of the Lord In the OT a day of retribution when Israel, hardened in sin, is to be punished. After the Fall of Jerusalem it becomes a day of hope when Israel's

oppressors are to be punished. The imagery becomes more and more lurid, including cosmic signs, earthquake, eclipse. In the NT it becomes the Day of Christ, when Christ the Lord will come as judge*, often amid similar imagery, to renew the world, requite the wicked, reward the just and hand over the kingdom* to his Father. Jl 2; Am 5:18; 8:9; Mt 24:29–31; 25:31–46; 1 Co 15:24; 1 Th 4:15–17.

deacon Seven officials are appointed *deaconein* in Ac 6. Notionally in charge of distributions to the needy, they in fact seem to be a hierarchy subordinate to the Twelve, and in charge of the Hellenist* Christians, but preaching and baptising just like the Twelve. Later, deacons seem to be authoritative officers, mentioned after presbyters*. Ac 6; Rm 16:1; Ph 1:1; 1 T 3:8–13.

death In early Israel death means 'being gathered to the forefathers', but soon the dead are thought to lead a shadowy existence in Sheol*. But the conviction that God cannot abandon his faithful ones eventually flowers in the concept of a life after death, vindication for the faithful and disgrace for the wicked. Paul sees death as a moment of coming even closer to Christ. Gn 25:8; Ps 6:5; 16:11; Jb 19:25–26; Is 53; Dn 12:2; Mk 12:27; Ph 1:21–23.

descent into hell In 1 P 3:18 Christ 'went to preach to the spirits in prison'. This is a flimsy basis for the belief that Christ descended into Sheol*. It is even uncertain who these spirits were, the chained demons of Jewish legend or the righteous dead. Rm 10:6 and Ep 4:8 merely declare the reality of Jesus' death.

desert In the thought of Israel the desert is the abode of evil spirits, into which the scapegoat is driven to its death. But it is also the place where Israel first became God's people and lived with him in a honeymoon period of faithful love. In the messianic renewal of the world the barrenness of the desert will turn to fertile blossom. Lv 17:7; Is 35:1; Ho 2:16; Am 5:25.

devil See 'spirits', 'Satan'.

divorce Permitted under the old Law, on condition that it be irrevocable, divorce is forbidden by Jesus with an appeal to the fusing of personalities envisaged by Gn.

Mt adds a clause allowing divorce in the case of 'illicit marriage', generally understood to mean marriages illicit by Jewish law but permitted in other codes. Dt 24:1; Mt 19:3–6.

dreams Despite the widespread ancient belief in dreams as a means of divine communication, they appear as such in the Bible rarely outside specific clusters, e.g. Gn 37–41; Dn; Mt 1–2; Ac 16–27. There are also warnings that dreams may contain deceptive messages, reflecting only the viewer. Dt 13:2–6; Si 34:1–8.

elders After the model of the 70 elders appointed by Moses, local Jewish communities wre governed by a committee of elders (*presbyteroi*). This structure was taken over by Christian communities. Elders were carefully selected and their office was seen to depend on the holy Spirit*. The president (*episcopos*) was probably chosen from among them. Ex 18:13; Ac 11:30; 14:23; 20:28; Ti 1:5–9.

eschatology The doctrine of the last things, usually referring to teaching about the Day of the Lord*, e.g. the eschatological discourse of Mk 13 par. Jn however displays a 'realised eschatology', i.e. with the coming of the Spirit* the last age of the world has already begun.

eternal life Christ himself is life, and gives life to those who believe in him. This life is eternal, in that the believer has already entered into this ageless, unchanging quality of God. It has only to be completed by the resurrection. Jn 1:4; 3:15, 36; 6:40, 54; 1 Co 15:42; 2 Co 4:17.

eucharist The rite instituted by Jesus at his last supper with his disciples and repeated by them on his instructions. It is the new Passover of Christ, at which he seals the new covenant* in his blood*, shed for the remission of sins. Christ's body* which is his members is portrayed and fed by sharing in his eucharistic body, the true bread from heaven which gives eternal life*. Mt 26:26 par; Jn 6:31–58; 1 Co 11:17–34.

expiation Expiation or atonement is a process by which sin is removed (the Hebr word is related to 'cover') in order to achieve reconciliation and peace with God or a fellow human. In the old Law there

was an annual Day of Expiation, on which the scapegoat was sent out and the high priest offered sacrifice* for the sins of all the people. Jesus' sacrifice of expiation is seen as the perfect fulfilment of this repeated rite. Lv 16; 2 Co 5:18–19; Heb 9:11–14; 13:11–12; 1 Jn 2:2.

faith Trust in and commitment to God in response to his promises. Christian faith is the acceptance of Christ as Lord* and Saviour*; it unites with Christ and makes the believer a child of God, who imparts his Spirit* to the believer. Faith is normally expressed in baptism* and the works of the Spirit. In contrast to the Law, faith is a reliance not on self but on God, but it requires strength and tenacity. Rm 3:21–5:11; Ga 3:2–9; 2 Th 3:2–8.

fall, the One seemingly historical account of the origin of human sin. It draws heavily upon the myths of the surrounding cultures but purifies them to teach its own lesson. The sin is perhaps represented as sexual, but certainly as consisting in arrogant disobedience, with which Christ's humble obedience is contrasted. Traces of other accounts of the origin of evil survive, e.g. in Ezk 28:11–19. Gn 3; Ws 2:22–25; Rm 5:12–21; Phil 2:6–11.

fasting A natural expression of grief, in the Law* fasting is prescribed only for the Day of Expiation. Other fasts were added to implore God's mercy, and fasting became one of the three principal good works of Judaism. The prophets and Jesus warn against hypocrisy* in this matter, and there is no evidence that Jesus encouraged fasting. Lv 16:29; 2 S 12:16; Is 58:1; Mt 9:14.

father See 'abba'.

fear of Yahweh The absolute holiness of God can inspire absolute terror as well as obedience, but there is also an awe at the majesty of God which is compatible with delight in him and love. Nevertheless, a sense of human unworthiness lays even the prophets prostrate before God. Dt 6:2; Ps 112:1; Is 2:6–21; Ezk 1:28; Rv 1:17.

fire A symbol of the presence of God, whose holiness makes him, like fire, unapproachable. Also the most radical purifying and refining agent, whence hell or Gehenna (a valley full of burning rubbish-dumps) is represented as fiery. The Baptist expected the Messiah* to come with fire. Ex 13:22; Is 6:7; Mt 3:11–12; Mk 9:43.

flesh Basically meat, animal or human, flesh comes to mean humanity as a whole, often what is frail and perishable in humanity, the natural human desires, inclinations etc, which need to be brought under the divine influence. Hebr has no word for 'body' as opposed to 'soul', for the spirit animates the flesh and gives it life. Gn 2:23; 6:17; Is 40:6; Jn 3:6; 6:63; Rm 8.

forgiveness A willingness to forgive is one of the salient characteristics of Yahweh from the earliest times. Forgiveness is an element in the messianic future. When Jesus forgives sin, he is judged to be assuming a divine prerogative. But he also stresses that fellow-Christians must forgive each other. Gn 18:26–32; Ex 34:7; Mt 6:14; 9:2–6; 18:23–35; Lk 7:36–50.

freedom Christ came to bring freedom from slavery to sin. The Christian now willingly serves a new master, God or Christ. Paul seems to have been indifferent to political freedom and to have accepted the institution of slavery without a qualm. Rm 6:15–22; 1 Co 7:21–22; Ep 6: 5–9.

fulfilment Jesus is the fulfilment of the Father's promises in the OT, completing his plan for Israel. He also brings the old Law* to completion by removing its imperfections. Mt particularly sets out to show Jesus deliberately fulfilling OT passages in exact detail. Mt 1:22; 5:17–48; Heb 11:40.

fullness This difficult term (*pleroma* in Gk) is used of Christ in Col and Ep. In him lives the fullness of divinity, and Christians too find their fulfilment in him. Further, all fullness is found in him, for all creation reaches its term and completion in him. Ep 1:23; 4:13; Col 1:19; 2:9.

gentile Anyone not a Jew. In later Jewish literature, even the gospels, they are sometimes judged harshly. Mt 5:47; 18:17; Rm 1:18–32; 1 Co 5:11. But after some controversy it was decided that gentiles too, not Jews only, could be Christians. Ac 10; 15:7; Ga 2:14.

glory Often an awesome visible manifestation of the unapproachable God in brightness and fire, conveying his majesty and splendour. To give glory to God is to recognise his divinity and omnipotence; so the earth is full of his glory. Jesus shares in and reveals this glory, and the Christian too is to share it. Ex 24:16; Lk 2:14; 19:38; Jn 1:14; 12:23; 17:22–24.

gospel The English 'god spell' = 'good news' mirrors the Gk *euangelion*. Originally used in the emperor-cult, where it denoted news of any great imperial event, victory, birth of an heir etc, the term was adopted already in Paul for the good news brought by Jesus and preached by Paul. Mk so uses the term, but from Mt onwards it comes increasingly to mean the text or a part of it. Mt 26:13; Mk 1:15; 2 Co 2:12; Ga 1:7–8.

grace A fluid term related to favour (Gk *charis*, whence 'grace'). It may be a quality of graciousness, loveliness which arouses favour, or the unearned favour of a powerful ruler who need give no account of his actions. Basically it is the pleasingness of the favourite or the pleasure of the favourer, but it may also be the favours bestowed. Pr 11:16; Jn 1:14, 17; Phil 1:2; Rv 22:21.

head In medical thought of Jesus' time the head is considered the superior guiding principle, and also the source of life for the body. So when Christ is designated the head of his body the Church, he is nominated its guiding authority and source of life. Ep 1:22; 4:16; 5:23; Col 1:18; 2:19.

healing Sickness was regarded as the grasp of evil on a person, so that healing is a sign that evil is being overcome. Jesus' cures are part of the triumph over evil expected for the renewal of the world in the last times. It is not necessary that all the cures should be miraculous in the sense of being scientifically inexplicable. Mt 4:23; 8:16; 11:2–5; Jn 5:14.

heart The source of thoughts, feelings, decision, the centre of religious awareness, through which God is perceived, sought, heard, praised and loved. Dt 6:5; Ps 51:10; Jr 31:31; Ezk 36:26.

heaven In the primitive Hebr conception of a three-tier universe heaven is the dwelling-place of God, and 'Heaven' is used as a reverent circumlocution to avoid using the sacred name of God (so in Mt 'the Kingdom of Heaven' = 'the Kingdom of God' elsewhere). The homeland of the Christian is in heaven, by which is meant that the Christian's thoughts, interests, etc are there centred. Gn 1:6–8; Jb 22:12–13; Ps 11:4; Mt 3:2, 16; 6:20; Phil 3:20.

hell See 'fire'.

Hellenists Jews from outside Palestine, who used Gk as their language of worship. The Hellenist Christians of Jerusalem soon became a distinctive group, with their own hierarchy, the Seven 'deacons'*, and were the first to be persecuted. Ac 6:1; 8:1.

high priest The high priesthood as such may not have existed until after the Exile; it includes politico-religious leadership from about 200 BC until 70 AD. Jesus is called 'priest' or 'high priest' only in Heb: his sacrifice is effective; he has access to the heavenly sanctuary; he is the perfect mediator*. 2 Mc 3:1; Jn 18:13; Heb 2:17; 7:26–28; 9:11–28.

holiness Awe, terror, fascination, reverence are human reactions to the otherness of God. He is so holy that no human being can see him and live; they can only be staggered and awestruck at experiencing him. Yet association with him demands some share in his holiness, moral purity and (in some circumstances) ritual purity, consisting in separation from the ordinary processes of life. God asserts his holiness by protecting his people from all enemies, and when their sins prevent this, it is a slur on his holiness. Ex 3:5; Lv 19:2; Is 5:16; 6:3; Ezk 36:23; Rv 4:8.

hope Closely allied to faith* as trust in Yahweh, hope is reliance on God's faithful love and confidence that his promises will be fulfilled. Abraham's hope is the model of Christian hope in that it relied on no human possibilities. Jr 17:5–8; Ho 2:17; Rm 4:18–5:11; Heb 11:1.

hour of Jesus In Jn the moment of Jesus' passion, death and resurrection, considered as the moment of exaltation and glorification. From Cana onwards Jesus and the reader are conscious of this goal to which the whole of Jesus' life is directed. Jn 2:4; 7:30; 12:23, 27; 16:22.

humility In the sense of 'lowliness' this

quality calls for God's mercy and favour; the humble are specially dear to him, for those who accept their own helplessness must rely only on God. This was very central to Jewish spirituality during the oppressed period after the Fall of Jerusalem. In the modern sense of self-deprecation it has little place in the Bible; especially Paul seems to offend against it. 1 S 2:1; Ps 113:7–9; Lk 1:46–55; 6:20–23; 1 Co 11:1.

hypocrisy The prophets castigate hypocritical religious observance, ritual without due dispositions or social justice. The gospels similarly warn against the hypocrisy of the Pharisees. Is 1:10–16; Ho 8:11; Am 5:21; Mt 6:1–18; 23; Jn 7:53–8:11.

immortality See 'death'.

intercession In all parts of the OT various figures are asked to intercede for those in spiritual and temporal need: Abraham, Moses, Job, Jeremiah. It seems to have been thought especially appropriate to those men of prayer, the prophets. After the last supper Jesus intercedes for his followers. At the end of the OT, sacrifice* and intercession for the dead occur. Gn 18:24; Jb 42:8; Jr 42:2; 2 Mc 12:38; Jn 17.

Israel Three meanings: **1.** A personal name given to Jacob, Gn 32:29, whence the other meanings. **2.** A politico-geographical name, the northern territories, 1 S 11:8, or the united kingdom, 1 K 11:42. **3.** The holy people of God, a religious entity, for God chose Israel to be his very own people, a consecrated nation, set apart from other nations by the covenant*, but destined to bring salvation to all. Jesus makes a new holy people for himself, to which the same theology is applied. Dt 7; Ex 19:5; Is 45:14–17; Rm 9–11; Ga 6:16; Heb 8:8–10; 1 P 2:9.

Jesus See under separate titles: 'Lord', 'messiah', 'prophet', 'son of David', 'son of God', 'son of man', 'truth', 'word'.

judge The judges of the 'period of the judges' immediately after the settlement of Israel in Canaan are of two kinds: charismatic leaders or warlike liberators raised up in crisis, and authoritative figures to whom people of a certain district bring lawsuits for decision. Jg 3:9; 10:2, 3; 12:7. God is the supreme judge of all nations, and of the oppressed, often in the sense of vindicator; he will judge all nations at the end. Dt 10:18; Ps 9:7–8; Is 2:4; Jl 4:12. But he gives all judgement to the Son. Mt 25:32; Jn 5:22; Ac 10:42.

justice God's saving justice consists in punishing, but also in pardoning the repentant sinner, because he is then just by fidelity to his promises of salvation. To this corresponds human justice, or 'uprightness' which may be gained only by trust in these promises, ultimately by faith★ in Jesus. Is 5:16; Ho 2:21; Rm 3:21; 4:1–25; Ga 3:8.

king/kingship Israel, God's people, has no king but Yahweh. But at a certain stage military necessity made an earthly king unavoidable. David, God's chosen king, became the ideal for the future king who would renew God's kingship in Israel, and thence over the whole world. Jesus preached that God's rule or kingship had been inaugurated, showing it by his triumph over evil in all its forms, sickness, demonic possession, moral evil, death itself. God's kingship was still to be completed. 1 S 8:1–9; Ps 93; 97; Is 11:1–9; Ezk 34:23; Mk 1:15; 4:26–32; 11:10; Mt 25:31.

korban =dedicated to God. The rabbis taught that nothing so dedicated could be given away for any other purpose, no matter how laudable. Thus the owner retained its use. Mk 7:11; Mt 15:15.

lamb A Johannine image for Christ, combining the idea of a sacrificial lamb with that of the Servant★ of the Lord who takes all sin on himself. Ex 12:5; Lv 14:10; Jn 1:29; 19:36; 1 P 1:19. The Lamb of Rv, slain and yet living and enthroned, is expressed in Gk by a different word. Rv 5:6; 17:14; 21:27.

Law The first five books of the Bible, the 'Pentateuch' formed the written Law of Israel, revered as the terms of God's covenant★ with Israel, so a source of life to Israel. Also a body of tradition had grown up which enjoyed equal status as the 'oral Law'. Jesus fulfills the Law by his life and teaching. Paul sees the Law at best as a temporary guide, or as showing the enormity of sin by making it formal and conscious; so Christ rescues from slavery to the Law those who believe in him. Dt 8:3; Ps 119; Mt 5:17; 15:1–9; Rm 7:7; Ga 3.

leprosy The word traditionally used far more widely than the modern medical term, to cover many forms of skin diseases, serious or trivial, or even signs of decay in clothing or on walls. See Lv 13–14.

levite A member of a group assisting the priests in the sanctuary, probably originally priests themselves, and claiming Levi as their ancestor. Gn 29:34; Nm 16–17; Dt 18:1–8; Ezr 2:40–42.

liberty See 'freedom'.

life Life is given by God and belongs to God, who remains master of life. The fullness of life is eternal life★, which Jesus, who is himself life, came to bring. The believer's life is hidden in Christ and implies holiness★ and living to God in the spirit. Gn 2:7; 9:4; Ps 104:29; Jn 10:10; Rm 8:1; Phil 1:21; Co 3:3.

light A feature of divine manifestations and a messianic title. God is light and his Servant★ is a light to the nations. God's Law★ is a light to the steps. In the NT Jesus is the true light. By contrast, darkness symbolises the reign of evil. Ps 27:1; Is 9:1; 42:6; 60:1; Jn 1:4–5; 8:12.

Lord In the Gk OT the divine name Yahweh★ is translated 'Lord'. But the expression can bear a far weaker sense, merely 'Sir!'. However in the early community to call Jesus 'Lord' was the test of faith, and Christians were 'those who invoke the name of the Lord', in the sense of the divine name. Mk 7:28; Lk 10:40; Ac 2:21; 9:14; 1 Co 12:3; Phil 2:11.

love The Hebr concept of love involves a generous, responsive, active self-giving, modelled on that of God. God's relationship to Israel is that of passionate married love; the Israelite must love God with his whole being, and similarly his neighbour. Jesus extends this obligation to love to all human beings, with Jesus' own selfless love as model. Dt 6:5; Ho 2:21; Ezk 16; Mk 12:28–34; Jn 13:34; 1 Co 13; 1 Jn 4:7–5:4.

marriage See 'bride', 'divorce'.

mediator Various figures in the OT act as mediators, see 'intercession'. In the NT

Christ is the one mediator. In him is the fullness* of divinity, yet he is the Head* of the Body*. Through him come grace* and truth*. He is the mediator of the perfect covenant*. Jn 1:16–17; Col 2:9; 1 Tm 2:5; Heb 8:6.

mercy See 'forgiveness'.

messiah ='anointed' (Gk *christos*), normally a royal title, see 'anointing'. In the decades before the Jewish revolts in 66 AD and 132 AD it was popular as a title of revolutionary leaders. Jesus was so hailed by his followers, by the crowds and by his opponents (to construct a charge against him). He, however, was non-committal in regard to it, probably because of its political implications. The tradition after him is more positive, and in Paul 'Christos' becomes part of Jesus' name. 2 S 7:12–16; Ps 2; Is 6–9; Mk 8:29; 12:35; 14:61; 15:32; Ac 2:36.

ministry Jesus' concept of ministry is one of service. The earliest Christian communities were governed by elders* but there were many other ministries, such as that of the apostles* to witness to Jesus' resurrection, and the Seven, deacons*, leaders of the Gk community in Jerusalem. Paul mentions also prophets, teachers, healers, etc. Mt 20:26; 23:11; Ac 1:15–22; 6:1–6; 1 Co 12:28–30.

miracle Not exactly a biblical concept, centred as it is on contravention of the laws of nature. The Bible speaks rather of the 'wonders of God', signs of his power exercised for the sake of his people, especially in delivering them from Egypt. So Jesus' works of power or wonders are signs of the outbreak of the kingship/kingdom* of God and the presence of God's power in a new way. Jos 3:5; Ps 9:1; 107:24; Mt 12:38–39; Mk 6:2, 5, 14; Jn 2:11, 18, 23; Ac 4:22.

mystery A concept borrowed by Paul from Jewish apocalyptic*, of the mysterious plan long hidden in God and finally revealed. He applies it to the climax of history, the cross and resurrection, salvation preached to all nations and the restoration of all things in Christ. Rm 16:25; 1 Co 2:8; Ep 1:9–10; 3:3–12.

name Names in the Bible determine the nature of what is named. When Adam names the animals he determines their nature. Similarly, by a new naming a person is given a new significance and a new power (Israel, Emmanuel, Peter). Hence many Hebr names are etymologised to show a special significance. God's name carries with it his power; so to speak his name invokes his power, to make his name known is to display his power. Those who call on the name of Jesus (e.g. in baptism*) submit themselves to his power. Gn 1:19; 32:29; Ps 54:1; Mt 1:23; 16:18; Ac 2:38; 10:43; Phil 2:9.

nazirite ='one set apart' ritually by a vow whose terms are given in Nm 6; Jg 13:5–7; Am 2:11; Ac 18:18.

numbers In the Bible numbers often have a set significance, e.g. 4 for the quarters of the world, so the whole universe, Gn 2:10; 7 for completion, Lk 8:2, so 6 for radical incompletion, Rv 13:18 (similarly 3½, Dn 7:25); 12 for fullness (so 144,000 for utter totality, Rv 7:4); 40 a round, large approximate number, Ex 16:34. Since in Gk letters are used as digits, a number may also be a cryptogram for a name whose digits add up to that number, Rv 13:18.

obstinacy The obstinacy of Israel is a frequent theme especially in the prophets. God will correct his people with punishment but not desert them. This obstinacy is given as the reason why Jesus speaks in parables. But Jesus' own disciples also are in Mk (softened in the other gospels) rebuked for their hardness of heart and failure to believe. Dt 9:13; Is 48:4; Mt 13:13; Mk 4:40; 7:18; Ac 28:25; Rm 11:7.

parable Short stories told for comparison or to illustrate a point, a method of teaching much used in popular teaching, in the OT and especially by Jesus in the gospels. The underlying Hebr term *mashal* includes also other imaged sayings, similes and riddles. The gospel parables are often adjusted by the evangelists to apply to their own situations. Jg 9:7–15; 2 S 12:1–14; Mt 13; Mk 4; Lk 15–16.

paraclete A helper, counsellor, advocate, Jesus, himself a 'paraclete', will send another 'paraclete' to guide his disciples into all truth. This will be the holy Spirit*. The term is used in Judaism, but in the Bible only in Jn 14:16, 26; 15:26; 16:7; 1 Jn 2:1.

Passover Originally an annual nomadic feast for the flocks at the first full moon of spring, it came to commemorate the liberation from Egypt. Later it was combined with the feast for the beginning of harvest, Unleavened Bread, and so acquires the symbolism of a fresh start, free from corruption. Jesus probably used a Passover supper to seal his new Covenant★. The name itself (Hebr *pessah*, Aram *pascha*) is obscure. Ex 12; 2 Chr 35:18; Mt 26:26; 1 Co 5:8.

peace 'Shalom!' is the normal Jewish greeting, but its realisation is a messianic blessing, presupposing justice and fidelity to God. So Christ is our bond of peace, and the gospel is the word of peace. Ps 122:6–8; Is 48:18; Jn 14:27; Ep 2:14–16.

Pharisees A party within Judaism, the strictest observers of the Law, both written and oral, sometimes prone to casuistry and hypocrisy, but also known for great warmth of devotion. Jesus' independence with regard to the Law often brought him into opposition with them. Mt 12:2; 15:1–20; 23; Lk 7:36; Ac 23:6.

poverty In the OT the poor are specially protected by Yahweh, and specially favoured if they call to him. He will punish their oppressors and render them justice. The remnant★ of God's people will be poor, and the messianic king★ a humble king. In the wisdom literature, however, poverty is regarded as a curse of idleness and folly. In the NT the poor are included among the outcasts to whom the gospel message is especially addressed; their misery will be reversed. Ex 22:21; Jb 24:2–12; Ps 22:26; Pr 6:11; Am 4:1; Lk 6:20; 16:19–31.

prayer The Psalms form the largest collection of prayers in the OT, but other intimate and confident prayers to Yahweh abound. In the NT Jesus is seen to be constantly praying to his Father, as he teaches his followers to do. Praise and thanksgiving, inspired by the holy Spirit, especially mark the early communities. Jr 15:10–21; Mt 6:5–13; Lk 22:39–46; Jn 17; Ac 2:42; 4:24; Rm 8:26–27.

priest The English word is derived from *presbyteros*=elder★. In primitive Israel any head of a family would offer sacrifice,

though there were priests of the various sanctuaries throughout the land. The Temple priesthood cannot predate Solomon's Temple, and its importance grows with the centralisation of cult there shortly before the exile. See also 'high priest'. In the NT only Christ is called priest or high priest★. Ex 12:6; 2 S 8:17; 1 K 8:6; Neh 10:3–9.

prophet The task of the prophet is not so much to foretell as to pronounce God's will, to mediate God's view of a situation, sometimes backing this up with predictions. Some professional court prophets are mentioned, but the prophetic movement was more often critical of the establishment. A final prophet was expected who would initiate God's renewal of all things, and Jesus is seen as this prophet. There were also prophets in the earliest Christian communities. Dt 18:15–18; 1 K 18:22; 19:16; 22:6; Lk 4:16–24; 7:15; Ac 11:27.

prostitution In the Bible an image of Israel's unfaithfulness to Yahweh, whose bride★ she is. Ex 34:16; Ho 1:2; Ezk 16.

punishment See 'anger'.

purity The concept of clean and unclean was most important in OT ritual, many (but not all) of the prescriptions being based on primitive health precautions for hot countries and reverence for life-processes. Such ritual uncleanness was not necessarily morally culpable but rendered a person unfit for the cult. Jesus removed the basis of such prohibitions, and this was applied more widely by the early community. Lv 11–22; Mk 7:14–23; Ac 10:9–16; 15:19–29; Rm 14:14.

recapitulation in Christ See 'head'.

redeemer A technical term of family law, the closest male relative, the *go'el*, who is bound to extricate his relative from disasters such as childlessness or debt. God is the *go'el*, so redeemer or saviour of his people. Of Christ the term 'Saviour' is used almost exclusively in the Pastoral Letters and 2 P. Jb 19:25; Ps 19:14; Is 41:14; Phil 3:20; Ti 1:3–4; 2 P 1:1, 11.

redemption A general term used in the OT for the deliverance of Israel from Egypt by God's mighty power, without any price or ransom being paid, to be his own possession; then for the deliverance from exile in Babylon, especially as an image of final deliverance from sin. Christ delivers the new Israel from slavery to the Law* and to sin, making her his own people. The mention of Christ's blood as a ransom-price is rare. Dt 7:6–8; Jer 31:11; Ps 44:26; Mk 10:45; Rm 3:24; 1 Co 6:20; Col 1:13; 1 P 1:18.

remnant An important theme in the prophets is that, though Israel will be punished for infidelity, a faithful remnant will be preserved and will be the spearhead of the messianic renewal. Is 10:19–21; Ezk 6:8–10; Am 9: 8–10; Zc 13:8–10.

resurrection By the mid 2nd century BC belief in a general resurrection after death* at the end of time, to glory or disgrace, is apparent. The resurrection of Jesus before the end of time is different, though Paul still sees it as the fulfilment of the hope of Israel. God raised him to new life as the glorious Lord with all authority in heaven and on earth, first-born from the dead and so the leader of a new humanity. Those who have entered into his death and resurrection by baptism* are raised and glorified with him, transformed into the sphere of the divine. Dn 2:12; Mt 28:18; Mk 16: Ac 23:6; Rm 1:4; 1 Co 15; Phil 2:9–11; Heb 2:10.

revenge See 'vengeance'.

rock An image for a reliable foundation which can be trusted, used of God, Ps 18:2; 95:1; of Christ, 1 Co 10:4; and of Peter, the rock on which Christ built his community, Mt 16:18.

Sabbath A weekly day of rest dedicated to Yahweh, but also to ensure human freedom to God. Of very ancient origin, it gained its full importance at the time of the Exile and became one of the touchstones of fidelity to Judaism. Gn 2:2; Ex 23:12; Neh 13:15; Mt 12:1.

sacrifice Laws and ritual for the various sacrifices which played such an important part in the OT are set out in Lv 1–7. The prophets, echoed by Jesus, strongly criticised the sacrificial practice as insincere, external rites at variance with dispositions and blindness to injustice. Jesus sealed his new covenant by the sacrifice of

his blood, fulfilling the purpose of OT sacrifices in a way which they could not. Ps 50; Is 1:10–17; Ho 6:4–5; Mt 26:26–29; Ep 5:2, 25; Heb 7–10.

Sadducees The traditionalist party of the Jews, mostly from the great priestly families, they sought and held political power. They kept to the written Law and rejected new developments such as angels* and the doctrine of resurrection*. Mt 22:23; Mk 12:18; Ac 23:6–8.

Samaritans Inhabitants of Samaria, the region midway between Galilee and Judaea, disliked and despised by the Jews for their mixed race and mixed religion. Of the Bible they accepted only the first five books. The dislike was mutual. But Jesus, especially in Lk, contrasts Samaritan openness with Jewish rigidity. Lk 10:30–37; 17:16; Jn 4; Ac 8:25.

Satan The Hebr word means 'adversary' and is used in a general sense, then in particular of one of the 'sons of God' who is responsible on God's behalf for testing and proving human beings. Only in 1 Ch 21:1 does it become a proper name. In the NT he is interchangeably called the 'devil' (Gk *diabolos*=accuser), and also actively promotes evil, claiming power over the world. In the Johannine writings the devil/Satan is a fundamentally evil entity. 1 K 5:18; Jb 1:6; 2:1; Zc 3:1–2; Mt 4:1; 13:19; 25:41; Jn 8:44; 1 Jn 3:8–10.

saviour See 'redeemer'.

scribes At the time of Jesus Jewish scholars learned in the Law and the scriptures, to whom people turned for authoritative guidance and interpretations. Many were Pharisees, and they opposed Jesus actively. But not all were hostile. Mt is often called a Christian scribe. Mt 12:38; 13:52; Mk 11:27; 12:28–34; Jn 8:3; Ac 4:5.

Second Adam Inverting Jewish legend that the Adam of Gn was preceded by a first, heavenly Adam, Paul teaches that the founder of the human race was the first Adam and Jesus the Second, heavenly, Adam. The first Adam fell by his sin of pride and disobedience, dragging down the human race. The Second Adam raises and renews the human race by his humility and obedience. Rm 5:12–21; 1 Co 15:21, 45; Phil 2:6–11.

servant In the Semitic world often a title of honour because of the confidential relationship between servant and master. The Servant of the Lord in Isaiah is a redemptive figure, perhaps Israel, perhaps an individual representing Israel, whose mission is, by suffering willingly borne, to free from sin and bring God's salvation to the nations. Subtle allusions suggest that Jesus, and certainly the evangelists, identified himself with this figure. Is 42:1–4; 49:1–6; 50:4–9; 52:13–53:12; Mt 3:17; 8:17; 26:28; Phil 2:6–11; 1 P 2:21–25.

Sheol In Hebr thought a place where the dead continue to exist in darkness, dust and helplessness, without wisdom and unable to know or praise God. Jb 17:13–16; Ps 88:3–12; Is 14:9–11; Rv 20:14.

shepherd A common image of kingship in the near East, used by Jr and Ezk to accuse the selfish rulers of Israel. Ezk also uses it to foretell a messianic shepherd who will pasture his people in Yahweh's name and renew the covenant*. Jesus uses it in his parable of the lost sheep and his own claim to be the good shepherd. Jr 23:1–6; Ezk 34; Zc 11:4–17; Mt 18:12–14; Mk 6:34; Jn 10.

sign The miracles of Jesus are signs of his messianic mission and of the Father's glory; Jn 1–12 is conventionally known as The Book of Signs. Jesus himself, however, prefers the expression 'the works of my Father' and at times refused to manifest the signs which the Jews demanded. Mt 12:38; Jn 2:11; 4:48–54; 10:32–38; 1 Co 1:22.

sin Consciousness of sin and failure is deep in Israel. But admission of guilt leads on always to confidence in God's forgiveness; the paradigm case is the sin of Eve and Adam, followed by the other stories of primitive sin till the Flood. Especially after Israel's infidelity is sealed by the Exile, this awareness is intensified. In Paul Sin (as a personification) has ruled over all people by solidarity with the sin of Adam*, and is overcome only by solidarity through faith* with the sacrifice of Christ. Gn 3; Ps 51; Bar 1:15–22; Rm 1:18–3:20; 5:8–21; 6:17–23.

son of David A messianic title stemming from the promise to David, and stressed thenceforth in the OT and at the time of Jesus. Mt especially shows Jesus being so hailed and emphasises its importance. Jesus himself was hesitant towards this title, perhaps because it suggested too human a notion of the Messiah*. 2 S 7:8–16; Ps 89; Is 11:1–5; Ezk 34:23–24; Mt 1; 9:23; Mk 12:35; Lk 1:32; Jn 7:42; Ac 2:30; Rm 1:4.

son of God A title expressing a special choice by God, a special mission from God and special protection by him. It is applied in the OT to the angels, to Israel, to its leaders and to other individuals. Jesus is so hailed by Satan and the possessed, by the voice from heaven at his baptism and transfiguration, and finally by the centurion. Jn and particularly Paul use the title more widely of Jesus. Jesus himself speaks only of 'the Son' with relation to his Father. Ex 4:22; Ps 2:7; Ws 18:13; Ho 11:1; Mt 3:17; 4:3, 6; 8:29; 11:27; 17:5; 26:63; 27:54; Jn 1:34; 11:4, 27; 17:1; Rm 1:3–4; Ga 2:20.

son of man An Aramaic expression by which a speaker self-effacingly points to himself. It was a favourite self-designation of Jesus. It is understood by the evangelists by reference to Dn as a title of glory*, but scholars dispute whether it could already have held this sense in Jesus' own lifetime. Dn 7:13; Mt 8:20; 13:13; 25:31; 26:64; Ac 7:56; Rv 1:13.

soul In the NT corresponds to the Hebr *nephesh*, meaning the life or the self, the centre of desire, emotions and loyalty. Mt 26:38; Lk 2:35; 12:19; Heb 10:39.

spirit In Hebr and Gk the same word means 'breath', 'wind', 'spirit', often the principle of life and activity in human beings, given by God and withdrawn by him. Prophets and charismatic leaders receive the spirit of God in a special way for a special task. In the last days the spirit is to be poured out on the whole people and on individuals, in a new covenant of the spirit. Gn 1:2; Nm 11:17; Jg 3:10; 6:34; Is 11:2; Ezk 37:1–14; Jl 3:1–2.

In the NT the Spirit comes upon Jesus at his baptism and upon the Apostles at Pentecost, after which every decisive move in the early community is seen to be guided by the Spirit. Similarly in Paul the Spirit, the Spirit of God or of Christ, makes Christians children of God and empowers them to all Christian activity, including prayer and love. Jn teaches especially that this Spirit, the Paraclete*, brings the continuing personal presence of Christ. That this Spirit of God or of Christ is a distinct person is implied also by the frequent triadic formulae in Paul. Mk 1:10; Jn 1:33; 14:16; Ac 1:8; 15:28; Rm 5:5; 1 Co 14:14–16; 2 Co 13:13; Ga 5:13–36.

spirits In Judaism spirits bulked large in the popular imagination. Various mental disorders were attributed to unclean spirits, and Jesus shows his conquest of evil by expelling them. There was also a range of cosmic spirits, intermediaries between God and the world, controlling events and nations ('principalities', 'powers', etc); the supremacy of the risen Christ is expressed by his command over them. Mk 1:23, 32; Ac 16:16; Ga 4:3; Ep 1:21.

suffering God tests his faithful by suffering. Job's endurance gives power to his prayer, and the Servant* of the Lord in Isaiah atones for the sins of others by his suffering. Christ teaches that persecution is part of the mission of apostles*, and Paul regards it as a sign of his apostolate. He attributes to the Christ who is in him the sufferings he bears. Jb 42:8; Is 53:4–7; Mk 13:9–13; 2 Co 11:23; Col 1:24.

temple The importance of the temple in Jerusalem was as the dwelling-place of God in the centre of his people. Already the prophets taught that in the new covenant* God would dwell in each individual heart, and Paul teaches that Christians are temples of the spirit*. In the final vision of Rv there is no temple because God fills his whole people. 1 K 8:10; Ezk 9–11; Jr 31:33; Jn 2:21; 1 Co 3:16; Rv 21:22.

tongues 'Speaking in tongues', a form of ecstatic speech inspired by the Spirit, is bursts of praise unintelligible to the ordinary listener and needing an interpreter. Paul recognises but does not fully encourage this phenomenon. At Pentecost Ac describes a similar happening, when the apostles preach intelligibly in tongues unknown to themselves. Ac 2:4; 1 Co 14:1–25.

truth In the NT truth is related to the divine. Jesus is the true vine, the true bread from heaven, the true shepherd, the true light, the fulfilment of these OT figures, promises of God. He is also the Truth itself, and his Spirit* will guide his followers into all truth, which will sanctify them and set them free. Jn 8; 14:6; 17:17–19; 2 Co 6:7; Ep 4:21.

vengeance In a society without police the law did not so much enjoin revenge as limit punishment to the equal of the damage caused. But in Israel the nearest relative was obliged to protect the living rather than to avenge the dead. Forgiveness within Israel was prescribed, and Jesus strongly demanded mutual forgiveness. Nb 35:33; Lv 19:17; Mt 5:38; 18:21.

vine An image for Israel, the vine or vineyard of the Lord, tended by him but unresponsive. Similarly the grape-harvest is an image of the final judgement. Jesus is the true vine fulfilling perfectly the vocation of Israel. Is 5:1–7; Jr 2:21; Jn 15:1.

virgin In the OT the virgin daughter of Zion is a symbol of Israel, emphasising her vulnerability and her dependence on Yahweh. It is the firm tradition of the gospels that Jesus was born of a virgin mother. Paul commends virginity in view of the pressing eschatological crisis. Lam 1:6; 2:1; Am 8:2; Mt 1:25; 1 Co 7:25.

witness A witness (Gk *martyr*) in the NT sense does not simply witness to an observed fact but bears personal testimony to a truth, putting personal weight behind it. So Jesus witnesses to the truth, and the Father, the scriptures and the Spirit witness to Jesus. The apostles witness to the resurrection in the sense of proclaiming it. The Gospel of Jn is laid out as a great trial scene, in which people reject or accept the witness to Jesus. Jn 1:7–8; 5:31–37; 18:37; Ac 1:8; 1 Tm 6:13.

word God created by his Word and reveals by it, so that the Word is an image of God at work in the world. The Word is distinct from God and yet divine, always united to him and dependent on him, sent by him in power to reveal his salvation. Si 42:15; Is 55:1; Jn 1:1; Rv 19:13.

Zion The holy mountain of Jerusalem, the dwelling-place of God and the symbol of his presence. All nations will flow thither to receive salvation and to revere God. It will be a city of joy and source of the river of salvation, the city of the Lamb. Ps 122; Is 60:1; 66:18–20; Zc 14; Rv 21–22.

CHRONOLOGY OF THE NEW TESTAMENT

GENERAL HISTORY

31 BC – 14 AD Augustus supreme

14–37 Tiberius emperor

37–41 Caligula

41–54 Claudius

54–68 Nero

69–71 Titus

81–96 Domitian

96–98 Nerva

98–117 Trajan

PALESTINIAN HISTORY

40–4 BC Herod king of Judaea

?6 BC–?30 AD *Jesus*

4 BC–6 AD Archelaus king of Judaea

4 BC–39 AD Herod Antipas tetrarch of Galilee

6–41 Judaea a Roman province

6–15 Annas high priest

26–36 Pontius Pilate prefect

18–36 Caiaphas high priest

Paul's letters

66–70 *Siege of Jerusalem*

Synoptic Gospels

John's Gospel

MEASURES AND MONEY

APPROXIMATE EQUIVALENTS

Length *cubit* = 50 cm (2 feet)

Weight talent = 30 kilograms (70 lbs)
mina = 50 grams (1 lb)
sheqel = 1 gram (½ oz)

Money 'silver piece' = 4 drachmas

drachma (Gk) = denarius (Roman) = day's wage of casual labourer

'penny' = cheapest coin available

INDEX OF PERSONS

Principal references are given, but the list is not exhaustive. Sometimes only the first verse of a passage is cited.